The
New Orleans
Garden

Franklin Adams

The
New Orleans
Garden

By Charlotte Seidenberg

Silkmont & Count 1990
New Orleans

PUBLISHED BY SILKMONT & COUNT

Copyright © 1990 by Charlotte Seidenberg

Cover Illustration & Photograph: Copyright © 1990 by Jacob Jean Seidenberg

Frontispiece: Copyright © 1990 by Franklin Adams

Illustrations: Copyright © 1990 by Jacqueline Bishop, Judy Burks,
Andree B. Carter, Betsy Ewing, Dorothy Furlong-Gardener,
Harriet Hazlett, Susan Openshaw LaRocca, Michael Ledet,
Allison Crutcher McAshan, Evelyn Menge, Harriet Quick,
Dara Rosenzweig, Pam Kelly Sills, Allison Stewart,
Kathleen Trapolin, Pat Trivigno, Nancy Weller.

DESIGNED BY EUGENIE SEIDENBERG-DELANEY

Library of Congress Catalogue Card Number 90-092025

ISBN 0-9627757-0-3

Manufactured in The United States of America

SILKMONT & COUNT
Post Office Box 15060
New Orleans,
Louisiana 70175-5060

Dedication

To my husband, Jean Seidenberg,
who's always had the courage to follow his dream
and has been unfailingly supportive of me
in the pursuit of mine;
he never once took my project less than seriously.

Acknowledgments

First, to Anne Bradburn who, on a birding trip to Aransas Wildlife Refuge, said I should write a book on gardening which presupposes that I COULD write a book on anything. It never would have occurred to me!!! To the Tulane University Herbarium which she and Steve Darwin curate.

To Anne Bradburn and Kent Prince who were the first outside my family to read the massive first draft and for their honest comments. To Faye Prince who generously volunteered Kent.

To my father, Joseph Conti, who gave me my first computer. Everybody said, "You can't write without a word processor." I couldn't have written WITH a word processor without extensive consultations with experts Robert Keim of Arizona State University (compliments of my sister, Judy Keim), and Bill Seemann of Ocean Springs (compliments of his wife, Wynn).

To my stepdaughter, Eugenie Seidenberg-Delaney, who's twice won prizes for graphic design in the New England Book Show (sponsored by the Book Builders of Boston) and to my friendship garden of artists for helping us to make a pretty book. To Michael Ledet for sharing his experience in designing and publishing. To Dorothy Furlong-Gardner for all kinds of support.

To those who shared their knowledge, research, years of expertise, secrets: Joseph Ewan of the Missouri Botanical Garden; Ann Kennedy, who told me about Joe Ewan; Bill Cullison and Susie Burkes of The Garden Library of the New Orleans Town Gardeners, Southeastern Architectural Archive, Tulane University Library; Gallier House Museum, Tulane University; Joan Caldwell and Ann Smith of the Louisiana Collection, Howard Tilton Memorial Library, Tulane University (without Joan, I never would have found the *Catalogue of the Lepidoptera of New Orleans and its Vicinity* by Ludwig von Reizenstein); Nancy Newfield, hummingbird expert (and tour guide extraordinare!); Skip Newfield (who noticed I'd left out mulberries); Stephen Hand of the Vieux Carre Commission; Sally Kittridge Reeves of the Notarial Archives; Suzanne Turner, Landscape Historian; Florence Schornstein, Brenda Pumphrey, Skip Treme', Keith Bleichner, Arlen Brunsen, of the Parkway and Park Commission of New Orleans; Dorothea Boldt, Hilda Latapie, Les Cambias, Camilla Bradley, Maureen Detweiler, Julia Sanders, Margaret Seale, Pat Boothby, Ernestine Hopkins, Louise Ewin, the late Dr. Will Sternberg and his wife, Tedda, Dr. Irma Overby, Shirley Heumann, Dorothy Dubourg (Kraak), Louise Kraak, Louise Hanchey, John Sanderford, Danny Wheeler, Mrs. John Minor Wisdom, Arlene Mmahat, George B. Atkins, George Schmidt, A. Reed Hayward of The Greenery, Rene Fransen, landscape architect; Paul Wells, Mrs. Edmund Wingfield, Dr. Severn Doughty, D. Clive Hardy; Louisiana Division of the New Orleans Public Library; Don Schmitz, of the Bureau of Aquatic Plant Management, Department of Natural Resources, State of Florida; Marie Caillet and Joseph Mertzweiller of the Society for Louisiana Irises; Celia Jones of Sisters' Bulb Farm; Dee Phillips of the Garden Study Club; and everyone else who's given me help and support.

To Leslee Reed and others who aren't too busy, important, or grown-up to look for frogs or monkey puzzles. When Jerome Lebo said, "I've never seen you at the City Park Botanical Garden, before," I didn't remind him of the time he caught two ladies with nets scooping tadpoles out of his lilypond! To Mike McClung of Four Seasons Landscape Maintainence and Kathy, his wife, who share orders of bullfrog tadpoles and don't mind toads singing under their bedroom window. To Eddie McLellan who eats worms. What more can I say? To Kit McLellan who stays married to him anyway.

To my partners in crime, Bob Skinner and Patty Friedmann!

To Camillo Ruiz and the clientele and staff of P. J.'s Coffee & Tea Co., Magazine Street, weekdays between 7:00 and 8:30 A.M., for early morning support.

About the Author

When Charlotte Seidenberg was a child, her father made a prediction that proved wildly unprophetic. "She'll grow out of this when she has children," he said of the young naturalist. A farm of pets in her bedroom, a grade school award in Jackson, Mississippi, for an arrangement of magnolias and honeysuckle: this was only the beginning. When Charlotte taught school, her classroom was full of snakes and toads and sweet potato vines, of dissected animal parts and hatching chickens--plus the reverberations of cries from cafeteria and janitorial staff over assorted reptiles creeping and slithering through heating ducts. Charlotte later had children, and the nurturing instinct grew as fast as the sweet potato vines: a profusion of plants and an abundance of animals arrived with her expanding family. When Charlotte changed professions, she went deeper into the taking-care-of role: an RN, she has worked in medical-surgical, pediatric, detoxification, and psychiatric units. Now she is a rehabilitation specialist, a medical services consultant working from a home office where she can, Candide-style, cultivate her garden. Artist husband Jean has a studio across the street. Between them they have made every square inch of their home a visual delight, outside and in. Altogether, theirs is a lusty, romantic life.

This book--like every other Charlotte Seidenberg project--has had a gentle, careful gestation. A serious gardener for over twenty years, Charlotte has been storing up facts, experiences, and anecdotes for a long time--on her shelves, in her steel-trap mind. "I like secrets, mysteries, gossip," she will tell you, and so her book is chock-a-block with stories, from her search for the monkey puzzle tree to her sleuthing about the origins of the hummingbirds that once graced the Hummingbird Bar & Grill. The writing itself took two and a half years. A happy result of Charlotte's probing is a strong historical focus--when plants were introduced, how they were used in earlier times. She has "unearthed" myths about creole box, creole camellias; she has put on paper reminiscences of better times, when New Orleans had the funds to put flowers out in spring, then greenhouse them for the winter.

An even-handed, thoroughly researched, comprehensive picture of New Orleans gardening, this book nevertheless has philosophical underpinnings. Wildlife gardening and the use of native plants are highlighted--to create awareness of how delicate the natural world outside of gardening is. Charlotte concedes that backyard habitats aren't the answer for many animals. She points out that the widespread spraying for buckmoths upsets many balances. And as for gardening in general, she says, "Aestheticism is enough. It should be fun, or you shouldn't do it."

With her book in print, Charlotte is still learning. She's traveled to Costa Rica and been enthralled by the begonias and bromeliads. She's been trying black-eyed Susan vines for ground cover, has let some plants go out of bounds to use her energies for other plants. Recently she built a new pond, with bog and water plants. Volunteers and traveling plants, johnny jump-ups, purple verbena and wild salvia, spiderwort and yellowtop, mock strawberry and Japanese climbing fern--plus frogs, toads, garter snakes, brown snakes, mosquito hawks: for Charlotte Seidenberg, creating a New Orleans garden is truly a growing process.

"It is not often that someone comes along who is a true friend and a good writer. Charlotte (is) both."
from *Charlotte's Web* by E. B. White

Patty Friedmann, Fall, 1990
author of *Too Smart To be Rich*
and *The Exact Image of Mother*

Harriet Quick

Foreword

What is the most characteristic art of New Orleans? Most people would consider the obvious answer to be cooking, or perhaps music, or even architecture. An equally strong case, however, can be made for gardening. From the first French settlement to the present day, the sub-tropical climate and rich alluvial soil have drawn New Orleanians of all races -- rich and poor alike -- to gardening. Architecture has been left to architects and builders, music to the musicians. Only cooking rivals gardening as an art for everyone in New Orleans.

And well it might! With little expenditure beyond perspiration, anyone can be an artist-gardener in this blessed climate. Here one scarcely needs to encourage plants to grow. They will anyway. Like the sculptor who described his art as "cutting away all the extra stone," the New Orleans gardener's challenge is as much one of subtraction as addition.

The New Orleans garden has never been a purely aesthetic enterprise. It has provided food, fruits, and herbs in abundance. Its blossoms have provided welcome olfactory relief from the stench of rotting organic matter that hovers over the city through the long hot months. Its arbors and shade trees have provided havens both from the blazing sun and the teeming bustle of a great city.

As much as any other art, gardening in New Orleans has absorbed the diverse cultures of the city's population. The geometric plan of early French and Spanish gardens spread uptown from the French Quarter to a few outposts in the Irish Channel and downtown through Faubourg Marigny. More informal landscaping -- along with appropriate flora -- made its debut with the Anglo-Saxon and German immigrants of the nineteenth-century. With the commercial wealth of the twentieth-century came a return to more formal plans, as epitomized by Mrs. Edith

Stern's extravaganza at her Metairie estate, Longue Vue.

New Orleans gardens have accurately mirrored the local economy. Expanding trade in the early nineteenth-century brought many new plants both from Europe and the Orient. Quickly absorbed into their new setting, these flowers and trees were soon believed by many to have been indigenous to Louisiana. Mid-nineteenth century prosperity created by cotton, trade and banking also brought professional gardeners, such as the Alsatian who developed the grounds of Mr. James Robb's now-demolished *palazzo* in the Garden District. Later, as the struggle for survival gave way to greater ease, gardening stores also made their appearance, enabling people of modest means to adorn their shot-gun homes with exotic gardens.

Except for food, no other art practiced in New Orleans is as evanescent as gardening. Even the culinary arts are preserved in recipes and cook books. Gardens, by contrast, fade away unnoticed and, with notable exceptions, undocumented. Because of this, the extraordinary wealth of New Orleans' gardening heritage is all but lost today. Gardening books available in the Crescent City speak about the United States as a whole or, at best, the South. The aspiring New Orleans gardener has little more to guide himself or herself than the example of neighbors or dinner-table hearsay.

Fortunately, this has begun to change in recent years. Professor Joseph Ewan of Tulane University [now of the Missouri Botanical Garden] conducted pioneering research -- some of it included herein -- on local flora. More recently Ms. Suzanne Turner has undertaken a doctoral dissertation on early gardens of the French Quarter. However important, these and other efforts are only a beginning. Rich archival sources, photographic collections, and oral history sources have barely been touched. Archaeology and allied fields in botany have yet to be exploited as tools for uncovering New Orleans' gardening tradition.

Doubtless, the art of gardening and its history in New Orleans would be better known by now had public

interest been greater. Social change over the last generation has discouraged this. The quickening pace of professional life -- not to mention the competition of television
and sports -- have left less time for gardening. The advent of two-career families has also taken its toll. The
purpose of the present book is to reverse this neglect, to
arouse new interest in the art of gardening, and to inspire
those who to now have been indifferent or passive to taste
its joys.

Charlotte Seidenberg's engaging writing style belies
the careful research that went into this book. Both the
novice and experienced gardener will find much sound
and intriguing advice in its pages. If this volume suc-
ceeds in its task, it should quickly be followed by a
second edition, one that continues to pay homage to the
past but which also includes a chapter on "the New Orleans Garden of the Twenty-first Century." In all likeli-
hood, that garden of the future will have deep roots in
the local past. Gardening, after all, is the most organic of
arts.

S. Frederick Starr
Oberlin, Ohio/New Orleans
September 6, 1990

Table of Contents

INTRODUCTION   17

BASICS   25

    Soil, 26, Modifying the Soil for Gardening, 28
    Climatic Considerations, 37, Microclimates, 41
    Seeds, 44, Cuttings, 47, Pest Control, 48

ROSES   51

    Roses for the New Orleans Garden, 65
    Old Roses, 65, Modern Roses, 67

EXOTIC TREES & SHRUBS   71

    Exotic Trees & Shrubs
      for the New Orleans Garden, 75
    Deciduous Trees, 75, Deciduous Shrubs, 85
    Evergreen Trees, 98 Evergreen Shrubs, 105
    Palms, Palmettos, Cycads, 123
    Trees for Fall Color, 125

VINES   127

    Vines for the New Orleans Garden, 130
    Vines by Season of Bloom, 149

ANNUALS   153

    Annuals for the New Orleans Garden, 157
    Annuals by Season of Bloom, 176

PERENNIALS   179

    Perennials for the New Orleans Garden, 182
    The Daylily, 209
    Perennials by Season of Bloom, 215

BULBS, CORMS, TUBERS, RHIZOMES   219

    The Louisiana Iris, 223, Bulbs, Corms, Tubers,
    Rhizomes for the New Orleans Garden, 225
    Bulbous Plants by Season of Bloom, 263

NATIVE TREES AND SHRUBS   267

    Native Trees & Shrubs
      for the New Orleans Garden, 275
    Deciduous Trees, 275, Deciduous Shrubs, 284
    Evergreen Trees, 289, Evergreen Shrubs, 294
    Palms, Palmettos, 298, Trees for Fall Color, 299

FERNS   301

    Culture of Ferns, 305
    Ferns for the New Orleans Garden, 308

WILDFLOWERS   313
    Wildflowers for the New Orleans Garden, 320
    Wildflowers by Season of Bloom, 337
LAWNS AND GROUNDCOVERS   341
    Ground Covers for the New Orleans Garden, 347
THE WILDLIFE GARDEN   349
    Water, 360, Shelter, 362, Plants, 363
    Plants for the Wildlife Garden, 366
    The Hummingbird Garden, 368
    Plants for the Hummingbird Garden, 373
    The Butterfly and Moth Garden, 376
    Moths, 380
    Plants for the Butterfly & Moth Garden, 383
    The Bee Garden, 386
    Bats in the New Orleans Garden, 389
SPECIAL GARDENS   393
    Container Gardens, 397, Water Gardens, 399
    The Fragrance Garden, 401
    The Shade Garden, 403
    The New Orleans Herb Garden, 410
HISTORIC GARDENING   421
    Plants in Traditional New Orleans Gardens, 427
    The Garden of 1799, 427
    Of the 1830's, 428
    Of the 1850's, 428
    Lelievre's Plant Recommendations, 1838, 431
    Border Plants for 1895, 433
    A History, 435
        Colonial Era: 1718-1803, 436
        Antebellum Era: 1803-1860, 440
        Cotton Exposition: 1860-1900, 453
        Modern Era: 1900-1990, 462
APPENDICES   485
    Notes, 486
    Bibliography, 495
    Botanical Names, 500
    Resources, 502
    Index, 514

Michael Ledet

Introduction

"New Orleans is different."

Hilda Latapie, April 13, 1989

New Orleans is different. Everybody knows that, not just Hilda Latapie. But with fifty years of gardening under her belt, she really knows the implications of the difference. She qualifies advice with the comment, "I'm only an amateur, but...." Not many amateurs have won The Herbert Medal of the American Plant Life Society. This honor was bestowed on her and her husband Walter in 1982 "for eminent service". Years of committed gardening culminated in their developing the first white double amaryllis. As Mr. Latapie was color blind, Hilda did all the cross-pollinating in their work. "Of course it didn't matter with the whites...."

On April 13, 1989 I did not really need a street address to find the Latapie garden on Elysian Fields Avenue. Its spring splendor called for the superlatives used for late Victorian English gardens. It was *"blazing with colour"*! I saw plantings in rounded beds both freestanding and edging the house and walks as well as in pots of every size and shape.

"I plant so much, I sometimes forget what I planted," Mrs. Latapie says. She recommends always sowing "easy" plants with the hard, so the glorious color of nasturtiums can console you when your ranunculus fails. Blooming was a collection of natives and exotics, traditional plants with new hybrids: orange flowered native azalea and Louisiana blue phlox, small-flowered Margo Koster polyantha roses, pink watsonia, freestanding orange and red gloriosa climbing lilies, new hybrid petunias and pansies, local favorite red geraniums. Potted pink Mandevilla vine, a souvenir of the 1984 World's Fair, climbed its trellis. Formosa lilies (a find! as few lilies repeat well in New Orleans) emerged for summer bloom in feathery-foliaged stands. She pointed out the narcissus, long since finished blooming, which were rescued from destruction from the grounds of the demolished Kolb home in Gentilly. The flowers "like paperwhites, but bigger" repeat yearly in ever enlarging clumps. She knows so much! I filled a notepad with pointers during my two-hour visit. Mrs. Latapie confided that she was one of Rachel Daniel's secret sources of "grassroots" information for the column "Green Gardens," in the *Times-Picayune* until 1988.

According to the National Gardening Association in 1988, 78 per cent of America's households gardened. Much of this enlarged market is inexperienced, yet heavily targeted for advertising of horticultural products. This makes for even more risks for the new gardener in New Orleans than in other years and other places. As fullfilling fantasies is so frequently part of the pleasure of planning as well as planting the garden, novices can be easy prey for the barrage of mail offering books and products which will "...make your gardening dreams come true," plants and bulbs which will "...bloom year after year with little care." They may in other parts of the country, but New Orleans is different. Experimenting is fun if you realize that is what you are doing. You can throw away a lot of money and suffer severe disappointment if your plans do not consider the peculiarities of this city when you order seeds and plants.

Because so many of the rules for other locales do not apply here, Mrs. Latapie and other long-time experimental gardeners are probably the most important source of information. Of the limited references available on New Orleans gardening, the most valuable are based on hands-on experience. "Ask the lady next door," can be the best advice. I should not leave out the men who are experienced gardeners; after all, the Men's Amaryllis Club does entertain entries from ladies! (Actually, according to Vincent Peuler, there used to be ladies in the Amaryllis Club. They left in 1958. "The women said it was because the men were too much trouble, but the men said it was because they won all the prizes!" The women formed their own club, now defunct.)

During a drive along Constance, Laurel, or Annunciation Streets you will see many shotgun houses fronted with small, fenced, "doorstep" gardens. Often they are no more than collections of potted plants, well tended. A talk with the gardener will give you all kinds of pointers on plant propagation, as many of their prizes originated from stealthily snatched or freely given cuttings from other gardens. Collected plants are common in doorstep gardens: natives from the swamps (iris and swamp lily), old plants from abandoned yards (St. Joseph's lily, 'Louis Philippe' roses), exotics from the more affluent gardens during the walk from the St. Charles streetcar stop to Annunciation closer to the River (Kahili ginger). Some plants (white rain-lily) which were exotic introductions escaped cultivation to be returned by a doorstep garden-collector.

Some imports introduced during the late Victorian era, or by wealthy botanist-plantation masters in the early 19th century or earlier travel from garden to garden.

Spores of maidenhair fern, the ladder brake (China), and the sword fern (Canary Islands) find moist, alkaline nitches such as are common in the masonry of our cemetaries and old brick walls and walks. They have earned the name "cemetary plants". A *Times-Picayune* garden columnist pen-named Lady Banksia noted in a 1935 article the "rock ferns" which grow in the "bricks of bygone centuries" revealed by "peeling stucco" in French Quarter gardens. The image has become one of the symbols of the French Quarter. The deterioration which allowed such ferny growth would not occur in a well maintained home. Wandering exotics may or may not be allowed to stay in a doorstep garden where plants are ageless, "bygone century" just means old and things which grow where they shouldn't could be considered weedy.

Flowers are the stars of the above little gardens, not landscaping, though some design ideas may have also been picked up during the walk from St. Charles towards the River. They are exclusive worlds even though shared; personal expressions of creativity. Though the gardeners respond to admiration, I think they would continue their labors completely unacknowledged because of the private rewards.

These are not the gardens described in tour guides and horticultural histories yet in a sense they contain all of gardening that has gone before and the germ of the future. They are here and I think they have probably always been even though their styles and magnitudes have changed through the years. They are the New Orleans versions of the English Cottage garden which dates to the Middle Ages and the French herb and vegetable garden, sources of food, medicines, scents to override daily odors in a less washed time, and the beauty of herbal flowers.

For aesthetic and ecological reasons, modern gardening interests are expanding into areas such as planting for birds and butterflies and growing wildflowers. More extensive use of native plants, planting for wildlife, redu-

cing lawn in favor of groundcovers and other low maintainence practices conserve energy and dwindling natural
resources. We may look to doorstep gardens for ideas.

I heard a story recently in P. J.'s Coffeehouse on
Magazine Street which illustrates the rapidly changing
world focus. In 1963 a local adventurer shipped one-
hundred rubythroated hummingbirds from Central America, home. The birds had been snatched by natives with
flashlights from branches where, in nighttime torpor, they
slept.

The contact in New Orleans who received the shipment asked:

"What do you want me to do with a hundred hummingbirds?"

"Sell them to the Hummingbird Bar and Grill!" he
was told.

And he did. Or did he?

Though the storyteller's eyes twinkled as he related
the tale, he admitted that the sense of unlimited natural
resources which would allow such a flamboyant act or
even such a tale so few years ago is a severe contrast to
attitudes engendered by today's world of endangered lists,
dwindling habitats, vanishing species, and organizations
such as the Nature Conservancy. Today's heroes are the
amateur and professional naturalists, who capture the wild
through photography, art, the printed word, story telling,
or maybe just keep it in their memories. Today's adventure can be found in far away places or as close to home
as your own back yard or your front doorstep when you
create a habitat for indigenous plant and animal life in
your garden.

Modern issues as well as the principles of a New
World identity in gardening and landscape design are
articulated by Carole Ottesen in *The New American Garden*,
1987. She says:

*Emerging all over the country, American style gardens brim
with soft, full, relaxed--often wild--plantings that complement
the local landscape, adapt to regional growing conditions, and
respond to seasonal change.   These are gardens that express
themselves in the vernacular, often using native plants and
drawing inspiration from the natural setting, rather than
from conventional gardening models.   They are nostalgic
gardens, restoring the unique flora of a new land.*[1]

To me, looking for a monkey puzzle now represents
all the mysteries, secrets, adventures of gardening.
Through the search for this Chilean oddity, popular with
botanical collectors during Victorian times, I found many
other plants in places I would not have otherwise gone,
met people who showed me their gardens and told me
their secrets.   People who remember the monkey puzzles
in New Orleans speak in wondrous terms of their shapes
and sizes.   Some such as Skip Treme' and Kevin Bleichner
of the Parkway and Park Commission, were as intrigued
as I by the mystery.   They remembered that before the
1983 freeze monkey puzzles grew on Robert E. Lee, and
Bunya-Bunyas (Australian *Araucarias*) on Farnum Place.

"There are monkey puzzle trees growing in botanical
gardens in Vancouver, British Columbia.   Why not here?"
they wondered.

Skip experienced the same disappointment as I when,
"...I thought I'd found one, but when I got up close, I
realized it was a Cunningham Fir."

Dr. Lawrence P. O'Meallie photographed one on a
birdwatching trip to Chile.   It towered over all the other
trees.   "It was big!" he said.

Dottie and Phillip Gardner found a monkey puzzle in
a botanical garden in New Zealand.   In the photo Phillip
took, a dot-like Dottie stood in front to demonstrate its
enormous size.

I hope this book will encourage you to see gardening
in New Orleans as an adventure.   I hope it will lead you
to explore the wealth of gardening resources found in our

city. I hope it will encourage you to support research to solve the mysteries of our local past and recreate historical gardens.

I hope you will enjoy the excitement of discovering new plants. I have shared my failures as well as successes to help you avoid some of the problems I encountered. Most of all, I hope to encourage you to look toward the future by planting for wildlife or growing wildflowers. I feel cultivation of these interests at home has to create a greater consciousness of the beauty and fragility of the natural world outside the garden.

The garden which is more conscious of nature and conservation issues will, I predict, have its own personality in New Orleans, maybe in each section of New Orleans. Its identity will blend the many identities which came before, yet allow them to remain separate, reflecting in our gardens the quality which, to me, is the appeal of New Orleans as a city.

There are many local experts with whom I make no effort to compete, and whose names I offer as resources. I am not the most knowledgeable amateur I know. I am more an exhuberant gardener than a careful one. If I seem to be dropping names throughout the text, I am. This book is also about friends and heroes: those who have taken the time to teach, to listen, to laugh, to share in many ways. If there are those whose experiences differ from mine, great! I am always willing to consider revising my point of view and to allow others their own. An important message I hope to get across is that gardening, learning about gardening, and every aspect in the evolution of my garden (from the first tropical effort which was smushed by a freeze, through the barnyard phase, to the present combination wildlife, ornamental, and sculpture garden) has been an immense amount of fun...as much fun as looking for a monkey puzzle! That is what I wish for everyone!

Dara Rosenzweig

Basics

"Earthworms will be America's salvation!"

Edward McLellan, September 7, 1988

The logical place to start a book on gardening is at the ground.

"Talk to Eddie," said my husband, Jean. Edward McLellan is a forester who has a knowledge of soil via his occupation and his interest in earthworms. But we didn't think he would eat one! He spoke fervently on the potential of worms as a garbage disposal system. Composted waste could be used as food for the earthworms which reproduce rapidly. There is a limited market for compost, but the worms, themselves, could be harvested in vast quantities to serve as a cheap but nutritious feed for catfish and other human food sources.

Eddie feels that humans, in our world of hunger, could more directly benefit from the nutrients in worms. Raw, or purged in salt and cooked (with crab boil, maybe?), they are a rich source of protein.

As his oratory reached a feverish pitch, he abruptly

stopped, raced to his front yard, returned with a medium sized, but plump and healthy-looking very wiggly worm which he popped into his mouth and swallowed in one gulp. Jean says he chewed, but I prefer to think that he didn't.

I asked his wife, Kit, what kissing someone with earthworm breath is like. Her answer is unprintable.

Earthworms   play an important role in creating the type of "ground" in which plants will flourish, but more about them later. The ground is very definately the place to start gardening. My neighbor, Mike McClung of Four Seasons Landscape Maintainence feels that all other money spent in installing a garden is wasted if soil preparation is not addressed first, especially   given the handicaps faced by New Orleans gardeners.   When he is landscaping a yard on a tight budget, Mike uses smaller plants rather than cutting back on proper soil preparation.

Mike is pessimistic about people's interest in this most important aspect of gardening.   "Very few people will read that chapter," he predicts.

I think understanding the geology of the area helps to see why soil preparation is so important.   Maybe it can make the subject more interesting, too. Maybe not....

THE SOIL

The ground on which Greater New Orleans rests is the floodplain of the Mississippi River.   Our soil is alluvial, deposited by the River as velocities slowed and during flooding through the centuries. A system of levees and the Bonnet Carre Spillway have changed those patterns, now, though sand and silt are still deposited upon the battures, riverside of the levees.

Other than the tops of the levees, which can reach twenty-six feet above sea level, the greatest elevations in our area are the actual banks of the river.   They are levees, too, natural as opposed to man-made.   The big "levees" maintained by the Corps of Engineers were built on top of the natural river banks which rise to 12 feet above sea level. The man-made levee along Lake Pontchartrain is 9 feet above sea level. Formations such as Gentilly and Metairie Ridges and Bayou des Famillies on the West Bank are the edges of former Mississippi River distributaries, 3 to 7 feet above sea level.

As the River overflowed during spring floods, it dropped its load of sediment heaviest particles first, leaving soils of differing character: sand to silt to clay; in slopes from the natural levees and flood plains of the Mississippi to swamps and marshes. As areas of marsh were drained and filled, some parts of the City actually became lower, as much as five feet below sea level near Lake Pontchartrain in Jefferson Parish. You can see this difference if you look toward land from the Causeway. The eaves of the houses beyond the levee appear Lake level!

In spite of all this discussion of elevations, we know the differences are not that great. New Orleans is a low City. But, Clair Brown says: *"Six inches of difference in elevation are more significant in changing the plant communities in Louisiana than 100 feet in the mountains."*[2] The plants which grew on the levees and in swamps and marshes, lived and died, adding organic matter to the soil as marsh grass muck, peat, or humus in small amounts or large which stayed or dissipated, depending on the water saturation of the soil in different locations.

Water, earth, and plant and animal life interact mechanically and chemically to create many different soil types. Poor drainage is common to all in New Orleans, due to soil makeup, underlying clay layers, and the low elevation. The mechanical drainage applied by the system of pumps which rids the city of excess water has lowered the water table. Because of all the changes man has made to build a city on swamps and marshes, soils can be different from one lot to the next.

The silty-loamy soils of the levees and floodplains of the river, including the spillway, source of much of the "river sand" used for landfill in the Greater New Orleans area, are alkaline. This is because of their mineral content and also the fact that underlying clay prevents the leaching of minerals which changes the pH.

In marshy or swampy areas, soils consist more of clay and accumulated plant material. When exposed to air, as by subsurface drainage, the organic layers begin to break down, either slowly or in dry weather, quickly, by burning. (When I was a teenager living in Jefferson Parish, I remember being told that certain seasonal smells were "Peat moss burning underground.") Breakdown of organic matter causes an acidic reaction, changing the pH in upper layers from its natural neutral or alkaline state.

When the Floral Trail project, begun in 1935, was threatened due to the expense of acid soil for the sixty miles of azaleas and camellias to be planted, the area was scouted for new sources. The New Orleans Floral Trail, Inc. purchased a once marshy tract in Kenner. Civic leader Sam Zemurray, donated ten acres in Little Woods. "Kenner" and "Little Woods" soils became synonomous with the rich, acidic earth which provides the perfect medium for New Orleans' favorite shrubs.[3]

The only non-alluvial deposits in the New Orleans area are those of shells of the marsh clam, *Rangia cuneata*, which line the bottom of the Lake and are found in large refuse piles called middens left by Indians from as early as 500 B. C. on. These and oyster shells deposited by modern man are found compacted in old yards just about any place you decide you want to dig to start a new garden!

MODIFYING THE SOIL FOR GARDENING

To be successful in growing anything other than the native species found in your yard, you will probably have to make some changes to compensate for the poor drainage and poor suitability of most soils found naturally in the area for gardening. One cynical gardener told me he doesn't know anyone who has achieved real success in New Orleans without complete soil replacement in planting areas.

Mr. Henry Lawrence addressed drainage problems with soil replacement in his 1841 garden as reported in the *"Daily Picayune"* (1866): *"...The very soil* (was) *brought from foreign climes....Kensington gravel on the walks. Soil of Devonshire forms the basis of many a flowerbed."*

French Quarter garden beds were raised to improve drainage in the early 18th century. Raised beds are still strongly recommended all over New Orleans. They are essential for best results from roses and camellias. Directions for camellia planting from the Magnolia Nurseries catalogue of 1859 aim to achieve the same conditions as today: *"...if the ground is wet, throw out the soil 2 or 3 feet deep, fill one foot of the bottom with brick rubbish. Fill up the bed with surface soil from the woods, let it settle,..."*

One modern option is "synthetic soil" made up of combinations of selected organic and mineral components in proper proportions. The "soil-less mixes" sold as potting soil are in this category. Some landscape men offer their own formulae of synthetic soil for use on a larger scale in outdoor beds. Most soil is not so far beyond help that it cannot be improved rather than completely replaced.

The first step in soil preparation should be to get your soil tested through the Cooperative Extension Service or test it yourself with a commercial kit to "get the dirt on your dirt". The Extension Service sends a little cardboard box for the sample. You mail it back. They analyze it, and send a report which tells you your problems and suggests remedies. If there seem to be several soil types in your yard, you will need to collect a specimen of each. For each sample, dig six inches deep in three to six locations within the soil type area and mix the soils well.

A soil report can tell you the texture of your soil, its fertility, pH, and information on special problems for old-home owners such as lead buildup from the scrapings of lead based paint after many years of home maintainence.

The best garden soil is one with proportions of sand, silt, clay, and humus to produce fertility, and a consistency which is workable, well-aerated, well-drained yet retentive of moisture and nutrients. You can tell by the "feel" of moistened soil when you rub it between your thumb and fingers whether it has too much clay (slippery with glutinous clumps) or too much sand (grainy). A more exact do-it-yourself method is to put soils from different parts of your yard into a quart jar two/thirds full of water with 1 teaspoon of Calgon (a dispersing agent). Particles will settle out in the same order as when dropping out of overflowing river water, heaviest to the bottom. You can see the makeup of your soil in the depths of the different layers. The desirable proportions form a textural class geologists call loam: 40 percent sand, 40 percent silt, 20 percent clay. You can add organic matter in amounts up to one-third of the final soil to correct imperfections.

Sand and silt contain the minerals needed for plant growth. Because silt is finer, it exposes more surface area for mechanical breakdown and chemical reaction, which are how minerals are released. Our "river sand", sold as "batture sand" by R. Maitre in 1875, is a productive medium for plant growth.

Organic matter is important because it affects the texture of the soil, but also because it decomposes to become the dark and gummy substance called humus. Humus provides a home for the microorganisms which cause decay of organic wastes and the release of nitrogen, carbon dioxide and mineral nutrients for plant growth. It also forms a moist coating around each soil particle, where dissolved minerals are held, readily available to plant's roots.

Peat moss, rotted animal manures, nitrogen fortified sawdust, ground bark, leaf mold, and compost are examples of organic matter. Decayed materials, not fresh, should be incorporated into the soil because the microorganisms which cause breakdown of fresh material use nitrogen at so rapid a rate during the early part of the process that they can deplete the soil of that element.

Humus must be replaced on a continual basis as it is used up. Organic materials for humus production should be placed on the surface or worked into the top layers of the soil, depending on your philosophy and your leisure/ gardening time. I put most on the surface.

A well managed compost heap is an ideal source of matter for soil improvement. Every gardening book but this one tells you how to construct one.[4]

My plans for the future have always included a compost. I put refuse such as tea leaves, coffee grounds, chopped banana peels and other vegetable and fruit waste from my kitchen which would go in a compost in spots around the garden. Each autumn, I collect fallen leaves from Chesne, the oak tree on the corner, for organic replenishment as well as winter protective mulch. It seems to work.

The finer the texture of organic matter, the faster it breaks down. Whether it is added to a compost or placed on the ground, it should be machine shredded or chopped manually. The nutrients taken from the soil by plants can be returned if end-of-season annuals and trimmed dead growth from perennials and shrubs are chopped or shredded. Be careful not to use diseased plants. Even though chopping pruned branches takes forever with our small machine, I feel virtuous when I see the results of my labor: uniformly sized pieces of freeze-dead angel's trumpet branches or black-eyed susan vines protecting then enriching the garden soil as mulch.

Different gardeners develop practices suited to their own lifestyles. Mike McClung says one of the healthiest gardens he knows belongs to the wife of a committed fisherman who buries fishheads and other debris of each catch in her flower beds. Mike says even buried "tin" cans are good, as they offer trace minerals to the soil. He does not understand or endorse the practice of one of his uptown gardening clients who buries old pantyhose among her azaleas.

A balanced soil, to which additional organic material for humus formation is added on a regular basis (at least once a year) should provide all the nutrients needed for healthy plant growth. A fertilizer can be added for additional nutrients if you must.

If plants are not thriving, test your soil to see if it may be deficient in one of the major nutrients needed for plant growth: Nitrogen, Phosphorus, Potassium. Their proportions are represented, in that order, by the numbers on fertilizer labels. Other nutrients, as well as smaller amounts of trace elements are needed, but the above three are the most important and the most often lacking.

A "complete" fertilizer contains amounts of all three essential macronutrients. (Examples are 8-8-8 or 5-10-10, etc.) For gardeners without specialized knowledge, these are safer to use than single nutrient fertilizers (0-0-60 or 0-10-10, etc.). Chemical fertilizers are quick acting and powerful and can be more damaging than helpful if they are overdone. Except for the special preparations I buy for roses and camellia/azaleas, 8-8-8 is the only chemical fertilizer I use. I don't use it too regularly.

Organic fertilizers are more expensive than chemicals, but their slow-release makes them safer. They do not concentrate in the soil to burn plant roots and harm earthworms and other beneficial organisms.

The most popular fertilizers of the last century were advertised in the *"Daily Picayune"* of December 1, 1860 by J. S. Holden & Co. at Poydras and Magazine Streets:

"Peruvian Guano, manipulated Guano (Peruvian Guano and Phosphate of Lime), Mexican Guano, Ground bones."

Except for guano (excrement of sea fowl or bats), the same organics are preferred today: blood and bone meals, fish emulsion, and manures. Bone meal is my favorite for bulb planting. I would love to be able to say I fertilized with bat droppings!

Most plants require a soil which is slightly acid (pH of about 6.5), though some, such as azaleas, camellias, and some hollies, require more acidic conditions and some need alkalinity. (A pH of 7.0 is neutral, below that is acid, above is alkaline.) The wrong pH prevents utilization of nutrients from fertilizers and from soil by your plants.

Most areas of New Orleans have alkaline or basic soil. A soil test can tell you your soil's pH for sure. Beds near house foundations are frequently alkaline, because lime from the mortar in brick piers and chain walls leaches into the soil. Our city's tap water is alkaline, too, so many waterings of corrected soil can cause it to return to a basic condition. Years of disposal of oyster shells in the back yards of homes either after seafood feasts or as landfill, has added a factor contributing to the alkalinity of already alkaline soil. Debris from old home renovation has left dangerously alkaline levels in foundation soil around these houses. Even if your home is in a formerly marshy or swampy area which has acidic soil, the fill added to make up for subsidence after drainage was probably alkaline.

Add sulphur or aluminum sulfate to your soil to increase acidity, lime to decrease acidity. Additions should be based on test results and not be overdone. Sulphur is slower acting than aluminum sulfate, but its use will not entail risk of a buildup of aluminum which can be toxic to plant growth. Other actions which counteract extreme alkalinity are the use of peat moss, which is

acidic, as a component of the soil during amendment.
Using pine leaves as a mulch helps keep soil on the acid
side. Oak leaves are acidic first but become alkaline as
they age. Fertilizers designed for acid-loving plants usually provide a pH-lowering agent.

The following chart summarizes pH information and
tells lots more if you read it carefully! I found it in *The
Culture of Azaleas and Camellias in New Orleans Soils* by
William M. Garic, published by the Parkway Commission
of New Orleans and reproduced in the *1949 Report.*

pH BASIC
    12.2 - Lime
    10.0 - Bone meal and ashes
     9.5 - New Orleans purified City Water
     8.6 - Mississippi River sand
     8.4 - Most animal manures, under N.O. conditions due to liming
          as required by health regulations
     8.4 - Untreated Mississippi River water
     8.4 - Charcoal Dust
8.4-8.2 - Soil conditions in most N.O. gardens caused by continued
          use of alkaline materials
     7.8 - Oakleaf mould
     7.4 - Natural New Orleans clay soil
     7.0 - Rain water, Neutral point--approximately
6.0-5.6 - Roses do best in soil of this value
     5.4 - Bagasse
     5.2 - Freshly fallen oak leaves
     5.0 - Lake Shore and Lake View District soils
5.0-4.5 - Best soil condition for azaleas and camellias
     4.5 - Coffee and tea grounds
     4.0 - Peat moss and cottonseed meal
     3.2 - Aluminum sulphate
     2.5 - Superphosphate--Manganese
     1.2 - Sulphur (It takes sulphur six months to become completely
          available)
pH ACID

Earthworms, insects, centipedes, millipedes, and, less
commonly in the home garden, crawfish, play an important part in aerating the soil through burrowing and tun-

neling practices. The tunnels allow for the movement of water, too, helping drainage.

The most common southern worm is the common field worm, *Allolobophora caliginosa*. *Lumbricus terrestris*, the night crawler, is the largest earthworm. Worms are not usually seen by day, but, by night, they come to the surface to dine on dead leaves and whatever other organic matter they find. These are carried deep into the soil by the worms, where they are deposited as wastes in the form of "castings" which are rich in bacteria and the essential elements needed by plants.

Mel Bartholomew in *Square Foot Gardening* compares earthworms to rototillers. In woodlands or open fields where old plant growth and fallen leaves accumulate to offer food for the worms, they tunnel up and down constantly, keeping the soil turned, loose, and light. The same conditions can be created in your New Orleans garden once you get rid of the oyster shells. One philosophy proposes leaving tilling completely to the worms, as turning the soil with garden tools causes destruction of earthworms, eggs, and burrows.

The use of mulches is an attempt to mimic nature in the garden and to obtain all the benefits of deteriorating organic material for the soil. There may be beds in which a permanent mulch would not be desirable, for instance, those where the plantings are changed each season.

In addition to enrichment, mulching can offer other benefits:
1. It helps keep the soil moist by slowing evaporation of water.
2. It helps regulate soil temperature, in our hot summers, keeping it cooler.
3. It helps control weeds by preventing them from sprouting. Those which do sprout in the mulch are easy to pull.

Black plastic, which is widely recommended to block weed growth, is not a good idea in the New Orleans area, as it can keep the earth too warm during our steamy summers.

Some good mulches are:

1.   Layers of newspaper. I soak the paper in water first, so the wind does not blow it away before I weight it with mulch. Six or seven layers of bark or leaves on top hide it and hold it in place. In a year's time, the paper, which is a wood product, has deteriorated. I rake back the mulch, add layers of paper, and replace the mulch.

2.   Barks of various kinds and sizes. Smaller size results in faster breakdown.

3.   Compost.

4.   Bagasse. This by-product of sugar production is readily available in Louisiana. It is slightly acidic as it breaks down.

5.   Leaves. Pine and fresh oak leaves help keep the soil acid.

6.   Grass clippings. Apply them loosely. They can stick together, forming mats which can heat up and harm plants as they decompose.

7.   Sawdust. Add Nitrogen to prevent the deficiency of that element which can occur in the soil as sawdust decomposes.

Now that the basic form of my garden is established, beds are raised, soil is replaced or amended, tons of oyster shells and archeological debris is removed, my main cultural practice is the addition of organic material as mulch, to enrich the soil, and to create the perfect environment for earthworms. The soil is tilled in the immediate vicinity of the new plants I introduce and when Ian Jordan comes with his Daddy, Jonny, to dig for worms. He finds the fattest, squirmiest earthworms, and more per square foot than anywhere else in the uptown area. Eddie McLellan knows it, too!

CLIMATIC CONSIDERATIONS

"Someone has facetiously remarked that New Orleans has no climate; it has only weather....we have some wonderful weather throughout the varying seasons; many days that make our City famous, and some that make it infamous,..."[5]

If you have ever used the *Time-Life Encyclopedia of Gardening* as a reference, you have seen this phrase in some plant descriptions: *"...grows in Zone 9 except in Florida and along the Gulf Coast."* [6]

The Zone 9 designation is from a hardiness map, which is based on average annual minimum temperatures alone. This map, which you see often in seed catalogs and gardening books, is devised by the U.S. Department of Agriculture and is based on records from the U.S. Weather Bureau. An updated version, newly available and more sensitive to regional differences, puts the New Orleans area in Zones 8b and 9a. The flaw in using these system is that more than just resistance to low temperatures determines a plant's hardiness. But, despite the limitations, the hardiness map should be your starting point for plant selection. Temperature is still the most useful criteria of whether a particular plant will make it in your garden.

Described as "semi-tropical" and "hot and humid", our climate is mild, but can offer some extremes of heat and cold. Temperatures are modified by the bodies of water which surround the city and by the proximity of the Gulf. We can experience winters without a freeze at all, or... remember the winter of 1962-63 when most camphor trees froze?[7] The snows and bad freezes are infrequent enough here that they become remembered milestones. My son David claims to remember the snowman he built during the winter of 1973 when his sister Dara was a newborn and he was two. Jean Seidenberg will never forget 1982 when, as my new husband, he had the opportunity to show off his sculptor's talents while repairing all the water pipes which split in the hard freeze of that year.

Two-thirds of the years, our lowest temperature is 24 degrees or above. Lowest temperatures reached are below 10 degrees, though thankfully not very often! The *Times-Picayune* reported on December 24, 1989, that the 12 degrees measured the morning before in Audubon Park was the lowest temperature recorded since the 7 degrees measured at the same site in 1899. Cold spells which can occur from mid-November to mid-March do not usually last over three to four days. Thirty-two degree temperatures can occur as early as December 5 and as late as February 20, but we don't usually see a freeze before Christmas. March 15 is considered the earliest truly safe date for planting caladiums, a standard for tender plantings.

I have heard people speculate after a freeze that the climate is changing. It may be, but sudden freezes, devastating to flora fooled into early spring performance have long been a part of the New Orleans experience. Sylvanus wrote in 1851 in *Notes on Southern Horticulture*:

> It was near the first of March, and--do not feel envious-- green peas were ready for the table; as I passed a coffeehouse, the fragrant scent of fresh mint, as some dry citizen was imbibing a julep, floated invitingly into the street, and--restrain your feelings--a bowl of fresh strawberries, the very first of the season, had that morning been announced as having been deposited in the sanctum of some lucky editor. The next day 'came a frost, a killing frost--pea blossoms wilted, strawberries soured, and mint-juleps gave way to hot toddies.' But this lasted only a few days.[8]

Grace Matt Thompson describes the winter of 1946 and her protective measures:

> Last year the winter was what you call severe; the ice on the pool would hold you up. I despaired; I could see the loss of all my garden. I banked all the roots with sharp sand, then I turned the hose on everything at 5 A.M., before the sun could shine on the plants. I did not lose a plant.[9]

Because of the inconsistency of our seasonal patterns, there will never be an absolutely fool proof method of choosing non-indigenous plants. Some need more cold and a longer dormant period than New Orleans provides (peonies). Others do fine with our heat, but need protection when a freeze threatens (*Hibiscus rosa-sinensis*). Still others handle the climate well until that occasional severe temperature drop, such as the one in 1982 which killed all the bottlebrushes.

Early experiences with sub-32 degree temps precipitated an increase in the number of evergreen items in my garden. My first inclination had been to create a tropical place fantasy: banana trees, elephant ears, split-leaf philodrendron, coleus, impatiens, etc. After the first freeze, all that was left was slime and mush. Of course, a lot grows back, but a little ivy and a few evergreen hollies and azaleas are nicer to look at than the bleakness of a frozen garden.

Plants can be protected to minimize the damage suffered when a freeze is expected.

1. Pile heavy mulch around the base of semi-tropical shrubs and tender bulbs at the beginning of winter to save last-minute running around when the forecast says: "freeze."

2. Place heavy paper cartons or black plastic nursery flower pots over tender bedding plants and lilies. Remove them as soon as the temperature rises above 32 degrees.

3. Water the soil heavily to drive cold-attracting air from the vicinity of plant roots. Lightly water plants to replace lost moisture as they begin to thaw. These measures help reduce evaporation from the plant, and, therefore, reduce the drying which is "freeze damage".

Once freeze damage has occurred, certain measures are recommended:

1. Remove the parts of the tropical bulbous and herbaceous perennials, such as crinums, spider lilies, amaryllis, bird-of-paradise and red hot poker, which are left mushy

after the freeze to prevent decay of the rest of the plant, then apply a mulch.

2.   Delay pruning of woody plants until new growth emerges in the spring. Dead tissue and even leaves offer protection for the rest of the winter and in the event of another temperature drop.

3.   Do not apply fertilizer containing nitrogen.

4.   Spray shrubs such as azaleas, camellias, pittosporums, ligustrums, Italian cypress, osmanthus, viburnums, boxwood, and Indian hawthorn with a fungicide soon after a dry freeze. Spraying can prevent infection which can result if surface fungi enter the microscopic fissures left on damaged stems and branches.

During our warm winters, many plants continue blooming beyond the time when, in areas which follow stricter patterns, they would have ceased. What is a plant to do if it "blooms until frost" and there is no frost? The sporadic bloom which appears on trees such as flowering pear when cold weather is late, result in a reduced intensity of spring display. Late freezes push the bloom of spring-flowering plants later.

In addition to the yearly variation in minimum winter temperature; the horticultural environment is affected by extremes in precipitation patterns, high humidity, tropical storms, and wind patterns, which together create the peculiar set of conditions which is New Orleans.

Hurricanes can upset plant patterns, causing unseasonable bloom. For example, the complete defoliation of trees caused by the strong winds of a storm stimulate the production of new leaves and flowers several weeks afterwards. The same effect can be produced by too heavy pruning after a storm, exposing the new growth and the plant as a whole to damage in an early freeze.

Even in a mild winter, Gulf breezes combined with high humidity make temperatures seem "bitter cold". The same humidity in the summer makes the heat seem more intense. My sister, Judy Keim, in Arizona loves to say that 105 degrees in Mesa is not as bad as 80 here because, "We don't have all that humidity in Mesa." These factors affect plants, too.

Our average yearly rainfall is approximately 60 inches, considered heavy, yet there can be very dry periods. We have rain for an average of 120 days. Mid-December to mid-March is a rainy period, but heavy rain can occur any time of the year--to as much as fourteen inches during a twenty-four hour period. Though snow is not common, it can occur.

Clair Brown best describes the effect the amount and distribution of rainfall have on native plant growth patterns:

> *There is the spring dry spell which starts about mid April and extends until the June rains (if they come). Our spring blooming plants start to mature and dry up. Thus the spring plants which reached their peak of bloom in March and April will be gone by June. There is a summer flora which is enhanced in volume when stimulated by the midsummer rains. This gives way to a more xeric fall flora of the usual September-October dry spell which may extend into November.*[10]

These patterns should be remembered when bedding plants are being chosen.

MICROCLIMATES

Sunlight, wind, rain, and temperature interact in the same way in your yard as they do in our geographical area as a whole to produce conditions which can support plants with a variety of climatic needs. Architectural elements such as walls, fences, buildings and deliberately placed plants can act in the same way, but on a smaller scale to influence air flow patterns, block or allow sunlight, direct or hold precipitation, therefore affecting humidity, temperature, light.

Combine manipulation of climatic elements with soil adjustment to greatly enhance your capacity to produce an array of microcosms. There are still the limitations of the climate as a whole, but the possibility of creating just the right setting for a plant which otherwise wouldn't do here can be a stimulus for experimentation. And, more basically, proper preparation and selection of a site gives you more control of your investment of time and money in the plants you place there. With creation of an appropriate environment, or proper selection of plants for the existing clime or climes in your garden, you maximize the chances of your plants surviving and thriving.

Man-made structures can be used in many ways to help form climatic microcosms. The phrases "southern" or "northern exposure" as indicators of sunlight intensity are familiar to most of us. Control of light can be achieved in other ways than selecting a proper spot in relation to one's home. Trees and shrubs can be planted in such a way as to block the sun's rays, creating shade. Ground covers and different colors and textures of paved and mulched surfaces affect reflection and absorption of light, and therefore temperature. Trees and shrubs or fences and walls which serve as screens to block wind and otherwise redirect air flow which alters evaporation patterns and influences moisture content in the air and ground.

Plant descriptions give you clues as to climatic needs, both with hardiness zone designation and other information, for example:

"Cleome prefers a hot, dry location, but will tolerate some shade."

"Cynoglossum thrives in full sun or partial shade, and tolerates both wet and dry locations."

"Gazanias grow well in windy places, need full sun, will prosper in dry soils. They grow best when summer temperatures are in the 80s and 90s."

I ordered seeds for *Jacaranda mimosifolia* which Park Seed Company described as a "pot plant". It grew very rapidly. On a trip to the San Diego Zoo, I found a small label which said *"Jacaranda mimosifolia"* in front of a 40 foot high tree. I knew then that the pot was not going to hold up for long. Reading gave me further information: "Zone 10. Used as ornamentals in all the tropical countries of the world and in southern Florida and southern California." When I saw a blooming *Jacaranda* in the botanical garden in Palermo, Sicily, I knew how badly I wanted its feathery textured leaves and beautiful clusters of blue flowers for my own garden. I took it out of the pot and planted it in the narrowest part of the yard where its lower trunk was shielded from wind and cold air by a wooden fence on one side, the house on another, and a structure containing a hot water heater on a third. The southern exposure maximizes solar radiation. The right microcosm? It became twenty feet high lasted six years, blooming the last three. It died in the freeze of December, 1989. By June of 1990 it was coming back from the roots. We can't wait to see blooms again!

I tried lavender in various spots in my yard several times. I have consulted with other gardeners through the years who also reported failure. In 1988, I visited the Irish Channel garden of Dan Davis, who showed me a huge clump of the blooming, scented herb. I am so programmed to exclude this plant from my mental register of what grows in New Orleans, that I couldn't even identify it. How did he do it? A combination of the right variety, good drainage and the right elements of climate to create a microcosm which do not exist further uptown? It didn't last, though. By early 1990 it had disappeared.

Bougainvillea planted in New Orleans may last or may not. When Arlene Mmahat moved into her house on First Street, she found an established plant with magnificent lavender blooms climbing all the way to a second floor gallery, its huge trunk indicating great age. She remembers it returning after several freezes over the years she lived there, 1973 to 1989. It had been planted in the

1950's by the John Minor Wisdoms. Perfect exposure was the secret. It was planted against the south side of a building whose heat afforded extra protection during a freeze. I called the current owner, Stan Rice, to see if the plant made it through the Christmas Eve, 1989 temperature drop. It did not. It has been replaced with native coral honeysuckle.

"No one is going to be able to grow everything," says Camilla Bradley.

SEEDS

There is a lot to know about seeds and plant reproduction. For the drama and theory, I refer you to *The Sex Life of Flowers* by B. Meeuse and S. Morris. For application to gardening, try *The New Seed Starters Handbook* by N. Bubel or Park Seed Company's *Success With Seeds.* I would like to make a few comments on information I find particularly useful.

The advantages of starting plants from seed over purchasing started plants at a nursery are:
1. A bed of flowers from seed costs a lot less than the same bed filled with nursery plants.
2. Selecting seeds from catalogues greatly expands your choices.

There are some tricks for success with seed. Continuous moisture in the right amount is important. There are lots of products available for starting seeds. My favorite has its own automatic watering system built in via capillary matting which draws up moisture from a rectangular, styrofoam box-well and feeds it to an open-ended grid of germination mix-filled cubes on which it is set. An adequate light source, preferably the sun, is important for the development of healthy seedlings. Special lighting systems are available as sun substitutes if you do not have an adequately sunlit spot. Good air circulation is important to prevent "damping off", the fungal disease which cuts off seedlings at the ground.

I find starting seeds in containers and transplanting allows me more control. It saves the step of thinning seedlings and prevents the wash out of seeds or tiny sprouts by unanticipated heavy rainfall. The larger, faster germinating seeds such as four o'clocks and sunflowers are easy no matter where you start them. Tiny ones, such as those of the petunia are better started in containers.

Some seeds should be placed directly in the ground because they do not transplant well. If you direct seed, it is important to water lightly to provide consistent moisture until germination takes place. When I plant seeds in rows, I cover them with a light layer of sand so I can remember where I put them. The contrasting sand also helps to separate the seedlings of flowers from those of weeds until you are experienced enough to know the difference. Of course, this system doesn't work with the tiny seeds such as poppies which are broadcast across a bed instead of planted in rows. Tiny seeds should be mixed with sand before broadcasting to prevent too heavy a concentration of seedlings.

Follow the directions for planting on the seed packet as far as depth, spacing, etc. Be careful about dates. There are cool weather annuals which must be planted in the fall in New Orleans to allow bloom before they are killed by hot weather. Planting dates given on seed packets do not always accurately reflect the peculiarities of gardening here. Seeds started the wrong time of the year may be wasted.

Study your seed catalogues carefully before ordering perennial seeds. Some may take a long time to germinate or require special treatment making them more of an effort than you are willing to invest.

I have heard that it is best to order seeds from a source which is in a climate similar to yours so the plants you grow are acclimated to your regional conditions. Of course that's rather difficult since most of the big seed companies buy seeds from growers in many different places. Local experimental gardeners will have opinions on sources of seeds and which companies' products they have had luck with. Ask.

You can harvest your own seed for replanting in your garden if you wish. Why? By selecting seeds of the "best" plants to plant the next year over a period of years, you can develop annuals more suited to our environment.

Flowers either pollinate themselves or cross pollinate with others of their own species naturally in what is called open-pollination. By controlling which plants pollinate which, man can intervene to keep strains pure or to create changes. Crossing takes place among plants of one species. Hybrids are plants of different species which are bred for certain characteristics. Good hybrids are dramatically improved over their parents. This characteristic is called hybrid vigor. It does not persist in plants grown from the first generation hybrids. They revert to recent highly inbred ancestors. Hybrids should be started from newly purchased seed each year. Hybrid seeds are usually sterile, anyway.

Some plants are said to reseed. They may drop seeds, but whether germination takes place depends on whether the proper environment in terms of light and moisture exist. If the ground is cultivated, dropped seeds may be disturbed in such a way that they will be covered too deeply, or uncovered and exposed, either encouraging or discouraging sprouting. Seeds dropped into a thick ground cover may not receive enough light to sprout. I have found it useful to plant reseeding annuals along my walk of bricks set in sand. The crevices of moist fill make the perfect sprouting spot for seeds which lie in wait for the right temperature: torenia, johnny-jump-ups, polygonum capitatum, Madagascar periwinkle, thyme, portulaca, wild salvia, perilla. I move them to other spots where they continue their growth.

Allowing modern garden varieties to revert to the wild may be a way to return to the past. Old plants are frequently wild or unimproved varieties of what we grow today. For those interested in growing historic varieties of plants, I have provided information with plant entries which will indicate the earliest date of listings in catalogues of the New Orleans area, listing in J. F. Lelievre's *Nouveau Jardinier de la Louisiane*, 1838, listing in Thomas Jefferson's Garden Book of species grown at Monticello as early as 1766, and other dates of interest. The Thomas Jefferson Center for Historic Plants offers an informative newsletter with sources of further information. See RESOURCES for more on finding antique plants.

CUTTINGS

Plants can be propagated by cuttings. When a doorstep gardener offers you a piece of a plant, take it. The following instructions apply to most of the cuttings the ordinary gardener will make. Root, leaf, and hardwood cuttings require more complicated procedures.

1. Cuttings should be 4 to 6 inches long.
2. Cuttings should made with a 45 degree angled cut.
3. Cuttings should be made one-half inch below a leaf node.
4. The bottom third to half of the leaves should be removed as well as any flower stems.
5. Some plants will root in water. Most require placement in well-drained soil.
6. Water the cutting well after planting to make sure the planting medium settles in around the stem.
7. Keep the medium moist as well as the air around the cutting. This can mean keeping your cuttings outdoors or making a mini-greenhouse by enclosing them in a clear plastic bag.

Why bother? You can save some money. You can obtain some plants for your garden which you can't find in nurseries. You can have fun and feel the sense of accomplishment I feel when I see the first new growth!

PEST CONTROL

I saw a runner in Audubon Park today chewing on a weed as he ran. I don't know what it is called. The stems are juicy. I remember chewing on them, myself, when I was little. Most of us have such memories from childhood. George Farnsworth admits to eating clover. Susan Lafaye tried lots of weeds. She liked a pink kind best.

Soon after I pulled up fond memories, my mental screen flashed an alarm: What is on the stem that man is chewing? Is it really safe for him to put it in his mouth? I visualized the garden section of the local hardware full of insecticides, fungicides, herbicides, miticides....

Awareness of the disruption of nature's balance of predators, plant-eaters, and pollinators by the use of chemicals in the garden is slowly dawning on a city which may save its live oaks from the buckmoth at the cost of natural insect predators of the caterpillar, as well as the beautiful monarch butterfly. See WILDLIFE GARDENING for more discussion of natural balances.

There is no easy answer. Many will feel the selective use of chemicals to be necessary. A return to old fashioned, less toxic means of disease control or the discovery of new, non-toxic means based on a greater understanding of nature are possible. Healthy plants are more disease-resistant. Match your plants with the appropriate environmental conditions by planting in appropriately altered and maintained conditions or using indigenous species.

Three sources of advice on plant disease and treatment are:

1.   The *Ortho Problem Solver*, available in many nurseries and gardening departments. Its photographs of diseased plants help you determine the exact chemical agent you need to treat the problem.

2.   *Rodale's Garden Insect, Disease & Weed Identification Guide*, the goal of which is to *"make you aware of the value of all garden insects and weeds, and... inform you of their life cycles, their growth habits, and the roles they play in the garden's ecology."*

3.   The *Bio-integral Resource Center's Commonsense Pest Control Quarterly*. The goal of B.I.R.C. is *"to provide practical information on the least-toxic methods of managing pests."* Its staff works to design alternative solutions to heavy poisons for pest problems.

Be Boe of Belle Chasse remembers visiting rural doorstep gardens of the poor of Plaquemines Parish with her first husband during the 1940's. There was always a beautiful, healthy old-fashioned rose bush. After dinner, the pan of soapy dishwater was always poured directly over it. Some of the answers may be in doorstep gardens!

Pat Trivigno

Roses

*"...Roses are the only flowers
that impress people at garden parties;
the only flowers that everybody is certain of knowing."*

The Garden Party by Katherine Mansfield

Isn't that so often true? I thanked Roger Green for recommending Mansfield's short story where I found the above quote. We were at a garden party given in honor of roses and art in Ida Kohlmeyer's spectacular Metairie rose garden. She has devoted the entire rear portion of her yard to raised beds full of lush, green, disease free, heavily flowered bushes--hundreds of them. They were "modern roses": Hybrid Teas, Grandifloras, Multifloras, Climbers, Miniatures. Each blossom was flawless, exquisite.

It was April, peak month in New Orleans for roses. It was easy to see why the flower is such a favorite. Our own Congresswoman, Lindy Boggs, led and won the fight in 1987 (against the marigold and others) to make it the national flower of the United States. The Hybrid Teas which now symbolize roses to most people were not easily grown in New Orleans before the 1930's and 1940's.

From their probable origin in Asia 60 million years ago, roses in various forms have spread worldwide. Fossils of roses found in California date to 32 million years ago. There are wild roses which are native to America and found in Louisiana: the prairie rose *(Rosa setigera* Michx.), a pink flowered climber and carolina rose *(Rosa carolina* L.), also pink flowered, mentioned in *Wildflowers of Louisiana*. Our southern dewberry and blackberries are also in the Rose family and have the characteristic single rose-like flower.

Garden cultivation of roses began at least 5000 years ago in China. The flower has persisted as a symbol of virtue or vice throughout the history of the western world; in Greek literature, Christian art and architecture, as the English national flower from the 15th Century War of the Roses, and as the emblem of many nations. A bouquet of roses continues to represent esteem during courtship and marriage though a single friend of mine issues a warning from her personal experience: "Never trust a man who gives you lavender roses!"

Empress Josephine of France was one of the most famous proponents of the flower. From 1804 until her death in 1814, she amassed a collection at Malmaison which included every species of rose then known, including the native American swamp rose *(R. palustris)*, which grows in moist soil. Her passion was contagious. Growing roses became high fashion among the rich of western Europe and spread to America, and of course, to Louisiana with its French ties.

Roses are a tradition in New Orleans. They were grown in the botanical garden built by the Ursulines in 1731. *"When the Americans took over Louisiana in 1803, the people of New Orleans could boast...of roses that grew in prodigal abundance, 'literally embowered in roses', as one visitor wrote in 1804."*[11]

In her *Retrospect of Western Travel* of 1837, traveler Harriet Martineau wrote of her visit to the Battlefield of

New Orleans: "...*Gardens of roses bewildered my imagination. I really believed at the time that I saw more roses that morning than during the whole course of my life before.*"[12]

Mark Twain wrote of his 19th century visits to the Garden District: "*These mansions stand in the center of large grounds and rise, garlanded with roses, out of the midst of swelling masses of shining green foliage and many-colored blossoms.*"[13]

Before World War II, West End Park on Lake Pontchartrain behind the Municipal Yacht Harbor contained "*...a rose garden with 6000 rose bushes in 16 varieties.*"[14] What a statement about gardening and roses!

Before you picture Hybrid Teas, let me clarify that most of the roses above were what are today called "old roses" or "garden roses". In 1867, a French hybridizer inspired by a desire for new forms and colors presented the product of his work, the first Hybrid Tea Rose. It was called 'La France'. By the end of 19th century, the modern romance with Hybrid Teas and other new groups had begun, the old species gradually fell to the wayside. In 1895 The New Orleans Horticultural Society reported a local trend toward "*everblooming teas*" and Hybrid Teas for flowers all year.[15]

We have some information as to which old species were used in New Orleans. A letter dated 1820 from Mrs. B. N. B. Latrobe to Mrs. C. Smith describes Musk roses growing around the City.[16] Lelievre, in his 1838 volume on gardening in Louisiana, recommends 'Sweet Briar' or 'Eglantine Rose'(*R. eglanteria*). It is an ancient European native represented by many species in 19th century catalogues. Other possibilities for early Louisiana gardens are 'French Rose'(*R. gallica*), or 'Double French Rose' (*R. gallica versicolor*), 'Rosa Mundi'(*R. gallica officinalis*), European natives of great antiquity. 'Austrian Briar' (*R. foetida*), and 'Austrian Copper'(*R. foetida bicolor*), early Asian introductions to Europe were offered by Affleck's Natchez nursery in 1854. 'Cherokee Rose'(*R. laevigata*), a Chinese native, was introduced to this country in the late 18th century, was widely used and is now naturalized in Louisiana.

John Nelson's Magnolia Nurseries 1859 catalogue listed many varieties of Bengal or China, Tea, Noisette, Bourbon, Moss Roses and Remontants, the Hybrid Perpetuals.

Roses recommended for local planting in the 1928 New Orleans Garden Society Yearbook included the 'Pink and Red Radiance' Hybrid Teas, but consisted mostly of Teas, Bourbons, and Hybrid Perpetuals. The authors of the list were Mr. Horace McFarland and Mr. George Thomas of the Parkway Department who experimented with soils for azaleas and roses in his Calhoun Street garden. In a January, 1933 publication by Reuter Seed Co., 'Radiance Roses', pink and red, Hybrid Tea favorites were offered at 3 for $.95.

Until sometime during the 1940's Kraak's Nursery on Central Avenue in Jefferson Parish grew roses to cut and sell for household use. The varieties were 'Marechal Niel', a Noisette, and 'Red and Pink Radiance' Hybrid Teas. Locally grown "field roses" were eventually replaced by refrigerated cut roses shipped from California.[17]

New Orleans Garden Society members of the 1930's remember garden consultant Harry Daunoy who performed soil testing in during that period to help derive the specific cultural techniques used today for growing roses. In an article written in 1936, he stated:

> The use in New Orleans gardens of lime, bonemeal, charcoal dust, ashes, WITHOUT THE ADDITION OF SOME A-CIDIFYING AGENT has done more damage to New Orleans gardens than any other factor. I repeat that statement in this article with more force and confidence than ever before.

He also presented guidelines for pest control and fertilization which, he said, had been "...worked out... after *many years of tests and after consultation with recognized Research Bureaus and Experiment Stations in various parts of the country."*

By 1952, Garden Society recommendations were predominantly "New Patented Roses," Hybrid Teas. Anne Bradburn remembers hearing her mother-in-law complain during the 1950's that roses had gotton to be too much trouble in contrast with "the old days" when they were easy and everybody grew them.

By 1989 there were no local commercial sources of "old roses." Until recent times and except in old gardens, doorstep gardens, and cemeteries, the old roses had been almost forgotton.

The climate and terrain of New Orleans present particular problems for roses, and especially the modern hybrids which have been weakened by excessive inbreeding: high humidity, heavy rainfall, poor drainage, intense summer heat. Against such odds, how are such gardens as Ms. Kohlmeyer's achieved? With a lot of work! Many people consider the effort worthwhile.

Here are some rules for modern roses. Then I will tell you Maureen Detweiler's secret for rose gardens which offer bloom all year round with limited disease and a whole lot less maintainence!

1. RAISED BEDS are important to provide the good drainage required for perfect roses, especially in the special conditions of New Orleans and given the special needs of roses. A minimum of eight inches above the ground is recommended so that plenty of moisture can be provided without allowing the root systems of the plants to stand in water. That can kill the bushes by depriving the roots of oxygen.

Raised beds devoted exclusively to roses, or roses and edging plants with similar requirements, are a good idea for ease of care. (We edged our bed with gerbera daisies and verbenas, which also benefit from the good drainage, and from the regular spraying which helps combat the mildew and spider mites to which those plants fall prey.)

Isolating the high-care plants which need spraying with pesticides from flowers intended to attract butterflies and other insects in a wildlife garden is essential. Isolating roses, with their specific care requirements, makes it easier to give them the care they need. Spacing three to four feet apart, depending on the habits of the particular cultivars you choose, in beds of their own will allow good ventilation to help prevent disease. Competition with tree and perennial roots, which roses do not handle well, can also be avoided.

If possible, beds should be narrow or have walkways to prevent the compacting of soil caused by foot traffic during maintainence chores. Narrow beds make reaching the plants for pruning, fertilizing, spraying, and harvesting the gorgeous blooms easier.

2.   PROPER SOIL PREPARATION for roses should create good drainage, yet moisture retentiveness; a slightly acidic pH (between 6.0 and 6.8-7.0 is neutral); and provide the nutrients needed for plant growth. Digging out the soil to a depth of 18 inches to 2 feet is recommended when preparing the bed, as rose roots extend deeply into the soil. Complete soil replacement or thorough amendment in raised beds is a good idea. Follow the guidelines in the chapter on BASICS.

Before excavating our bed, we turned over the sod within the area where the bed was to be laid. We placed the pieces of sod upside-down in the pit from which soil was removed. Once the railroad tie border was in position, we shovelled into the bed a mixture of soil and organic materials (peat moss, bags of leaves from Betsy Ewing's rental property, and dried cow manure), with superphosphate added for strong root growth. The above technique assures the availability of nutrients deep in the soil where the plant roots extend. Since the additions take time to break down and act on the soil, the bed should be allowed to sit for two to three months before planting is done.

3. PLANTING of roses is best done in New Orleans in late December and January, during the dormant season. Planting too early can result in growth spurts if a warm spell occurs. Container-grown roses can be planted any time of the year, but the best times are winter and spring. A wider selection of plants is available during the winter, also.

I have had success with bare-rooted plants from mail order companies which ship bushes at the appropriate time for planting. The selection is very large, and the plants seem to be more disease-free than the ones I have purchased locally. It does not seem to take long for black spot to take hold once the barerooted roses are planted in pots and set out in our climate with overhead watering and without frequent spraying.

The proper technique for planting is as follows:
A. Dig a hole 18 inches deep.
B. Mound soil back into the center in the shape of a cone.
C. Place the bush on the peak of the cone so that its bud union (the swollen lump which marks the joining point of the decorative hybrid onto more vigorous rootstock) is above the level of the ground and spread the roots around the mound.
D. Add soil to cover the roots.
E. Tap the soil down with your feet.
F. Fill the hole with water.
G. After the water has soaked in, add the rest of the soil.

4. Choose and carefully follow a PLAN OF CARE which includes regular spraying for pests, fertilization, and water-

ing. The above soil preparation is not in lieu of the FER-
TILIZATION needed by vigorous roses during the growing
season if heavy bloom is to be achieved. We fertilized
monthly after the first show of leaves, alternately with a
granular rose food which contains a systemic insecticide,
and fish emulsion. Different formulae are offered by
different rosarians. There is, however, agreement on one
fact: roses need lots of feeding. Mark the date of fertilizer application and the type used on a calendar. If you
don't, you risk doing what I do. I find myself imagining
that I just completed that chore last week and can't possibly need to do it again so soon until a whole month has
been missed. Do not feed roses after the month of October, as you risk stimulating growth during the time that
the bushes approach dormancy.

SPRAYING WEEKLY from the time the first leaves
appear on the bushes in the spring is your only hope of
avoiding black spot, a fungus which, once established, can
cause all the leaves to fall off each bush. Powdery mildew and rust are two other fungal evils. The magic
ingredient, say several sucessful rosarians, is Triforine,
active agent in several products on the market. I find the
most convenient means of application to be by the type of
sprayer which attaches to your garden hose. It allows for
a forceful spray to be easily directed so that all the leaves
can be reached, top and bottom. Supposedly, with religious preventive use of the above, the fungal diseases can
be greatly reduced and controlled.

Aphids, mites, thrips, leafhoppers are among the pests
which can attack roses. Again, prevention is recommended. Miticides and insecticides are available as sprays or
dusts. Spraying is supposed to be slightly more effective
than dusting. I find it much easier, too. I suggest reading
labels and asking your friends or nurseryman which
brands they use. If a particular pest becomes established
in spite of preventive efforts, specific measures may be
required. Take an affected piece of the plant to an expert

for advice. Gardening departments and nurseries frequently display a reference volume with pictures of diseased plants and recommendations for cure which make diagnosis and treatment of the problem easier. I have talked to people who have one or two rose bushes in containers or in raised beds as specimen plants. They bemoan the difficulty of providing adequate preventive care for so few plants. Fungicides and insecticides are available in spray bottles for spot use. Though this would be too expensive a form in which to purchase enough chemicals for spraying a whole garden, they make provision of adequate preventive care for one or two bushes easy.

Roses need lots of WATER during the growing season to assure steady and even growth. Though our rainfall is heavy, it is not always even. The hot, dry spells experienced during our summers can be very stressful to roses. Stressed plants are more susceptible to diseases. Some form of irrigation is required. It can be provided by a garden hose which is moved from bush to bush after allowing enough water at each spot to soak the soil to a depth of eight to ten inches. Soaker hoses are also good for this task. I had an underground irrigation system which worked well when I remembered to turn it on regularly. The ultimate would be such a system set to timers which automatically turn the water on and off on whatever schedule was desired.

Overhead sprinkling is not recommended as wet foliage predisposes the plants to diseases.

5. MULCH as recommended in BASICS, to conserve moisture and prevent competitive weeds. The system which worked beautifully in my rose bed is layers of newspaper weighted and disguised with bark chips.

6. PRUNE your roses in January or February, and again in August to promote healthier, more attractive, and more plentiful blooms and more attractive bushes. Use sharp shears. Make your cut at a 45 to 65 degree angle either one fourth inch above an outside bud or at the point of origin of the cane. Remove any stem growth from below the bud union.

Experts differ on moderate versus light pruning. In moderate pruning, leave 5 to 12 canes, 18 to 24 inches high, and remove dead wood and cross-branched stems or canes. Remove canes from the center of the bush to allow good air circulation and reduce disease. Light pruning entails minimum cutting, to a height of 3 to 4 feet.

In either case, pruning should be specific to the individual plant to enhance its natural form. Modern roses have little enough to offer as shrubs without being given crew cuts! Weekly removal of spent blooms and dead leaves is important, but can be done while you are cutting for indoor arrangements.

Old Roses and Climbers are pruned right after blooming. Old canes should be thinned, not the new ones as flowers form on the new ones. Groom to remove spent blooms and dead growth any time it is needed.

7. METICULOUS HOUSEKEEPING is important. Remove old blooms and leaves from the ground around the bushes. They can be a home for the spores which cause disease.

Sounds like a lot of work? It doesn't have to take much time once a routine is established. But once you start, don't ever stop... or else!

One July, I strolled through my garden noting that heat and neglect had not made that season one of the better ones for roses. I sought a bloom from the sparse numbers available on the twenty or so bushes in my garden. In addition to there being fewer flowers produced during the hot months, the ones that do grow seem to progress from bud to open and aging flower in two days time.

I picked a 'Medallion', a Hybrid Tea, the best specimen I could find. As small and thin as it was due to its
stressful environment, it had a fragile beauty. The light
through its translucent petals played up the subtle blend
from yellow to apricot. It emitted a slight "rose" fragrance;
a special flower at its worst.

My rose garden had good years and bad. At its
worst we loved the blossoms we got. Seeing other people's successes spurred us on to more intensive efforts.
One spring we took bouquets to all our friends here rather
than leave them on the bushes unenjoyed when we went
to New York for a week. We cut enormous numbers of
blooms. The following year, pickings were sparse and we
lost three bushes to disease. My husband Jean thinks that
colder winters produce rosier springs. I think forgetting
to spray caused those bad years.

Eventually, the compulsion to mind roses wore off.
One year of no care as we turned to other interests was
all it took for us to, for all practical purposes, lose our
roses--except 'Lady Banksia'.

'White Lady Banksia' is a species rose first introduced
from the Orient in 1807, 'Yellow Lady Banksia' in 1824.
They have long been found in many New Orleans gardens. They bloom clusters of small yellow or white blossoms in the spring, usually with the azaleas. The yellow
has lasted in my garden for 15 years, blooming heavily
and reliably with no care but the yearly addition of organic material as a mulch and pruning when it moves to
far into a neighbor's yard. I don't usually even think of it
as a rose.

Eudora Welty, in *The Optimist's Daughter*, captures the
mystique of the old rose:

> *"I'd give a pretty to know what exactly that rose is!"*
> *Laurel's mother would say every spring when it opened its*
> *first translucent flowers of the true rose color. "It's an old*
> *one, with an old fragrance, and has every right to its own*
> *name, but nobody in Mount Salus is interested in giving it to*

*me. All I had to do was uncover it and give it the room it
asked for. Look at it! It's on its own roots, of course, utterly
strong. That old root there may be a hundred years old!"
    "Or older," Judge McKelva had said, giving her, from
the deck chair, his saturnine smile. "Strong as an old
apple tree."*[18]

For many years, New Orleans has forsaken its "old
roses". I did not know much about them until I talked to
Maureen Detweiler. I assumed that the lack of local availability probably meant fewer blooms, shorter bloom season, or some other such negative.

"NO," said Maureen. She feels the obsession with the
new caused people to loose sight of the values of the old.

There are Old Roses which bloom almost all year
round. Their toughness and disease resistance are demon-
strated by the fact that specimens are found growing and
thriving with absolutely no care in old cemetaries and
abandoned homesites. Maureen helped revitalize a rose
which has been tentatively identified as 'Climbing Old
Blush,' a China Rose, still thriving in the French Quarter
courtyard of Gallier House on Royal Street and believed to
have been planted there in 1857.

Roses propagated from cuttings from unidentified old
plants, such as 'Nachitoches Noisette' are called "found
roses". They are offered for sale through sources such as
the Antique Rose Emporium. As accurate identity of roses
which have been out of commerce is determined, changes
are made in the Emporium catalog to reflect the original
commercial name and date of introduction.

In her column, "A Bed of Roses" in *New Orleans Plants
and Gardens* magazine, Ms. Detweiler says:

> *In the nineteenth century, antique roses bloomed all over New
> Orleans. The Vieux Carre, the Garden District, Uptown and
> quaint neighborhoods were filled with their scent and beauty.
> Even the public green spaces were planted with such hardy
> roses as 'Louis Philippe,' 'Cecile Brunner,' and 'Seven Sisters'.*

She has made a commitment *"...to promote the cultivation, the study and the love of these historic roses and to return them to the gardens of New Orleans."* During restoration of an old home, she suggests planting varieties which were introduced in the same year the house was built.

The planting rules for modern roses should be used for antiques. The difference in old rose culture is that because they are more disease resistant, they can be sprayed only as needed for cosmetic reasons when blackspot or insect pests appear. A well planted, healthy old rose, though it may still be attacked, will not be crippled by disease.

The old roses are more noted for fragrance than the new. They also *"...billow, creep, arch, and sprawl in ways that few modern cultivars can imitate....The vast majority of modern rose hybrids,...aren't particularly notable as bushes."*[19] Rosarians hope the English Roses developed by David Austin present a whole new race, combining the *"...recurrent flowering habits and wide color range of modern hybrids with the form, growth habits, and fragrance of old garden roses."* There is room for all interests!

Roses can be seen at the L.S.U. All-American Rose testing garden in Baton Rouge and at the American Rose Center Gardens in Shreveport, home of the American Rose Society. Thousands of roses are grown there, including 100 old roses. The A.R.S. publishes a *Handbook for Selecting Roses,* which rates (on a 1 to 10 scale) 1000 available roses.

As in all New Orleans ventures, the most important recommendations of varieties should come from other New Orleans gardeners. Longue Vue Gardens and the City Park Botanical Garden have collections of roses where you can observe rose performance.

Members of the New Orleans Rose Society and non-joiner rosarians are usually delighted to "talk roses" and share their experiences.

Plants can be purchased at local nurseries, though I have had my best experience ordering bare-rooted bushes to be delivered via mail. Old roses must be obtained mail order, though they should be available soon from a local nursery. (Follow Maureen Detweiler's column in *New Orleans Plants and Gardens* magazine to find out when and where.) Making your own cuttings is easy with old roses, though illegal with new, patented hybrids.

The sources of the following recommendations are the New Orleans Rose Society, Inc., Maureen Reed Detweiler, The New Orleans Garden Society, Inc., 1952 and 1928, an 1894 *Southern Garden* article by Georgia Torrey Drennan,[20] and my own experience. The date of introduction of the species or cultivar is included.

ROSES FOR THE NEW ORLEANS GARDEN

*   Indicates roses which were available in the 1859 catalogue of the Magnolia
    Nurseries, Metairie Ridge and at the Plant Depot, Corner of Camp Street
    and Lafayette Square in New Orleans.
**   Indicates G. T. Drennan's recommendations for cemetery plantings, 1895.
*** Indicates 1928 recommendations of George Thomas and Horace McFarland
    in the *New Orleans Garden Society* yearbook.

OLD ROSES

The two Garden Groups most likely to thrive in New
Orleans are Chinas or Bengals and Teas, both known for
their continuous flowering habits (remontancy).   Teas have
the fragrance of tea; Chinas have a banana-like scent. Both
are less hardy than other roses.

CHINA OR BENGAL ROSES

*   'Agrippina' (1859)
*   'Archduke Charles' (before 1837)
    'Climbing Old Blush' (date unknown, though it is a sport or
        mutation of Old Blush, 1752.)
    'Hermosa' (1840)
*   'Louis Philippe' (1834)
        Frequently found in New Orleans, called "The Cemetary Rose".
    'Old Blush' (1752)

TEA ROSES

*   'Bon Silene' (before 1837)
    'Duchesse De Brabant' (1857)
***'Etoile de Lyons' (1881)
***'Lady Hillingdon' (1910)
***'Madame Lombard' (1878)
    'Maman Cochet' (1893)
***'Marie Van Houtte' (1871)
** 'Niphetos' (1843)
    'Souvenir de Therese Lovet' (1886)
    'William R. Smith' (1908)

ROSA MULTIFLORA "PLATYPHYLLA"

'Seven Sisters' (1817)

BOURBON ROSES

'Boule de Neige' (1867)
Blooms round the year in the Detweiler garden.
'La Reine Victoria' (1872)
* 'Souvenir De La Malmaison' (1843)
Year-round bloom, fifteen buds on Christmas day, 1989, in
Maureen Detweiler's garden.
*** Horace McFarland recommended all the Bourbon Roses for the
"Far South."

HYBRID PERPETUALS OR REMONTANTS

'American Beauty' (1875)
'Frau Karl Druschki', 'Snow Queen' or 'White American Beauty'
(1901). Only bloomed once a year for me, spring.
***'General Jacqueminot', 'General Jack' (1853)
* 'La Reine' (1842)
** 'Mabel Morrison' (1878)
'Reine des Violettes' (1860)
Everblooming and ever-fragrant in Susan LaRocca's garden.

NOISETTES

'Nachitoches Noisette'
A "found" rose grown from cuttings from a gravesite rose
bush at the old fort in Natchitoches, Louisiana.
* 'Aimee Vibert' (1828)

MOSS ROSES

* 'Salet' (1854)
Though moss roses do not generally do well here, this is one
is a classic, available before the Civil War.

POLYANTHAS

Very small clusters of flowers, profuse, continuous bloom.

'Cecile Brunner' (1881)
    The "Sweetheart Rose."
'Margo Koster' (1931)
'The Fairy' (1941)

MODERN ROSES

CLIMBERS

Many types and bloom patterns.   Some of these are old, some modern.

'America' (1976)
'Don Juan' (1958)
***'Dr. W. VanFleet' (1910)
'Joseph's Coat' (1964)
'White Banksia' (1807)
'Yellow Banksia' (1825)
***'Madame Butterfly' (1918)
'Mermaid' (1918)
    Hybrid of *Rosa bracteata* Wendl., 'Chickasaw Rose', an Asian
    Rose naturalized in parts of Louisiana.
'Peace' (1950)

FLORIBUNDAS

Clusters of medium-sized, short stemmed flowers, continuous bloom.

'Angel Face' (1968)
'Betty Prior' (1935)
'Cherish' (1980)
'Else Poulsen' (1924)
'Europeana' (1963)
'Fashion' (1950)
'First Edition' (1977)
'French Lace' (1982)

'Iceberg' (1958)
'Red Pinocchio' (1947)
'Show Biz' (1985)
'Simplicity'
'Sun Flare'
'Sun Sprite'
'Vogue' (1951)

HYBRID TEAS

Large flowers, continuous waves of bloom. The most popular type used in modern gardens. Good for cutting.

The older hybrid teas may be harder to find, but I have found most of those listed below in recent catalogs if not in local nurseries. Some of the earlier introductions are hardier and more disease resistant than the new which have been weakened by genetic manipulations aimed toward "improved" flower form.

'Dainty Bess' (1925)
'Dame Edith Helen'(1926)
'Etoile de Hollande'(1919)
'Kaiserin Auguste Viktoria'(1891)
'La France' (1867)
    The first Hybrid Tea.
***'Ophelia' (1912)
***'Radiance' (1901)
    Has withstood the ravages of time and Buster, the dog, in
    Phil and Karen Martin's old garden off Esplanade.
***'Red Radiance'(1916)
    Both 'Radiances' are long lasting, highly recommended for
    New Orleans.

'Brandy' (1982)
'Charlotte Armstrong'(1940)
'Chrysler Imperial' (1952)
'Crimson Glory' (1935)
'Double Delight' (1977)
'Eclipse' (1935)
'First Prize' (1970)
'Forty-Niner' (1949)
'Fragrant Cloud' (1968)
'Garden Party' (1959)
'Granada' (1963)
'John F. Kennedy' (1965)
'Katherine T. Marshall'(1943)
'Lady X' (1966)

'Lowell Thomas'(1944)
'Medallion'(1973)
'Peace'(1945)
'Pristine'(1978)
'Royal Highness'(1962)
'Mirandy'(1945)
'Mister Lincoln'(1964)
'Olympiad'(1984)
'Sutter's Gold'(1950)
'Talisman'(1929)
'The Doctor'(1936)
'Tiffany'(1954)
'Tropicana'(1960)
'White Masterpiece'(1969)

GRANDIFLORAS

Large flowers on long stems, continuous bloom.

'Montezuma' (1955)
'Ole' (1964)
'Pink Parfait'
'Queen Elizabeth' (1954)
    Highest rated by the A.R.S. My first rose. I was wearing one from my garden when I met my husband. It flourishes when cared for, but withstands neglect better than any other modern rose I've grown.
'Sonia' (1975)

MINIATURES

Tiny flowers on bushes to 18 inches, continuous bloom.

'Beauty Secret'
'Cinderella'
'Cupcake'
'Minnie Pearl'
'Magic Carousel'
'Over the Rainbow'
'Poker Chip'

'Rise 'n Shine'
'Red Beauty'
'Snowbride'
'Starina'
'Starglo'
'Toy Clown'

DAVID AUSTIN'S ENGLISH ROSES

To be announced...

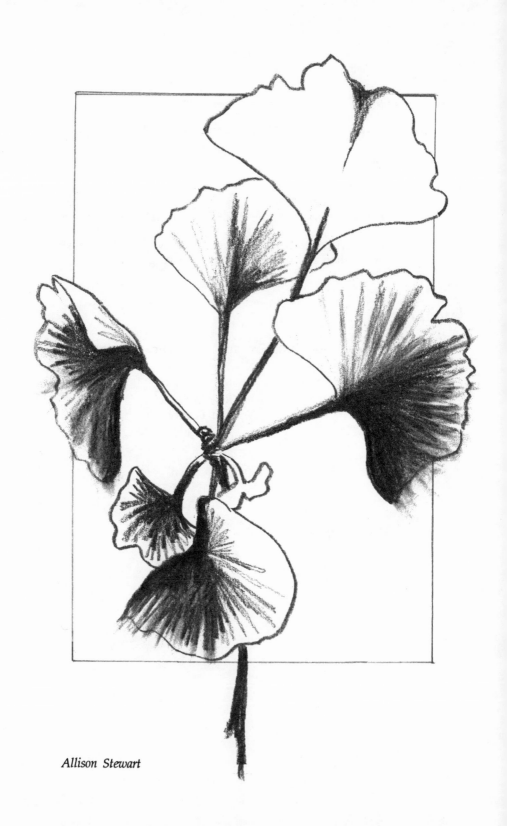

Allison Stewart

Exotic Trees and Shrubs

"We'll sip the orange wine and I'll ask you to be mine,
Julie, dear.
We'll dance and then we'll dine at the famous Antoine's
In the land of the fragrant Jasmine.

When I think, my eyes go drippy
With thoughts of you, and the dear old Crescent City.
The years will pass away, but you and I will still be gay.
When we stroll together in the old Vieux Carre.
Down Louisiana Way."

from "Down Louisiana Way"
A Garden Book of Old New Orleans
by Grace Matt Thompson (1947)

I discovered *A Garden Book of Old New Orleans*, by Grace Matt Thompson, in the Louisiana section at the Latter Branch of the New Orleans Public Library. It is the collection of poetry, personal gardening records and recollections of a lady who, in contrast to her ability as a poet, appears to have been a serious and knowledgeable gardener. She experimented with many sub-tropical plants. A visit to her patio in 1947 would have allowed one to view many flowering shrubs, bulbs, and perennial plants which she says she grew successfully, but which I have never seen grown in New Orleans. My mouth watered for a look at her patio today, in 1989. I wonder what is still there? How much has endured?

I found the Cottage Flower Shop, which she formerly owned, listed in the 1946 City Directory on 4609 Freret Street (phone number UPtown 0422). If her patio was there, it is gone, now. The building did not look lived in.

I drove around the block to investigate, but was only able to see what appeared to be a large clump of elderberry over the top of an unpainted wooden fence. Elderberry is not usually a strong indicator of a well tended exotic garden.

I researched the *Times-Picayune* index at the Public Library hoping to find articles or an obituary notice which would give me more information about Mrs. Thompson and her patio. I found no more leads. Were past gardeners more venturesome than those of today? Where are the ornamental shrubs Mrs. Thompson and, undoubtedly, other past gardeners planted? I found the answer while I was looking for a monkey puzzle tree.

Once I read about the Araucaria family member which inspired, in my references, an array of adjectives from *"strikingly peculiar," "weird,"* and *"fascinating,"* to *"reptilian,"* I had to see one. According to information in several general sources, it should be hardy all the way to Zone 7, much farther north than New Orleans.

I followed leads on the west bank and east: to the Overby's house, to Tulane University's campus, to several sites in Audubon Park, to a Leontine Street residence where I found Miss Olive Carriere, who taught me Spanish at East Jefferson High School over 25 years ago. There were no monkey puzzle trees anywhere I looked. I did find Cunningham firs.

The monkey puzzle tree Dottie and Phillip Gardner remembered from Tulane's campus was a dawn redwood (*Metasequoia glyptostroboides*), described from fossils before it was discovered in China. It was introduced into cultivation from seed sprouted at the Arnold Arboretum of Harvard University in 1948. A specimen was planted between the Richardson Building and Dinwiddie Hall in 1959. It is still there today, between a gingko and a bald cypress.

Anne Bradburn remembered that Dr. Will Sternberg had grown a monkey puzzle in his garden on Audubon

Street near St. Charles. When it fruited, staff from the Herbarium at Tulane collected a specimen and made a positive identification.

I called Dr. Sternberg, who had moved to an apartment. He and his wife Tedda bought the plant at Guillot's Nursery in the early 1960's. They were told that the seedling would grow to about 6 feet. They watched it reach the height of their 2 story house over a 10 to 15 year period. Its prickly basal foliage had to be trimmed for safe passage through the side yard.

The tree developed cones which, Dr. Sternberg said were "...solid like a pineapple, and very heavy. We were amazed when one came crashing down!" He described it as yellow on the outside, composed of pie-shaped green segments into which it split on impact. A dried cone displayed on a coffee table as a curiosity once noisily exploded, flinging its segments every-which-way.

"I have to see it!" I exclaimed.

"Oh, it's not there anymore. It was nearly killed during a very cold spell in the late 1970's...1976? It came back after the freeze, but was not decent looking. There were just tufts here and there. We cut it down."

My last lead was to a little house on Atherton Drive in Metairie where a friend said she planted a monkey puzzle tree in the backyard 15 years ago. She lived there and gardened while she waited for her love to be free to marry her. When he did, they moved uptown. No one was home, but the yard was open. I searched. Someone had cut down three oak trees. The monkey puzzle was gone. Apparently, it didn't last. (Neither did the marriage.)

I called nurseries. "It won't do good here, but I can order you one from California," I was told on the west bank.

Another gave me the following history: "Nurseries years ago used to stock a lot of these things. They don't make it in a bad freeze and are hard to hold over. A hibiscus won't make it either, but at least it blooms all summer."

There was an answer. Monkey puzzle trees do not last in New Orleans due to some peculiarity of the climate. The changed economy has made the risk of loss of nonhardy and unsold stock too great for the nurseries. But, for those ready to continue Mrs. Thompson's experimentation, these plants can be ordered, if not found locally. Though to my knowledge, there are no monkey puzzles in New Orleans, there can be again! Read the ads in gardening magazines for sources.

The following trees and shrubs are those which may make it in your patio garden or other perfect spot, or may last only a few years. The risk of planting them may lead to utter failure or delight beyond belief. This list is only for adventurous gardeners!

I have not listed specific wildlife offerings of each of these plants. Many of them are notable for floral performance, therefore offering nectar for bees, moths, butterflies, and hummingbirds. General planting and cultural information for trees and shrubs is found in NATIVE TREES & SHRUBS.

EXOTIC TREES & SHRUBS
FOR THE NEW ORLEANS GARDEN

1859 Indicates listing in the catalogue of plants offered for sale by John M. Nelson at Magnolia Nurseries at Metairie Ridge and at his Plant Depot, Corner of Camp St. & Lafayette Sq., New Orleans.

1885 Indicates listing in the 1885 *Maitre & Cook Catalogue of Southern Grown Plants*, nurseries on St. Charles at Lower Line.

1918 Indicates listing in Bollwinkle Seed Co. Ltd., *Catalogue & Garden Guide*, 510 Dumaine St., New Orleans.

1921 Indicates inclusion in lists of recommended plants by the New Orleans Garden Society, Inc. in *Notes on Gardening in New Orleans*. From Stephen Hand, pp. 183-187.

1935 Indicates listing in "The Aristocrats of the New Orleans Gardens" compiled by Landscape Architect William A. Wiedorn. From Stephen Hand, pp. 188-192.

1947 Indicates listing in *Trees, Vines, and Shrubs of New Orleans* which described plants used in City Parks, Parkways.

DECIDUOUS TREES

Ailanthus altissima (Mill.) Swingle **TREE-OF-HEAVEN, VARNISH TREE** Quassia family. China. Deciduous, fast growing to 60 feet. Short lived. Sun, shade. Any soil, wet or dry. Grows in high stress conditions. Dioecious. The male trees produce yellow pyramidal clusters of vile smelling flowers. Females produce clusters of samaras which turn reddish in fall. Common in inner cities where it spreads like a weed. Introduced in this country from the Orient via Kew Gardens in 1784 by horticultural patron William Hamilton of Philadelphia. 1859.

Albizia julibrissin Durazz. **MIMOSA, SILK TREE** Pea family. Asia. Deciduous tree, to 40 feet. Almost any soil, moist or dry. Fern-like leaves close at night, like the sensitive plant. Flowers in May and June are globular pink puffs of extruded stamens, followed by 6 inch long seed pods. Lives under 25 years, self-seeds readily, a messy tree. Common in New Orleans gardens, today. Hummingbirds like it. Subject to sudden death from wilt, but disease resistant species are hoped for soon. Introduced to Charleston by Michaux before 1803, grown by Thomas Jefferson at Monticello, 1811. 1859. *Southern Gardener* magazine in 1895 described the SILK TASSEL TREE as *"...almost forgotton in New Orleans...."*

Bauhinia L. species ORCHID TREE Tropical shrubs and trees of the Pea family with two-lobed leaves and orchid like flowers followed by long seed pods. Sun to partial shade. Any well-drained, slightly acid soil; lots of moisture. Plant in a protected spot. They may die back in a freeze.

B. blakeana S. T. Dunn HONG-KONG ORCHID China. 25 feet. Pink to deep wine and purple, orchid like blossoms fall to spring.

B. forficata Link HARDY ORCHID TREE South America. Evergreen, 25 feet. Flowers in March and April are 5 inch white, orchid-like. See one on Jefferson Avenue close to the lake side of Prytania.

B. punctata C. Bolle or *B. galpinii* NASTURTIUM BAUHINIA Africa. Vining shrub in form. Flowers are salmon to orange red, spidery orchids, 2 to 3 inches each in clusters; late summer to fall, very showy. Hardy only to 28 degrees.

B. purpurea L. BUTTERFLY TREE, ORCHID TREE India. 25 feet. Lavender flowers November through late spring. 1947.

Brachychiton acerifolius (A. Cunn.) F. J. Muell. AUSTRALIAN FLAME TREE Australia. Sterculia family. Deciduous, fast growing to 60 feet. Sun. Deep, well-drained soil, moist or dry. 5-7 lobed 10 inch long leaves drop before the blooms appear or during cold. Flowers in spring. Small, tubular orange to red blossoms are profuse, followed by clusters of showy seed pods. Grown by Grace Thompson, 1946. This tree likes our hot weather, but is hardy only to 25 degrees.

B. discolor (F. J. Muell.) PINK FLAME TREE, PINK STERCULIA 6 inch maple-like leaves, wooly white below, dark green above, drop before the axillary clusters of rose to pink spring blooms. Good for street planting. Skip Treme' remembers them here. Hardy to 25 degrees.

Broussonetia papyrifera (L.) Venten. **PAPER MULBERRY** Temperate East Asia. Mulberry family. Deciduous, fast growing to 30 feet. Sun, part shade. Adaptable as to soil. 8 inch, hairy leaves, deeply lobed in young trees, entire in mature, olive-green with gray undersides. The inner bark was used to make paper by the Chinese. Pollen is released explosively by male flowers, causing what looks like a puff of smoke. The fruit is a globe of pointed, reddish orange seed capsules. Colorful, good food for birds. Of course, considered messy by some. Self seeds, has naturalized widely. Reputedly introduced in New Orleans gardens from European sources before 1800.

Calodendrum capense (L.f.) Thunb. **CAPE CHESTNUT** South Africa. Rue family. Tree, evergreen to deciduous depending on the temperature; 40 feet. Sun, part sun. Very well drained, deep soil, lots of water. 5 inch, spotted leaves; profusion of fragrant clustered blossoms; white, rose, lilac curled petals with long stamens spring or summer. Young trees do not bloom, need protection. Hardy to 22 degrees.

Cercis chinensis Bunge **CHINESE RED BUD** Pea family. China. 8 feet. Sun, part shade during the hottest part of the day. Well-drained, fertile, acid soil. Bushy shrub whose leafless stems and branches are covered in spring with thick clusters of rosy purple flowers. Leaves are yellow in fall.

C. siliquastrum L. **JUDAS TREE** Southern Europe. Pea family. Deciduous, to 40 feet. Sun. Rich, sandy loam. Branches are very heavily covered with purplish-red or white flowers in early spring. Less common in this country than in southern Europe and western Asia.

Cydonia oblonga Mill. **COMMON QUINCE**, *C. sinensis* Thouin. Asia. To 20 feet, deciduous. Sun, shade. Well-drained, fertile, slightly acid soil is best; is adaptable if

drainage is good.   Attractive form; colorful leaves in autumn.   Blooms are pink, sparse, in spring.   Fruit forms in
late fall; is apple sized, aromatic, yellow; used for making
jelly. 1859.

Erythrina crista-galli L. **CORAL TREE, CRY-BABY
TREE** Brazil, Argentina.   Pea family, deciduous, 20 feet.
Sun.   Well-drained soil, poor and dry for best flowering.
Leaves of 2 to 3 greenish-yellow leaflets, each 3 inches
long; thorny branches.   Pendulous clusters of tubular,
orangish 2 inch flowers cry nectar tear-drops May to frost.
Branches which die back after bloom should be removed.
Becomes untidy after several years of freeze damage,
regrowth.   I found two explanations for the name CRY-
BABY TREE.   One is because the flowers drip nectar.   The
one I like best is: *"Its flowers emit a peculiar cry when
crushed."*[21]   I didn't believe it at first.   I saw a coral tree
blooming in the garden of Our Lady of Lourdes church on
LaSalle Street off Napoleon.   I stopped and asked the
gardener if I could squeeze some of his flowers.   He
looked ready to call for help.   Thank goodness the first
flower I pinched cried!   Thank goodness he heard it, too!
The sound was just like that of a cry baby doll when it's
turned over.   Unfortunately, I couldn't make any others
flowers cry.   It must require the perfect technique.   Hummingbird and oriole plant.   Alexander Gordon reported
Erythrinas growing in New Orleans in 1849. 1921.

Ficus carica L. **FIG TREE** Mediterranean.   Mulberry
family tree, deciduous, 30 feet.   Sun, part sun.   Rich,
moist, deep, well drained soil.   Spreading form.   Large,
thick, rough, lobed leaves; dark green.   Fruit is green to
brown, pear-shaped, delicious for people or wildlife.
Planted in the Ursulines Convent garden, 1731.

F. elastica Roxb. ex. Hornem. **INDIA RUBBER TREE,
RUBBER PLANT** Ten feet.   Sun, part shade.   Loose,
well-drained soil.   Foot long, glossy leaves make this tree
a favorite for pots.   Fast growing outdoors.   Though

tender, specimens can last, with protection in New Orleans in the right spot and until a severe freeze. 1918.

Firmaina simplex (L.) W. F. Wight [*F. platanifolia* (L.F.) Marsili; *Sterculia platanifolia* L. f.] **CHINESE PARASOL TREE, JAPANESE VARNISH TREE, VARNISH TREE** Eastern Asia. Sterculia family. Deciduous, medium to fast growth to 60 feet. Sun, part shade. Any well-drained soil. 3 to 5 lobed leaves up to 12 inches across which turn bright yellow in fall. Shiny gray-green trunk and branches. Summer flowers are foot-long spikes of tiny greenish flowers followed by attractive 4 inch seed pods in fall. These I have seen in New Orleans are coarse textured, straggly looking.

Ginkgo biloba L. **GINKGO, MAIDENHAIR TREE** China. Ginkgo family, 120 feet, deciduous tree. Sun. Any soil. 4 inch light green leaves similar to Maidenhair fern, yellow in fall. Female trees are considered undesirable because the fruit which forms stinks (though raccoons like it), usually only males are sold. This tree only exists in cultivation, was found in Chinese temple gardens by Western travelers, brought to this country after 1800. It is called a "living fossil," as it has existed unchanged for 125 million years; is only remaining member of a family which used to dominate the plant kingdom, worldwide. Considered a good city tree, attractive, with few negatives. On the Parkway and Park recommended list in 1949, though less commonly used than others. Long lasting in New Orleans. See one on St. Charles near Jena. Nestsite for birds. Introduced by Andre' Michaux to Charleston before 1803.

Jacaranda mimosifolia D. Don **JACARANDA** Argentina. Bignonia family tree, 50 feet, deciduous midwinter, or earlier with significant frost. Sun for best bloom, grow in light shade. Light, well-drained soil. Leaves are mimosalike but finer. Flowers on bare branches in April, May are a profusion of 2 inch, blue bignonia-funnels with ruffly, folded back ends. Hardy to 25 degrees. Plant in a sheltered spot. Mine bloomed with a tall magenta-flowered mallow intertwined for several years, until the freeze of Christmas Eve, 1989. It is returning from the roots.

Koelreuteria bipinnata Franch. **GOLDEN RAIN TREE** China. Deciduous tree, 60 feet, Soapberry family. Sun. Rich, loose soil. Leaves of 7 to 12 oblong, pointed leaflets with toothed edges, fernlike, yellow in fall. Delicate yellow flowers rain from foot long branch-tip clusters, carpeting the ground below in September, October. Papery seedpods change from pink to brown through winter. Subject to freeze damage, death, every few years in New Orleans. Popular for street plantings by Parkway and Parks from the 1940's until the 1983 freeze. So many people are fond of this tree, I predict it will always be found somewhere here, in spite of its problems. *K. elegans* (Seem.) A.C. Sm.,[*K. formosana*] **FLAMEGOLD** Taiwan, is more colorful, common here, easy from seed. *K. paniculata* **NORTHERN GOLDEN RAIN TREE** June bloom, better for the north, grows here with superb drainage.

Lagerstroemia indica L. **CRAPE MYRTLE** China. Loosestrife family trees, shrubs, groundcover, deciduous, 20 feet. Sun. Moist, well-drained soil is best, tolerates less than perfect conditions. Small, rounded, dark green leaves turn yellow, orange, red in fall. Bloom for three months in summer at the tips of current growth is 6 to 12 inch clusters of one and a half inch crepy, crinkly flowers in white or shades of pink, red, lavender, purple-red. Modern cultivars are available in all sizes, from tall (over 15 feet), medium (to 12 feet), semi-dwarf (to 6 feet), to the "miniature" (18 to 24 inches) which was developed by horticulturist David Chopin of Baton Rouge. It was the star of the 1984 World's Fair in New Orleans where the crape myrtle was the official flower. Make sure you know what size your crape myrtle will become when you purchase it. Long lived. Hummingbird plant. Brought to Charleston by Michaux before 1803, grown in New Orleans since before 1837. 1859, 1885, 1918, 1921, 1935, 1947.

Magnolia heptapeta (Buc'hoz) Dandy **WHITE SAUCER MAGNOLIA, YULAN MAGNOLIA** China; *M. quinquepeta* (Buc'hoz) Dandy **TULIP MAGNOLIA** China; *Magnolia X soulangiana* Soul.-Bod. **ORIENTAL** or **SAUCER MAGNOLIA** Hybrid of two Chinese species, *M. stellata* (Siebold & Zucc.) Maxim. **STAR MAGNOLIA** Japan. See *Magnolia*, NATIVE EVERGREEN TREES.

Melia azedarach L. **CHINABERRY** Mahogany family tree, deciduous, 40 feet. Sun. Rich sandy soil, deep, well-drained, any pH. Dark green leaves to 3 feet are composed of many 1 to 3 inch leaflets. Spring flowers are delicate clusters to 8 inches, lilac colored, fragrant. Marble sized green berries follow, they become yellow, wrinkled, and sticky; last through fall. The pits are sometimes used to make rosary beads. This fast growing tree is good for shade. 'Umbraculifera' is recommended for its form. This is not a good wildlife tree, as its berries can cause intoxication in birds and are possibly poisonous to some animals. Introduced by Andre' Michaux to Charleston around 1787. 1885.

Morus alba L. variety *multicaulis* (Perrotet) Loud **WHITE MULBERRY** China. Mulberry family. Deciduous, fast growing to 80 feet. Sun, part sun. Rich, moist soil. The simple leaves, 3 to 9 inches long, some lobed. Introduced in the U. S. in 1826 by a William Prince of Long Island who propagated them for sale and use in a silk industry which never materialized. Hedrick says during this time nearly every garden had a mulberry. There are records of shiploads of the trees passing through New Orleans. Now widely naturalized. Berries are good food for birds.

Musa species L. **BANANA** Asia. Banana family, tree-like rhizomatous perennial, 5 to 15 feet depending on the species. Sun, part sun. Moist, but well drained soil. Large, simple leaves grow from atop thick trunks which form clumps. The flowers are pretty, in shades of pink, maroon, red, depending on the species. The fruit which follows is insignificant in some species; edible, but not high quality in *M. X paradisiaca* L., **PLAINTAIN**. Once established, their spread is rapid and insidious. To get rid of them, every piece must be laboriously dug from the depths to which the heavy, water-laden trunks sink. Containment is advised. The plaintain and *M. ornata* Roxb., **ROSE BANANA**, which are the two most commonly grown in New Orleans, return after freeze damage. Hummingbirds may visit their flowers. Probably grown in New Orleans since the 1840's. 1947.

Parkinsonia aculeata L. **MEXICAN PALO VERDE, JERUSALEM THORN** Tropical America. Pea family, 20 feet, deciduous tree. Sun. Rich, well-drained soil. 12 to 18 inch leaves with many tiny leaflets, fern-like, thorny branches, open form. Fragrant, pendulous, yellow flowers in spring, summer. Ann Morcos of Kenner, who had one grown from a cutting, said it seemed to be producing its beautiful blooms all the time. She recommends planting it clear of walkways where its low thorny branches and the bees who love its flowers can worry pedestrians. Hers was blown down in a storm. 1921, 1947.

Prunus campanulata Maxim. **TAIWAN CHERRY** Japan. Deciduous, 25 feet. Sun. Rich, well-drained soil. Attractive foliage. One inch rosy-red, bell shaped blossoms coat the leafless branches in January-February. Half inch dark red fruits follow. Blooms third year from seed, lifespan in the deep south is only ten years.

P. cerasifera J. F. Ehrh. **PURPLE LEAF PLUM** Asia. Deciduous, 25 feet. Sun. Well-drained soil. Grown for its foliage, reddish-purple, 1 to 3 inch leaves. Flowers on the bare branches in early spring are delicate, pale pink. 1 inch fruit follows. Not long lived in New Orleans. Several varieties available in different sizes and with flowers from white to pink. Notable is 'Altropurpurea', sometimes called 'Pissardi' after a gardener to the Shah of Persia.

P. serrulata Lindl. **JAPANESE FLOWERING CHERRY** Asia. Deciduous, 80 feet. Sun. Rich, well-drained soil.

Attractive foliage.   White or pink clusters of one and a half inch flowers before foliage in spring.   Inconsistent performance and short life here.   This plant is better suited for colder places. Many varieties exist.   It is best to buy from local nurseries, not mail order, to make sure you get the ones most suited (or least unsuited) for New Orleans. 'Kwansan' is one of the better known.

Pyrus calleryana 'Bradford' **BRADFORD FLOWERING PEAR** China. Sun. Rich, moist, well-drained soil. Bright green, leathery, glossy leaves to 4 inches (coppery when new).   A profusion of small, white flowers coat the branches with the new leaves for a brief, but glorious, period in mid-spring.   Terry Gauthier on Constance Street brought me a branch from his flowering tree so I could see it up close. They do not smell as good as they look: I had to put the vase on the back porch. I have heard that if flowering branches are cut before the blooms open and are pollinated, they will not smell bad. Fruit is half inch sized. This variety is least susceptible to pear blight and best suited to the South. *P. communis* L., Europe and Western Asia is the **COMMON PEAR**.

Salix babylonica L. **WEEPING WILLOW** China. Willow family tree, deciduous, 30 feet. Sun.   Adaptable to soil conditions though moist is best.   Narrow leaves to 6 inches on gracefully arched and drooping branches. Early spring flowers, 2 inch fuzzy catkins, appear with new leaves; hungry-from-winter bees love their pollen and nectar. Leaves are the larval food of the mourning cloak butterfly; good nesting sites for birds. "Weeping" forms of trees were popular nationally in the 1850's, especially for cemetary planting.[22]

Sapium sebiferum (L.) Roxb. **CHINESE TALLOW, POP-CORN TREE** Spurge family tree, deciduous, 40 feet. Sun. Almost any soil. Delicate, light green leaves to 3 inches; red and yellow in fall.   Flowers in spring are yellow catkins which rain pollen; fruit is a hard-shelled half inch nut which splits open to expose 3 shiny, white seeds.

Lifespan of about 20 years, but the one in my front yard is older than that and going strong. Bees and wasps love its flowers. Food for many birds, including masses of robins in early spring, yellow-rumped warblers. Downy woodpeckers love to run up, down, and out its limbs looking for bugs. It does drop a lot of "trash", but it has a different beauty each season; from the red and gold of autumn leaves to the popcorn-seeds which dot the tree with white in winter. In 1851, Sylvanus commented that it had been introduced into New Orleans *"within the last few years."* Was it the *Stillingia sebifera*, **TALLOW** or **CROTON TREE** listed 1859, 1885?

Sophora japonica L. **JAPANESE PAGODA TREE, CHINESE SCHOLAR TREE** Pea family. Deciduous, fast growing to 60 feet. Sun. Very well-drained, deep soil. Attractive, medium textured ferny leaves, scaly bark. Unreliable bloom, lightly scented foot long clusters of tiny, yellowish-white flowers in summer, followed by 3 inch seed pods which last into winter. Though popular with landscape architects in the 1970's, available from Maitre and Cook in 1885, it is better suited to cooler environments than ours.

Ulmus parvifolia Jacq. **CHINESE ELM** China, Japan; and *U. pumila* L. **SIBERIAN ELM** China, see *Ulmus*, NATIVE DECIDUOUS TREES.

Vitex agnus-castus L. **CHASTE TREE, SUMMER LILAC, VITEX** Europe. Deciduous, 20 feet. Sun, light shade. Any well-drained soil. Gray-green leaves of 5 to 7 five inch leaflets, sage-like odor when crushed or when wet. Spikes of lavender, pink, or white blossoms, also scented, in April, fall. A traditional New Orleans garden shrub. Beautiful in bloom in rows along the Courthouse at Tulane and Broad. A story is that, one year, as the leaves resemble marijuana, some westbankers believed it was and denuded all the trees on that side of the River. Bumblebee and butterfly plant. Reputedly grown in New Orleans before 1800. 1947.

Ziziphus jujuba Mill. **JUJUBE, CHINESE DATE** China. Buckthorn family tree, deciduous, 20 feet. Sun. Native of hot, dry settings, though it likes moisture, good drainage is important; likes alkaline soil. Oblong, 1 to 2 inch leaves, dark green and glossy. Oblong, datelike fruit, dark red to black in color, edible, ripens late summer. Hardy to 22 degrees. Grown in Henry Lawrence's garden 1841-1866. Grown by Grace Matt Thompson, 1946. Does not really thrive here as it does in California.

DECIDUOUS SHRUBS

Abelia X grandiflora (Andre) Rehd. **GLOSSY ABELIA** Hybrid of two Chinese species. Honeysuckle family, semi-evergreen, shrub, 6 feet. Full sun best; flowers less in partial shade. Well-drained, fertile, humusy soil best, but is adaptable. Foliage is reddish to purplish bronze, (depending on the season) on arching branches; flowers May to frost are small, tubular, pink to white depending on the cultivar. Old canes should be thinned each winter. Dwarf forms available. Offers long period of bloom for nectar-feeding wildlife. Thought to have been introduced to New Orleans between 1848-1860.

Abutilon pictum (Gillies ex Hook. & Arn.) Walp. **FLOWERING MAPLE** Brazil. Mallow family, shrub, 15 feet. Best in full sun. Fertile, moist, humusy, loose soil. Flowers summer to frost, or year-round if it does not have to regrow from the roots after a freeze. Leaves are similar in shape to maple leaves. Blooms are exotic: bellshaped and orange in color with red veins. Yellows and reds available, too. The fuzzy stamen hangs below the petals like the clapper in the bell. Not reliably hardy in a severe freeze. Roots very easily from cuttings. Hummingbird plant. Small forms. Grown in bedding plant exhibitions during the World Industrial & Cotton Centennial, 1884.

Bauhinia punctata or *B. galpinii* **NASTURTIUM BAU-HINIA**. See *Bauhinia*, EXOTIC DECIDUOUS TREES.

Brugmansia X candida Pers. (*Hortus Third* says plants sold as *B.* or *Datura arborea* are frequently this hybrid) **ANGEL'S TRUMPET** Ecuador. Nightshade family, to 15 feet. Sun. Well-drained soil. Large, velvety light green leaves; flowers 10 inch long inverted trumpets with flared mouths, usually white, yellows and pinks available, too. Mine is peach colored. Bloom comes in continuous waves from late summer to frost. Wonderfully fragrant at night. Will usually come back from the roots after a freeze. Roots very easily from cuttings. All parts of the plant are poisonous. There's been a white one on the corner of Broadway and Leake Avenue for years. Joe Ewan feels it was introduced to New Orleans between 1830-1840. 1947.

Buddleia alternifolia Maxim., *Buddleia asiatica* Lour., *Buddleia davidii* Franch. **BUTTERFLY BUSH** Asian tropics and subtropics. Logania family, deciduous shrub, to 12 feet. Sun. Rich, well-drained soil; tolerant, except of extremes: drought or wetness. Tiny fragrant flowers, white to shades of purple and pink, form in clusters on long spikes at the tips of arching branches in midsummer to fall. Can be cut to the ground each year to encourage growth of larger flowers, since blooms form on new growth. In *B. alternifolia*, flowers develop on last season's growth; these should be cut back after bloom, to about two-thirds of their original height. Butterflies, moths, bees like the blooms. *B. lindleyana* Fort. ex Lindl. was offered by Magnolia Nurseries, 1859.

Caesalpinia gilliesii (Wallich ex Hook.) Benth. or *Poinciana gilliesi* **BIRD OF PARADISE** Argentina. Pea family shrub or tree, 10 feet. Sun or light shade. Well-drained, humusy, slightly acid soil. Light green, feathery leaves with round-edged leaflets; orange-red flowers with prominent, red stamens in clusters eight inches across May through September. Hardy to 27 degrees.

C. pulcherrima (L.) Swartz **PRIDE OF BARBADOS, FLOWER-FENCE** West Indies. Shrub, 10 feet. Sun or light shade. Well-drained, humusy, slightly acid soil. Clusters of five petaled, bright red and yellow flowers with long red stamens year round. Hardy to 28 degrees. Lelievre's list for Louisiana gardens, 1838.

Calliandra guildingii Benth. **TRINIDAD FLAME BUSH** Trinidad. Pea family tree, 30 feet. Well-drained but moist soil. Mimosa like leaves. Brilliant red puffball flowers in spring and summer. Hummingbirds like the flowers of Calliadras.

C. tweedii Benth or *Inga pulcherrima* Cerv. ex Sweet **MEXICAN FLAMEBUSH** Brazil. Shrub, 6 feet. Sun. Well-drained, moist garden soil. Foliage similar to mimosa leaves. Red puffball flowers autumn to spring. One is growing in Mrs. Montgomery's front yard on Prytania Street near Napoleon. 1885.

Cassia alata L. **CANDLESTICK** American tropics. Pea family, shrub, 8 feet. Sun. Fertile, moist, humusy soil. Beautiful, golden-yellow flowers in spikey stalks in late summer and fall. Grown as an annual here due to lack of hardiness and unattractive appearance after one season. Butterfly attracter.

C. corymbosa Lam. **SENNA** South America. Semievergreen shrub, 10 feet. Sun. Moist but well-drained, fertile soil. Dark, blue-green leaves; clusters of yellow flowers July to frost, followed by 6 inch, cylindrical seed pods which remain on plant. Will suffer damage in a freeze.

C. splendida Vogel. **GOLDEN WONDER** Brazil. Semievergreen shrub, 10 feet. Sun. Fertile, well-drained soil. Spectacular display of yellow flowers in autumn. Not fully hardy.

Ceratostigma willmottiana Stapf. **CHINESE PLUMBAGO** China. Leadwort family, deciduous shrub, 4 feet. Sun. Can handle poor soil; needs good drainage. Brilliant blue flowers during summer. Hardy to 15 degrees.

Chaenomeles speciosa (Sweet) Nakai **FLOWERING QUINCE** China. Rose family, deciduous shrub, 10 feet. Sun. Loose, well-drained soil. Foliage is bronze in spring; dark, glossy green when mature. Four-petaled, waxy flowers in colors from pink to peach to red (depending on the cultivar) over a long period in spring; followed by 2 to 4 inch fruit which turns yellow in fall, is used in jellies. Subject to diseases which can cause leaf drop. Early flowers offer nectar to bees, hummers, orioles.

Chamelaucium uncinatum Schauer. **GERALDTON WAX PLANT** Australia. Myrtle family, 15 feet. Sun. Needs very good drainage. Delicate sprays of waxen flowers in shades of pink and lavender; blooms 3 months, winter to spring. Should be cut back one third of its height after flowering to maximize bloom. Hardy to 27 degrees. A 1946 recommendation of Grace M. Thompson.

Chimonanthus praecox (L.) Link **WINTERSWEET** China. Calycanthus family, deciduous shrub, 10 feet. Sun. Any soil. Leathery leaves. Fragrant, yellowish flowers, one inch in size appear winter to early spring.

Clerodendrum L. species **CLERODENDRUM** Asia. Verbena family, shrubs. Sun, part shade. Moist, but well-drained; fertile, loose soil. Clerodendrums were reported in New Orleans gardens in 1849 by Alexander Gordon.

C. bungei Steud. **CASHMERE BOUQUET** 5 feet. Spreads by suckers. Large heart-shaped leaves which give off a bad odor if bruised. 8 inch wide, flat topped, dense clusters of deep rose red flowers form during summer from May atop the tall stems. Relic of an earlier garden, this plant was thriving in the overgrown back yard of my house, abandoned for five years when we purchased it in 1972. I got rid of it because it attracted ants. My neighbor, Miss Maude, told me it was cashmere bouquet. It was available mail-order through Langdon Nurseries of Mobile, listed in their 1874 catalogue. Reputedly grown before 1860 in New Orleans.

C. indicum (L.) O. Kuntze. **TUBEFLOWER, TURK'S-TURBAN** Shrub, to 8 feet. Spidery white flowers followed by purplish fruits on red calyces form at the tops of evergreen leafy stems in late summer-fall. Naturalized in parts of New Orleans. I saw my first one in bloom in a door-step garden on Constance Street. "It just grew there on its own," the gardener told me. Jerome Lebo likes the way the clumps of flowered stems wave in the wind, grows them at City Park Botanical Garden in spite of their invasiveness. Reputedly introduced in the New Orleans Garden District 1898-1910 by Ida Richardson.

C. philippinum Schauer or *C. fragrans* variety *pleniflorum* **CASHMERE BOUQUET, GLORY BOWER** Eight feet. Leaves 10 inches long. One inch, double, white or pinkish flowers in tight clusters; summer.

C. speciosissimum Van Geert., or *C. paniculatum* L. **PAGODA FLOWER, GIANT SALVIA, JAVA SHRUB** There is name confusion in my references. Four feet. Leaves 6 to 12 inches wide. Flowers are scarlet, on one and a half foot stalks which extend above the leaves; followed by dark colored berries. I first saw one growing in an old garden in Covington. It does look like a huge salvia! Hummingbirds like it.

Coronilla valentina L. **CROWN VETCH** Mediterranean. Pea family, shrub, 4 feet. Part shade. Any soil, well-drained. Flowers are fragrant, yellow, pendulous, pea-family blooms. In the same genus as the ground cover, crown vetch.

Coleonema pulchrum Hook. **CONFETTI BUSH, BREATH OF HEAVEN** South Africa. Rue family. Sun. Welldrained soil. Branched shrubs with heath-like, aromatic foliage. Blooms fall to spring. Hardy to low twenties. *C. album* (Thunb.) Bartl & H. L. Wendl. has star-like white flowers. *C. pulchrum* Hook. has flowers of red or pink.

Cuphea micropetala HBK. **MEXICAN CIGARFLOWER, CIGARETTE PLANT** To 5 feet. Sun or part sun. Well-drained soil. Fine, shiny, green leaves. Small, orange, tubular flowers with yellow tips (like the burning ash) in summer to autumn. In the absence of a freeze, it blooms year round in my garden. Hardy to 25 degrees. Foliage burn with frost. Mulch to protect the roots. It should return after most freezes. Easy to propagate from cuttings. Specimens can be seen in Audubon Park in front of the Heymann Memorial Conservatory. (Look for humming-birds there, too!)

Cytisus L. hybrids **BROOM** Pea family. Shrubs native to the Mediterranean and the Canary Islands, Great Britain. Sun. 6 to 8 feet. Dry soil, not too rich, on the acid side, extremely well-drained. Twiggy, green leaves; some varieties used to make brooms. Showy spring to fall blooms; used in florist's bouquets. Though I found only one report of local cultivation of this plant in my refer-ences, it sounds worth the effort. 'Pomona' is described by Thompson thus: *"Very showy. Orange-apricot sweet-pea like flowers, followed by silvery, red, berries."* I found *C. racemosa* identified as *Genista racemosa* dying in pots in the back lot of one local nursery. Genistas were offered in 19th century nursery catalogs in New Orleans.

Datura metel L. **HORN-OF-PLENTY, DEVIL'S TRUM-PET** Chinese and Indian native. Annual, to 5 feet. Sun. Moist but well-drained, fertile soil. Coarse foliage, 8 inch leaves. Trumpet shaped flower to 7 inches with twisted, upturned petals; white, yellow, and purple forms, singles and doubles. Source of the drug scopolamine. Frequently reseeds.

Deutzia Thunb. species **DEUTZIA** Natives of temperate Asia. Saxifrage family deciduous shrubs. From 4 to 10 feet. Sun to part shade. Any moist, well-drained soil. Profuse spring flowers, no fruit, no autumn color. Because of their growth habits, they need a lot of pruning to look good. Less vigorous in areas with mild winters, like New Orleans? Paul Keith, Audubon Park horticulturist, has tried several, says they last about 3 years, then die. New

Orleanians keep trying: 1859, 1885, 1921. *D. gracilis* Siebold & Zucc. **SPREADING DEUTZIA** Japan. 6 feet. Arching foliage; double, white flowers. *D. scabra* Thunb. To seven feet. Mounding form with arching branches; flowers in white, shades of red.

Eleagnus angustifolia L. **RUSSIAN OLIVE** Deciduous, to 20 feet. Sun. Well-drained soil. Leaves are silvery underneath, stems spiny; fragrant yellow flowers are followed by fruit. Bee and bird plant.

Eranthemum pulchellum Andr. **BLUE SAGE** India. Acanthus family shrub, 4 feet. Sun, shade. Light, rich soil; lots of moisture. Deep blue, 5 petaled flowers bloom from a lasting white and green veined bract several inches long; leaves to 8 inches. Will bloom in New Orleans in early spring with the midseason azaleas if it has not been frozen back. Hardy to 32 degrees, protect. May return from the roots. Take cuttings before a freeze to be sure. 1935 as *Daedalacanthus nervosa*.

Euphorbia pulcherrima Willd. ex Klotzsch **POINSETTIA** Mexico, Central America. Spurge family shrub, 15 feet. Sun. Rich soil, moist but well-drained. Small yellow flowers surrounded by leaf-like bracts in red, pink, or white; winter bloom. Southern exposure, protection are your best bets outdoors, here. Hardy to 25 degrees. Most newer cultivars were developed for indoors. My neighbor has one grown from a cutting from Mexico which lasted in his garden for years, died with the 1989 freeze. Introduced to Charleston in 1833 by Joel Poinsett. 1918.

Felicia fruticosa (L.) Nichols. **ASTER BUSH** South Africa. Composite family shrub, 2 and one-half feet. Sun. Dry, well-drained gravelly soil, enriched with organic matter. Spring flowers are aster form in purple, pink or white. Hardy to 26 degrees.

Galphimia glauca Cav. **SHOWER OF GOLD, THRYALLIS** Mexico. Malpighia family shrub, semi-evergreen, 6 feet. Sun. Well-drained, fertile soil. Green leaves, new stem growth is red. Loose clusters of yellow flowers in summer are so profuse as to almost hide the foliage. Hardy to 28 degrees.

Hibiscus mutabilis L. **CONFEDERATE ROSE, COTTON ROSE** China. Mallow family, shrublike perennial, 15 feet. Sun. Fertile soil, lots of water. 4 inch wide flowers are white when they open in the morning, change to pink to red to maroon through the day until they fall at night. Bloom June to October, longer in mild weather. Found in old gardens. 1947.

Hibiscus syriacus L. **ALTHAEA, ROSE-OF-SHARON** Asia. Mallow family shrub, deciduous, 12 feet. Sun. Fertile, well-drained soil. Summer to fall flowers are showy, single to semi-double to double in white and shades of red, pink, purple, blue. Prolific bloom on plants which can get rangy, but can be pruned heavily to increase flowers and keep in bounds. Single blossoms more appealing to hummingbirds. Due to limited selection in any one local nursery and the large number of varieties available, I suggest ordering them from a source with lots of choices or taking cuttings from your favorites in friends' gardens. Hardy here. Grown since 1820 or before in New Orleans.

Hydrangea macrophylla (Thunb.) Ser. **GARDEN HYDRANGEA** Japan. Saxifrage family shrub, deciduous, 5 feet. Shade, part sun. Fertile, moist but well-drained soil, mulch. Needs extra water during hot months to keep from wilting. Large, shiny leaves with serrated edges; rounded clusters of flowers from 4 to 15 inches across, depending on the variety, in May and June; white, blue, pink. To change flower color (takes 2 years), add lime to the soil for pink; add iron or aluminum sulfate for blue. Prune right after flowering. Mulch for winter protection. Many new cultivars. Introduced to New Orleans before 1800. 1859, 1935.

Itea illicifolia, I. yunnanensis, **SWEETSPIRE** See *Itea,* NATIVE DECIDUOUS SHRUBS.

Indigofera kirilowii Maxim. ex Palib. **INDIGO** China. Pea family, deciduous, to 4 feet. Part shade. Moist, fertile soil. Delicate, fernlike foliage on stems which rise from underground suckers to form clumps; rose tinted pea-like pendulous clusters of flowers 5 inches long, spring through fall. Hardy. Mine is loosely clumped with arching branches.

Jasminum floridum Bunge **FLORIDA JASMINE** China. Semievergreen, 4 feet. Sun, part shade. Fertile, well-drained soil. Branches arch from a central clump. Fragrant, star-shaped yellow flowers form in clusters during spring. May not last through the severe freezes which we occasionally experience. *J. polyanthum* Franch. **PINK JAS-MINE** Scrambling shrub, used as vine or shrub. For other jasmines, see VINES.

Kolkwitzia amabilis Graebn. **BEAUTY BUSH** China. Deciduous shrub, Honeysuckle family, 10 feet. Sun, part shade. Any well-drained soil, poor better. In spring, clusters of tiny yellow throated, pink flowers form so thickly on the arched branches that the slender, grayish green leaves are hidden. Hairy seed pods remain on plant through winter. Foliage reddish in fall.

Lantana camara L. **HAM AND EGGS** Tropical America. Verbena family, perennial shrub, 4 feet. Sun. Any soil, can handle dry. Sprawling, irregular form. Hairy, 5 inch, toothed, yellow-green leaves, aromatic when crushed. 2 inch clusters of tiny red and yellow flowers, summer to frost. Cultivars flowers in combinations of white, vivid pinks, yellows, orange-reds as well as solids. Dark berries in fall. Used as a ground cover, too. Grown here since the early 19th century. Flowers are attractive to bees, butterflies, hummingbirds. 1921.

L. montevidensis (K. Spreng.) Briq. **WEEPING, TRAIL-ING LANTANA** Sun. Well-drained soil, but adaptable. Sprawling, mounded form; frequently used as a ground cover. Profuse rosy-lilac flowers in 1 inch cluster heads summer and fall, year-round if winters are frostless. On

Daneel Street, I saw several plants woven into an 8 foot page fence, forming a wall of purple and green. 1935.

Magnolia quinquepeta (Buc'hoz) Dandy **TULIP MAGNOLIA** China.   See *Magnolia*, NATIVE EVERGREEN TREES.

Malvaviscus arboreus variety *Drummondii* **TURK'S CAP, SULTAN'S TURBAN** Old World tropics.   Mallow family shrub, evergreen, 8 feet.   Shade, part sun.   Moist, sandy, alkaline soils.   Light green leaves with toothed edges on a vine-like shrub which needs propping by a fence or another shrub to maintain somewhat erect posture.   Blooms are bright red, twisted petals, protruding stamens, summer to frost.   (Judy Burke's mother calls them "Chinese earrings" or "earring plant.")   Will freeze back, return from the roots.   Easy to grow.   Can be trained as a groundcover, also.   Hummingbird plant.

Manihot esculenta Crantz **CASSAVA** Brazil.   Deciduous due to frost sensitivity, 9 feet, Spurge family shrub.   Sun, part sun.   Rich, moist, sandy soil.   Leaves to 16 inches, deeply cut into finger-like lobes.   Flowers insignificant. Known for its edible roots which resemble sweet potatoes: tapioca is the product after a poisonous sap is removed.

Odontonema strictum (Nees) O. Kuntze **FIRESPIKE** Central America.   Perennial shrub, Acanthus family, 6 feet. Sun, part shade.   Does best in moist, fertile   soil, but is adaptable.   6 inch long, wavy edged leaves.   Clumping stems which are erect or lean towards more sun give this plant a sprawling look.   Flowers appear in June, last through fall, are stem tip spikes of one inch scarlet flowers, only a few in bloom at one time.   The hummingbirds which the flowers attract are more ornamental than the plant, itself.   Some people call it "the hummingbird plant." Roots very easily from cuttings.   I've seen it in old gardens, in the wild garden at Long Vue.   Mine came from Norma Harmison's garden near the parish line.

Philadelphus coronarius L. **MOCK ORANGE** Europe, Asia.   Saxifrage family shrub, deciduous, 10 feet.   Sun, part shade.   Good drainage essential; rich, moist soil is best though it can handle dryer soil.   Arching branches, 3 inch oval leaves; studded with fragrant, 4 petaled, creamy white flowers with yellow in April to May.   Removal of non-flowering canes after bloom keeps it from becoming rangy.   Found in old gardens.   Double varieties as well as other species and hybrids of *Philadelphus* are available. Flowers attract bees, butterflies, hummingbird moths. 1885.

Plumbago auriculata Lam. or *P. capensis* **PLUMBAGO, CAPE LEADWORT**   South Africa.   Leadwort family, shrublike perennial, to 10 feet.   Sun.   Well-drained, rich, moist, loose soil.   Vining shrub with arching branches; best against a structure, for both support and winter shelter. Pale blue clusters of phlox-like flowers from March to December, peak May to November.   Pruning yearly is recommended.   Hardy to 25 degrees.   When well planted, protected, will return from the ground after freeze-back. Camilla Bradley said in "New Orleans Garden," May, 1980: *"When I think of plumbago I am reminded of the End Zone plantings that once adorned the now demolished Tulane Stadium. They provided the blue component of the traditional olive and blue Tulane colors."* 1918, 1921.

Plumeria L. species **FRANGIPANI** Dogbane family. Sun, light shade.   Any soil.   Gorgeous flowering shrubs or trees with slender trunks and large, simple, leathery green leaves which are becoming popular as potted plants in local gardens.   The richly colored and fragrant periwinkle shaped flowers (spring to fall) are in 6 inch clusters, are used to make leis in Hawaii.   Hardy to 30 degrees, so must be brought indoors through most of our winters, though Dan Davis' lasted the winter of 1988 outdoors. Cuttings root easily, will bloom in a year if fertilized (recommended formula is 5-30-5).   Size and form of plant can be controlled by root pruning and judicious pruning of branches.   Improved hybrids, including evergreens, are available, but the basic parents, both   deciduous, are

P. obtusa L. Carribean. 24 feet. Leaves 7 inches. Inch or more wide, 5 petalled, fragrant white flowers with yellow eyes. *P. rubra* L. Mexico to Panama. 25 feet. Leaves to 20 inches. 4 inch flowers in pink, red, yellow, white, with yellow centers, fragrant.

Polygala apopetala Brandeg. **POLYGALA** Baja California. Milkwort family shrub, to 15 feet. Sun, part shade. Well-drained dry or moist soil. Clusters of pinkish-purple flowers on stem tips during summer. Hardy to 20 degrees. A specimen was growing in Jackson Square until recently.

Punica granatum L. **POMEGRANATE** Europe, Asia. Pomegranate family, deciduous, to 20 feet. Sun, part shade. Rich, moist, deep, well-drained soil. Smooth, leathery, 3 inch, oblong leaves, coppery when new, yellow in fall. April to September blooms are 2 inches, have orange-red crinkled petals; varieties with white and yellow or blended and streaked flowers, also. Edible fruit is deep-yellow to red, 4 inches, contains pulp encased seeds. Some varieties produce no fruit. 'Wonderful' and 'Sweet' do. Longtime popular plant in New Orleans. Grown in the Botanical Garden of the Ursulines in 1731. 1947.

Russelia equisetiformis Schlechtend. & Cham. **CORAL PLANT, FOUNTAIN PLANT, PTERIS FERN** Mexico. Figwort family shrub to 4 feet. Sun. Rich, well-drained soil. Clumps of arching, rush-like, many-branched stems with needle like leaves. Tubular, red flowers in profusion late spring through cool weather. Hardy to 28 degrees. There are some long established specimens in this area which have returned from the roots after many freezes. Mulch and protect. Hummingbird plant. 1947.

Salix discolor Muhlenb. **PUSSY WILLOW** Eastern North American swamps. Deciduous shrub, Willow family, 8 feet. Sun. Humusy soil, lots of water. Grown for its soft and silvery male catkins, the pollen producing flowering part of this dioecious plant, which appear on the shrubs in early spring and are used by florists in displays. Need colder winters than ours, so will not last in New Orleans. Another plant for experiments.

Sesbania punicea (Cav.) Benth. **RATTLE BOX** Brazil, Argentina, Uruguay. Pea family, deciduous shrub, to 6 or more feet. Sun. Moist, heavy clay soils. Feathery foliage, sparse, irregular form. Blossoms June to September are pea family dense, pendulous clusters of dark red to orange-red blooms followed by 4 inch seed pods within which dried seeds rattle. I have seen red and yellow varieties for sale, have found the plant growing wild in the marshy areas around Lake Pontchartrain off Highway 51. Grow easily from seeds, which are poisonous. Can be weedy.

Tecomaria capensis (Thunb.) Spach **CAPE HONEY-SUCKLE** Africa. Bignonia family shrub, 6 feet. Sun. Any soil, dry, wet, heavy, light. Form can be vinelike, used as ground cover, hedges, also; needs pruning to stay in bounds. Shiny, dark green leaves. Summer-fall blooms are tubular clusters in yellow or red-orange. Hardy to 25 degrees. Hummingbird plant.

Tetrapanax papyriferus (Hook.) C. Koch **RICE PAPER PLANT** China. Aralia family, semi-evergreen shrub or tree, 15 feet. Sun, part shade. Rich, moist but well-drained soil is best. Becomes tree-like as it ages, trunk is slender, gray, topped by foliage: foot or two wide leaves divided into 5 to 7 pointed lobes; dark or grayish-green above, fuzzy below. Flowers are one inch, white, globes, on 3 foot spikes in fall, winter; followed by small green berries which turn black. A mature plant in bloom is dramatic. Plants can die to the ground in a freeze, come back. Spread by underground runners which must be continually pulled unless spread can be physically restricted. I think the plant is worth the trouble. Bees love the flowers, birds the berries. Reputedly introduced in New Orleans between 1848-1860. 1921.

Weigela florida (Bunge) A. DC. **OLD-FASHIONED WEIGELA** Many species, cultivars. China, Korea. Decid-

uous shrub, Honeysuckle family, 10 feet. Sun, light shade.
Any soil, rich is better, good drainage is essential, but so
is moisture retention.   Open, spreading graceful form,
pointed leaves to 4 inches. Funnel shaped 2 inch rosepink
flowers in clusters of 3 and 4 appear along the stems right
before the new leaves in spring.   Prefers colder winters
than ours. Not long lasting in New Orleans--4 to 5 years
estimates Nancy Newfield.   Beautiful while it lasts.   Red
flowered CARDINAL SHRUB is frequently advertised. Its
brief but stunning bloom is appreciated by hummingbirds,
other nectar drinkers. 1885.

EVERGREEN TREES

Acmena smithii (Poir.) Merrill & L.M. Perry LILLY-
PILLY TREE Australia. Myrtle family. 25 feet. Sun, part
shade. Any soil. Bronze green foliage, evergreen. Clusters
of small whitish to purplish flowers in May to July followed by showy, purple berries in winter.   Not reliably
hardy here, so plant in protected spot.
     Araucaria araucana (Mol.) C. Koch MONKEY-PUZZLE
TREE, CHILEAN PINE (Formerly *A. imbricata*) Araucaria
family. Chile. Evergreen conifer, 50 feet. Sun. Moist,
well-drained soil; high humidity.   Twisted form; 2 inch,
leathery, needle-like leaves are pointed up on down drooping branches which are upturned at the tips. (Coming
down unstuck would be a puzzle for a monkey who
climbed up smoothly; hence, the name.)   One nursery
catalog calls it "uniquely strange" and "commanding" in
appearance, with "snaky branches."   Magnolia Nurseries
Catalogue of New Orleans, 1859, called it "very distinct".
Cones have edible seeds, are 3 to 7 inches high. According to references, it should be hardy to Zone 7.   There
were huge specimens on Robert E. Lee before the 1983
freeze and in other places. Sometimes confused with the

Cunningham fir. Paul Wells tells of a tree the cajuns call a "monkey tree." One grows somewhere in Folsom. I wonder if it's the same as a monkey puzzle?

A. bidwillii Hook. **BUNYA-BUNYA** Australia. Evergreen tree, 80-150 feet. Sun. Rich, moist, well-drained, acid soil. Needles are dark green, shiny, 2 inches, sharply pointed and spirally arranged on young trees. Mature foliage is oval, one-half inch. Cones on older trees are 10 inches and pineapple-like. Not reliably hardy. Available 1885, Maitre & Cook Nurseries of New Orleans. Specimens could be seen in the Australian exhibit at Audubon Zoological Garden and on General Haig across from Joy Peterson's house until the freeze of 1989.

A. heterophylla (Salisb.) Franco. **NORFOLK ISLAND PINE** Norfolk Island. Evergreen, 10 feet; to 200 feet in native setting. Sun. Rich, well-drained soil, humidity. Open form; loose branches with short, evergreen needles are horizontal, sometimes pendulous, from the main trunk. Familiar as a pot plant. Not reliably hardy here, but in the right spot....

Azara microphylla Hook.f. **BOXLEAF AZARA** Chile. Flacourtia family, evergreen shrub or tree, 18 feet. Shade. Well-drained soil, plenty of moisture. One inch, glossy, dark-green leaves; pendulous sprays of dainty, vanilla-scented greenish flowers with conspicuous stamens, followed by orange berries. Fragrance way out of proportion to size. Best results when fed. Popular in California. Other varieties available. This is another 1946 recommendation of Grace M. Thompson.

Cedrus atlantica (Endl.) G. Manetti ex Carriere **ATLAS CEDAR**, *C. deodara* (D. Don) G. Don. **DEODAR CEDAR**. North Africa and Asia. Pine family evergreens, 100 or more feet. Sun. Well-drained clay-loam soil. Leaves are short, narrow needles on stiff or pendulous branches, irregularly formed trees. Long lived. Though supposedly better adapted to more northern areas than New Orleans, the several specimens I have seen uptown, including one on Jefferson Avenue near St. Charles, are straggly but interesting. *C. libani* A. Rich., is the biblical **CEDAR OF LEBANON.** Though not common, it was used in New Orleans as early as 1840 when planted in Henry Lawrence's estate, Louisa Street fronting on Desire. *C. deodara* and *C. libani* both were offered by Magnolia Nurseries, as listed in the 1859 catalogue.

Cinnamomum camphora (L.) J. Presl. **CAMPHOR TREE** China, Japan. Laurel family, evergreen tree, 100 feet. Sun, part shade. Adaptable; though rich, moist soil is best. Glossy, dark green leaves smell of camphor when bruised. Pea-sized, black berries are good wildlife food. Drawbacks: other plants will not grow beneath it due to its competitive roots; leaves do not break down quickly. Reputedly brought to Louisiana during the 1840's. *Southern Garden* magazine, December, 1894, says *"Of late the Laurus camphora or Camphora tree has been added to our list of shade trees...."* Common here until severe freezes in 1963, 1983. Listed 1918, 1947.

C. Cassia (Nees) Nees & Eberm. ex Blume. **CASSIA BARK TREE, CHINESE CINNAMON** Burma. To 40 feet. 6 inch long leaves. Recommended by E. A. McIlhenny in 1928. Grace Thompson called it *"A great improvement over the common camphor tree"* in 1947. Bark is used like cinnamon.

Citrus species **CITRUS** Oranges were among the first imported plants grown in New Orleans, 1718. The varieties used for street plantings were grown for their fragrant spring blossoms, not their sour fruit. Many varieties of oranges, lemons, limes, grapefruit, and shaddock, similar to the grapefruit but a separate species, have been grown here through the years. A good source of information on citrus varieties for our climate is the Louisiana Cooperative Extension Service.

C. reticulata Blanco **SATSUMA, MANDARIN ORANGE** Asia. Rue family, evergreen tree, 10 feet. 6 hours of sun daily. Highly organic, loamy, slightly acid to neutral soil. Thick growth of glossy green leaves in a rounded crown, low branches. Fragrant, white, waxy blossoms in March and April; followed (in December) by mature satsumas. Not completely hardy, should be planted in a position which is physically protected: by a building, hedge, etc. Wrap young trees when freeze expected. Subject to attack by several pests and diseases which can be controlled by spraying. Flowers offer nectar to bees, hummers, butterflies.

Cunninghamia lanceolata (Lamb.) Hook. **CUNNING-HAM FIR, CHINA FIR** Asia. Taxodium family, evergreen, 120 feet. Sun. Well-drained, loose, acid soil. Pointed, light green needles with whitish undersides. Drooping branches, overall conical shape, though interestingly irregular. Foliage is similar to that of the Araucaria family. It is sometimes mistakenly called monkey-puzzle tree by New Orleanians. The leading clue to the difference if you are not sure is the cones: male are small clustered catkins, female, 2 inches; far from the 5 to 7 inches of *A. araucana*. Healthy specimens can be found on Leontine off Prytania and in the Heymann Conservatory. They are reportedly not reliable here, consistent with one tale of sudden death in an apparently thriving tree.

Eriobotrya japonica (Thunb.) Lindl. **JAPANESE PLUM, LOQUAT** traditional local name, **MESPILUS JAPONICA** Japan, China. Rose family tree, evergreen, 25 feet. Sun, part sun. Rich, loose, well-drained soil. 10 inch veined leaves, leathery in texture; dark green tops, lighter with a rusty colored fuzz underneath. Small, creamy-white, fragrant flowers in fall, winter provide nectar for wintering hummingbirds. Yellow-orange pear shaped fruit in spring attracts birds, squirrels, and hordes of small children. I'm glad mine can't be seen from the street anymore. Easy to grow from dropped seeds. Can be killed in severe freezes. It has been grown here since the early 18th century. Journalist Sylvanus described it as a local favorite in 1851, but denigrated its fruit. 1921, 1935.

Eucalyptus cinerea F. J. Muell. ex Benth. **SILVER DOL-LAR TREE** Australia. Myrtle family tree, evergreen, 25 feet. Sun. Fertile, well-drained soil; root rot will occur if drainage is not perfect. Aromatic, attractive foliage consisting of pairs of round leaves along thin stems is the reason for growing this plant. The scent is long lasting in stems cut and used in arrangements indoors. Subject to freeze damage; protect until established. Other species to try: *E. camphora* R. T. Bak., *E. neglecta* Maiden.

Grevillea banksii R. Br. **SPIDER FLOWER** Australia. Protea family shrub or tree, evergreen, 20 feet. Sun, part shade. Loose, well-drained soil. Attractive fernlike leaves. The 6 inch flowers are dense, spidery projections in red, bloom year-round. Protect when young. Severe enough freeze may kill it.

G. robusta A. Cunn. **SILK OAK** Australia. Evergreen tree, to 100 feet, 25 is average. Sun, part shade. Loose, well-drained soil. Fernlike leaves; olive green above, silver beneath. Bristly 6 to 10 inch orange-yellow flowers in spring. Hardy to 20 degrees. My husband grew a beautiful silk oak in his Short Street yard which was killed in the freeze of 1963.

Ilex cornuta Lindl. & Paxt. **CHINESE HOLLY** China. See *Ilex*, NATIVE EVERGREEN SHRUBS.

Juniperus L. species **JUNIPER** Cypress family evergreens from prostrate ground cover to upright shrub or tree in form, with needle- or scale-like leaves, gray or green berry-like cones on the female trees, a reputation for handling tough environmental conditions, some known as cedars. Many are available. Depending on the specific form, can provide food, cover, nest sites for birds.

J. chinensis L. 'Pfitzerana' **PFITZER JUNIPER** Asia. To 6 feet. Sun. Moist, sandy or loamy soil; tolerates dry, gravelly conditions. Broad, horizontally spreading form, feathery, gray-green foliage.

Leptospermum scoparium J.R. Forst & G. Forst **TEA TREE** New Zealand. Myrtle family, evergreen, 6 feet.

Sun. Sandy, well-drained, slightly acid soil. Half inch long, rigid, fragrant leaves from which Captain Cook brewed a "tea". Half inch flowers, single or double, white, pinks, reds, in profusion in spring-summer. Hardy to 25 degrees so protect.

Metrosideros excelsus Soland, ex Gaertn. **NEW ZEAL-AND CHRISTMAS TREE, IRONWOOD** Myrtle family, 30 feet, evergreen tree. Sun. Well-drained, acid soil. 4 inch oval leaves, lustrous dark green on top, fuzzy gray below. Another of the "bottlebrushes", its flowers are "pincushions" of brilliant scarlet stamens 1 or more inches in length on white stalks; summer bloom here. Hardy only to 25 degrees. Recommended for pot culture. Advertised for sale in 1855 *Daily Picayune* ads. Two species offered 1859. According to E. A. McIlhenny in 1927, the plants called *Metrosideros* by nurserymen *"for many years"*[23] are usually erroneously identified *Callistemon* species.

Persea americana [*P. gratissima* C. F. Gaertn.] **AVOCA-DO, ALLIGATOR PEAR** Mexico, Guatemala, West Indies. Laurel family, evergreen tree, 60 feet. Dark green, oval leaves to 8 inches. Considered a foliage house plant by those who spear seeds from grocery bought avocadoes (the fruit from this tree) with toothpicks, hang them over glass rims with their bottoms in a half inch of water, and watch them root; then transplant them to a pot. Bob Tannen's garden on Esplanade had a 40 foot tall avocado tree growing in an unprotected spot when he moved there 15 years ago. The tree bore fruit, a small, dark skinned variety, but only for two years. He said it was damaged by one of our hard freezes, had to be cut back some, but is still there! The variety 'Duke' is hardy to 20 degrees. Avocadoes are a wildlife hazard in some parts of the world where they flourish; I read a report of squirrels plummeting to their deaths under car wheels while trying to carry the heavy fruits in their mouths over electric and telephone wires above auto traffic. Reputedly introduced in New Orleans 1830-1840.

Royena lucida L. **AFRICAN EBONY TREE** South Africa. Ebony family evergreen, 12 feet. Sun. Well-drained
soil. Blossoms in spring are fluffy, white to yellowish,
lemon scented; can be followed by 1 inch long, red or
purple, white-fleshed fruit. A tropical for protected spots
such as the Toulouse Street patio where one is pictured in
Walled Gardens of the French Quarter, 1974.

Schinus terebinthifolius Raddi. **BRAZILIAN PEPPER
TREE, CHRISTMAS-BERRY TREE** Cashew family, evergreen tree, 20 feet. Sun. Dry soil. Lacey foliage, oblong
2 and a half inch leaflets; dark green above, lighter below.
Small greenish-yellow flowers followed by bright red
berries which cover the plant in late summer. Can be
damaged by freeze, should return. This bush has negatives as a wildlife plant: the berries make birds such as
cedar waxwings and robins drunk, victims of collision
with automobiles, easy targets for predatory cats. It was
introduced in Florida by Henry Nehrling in 1898, has now
become an environmental hazard there due to invasiveness. It can cause allergic reactions and illness in people
who ingest the berries or come into contact with sap,
blooms. CHRISTMAS PEPPER was listed in 1918. Is it
the same plant? *S. molle* L., **CALIFORNIA PEPPER TREE,
PERUVIAN PEPPER TREE** is safe for birds.

Syzygium paniculatum Gaertn. **AUSTRALIAN BRUSH
CHERRY** Australia. Evergreen tree, Myrtle family, 40 feet.
Sun. Any well-drained soil, moisture. Glossy, green, 3
inch leaves; red-tinged when new. Half-inch white flowers, conspicuous stamens, in sparse clusters fall and winter. Rose-purple three-quarter inch edible berries follow.
More compact varieties available. Hardy to 26 degrees.

EVERGREEN SHRUBS

Acacia baileyana F. J. Muell. **GOLDEN MIMOSA** See *Acacia*, NATIVE EVERGREEN SHRUBS.

Ardisia crenata Sims **CORALBERRY** Malaysia. Myrsine family, evergreen shrub, 3 feet. Partial shade; no direct sunlight. Fertile, well-drained but moist soil. Glossy, dark green leaves. Small, white, scented flowers in spring are followed by red berries which last 6 months or more, droop in clusters below the foliage. Protect if freeze to low twenties predicted. 1885. *A. crispa* (Thunb.) A. DC is thought to have been grown in French Quarter gardens before 1860.

A. japonica (Hornst.) Blume **MARLBERRY** Japan, China. Evergreen, to 18 inches. Shade, part shade; direct summer sun can burn leaves. Rich, loose, well-drained soil; mulch. Spreads by underground runners. Long used in New Orleans gardens, it is again becoming popular as a groundcover. Glossy, 4 inch, finetoothed edged leaves; tiny pinkish-white flowers through summer-fall are followed by berries which turn red in November.

Aucuba japonica Thunb. **AUCUBA** Japan. Dogwood family, evergreen shrub, 5 feet. Part shade, protect from noon sun. Acid soil; humusy, porous, moist but well-drained is best; but they will tolerate drought and almost any soil. Leaves are shiny, green and bright yellow variegated or solid, depending on the cultivar. Inconspicuous flowers are produced in spring followed by clusters of red berries on female plants, but only if plants of both sexes are available. 1859.

Brunfelsia australis Benth., *B. parciflora* (Cham. & Schlechtend.) Benth. sometimes called *B. calycina floribunda* **YESTERDAY, TODAY, AND TOMORROW** South America. Nightshade family, evergreen shrub, 9 or 12 feet. Part shade, sun. Fertile, moist, acid soil. Glossy, dark green leaves; flowers in spring are rich violet which fade to blue-lavender, to white over 2 to 3 days time. All three colors are present on the bush at the same time, hence the name. Some varieties bloom intermittantly through the year. Bloom is more profuse if the roots are crowded: they do well in pots. Said to be hardy only to 27 degrees, so planting in a protected spot would be prudent, however, mine has lasted outdoors for 5 years. There is one in full sun and exposure in the garden on the corner of St. Charles and Dufoussat which I have admired for years. The gardener told me it grew from a cutting given by a friend sometime during the 1970's. She says it has thrived and been through severe freezes without being "wrapped, fed, or talked to." Possibly introduced in New Orleans around 1840.

Buxus microphylla variety *japonica* Rehd. & E. H. Wils. **JAPANESE BOX** Box family, evergreen shrub, to 6 feet. Sun, part shade. Well-drained soil. Small leaves, fine texture, tolerates shearing and pruning, making it a favorite for hedges and edging. This variety is traditional in New Orleans, is called **CREOLE BOX** here though it was not introduced to this country from Japan until 1860, so could not have been used in earlier creole gardens. *Buxus japonicum* was offered by Langdon Nurseries of Mobile, 1874. Variety *koreana* Nakae. **KOREAN BOX** is more spreading, to two feet high. Cultivar 'Compacta' grows to two feet.

B. sempervirens L. **COMMON BOX** Europe. Shrub or tree, 6-15 feet. This is the first boxwood hedging, brought to this country from England in early Colonial times. It tends not to last in our area due to susceptibility to root fungi. It was used, however. The tree form, 'Arborescens', and 'Dwarf Box' were both offered by Magnolia Nurseries in 1859. 'Argentea' and 'Suffruticosa', **EDGING BOX**, by Langdon Nurseries of Mobile, 1874.

Callistemon citrinus (Curtis) Stapf [*C. lanceolatus*] **CRIMSON** or **LEMON BOTTLEBRUSH** Australia. Myrtle family, evergreen, 25 feet. Sun. Well-drained soil; can

tolerate alkaline conditions, drought. Elongated, bright red
flowers with long stamens like the bristles on a bottlebrush, heavy in spring to summer with a few to late
autumn. Hardy to 24 degrees. Felicia Kahn had one in a
brick planter by her front door until the bad freeze of
1983 when many New Orleans specimens were lost.
Pretty ones can be seen on Dublin Street near the corner
of Birch and in the Australian exhibit at Audubon Zoo.
Callistemon rigidus R. Br., from New South Wales is available, too. If E. A. McIlhenny is correct in his 1927 statement that this genus has erroneously been called *Metrosideros* for years, this plant was offered in 1859 by Magnolia
Nurseries.

Camellia L. species **CAMELLIA** Asia.   Tea family.
Evergreen shrubs.   Part shade, sun; small plants need
shade. Rich, slightly acid soil; high in organic matter and
sand for good drainage, yet constant moisture. Additional
watering may be necessary during dry months.   Raised
beds and soil replacement (with 1 part azalea-camellia soil,
1 part peat moss, 1 part sharp sand) is recommended.
When planting, set so the level at which the plants grew
in the container is 1 inch above soil line, so the plant can
settle in properly, its shallow roots at the surface. 2 to 3
inches of mulch for root protection and moisture conservation is important. Oak or pine leaves will help maintain
acidity, as will an azalea-camelia fertilizer applied after
bloom each year.   These trees are slow growing, under-
feeding is better than over. If needed, pruning should be
done immediately after bloom. The best protection against
disease is the health assured by good growing conditions.
Some problems you may see in New Orleans camellias
are:
1.   Scale, an insect infestation detected by a whitish coating on the bottoms of leaves. Treat it with an oil emulsion spray during spring and fall, when the temperature is
under 80 degrees in the shade and over 50 degrees.

Application during extremes of temperature can cause damage to the plant.

2.   Aphids and other chewing insects, which can be killed by Malathion.

3.   Flower blight, which causes discoloration of the petals; can be controlled by spraying under the plants with a fungicide; old blossoms which can harbor the fungus should be collected and destroyed, not allowed to accumulate on the ground.   Hummingbirds may visit the blossoms for nectar.

C. japonica **CAMELLIA** 15 feet.   Glossy green leaves. Flowers late fall through spring, depending on the cultivar; single or double in colors pink, red, variegated, white; to five inches across.   Choose from a nursery with a large selection during bloom season so you can see what you are getting.   A traditional New Orleans garden tree since antebellum days.   Do well in pots.   Blossoms are pretty floating in a bowl of water.

C. reticulata Lindl. 35 feet in native settings in China. More tender here than other varieties.   Called *"one of the most beautiful of all camellias,"* by Pizzetti.[24]   Rose colored, semi-double flowers; bloom from late November to February in mild winters.   1947.

C. sasanqua Thunb. **SASANQUA** 15 feet.   Frequently used as hedges.   Smaller leaves than those of *C. japonica*. Flowers, to 4 inches, are present in fall and winter; some varieties are fragrant.

C. sinensis (L.) O. Kuntze **TEA PLANT** 30 feet.   Shade. Leaves 2 to five inches.   Single, white flowers in large quantities in the fall.   This is the plant from whose leaves commercial tea comes.   Not common as a garden plant; recommended for our area.

Carissa grandiflora (E.H. Mey.) A. DC. **NATAL PLUM** South Africa.   Dogbane family, evergreen, lowgrowing spreading shrub or erect shrub to 18 feet.   Sun.   Rich, loose, well-drained soil.   Leathery, dark green, oval, spine-tipped leaves.   2 inch white starshaped flowers in spring have an orange-blossom fragrance; red, 2 inch, edible fruits follow, like cranberries in taste. Hardy to 26 degrees. May be killed in a bad winter. 'Green Carpet,' 'Prostrata,' and 'Tomlinson' are suitable as ground covers.

Cestrum diurnum L. **DAY BLOOMING JESSAMINE** West Indies. Nightshade family, 15 feet, evergreen shrub. Sun, part shade. Fertile, well-drained soil. Clusters of fragrant, creamy, white flowers during summer. Hardy to 25 degrees; best in a protected spot. Reported in New Orleans gardens in 1849 by Alexander Gordon. Has become an invasive pest in Florida. Fruits and foliage are poisonous to animals, children.

C. nocturnum L. **NIGHT BLOOMING JESSAMINE** West Indies. Evergreen shrub, 12 feet. Sun, part shade. Fertile, well-drained soil. Greenish white clusters of incredibly fragrant flowers which open at night and are present off and on throughout the summer to frost. Should return from the roots after a freeze if in a protected spot. Grown here since the 18th century.

Choisya ternata HBK. **MEXICAN ORANGE** Mexican native. Rue family, evergreen shrub, 10 feet. Sun, part shade. Sandy, rich, acid soil. Aromatic leaves; very fragrant white flowers in spring.

Chorizema varium Benth. **FLAME PEA** Australia. Pea family, evergreen shrub, 6 feet. Sun or part shade. Any well-drained soil. Orange and purple-red pealike flowers, spring and summer. Can handle light frost.

Cistus X hybridus Pourr. **ROCK ROSE** Mediterranean. Rock Rose family, evergreen, bushy; to 30 inches. Sun. Any very well-drained soil; mature plants are subject to root rot with too much water. One and a half inch flowers are white, yellow-centered; present in summer. Hardy to 20 degrees.

Cotoneaster Medic. species **COTONEASTER** Old World temperate regions. Rose family. Evergreen shrubs, heights from 18 feet to 18 inches, sprawling and prostrate in form. Sun. Well-drained, alkaline soil. Flowers are clusters of small pink or white blossoms in early summer. Plants are grown more for their fall foliage which turns bright colors, and their berries. Can take a year or more after planting to become attractive. Many cultivars are available. Birds eat the berries, bees like the flowers.

C. apiculatas Rehd. & E. H. Wils. **CRANBERRY CO-TONEASTER** China. Low and spreading, irregularly branched. Pink flowers, large, scarlet berries.

C. congestus Bak. **COTONEASTER** Himalayan. Low, spreading; gray leaves. Flowers pinkish.

C. horizontalis Decne. **ROCK COTONEASTER** Chinese. To 3 feet, spreads horizontally across the ground. White to pink flowers, scarlet to black berries.

C. lacteus W. W. Sm. **RED CLUSTERBERRY** China. 12 feet. Attractive foliage. Many clusters of white flowers, followed by red berries. Good for espalier.

Cocculus laurifolius (Roxb.) DC. **COCCULUS, MOON-SEED** Himilayas. Moonseed family, evergreen shrub. Sun, part shade. Moist, well-drained soil. Attractive foliage. Not reliably hardy here. Many old specimens in New Orleans were killed in the freeze of 1983. Reputedly introduced in New Orleans gardens 1898-1910.

Daboecia cantabrica (Huds.) C. Koch **IRISH HEATH** Europe. Heath family, evergreen shrubs, to 2 feet with equal spread. Shade. Humusy, acid, well-drained soil; plenty of moisture. Clusters of tiny, waxy, bell-shaped flowers; late spring to fall. Not a heath or heather, though it is related to both. It is another plant which, according to references, should not grow here. One source reports success. When you are ready for experimentation, you may want to try it in an azalea spot.

Duranta repens L. **GOLDEN DEWDROP** Brazil, southern Florida. Verbena family tree-shrub, evergreen, 18 feet. Sun. Well-drained, fertile soil. Bloom begins in spring: small, bluish-lilac flowers which cluster along 6 inch stems are still present when golden berries are formed. Arching foliage becomes pendulous with the weight of the berry clusters in fall. Branches have sharp spines. Hardy to 25 degrees, protect. Usually returns from the roots after freeze damage. See one in front of Heymann Conservatory. 1947.

Eleagnus pungens Thunb. **THORNY ELEAGNUS** China, Japan. Oleaster family shrub, evergreen, 15 feet. Sun. Well-drained soil. Adaptable to tough environmental conditions. Spreading form, spiny branches; leaves are wavy edged, 2 to 4 inches; can be solid olive color or variegated. Fragrant, silvery white pendulous blossoms in fall smell like gardenias, are followed by red berries which are silvery and brown when new. Several varieties are available. Flowers provide fall nectar for bees, berries are spring bird food.

Escallonia mutis ex L.f. **ESCALLONIA** South America. Evergreen shrubs or small trees, Saxifrage family. Sun, light shade. Any well-drained soil. Rich, glossy foliage; large clusters of fragrant, tubular flowers in white or shades of red during fall, winter. Hardy to 20 degrees. Popular in California. Most garden plants of today are hybrids. *E. bifida* Link & Otto was on a list of plants (as *E. floribunda*) purchased for Jackson Square in the 1850's. Cultivars offered by Magnolia Nurseries, 1859.

Euonymous L. species **EUONYMOUS** Species found on most continents though most are Asian, *E. americana* L. is found in Louisiana. Staff-tree family. Most are evergreen; trees or creeping shrubs. Sun or partial shade. Tolerant of most soil; for best results, provide moist, fertile, well-drained. Moisture is especially important for the low, spreading types. Solid and variegated forms have attractive leaves; flowers in spring are insignificant, pink to orange berries follow in the fall, but not reliably. These plants are widely available in spite of the fact that they are susceptible to several diseases and pests which are even greater problems in our climate. *E. japonica* was offered 1859.

Euryops pectinatus Cass. **GOLDEN SHRUB DAISY**
South Africa. Composite family, evergreen shrub, 3 feet.
Sun. Well-drained soil. Silver gray or green foliage (the
green better tolerates our humidity); bright, golden daisy-
like flowers all year. Can survive light frost.

Fatsia japonica (Thunb.) Decne. & Planch. **JAPANESE
ARALIA** Japan. Aralia, evergreen shrub, 6 feet. Part
shade. Loose, moist but well-drained soil. Glossy, blue-
green leaves are large and fan shaped, cut into 7 to 9
lobes, grow at the tops of long stems giving the plant a
rounded shape. Blooms in winter are rounded heads of
creamy-white flowers followed by small blue berries in
spring. *Aralia spinosa* L. DEVIL'S WALKING STICK was
available in 1859.

Feijoa sellowiana O. Berg. **PINEAPPLE GUAVA** Argentina. Myrtle family shrub, 18 feet, evergreen. Sun. Humusy, sandy, well-drained soil. 3 inch green leaves are
fuzzy white underneath. Flowers are 1 to 2 inches, showy
fuschia-like; white on the outside, purplish in, dark red
stamens, March and April. Redtinged green fruit, 3 inches, with white pulp; edible. Tender, though can stand a
little frost; protect. 1935.

Fortunella japonica (Thunb.) Swingle. **KUMQUAT**
Asia. Rue family shrub, evergreen, 10 feet. Sun, part
shade. Fertile, well-drained soil. Yellow green, attractive
leaves; small, white, very fragrant flowers in March and
April; one inch, edible, yellow-orange fruits which are also
used in preserves. Will be damaged by a severe freeze,
best planted in a protected spot. Grown in New Orleans
gardens before 1860.

Galvezia speciosa (Nutt.) A. Gray **ISLAND SNAPDRA-
GON** California. Evergreen vining shrub, Figwort family,
7 feet. Shade. Any moist, very well-drained soil. Spring
flowers are carmine red, like snapdragons. Needs cold
protection when young here.

Gardenia jasminoides Ellis **CAPE JASMINE, COMMON
GARDENIA** China. Madder family shrub, evergreen, 6

feet. Sun, part shade. Fertile, acidic soil, moist but well drained. Leathery, glossy, dark green leaves; waxy, white, wonderfully fragrant blooms, early summer with sporadic bloom in fall. Susceptible to whitefly, mold, scale, for which spraying is necessary. Fewer problems with a well-grown plant: drainage and pH are very important. A traditional shrub probably used in New Orleans gardens before 1800. 1859, 1947.

Halimium ocymoides (Lam.) Willk. & J. Lange. **HALIMIUM** Mediterranean region. Rock Rose family, evergreen, subshrub, 3 feet. Sun. Well-drained, alkaline, dry soil. Hairy leaves, gray and green foliage, yellow flowers with brown basal splotches on each petal, profuse in spring. Hardy to 24 degrees.

Hibiscus rosa-sinensis L. **CHINESE HIBISCUS** Asian. Mallow family, evergreen shrub, 5 feet. Sun. Moist but well-drained, fertile, alkaline soil. Single and double, funnel shaped, gorgeous showy blossoms in white, all shades of yellow, orange, red, pink; singles, doubles; bright yellow column of pistil, stamens protruding from its central depths. Foliage is shiny, attractive. I have never had them come back from the roots after a freeze as one source says they will. All the true enthusiasts I know grow them in pots and drag them in when the temperature drops. Maybe wrapping them will work. They're worth some trouble. Reputedly planted here before 1800. 1921.

Illicium anisatum L. **JAPANESE ANISE** For culture and more information, see *Illicium*, NATIVE EVERGREEN SHRUBS.

Justicia carnea Lindl. **FLAMINGO PLANT** South America. Acanthus family, evergreen, 6 feet. Shade, part shade. Moist, fertile soil. Attractive, deeply veined, green leaves with purplish undersides on clump-forming stems; fluffy, 8 inch clusters of densely packed, pink flowers form at the tips, summer. Cut back each stem after flowering to encourage repeat bloom. Hardy to 28 degrees, plant in protected spot, mulch. Mine came back after the freeze (to 10 degrees) of Christmas, 1989, was blooming in May.

Laurus nobilis L. **LAUREL, SWEET BAY, FRENCH BAY TREE** See *Persea*, NATIVE EVERGREEN TREES.

Ligustrum L. **PRIVET** Most are Asian. Olive family shrubs or small trees, evergreen. Fast growing, adaptable to many conditions. Most common of all plants offered by nurseries, main use is in hedges. If not clipped before flowering, they offer nectar to bees and butterflies, then berries to birds. L. species are listed 1859, 1885, 1935.

L. vulgare L., **COMMON PRIVET**, has many cultivars, including dwarfs. It is European, has been cultivated as a hedge plant for centuries. Subject to problems here.

L. amurense **AMUR PRIVET** China. Semievergreen, 15 feet. Sun best, part shade. Adaptable; but welldrained and fertile soil best. 2 inch leaves; clustered white flowers with a strong aroma in summer. First grown in this country at Berckman's Nursery, Atlanta, 1860. 1918.

L. japonicum Thunb. **WAX LEAF LIGUSTRUM** Japan. Evergreen, 10 feet. Sun, part shade. Fertile, loose soil best, though adaptable; good drainage important. Glossy dark green leaves with light undersides. Clusters of white flowers, heavy scented; offensive and allergenic to some. Dark berries follow. 1918.

L. lucidum Ait. **TREE LIGUSTRUM** China, Japan. Evergreen, 30 feet. Will grow in almost any conditions. Slightly glossy, 5 inch long leaves. White cluster flowers with characteristic ligustrum odor, late spring to summer; berries. Can be grown as a single trunked tree. 1859, 1885.

L. sinense Lour. **CHINESE PRIVET** China. Semievergreen, to 12 feet. Arching branches, dark green leaves. 4 inch clusters of white flowers in late spring, berries.

Mahonia bealei (Fort.) Carriere. **OREGON GRAPE HOLLY, LEATHERLEAF MAHONIA** China. Barberry family shrub, evergreen, to 7 feet. Shade to part shade. Welldrained but moist, humusy soil. Tough and leathery, hollylike leaves; green above, yellow below. Flowers in winter-spring are yellow, fragrant spikes which protrude above foliage. Clusters of bluepurple berries follow, persist on the plant. If flowers and berries form, they are of value to bees and birds.

M. aquifolium (Pursh) Nutt. **OREGON GRAPE** Northwest U.S. native. 3 feet. Performance variable in our heat. Brought from the West by Lewis & Clark in 1814.

M. fortunei (Lindl.) Fedde. **MAHONIA** China. To 6 feet. Narrow, serrated leaflets, creating finer foliage than other Mahonias; spreads by clumping. Spring flowers are 6 inch, yellow clusters.

Malpighia glabra L. **BARBADOES CHERRY** West Indies. Malpighia family, evergreen shrub, 10 feet. Sun, part shade. Any soil. Glossy green leaves, 3 inches long and oval. Clusters of one-half inch, five petaled, rose to red flowers during summer; followed by cherry sized bright red berries. Hardy to 28 degrees; plant in protected spot.

M. coccigera L. **DWARF HOLLY** Shrub, 3 feet. Sun. Moisture. Spiny edged, glossy topped green leaves, dainty shrub. Small, rose colored, fringed-petaled flowers are profuse during summer; followed by one-half inch red berry. Not hardy below 30 degrees; plant in protected spot or in a pot.

Malvaviscus arboreus variety *mexicanus* or *M. arboreus grandiflorus.* **TURK'S CAP** Evergreen shrub, 15 feet. Sun. Adapts to many conditions, though well-drained, fertile soil and moisture is best. Upright form, heart shaped, toothed leaves. Audubon Park specimens are huge clumps. It looks as attractive cut back and kept in bounds. It blooms from summer to fall. The pendulous, scarlet flowers are two and one-half inches long with protruding stamens which never open fully, hence another name: **SCOTCH PURSE.** Hardy to 25 degrees. Will usually return after freeze damage. Important winter hummer plant.

Melaleuca lateritia Otto. **ROBIN-REDBREAST BUSH**
Western Australia. Myrtle family shrub, evergreen, 10 feet.
Sun. Any soil. Slender leaves, bottlebrush shaped, honey
scented stameny flowers, scarlet red in color, long period,
spring to summer. Hardy to 25 degrees. E. A. McIlhenny
recommended *M. armillaris, M. hypericifolia, M. nesophylla* in
1927. *M. quinquenervia*, introduced in Florida in 1906, has
become a severe hazard there due to its invasiveness.

Michelia figo (Lour.) K. Spreng, *M. fuscata, Magnolia
fuscata* **BANANA SHRUB** Asia. Magnolia family shrub,
evergreen, 15 feet. Sun, part shade. Fertile, moist and
humusy but well-drained slightly acid soil. Oblong, 3
inch, shiny, dark green leaves on fuzzy branches; maroon
edged, creamy yellow, one and a half inch flowers which
smell like banana in spring, profuse; from fall-winter
velvety buds. Traditional "creole garden" plant grown
before 1860, probably before 1800. 1918.

Myrtus communis L. **MYRTLE** Europe. Myrtle family
shrub, evergreen, fast-growing to 15 feet. Sun, part shade.
Any soil if well-drained. Shiny, dark green, aromatic
leaves; three-quarter inch fuzzy pinkish or white flowers,
single and in clusters, May and June; followed by half
inch bluish berries. A traditional European garden plant
for centuries. 1859, 1885.

Nandina domestica Thunb. **NANDINA, SACRED BAM-
BOO** Asia. Barberry family, evergreen shrub, 8 feet. Sun,
part shade; more sun, more color. Rich, humusy, moist
soil. Delicate red-tinged to wine red foliage. 6 to 12 inch
clusters of white flowers in April; bright red berries in fall
and winter, more in cooler climates than ours. Dwarf
varieties available. Berries offer winter food for birds.
Grown in New Orleans in the 1850's, 1885.

Nerium oleander L. **OLEANDER** Mediterranean to
Japan. Dogbane family shrub, evergreen, 20 feet. Sun
for heaviest flowering, part shade. Any soil, moist but
well-drained is best. Rounded form, dense foliage. 6 inch
thin, shiny, dark green leaves; clusters of single or double,

2 inch flowers heavy April-June, sparser through fall, in colors yellow, red, pink, purple, salmon; some fragrant. All parts are poisonous if eaten. Hardy to 20 degrees; will return from roots. Beautiful in plantings along I-10 where they have room to spread. Reputedly brought to New Orleans during Spanish colonial times (1769-1802). 1859, 1947.

Osmanthus fragrans (Thunb.) Lour. **SWEET OLIVE, TEA OLIVE** Asia. Olive family, evergreen shrub, to 30 feet. Sun, part shade. Rich, moist soil is best, good drainage essential. 4 inch shiny green leaves with finely toothed edges, coppery colored when new. Drooping clusters of tiny white flowers, incredibly fragrant and in profuse quantities, bloom fall and spring in cycles. A very slow growing shrub. Can be damaged by a severe enough freeze. Traditional in old New Orleans gardens. Grown here before 1800. Offered in 1859 by Magnolia Nurseries. 1885, 1918, 1947.

Photinia serrulata Lindl. **CHINESE PHOTINIA** China. Rose family shrub, evergreen, 40 feet. Sun. Good drainage important, rich soil best. Lustrous, 8 inch, dark green leaves, lighter undersides; which are reddish bronze upon spring emergence. Prune in February before new growth appears. April bloom, six inch clusters of white flowers, red berries can follow in fall and winter, but not predictably in our climate. Several species available. All are longer lived and have fewer problems further north, but that is not to say they do not perform creditably in New Orleans. Used in Audubon Park and in City plantings along Carrollton Avenue. If the berries do form, Dennis says only cedar waxwings find them attractive. 1859, 1885.

Pittosporum tobira (Thunb.) Ait. **JAPANESE PITTO-SPORUM** China, Japan. Evergreen shrub or tree, 18 feet, Pittosporum family. Sun, part shade. Good drainage essential; rich, moist soil. Dense foliage; 4 inch, rubbery, dark green leaves with rounded tips; fragrant, creamy-white, one-half inch flowers in small clusters, March and April. Damage in severe freezes. Variegated and dwarf forms available. One of my favorite evergreens. 1859, 1885.

Podocarpus macrophyllus (Thunb.) D. Don **SOUTHERN YEW, JAPANESE YEW** China. Podocarpus family, evergreen, to 45 feet. Part shade best, sun. Moist, rich, well-drained soil. 3 to 4 inch long, three-eights inch wide, dark green, flat leaves, lighter underneath; in dense clusters. Dioecious; if a male is present, its yellowish flowers provide pollen for the female, purple berries are produced. 1885. *Torreya taxifolia*, FLORIDA YEW, STINKING CEDAR was offered by Magnolia Nurseries, 1859.

Pyracantha coccinea M. J. Roem. **PYRACANTHA, SCARLET FIRETHORN** Europe, Asia. Rose family, evergreen, to 15 feet. Sun. Rich, well-drained soil. One and one-half inch dark green, oval leaves; grayish, thorny branches with arching form if free-standing; good for espalier, too. Small white flowers in April, brilliant red-orange or yellow round berries in profuse clusters, fall through early spring. Many varieties, including dwarf and with variegated leaves. Is this the same plant as the *Mespilus piracantha* listed 1859 by Nelson's Nurseries? 1935.

Raphiolepis indica (L.) Lindl. **INDIAN HAWTHORNE** China. Rose family, evergreen, 5 feet. Morning sun, several hours of direct sun each day. Rich, moist, well-drained soil. Leathery, glossy leaves to 3 inches, coppery colored when new. Pinkish to white clusters of flowers, spring, intermittant bloom after; followed by blackish berries. Inconsistent performance in New Orleans except under perfect conditions. 1859, 1885.

R. umbellata (Thunb.) Mak. **YEDDA HAWTHORNE** is similar to the above. Hybrids are available offering variety in color and size, including dwarfs.

Rhododendron L. species **AZALEA** Azalea family. Though classified as rhododendrons by botanists, azaleas

differ from their cooler-climate cousins in having 5 stamens to the 10 or more in a rhododendron. When I think
"southern flowering shrub," I think azalea. They were
introduced in Charleston as early as the 1790's, grown at
least as early as the 1830's in Louisiana, achieved their
peak of popularity during the 1930's and later. No matter
how the character of my garden changes, there will always
be a place for azaleas, if not the lush flowered, evergreen
imports, then the more delicate native varieties, which are
deciduous. The brief but brilliant bloom season can be
lengthened by mixing varieties with different lengths of
bloom. Basic cultural requirements for all are the same:

Azaleas grow in full sun or partial shade, but enough
sun is crucial to full flowering. The best setting is the
shade such as is found under trees whose branches are
high or whose canopy is thin. Proper soil preparation is
important. Good drainage is essential, as is acidity (pH of
5.0 to 6.0). The surest way to achieve these conditions is
by planting your shrubs in raised beds in which existing
soil has been replaced with a mixture of equal parts of
peat moss and azalea-camellia soil (which can be purchased in sacks or by the yard from Reliable Soil Co.),
with sharp (builder's) sand added in quantities great
enough to ensure drainage. A mulch should be added to
conserve moisture around the shallow roots of the shrubs.
Acidic oak or pine leaves are best for this purpose.

The soil should be constantly moist. Watering is
necessary during dry spells. Soaker hoses are helpful. To
counteract the effects of watering with our alkaline tap
water, feed azaleas in late winter with a fertilizer designated for azaleas-camellias or acid-loving plants, as these
are acid in their reaction with the soil.

Conditions which will keep your azaleas strong and
healthy are the best preventative of dieback, petal blight,
spider mites, and several fungal diseases which can attack.
Bees and hummingbirds visit the blossoms for nectar.

Wild azaleas may also attract butterflies and hummingbird moths.

R. austrinum (Small) Rehd. **FLORIDA FLAME AZA-LEA** Florida, Georgia. Deciduous, 10 feet. Needs lots of sun for profuse flowering. Open form. Clusters of tubular flowers widen to ruffled openings from which long stamens protrude, brilliant orange to golden yellow with reddish tints. March, April bloom preceeds reappearance of foliage. Hilda Latapie's thrives on the northern side of her house, in sun.

R. canescens (Michx.) Sweet **WILD AZALEA, NATIVE AZALEA, HONEYSUCKLE AZALEA** Southeast U.S., Louisiana. Deciduous, 15 feet. Loose, open form. Flowers, March to April, are similar in form to the flame azalea, open before and with spring foliage. Fragrant, delicate pinkish shades to white clusters of tubes with spidery stamens; heavier when water supply is plentiful while the buds are forming in July. 1859.

R. serrulatum (Small) Millais **SWAMP AZALEA** Louisiana to Florida. Deciduous, 20 feet. Fragrant, thin, white tubular blossoms form in few flowered clusters in June and July, after leaves are formed.

R. indicum (L.) Sweet **INDIAN AZALEA** Japan. Deciduous, 6 feet. Attractive blue-green to light green foliage in mounded form, density determined by the amount of sun received. Flowers in spring are 2 to 3 inches, single or double, white, pink, magenta, orange-red; can be profuse enough to hide foliage. 1885, 1947.

R. obutusum (Lindl.) Planch. **KURUME AZALEA, DWARF AZALEA** Evergreen, 3 feet. Small, rounded, shiny green leaves. Clusters of one inch flowers, early to mid-spring; orange-red to bright and purple-red colors. Follow directions for bed preparation and care exactly for good results.

Most of the azaleas grown in gardens are hybrids. Bloom times vary. Plants can be selected for a prolonged season of bloom. Major groups and some examples of each are:

SOUTHERN INDIAN HYBRIDS

'Fielder's White'
  White, early midseason.
'Formosa'
  Rose-purple, midseason.
'George L. Taber'
  Pale lavender with darker markings, early midseason.
'Pride of Mobile'
  Watermelon red, midseason.
'Pride of Dorking'
  Carmine red, late.
'Southern Charm'
  Rose pink, midseason.

KURUME HYBRIDS

'Apple Blossom'
  Pink with white, late.
'Christmas Cheer'
  Bright red, midseason.
'Coral Bells'
  Salmon pink, early.
'Sherwood Red'
  Vivid orange-red, midseason.
'Snow'
  White, midseason.

PERICAT HYBRIDS

'Hampton Beauty'
  Pink, late mid-season.
'Pinocchio'
  Rosy-red, early.
'Sweetheart Supreme'
  Light pink, late midseason.

BELGIAN HYBRIDS

'Red-Wing'
  Brilliant red, ruffled petals.
'Albert Elizabeth'
  White with an orange edge.

GLENN DALE HYBRIDS

'Eros'
   Reddish pink, late.
'Fashion'
   Salmon to orange.
'Glacier'
   White with a green throat, midseason.

Tabernaemontana divaricata (L.) R. Br. **CRAPE JASMINE**
India. Dogbane family shrub, evergreen, 8 feet. Sun, part
shade. Rich, moist, well-drained soil. Attractive glossy
leaves, many branched form. One and a half inch waxy,
white, tubular flowers, nocturnally fragrant, year round
bloom. The double-flowered variety, called *fleur-d'amour*,
'Grandifolia' was traditional in pre-1860 Vieux Carre gardens. Hardy to 10 degrees.
   Viburnum tinus L. **LAURUSTINUS VIBURNUM**
Mediterranean. Honeysuckle family shrub, evergreen, 10
feet. Sun, part shade. Rich, porous soil, good drainage
essential. Leathery, lustrous, dark green, oblong leaves to
3 inches long. Oval form. White or pinkish 3 inch clusters of fragrant blossoms from very early spring to summer. Black berries. 1859, 1885. Bee and bird food.
   Many species are available, some native, with the
characteristic clustered flower. Some are:
   V. dentatum L. **ARROWHEAD** Eastern U.S., Louisiana. Deciduous, 15 feet. Sun, part shade. Rich, humusy,
moist, sandy, acid soil.
   V. nudum L. **SWAMP VIBURNUM** Eastern U.S.,
Louisiana. Deciduous, 15 feet. Sun, part shade. Sandy
but humusy, slightly acid soil.
   V. odoratissimum Ker-Gawl. **SWEET VIBURNUM**
Orient. Evergreen, 20 feet. Part shade. Loose, moist, rich
soil. Flowers less showy than other species; fruit not
consistently present. During severe freezes, can be damaged; prepare, protect. 1885.

V. suspensum Lindl. **VIBURNUM SUSPENSUM** Orient. Evergreen, 6 feet. Part shade. Moist, rich and humusy, well-drained soil.

PALMS, PALMETTOS, CYCADS

Butia capitata (Mart.) Becc. **COCOS PALM, BUTIA PALM** South America. Palm family, to 20 feet, trunk to 18 inches thick and covered with the bases of old leaves which form large, prickly scales. Sun. Well drained soil. Produces an edible fruit. Hardy to 15 degrees. Graceful, arching feather foliage.

Chamaerops humilis L. **MEDITERRANEAN FAN PALM** Europe, Mediterranean area. Palm family, 3 to 20 feet. Best in full sun, mine is fine in part shade. Well-drained soil. 2 to 3 foot, stiff and erect, fanshaped leaves on thick stalks which form clumps. Hardy here. I liked it because it is a miniature of the Louisiana palmetto for which I don't have room. It was killed by the 1989 freeze.

Cycas revoluta Thunb. **SAGO PALM** Japan. Cycad family, to 10 feet. Sun, part sun. Rich, moist soil, slightly acid. Very slow growing. Though most specimens I have seen appear to be trunkless rosettes of shiny, stiff palm-like leaves, eventually a thick trunk emerges. Dioecious, the different sexes produce their "flowers" in summer. Not reliably hardy in our most severe freezes. This has long been a popular ornamental in New Orleans. 1859, 1885.

Dioon edule Lindl. **CHESTNUT DIOON** Mexico. A cycad in the Zamia family, to 6 feet. Part shade. Rich soil. Stocky trunk, stiff 3 to 6 foot long leaves. Paul Wells, local member of the International Cycad Society feels that this plant is hardier in New Orleans than *Cycas revoluta* which it resembles and which is much more common in local gardens.

Livistonia chinensis (Jacq.) R. Br. ex Mart. **CHINESE FAN PALM** Japan, China. Palm family tree, to 30 feet. Sun, part shade. Moist, rich, well-drained soil. The trunk can be slow to develop under the clump of fan-leaves. Not reliably hardy, but it can take two seasons to return after freeze damage, so do not cut it back too soon. It may not have bitten the dust, yet! Introduced to New Orleans during the 1850's.

Phoenix canariensis Hort. ex Chabaud. **CANARY IS-LAND DATE PALM** Canary Islands. Palm family tree, to 50 feet or more, stout trunk to 3 feet in diameter. Bears decorative fruits if male and female present. Damaged in freezes below 20 degrees.

P. dactylifera L. **DATE PALM** North Africa. To 100 feet, slender trunk. Sun. Rich, well-drained soil. Source of edible dates if male and female trees are present. Not reliably hardy here. Both date palms have umbrella-like clusters of feather-form foliage gracefully perched at the tops of tall trunks. "Date palms" were among the first plants brought to New Orleans in the early 18th century. They did not produce fruit well here. In his 1851 article, Sylvanus described the largest "Date palm" in New Orleans at that time: 30 to 40 feet high, 18 inches in diameter, planted in a stable yard by the Jesuits 60 years earlier. There were only two others in New Orleans at that time, one 30 feet high, 10 inches thick, 20 years old. I am not sure which species he meant. *"It resists the cold weather, grows with remarkable rapidity, and yet is rarely planted, or to be found in the nurseries,"* he complained. There are New Orleans Garden District palms of today reputed to be greater than 100 years old. *P. dactylifera* was offered 1885. *P. canariensis* listed, 1935.

Trachycarpus fortunei (Hook.) H. Wendl **WINDMILL PALM** China. Palm family, 40 feet. Sun, part shade. Well-drained soil. Clusters of fan-shaped leaves are three feet or more across. Yellow flowers on stalks within the leaves are followed by pea like berries.

Washingtonia filifera (L. Linden) H. Wendl. **DESERT FAN PALM** California. Palm tree to 80 feet, thicker trunk than:

W. robusta H. Wendl. **THREAD PALM, MEXICAN WASHINGTON PALM** from Mexico. Palm family tree, 80 feet, slender trunk. Both are called WASHINGTONIAS. Sun. Well-drained soil. Both are commonly used in New Orleans street plantings. Skip Treme' and Keith Bleichner remember a pre-1962 national contest for the tallest Washingtonia which was won by a New Orleans palm.

TREES FOR FALL COLOR

Ginkgo biloba GINKGO, MAIDENHAIR TREE
Firmiana simplex CHINESE PARASOL, JAPANESE VARNISH TREE
Koelreuteria bipinnata GOLDEN RAIN TREE
Lagerstroemia indica CRAPE MYRTLE
Sapium sebiferum CHINESE TALLOW, POPCORN TREE
Clethra alnifolia SWEET PEPPERBUSH, SUMMERSWEET,
    WHITE ALDER

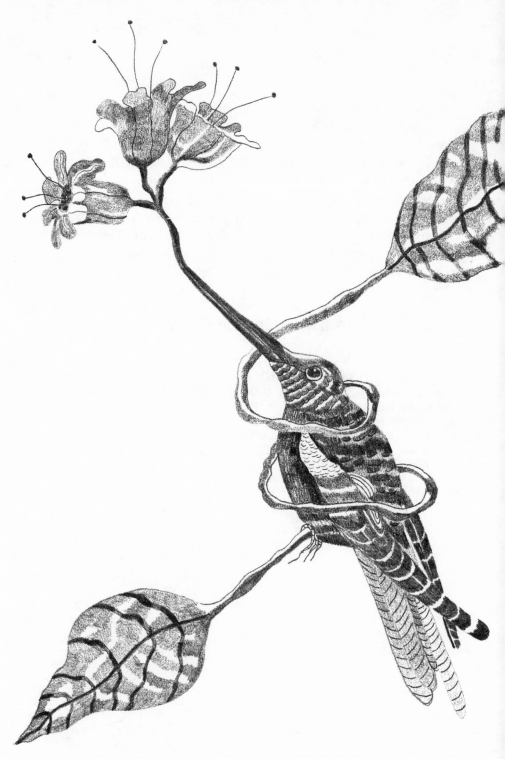

Jacqueline Bishop

Vines

"I've been to the Brazilian jungles...as a geologist.
That was in another life...."

McLain J. Forman, 1989
at P. J.'s Coffee & Tea Co., Magazine Street

I have always loved to hear tales of travel and adventure. Gardens, with their ornamental plants from faraway places, can be the perfect setting for bringing out well-traveled guests.

Larry O'Meallie describes birding trips to South and Central American rainforests where he saw the giant hummingbird, over twice the size of the rubythroats in my garden. He tells of climbing by rope high into the jungle where a biologist, perched on a platform, studied life in the canopy. He has toured the world, from Iceland to the Phillipines photographing birds: from great frigate birds and fairy terns on Christmas Island, to a nesting black skimmer on the Louisiana coast. He shares his photographs with friends, and his adventures...like the time he was so engrossed in watching birds that he didn't see Nia's car disappear into the quicksand beach at high-tide in Cameron... or the time he tested his climbing ropes from the fourth floor of his apartment building in New Orleans early in the morning when no one would see and was still met by an alarmed crowd at the ground!

Stephanie Dinkins said, on seeing my *Jacaranda mimosifolia* in bloom: "I consider the Jacaranda to be THE most romantic tree!"   During a trip to North Africa she contemplated sewing its seeds into the hem of her dress to smuggle them into New Orleans. She has a travel wound from one of her journeys, a finger dislocated while dismounting from a   camel in Egypt. Her desert host insisted that all his guests be involved in activities. He gave her the choice of volleyball or a camel ride. Not a difficult choice! She has traveled all over the world as a professional photographer: of Canary Island tourists pocketed aside camel humps, frosted New Zealand willows weeping crystalline foliage, Appalachian oldfolks.

Donald Bradburn says the fragrant white alyssum in my garden reminds him of Midway Island where that plant has escaped cultivation and grows wild. He has been all over the world photographing nature, from Africa to Midway Island to the the swamps of Louisiana and the islands of the Mississippi coast (which he likes best); from African weaverbirds to American bitterns. His photographs, eloquent records of the untouched beauty of Horn Island over a thirty year period were instrumental in obtaining protection for the Gulf Coast Barrier Islands under the Wilderness Act. His most fascinating tale, hard to extract, is of the eight year political committment which accomplished this coup.

Such efforts as his may not be enough to save fast disappearing wilderness worldwide. Green areas, especially belts of tropical jungle, profusely vegetated, benefit the whole earth by serving as "carbon dioxide sinks" to reduce the greenhouse effect.

To me, the word "jungle" elicits images of vines, hanging in tangled masses and great lengths from somewhere above. They bring back childhood movie memories of Tarzan swinging through tropical forests which teemed with plant and animal life. (Not always African animal life, if you watched the movie screen closely.) Those woody jungle vines are called lianas and are so thick they can hold a man's weight. I knew that from reading Ivan Sanderson's *Book of Great Jungles*.

My adventures are probably a little tamer than Tarzan's, but not to me. This year I visited the rainforests of Costa Rica. They were all that I had imagined and more. In remote Rara Avis, accessible only by foot or tractor, naturalist Amos Bien, Leslee Reed, Tara McCartney and I inched along trails in the night booted against the muck. We saw the glow of foxfire, heard howler monkeys and click-frogs. We scanned the darkness with flashlights to find wildlife by its eyeshine! Tara and I signed releases which warned: "THIS EXPERIENCE IS INTRINSICALLY DANGEROUS," strapped on rope harnesses, and were carried though and over the canopy, 50 meters above the jungle floor. Amos pointed out moss-covered pathways atop the branches, the aboreal highways along which animals travel. There were epiphytes, airplants, clustered along and clinging to tree trunks and limbs, some dripping sprays of flowers: the begonias, peperomias, bromeliads, philodendrons, orchids which we know as houseplants. And there were vines!

Vines are a long-time tradition in New Orleans. They were used in previous centuries for their flowers as heavily as annuals are used today. A look at the watercolors of the Notarial Archives will show examples of arbors, trellises, and frames on which vines were grown in the last century. They climbed the columns and draped the rails of balconies, creating "hanging gardens." They served as green shields from the hot sun which, if deciduous, dropped their leaves in winter to allow light and warmth access.

While researching the vines which flourish in our climate, it occurred to me that through selective planting, I

can experience all the ends of the earth including what I
like best about the Louisiana wilderness, and New Orleans' past without ever leaving my garden. I hope you
are as struck by the possibilities for vicarious travel as
well as our debt to the rainforests of the world as you
read the origins of the vines you can choose for your
fence, wall, trellis or original garden structure which I
can't begin to imagine!

VINES FOR THE NEW ORLEANS GARDEN

1766 Indicates species grown in Thomas Jefferson's Monticello garden.
1838 Indicates listing in Lelievre's *New Gardener of Louisiana*.
1859 Indicates listing in the catalogue of plants offered for sale by John M.
     Nelson at Magnolia Nurseries at Metairie Ridge and at his Plant Depot,
     Corner of Camp St. & Lafayette Sq., New Orleans.
1875 Indicates listing in *R. Maitre's Catalogue*, Magazine Street, New Orleans.
1883 Indicates listing in *Almanac and Garden Manual for the Southern States*, by
     Richard Frotscher, New Orleans seed merchant.
1916 Indicates listing in *Reuter Seeds for the South*, Spring, New Orleans.
1918 Indicates listing in Bollwinkle Seed Co. Ltd., *Catalogue & Garden Guide*, 510
     Dumaine Street.

Akebia quinata (Houtt.) Decne. **AKEBIA, FIVE LEAF
AKEBIA**   Orient. Lardizabala family, twining, herbaceous
vine evergreen in our area.   Can reach 30 feet as a vine.
As a ground cover, forms a plush mat.   Sun, light shade.
Well-drained soil, drought tolerant.   Fragrant clusters of
non-showy purple flowers in April.   Can be followed by 3
inch edible fruits. Though attractive, one source describes
it as a *"vicious grower"* which will smother all other
growth with which it comes in contact. Beware!   1875.
Allamanda cathartica L. **ALLAMANDA** Brazil.   Dogbane family, tropical non-clinging evergreen vine to 50
feet.   Full sun for profuse flowering.   Rich, well drained
soil, moisture. Likes our heat and humidity.   Bell-shaped
yellow flowers present intermittantly during warm and hot

months. Needs protection to overwinter here. Will come back from the roots after a light freeze. Can be trained on a trellis or fence. Grown at the 1984 World's Fair, where many people misidentified it as yellow mandevilla. There is a purple ALLAMANDA (*Allamanda violacea* G. Gardn. & Fielding), a climbing shrub.

Anredera basselloides (HBK) Baill. [*Boussingaultia basselloides*] MADEIRA VINE, MIGNONETTE VINE Brazil, Argentina, Paraguay. Basella family, perennial twining vine to 20 feet, rapid growth. Forms 1 foot racemes of tiny white fragrant flowers, late summer. Small tubers form in the axils of the leaves. 1875.

Antigonon leptopus Hook. & Arn. ROSE OF MONTANA, CORAL VINE, CHAIN OF LOVE, CADENA DE AMOUR Mexico. Herbaceous twining vine, fast growing to 40 feet, Buckwheat family. Sun. Rich, welldrained soil. Vivid pink masses of flowers in summer-fall. Hardy to 15 degrees. Dies to ground in the winter, up again in the spring. There is a white variety, also, not as pretty. Common today though described in *Southern Garden* magazine as scarce in New Orleans, 1895.

Aristolochia durior J. Hill DUTCHMAN'S PIPE Central U.S. Birthwort family, twining woody perennial vine which grows rapidly to 30 feet, crowds out other vines. Sun, shade. No special soil requirements though they are found naturally in rich, moist woods. Blooms, April through June; are mahogony, green and white, look like little, curved Meershaum pipes, to 1 and one-half inches long. Leaves are heart-shaped and 6 to 15 inches long.

A. elegans M. T. Mast. DUTCHMAN'S PIPE, CALICO FLOWER Brazil. Perennial climbing vine to 8 feet. Rich soil, plenty of moisture; likes warm, moist climates. Large, heart shaped leaves. Blooms in summer are 3 inches wide, white and purple, with the same pipe-shape as the above, called "unbelievable" by one source. Interesting fruits follow. Hardy to 28 degrees; provide mulch, it should return from the roots after a freeze.

Asarina barclaiana (Lindl.) Penn [*Maurandia barclaiana*] **CLIMBING SNAPDRAGON** Mexico Figwort family, tender perennial twining vine to 10 feet or more. Fast blooming, can be grown as an annual. Moist, well-drained soil. Showy pink to deep purple, snap-dragon like blooms in profusion. Good in hanging baskets. 1918, 1883

Bignonia capreolata L. **CROSS VINE, TRUMPET FLO-WER** North America, Louisiana. Bignonia family, evergreen perennial climber, attaching itself with tendrils; fast growing to 60 feet. Sun, shade. Acid soil. Clusters of yellowish-red trumpet-shaped blooms are profuse in spring and early summer. Hardy. 1859, 1875.

Bougainvillea glabra Chois, B. spectabilis Willd. sometimes called *B. brasiliensis, B.* hybrids **BOUGAINVILLEA** Brazil. Four O'clock family, climbing shrub or evergreen vine. Full sun, hottest possible exposure. Very well-drained, sandy alkaline soils. Likes dryer conditions, tolerates drought well. Blooms best when root bound and in poor soil, especially in New Orleans where heavy rain encourages vegetative growth at the expense of flowers. Planting in pots is a good idea. Best planting location is against a protected, sunny wall. Bloom is profuse, spring through summer. Colors intense. The actual flower is insignificant though surrounded by intensely colored bracts (a modified leaf) in magenta to purple to red to violet to orange and yellow and white. Not reliably hardy in New Orleans. Plant in a protected spot, mulch heavily, and pray. One source says the plant will come back from the roots after a temperature drop to 27 degrees. A bougainvillea grew on the chain link fence by the Dante Deli several years until the freeze of 1989 got it.

Campsis radicans Seem. **TRUMPET VINE, TRUMPET CREEPER** Louisiana, North America. Bignonia family, perennial deciduous clinging vine, rampant grower to 30 feet. Sun. Moist, well-drained soil. Orange, trumpet-shaped blooms April through September. Hardy, of course. Problems: blossoms attract ants, dermatitis caused in some by handling of flowers or leaves, invasive. 'Flava' has yellow flowers. *C. radicans X tagliabuana* 'Madame Galen' is recommended over the native variety as it has larger, showier orange-scarlet flowers and less rampant growth. Hummingbird and bee plant.

Cardiospermum halicacabum L. **BALLOON VINE, HEART-SEED, LOVE IN A PUFF** Tropical America. Woody perennial vine to 10 feet, grown as an annual, may last through mild winters. Small white flowers are followed by one-inch green fruits: 3 sectioned, inflated puffs, enclosing dark, pea-sized seeds stamped with white heart shaped marks. Can reseed. 1916, 1883

Celastrus scandens L. **BITTERSWEET** North America, not found in South Louisiana. Staff-tree family, deciduous, vigorous grower to 20 feet. Twines along fences or can be used as a ground cover. Valued for its orange-yellow berries which appear in the fall on the female plants, male plant is required for fertilization. Unfortunately, berry production is sparse in our heat and humidity, and the vine is quite invasive and hard to get rid of as it spreads by underground roots.

Clematis L. species **CLEMATIS** Try the gorgeous, largeflowered varieties you see in the catalogues, but do not count on them to flourish here and don't be too disappointed if you fail. One optimist feels planting in a raised bed in slightly limed soil, shading the roots, and giving the plant several years to become established may work.

C. X jackmanii T. Moore **CLEMATIS**, hybrids of Asian and European species are the vines to 10 feet which produce the stunning 4-sepaled, 6 inch flowers in white, shades from blue to purple to red which you will find enticing in catalogs. While you wait for them to succeed, try the two more certain for New Orleans. There is confusion in my references as to whether one of those is two separate species or one species sometimes incorrectly called. I refer to **JAPANESE CLEMATIS** *C. dioscoreifolia* Levl. & Van., Korea, or *C. paniculata* J. F. Gmel., New Zealand. Ranun-

culus family, deciduous climbing vine, to 30 feet. Sun.
Moist, rich, humusy soil. The base of plant and roots
should be shaded, such as by overplanting, to keep them
cool as in a woodland setting. Bloom is a profusion of
fragrant, four-sepaled, white flowers July to September.
1875.

C. virginiana L. **VIRGIN'S-BOWER** Eastern U.S., North
Louisiana. Semi-evergreen twining vine, to 20 feet. Male
and female flowers are on different plants. Bloom in
August, small fragrant, white, starshaped followed by
fluffy fruits.

Caroline Dorman says that the flowers of the native
clematis are almost exactly like the ones of the oriental
except not as white, but that the native wins for beauty
when its feathery seed pods form. 1875.

Clerodendrum thomsoniae Balf. **CLERODENDRUM,
BLEEDINGHEART** West Africa. Verbena family, twining,
evergreen vine to 12 feet. Sun. Rich, well-drained soil;
likes our warm, humid atmosphere. Tiny red flowers surrounded by white calyxes form in the spring and summer.
Should be planted in a protected spot. Not reliably hardy
but may come back from the roots after a freeze. There is
a beautiful specimen in the 1200 block of Phillip Street.

Clitoria mariana L. **CLITORIA, BUTTERFLY-PEA** Dryer
areas of the U.S. Pea family perennial twining vine, 1 to 3
feet. Sun. Sandy, well-drained soil. Characteristic legume
family flower, 2 inches long, in beautiful lavender clusters;
blooms throughout summer are followed by seed pods.

C. ternatea L., also called **BUTTERFLY-PEA** Tropical
perennial twining vine grown as an annual. Sun, part
shade. Sandy soil. Low growing plant. Blooms are clustered, bright, dark blue, with light blue and yellow markings. Like the native *Clitoria*, but showier. A double form
is now available, showier, still.

Clytostoma callistegioides (Cham.) Bur. **BIGNONIA, AR-
GENTINE TRUMPET VINE** Argentina, Brazil. Bignonia
family, evergreen twiner fast spreading to 15 feet with

height twice that. Sun, part shade. Rich soil. Shiny
leaves; showy, lavender, trumpet-shaped flowers in April,
May. Will die to the ground at 20 degrees but should
return from the roots. Should be woven into the fence or
trellis to distribute the growth which otherwise can become a heavy mass which shades out flower growth.
Easily controllable, pruning after flowering helps keep the
plant in bounds. Usually called bignonia in local nurseries, this plant is in the family Bignoniaceae, as are other
plants with trumpet shaped flowers, but in the genus
Clytostoma. Some name confusion relates to reclassifica-
tions by botanists. Today, the genus Bignonia is represented by only one species: *Bignonia capreolata* L., crossvine, which is described above.

Cobaea scandens Cav. **CUP & SAUCER VINE, CATHE-
DRAL BELLS** Mexico. Phlox family, perennial climbing
vine fast growing to 25 feet, recommended as an annual
as flower numbers diminish after first season. Sun. Rich,
moist, well-drained soil. 2 inch flowers turn mauve to
lavender as they open into bell shapes, cup and saucers if
inverted, summer. 1883

Cocculus carolinus (L.) DC. **COCCULUS, CAROLINA
MOONSEED** Southeast U.S., parts of Louisiana. Moonseed family, evergreen twining vine which rapidly grows
to 30 feet. Sun, part shade. Not fussy about soil, found
along streams. Flowers in spring are nonshowy, greenish-
white clusters followed summer-fall by very attractive,
bright red, six inch long clusters of berries. Foliage is
sparse; berries, which are good wildlife food, do not form
until the plant is several years old.

Curcurbitaceae species Juss. **GOURD FAMILY** Tropics,
subtropics. The same family as melon, pumpkin, squash,
and cucumber includes vining plants which produce the
usually hardshelled, colorful, smooth-skinned or warty
fruits of all sizes and shapes which are dried, shellacked,
and used as ornaments. The luffa sponge is a gourd.
Some have shapes which allow them to function, when

dried, as dippers and bird houses. The vines are fast growing and attractive; can be grown on a trellis or the ground. Sun. Any well-drained garden soil, lots of water. Plant in spring for fall fruit. 1883

Dolichos lablab L. **HYACINTH BEAN** Old World Tropics. Pea family. Twining vine, perennial and evergreen when winters are mild, can be grown as an annual. Rapid growth 10 to 30 feet. Sun. Well-drained soil. Oval leaves. Purple or white flowers summer-fall. Flat, maroon seed pods follow. Volunteers from dropped seed. Easy to grow, attractive. 1776, 1838, 1883

Dioscorea alata L., *D. bulbifera* L. **POTATO VINE, AIR POTATO** India, East Asia. Twining vine, yam family. Sun, shade. Well-drained soil. Large, heartshaped, green leaves are very ornamental. Warty tubers, some quite large, form along the vines during the fall. Vines return in spring from fallen "potatoes". One year my vine climbed high into my Chinese tallow tree. Plumetting "potatoes" were a hazard. Introduced in Florida by the U.S.D.A., 1905, distributed by Henry Nehrling.

Ficus pumila L. **FIG VINE** Australia, China, Japan. Mulberry family. Clinging evergreen vine climbs to 60 feet or more, medium rate of growth until established, then rapid. Sun, shade. Any soil. Fine-textured leaves, which should be kept trimmed, form a thick mat over wood or brick. Eventually, if not removed by pruning, mature branches with larger leaves form and inedible figs grow. Not completely hardy, the 1983 freeze got most of mine. Reputedly grown in New Orleans gardens before 1860.

Gelsemium sempervirens (L.) Ait. **CAROLINA JESSAMINE** Southeast U.S. Logania family, semi-evergreen twining vine, rapid growth to 20 feet. Part shade, sun; less bloom in shade. Moist, well-drained soil. Flowers are scented, yellow; can be present in fall to profusely in spring. Easy to control though does need pruning.

Weave into fence, trellis or use as a ground cover. Entire plant is toxic. 1859, 1875.

Hedera canariensis Willd. **ALGERIAN IVY** North Africa, has more rounded leaves, is faster growing than:

H. helix L. **ENGLISH IVY** Europe, western Asia, north Africa. Both are Aralia family members, evergreen vines which climb walls or trees or ramble as ground covers. Sun or shade. Rich, moist soil is best. Can take three years for full coverage. Easy to increase from stem cuttings. 1875.

Hydrangea anomala petiolaris (Sieb. & Zucc.) McClint. **CLIMBING HYDRANGEA** Japan. Saxifrage family, deciduous climber which attaches itself to surfaces as does ivy, with aerial roots, up to 60 feet. Shady northern exposure recommended for success in New Orleans. Rich, humusy soil, lots of moisture. Flowers in summer, 6-8 inch white clusters.

Ipomoea alba L., *Calonyction aculeatum* **MOONFLOWER** Tropical American twining vine. Bindweed family, tender perennial, usually grown here as an annual. Grows rapidly to 20 feet. Sun. Rich soil, moisture. Seeds are hard, should be nicked and soaked to speed germination. In my garden the plants grow from seeds dropped the previous season. Flowers begin in July, spiral open while you watch in the evening, night, and on cloudy days. Huge, luminous, fragrant white blooms which almost glow in the night.

I. purpurea Lam. **MORNING-GLORY** American tropics. Annual twining vine. To 40 feet, rapidly. Sun. Best in a fertile, moist soil, preferably alkaline. Nick and soak seeds before planting in spring. Trumpet-shaped blooms open in early morning, close midday except on cloudy days, May through September. The original was dark purple flowered. Hybrids available today in all colors from white, blue, and red, to purple; all sizes from small to large and showy. Have escaped cultivation and become pests.   Will reseed themselves, becoming smaller flowered with time. Hybrids must be replanted each year. 1883.

I. purpurea var. *diversifolia* (Lindl.) O'Don. [*I. Mexicana batatoides*]   Annual twiner with purplish-pink flowers. Naturalized in U. S., in New Orleans since at least 1895.

I. acuminata (Vahl) Roem. & Schult. **BLUE DAWN VINE** Mexico. Perennial vine with showy white throated blue flowers.

I. coccinea L. **RED MORNING GLORY, STAR MORNING GLORY** North America. Annual twining vine to 10 feet. Sun, part shade. Summer, autumn blooms are small, crimson-scarlet,   yellow-throated   trumpets   which humming- birds love.

I. digitata L.-D.C.[*I. paniculata*] Tropics of both hemispheres.   Tuberous-rooted perennial climber.   Flowers in the summer, fall are pinkish-purple or pink, darker at the throat.   Brought to New Orleans via London from India by Dr. Tobias Richardson, around 1879.

I. quamoclit L. **CYPRESS VINE, CARDINAL CLIMBER** American Tropics. Annual twining vine growing fast to 20 feet.   Feathery leaves.   Bright red funnel-shaped flowers. Heaviest bloom summer-fall. Reseeds. Hummingbird plant. 1883, 1766

Jasminum L. species   The true **JASMINES** are members of the olive family, Oleaceae. Known for their fragrant, frequently star-shaped flowers, they originate in many parts of the world and have been cultivated in gardens for centuries.   One of my favorite garden references (Pizzetti, Cocker) considers it "incomprehensible" that a garden could be without a representative of this plant.

They should be evergreen in our climate, will lose leaves if the winter is severe enough, are called "clambering shrubs" so can be fastened to a fence or trellis or left free. Pruning should be done in early spring. Moist but well-drained, rich soil and partial shade are recommended. The following is not an exhaustive list of possibles for New Orleans. 1838.

J. fruticans L. **JASMINE** North Africa, Asia Minor. 10 to 20 feet. Yellow, fragrant flowers in summer followed by shiny black pea-sized berries.

J. humile L. **ITALIAN JASMINE** China. Imported from Italy to England before 1656, hence the name. To 7 feet with a spread of 4 to 5 feet. Fragrant yellow flowers in clusters during June and July.

J. humile 'Revolutum' **ITALIAN JASMINE** To 8 feet. Large, fragrant yellow flowers June, July. Hardy to 10 degrees. 1875, 1885, 1918.

J. nudiflorum Lindl. **WINTER JASMINE** China. Deciduous, to 18 feet with spread of 15 feet. Hardy. Inch wide vivid yellow blooms November through March, needs sun for best bloom. Introduced in 1840's.

J. officinale L. **COMMON WHITE JASMINE** Common in China, originally from Iran. Fast growing to 40 feet. Very fragrant clusters of white flowers May to June, intermittent bloom to October followed by black berries. This was the one jasmine listed by Magnolia Nurseries' 1859 catalogue. 1875.

J. officinale 'grandiflorum' is a cultivar of the above with even larger white flowers (one and three/quarters inches wide).

J. grandiflorum L. **SPANISH JASMINE** India. Similar to *J. officinale* though needs protection from frost. To 6 feet. Very fragrant single flowers are pink as buds to white when open, profuse June to October.

J. polyanthum Franch. **CHINESE JASMINE** China. To 25 feet. Hardy to 20 degrees. Fragrant, profuse flowers, April to June; pink when bud, white in bloom.

J. sambac (L.) Ait. **ARABIAN JASMINE** Probably Asian. Clusters of white, cauliflower-like, fragrant flowers spring to fall. 'Grand Duke of Tuscany' (according to Bradley, "N. O. Garden," August, 1975) used to be found in almost every New Orleans garden. W. H. Coleman described it as commonplace in 1872. 1918.

Lathyrus latifolius L. **PERENNIAL SWEET PEA** Southern Europe. Pea family vine, 9 feet. Sun, part shade. Any well-drained soil. Rose, carmine, white flowers, spring or summer. Not as showy as annual sweet peas. One source says they are easy to grow here. Another says they are better suited to north Louisiana. They are naturalized as wildflowers in parts of the U.S. 1766.

Lonicera japonica Thunb. **JAPANESE HONEYSUCKLE** Eastern Asia, naturalized in U.S. Honeysuckle family, twining vine, evergreen. Sun, shade. Any soil. 'Halleriana,' **HALL'S HONEYSUCKLE**, is the most often available variety. Flowers spring, summer are fragrant; white, turning yellow, followed unreliably by purple berries. Invasive; needs some work to control. It's easy to find out why nectar loving creatures love the flowers: pick a flower, pinch off the trumpet at its base just above the calyx, pull the style through. The stigma, its head, will be preceded by a sweet drop. But then most of us learned how to taste honeysuckle nectar as children. 1875.

L. sempervirens L. **CORAL HONEYSUCKLE** Eastern U.S. Evergreen, twining vine to 50 feet. Sun. Any soil. Reddish or coral colored tubular flowers during spring, summer. Not as rampant a grower as other honeysuckles. Hummers love it. Available from Magnolia Nurseries, 1859, 1838.

Macfadyena unguis-cati, formerly *Doxantha unguiscati*, *Bignonia tweediana* **CAT'S CLAW, YELLOW BIGNONIA** West Indies. Bignonia family, evergreen vine which climbs to great heights with tropical rapidity, clinging with clawlike tendrils. Prefers sun. Any soil. Has the characteristic Bignonia family trumpet shaped flowers in yellow; blooms in March, April. It is my feeling that this plant's beautiful flowers do not come remotely close to redeeming it for its destructiveness. Its seeds are spread by the wind and sprout anywhere. Large tubers which extend deep into the ground form on the roots and are difficult to dig out. The "claws" damage the surfaces on which they climb in addition to holding rain moisture, encouraging wood rot. The vine will smother other growth which tries to compete. I found one which had crept under my house and was growing up my livingroom fireplace chimney! Persistant pulling and the selective use of an herbicide will keep the beast somewhat under control until you get a new neighbor who sees it on his side of the fence and says: "What pretty flowers! I think I'll let it grow." Unfortunately, cat's claw is very common in the New Orleans area. The New Orleans Garden Society actually recommended it (as *Bignonia unguis-cati*) in 1928. Probably introduced through the U.S.D.A. in Florida, this century.

Mandevilla X amabilis (Hort. Backh.) Dress, also called *M. splendens* or *Dipladenia spendens*. **MANDEVILLA** Argentina. Evergreen twining vine. Rapid growth to 20 feet. Sun. Fertile soil with excellent drainage, lots of moisture. Fragrant pink funnel-shaped flowers which grow from 2 to 4 inches, last 3 to 4 days, summer to frost. Hardy to 33 degrees, so, either protect it and pray or grow it in a tub and drag it in each year. *Flower & Garden* (December, 1988) has an article with particulars of tub culture. Became popular here after New Orleanians saw it in gorgeous flower at the 1984 World's Fair. Cultivar 'Alice du Pont' is recommended. *M. laxa* (Ruiz & Pav.) **CHILEAN JASMINE** has 2 inch white to pinkish flowers. *M. splendens* (Hook.f.) Woodson, *Dipladenia splendens* has pinkish white blooms to 4 inches. Others, called *Mandevilla* or *Dipladenia* depending on the reference, are in various shades of pink from rose to salmon. The so-called **YELLOW MANDEVILLA** is usually **ALLAMANDA**, though Louisiana Nurseries catalogue lists a *Mandevilla X* 'Yellow'.

Manettia cordifolia Mart. **FIRECRACKER VINE** South America. Madder family, evergreen, twining to 15 feet. Part sun. Sandy, acid soil, enriched with organic matter is best. Scarlet-crimson tubular flowers are present from late spring to frost. May be frozen to the ground, but should return from the roots. Hummers love it! "Manettia" was described in New Orleans gardens in 1849 by Alexander Gordon. *M. coccinea* was listed 1875. The same?

Merremia tuberosa (L.) Rendle **WOOD ROSE** Tropical. Bindweed family, perennial climber to 15 feet. Small yellow morning-glory like flowers form in fall followed by a fruit which hardens into a wooden, rose-like form. Called a "wood rose," they are prized for dried flower arrangements, but, as they take three months to develop and as the plant is hardy only to 35 degrees, it cannot be relied upon to mature in New Orleans.

Millettia reticulata Benth. **EVERGREEN WISTERIA** China. Pea family, twining, woody vine. Sun. Moist, rich, well-drained, slightly acid soil is best. Dark green, glossy foliage. Part evergreen during mild winters. Deep wine-purple 10 inch clusters of flowers are produced spring through summer. Fragrant, sometimes hidden by foliage, the blooms drop over a long period. Followed by seed pods. Mike McClung uses it a lot in local gardens.

Momordica balsamina L. **BALSAM APPLE** Africa, Asia. Gourd family, perennial grown as an annual, to 20 feet long, twining. Full sun. Rich, moist soil. Small yellow flowers bloom all summer, followed by 3 inch long, egg-shaped, warty, green fruit which turns orange and bursts open when ripe to reveal red seeds and pulp. Needs hot summers like ours to set fruit. 1883, 1766

Monstera deliciosa Liebm. **MONSTERA, SPLIT-** or **CUT-LEAVED PHILODENDRON** Tropical American jungle vine which clings with aerial roots. Rapid growth, usually to 8 feet, can reach 30. Needs several hours of sun each day. Well-drained but moist, fertile soil. The flower is 10 inches long, calla-like; develops into an edible fruit. Not freeze-hardy, though if planted in a protected spot with a heavy mulch, may return from the roots.

Parthenocissus quinquefolia (L.) Planch. **VIRGINIA CREEPER** North America. Grape or Vine family, deciduous clinging vine, fast growing to 25 or more feet. Sun, shade. Any soil. Attractive foliage with five leaflets, red in autumn, similar to and found in association with poison ivy. Berries are dark blue, small, form long clusters; poisonous. Widely advertised. It will not do well in New Orleans. 1875.

Passiflora caerulea L. **BLUE PASSION FLOWER** Brazil. Passionflower family, vigorous climbing shrub which clings with tendrils to 18 feet. Sun for heavier bloom. Well-drained, not-too-rich soil. Blooms July to September are scented blue, purple, and white. The elaborate and unusual arrangement of flower parts was interpreted in terms of religious symbolism by European visitors to the New World during the 17th century; hence the name; followed by orange egg-shaped and sized fruits. Will freeze to the ground, return from the roots if the freeze is of brief duration; mulch to be sure.

P. incarnata L. **MAYPOP, PASSION FLOWER** Eastern U.S., including Louisiana. Perennial vine, to 28 feet. "Passion flower" is purple and white, summer blooming, yellow fruits are edible. Hardy. Attracts caterpillars; is the larval food of the Gulf fritillary butterfly. 1838, 1875.

Phaseolus coccineus L. **SCARLET RUNNER BEAN** Tropical America. Pea family, annual, fast-growing twining vine to 8 feet. Sun. Rich, well-drained soil. Sow in early spring. Clusters of bright red flowers, spring, summer, followed by edible beans. Hummers like its flowers. 1766.

Quisqualis indica L. **RANGOON CREEPER, HEART-OF-MAN** Southeast Asia. Combretum family, fast growing perennial twining vine, to 30 feet. Sun, part sun. Moist, well-drained soil. Proper conditions are important for successful culture. Flowers are fragrant clusters in pink to red, summer, fall. Hardy to 34 degrees. Usually comes back from the roots after a freeze. Needs vigorous pruning to keep it in bounds if it does not freeze. Reputedly introduced in New Orleans by Ida Richardson between 1898 and 1910. Those who have grown it find it memorable for its beauty and fragrance.

Rubus trivialis Michx. **SOUTHERN DEWBERRY** Louisiana. Rose family, prostrate prickly shrub or "bramble;" can be invasive. Sun. Moist but well-drained soil. White flowers with yellow centers are followed by blackberry-like fruit which ripens in April and May.

Rubus...several species. **BLACKBERRIES** Information same as southern dewberry, above, except that fruit ripens July and August. 'Brazos' is one variety recommended for the Gulf Coast. It has done well for Hilda Latapie.

Sechium edule (Jacq.) Swartz **MIRLITON, ALLIGATOR PEAR** American tropics. Gourd family, climbing vine, perennial but usually killed by frost, here. Sun. Well drained garden soil. Attractive, fast growing vines produce the edible fruits spring, but mostly in fall. Be and Mitch Boe produce huge crops of the vegetables which they use in wonderful seafood recipes. 1883

Senecio confusus (DC.) Britten. **CONFUCIOUS VINE, MEXICAN FLAME VINE** Mexico. Composite family, perennial climber to 25 feet. Plant where roots are shaded, top of plant gets at least half a day's full sun. Well-drained soil; likes our moist air. Its red-orange daisy-flowers are profuse spring to fall. Hardy to 32 degrees. Plant in a protected spot and mulch heavily. Cut back hard after blooming.

S. tamoides **CANARY CREEPER** South Africa. Climbing evergreen shrub, to 20 feet. Sun for best bloom. Well-drained soil, drought resistant. Blooms are like clusters of yellow daisies, fall to winter. Hardy to 25 degrees.

Solanum jasminoides Paxt. **POTATO VINE, VIRGIN'S BOWER** Brazil. Nightshade family, vigorous deciduous perennial climber to 20 feet. Sun, part-sun. Moist, well drained, fertile soil. Star-shaped one inch flowers, pale blue with yellow centers; May through October. Hardy to 20 degrees. Though of the same family as the practical potato and eggplant, this vine and its relatives, below, are much more ornamental than functional. 1875.

S. seaforthianum Andr. **POTATO VINE, JASMINE NIGHTSHADE** Tropical America. Star-shaped lilac colored flowers during summer, followed by yellow berries. Hardy to 30 degrees. Plant in a protected, sunny spot and mulch. Not for the wildlife garden: the berries sometimes intoxicate birds.

S. wendlandii Hook.f. **POTATO VINE, PARADISE FLOWER** Costa Rica. Prickly, shrubby climber with gorgeous lilac-blue clusters of 2 inch flowers during warm weather; red berries may follow. Hardy to 25 degrees. Protect and mulch.

Stigmaphyllon ciliatum (Lam.) A. Juss. **BUTTERFLY VINE** Tropical America. Malpighia family, twining vine, rapid growth to 20 feet. Shade, part shade. Any garden soil not too alkaline. Glossy, dark green leaves on slender vines; flowers summer to fall are yellow and orchid-like, in clusters. Butterfly shaped seed pods follow which change from bright green to tan, persist on the vine. Hardy to 25 degrees. Needs protection to return after freeze.

Thunbergia alata Bojer **BLACK-EYED SUSAN VINE, CLOCK VINE** Africa. Acanthus family, tender perennial grown as an annual here, a twining vine to 6 feet. Sun, light shade. Moist, rich soil. Grow on fence, trellis, or as ground cover. Start from seed in spring for profuse bloom from summer to frost. It volunteers from dropped seed each year by my front fence. Flowers are golden yellow funnels with dark throats, one to two inches in diameter. Unusual, they stimulate more comment than anything else growing in my front yard. Varieties in white, buff, and orange both solid and with dark centers. 1883

T. grandiflora L. **BLUE THUNBERGIA, BENGAL TRUMPET VINE, BLUE SKY VINE, BENGAL CLOCK-VINE** India. Tender twining perennial which usually returns from the roots after a freeze here, but is fast maturing enough to be grown as an annual. To 10 feet, needs lots of space to spread. Sun. Rich, well-drained, alkaline

146 THE NEW ORLEANS GARDEN

soil and abundant summer watering (to simulate the rainy season in Calcutta). The plant in bloom is called unsurpassable in beauty, with 3 inch periwinkle blue trumpet-shaped flowers whose throats are yellow and veined and which hang in 2 foot long pendulous clusters. Blooms summer into fall here. (Define "fall" loosely. In December of 1988 one was blooming on the fence by the Absolute Restaurant on Tchoupitoulas Street. It was gone after the freeze of 1989.) Likes our heat. White variety available.

Trachelospermum asiaticum (Siebold & Zucc.) Nakai **DWARF CONFEDERATE JASMINE, ASIAN JASMINE** China. Dogbane family, evergreen vine to 25 feet, ground-cover mat to 18 inches. Sun, shade. Rich, moist soil. Small, dark-green, leathery leaves can form luxuriant carpet in 2 years if clumps are planted every 20 inches. Growth is so thick that once established, only DOORSTEP FLOWERS can make it through. Non-flowering, though mixing in a few clumps of Confederate jasmine is suggested to make up this deficit.

T. jasminoides (Lindl.) Lem. *Rhynchospermum jasminoides* **STAR JASMINE, CONFEDERATE JASMINE** China, Japan. Dogbane family, evergreen twining vine, fast growing to 20 feet. Sun, part shade. Rich, moist but well-drained soil. White star-shaped clusters of very fragrant flowers April, May. Not completely hardy.

Tropaeolum peregrinum Jacq., *T. canariensis.* **CANARY-BIRD VINE, CANARY CREEPER** Peru, Equador. Nasturtium family, annual vine, fast growing to 15 feet. Part shade, especially at midday. Average to moist soil, sandy, on the poor side in nutrients. Like other nasturtiums, it does not really like our hot summers. Blooms late summer, fall are feathery, yellow.

Vinca major L. **GREATER PERIWINKLE** Europe. Dogbane family, evergreen trailing subshrub used as a ground cover, to 12 inches. Part shade. Rich, loose soil. Its lack of density makes it suitable for a natural rather than manicured setting; also make it require more maintainence than other ground covers. Two inch blue-violet blooms in spring and sporadically through summer, sparse in deep shade.

V. minor L. **COMMON PERIWINKLE** Smaller leaves, flowers than *V. major*. Considered one of the "finest evergreen groundcovers" for many parts of the country, you will find it touted in many catalogs, offered in many "specials". Though I have heard people say they have grown it successfully, it is not a sure thing for New Orleans. I have heard more reports of failure, which has been my experience.

Vitis L. species **GRAPES** Natchez nurseryman Thomas Affleck explained in his 1854 *"Almanac"* that the European vines so desired for wine *"dwindled"* or did not ripen its fruit after a few years. He blamed failure more on *"defects of the soil than climate"* but recommended improved scuppernong, the native species, instead.

V. rotundifolia Michx. **MUSCADINE GRAPES, SCUPPERNONG** South U.S., Louisiana swamps. Grape or Vine family, deciduous perennial vine clinging with tendrils. Sun, part shade. Well-drained soil. Needs a trellis or will climb on anything in its path. Pruning is required to train vine to desired shape and to maintain a high level of berry production. Be sure to buy a self-pollinating variety, otherwise you will need male and female plants. Berries ripen in the fall. My grapevine is on a trellis over a deck. The first year, the grapes dropped, leaving a slimey, but sweetsmelling mess. The second year, the birds found them. Very few made it to the deck.

Wisteria sinensis Sweet **WISTERIA, CHINESE WISTERIA** China. Legume family, deciduous twining vine which can grow to 100 feet though average is 30. Sun, part sun. Moist, well-drained, fertile soil. Beautiful blue clusters of fragrant flowers six to twelve inches long appear in profusion in spring before the new leaves sprout and occasionally through the summer. Seeds follow in large, light brown suede pea pods. Very vigorous grower with twining branches. Needs frequent pruning to restrict its rampant growth and a strong framework to support it. Can be trained into tree form (as in Be Boe's Belle Chasse garden). Its beauty makes it worth all the efforts at control. One of the best known specimens is on the closed and deteriorating old building which was Maylie's Restaurant on Poydras Street. Wisteria is long familiar in New Orleans gardens. Obtain vegetatively reproduced plants as bloom from seed can take several years. Cultivars in white, also. 1875.

W. floribunda D.C. **JAPANESE WISTERIA** Japan. Flowers later than Chinese, does not present the same burst of color; but clusters of white, pink, and purple blossoms are spectacular, twenty inches or more long.

VINES BY SEASON OF BLOOM

SPRING BLOOMING VINES

Akebia quinata AKEBIA, FIVE LEAF AKEBIA
Allamanda cathartica ALLAMANDA
Aristolochia durior DUTCHMAN'S PIPE
Bignonia capreolata CROSS VINE, TRUMPET FLOWER
Bougainvillea species and hybrids BOUGAINVILLEA
Campsis radicans TRUMPET VINE, TRUMPET CREEPER
Clerodendrum thomsoniae CLERODENDRUM, BLEEDINGHEART
Clytostoma callistegioides BIGNONIA, ARGENTINE TRUMPET VINE
Cocculus carolinus COCCULUS, CAROLINA MOONSEED
Gelsemium sempervirens CAROLINA JESSAMINE
Ipomoea purpurea MORNING-GLORY
Jasmine nudiflorum WINTER JASMINE
Jasmine officinale COMMON WHITE JASMINE
Jasmine polyanthum CHINESE JASMINE
Jasmine sambac ARABIAN JASMINE
Lathyrus latifolius PERENNIAL SWEET PEA
Lonicera japonica JAPANESE HONEYSUCKLE
Lonicera sempervirens CORAL HONEYSUCKLE
Macfadyena unguis-cati CAT'S CLAW
Millettia reticulata EVERGREEN WISTERIA
Phaseolus coccineus SCARLET RUNNER BEAN
Rubus trivialis SOUTHERN DEWBERRY
Senecio confusus CONFUCIOUS VINE,
    MEXICAN FLAME VINE
Thunbergia alata BLACK-EYED SUSAN VINE, CLOCK VINE
Trachelospermum jasminoides STAR JASMINE,
    CONFEDERATE JASMINE
Vinca major GREATER PERIWINKLE
Wisteria sinensis WISTERIA, CHINESE WISTERIA
Wisteria floribunda JAPANESE WISTERIA

SUMMER BLOOMING VINES

Allamanda cathartica ALLAMANDA
Anredera basselloides MADEIRA VINE, MIGNONETTE VINE
Antigonon leptopus ROSE OF MONTANA, CORAL VINE
Aristolochia durior DUTCHMAN'S PIPE
Aristolochia elegans DUTCHMAN'S PIPE, CALICO FLOWER
Asarina barclaiana (Maurandia barclaiana)
    CLIMBING SNAPDRAGON
Bignonia capreolata CROSS VINE, TRUMPET FLOWER
Bougainvillea species and hybrids BOUGAINVILLEA

Campsis radicans TRUMPET VINE, TRUMPET CREEPER
Cardiospermum halicacabum BALLOON VINE, HEART-SEED,
    LOVE IN A PUFF
Clematis dioscoreifolia, Clematis paniculata JAPANESE CLEMATIS
Clerodendrum thomsoniae CLERODENDRUM, BLEEDINGHEART
Clitoria mariana CLITORIA, BUTTERFLY-PEA
Cobaea scandens CUP & SAUCER VINE, CATHEDRAL BELLS
Cocculus carolinus COCCULUS, CAROLINA MOONSEED (berries)
Dolichos lablab HYACINTH BEAN
Hydrangea anomala petiolaris CLIMBING HYDRANGEA
Ipomoea alba, Calonyction aculeatum MOONFLOWER
Ipomoea purpurea MORNING-GLORY
Ipomoea coccinea RED MORNING GLORY,
    STAR MORNING GLORY
Ipomoea quamoclit CYPRESS VINE, CARDINAL CLIMBER
Jasmine fruticans JASMINE
Jasmine humile ITALIAN JASMINE
Jasmine officinale COMMON WHITE JASMINE
Jasmine grandiflorum SPANISH JASMINE
Jasmine sambac ARABIAN JASMINE
Lathyrus latifolius PERENNIAL SWEET PEA
Lonicera japonica JAPANESE HONEYSUCKLE
Lonicera sempervirens CORAL HONEYSUCKLE
Mandevilla X amabilis MANDEVILLA
Manettia cordifolia FIRECRACKER VINE
Millettia reticulata EVERGREEN WISTERIA
Momordica balsamina BALSAM APPLE
Passiflora caerulea BLUE PASSION FLOWER
Passiflora incarnata MAYPOP, PASSION FLOWER
Phaseolus coccineus SCARLET RUNNER BEAN
Quisqualis indica RANGOON CREEPER
Rubus...several species BLACKBERRIES
Senecio confusus CONFUCIOUS VINE, MEXICAN FLAME VINE
Stigmaphyllon ciliatum BUTTERFLY VINE
Thunbergia alata BLACK-EYED SUSAN VINE, CLOCK VINE
Thunbergia grandiflora BLUE THUNBERGIA, BLUE SKY VINE,
    BENGAL TRUMPET VINE, BENGAL CLOCK VINE
Tropaeolum peregrinum CANARY-BIRD VINE, CANARY CREEPER
Solanum jasminoides POTATO VINE

FALL BLOOMING VINES

Allamanda cathartica ALLAMANDA
Antigonon leptopus ROSE OF MONTANA, CORAL VINE
Asarina barclaiana (Maurandia barclaiana)
    CLIMBING SNAPDRAGON
Campsis radicans TRUMPET VINE, TRUMPET CREEPER

Cardiospermum halicacabum BALLOON VINE, HEART-SEED,
     LOVE IN A PUFF (seed pods)
Clematis dioscoreifolia, Clematis paniculata JAPANESE CLEMATIS
Cocculus carolinus COCCULUS, CAROLINA MOONSEED (berries)
Curcurbitaceae species GOURD FAMILY
Senecio confusus CONFUCIOUS VINE,
     MEXICAN FLAME VINE
Senecio tamoides CANARY CREEPER
Thunbergia alata BLACK-EYED SUSAN VINE, CLOCK VINE
Tropaeolum peregrinum CANARY-BIRD VINE,
     CANARY CREEPER
Solanum jasminoides POTATO VINE
Solanum seaforthianum POTATO VINE,
     JASMINE NIGHTSHADE
Solanum wendlandii POTATO VINE, PARADISE FLOWER
Vitis rotundifolia MUSCADINE GRAPES, SCUPPERNONG

Susan Openshaw LaRocca

Annuals

*"The point here is really flowers--
gorgeous and abundant flowers..."*

Lee Bailey's *Country Flowers*

"Look at this flower!" I heard. I was waiting in the checkout line at the westbank nursery which is a tradition for economy minded New Orleans gardeners. People stood ahead and behind guarding yellow wagons laden with flats and pots of plants.

"I wonder what it is?"

I looked over my shoulder to see a woman proudly holding her find: of all things, a zinnia! My first response was a condescending smile at the thought that someone could be so inexperienced in gardening as not to recognize the most common of cultivated flowers.

Then I thought, "When was the last time I really looked at a zinnia? It is beautiful!" It was pink, one of the "mammoth dahlia types" as a seed catalog would say; not really the generic zinnia a novice would picture.

I mentally reviewed my experience with zinnias: they are very easy to grow from seed, sprouting in 3 to 5 days and blooming from 6 to 8 weeks later. Many varieties are available, offering a huge selection of forms, colors, sizes. Flowering is over a long period of time. The border and edging zinnias are full and attractive plants. The taller ones offer beaucoup long stemmed and long lasting cut flowers which make the necessary staking worth the effort.

I was in the year of my "red bed". I had turned up my nose at the common annuals in favor of more esoteric plants. I planned red *Abelmoschus* hybrids interspersed with *Cuphea miniata* 'Firefly' and edged all around with 'Blaze' verbena. Unfortunately, only one verbena sprouted and a few cupheas. The *Abelmoschus*, many of which germinated, didn't bloom until July and then became rangy. The lobed-leaved foliage was "interesting", the flowers delicate and lovely but not as numerous as I had hoped. To fill in, I found three red verbena plants at Weber's nursery, but only one 'Blaze' was available. They and the sparse cupheas fell far short of the image conjured up over a Park Seed Company catalog the previous fall when I ordered the seeds.

On the way home, I decided what I had to do. My order for 'Dreamland' hybrid zinnias in scarlet arrived from Park a week or so later. I sowed the seeds along the edge and in the gaps. By the fall, my red bed was a reality.

Annuals are plants which sprout, mature, flower, bear seed, and die in one season. The flowers are their reason for being. The more prolific bloom production, the greater the assurance of producing enough seed to continue the species. Annuals are the best choice for *"gorgeous and abundant flowers"* over a long period of time. They do have to be replanted seasonally. But enough are easy and quick from seed and rewarding in their display of blooms that I could hardly imagine a garden without them.

Annuals from seed make possible selection from a wider variety of species and hybrids than are available as nursery-grown plants. I recommend ordering from catalogues rather than local seed racks to expand your choices. Of course the advantages of nursery started annuals in spite of their higher price are obvious. A few potted annuals tucked into colorless spots in the garden or at the edge of the walk are an easy way to decorate. They can be replaced when they fade, or moved around for variation. See BASICS for more on seeds.

Another annual so common that its value can be underestimated is the marigold. Its long popularity nationwide is deserved, due to its beauty, productivity, and its ease of cultivation. My husband, Jean, remembers a yearly flower show in New York City with a category for grammar school children called "Marigolds in Beanpot." He won the medal in 1942, at age 12, with an arrangement in his mom's brown glazed beanpot. He grew them himself.

Growing marigolds from seed is foolproof. Ordering from seed catalogs vastly expands your selection, so that, even though you have planted the most common garden flower you may have beds like no one else's. The bicolored French edging marigolds, such as the maroon and gold 'Flame', are my favorites. Their disease and insect resistant foliage looks good and they flower for long periods of time.

Tall African marigolds come in shades of yellow, orange, gold. The carnation-like blooms are so large on some varieties, the plants need staking to support them. My favorite bouquet is a mixture of these giants in pale yellow, orange, and gold in the brown pottery vase which was a wedding present.

New Orleans' mostly mild winter weather makes possible the fall planting of annuals which bloom during summer and fall in cooler places but cannot tolerate our hot summers. If it works, the result is year-round flowers.

The secret of winter annuals has been known for a long time. W. H. Coleman in 1885 described what experienced New Orleans gardeners know today:

*Now as to the facts: Some of the plants in New Orleans'
gardens are occasionally killed or injured by cold, but after all a
very small proportion, and so little penetrating effect has the
cold that there have been geraniums, and even more delicate
plants saved by a covering of a few newspapers.....As to the time
for planting seed, October and November might really be called
spring months, that is to say, the influence of this climate
during those months upon the germination of seeds and the
growth of young plants of many kinds is equivalent to the real
spring time further north. It is also provided by nature that
such as should be planted shortly before the advent of cold
weather are sufficiently hardy to withstand the coming winter,
and few will be killed, though afforded no protection whatever.
Reference is made to a number of annuals and perennials whose
proper season for bloom in this climate is from the first of
January to the end of April. So, under the impression that
spring is the time for planting, many persons wait until they
see pansies, asters, or others in bloom in a florist's hands,
before they plant the seed, and being about three months behind
the proper time they have very little success....*

My experience has been that results from fall plantings vary with the species planted. Even though plants
are said to be hardy, if one of our freaky winters comes
along with a steep drop in temperatures, some little
seedlings which sprout in fall may be frozen. In a mild
year, with the use of annuals from both the lists at the
end of the chapter, you can enjoy gorgeous and abundant
flowers almost all year round!

City Park Botanical Garden, and Longue Vue Gardens
are good places to see annuals.

ANNUALS FOR THE NEW ORLEANS GARDEN

References to J.B. Russell and Joseph Breck Boston catalogues are from the brochure from *Select Seeds, Fine Seeds For Old-Fashioned Flowers.*

1766 Indicates species grown in Thomas Jefferson's Monticello garden.

1838 Indicates listing in Lelievre's *New Gardener of Louisiana.*

1859 Indicates listing in the catalogue of plants offered for sale by John Nelson at Magnolia Nurseries at Metairie Ridge and at his Plant Depot, Corner of Camp St. & Lafayette Sq., New Orleans.

1883 Indicates listing in *Almanac and Garden Manual for the Southern States,* by Richard Frotscher, New Orleans seed merchant.

1916 Indicates listing in *Reuter's Seeds for the South,* Spring, New Orleans.

1918 Indicates listing in Bollwinkle Seed Co. Ltd., *Catalogue & Garden* Guide, 510 Dumaine St., New Orleans.

Abelmoschus moschatus Medic. **ABELMOSCHUS, MUSK MALLOW** Asia. Mallow family, tender perennial used as an annual, 18 inches. Sun. Red or pink, white centered, hibiscus like flowers with skinny, rodlike stamens which curve from their centers. Like hot weather. Easy from seed started in early spring for bloom from July. Reseed. Newly available from seed companies. Becoming more common in New Orleans gardens.

Ageratum houstonianum Mill. **AGERATUM, FLOSS FLOWER** Mexico. Composite family, 6 inches to 2 feet. Sun, part shade. Rich, moist, well-drained soil. Clusters of fuzzy blue flowers cover plants mounding and spreading in form; white and pink available, too. Die back with heat or frost, but with two plantings, you can enjoy them spring and fall. I have had them volunteer in my garden a second season. Dwarf varieties are more heat-resistant.

Alcea rosea L. *(Althea rosea)* **HOLLYHOCK** Asia minor. Mallow family biennial or annual, annual strain 'Indian Spring' is better for New Orleans, 2 to 5 feet. Sun. Average soil. Flowers in red, rose, pink, white are 2 to 4 inch double or semi-double, profuse along tall spikes. Plant in the fall for spring bloom. Someone on Magazine Street near Audubon Park grows them every year. They are so spectacular in appearance that you want to tell everyone about them! 1766, 1838.

Amaranthus caudatus L. **LOVE-LIES-BLEEDING, TAS-SELFLOWER, PRINCES FEATHERS** India.   Amaranth family, 3 to 5 feet.   Sun.   Best appearance in poor, dry soil.   Red foliage, drooping, tassel-like flower spikes. Summer, fall bloom.   Grown as a food plant in India. 1766, 1838, 1883.

A. tricolor L. **JOSEPH'S COAT** 1 to 4 feet. Grown for its yellow, green, crimson foliage; summer, fall. 1766, 1838.

Anchusa capensis Thunb. Bien. **BUGLOSS, CAPE FOR-GET-ME-NOT** South Africa.   Borage family, 8 inches to 2 feet.   Sun, light shade.   Any moist, well-drained soil. Clusters of white-centered flowers in unusual shades of blue; pink and white available, too.   Sow in the fall for spring bloom, will not withstand freeze.

Antirrhinum majus L. **SNAPDRAGON** Mediterranean. Figwort family, 6 inches to 4 feet, perennial grown as annual. Sun, part shade.   Rich, organic, well-drained soil; pH neutral to alkaline.   Spikes of flowers in many colors. Individual blooms have little dragon mouths which open when squeezed (say my kids).   Tall varieties need staking. Set out in fall for winter and spring bloom.   Usually die back with heat, but I have had dwarf varieties last two years. 1766, 1838.

Arctotis stoechadifolia Bergius. **AFRICAN DAISY** South Africa.   Composite family, 2 feet, dwarf forms shorter. Sun.   Light, sandy, well-drained soil.   Can withstand drought.   Long stemmed, daisy-like flowers have white petals, purplish underneath, lavender centers; hybrids in yellow, white, pink, red, orange.   Like cool nights, so sow in fall for spring bloom.

Bellis perennis L. **ENGLISH DAISY** Europe.   Com-posite family, biennial grown as annual, 6 inches.   Sun, light shade.   Any moist soil.   Bushy plants with lots of 1 to 2 inch flowers, bushy balls of white, pink, or red petals. Cool weather plants which should be sown in fall for early spring bloom. 1766, 1883.

Browallia speciosa Hook. **BROWALLIA** Colombia. Nightshade family, annual, trailing form, height and spread of 12 to 15 inches. Sun, part shade. Average to rich soil. Blue or white star-shaped trumpets, velvety petaled, 2 inches across. Related to the petunia. Cultivar 'Major' is recommended. Tender. Sow for bloom 12 weeks later. Good in hanging baskets, pots. Planted in fall for spring bloom in 1885 New Orleans gardens. Protect from freeze. *B. americana* L. 'Major' recomended for use in borders, 1895.

Calendula officinalis L. **CALENDULA, POT MARI-GOLD** Southern Europe. Composite family, 10 inches to 2 feet. Sun. Rich, moist, well-drained soil; cooler weather. Abundant blossoms in creams, yellows, oranges. Included in traditional herb gardens for its use in dyes, medicinal value. 1766, 1883.

Callistephus chinensis (L.) Nees **CHINA ASTER, AN-NUAL ASTER** China. Composite family, 6 inches to 3 feet. Sun, light shade. Rich, well-drained, neutral to alkaline soil. Varied flower forms in a rainbow of colors, long stems. Plant in early spring here. The bloom period, about one month, can be prolonged with successive plantings. Unlike most other annuals, they do not rebloom when cut. Need mulch to protect and cool their shallow roots. Should not be planted in the same spot successive years due to susceptibility to fungus diseases found in the soil. 1883.

Campanula medium L. **CANTERBURY-BELLS** Southern Europe. Bellflower family, 1 to 3 feet. Sun. Rich, moist soil. Large, bell-shaped pink and blue flowers cluster along the flexible spikes which require staking or mass planting for support. Sow seed in fall for bloom 6 months later. 1766, 1838.

Capsicum annuum L. **ORNAMENTAL PEPPERS** Sub-tropical North and South America. Nightshade family, 6 to 30 inches, perennials used as annuals. Sun, light shade. Rich, moist, well-drained soil. They like our hot summers.

Many varieties grown for their fruits, mostly red or orange, though also black, purple, yellow, green, white. I received as a gift a potted specimen which had peppers in all the above colors at once! Edible in spicing food but only if you like it hot! Birds like them.

Carthamus tinctorius L. **SAFFLOWER** Eurasia. Composite family, 3 feet. Sun, part shade. Well-drained soil. Source of the seeds used for oil, birdfood is also a beautiful ornamental, good for drying. You may have bought a bunch from a flower shop. Cool weather plants. Sow seed in fall or very early spring for spring bloom. I have only grown them by accident, from dropped parrot seed, but with good results after a cold winter, cool spring.

Catharanthus roseus (L.) G. Don, *Vinca roseus* **MADAGASCAR PERIWINKLE** Madagascar, India. Dogbane family, perennial grown as an annual, 10 to 18 inches. Sun, part shade. Rich, moist but well-drained soil, lots of water. Glossy green leaves on bushy, spreading plants. Prolific blooms in rose, white, pink or red eyed white, summer to frost. With our mild winters, they frequently act as perennials. If not, they return from dropped seed, but not until the weather gets hot. They are easy, always look good. Do without them? No way!

Celosia cristata L. **COCKSCOMB** Tropical Africa. Amaranth family, 6 to 36 inches. Sun. Soil is best rich, organic, well-drained; tolerates poor, dry conditions. Unusual flowers in yellow, orange, red, pink, purple are formed variously as plumes, feathers, or cockscomb-like crests. Sow in spring for summer, fall bloom. 1766, 1838.

Centaurea cyanus L. **CORNFLOWER, BACHELOR'S-BUTTON, BLUE-BOTTLE** Europe. Composite family, 1 to 3 feet. Sun. Any well-drained soil; rich, moist is best. Flowers in blues, pink, white. Fall sowing directly into the ground is recommended for bloom in spring. Hardy. 1766, 1838.

C. cineraria L., *C. gymnocarpa* **DUSTY MILLER** are both of Mediterranean origin, have hairy-white foliage, purple flowers, grow to three feet. *C. cineraria* was reputedly used in New Orleans gardens before 1860.

C. montana L. **MOUNTAIN BLUET, MOUNTAIN BLUE-BOTTLE** Central Europe. 1766.

C. moschata L. **SWEET SULTAN** 2 feet. Flowers in white, yellow, pinks, purples. Sow where to grow in fall for spring bloom. 1766.

Cheiranthus cheiri L. **WALLFLOWER** Southern Europe. Mustard family, from 6 to 18 inches. Sun, light shade. Well-drained, neutral soil. Fragrant spikes of blossoms in gold, yellow, red, mahogany present in spring. Thrive in cool, damp climates; die in heat. Start from seed in fall. 1766, 1838.

Chrysanthemum carinatum Schousb., *C. coronarium* L., *C. segetum* L. and their hybrids **ANNUAL CHRYSANTHE-MUM** Europe, Africa, Asia. Composite family, 6 inches to 2 feet. Sun, light shade. Well-drained soil. Single and double daisy and other formed flowers in white, yellows, oranges, bronzes, maroons; solid or zoned. Sow in early spring for summer,fall bloom. Easy from seed.

C. parthenium (L.) Bernh., *Matricaria capensis* **FEVER-FEW** Europe. Tender perennial used as an annual, 2 feet. Three-quarter inch yellow-centered white daisies stud aromatic bushes during summer. Reseed. 1883.

Clarkia unguiculata Lindl. **CLARKIA, GODETIA** California. Evening Primrose family, 18 to 24 inches. Part shade to compensate for our heat, prolong bloom. Very good drainage; light, sandy, infertile soil. Delicate 1 inch flowers which grow along erect stems are shades of red, pink, salmon, and white. Start from seed in fall here for spring bloom. Hardy. Bloom season will be short in our hot, wet climate, as opposed to the west coastal and mountain summers these natives love. Used in Parkway plantings during the 1940's.

Cleome hasslerana Chodat **CLEOME, SPIDER FLOWER** South America. Caper family, 3 to 4 feet. Sun. Any well-drained soil, lots of water, though they can stand drought. White, pink, red flowers with long whiskery stamens, strong fragrance; leaves look like marijuana. Warm weather plants, easy from seed sown in spring; reseed. Hummingbirds like them. Introduced to the U.S. 1817-1840

Coleus blumei Benth. **COLEUS** Java. Mint family, 3 to 36 inches, tender perennial grown as annual. Sun, shade. Moist, well-drained soil. Known for foliage, ornamental in form and color: pink, red, bronze, yellow, maroon, green, chartreuse. Flowers do form, sparse purply spikes, which should be pinched to keep the plants bushy. Easy from seed. Plant in early spring for color until frost. Grown in Cotton Centennial Exhibitions 1884. 1918.

Consolida orientalis (J. Gay) Schrodinger (*Delphinium ajacis*) **LARKSPUR, RABBIT EARS, ANNUAL DELPHINIUM** Mediterranean region. Ranunculus family, 1 to 2 feet. Sun. Rich, well-drained, moist, organic soil, slightly alkaline in pH. Spikes of delphinium like flowers in white, pink, blue, purple; lacy foliage. Sow in the ground in November for spring bloom. Hardy. Volunteer year after year, as in Frank Kennett and Bob Gordy's Bell Street garden. The purple is most commonly seen in New Orleans. Their local nickname is "Rabbit ears." Skip Treme' seeded his St. Augustine lawn with purples and pinks. They provide their lovely display and drop their seed for next year before time for the first spring mowing. 1766, 1838, 1883.

Coreopsis tinctoria Nutt. **CALLIOPSIS, NUTALL'S WEED** North America. Composite family, 6 inches to 3 feet. Sun. Good drainage, light, sandy soil. Cultivated varieties of the native wildflower have the same daisy form, dark centers, toothed petals either solid or bicolored in shades of yellow, purple-red, brown. Profuse bloom over a long period. Reseed. Available from Joseph Breck's seed catalogue, 1838.

Cosmos Cav. species **COSMOS** Tropical America. Composite family, 18 to 48 inches. Sun. Well-drained, dry, infertile soil promotes most bloom. Sow where to grow in spring for summer, fall bloom. Tall varieties need staking. Recommended for New Orleans use by nurserymen, 1895.

C. bipinnatus Cav. **EARLY COSMOS** Daisy-styled flowers with yellow centers, notched petals of lavender, pink, magenta, white. Floppy plants with delicate foliage. This is Dr. Warren Trask's favorite flower. Plant in early spring for spring-summer bloom.

C. sulphureus Cav. **YELLOW and ORANGE COSMOS** Flowers as above but vivid golds, yellows, orangescarlets, on plants with fern-like leaves. Sow in spring for a profusion of summer-fall bloom. Reseeds if given half a chance.

Cuphea platycentra A. DC. **CIGAR FLOWER, FIRE-CRACKER PLANT** Mexico, Jamaica. Loosestrife family, shrubby to 1 foot. Sun, part sun. Any soil. 1 inch flowers are bright orange tubes with violet and white tips. 1859.

C. X purpurea Lem or *C. miniata* 'Firefly' **CUPHEA** Tropical America. 20 inches, perennial grown as annual. Spreading or erect plants with small, striped tubular flowers whose ends open into vividly colored red to purple-violet ruffles. Blooms appear 4 to 5 months after seeds sown, so start early. They will reseed readily. In my garden, I see blooms in late June from plants sprouted between the bricks. They hang over edges nicely, of raised beds, pots.

Cynoglossum amabile Stapf & J. R. Drumm **CHINESE FORGET-ME-NOT** Asia. Borage family, biennial grown as annual, 2 feet. Sun, part shade. Wet or dry soil, average fertility. Tiny blue flowers similar to real forget-me-nots; pink and white varieties are not as pretty. Hardy. Sow seeds in the fall for spring bloom.

Delphinium grandiflorum L. **SIBERIAN LARKSPUR** China. Ranunculus family, 2 to 3 feet, perennial grown as an annual. Flowers on tall spikes in wonderful blues,

white if you must. Cold hardy, but when our nights get
hot, they go. Sow seeds in fall for spring bloom.

Dianthus L. species **PINKS** Eurasia. Pink family, 4 to
18 inches, biennial or perennials grown as annuals. Sun,
light shade. Well-drained, alkaline soils. Showy flowers
of different sizes in pink, rose, purple, white, or blends
with characteristic "pinked" edges. Sow in fall, or set out
plants in fall, winter for winter-spring bloom. Though
they usually go with the heat, I have had them last a
second year. I plant them in cinder blocks, for drainage
and alkalinity. *D. barbatus* **SWEET WILLIAM** L., 1766,
1838, 1883.

Digitalis purpurea L. 'Foxy' **FOXGLOVE** Spain. Figwort family, perennial grown as an annual, 3 feet. Shade,
part shade. Moist, but very well-drained soil. Spikes of 3
inch, thimble-shaped flowers in cream, yellow, rose, red
with flared, ruffled openings and spots inside. Blooms in
five months from seed, hardy. If planted in fall, the
amazingly showy flowers can be enjoyed in spring before
they succumb to our heat.

Eschscholzia californica Cham. **CALIFORNIA POPPY**
California. Poppy family, to 2 feet, perennial wildflower
grown as an annual. Sun. Well-drained, sandy soil. 3
inch, poppy-like flowers in original gold, and new shades
of orange, pink, white in spring. Plant in fall in the
ground as they do not transplant well. They can reseed
and repeat in the right spot here. Offered as "new and
rare" in an 1833 seed catalogue, 1883 by Frotscher in New
Orleans.

Gazania rigens (L.) Gaertn. **TREASURE FLOWER, GA-
ZANIA** Africa. Composite family, 6 to 15 inches, perennial grown as an annual. Many of the plants available are
hybrids of annual and perennial species, may perform as
annuals. Sun. Light, sandy, very well-drained soil. Large
centered, daisy-like flowers; patterned or solid in cream,
yellow, golden-orange, bronze, pink, red. Does not do as
well in our hot, wet summers as in dry conditions. Sow

in early spring. Division of clumps is suggested after several years. I have never had them last that long.

Gomphrena globosa L. **GLOBE AMARANTH** Oriental tropics. Amaranth family, 9 to 30 inches. Sun. Well-drained soil. Like hot weather, tolerate our humidity. Blooms are like clover flowers with stiff, straw-like petals, in purples, white, pink, orange, yellow. Good for drying. I have found them easy and satisfying plants from seed sown early spring. The taller ones need staking. 1766, 1838, 1883.

Gysophila elegans Bieb. **BABY'S BREATH** Eurasia. Composite family, 8 to 24 inches. Sun. Well-drained, infertile, neutral to alkaline soil. Fine foliaged plant covered during spring with tiny, white flowers; good for drying. Hardy, sow seeds in fall in the ground for spring bloom here. A wire basket inverted over the taller varieties when small rather than stakes are recommended to preserve the airy quality of the plant. 1883.

Helianthus L. species **SUNFLOWER** New World natives. Composite family, 2 to 6 or more feet. Sun. Any soil, though light, well-drained is best. Flowers from small to huge, many to one per plant, single row of petals to many petaled fuzzy balls; colors yellow, gold, cream, orange, mahogany, with centers of red or purple or brown, huge to small in size. Some produce the seeds loved by birds. Very easy to grow from seed sown spring or summer. See WILDFLOWERS. 1883.

H. annuus L. **COMMON SUNFLOWER** or **MIRASOL**, 1766, 1838.

H. divaricatus L. **SUNFLOWER** 1766.

Helichrysum bracteatum (Venten.) Andr. (*H. monstrosum*) **STRAWFLOWER** Australia. Composite family, 18 to 36 inches. Sun. Moist, light, well-drained soil; slightly alkaline in pH. Do not overwater. Small, yellow flowers are surrounded by rows of petal-like, stiff bracts in white, orange, red, salmon, yellow, pink, purple; striking in appearance; good for drying. Taller plants need staking.

Sow seeds in very early spring for summer-fall bloom.
Likes hot summers. 1883.

Heliotropium arborescens L. HELIOTROPE Peru. Borage
family, perennial grown as an annual. Sun, part shade.
Rich soil. To 2 feet or more. Flower clusters as large as
1 foot in diameter in shades of purple to white. Known
for its incredible fragrance. Sow seed in flats in midwinter, set out plants in spring. 1766, 1838, 1859, 1883.

Iberis L. CANDYTUFT Europe. Mustard family. Sun,
light shade. Moist, well-drained soil. Hardy; sow seeds
in fall in the ground for bloom (6 to 10 weeks later) in
winter and early spring before our heat and humidity
causes their demise. 1838.

I. amara L. ROCKET CANDYTUFT One foot. One
inch white flowers, fragrant clusters in profusion. 1883.

I. umbellata L. GLOBE CANDYTUFT Flat-topped clusters of tiny flowers in rose, lavender, white; unscented.
Low, spreading plants. 1883.

Impatiens balsamina L. GARDEN BALSAM, LADY'S
SLIPPERS China. Balsam family, 1 to 3 feet. Sun, part
shade. Well-drained soil high in sand and organic matter.
Flowers in reds, white, yellow are in clusters close to the
stem; singles, doubles. The   newer camellia flowered
varieties are recommended. Sow in the ground in spring.
Likes our hot summers. Reseeds. Old cultivars, called
lady's slippers, found in old local gardens. 1766, 1838.

I. wallerana Hook.f. IMPATIENS, SULTANA Africa.
Balsam family, tender perennial grown as an annual, 6 to
18 inches. Shade. Rich, light, moist soil, sandy and organic; lots of water. Mounding form, profusion of spurred
flowers in pinks, purples, reds, yellow, and white. The
NEW GUINEA HYBRIDS are larger, have larger flowers
and variegated foliage. Impatiens will last through a mild
winter in New Orleans. I always find they drop bottom
leaves and get rangy toward the end of a rainy summer.
Cutting them back will rejuvenate them.

Kochia scoparia variety *trichophylla* (Schmeiss) Schinz & Thell. **SUMMER CYPRESS** Southern Europe. Goosefoot family, 3 feet. Sun. Well-drained, sandy soil. Bushy green plant with feathery foliage which turns red in fall. Inconspicuous flowers. Sow in spring. Likes our heat.

Lathyrus odoratus L. **SWEET PEA** Italy. Pea family, vine to 6 feet. Sun. Rich, well-drained, slightly alkaline soil, high in organic matter. Recommended procedure is to plant seeds in a 6 inch deep trench under 2 inches of rich, organic, slightly alkaline earth with sand added for good drainage; then to backfill for support as the vines grow. The vines should be well watered, and mulched. Planting, of course, should be near a fence or trellis of wire or string netting. They should be started in the ground. The fragrant, showy flowers (my husband's favorite) are blue, lavender, purple, pink, salmon, red, white. They must be started in fall here to beat the heat which will stop their blooms. Though they are cool weather plants, they are not necessarily freeze hardy, and therefore not a sure thing in New Orleans. 1766.

Limomium sinuatum (L.) Mill. **STATICE** Mediterranean region. Plumbago family, biennial grown as an annual, 12 to 30 inches. Sun. Very well-drained soil. Tiny white, blue, lavender, pink, red flowers in showy clusters; frequently seen as dried flowers. Sow in spring for summer bloom. Drainage is critical for success, as this plant is very prone to root rot. It is difficult to grow well in New Orleans. See it at City Park Botanical Garden.

Linaria maroccana Hook.f. **TOADFLAX** Morocco, naturalized in parts of U.S. Snapdragon family, 18 inches. Sun. Any well-drained soil. Narrow leaved plants produce spikes of flowers like miniature snapdragons in yellow, blue, lavender, pink, red, salmon, bronze, white, multicolors. Sow in the ground fall, winter to bloom winter, early spring. Does best in cool summer climates, but, as a snapdragon substitute, it is more heat resistant, may last longer than the the more often used snaps.

Lobelia erinus L. **EDGING LOBELIA** South Africa. Lobelia family, 8 inches. Part shade. Rich soil high in sand and organic matter. Profusion of tiny, intensely blue flowers on low, trailing plants. Sow seeds in the fall for spring bloom, which can be extended by cutting back after the first wave of flowering and planting in the shade. They will eventually succumb to our heat. 1883.

Lobularia maritima (L.) Desv. **SWEET ALYSSUM** Europe. Perennial used as an annual. Mustard family, 12 inches. Sun, light shade. Well drained, average to poor soil. Tiny white, purple, or rose flowers cover the plants, hiding foliage, exuding a honey-like fragrance. Bloom ceases with heat and frost. In mild winters, it lasts all year round, but is not particularly attractive when heat stops its bloom. Volunteers readily from dropped seed. When I worked at New Orleans Mental Health Center, I told psychiatrist, Dr. Ed Fuchs, about a dream of white alyssum. "Those images are sexual," he said. I was too embarrassed about what I may have revealed to ask what the flower had to do with sex, but that is what I am reminded of when I see the plant's billowing, scented mounds. 1838, 1883.

Malva sylvestris L. **ZEBRINA, FRENCH MALLOW** Europe. Mallow family, 3 feet, biennial grown as an annual. Sun, part shade. Average, well-drained soil. Flowers are noticeably hibiscus-related, rose-purple petaled with darker veins, on bushy plants. Sow in the ground in fall for early spring through summer bloom. 1766

Matthiola incana (L.) R. Br. **STOCK, GILLYFLOWER** Southern Europe. Mustard family, perennial grown as an annual, cultivar 'Annua' is recommended for quick bloom, 30 inches. Sun, light shade. Moist, organic, well-drained soil. Heavily flowered fragrant spikes in white, ivory, purples, pinks, reds. These traditional southern garden plants are hardy, started in early fall for winter-spring bloom. Heat brings their demise. 1838, 1883.

Mesembryanthemum crystallinum L. **ICE PLANT** South Africa. Carpetweed family, prostate branches to 2 feet. Sun. Well-drained, dry soil. Mat-forming fleshy leaves, small white to rose colored daisy-like flowers. Sow in spring for summer-fall bloom. Tender. 1838, 1883.

Myosotis sylvatica Hoffm. **GARDEN FORGET-ME-NOT** Europe, Asia. Borage family, biennials grown as annuals, 6 to 12 inches. Part shade. Moist soil. Clusters of tiny gentian blue flowers on erect plants herald spring for some. Bloom stops with hot weather. Seeds can be started in the ground or in flats in fall for spring bloom. Reseed. *M. scorpioides* L. (*M. palustris*) offered 1883.

Nicotiana alata Link & Otto (*N. affinis*), *Nicotiana* hybrids **FLOWERING TOBACCO** South America. Nightshade family, perennial grown as an annual, 1 to 3 feet. Sun, light shade. Moist, well-drained soil. The clusters of star-shaped blooms are in white, creams, yellows through shades of red to maroon. Though all flowering tobaccos are said to be fragrant, I have not found the hybrids to be very much so. Easy from seed sown in early spring for summer bloom. I have had plants last 2 to 3 years through mild winters. *N. sylvestris* Speg. & Cornes, from Argentina, is also available.

N. glauca R. C. Grah. **TREE TOBACCO** South America. 10 to 30 feet. Sun. Well-drained soil. Leathery, grayish leaves on sparsely branched, tree-like plant. Clusters of waxy, yellowish, tubular blooms which are attractive to hummingbirds.

Nigella damascena L. **LOVE-IN-A-MIST** Mediterranean region. Ranunculus family annual, 2 feet. Sun. Well-drained soil. Feathery foliaged plants produce intensely colored cornflower-like blooms in white, blues, purples, pinks to reds which are followed by seed pods good for dry arrangements. Plantings can be staggered to prolong short bloom period. Should be sown in the ground in late fall or early spring. 1766.

Papaver L. species **POPPY** Poppy family. All should be planted in rich, perfectly drained soil high in sand and organic matter. All should be sown in the ground in fall for winter, early spring bloom. All are cool climate plants which will expire with arrival of our summer heat. All are spectacular while they last! *P. somniferum* L. **OPIUM POPPY** was available in 1883, though not today.

P. nudicaule L. **ICELAND POPPY** North American, Eurasian Arctic regions. Perennial grown as a hardy annual, 1 foot. Sun. Fragrant, crepy textured blooms to 3 inches in yellow, pink, orange, greenish, red; fernlike foliage.

P. orientale L. **ORIENTAL POPPY** Asia. Perennial grown as a hardy annual, 3 feet. Sun. Orange, red, pale pink flowers, single or double, showiest of the poppies. Offered as "new and rare" by J. B. Russell, 1833.

P. rhoeas L. **FIELD, FLANDERS, SHIRLEY POPPY** Europe, Asia. Annual, 3 feet. Sun, part shade. 2 inch flowers are reds, purple, white, single, double. Easy in a raised bed. 1766.

Perilla frutescens (L.) Britt. **PERILLA** Asia. Mint family, 3 feet. Grown for its rich purplish-green, wrinkly edged, toothed leaves; aromatic. Spikes of small white flowers become seeds which my caged birds will kill for. Sow in spring. Rampant reseeder.

Petunia X hybrida Hort. Vilm.-Andr. **PETUNIA** South America. Nightshade family, 10 to 18 inches, derived from annuals and perennials, used as annuals though may sometimes last more than one season. Sun. Rich, light, moist but well-drained soil; lots of water. Flowers are funnels which flare into smooth to ruffly edged, 2 to 7 inch, velvety blooms in every color but true blue, some blends, edged or striped white. Multifloras are smaller, more heavily flowered, and less susceptible to the blight which causes blossom drop during damp weather; grandifloras produce fewer enormous blooms. Cascade types are good for raised beds, hanging baskets. Some are scented (usually the purple ones).   Cutting them back when they get rangy can rejuvenate them and bring another wave of bloom.   They are called hardy, perennial types will last through a mild winter here.   Shielding them from direct sun on hot afternoons can help promote bloom all summer.   Easy from seed started in fall, winter, for beaucoup flowering the rest of the year with proper care.   I have not had luck with them, myself, but I am not really a careful gardener.   Ernestine Hopkins has an old-fashioned pale pink multiflora variety that has repeated in her garden for years.   1859

Phlox drummondii Hook.   **ANNUAL PHLOX**   See WILDFLOWERS.

Portulaca grandiflora Hook.   **MOSS ROSE** South America.   Purslane family, forms mats to 6 inches high.   Sun.   It really likes poor, dry soil.   Fleshy, needle-like leaves; rose, salmon, pink, scarlet, orange, yellow, white single or double; the fragile, profuse, brilliantly colored flowers close on sunny days, and after bees have visited.   Easy from seed sown in early spring, bloom through fall, reseeds.   1883.

P. oleracea L.   **PURSLANE** India.   Purslane family, prostrate, mat forming.   Sun.   Any soil.   Larger succulent leaves than Moss Rose.   Larger flowered cultivars of this persistant weed are offered as garden plants.   Very attractive and well-behaved as a ground cover or in hanging baskets.   Can reseed.

Reseda odorata L.   **COMMON MIGNONETTE** North Africa.   Mignonette family, annual, to 18 inches.   Six to 10 inch spikes of yellowish-white flowers.   Intensely fragrant.   Plant in the fall or winter for spring bloom.   Must be sown in the ground.   Does not transplant well.   1766, 1838, 1883.

Salpiglossis sinuata Ruiz. & Pav.   **SALPIGLOSSIS, PAINTED TONGUE** Chile.   Nightshade family, 15 to 36 inches.   Sun, part shade.   Rich, moist soil with lots of sand and organic matter for very good drainage; slightly alkaline pH.   Flowers are trumpet shaped, velvety textured, in combinations of purple, yellow, red, bronze, blue, pink with deep veins which create interesting patterns through the areas of color. They like cool summers, but can not tolerate a freeze. For success in New Orleans, seed must be sown in flats in winter to be set out as soon as possible after our last freeze for bloom in spring and before the heat hits. One source says they are tricky to grow. I have not tried them.

Salvia splendens F. Sellow ex Roem. & Schult. **SCARLET SAGE** Brazil. Mint family, 6 inches to 8 feet, tender perennial grown as an annual. Sun, part shade. Well-drained, rich soil, high in organic matter. The large, showy, spikes of red flowers are the most commonly seen of the salvias, others of which are listed as wildflowers and herbs. Varieties in white, shades of pink, purple. Sow seeds or set out plants in early spring for bloom from summer to frost. Salvias can reach 8 feet when not killed by a freeze. Even if they appear dead, leaving them in place after a mild frost may reward you with return growth. They are shrubby and rangy in appearance when larger, so you may wish to start new plants each year. Hummingbirds love them. "Salvias" were offered 1859, 1883, 1918.

Sanvitalia procumbens Lam. **CREEPING ZINNIA** Mexico. Composite family, prostate plant to 6 inches. Sun. Light, well-drained soil; likes heat. Studded with 1 inch, dark purple centered, yellow to orange petaled flowers summer, fall. Sow seeds where they are to grow in fall.

Scabiosa atropurpurea L. (*S. nana*) **PINCUSHION FLOWER** Southern Europe. Teasel family, 2 feet. Sun. Rich soil, well-drained, alkaline, high in organic matter. The flower is a cluster of smaller flowers, each with prominent, light colored stamens, long stems; blues, purples, reds, pinks, white. Taller ones may need staking. Sow seeds in early spring for bloom in summer. 1766, 1838, 1883.

Tagetes L. species **MARIGOLD** Western hemisphere. Composite family. Sun. Well-drained, moist or dry garden soil. Easy from seed sown in the ground or flats in spring through summer for summer, fall bloom. Heavy flowering plants with attractive, ferny, scented foliage which I have found stays attractive for long periods. 1838.

T. erecta L. **AFRICAN** or **AZTEC MARIGOLD** To 3 feet. Flowers are globes of yellow, gold, orange up to 5 inches, depending on the variety. Need staking. Make the most wonderful bouquets of long-lasting cut flowers! 1766, 1883.

T. patula L. **FRENCH MARIGOLD** 6 to 18 inches. Bushy plant with lots of small single or double flowers in yellows, golds, bronze, mahogany and my favorites, the bicolors. Good edging plants. 1766, 1883.

T. tenuifolia Cav. **SIGNET MARIGOLD** The 'Pumila' cultivars are 1 foot or less. The single blossoms are single, yellow or golden-orange flowers on mounded plants with even finer ferny foliage than the above marigolds.

Tithonia rotundifolia (Mill.) S. F. Blake **MEXICAN SUN-FLOWER** Mexico, Central America. Composite family, to 6 feet. Sun. Well-drained soil. Tolerates heat and drought better than overwatering. Floppy, sprawling plants, even 'Goldfinger' which is touted to be the most compact at 3 plus feet. Need staking. The flowers are numerous, yellow centered daisies, brilliantly colored: scarlet-orange say the most accurate descriptions. Easy from seeds sown in spring for summer-fall bloom.

Torenia fournieri Linden ex E. Fourn. **TORENIA, WISHBONE FLOWER,** BLUEWINGS South Vietnam. Figwort family, 1 foot. Deep to light shade. Rich, moist soil. Lots of purple and violet flowers with yellow throats, wishbone shaped male parts. Rarer are the yellow throated white and pink or the purple throated yellow varieties. Very easy from seed planted in spring for summer-fall bloom. Reseed readily. I transplant the volunteers which sprout in between bricks in the front walk each July from seed dropped the year before.

Tropaeolum majus L. **NASTURTIUM** South America. Nasturtium family, 12 inches. Well-drained, sandy, dry, poor soil. High fertility will encourage foliage at the expense of flowers. Round leaves on trailing or vining plants. Spurred flowers; solid, striped or spotted; yellows, orange, reds; singles and doubles. Cool weather plants, but tender. Large seeds, should be planted in the ground where they are to grow. I usually plant fall and spring crops. If there's no freeze, we get to enjoy an extra long season of bloom. They do poorly with the arrival of summer. Their leaves and flowers are tasty (though startling to find) in salad. Easy. 1766, 1838.

T. peregrinum L. **CANARY-BIRD FLOWER** Green spurred, feathery petaled yellow flowers on vines which grow rapidly to 10 feet. Like common nasturtiums, they like cool weather; shade them during the hottest part of the day. 1916.

Verbena X hybrida Voss **GARDEN VERBENA** Hybrid of *V. peruviana* (L.) Britt. and other species, all North and South American natives. *V. bonariensis* L. **PURPLETOP**, *V. canadensis* (L.) Britt. **ROSE VERBENA**, *V. peruviana* (L.) Britt. **PERUVIAN VERBENA** are species frequently available. Vervain family; tender perennials grown as annuals; some mound to 12 inches, others form carpets. Sun. Rich, well-drained, sandy soil. Cluster flowers in white, pink, red, blue, lavender, purple; profuse bloom from early spring to winter. Mine act as perennials, but they do need cutting back periodically to look good; they get rangy with age, and even with the best care in New Orleans they mildew. I find them hard to grow from seed. Verbena of some species was recommended by Lelievre, 1838; *V.* hybrids, 1883, 1918.

Viola cornuta L. **VIOLA**, *V. X wittrockiana* Gams. **PANSY** *Southern Garden* magazine, 1895, 1918; *V. tricolor* L. **JOHNNY-JUMP-UP** 1766, 1838. Europe, Asia minor.

Violet family, 4 to 9 inches, perennials, biennials grown as annuals. Sun, part shade. Rich, moist, well-drained, organic soil. Solid, blotched or lined, velvety blossoms from tiny to larger; blues, lavenders, rich purples, maroon, black. Cool weather plants, hardy. Refrigerate seeds several weeks before sowing in August; set plants out in November. Heat brings their demise. I like masses of pansies of varieties and colors which cannot always be found in nurseries, so seeds are economical and allow a huge increase in selection. Johnny-jump-ups are the tiny bloomed violets, most commonly yellow and purple; named because of their reseeding tendency. They are prettiest heavily planted; so hundreds of their tiny flower-faces look upward at the sun in unison.

Xeranthemum annuum L. **IMORTELLE** Southern Europe. Composite family, to 2 feet. Sun. Light, well-drained soil. 1 to 2 inch-papery textured single and double flowers in pink, rose, purple, white. Used as dried flowers. Sow seeds in the ground in spring for summer, fall bloom. 1838.

Zinnia L. species **ZINNIA** Central, South America. Composite family, 6 to 40 inches. Sun. Rich, well-drained garden soil. Prolific, lovely flowers bloom over a long period of time which can be extended by cutting. Flower heads from tiny to a huge 6 inches across in several forms; usually solid colors though some are bicolored; in every color there is but blue. My daughter, Dara, loved to plant green zinnias. They are not that showy, but quite a novelty to point out to friends. Taller varieties need staking, have longer stems for long lasting bouquets. The leaves are susceptible to mildew in our humidity. Good air circulation, planting in full sun, spray with fungicide, and ground watering can help. Seed sown in the ground April to August will quickly produce bloom until frost. They volunteer year after year in the back of my garden, in shades of pink, reverted to smaller, single form. They look like wildflowers. 1838. *Z. peruviana* (L.) L. 1766.

ANNUALS BY SEASON OF BLOOM

SOW SEEDS OR SET OUT PLANTS IN FALL
FOR WINTER, SPRING BLOOM

Ageratum houstonianum　AGERATUM, FLOSS FLOWER
Anchusa capensis BUGLOSS, CAPE FORGET-ME-NOT
Antirrhinum majus SNAPDRAGON
Arctotis stoechadifolia AFRICAN DAISY
Bellis perennis ENGLISH DAISY
Calendula officinalis CALENDULA, POT MARIGOLD
Campanula medium CANTERBURY-BELLS
Carthamus tinctorius SAFFLOWER
Centaurea cyanus　CORNFLOWER,　BACHELOR'S-BUTTON
Centaurea moschata SWEET SULTAN
Cheiranthus cheiri WALL-FLOWER
Clarkia unguiculata　CLARKIA, GODETIA
Cynoglossum amabile CHINESE FORGET-ME-NOT
Delphinium grandiflorum SIBERIAN LARKSPUR
Dianthus species PINKS
Digitalis purpurea 'Foxy' FOXGLOVE
Eschscholzia californica　CALIFORNIA POPPY
Gysophila elegans　BABY'S　BREATH
Iberis amara　ROCKET CANDYTUFT
Iberis umbellata　GLOBE CANDYTUFT
Linaria maroccana TOADFLAX
Lobularia maritima SWEET ALYSSUM
Lathyrus odoratus SWEET PEA
Lobelia erinus EDGING LOBELIA
Malva sylvestris ZEBRINA
Matthiola incana STOCK
Myosotis sylvatica GARDEN FORGET-ME-NOT
Nigella damascena LOVE-IN-A-MIST
Papaver nudicaule ICELAND POPPY
Papaver orientale ORIENTAL POPPY
Papaver rhoeas FIELD, FLANDERS POPPY, SHIRLEY POPPY
Reseda odorata　COMMON MIGNONETTE
Salpiglossis sinuata SALPIGLOSSIS, PAINTED TONGUE
Sanvitalia procumbens CREEPING ZINNIA
Tropaeolum majus NASTURTIUM
Verbena Xhybrida GARDEN VERBENA
Verbena bonariensis PURPLE-TOP
Verbena canadensis ROSE VERBENA
Verbena peruviana PERUVIAN VERBENA
Viola cornuta VIOLA
Verbena Xwittrockiana PANSY
Verbena tricolor JOHNNY-JUMP-UP

SOW SEEDS OR SET OUT PLANTS IN SPRING
FOR SUMMER, FALL BLOOM

Abelmoschus moschatus ABELMOSCHUS, MUSK MALLOW
Ageratum houstonianum AGERATUM, FLOSSFLOWER
Alcea rosea HOLLYHOCK
Amaranthus caudatus LOVE-LIES-BLEEDING
Amaranthus tricolor JOSEPH'S COAT
Browallia speciosa BROWALLIA
Callistephus chinensis CHINA ASTER, ANNUAL ASTER
Capsicum annuum ORNAMENTAL PEPPERS
Catharanthus roseus, Vinca roseus MADAGASCAR PERIWINKLE
Celosia cristata COCKSCOMB
Chrysanthemum hybrids ANNUAL CHRYSANTHEMUM
Chrysanthemum parthenium or *Matricaria capensis* FEVERFEW
Cleome species CLEOME, SPIDER FLOWER
Coleus blumei COLEUS
Coreopsis tinctoria CALLIOPSIS
Cosmos bipinnatus EARLY COSMOS
Cosmos sulphureus YELLOW and ORANGE COSMOS
Cuphea platycentra, C. X purpurea, C. miniata 'Firefly' CUPHEA
Gazania rigens TREASURE FLOWER, GAZANIA
Gomphrena globosa GLOBE AMARANTH
Helianthus species SUNFLOWER
Helichrysum bracteatum STRAWFLOWER
Heliotropium arborescens HELIOTROPE
Impatiens balsamina GARDEN BALSAM, LADY'S SLIPPERS
Impatiens wallerana IMPATIENS, SULTANA
Kochia scoparia variety *trichophylla* SUMMER CYPRESS
Limomium sinuatum STATICE
Mesembryanthemum crystallinum ICE PLANT
Nicotiana alata FLOWERING TOBACCO
Perilla frutescens PERILLA
Petunia X hybrida PETUNIA
Phlox drummondii ANNUAL PHLOX
Portulaca grandiflora MOSS ROSE
Portulaca oleracea PURSLANE
Salpiglossis sinuata SALPIGLOSSIS, PAINTED TONGUE
Salvia splendens SCARLET SAGE
Scabiosa atropurpurea PINCUSHION FLOWER
Tagetes species MARIGOLD
Tithonia rotundifolia MEXICAN SUNFLOWER
Torenia fournieri TORENIA, WISHBONE FLOWER
Tropaeolum species NASTURTIUM
Tropaeolum peregrinum CANARY-BIRD FLOWER
Xeranthemum annuum IMORTELLE
Zinnia species ZINNIA

Dorothy Furlong-Gardner

Perennials

*"Among the most rewarding traits of perennials is the fact
that they come up unprompted year after year to offer the garden masses
and highlights of color in uninterrupted but everchanging patterns from
April to November."*

from *The Time-Life Encyclopedia of Gardening: Perennials*
By James Underwood Crockett and the Editors of *Time-Life Books*
© 1972 Time-Life Books, Inc.

A plant which lives two years is a biennial, more than
two years, a perennial. This includes trees and shrubs.
By "perennials", I mean herbaceous, nonwoody plants,
excluding bulbs-rhizomes-tubers-corms. Some perennials
are evergreen. Some die down to the ground in the
winter and come back from the roots in succeeding
springs. They don't always come back in New Orleans
even when you plant the right ones and do all the right
things to make them succeed! Our hot, humid summers
may cause even the best suited to rot; our unpredictable
winters with too short a cold span to provide a proper
dormant period overcome garden plants which do well in
other regions.

If you are willing to go to the trouble, you can grow
almost anything, even peonies, as Grace Matt Thompson
demonstrates: *"Peonies blooming, quite a red letter day. I put
a tin bucket over the place the Peony roots were planted, filling*

the bucket with ice-thru the cold days of winter. So here is the picture to prove that peonies will bloom in old New Orleans."[25] Can you imagine the effort required to produce a whole garden of peonies using that technique?

The picture painted above by the *Time-Life* series describes the other end of the spectrum. Without careful planning, selection of plants suited to New Orleans and careful maintainence it, too, is unrealistic.

Though annuals, vines, and shrubs have historically been used here for garden color, a few perennials such as four o'clocks, daylilies, chrysanthemums, shasta daisies, and violets are traditional in New Orleans gardens since pre-Civil War days. I have expanded the list of perennials for New Orleans for those who want to deviate from tradition and to enjoy the advantages of repeating plants.

It's hard not to be drawn to the extravagant claims and recommendations made for perennials in catalogues and literature. Trial and error can be an expensive proposition for choosing mail-order plants. They are expensive! New introductions are advertised all the time. If you know you are experimenting, that's fine. If that's not what you want to do, the Botanical Garden at City Park is a good resource. There you can see an extensive collection of plants which will grow here, including many of those listed below. Horticulture director, Jerome Lebo can update you on his experiments with new introductions.

Some rules of culture for perennials in New Orleans:

1. I again stress good drainage as the most important factor for success with perennials. Plant perennials in raised beds. Pay close attention to soil improvement suggestions and mulching as described in the chapter on BASICS.

2. Plants can be started from seed, or purchased from local or mail order nurseries. Read culture information carefully before deciding which perennial seeds to order. Some require long times or special procedures for germi-

nation. You may decide on cuttings, mail-order, or local nursery plants for these. For barerooted perennials ordered through the mail, the best planting time is usually the fall. Beware of perennial garden catalogs which only ship in spring. I have had some ordered plants fail to become established before being overcome by early summer heat.

3. Plant bare rooted perennials at the same depth from which they came, the roots spread over a mound of soil created at the bottom of a hole big enough to allow for expansion. At the time of planting, the soil should be packed down and watered to eliminate air pockets.

4. Label your plants. There are several products sold for this purpose. Tags will mark the location of a plant so that you do not damage its roots inadvertently during the dormant stage when foliage has died back. Labeling helps when you want to divide and rearrange dormant or non-blooming plants by height or color.

5. Staking is recommended for some plants. Depending on the form of the plant, several methods can be used including, purchased bamboo stakes and wire rings to twiggy branches pruned from shrubs and placed within floppy-stemmed clumping plants such as coreopsis. Stakes can be put in place and situated so that they are hidden by foliage with most plants.

6. Removing faded blooms, or deadheading, can delay a plant's going to seed, and in perennials such as coreopsis, produce another wave of bloom. Other advantages are improved appearance, diversion of the plant's energy into root development rather than seed production, and the prevention of volunteers from dropped seed which will crowd the parent plant and require weeding.

7. "Maintainence-free" is a myth. Division is necessary at some point to maintain vigor and assure a continued high level of bloom. For most plants the best time to divide is opposite their period of bloom, when they're dormant, though some have individual peculiarities. Even

more frequent division may be required in New Orleans with its warm weather and long growing season.

One of the best suited perennials for New Orleans gardens is the daylily. It comes close to the ideal: the carefree repeating plant with a long blooming season. When it is not blooming, it presents attractive clumps of arching, green foliage. After reading in several places about the possibility of achieving almost three seasons of bloom with the right daylily cultivars, I decided I had found my plant! Daylilies deserve their special section. They are covered in depth after the following list.

PERENNIALS FOR THE NEW ORLEANS GARDEN

References to listings in Joseph Breck and J.B. Russell of Boston seed catalogues are from the brochure for Select Seeds, *Fine Seeds for Old Fashioned Flowers.*

1766 Indicates species grown in Thomas Jefferson's garden at Monticello.

1838 Indicates listing in J. F. Lelievre's *New Gardener of Louisiana.*

1859 Indicates listing in the catalogue of plants offered for sale by John M. Nelson at Magnolia Nurseries at Metairie Ridge and at his Plant Depot, Corner of Camp St. & Lafayette Sq., New Orleans.

1883 Indicates listing in *Almanac and Garden Manual for the Southern States,* by Richard Frotscher, New Orleans seed merchant.

1916 Indicates listing in *Reuters Seeds for the South,* Spring, New Orleans.

1918 Indicates listing in *Bollwinkle Seed Co. Ltd., Catalogue & Garden Guide,* 510 Dumaine Street.

Achillea filipendulina Lam. **FERN-LEAF YARROW** Asia minor. Composite family, 4 feet. Sun. Average, well-drained soil, moderate watering. Erect plant which appears bushy if planted in groups. Leaves are fern-like, summer blooms are shades of yellow, gold; large, flat clusters of tiny flowers which make good dried flowers. May repeat bloom if flowers cut. Stakes may be necessary. Humidity may bring mildew. Yarrows have a long history of European garden use.

A. millefolium L. **COMMON YARROW** See WILD-FLOWERS.

A. ptarmica L. **SNEEZEWORT** Blooms in summer, tiny white globes on plants which become loose mounds.

A. tomentosa L. **WOOLY YARROW** Forms wooly mats of foliage which make a good ground cover. Flat clustered yellow flowers on stems to one foot in summer.

Agave L. species **CENTURY PLANT** New World. Agave family. Sun. Susceptible to root rot without very well-drained, sandy soil. Species listed below can handle our humidity. The plant reaches a slow maturity, blooms, then dies, succeeded by offsets which develop around its base. Though species vary and environmental conditions are a factor, the plants do not take a century to bloom. The appearance of flowers is rare enough that agave should be considered a foliage plant. The clumps of leathery leaves make dramatic specimens, can be dangerously spiny or smooth-edged, solid or variegated, in colors from gray to green. The tubular flowers, clustered on stalks which can be very tall and thick, are attractive to hummingbirds. Though usually hardy, a severe enough temperature drop, such as the one in 1983, can kill agaves.

A. americana L. **CENTURY PLANT, MAGUEY** Ten inch wide gray, margin-toothed leaves to 5 feet long, arch from a central clump; pale yellow flowers form in clusters along a stalk to 25 feet high. Cultivars offer varied foliage forms. This is the most common agave seen in New Orleans. Gallier House garden, 1850's. Noted by Coleman on the Cotton Centennial grounds, 1885.

A. filifera Salm-Dyck. Dark green to purplish leaves to 20 inches; greenish flowers which become maroon form on a 6 to 8 foot spike.

A. stricta Salm-Dyck. **HEDGEHOG** 14 inch leaves, red to purple flowers on a spike to 8 feet.

A. victoriae-reginae T. Moore 6 inch leaves form a rounded clump which resembles an artichoke; greenish flowers form on a stalk which can reach 15 feet.

Ajuga reptans L. **AJUGA** Europe. Mint family, perennial, 10 inches. Shade, part shade best in New Orleans. It will wilt in our heat. Very well-drained, but moisture-retentive soil. Grown as a ground cover, its elongated leaves are variegated or solid in bronzes, purples; form mats from which spikes of blue or white flowers arise in spring. Spreads quickly by stolons. Returns after freeze damage. Not exceptionally competitive against weeds, therefore, not very good for large areas. Susceptible to crown rot which can destroy a whole planting rapidly. I think it is very attractive. My garden has always included a patch of it somewhere.

Aquilegia L. species **COLUMBINE** Northern Temperate Zone. Ranunculus family, 18 to 36 inches. Light shade. Deeply moist, light, very well-drained soil. A short-lived perennial, even in the cool climates it likes. I find even one season of bloom worth the effort. Delicate, airy foliage grows in clumps which in spring emit unusual spurred flowers in bicolors or solid white, blue, purple, red, pink, yellow, orange, or red. I have had them reseed. Volunteers of hybrids revert to a smaller, less colorful form. Hummingbirds like them. Species and hybrids are available as plants or seed to placed or sown in the fall. In plants grown from seed, you will not see flowers until the second spring. 1838, 1883, 1916.

A. canadensis L. **WILD COLUMBINE** is an Eastern American native which I found very easy to grow from seed. 1766.

A. X hybrida 'McKanna Giants' are long spurred, large flowered, many colored. We ordered plants one fall, were delighted with the spring blooms. They almost lasted to bloom again, but were "weeded" by my husband.

Asparagus densiflorus 'Sprengeri' **ASPARAGUS FERN** South Africa. Lily family, 3 feet. Arching branches with short, green needle-leaves. Red berries may form on an established plant, especially if rootbound. The clumps are especially attractive in raised beds, containers. Need protection to last through winter freezes. Not a fern. *Asparagus officinalis* L. is the vegetable asparagus. 1916.

Aspidistra elatior Blume **CAST-IRON PLANT** Japan. Lily family, 30 inches. Shade. Rich, loose soil is best, though this plant will grow almost anywhere. The dark green, solid or variegated, oblong leaves form clumps of foliage which are traditional in New Orleans gardens. Small flowers, very obscure. We found them recently, for the first time, when thinning a clump of aspidistra. They look like a latex creation of extraterrestrial plant life for a science fiction movie. Because the plant takes a lot of abuse, people seem to abuse aspidistra. So many stands of it are poorly grown and poorly groomed. Selective thinning of ratty leaves, or mowing the whole stand just before new growth appears in spring will turn the shiny green leaves into a valuable asset in the deeply shaded spots where little else grows well. Reputedly grown locally before 1860.

Bambusa Schreb. species **BAMBOO** Old World tropics. Grass family, average 10 to 25 feet. Sun, part shade. Dry to moist but well-drained, rich soil. Varied species are available. Some form clumps, some spread by runners. Slow to become established, beautiful and imposing when it is. The running form can be difficult to contain and difficult to eradicate. Neither is really suitable for small yards. Good wildlife cover. Forms an attractive screen. Freeze tolerance varies with species. Clumping variety described in a New Orleans garden from 1875. 1885. E. A. McIlhenny of Avery Island introduced many oriental varieties to southwest Louisiana during the early 1900's. Included in landscape architect William Wiedorn's 1935 list of "Aristocrats of New Orleans Gardens."

Begonia L. species **BEGONIA** Tropics and Subtropics, worldwide. Begonia family. Shade, part shade. Humusy, moist but well-drained soil (poor drainage = root and leaf rot). Most are tender perennials which may last through a mild winter or a harsher one if protected. The many species are divided into 3 basic groups: fibrous-rooted, rhizomatous, and tuberous-rooted begonias. Featured in exhibitions at the Cotton Centennial, 1884. 1918.

The fibrous-rooted group includes the **WAX BEGONIAS** such as *B. cucullata* variety *Hookeri* (*B. semperflorens*) and other hybrids, and the **CANE** or **ANGEL-WING BEGONIAS** such as *B. corallina* Carriere and hybrids.

The succulent stemmed wax begonias are familiar to everyone, as hanging basket as well as bedding plants for the shade. Their solid and variegated leaves are found in shades of bronze, red, pink, green. The everpresent blossoms are white, pink, red with bright yellow stamens; singles and doubles; tiny to large. Cutting back and heavy mulching will help these plants last through winter; will also improve appearance, as the foliage tends to get ratty and the form rangy during the other seasons.

The tuberous rooted group includes the largest, most elaborately and colorfully flowered of all begonias which are also the most impossible to grow here. It also includes *B. grandis* Dryand. (*B. Evansiana*), the **HARDY BEGONIA**, which tolerates winters to New York and can reputedly handle our hot, wet summers. I have not grown them. The beautiful camellia flowered "Tuberous Begonias" are occasionally offered in hanging baskets by local nurseries. I do not know how long they last after people take them home. We saw incredible beds of them in West Germany which has the cool, humid climate needed for their bloom; unfortunately not what New Orleans has to offer, indoors or out.

Rhizomatous-rooted begonias include *B. X rexcultorum* L. H. Bailey, the **REX** and **BEEFSTEAK BEGONIAS** Grown for their foliage, usually pot or greenhouse plants, they are not supposed to be hardy, but I know a yard on Coliseum Street which hosted tons of green and red starleaved plants for several years. They were on a southern exposure near a brick wall and tucked among other plants for protection.

Chrysanthemum L. species **CHRYSANTHEMUM** Composite family. Full sun, except for shastas, which can handle part sun, also. Perfect drainage in soil enriched with organic matter is essential, especially in winter, when soggy soil is deadly.

C. *frutescens* L. **MARGUERITE** Canary Islands. Bushy plants to 3 feet. 2 inch yellow-centered flowers are white or yellow-petaled, present spring to frost.

C. *leucanthemum* L. **OXEYE DAISY** Europe, Asia, naturalized in North America. 3 feet. 1 to 2 inch yellow-centered white daisies grow on a stem which protrudes from a basal rosette of leaves, summer bloom. Considered a weed because it spreads so rapidly by underground rhizomes and reseeds readily. Tolerant of varied conditions, including poor drainage.

C. X *morifolium* Ramat. **FLORIST'S** or **GARDEN CHRYSANTHEMUM** China. 15 inches to 3 feet, depending on variety and cultural practices. Hundreds of types are available in every color but blue; sizes from small to mammoth; many flowers forms. Manipulation of chrysanthemums is traditional: through forcing into spring flower by florists, to disbudding and pinching by home gardeners. Disbud large flowered chrysanthemums to produce enormous blooms. Pinch back terminal growth to stimulate branching, make bushier plants and more buds. Pinch off new growth as it reaches four inches in length from spring planting until the end of July. Bloom is over a long season in autumn, can be so profuse as to hide foliage. Larger plants may need staking. Divide clumps every spring. Details of care are free in *Chrysanthemums* (Cooperative Extension Service). 1838, 1859 "Pompone and Daisy varieties." A favorite in flower exhibitions held by the New Orleans Horticultural Society in 1895.

C. *nipponicum* (Franch. ex Maxim.) Sprenger. **NIPPON DAISY, NIPPON OXEYE DAISY** Three foot shrubby plant whose lower third is frequently devoid of leaves, should be planted behind other plants. 3 inch greenish-tinged yellow centered flowers with white petals are similar to shastas, prolific in fall.

C. X superbum Bergmans ex J. Ingram **SHASTA DAISY** 2 to 3 inch yellow-eyed white daisies are single or double on bushy plants from the foot high 'Little Miss Muffet' to 3 foot specimens. Many hybrid varieties are available. Bloom in May. I should follow the example of the gardener on Upperline Street near Prytania whose narrow brick-lined raised bed between his house and sidewalk has profuse shasta bloom every year. Every year he divides and replants his Shastas. Not a plant rots as some of my undivided clumps consistently do during wet winters (even in the best drained beds). 1859.

Chrysogonum virginianum L. **GOLDEN STAR** Eastern U.S., Louisiana. Composite family, evergreen; low growing, spreads to 1 foot. Sun, part shade. Average, well-drained but moist soil. 5 petaled golden flowers spring to fall. Recommended as an edging plant or ground cover. I have not tried it.

Coreopsis L. species **COREOPSIS** North America. Composite family. Sun. Moist, well-drained soil; rich or infertile.

C. auriculata L. cultivar 'Nana' **DWARF COREOPSIS** A low growing plant whose clumps can be used as ground cover; flowers are golden daisies with toothed-edged petals on stems 4 to 6 inches above the plant.

C. grandiflora Hogg ex Sweet. **BIG FLOWER COREOPSIS** Two feet. Clumps of elongated leaves are floppy and spreading, especially if they are not in full sun. Tons of gold-orange flowers with cerrated petals are produced over a long period in summer. 'Sunray' has double flowers. Will rebloom if old flowers cut back. Volunteer readily from dropped seeds. They do belong in an unmanicured setting. Easy, rewarding to grow. Flowers are long lasting cut. A beautiful display of Coreopsis can be seen in Bob Biery's garden on Camp Street and Bellecastle. They grew from volunteers from my garden. 1916.

C. lanceolata L. **LANCE-LEAVED COREOPSIS** See WILDFLOWERS.

C. verticillata L. **THREAD-LEAF COREOPSIS** Bushy plants to 3 feet have fern-like foliage, 2 inch golden daisies during a long summer bloom period.

Cortaderia selloana (Schult. & Schult.f.) Asch. & Graebn. **PAMPAS GRASS** South America. Grass family, 10 feet or more. Sun. Any well-drained soil. Forms very thick clumps of arching foliage. The blooms are white (sometimes pink) plumes which form in fall. Flowers are gynodioecious: complete on some plants, female only on others. Prettiest blooms are on female plants. Pampas grass is common on neutral grounds in the New Orleans area. They offer the space it needs to spread and look its best. Though available in New Orleans before, it became popular through its use on the grounds of the Cotton Centennial, 1884.

Cuphea hyssopifolia HBK **MEXICAN HEATHER** Central America. Loosestrife family, 1 foot. Sun. Moist, rich soil is best; poor is O.K. if drainage is good. Tiny leaved, shrubby plants covered with tons of small, 6-petaled purple, pink, or white flowers except in winter. They will die back in a freeze, usually return. They reseed prolifically in my garden.

Dichorisandra thrysiflora Mikan.f. **BLUE GINGER** Brazil. Dayflower family, 3 feet. Part sun, shade. Well-drained, rich, moist soil. Shiny, green leaves spiral around stems which send up deep blue-violet flower spikes in October. Tender, but it's lasted through several winters under pine trees and mulched heavily in Dottie Gardner's New Orleans garden, and in her sister-in-law's garden, north of Lake Pontchartrain, where it gets colder.

Echeveria secunda W. B. Booth. **HENS AND CHICKENS** Mexico. Orpine family, succulents, low-growing. Full sun. Dry, well-drained soil. Basal rosettes of succulent grayish leaves which spread by forming offsets, bloom on spikes which rise above the plant. Suitable for containers, raised beds, ground cover for small areas. Used in the "carpet bedding" schemes of the latter 19th century.

Echinacea purpurea (L.) Moench **PURPLE CONE-FLOWER** North America. Composite family, 3 feet. Sun, light shade. Very well-drained, neutral to alkaline soil; winter sogginess can be deadly. Garden varieties of this native wildflower come in white as well as purple. Blooms May, June. J. B. Russell's 1827 seed catalogue.

Echinops exaltatus Schrad. **GLOBE THISTLE** Russia. Composite family, 3 feet. Sun. Very well-drained soil. Dark green leaves are wooly underneath. 3 inch blue or white, globular flower heads, summer, do well as dried flowers.

Evolvulus nuttallianus Roem & Schult. **EVOLVULUS** North America. Bindweed family, 12 inches. Sun. Moist, well drained soil. Prostate, spreading form thickly covered with small gray-green leaves. Good as a ground cover, or in raised beds over whose edges it can drape. Many small, blue flowers are present along the stems almost year round in the absence of frost. 'Blue Daze' is the variety available in local nurseries. A relatively new introduction.

Gaillardia X grandiflora Van Houtte **BLANKETFLOWER** North America. Composite family, 1 to 3 feet. Sun. Light, well-drained soil. The flowers are cerrated edged daisies, solid or in bicolors of yellow, orange, red, maroon; bloom spring to winter. 'Goblin' is low-growing, my favorite. Though perennials, because these plants are hybrids of perennial and annual wildflowers, *G. aristata* and *G. pulchella*, they are short-lived. I have found them to reseed readily, and (in well-drained spots) to form clumps which spread. From first planting, I have had them at least four years; whether the original plants or vegetative or seed relatives, I do not know. *Gaillardia bicolor* was listed by Frotscher in 1883.

Geranium L. species **CRANESBILL, HARDY GER-ANIUM** You will see plants of this genus described in seed catalogues. They will not tolerate our heat and humidity. The geranium so popular in New Orleans gardens is of the genus *Pelargonium.*

Gerbera jamesonii H. Bolus ex Hookf. **GERBERA DAI-SY, TRANSVAAL DAISY** Africa. Composite family, 18 inches. Sun, part sun. Very well-drained soil amended with peat, organic material. They like to go dry between waterings. Raised beds are best in New Orleans. Should be placed with their crowns above ground. Attractive clumps produce thin-petaled daisies on slender stems most of the year. Flowers are single, double; in cream, white, yellow, pink, salmon pastels, or vivid rose, red, orange. Long lasting in bouquets. Seeds will bloom 9 months after sowing, sprout easily if you plant with the tufted end protruding from the soil. Interesting new varieties are available, but expensive. If masses of the plants are desired, such as I have around the entire perimeter of my rose bed, they are possible from seed without enormous expense. Division of the clumps in October or November is another way to increase plants. Will freeze to the ground, but come back. Reuter Seed Co. magazine, March, 1933 says *"We would like to see gerberas...more extensively used."* Were they recent introductions then?

Gramineae Juss. species **ORNAMENTAL GRASSES** Grass family. Distribution, worldwide. Sun, some in shade. Any well-drained soil, some tolerate wetness. Bambos and pampas grass are examples of ornamental grasses mentioned elsewhere in this chapter. Small to very tall, most grasses are clump-forming, produce attractive flowers or seeds which usually rise above the foliage. Some grasses were used in plantings for the 1984 World's Fair in New Orleans. I have heard differing opinions on performance. Grasses are gaining in popularity, your experimentation will add to the list for New Orleans gardens. See HERB GARDENS for a discussion of *Vete-*

veria zizanioides (L.) Nash, a grass traditionally grown in New Orleans for its scented root.

Hemerocallis species and hybrids **DAYLILY**   See page 209 for a discussion of this important perennial.

Hibiscus coccineus (Medic.) Walt. **SCARLET ROSE MALLOW, TEXAS STAR HIBISCUS** Coastal S.E. U.S. Mallow family, 6 feet. Sun. Rich, moist, well-drained soil. Delicate, open form, pointed lobed leaves like hands with spread fingers.   Brilliant red flowers with spread petals which touch only at their bases; stamen protruding in the usual hibiscus form, June-September.   Easy from seed. Dies back in winter.

H. moscheutos L. subspecies *moscheutos* and *palustrus* (L.)R. T. Clausen and hybrids **ROSE MALLOW** Eastern U.S. 2 to 8 or more feet. This group accounts for many of the native hibiscus found in older New Orleans area gardens. Sun, light shade. Moist, rich soil. White, pink, rose, crimson flowers as large as 10 inches in size from spring to winter. Die to the ground in winter. Return in spring. The hybrid 'Disco Belle' is easy from seed, an attractive, 2 foot plant with stunning 9 inch flowers. Specimens can be admired at City Park Botanical Garden or my garden.

Hosta Tratt. species **PLANTAIN LILY** Orient.   Lily family.   Shade.   Rich, moist, well-drained soil.   Coolest possible conditions during hot weather.   There are many varieties of this low growing plant which form thick clumps of smooth or textured, solid or variegated, large or small leaves, but not in New Orleans.   Do not believe performance claims in the literature you are sure to receive as soon as you get on a few mailing lists, or the descriptions you read in books on shade gardening. Those statements are all true for Vermont where I saw glorius hostas in massive clumps.   Hunter and Cathy Pierson have beautiful hostas--for New Orleans.   Hostas will grow and bloom here, but my experience and that of the New Orleans gardeners I have interviewed is that you can not count on them and should not invest too much money in them, or expect them to function as ground cover. I have found them attractive as specimens in a bed of ajuga. They do send up spikes of trumpet-shaped, sometimes very fragrant, lavender to white blossoms in summer or fall. Plant them in soil and conditions described above for best results. May need protection from snails and slugs.

Houttuynia cordata Thunb. **HOUTTUYNIA** East Asia. Lizard's Tail family; dense, low-growing ground cover, 6 inches to 2 feet. Sun, shade. Moist soil. Heart-shaped leaves, green or variegated depending on the variety. Flowers are white, half to one inch spikes projecting from the center of four petal-like bracts, summer. Forms a thick cover which will block weeds around perennials, bulbs.

Justicia brandegeana Wassh. & L. B. Sm. or *Beloperone guttata* **SHRIMP PLANT** Mexico. 3 feet. Sun or shade, thicker form, heavier bloom with more sun. Fertile, well-drained but moist soil best; but is adaptable. Short, hairy leaves on loosely spreading branches; small, white tubular flowers spotted purple extend from reddish-brown bracts on shrimpy-looking spikes, summer and autumn; mine bloom year round in the absence of a freeze, during which they will die to the ground, usually return. Cultivar 'Yellow Queen' has yellow bracts, is not attractive to hummingbirds, not winter hardy here; grow in containers. Grown in antebellum New Orleans gardens.

Kniphofia uvaria (L.) Oken **RED-HOT-POKER, TRITOMA** South Africa. Lily family, 2-3 feet. Sun. Well-drained soil. Clumps of coarse, floppy, grass-like leaves. Blooms are drooping tubular flowers clustered densely around the tips of stems which rise, lance-like, from the foliage in any season; depending on the variety and on the weather here. Bi-colored or solid in white, yellows, oranges, reds. The very large leaved variety which is available at many local plant sales is a winter-bloomer, may be frozen back before it flowers. Smaller, earlier blooming varieties are very easy from seed, though they may not flower the first year. Even though the foliage is not particularly attractive, the flowers are so unusual as to make this plant worth growing. I have two types in my garden. Hummingbirds love them. 1874, Langdon Nurseries of Mobile.

Kalanchoe Adans. species **KALANCHOE** Africa, Asia. Stonecrop family, usually under 2 feet. Sun. Rich, very well-drained, sandy soil. Succulents with varied foliage, flowers; several of which are popular as pot plants. Tender, but will last outdoors through a frost-free winter, or in a protected spot. *K. blossfeldiana* Poelln. is the one most commonly available in New Orleans. It produces masses of flowers clustered atop elongated stems in yellow, orange, salmon, shades of red, over a long period of time in winter.

Leonotis leonurus (L.) R. Br. **LION'S EAR** S. Africa. Mint family, to 6 feet. Sun. Rich, well-drained soil. Needs water during hot weather, though drought tolerant otherwise. Flowers are clusters of velvety orange tubes which develop around the stems in successive tiers in summer and fall. Should be cut back after bloom. Unusual looking. Hummingbirds like its blooms. See it at City Park.

Liatris elegans (Walt.) Michx., *L. pycnostachya* Michx., *L. spicata* (L.) Willd. **BLAZING STAR, GAYFEATHER** United States. Composite family, 18 inches to 3 feet. Sun, part sun. Rich or average, light, very well-drained soil. Spikes of fluffy flowers in shades of purple, white bloom from the top down in August, September. Named cultivars of some species of this wildflower are available, as well as hybrids. Not easy to grow here. Winter wetness and heavy soil are major threats.

Libertia K. Spreng. species **LIBERTIA** Iris family. Sun, part sun. Average, well-drained but constantly moist soil. Leaf tips will brown if not kept moist. Fan-like clumps of blade-like leaves from which erect stalks bearing sprays of white flowers, like miniature irises, rise in spring, summer. Followed by pods of yellow or orange seeds.

L. formosa R. C. Grah. Chile. Clumps to 18 inches, ivory and greenish-brown flowers on stalks 2 to 4 feet tall.

L. grandiflora (R. Br.)Sweet. **NEW ZEALAND IRIS** New Zealand. Foliage to two and one-half feet, stalks to three feet. White flowers.

L. ixiodes (J. R. Forst.) K. Spreng. Clumps to 1 foot; flower stalks 2 feet. White flowers.

Ligularia tussilaginea (Burm.f.) Mak. **LIGULARIA** Orient. Composite family, 2 feet, evergreen. Shade, part sun. Deep, rich, moist soil. Forms clumps of leathery, evergreen, kidney-shaped leaves to 12 inches wide, on long stems. Grown mostly for the foliage. Flowers are 2 inch, yellow daisies in clusters on bare stems to 2 feet; summer and fall. Several cultivars are available, including 'Argentea', green, gray, white foliage; 'Aureo-maculata', **LEOPARD PLANT**, whose leaves are spotted yellow; 'Crispata', **PARSLEY LIGULARIA**, ruffly leaves. Other species than *L. tussilaginea* are available, less likely to thrive in our humidity. If it dies back in a freeze, it should return from the roots in spring.

Linaria Mill. species **TOADFLAX** Perennial versions of this snapdragon relative will probably not adapt to our hot, humid summers. See ANNUALS.

Liriope Lour. species **LILYTURF, LIRIOPE** Orient. Lily family, evergreen. Shade, part shade; foliage can burn in full sun. Rich, moist but well-drained soil is best; can handle drought. Clumps of arching, thick, grasslike foliage, green or variegated, send up flower spikes in shades of lavender, white in summer. Followed by dark berries. Spreads by underground rhizomes. For best appearance, shear off old leaves as the new growth emerges in spring. Many people make the mistake of planting clumps which are too large. This prevents the even coverage desired in borders or ground cover. Nursery plants, or divisions thinned from established plants, should be broken into units of 3 to 4 plants and placed 8 to 10 inches apart. Division is such an easy and rapid way to increase this plant, I cannot imagine anyone needing to purchase them more than the first time. This is one of the ground covers which does so well here, it is almost too common. A well-grown stand of liriope in bloom is lovely. Reputedly grown in New Orleans gardens before 1860.

L. muscari (Decne.) L.H. Bailey **BIG BLUE LILYTURF** 18 inches. Best for borders. Flowers project high above the clumps.

L. spicata Lour. **CREEPING LILYTURF** Ten inches. Invasiveness makes it more appropriate for ground cover than edging, where it quickly gets out of hand. Flowers do not project as high above foliage as in *L. muscari.*

Lisianthus nigrescens Cham. & Schlectend. **LISIAN-THUS** Central America. Gentian family, 6 feet. Sun, shade. Well-drained, alkaline soils. Called "a funereal curiosity" by one source, this plant is not the lisianthus of current popularity. That, you will find under *Eustoma grandiflorum* in the WILDFLOWERS chapter. This plant produces clusters of two inch purple black flowers, should do well in our heat and humidity. Seeds are not commonly available, but I do not think I could pass them up if I found them!

Lythrum salicaria L. **PURPLE LOOSESTRIFE** Old World; naturalized in the northern U.S. Loosestrife family, 6 feet. Sun, light shade. Any garden soil. Though found in wet places, Welch (*Perennial Garden Color*) reports losing plants from apparent overwatering in the heat of summer. Willow-like leaves. One-inch, purple blossoms on spikes to 1 foot from late spring to September. Deadheading will prolong bloom. Though this plant is not supposed to do well in our heat and humidity, one reference raves about its local performance. Sale of loosestrife was banned in 1989 in Minnesota because of invasive growth in wetlands and the threat to native plants important to wildlife.

Hopefully, our less-than-perfect climate will set limits on
such behavior by loosestrife in New Orleans.   In Joseph
Breck's 1838 seed catalogue.

Melampodium cinereum DC **MELAMPODIUM** Texas,
Colorado, New Mexico.   Composite family, 1 foot.   Sun.
Well-drained soil.   Gray-green leaves, bushy plant covered
with little yellow flowers over a long period, including
summer.   Newly available in New Orleans nurseries.   It
has already reseeded in my brick walk.

Melianthus major L. **HONEYBUSH** South Africa, India.
Melianthus family, 10 feet.   Sun.   Rich, well-drained soil.
Grown from seed for its blue-green foliage, one foot leaves
of 6 to 9 oblong toothed leaflets.   Flowers in spring are
erect, red-brown clusters on one foot spikes followed by
papery seed-pods.   Shrub-like in form and invasive.
Should be confined.

Mirabilis jalapa L. **FOUR O'CLOCK** Tropical America.
Four O'Clock family, 3 feet.   Sun, part shade.   Rich or
poor soil, well-drained.   Grows taller in rich soil.   Erect
and shrub-like in sun.   In part shade, the plants flop
toward the sun.   White, pink, magenta, yellow, or bicolored trumpet shaped blossoms open in the afternoon,
fragrant at night; bloom spring until almost winter.   Plants
last forever, and reseed heavily.   Once established in a
spot, they require extensive effort to eradicate.   Hummingbirds and moths like the flowers.   Birds eat their seeds.
Popular for years in New Orleans as evidenced by the
stands of them in old and even abandoned gardens.   1766,
1838, 1883.

Mitchella repens L. **PARTRIDGEBERRY** North America, Louisiana.   Madder family, evergreen trailing herb.
Shade.   Dry, well-drained and humusy acid soil.   Forms
thin mats of leathery leaves.   Pairs of white, fragrant
flowers May to July are followed by half inch red berries
in fall and winter.   Not usually available for purchase.
Difficult to establish in settings not duplicates of the rich,
organic layered forest floor in which it is found.   A chal-

lenge for the mossy spot where ferns, jack-in-the-pulpit and violets thrive. Wildlife likes its fruit.

Monarda didyma L. **BEE BALM, BERGAMOT** Eastern North America. Mint family, 3 feet. Sun, light shade. Rich or average, moist but well-drained soil. Aromatic leaves, used to flavor Earl Grey Tea. Flowers are slender tubes clustered together in whorls; shades of red, pink, violet; June to August. Many cultivars of this native wildflower are available. It spread like crazy in my garden, but only flowered one year. Nancy Newfield's experience is also negative. Leslee Reed and others report yearly bloom but variable and not prolific performance from year to year. If yours lasts, division is recommended every 2 years. If it flowers, it will attract bees, hummers, butterflies, and hummingbird moths. Don't count on it! In J. B. Russell's 1827 seed catalogue. (See WILD-FLOWERS for *Monardas* native to Louisiana.)

Nierembergia hippomanica variety *violacea* Millan **CUP-FLOWER**, *N. scoparia* Sendtn. **TALL CUPFLOWER** Argentina. Nightshade family, 6 to 36 inches. Light shade. Rich, moist but well-drained soil. 1 inch violet to violet-blue, yellow-centered flowers in profusion summer through fall. Removing spent blossoms, deadheading, prolongs bloom. Cut back after flowering. 1883

Oenothera L. species **EVENING PRIMROSE, SUN-DROP** New World. Sun. Well-drained, dry soil. The same genus which contains the Louisiana native (*O. speciosa*, see WILDFLOWERS) offers other species with flowers in yellows and pinks. Most commonly available species is *O. missourensis* Sims., **MISSOURI PRIMROSE, OZARK SUNDROP** Different references offer differing reports on their viability in our climate. Worth a try. *O. biennis* available 1827, Russell.

Ophiopogon japonicus (Thunb.) Ker-Gawl. **MONKEY GRASS, MONDO GRASS** Japan. Shade, sun, though foliage-burn can occur in full sun. Rich, moist, high organic soil. Lily family, evergreen ground cover, 12 inches. Often confused with liriope, this plant is finer textured. It has similar spikey, blue blooms which are short, hidden by the grass-like foliage. As with liriope, it will not achieve full coverage if planted in clumps. Batches of 3 to 4 plants set 6 inches apart will allow even spread over a 2 year period. Reputedly used in antebellum New Orleans gardens.

Opuntia Mill. species **PRICKLY PEAR CACTUS** North and South America, Louisiana. Cactus family. Sun. Well-drained soil. *O. ficus-indica* (L.) Mill., grown for its fruit, was one of the first plants taken to Europe by the early Spanish explorers in the New World. Reputedly used in early New Orleans gardens. The fleshy segmented plants are spiny and more "interesting" than attractive, though the blooms are pretty.

Pachysandra terminals Siebold & Zucc. **PACHYSANDRA, JAPANESE SPURGE** Japan. Spurge family, evergreen, used as a ground cover, 8 inches. Shade, part shade. Rich, well-drained, loose, acidic soil. Green or variegated saw-toothed leaves on stoloniferous stems form an 8 inch carpet. Spikes of 4 inch white flowers appear in spring, sometimes followed by white berries. Though it does well when perfect conditions are provided, it is an inconsistent performer in New Orleans.

Pelargonium L'Her. ex Ait. species **GERANIUM** South Africa. Geranium family, 2 feet. Sun, with protection at midday. Extremely good drainage, rich soil. Too much water, from natural or artificial sources, is not good. Our high humidity coupled with hot summers do not create the ideal setting for these plants. However, rot or not, they are the favorite garden and pot plant of many New Orleans gardeners. Best bloom is in spring, fall when temperatures are below 80 degrees. Flowers are white, shades of red, pink, purple. *P. zonale* (L.) L'Her. ex Ait. is the **ZONALE GERANIUM**, principal parent of the hybrids which is probably not even cultivated any more. This was the most popular flower for use in pots in the antebellum

Carolinas. New Orleans? In addition to the **COMMON GERANIUM,** *P. X hortorum* L. H. Bailey, there are many other species and hybrids with a variety of leaf and flower types--some you would never recognize as "geraniums." Unfortunately, the fragrant ones do not do well in New Orleans. Tender, but common geraniums last through many of our winters. New plants can be begun as cuttings each year if the old ones become too rangy, even with pruning. May need slug and snail protection. 1838, 1883, 1918.

Penstemon species. See WILDFLOWERS.

Pentas lanceolata (Forssk.) Deflers **EGYPTIAN STAR-CLUSTER, PENTAS** Africa. Madder family, 4 feet. Sun. Rich, moist, well-drained soil. Shrub-like, fast growing plant which sprawls toward full sun if placed in the shade. Pretty green leaves; continuously produced magenta, pink, lilac, white, red flowers which are as named, 4 inch clusters of tubular five pointed stars. One source says they will return from the roots after a freeze. Though I have had them return, this is not my usual experience. I recommend taking cuttings before the first freeze to set outside in spring. Another reason for cuttings is that I have not found a source of red-only seeds. Red is my favorite as well as the favorite of hummingbirds. Potted pentas put outside on cold days bring winter hummers to my back porch. Bees, butterflies like the purples and pinks, too.

Phlox divaricata L. **LOUISIANA PHLOX, WILD BLUE PHLOX** See WILDFLOWERS.

P. paniculata [*P. decussata* Lyon ex Pursh]. **PERENNIAL PHLOX, SUMMER PHLOX** Eastern U.S. Phlox family, 2 feet. Sun, part shade. Moist, light, well-drained soil. Water well during bloom period. Clumps of stems are formed at whose tips clusters of 6-petaled flowers bloom over a long period in summer-fall. Most commonly seen in New Orleans are the magenta-colored varieties which are the vigorous parents of the cultivated strains. It and a white are the only ones which really last in our hot and humid climate. I bought a 5 plant collection of which 3 died; 'Bright Eyes' (red-centered pink) and 'Fairy's Petticoat' (dark pink) have bloomed several years, but have not increased dramatically. Cutting old blooms will stimulate repeat bloom. Volunteers from dropped seed revert to the original magenta. Thinning each plant to 3 or 4 stalks in spring is recommended to produce stronger growth. Spacing for good air circulation and ground watering are essential to help avoid the molds and fungi to which the plants are very susceptible.

P. sublata L. **MOSS PINK, THRIFT** Sun. Poor soil, sandy and extremely well-drained; need lots of water during bloom, but is very susceptible to rot. Forms mats of needle-like leaves to 6 inches. Foliage is hidden by spring bloom white, shades of pink, red, blue, lavender. It does not usually last long in New Orleans due to our heavy rainfall and humidity. This is one of the plants sometimes advertised by mail-order nurseries in the Sunday newspaper magazines with full color spreads and extravagant claims.

Phormium colensoi **MOUNTAIN FLAX,** *P. tenax* **NEW ZEALAND FLAX** New Zealand. Agave family, to 6 feet. Sun, part shade. Any well-drained soil. Clumps of stiff to arching, sword-shaped leaves; solid or striped in white, greens, bronze, reds, purple. Flowers in late spring are tubular, rusty-red or yellow, on a stalk which rises to 2 feet above the plant. Hardy to 20 degrees. Size can be kept small by growing in containers, division every few years.

Physalis alkekengi L. **CHINESE LANTERN PLANT** Europe, Asia. Nightshade family, 2-4 feet. Sun, light shade. Any well-drained soil. Shrubby plant produces small white flowers in summer, 2 inch orange, inflated pods which enclose red, cherry-like fruits in fall. They make good dried flowers: Pick stems before the lanterns turn orange, strip off the leaves, hang upside down.

Spread by underground roots, can be invasive. The authors of *Perennials for American Gardens* depart from their usual style to editorialize heavily about this plant: "*A good plant for a child's garden, but an adult's sense of aesthetics should be mature enough to avoid it.*"[26]

Physostegia virginiana (L.) Benth. **OBEDIENCE PLANT** Cultivated varieties of this native are available in pale pink or white. See WILDFLOWERS.

Plantago lanceolata L., *P. major* L. **PLANTAIN** Europe, Asia. Plantain family, 12 inches. Sun. Any soil. Grown for the green to red and purple solid or striped foliage. Flowers in late spring, summer are thin spikes. These are horticultural varieties of the common weed which are much more attractive and better behaved.

Platycodon grandiflorus (Jacq.) A. DC. **BALLOON FLOWER** Japan. Bellflower family, 2 feet. Sun, part shade during hot afternoon. Rich, well-drained soil. I have not tried this plant, though I have seen it growing in a garden on Marengo Street. It is not there now. Sources differ on its adaptability to our climate. Even a brief fling with its unusual flowers would be worthwhile. The balloon-like buds burst at suture-lines to become blue, pink, or white cupped star flowers present in late spring, summer. Bloom can be prolonged by removing spent blossoms. Begins new growth from dormancy late; markers will prevent digging by mistake. Recommended for containers. Bloom from seed in 2-3 years; buy plants.

Polygonum capitatum Buch.-Ham ex D. Don. Per. **KNOTWEED** Himalayas. Buckwheat family, mat forming to 8 inches. Sun, shade. Any well-drained, moist soil. Pinkish-green leaves on fast growing stems form a loose, tangled looking mass whose globular, pink, three-quarter inch flowers are present year round in sunny spots. Not neat. Though my first efforts to grow it from seed were unsuccessful, I now find it growing from between bricks where its seed dropped. Hardy to between 20 and 28 degrees (sources differ). Should return from dropped seeds as it has in my garden even after the 1989 freeze. See a beautiful planting of it at City Park Botanical Garden in full sun, raised bed.

Pseuderanthemum alatum (Nees) Radlk. **CHOCOLATE PLANT** Central America. Acanthus family. Part shade, morning sun. Moist, rich, loose soil. Low growing foliage plant with silver-blotched chocolate brown leaves; small purple flowers. I first noticed it in greenhouses. Though tender, it should return from its taproot in south Louisiana as it did in Leslee Reed's yard after the 1989 freeze. Reseeds rampantly in Dr. Rise Ochsner's patio garden.

Reinwardtia indica Dumort. **YELLOW FLAX** China, northern India. Flax family, evergreen, 3 feet. Sun, part sun. Rich, moist but well-drained soil. Elliptical leaves with pointed tips on a shrubby plant which should be pinched for compactness, cut back in late winter. Bloom is profuse, over a long period in late fall; widely flared, five petaled golden blossoms to 2 inches. Hardy to 24 degrees.

Rudbeckia L. species **CONEFLOWER** North America. Composite family. Sun, light shade. Well-drained soil. The varieties available in seed catalogs and nurseries are descendents of these natives. See WILDFLOWERS for further information:

R. fulgida Ait. **BRACTED CONEFLOWER** Cultivar 'Goldsturm' is my favorite, widely available and highly recommended. Its rosettes of hairy leaves develop into low clumps which, each August, send up golden coneflower-tipped stems. They have survived in a part sunny space in my garden for several years with no effort from me but occasional battle with wandering sword ferns and dayflowers. In Joseph Breck's 1838 seed catalogue.

R. hirta L. **BLACK-EYED SUSAN** Cultivars 'Gloriosa Daisy' and 'Double Gloriosa Daisy' are short-lived perennials frequently used as annuals. They are very easy to grow, reseed readily. Flowers are solids or bicolors in yellow, orange, mahogany. Spring-summer bloom. The foliage mildews. This does not detract from the beauty of the large, striking blooms which are longlasting cut.

R. laciniata L. **CUTLEAF CONEFLOWER** Cultivars 'Hortensia', available as 'Golden Glow'; and 'Golden Globe' are showy, double flowered, vigorous. Bloom summer, fall. Aphids, mildew can be problems. Breck, 1838.

Ruellia ciliosa (L.) Vahl. **WILD PETUNIA** Southeast U.S. Related to and similar to *R. caroliniensis* (See WILD-FLOWERS). Plants offered by garden catalogs. It seems silly to pay over $4.00 for a plant which is so common growing wild in this area.

Salvia L. species **SAGE** Mint family. The most commonly available perennial sage which is grown as a perennial is *S. farinacea* Benth. **MEALY-CUP SAGE**, Texas. There are cultivars in white, purples, blues. I have had 'Victoria' and 'Blue Bedder' for several years. They were both easy to grow from seed. Sun for heaviest bloom, part shade. Any well-drained soil. It dies back in the winter, returns in the spring from the roots. The spikey blooms are present from spring through summer, bloom can be prolonged by cutting the plant back in late summer. Bees love the flowers.

Many salvias, species and hybrids are available and easily grown in the New Orleans area. All are important bee and/or hummingbird plants. Do not limit yourself to the ones mentioned here and in WILDFLOWERS, AN-NUALS, and HERBS. See RESOURCES for catalogues. 1859, 1918.

S. guaranitica St.-Hil. ex Benth. **ANISE SAGE** South America. 3 feet. Intense blue-violet flowers in summer-fall. Not reliably hardy here. Easy from cuttings. A wintering calliope hummingbird was seen feeding at an anise sage in Reserve, Louisiana in recent years. Was it on its way to New Orleans?

S. greggii A. Gray **AUTUMN SAGE** Texas, Mexico. 3 feet. Shrubby plant which may not die back in winter. Showy red to purplish-red flowers spring to fall.

S. leucantha Cav. **MEXICAN BUSH SAGE** Mexico. 4-5 feet. Wooly leaves, bushy spreading plant, violet-purple flowers in fall. Another hummer favorite.

Saponaria ocymoides L. **SOAPWORT** Europe. Pink family, to 10 inches. Sun. Very well-drained soil. Evergreen mat-forming plant with trailing stems, one-quarter inch flowers in late spring in white or pink with purple anthers. Should be trimmed back after bloom to encourage new growth. Use as an edger in raised beds where it can drape over sides is suggested.

Saxifraga stolonifera Meerb. **STRAWBERRY GERANIUM** East Asia. Saxifrage family, 6 inches. Part shade, morning sun. Sensitive to direct sun during our hottest months. Rich, loose, moist but very well-drained soil. Non-competitive ground cover for small areas. Roundish, grey-green, white-veined hairy leaves which are reddish underneath, spread by stolons, forming mats from which rise 10 inch spikes of delicate white flowers in spring.

Sedum L. species **STONECROP** Northern Temperate Zone. Orpine family. Sun. Very well-drained soil. Species of two groups of this very large family of succulent plants grow well in New Orleans gardens if given proper conditions. Some examples are:

S. spectabile Boreau. **SHOWY SEDUM** 18 inches. Three inch, oval, leathery, gray leaves on plants which send up 4 inch, flat headed clusters of flowers in shades of red and pink in late summer. Reputed to be a good bedding plant, though 'Autumn Joy' did not bloom well for me. I think it did not get enough sun. Attracts butterflies.

S. acre L. **GOLDMOSS** and *S. album* L. **WHITE STONECROP** Europe, Asia, N. Africa. Mat forming succulents used as a ground cover, to 4-6 inches of height, in small plantings, along edges of raised plantings, in pots.

One has half inch yellow flowers in March; the other, smaller white blooms later.

Senecio cineraria DC. [*Centaurea maritima* cultivar 'Diamond'; *Cineraria maritima* L.] **DUSTY-MILLER** Mediterranean region. Composite family, 2 feet. Sun. Dry, well-drained soil. Grown for its foliage which is covered with long white hairs, making it appear silvery-white. Small clusters of yellow to white blooms appear in spring. The plant should be cut back in late winter to help its appearance. It will not be as attractive or as long lived in our heat and humidity as in dryer areas. Listed as a border plant for New Orleans gardens, 1895 magazine article.

Setcreasea pallida Rose. 'Purple Heart' **PURPLE HEART** Mexico. Dayflower family, 16 inches. Sun to shade. Loose, moist, well-drained soil best, though adaptable. Sprawling, succulent, purple foliage, more vividly colored in sun becoming green-tinged in shade. Small, purple flowers are present constantly in warm weather. Root readily from cuttings: shove a piece into the ground and watch it grow. Will die to the ground in a freeze, return from the roots.

Solidago L. species **GOLDENROD** Hybrids of this wildflower have been developed for the garden. See WILDFLOWERS.

Stokesia laevis L'Her. **STOKES' ASTER** Cultivars of this native flower are available as garden plants. See WILDFLOWERS.

Strobilanthes isophyllus (Nees) T. Anderson. **BEDDING CONEHEAD, MEXICAN PETUNIA** Assam. Acanthus family, shrubby perennial, to 3 feet. Sun, part shade. Moist, well-drained soil. Likes our hot weather. Willow-like leaves on a plant which may become weedy. Flowers are clustered, 1 inch long, pink, blue, white. Said to be sometimes confused with the *Ruellias* (See WILD-FLOWERS). I found this plant on a 1921 list of the New Orleans Garden Society and in a 1935 compilation of

"Aristocrats of the New Orleans Gardens" by Landscape Architect William Wiedorn in Stephen Hand's thesis. Maybe it will become popular again. I am growing *S. anisophyllus* (Wallich ex Lodd.) T. Anderson now. Its foliage is deep purple, beautiful. Tender.

Trachelium caeruleum L. **THROATWORT** Mediterranean region. Campanula family, 3 feet. Sun, part shade. Very well-drained soil. Produces 6 inch flowerheads, clusters of small blossoms in violet-blue or white from spring to fall. Good cut flowers. See specimens at City Park Botanical Garden.

Tradescantia albiflora Kunth. **WANDERING JEW** Brazil. Spiderwort family, ground cover, fast growing, 6 to 24 inches. Sun, shade. Moist, well-drained soil. There are lots of varieties of this fleshy-stemmed, striped-leaved plant, the most familiar to me being the purple and green. Roots easily from cuttings. Not reliably hardy.

Verbascum L. species **MULLEIN** Mediterranean region, naturalized in parts of U.S. Figwort family, 3-5 feet. Biennials and perennials, species and hybrids are offered for garden use. Sun. Very well-drained soil is important, especially during cold, wet weather. Foliage is in big, fuzzy clumps which send up branched spikes heavily flowered in 1 inch white, pink, yellow, lavender, red blooms, solid or bicolored in summer. Bloom can be extended by deadheading. Plants sometimes die after flowering, but reseed. Can need staking. See them at Jerome Lebo's City Park Botanical Gardens.

Verbena L. species **VERBENA** Though many of the verbenas available are perennials, they are frequently used as annuals. Coverage of the major garden species is under ANNUALS, WILDFLOWERS.

Veronica L. species and hybrids. **VERONICA, SPEEDWELL** Northern Temperate Zone. Snapdragon family, 12-30 inches. Sun. Very well-drained soil, average to rich in fertility. Clumping or mat forming foliage produces 6-8 inch spikes of tiny flowers during summer. Bloom can be prolonged by removing old flowers. White, pinks, and blues are available. One source says the blues, though most common and very beautiful, are least likely to live through our summer heat. Our humidity is a threat, too, as *Veronicas* are very susceptible to fungal diseases and leaf spot.

Viola odorata L. **SWEET VIOLET** Europe, Africa, Asia. Violet family, 8 inches. Sun, part shade. Rich, moist but well-drained, loose, humusy soil, slightly acid. The clumps of heart-shaped leaves spread by runners. Many varieties, single and double flowers, some fragrant, bloom in early spring in colors from white to shades of purple, red. Can be used as a border plant or to edge beds, though its foliage does not look its best during our hottest months. 1838.

Yucca L. species **YUCCA** North America. Agave family succulents. Sun. Very well drained soil; cold, wet soil will cause rot. Clumps of sword-like, sharply pointed leaves, either stemless or on trunks of varying lengths. Flowers are waxy, pendulous, arranged along a stalk which rises from the center of the clump. Bloom times vary, usually summer.

Y. aloifolia L. **DAGGER PLANT** Southern U.S. Trunk to 25 feet, leaves 32 inches wide, flower stalk to 2 feet.

Y. filamentosa L. **ADAM'S NEEDLE, NEEDLE PALM** Southeast U.S. Leaves to 32 inches. Flower stalks to 15 feet. On the recommended list of the N.O. Garden Society in 1921.

Y. gloriosa L. **SPANISH-DAGGER** Though it is on Joseph Ewan's list of natives introduced into Louisiana gardens between 1718 and 1800, this is not one of the yuccas noted by Clair Brown as found in Louisiana, today. 1885.

Y. louisianensis Trel. **YUCCA, BEAR-GRASS** Found in dry, sandy soils in Louisiana. Leaves 2 feet; Flower spike to 3 feet. Blooms April to June. Does not form fruit

unless pollinated by the yucca moth. Sometimes confused
with *Y. filamintosa.*

DAYLILIES

Hemerocallis L. species **DAYLILY** Lily family, fibrous
rooted perennial. A favorite garden plant for centuries,
the daylily is originally from the Orient. It is so called
because each bloom lasts for a day, though numerous
buds form on the several scapes produced each season.

H. lilioasphodelus L. [*H. flava*], the familiar **YELLOW** or
LEMON DAYLILY and *H. fulva* L., **ORANGE** or **TAWNY**
DAYLILY were grown in Europe before 1600. Both were
brought to the the United States, probably both to Louisiana, by early colonizers. During the 19th Century, additional species were imported from the orient. Through
hybridization and selective breeding, most done in the
twentieth century, dramatic changes have taken place,
increasing the range of color from yellow, orange, red to
blends and solids of the whole spectrum except true blue;
increasing the variety of forms; extending the bloom period.

For several years after I began gardening, I had not
found the source of the hybrids. I found only yellow
daylilies. They bloomed once, in May. The nurserymen I
spoke to couldn't help. My breakthrough came during a
"What have you been doing lately?" conversation with
Dottie Gardner. She had been planting daylilies!

She told me the secret: how to join the American
Hemerocallis Society and its local affiliate, the Delta Daylily Society. Dorothea Boldt founded Delta Daylily in
1982. There had been an earlier active New Orleans
Hemerocallis Society which dated to at least the 1940's
and had as members such accomplished gardeners as
Daisy Buckman Turman (died, 1986) who loved the yellows, and C. William Mackie III. Mr. Mackie's daylilies

on Exposition Boulevard are one of the joys of a walk in
Audubon Park! The most exciting disclosure by my new
associates was that several of the most active daylily
hybridizers and best nurseries and sources of new cultivars are in Louisiana, some in the New Orleans area!

Edna Spalding was a noted hybridizer in southwest
Louisiana. The same W. B. Macmillan of Abbeville who is
noted for his amateur work with Louisiana irises during
the 1950's visited Miss Spalding, bought some of her
daylilies and caught her enthusiasm. By the 1960's he had
become internationally known for the daylilies he introduced. He eventually gave up the work with irises.
After his death, "Mr. Mac's" work was carried on by his
gardener, Olivier Monette and his nurse, Lucille Guidry,
who became noted hybridizers in their own rights. The
Monette and Guidry nurseries became sources of Macmillan cultivars and their own nationally known flowers. Mr.
Monette died in 1985. The Guidry family continues to
produce daylilies.

Daylily nursery catalogues identify the hybridizer's
name next to the name of the cultivar. Other "famous
names" to look for in Louisiana hybridizers besides
Spalding, Macmillan, Monette, and Guidry are Crochet,
Gates, and Durio. Though you will find some excellent
growers in Florida and other places, try Louisiana sources
first.

What a change the new flowers made in my garden!
I visited private gardens and nurseries in the Lafayette,
Baton Rouge and New Orleans areas in May, peak month
for daylily bloom, to choose my favorites from among the
profusely flowering plants. The full, lush, richly colored,
ruffled blooms of cultivars 'Eternal' (Monette), dark pink
with a green throat, and 'Harry Barras' (Monette), pale
yellow with the sparkles called diamond dusting are as
elaborate as orchids. 'Linda Guidry' (Guidry) is a striking
purple with a green throat. I will of course share sources
See RESOURCES for a list of local daylily nurseries!

Though named varieties are beginning to appear in local nurseries, until very recently daylilies were sold unnamed. The simple yellow daylily or lemon lily is still the most commonly seen form in this area. I grow the original orange species, *H. fulva,* in front. I like its simplicity. It blooms profusely in early April-May and again lat er in June-August.

The most important information for New Orleans gardeners:
1. Daylilies have three types of foliage habit: dormant, semi-evergreen, and evergreen. Dormant daylilies WILL NOT LAST in New Orleans. Many of the national garden catalogues do not specify habit. One of the most popular and heaviest blooming plants advertised heavily by mail-order houses is 'Stella d'Oro', a dormant form. If you are ordering daylilies from a catalogue, make sure foliage habit is designated and that you only order evergreen or semi-evergreen plants.
2. The good news is, succession of bloom over a long period of time can be attained by choosing the right cultivars; the bad, no one can give you a list of what they are. Daylilies are described by their season of bloom, from early to midseason to late, season being designated b y initials including V for very and E for early: EE, E, EM, M, ML, L, VL. Unfortunately, there is little standardization of use of these terms from catalogue to catalogue. Even if there were, there are variations in the calendar date of bloom in different geographical areas and even within microcosms in the same garden, though the sequence of bloom is usually consistent. Rebloom and continuous bloom are other traits to look for in daylilies. Factors other than genetics also affect these qualities.
3. The definitive source on daylily culture and history is a booklet from the American Hemerocallis Society, *"Daylilies, Everything You've Always Wanted to Know About Daylilies."* The Society's *"Daylily Journal,"* published four

times a year for members is beautiful and a valuable source of information on daylily culture and cultivars. It offers the latest research on such issues as succession, rebloom, and continuous bloom, some specific to geographical area. Informative publications are also offered with membership in local and regional societies. See RESOURCES for how to join.

4. Bloom sequence studies have been done for other parts of the country, but not New Orleans. The best way to find out which cultivars perform well in New Orleans and when they perform is to trade secrets with other daylily enthusiasts. The Delta Daylily Society is a good place to find them. Meetings are held in local daylily gardens and nurseries during peak bloom season, April through May. With enough information and through trial and error in your own garden, maybe you can achieve *"...uninterrupted profuse bloom from early April through September!"*[27]

Very late and very early cultivars are the rarest. When you see a daylily blooming out of peak season, find out what it is! 'Olive Bailey Langdon' (Munson), a red, blooms in May and reblooms in DECEMBER in my garden; pale orange 'Valedictorian' (Kirchoff) blooms in May, reblooms in July. Dottie Gardner finds wine colored 'Little Wine Cup' (Carter-Powell) a long bloomer. 'Bitsy' (Lucille Warner), a little yellow, is a continuous bloomer for Dorothea Boldt. Neither Dottie Gardner nor myself have been able to get the famous yellow 'Hyperion' (Franklin Mead) to bloom at all, but Dorothea knows someone in New Orleans who has. In 1986, members of Delta Daylily supplied cultivars of 'Music Man' (Wild), lemon-throated red, for neutral ground planting by Parkway Partners at Howard and Loyola Avenues in Downtown New Orleans. You can see them in heavy and long flower there.

Some rules for Daylilies in addition to the general ones for perennials are:

1. Daylilies perform best if they receive six hours of direct sun a day.

2. Do not cut back daylily scapes, as you will destroy the rest of the season's buds. Do removed faded blooms.

3. Plants should be spaced between eighteen and twenty-four inches apart to allow for multiplication of clumps which occurs fast but not instantly. The masses of flowers in huge clumps finally appear in the third and fourth years after planting.

4. Early spring or late fall are the best times for dividing and replanting daylilies or for planting purchased divisions. If plants are put into the ground when the temperature and humidity are very high (July, August, or September in New Orleans), there is said to be a possibility of them rotting. I have bought and planted divisions during those months with no problems. Undivided plants can be safely moved anytime during the growing season.

5. When your clumps seem to be blooming less, it it time for division. This can be every four to five years. My oldest clumps are six years old and going strong. One source says that if the soil surrounding the clump is kept loose and pliable to allow outward growth rather than crowding, the plant can be left undivided for twelve to fifteen years. To divide, pull the clump apart. Cut back the foliage in each "fan" to six inches in an inverted "V" shape and replant per the general directions for perennials.

6. Though daylilies are remarkably disease and pest-free, there can be problems: aphids in the early spring, spider mites in dry weather, and thrips during bloom season. The only one I address with poison is aphids, and only when the plants appear severely threatened. I use malathion once, sparingly.

Dottie Gardner says she has had most consistent luck in her New Orleans garden with MacMillan daylilies. The following list includes some of her and my favorites, in addition to the ones mentioned in the text:

'Sally Lake' (Macmillan)
'Zaidee Williams' (Macmillan)
'Moment of Truth' (Macmillan)
'Agape Love' (Elsie Spalding)
'Becky Lynn' (Guidry)
'Petite Musette' (Crochet)
'Raspberry Frills' (Williamson)
'Mountain Violet' (Munson)
'Gauguin' (Munson)
'King's Cloak' (Munson)
'Little Business' (Maxwell)
'Harry Barras' (Monette)
'Cupid's Dart' (Kirchhoff)
'Sari' (Munson)
'Little Wine Cup' (Carter-Powell)
'Hope Diamond' (Macmillan)
'Clarence Simon' (Macmillan)

PERENNIALS BY SEASON OF BLOOM

SPRING BLOOMING PERENNIALS

Ajuga reptans AJUGA
Aquilegia species and hybrids COLUMBINE
Begonia hybrids BEGONIA
Chrysanthemum frutescens MARGUERITE
Chrysanthemum X superbum SHASTA DAISY
Chrysogonum virginianum GOLDEN STAR
Cuphea hyssopifolia MEXICAN HEATHER
Echinacea purpurea PURPLE CONEFLOWER
Gaillardia X grandiflora BLANKETFLOWER
Gerbera jamesonii GERBERA DAISY, TRANSVAAL DAISY
Hemerocallis species DAYLILY
Hibiscus coccineus SCARLET ROSE MALLOW,
    TEXAS STAR HIBISCUS
Hibiscus moscheutos ROSE MALLOW
Libertia species LIBERTIA
Mirabilis jalapa FOUR O'CLOCK
Pelargonium hybrids GERANIUM
Saponaria ocymoides SOAPWORT
Viola odorata SWEET VIOLET

SUMMER BLOOMING PERENNIALS

Achillea species YARROW
Coreopsis species COREOPSIS
Begonia hybrids BEGONIA
Chrysanthemum frutescens MARGUERITE
Chrysanthemum leucanthemum OXEYE DAISY
Chrysogonum virginianum GOLDEN STAR
Cuphea hyssopifolia MEXICAN HEATHER
Echinacea purpurea PURPLE CONEFLOWER
Echinops exaltatus GLOBE THISTLE
Gaillardia X *grandiflora* BLANKETFLOWER, GAILLARDIA
Gerbera jamesonii GERBERA DAISY, TRANSVAAL DAISY
Hemerocallis species DAYLILY
Hibiscus coccineus SCARLET ROSE, TEXAS STAR HIBISCUS
Hibiscus moscheutos ROSE MALLOW
Justicia brandegeana SHRIMP PLANT
Leonotis leonurus LION'S EAR
Liatris elegans BLAZING STAR, GAYFEATHER
Libertia species LIBERTIA
Liriope species LILYTURF, LIRIOPE
Lythrum salicaria PURPLE LOOSESTRIFE
Mirabilis jalapa FOUR O'CLOCK
Monarda didyma BEE BALM, BERGAMOT
Nierembergia hippomanica CUPFLOWER
Pelargonium species GERANIUM
Pentas lanceolata EGYPTIAN STAR-CLUSTER
Phlox paniculata PERENNIAL PHLOX, SUMMER PHLOX
Platycodon grandiflorus BALLOON FLOWER
Rudbeckia fulgida 'Goldsturm' BRACTED CONEFLOWER
Rudbeckia hirta 'Gloriosa Daisy'BLACK-EYED SUSAN
Rudbeckia laciniata CUTLEAF CONEFLOWER
Salvia farinacea MEALY-CUP SAGE
Salvia guaranitica ANISE SAGE
Salvia greggii AUTUMN SAGE
Sedum spectabile SHOWY SEDUM
Trachelium caeruleum THROATWORT
Verbascum species MULLEIN
Veronica species VERONICA, SPEEDWELL

FALL BLOOMING PERENNIALS

Begonia hybrids BEGONIA
Chrysanthemum X *morifolium* GARDEN CHRYSANTHEMUM
Chrysanthemum nipponicum NIPPON DAISY, NIPPON OXEYE DAISY
Cortaderia selloana PAMPAS GRASS
Cuphea hyssopifolia MEXICAN HEATHER
Dichorisandra thrysiflora BLUE GINGER
Hemerocallis species DAYLILY
Hibiscus coccineus SCARLET ROSE MALLOW,
    TEXAS STAR HIBISCUS
Hibiscus moscheutos ROSE MALLOW
Justicia brandegeana SHRIMP PLANT
Liatris elegans BLAZING STAR, GAYFEATHER
Lythrum salicaria PURPLE LOOSESTRIFE
Mirabilis jalapa FOUR O'CLOCK
Nierembergia hippomanica CUPFLOWER
Nierembergia scoparia TALL CUPFLOWER
Pelargonium species GERANIUM
Pentas lanceolata EGYPTIAN STAR-CLUSTER
Phlox paniculata PERENNIAL PHLOX, SUMMER PHLOX
Physalis alkekengi CHINESE LANTERN PLANT
Reinwardtia indica YELLOW FLAX
Rudbeckia laciniata CUTLEAF CONEFLOWER
Salvia guaranitica ANISE SAGE
Salvia greggii AUTUMN SAGE
Salvia leucantha MEXICAN BUSH SAGE

Kathleen Trapolin

Bulbs, Corms, Tubers, Rhizomes

"Hey Mom! I saw a naked lady in the garden!" my children,
David and Dara Rosenzweig used to tease. To me, there's only one
meaning to that announcement: fall has come to the New Orleans
garden. The naked ladies (*Lycoris*) are blooming!

Bulbs are technically perennial plants because they repeat year after year. What makes them different from the
herbaceous perennials is their mechanism for food storage
through their semi-dormant phase. There are bulbous
plants for a variety of settings, from wet to dry, shady to
sunny, for all qualities of soil, and for a range of conditions: harsh to lush, and for all seasons. The plants
which are loosely classified as "bulbs" take five different
forms: true bulbs (such as tulips), corms (such as gladiolus), tubers (such as caladiums), tuberous roots (such as
dahlias), and rhizomes (such as cannas).

When many people think of bulbs, the first image
which comes to mind is the spring-flowering hardy bulbs:
tulips, hyacinths, and large, golden trumpeted daffodils.
Flyers come through the mail in the fall showing huge
fields of naturalized flowers, which, of course are not
found in the New Orleans area. My favorite is the crocus

bloom protruding through the snow in the early spring. The bulbs offered in a December, 1857 *"Daily Picayune"* ad showed the same tastes for northern bulbs as today: hyacinths, double tulips, anemones, ranunculus, narcissus, jonquils, crocus, snowdrops, lilies, crown imperials, (and southern bulbs double tuberoses and double dahlias). Wit h the right preparation, the above bulbs can be grown in New Orleans, but most, only as annuals.

We think tulips are worth the trouble. We usually grow several hundred which must be planted individually each December. For such a huge task, a bulb planter with a spring action handle and team effort is essential.

For those gardeners willing to put out extra efforts digging, storing, and replanting bulbs each year, options increase. But, no matter what you do, you are going to come face to face with the same fact which surfaces in every aspect of horticulture here: conditions in New Orleans are different. The poor drainage, hot sun following heavy rains, short winters stimulate an overabundance of foliage growth and, worst of all, cause rot!

For the New Orleans gardener who wants low maintainence and repeat bloom in relatively disease-free plants, selected tropical bulbs from A to Z (*Amaryllis* to *Zephyranthes*) can provide those admirable traits. The bulbous flowering plants from southern parts are a relatively untapped source of ornamentals for cultivation.[28] Many bulbs (or tubers, corms, and rhizomes), such as gladioli, cannas, and tuberous begonias which are called "summer flowering" fall into this category. So do many of the spidery formed exotica (*Nerine* and *Lycoris*) and others such as the Aztec lily, an Amaryllid which inspired the following prose in *McClure and Zimmerman, Flowerbulb Broker's* catalog: *"The curious, solitary orchid-like flowers perch on their stems like exotic birds, astonishing every passerby with their gorgeous velvety crimson petals and golden, protruding stamens."* Irresistable?

The main difference between the bulbs of northern climates and the tropicals is that bloom is triggered in the former by a period of cold, and in the latter by a period o f drought. The dry spell is during the summer for some plants, the winter for others, whereas others are adaptable. These requirements are reflected in the instructions for forcing bloom for potted tropical bulbs, for example, the amaryllis (*Hippeastrum*) in which Christmas bloom can be induced by restricting water three months through the fall until the end of November.

New plant discoveries and developments are covered i n gardening periodicals as well as seed and plant catalogues. Some of the presently unknown tropicals may be available in the future for trial in our gardens. Some genera to look for (according to Alan Meerow) are: *Urceolina, Eucrosia, Phaedranassa, Stenomesson, Chlidanthus,* and *Neomarica.*

The basic rules for growing bulbs (corms, tubers, rhizomes) in New Orleans culled from several sources, including Louisiana Cooperative Extension's handout on growing bulbs in this area and personal experience follow. Differing cultural requirements will be noted in the plant descriptions.

1.   Provide good drainage, either by raising your beds, amending the soil, or both. A good soil would be made up of one-third sand, one-third peat moss, and one-third good garden soil and shredded pine bark.
2.   Plant bulbs close to the surface, regardless of planting instructions unless you are positive your drainage is excellent.   Then still plant as shallowly as possible for the bulbs to have enough support. I find that my tulips tip over if they're not planted deep enough. I plant in raised beds.

Placing a small amount of sand at the base of each bulb in its planting hole is another suggestion for improving drainage. I forgo that procedure now, except for true lilies. It is time consuming when you are planting large numbers of bulbs.

3. I use bone meal worked into the soil at the bottom of each planting hole as fertilizer. The layer of sand under each bulb suggested in #2 can prevent burn from the meal or other fertilizer which may have been used if you are concerned. I have never had fertilizer burn problems with bone meal. Use azalea-camellia or other acid fertilizers for Louisiana irises.

Animal manures have long been reputed to be good fertilizers for flowering bulbs. But, they can cause rot unless worked into the soil four to six months before planting the bulbs. Rotted manure is recommended for Louisiana irises.

4. Plenty of moisture is important during the natural growing season of the plant. Too much can cause rot.

5. Unless you are planning to discard the bulbs after blooming is finished, allow the foliage to mature and die back on its own. It is during this green period that nutrients are manufactured and stored to provide for the next season's growth.

6. If bulbs are to be stored, pull them after the foliage dies down; allow them to air-dry in a shaded place; dust them with a fungicide and insecticide; and store them in dry peat moss or an old nylon stocking.

7. Cutting flowers of bulbous plants is fine as long as the leaves are left intact. Removing the spent flower will prevent the plant from wasting energy going to seed and make the bulb stronger for the next year. Going to seed will not "make the bulbs useless for next year" as some sources say. If you are growing the bulb as an annual, it doesn't matter.

STATE FLOWER OF LOUISIANA, THE LOUISIANA IRIS

Before looking in exotic places for bulbous plants, examine what is uniquely ours, the Louisiana iris. Probably the original collected, native doorstep garden plant, the swamp iris has grown in New Orleans gardens at least since the early 1800's. John James Audubon first used the term Louisiana iris in reference to one illustrated in the background of his painting of a parula warbler. Four of the five different native species which constitute the class were officially described and named botanically between 1799 and 1817. The rust colored *I. fulva* created a sensation when taken to England in 1812.

Camilla Bradley remembers Mrs. B. Stanley Nelson of Carrollton (7319 Panola Street) and her twin sister, Mrs. Ethel Rollins nee' Hutson (7321 Panola Street) who, in the early 1900's, collected and saved native irises which faced destruction as swamps were drained so the city could spread into what is now Gentilly. In *The Louisiana Iris*, published by the Society for Louisiana Irises, 1988, Mrs. Nelson is quoted: *"until very recent years we gathered many shades of blue ones from the dump near Broad street and the new basin canal, but old Bayou Savage which runs along Gentilly highway was our favorite place, for all the colors grew there."*

The authors comment further: *"It is difficult for us who are familiar with present day New Orleans, to visualize the abundance and variety of Louisiana irises growing and blooming near the heart of the city."* [29]

George Thomas, Superintendent of Parks for New Orleans, was an early collector of irises who discovered the first yellow *I. fulva*. Native iris grew along the iron fence in his garden at 3038 Calhoun long after his death in 1934. They are gone, now.

Mr. and Mrs. Clifford Lyons were other early and extensive collectors. Mrs. Lyons was an early member of the

New Orleans Garden Society, as were Thomas, Mrs. Nelson, and Miss Hutson.

Collection of irises from the swamp reached a peak in the 1930's and 1940's after publicity was given the plant by John Kunkel Small of the New York Botanical Gardens and Percy Viosca, Jr. of Gentilly.[30] The heavy hybridization which occurred in natural settings, helped by bumblebee pollinators and the close proximity of species, created a remarkable variety of flower form and color, but made identification difficult.[31] Viosca did most of the observation and study which helped Small sort the species from the hybrids. He wrote *Delta Irises and Their Culture* and *The Irises of Southeastern Louisiana.* According to the *W. P. A. Guide*, his large experimental iris garden was at 2940 Dreux Avenue, in Gentilly.[32]

Pioneer efforts in hybridizing and growing the irises were conducted primarily by enthusiastic amateurs, notably by W. B. MacMillan of Abbeville, whose work with daylilies is also known. Now the adaptable flowers are known and grown by gardeners worldwide, hybridization continues on professional and amateur levels. The recognition they've received elsewhere has finally come in Louisiana. During the legislative session of 1990, the Louisiana iris was voted the state flower!

Though the bloom period is short, March-May, the incredible beauty and diversity of the flowers and the attractiveness of the foliage make these special New Orleans flowers worth growing. **You can see them in bloom at:** Audubon Park, City Park Botanical Garden, Jean Lafitte National Park, Longue Vue Gardens, Louisiana Nature and Science Center, the Parkway Partners planting on Loyola Avenue at Tulane which was donated by the Society for Louisiana Irises, native habitats though in fewer numbers because of wetlands drainage and development.

Buy them at nurseries, from plant sales at the above parks and gardens and sources listed in RESOURCES.

See RHIZOMATOUS IRISES for culture.

BULBS, CORMS, TUBERS, RHIZOMES
FOR THE NEW ORLEANS GARDEN

1838 Indicates listing in J. F. Lelievre, *New Gardener of Louisiana.*
1857 Indicates listing in *Daily Picayune* ad of December, 1857.
1875 Indicates listing in R. Maitre's *Catalogue,* Magazine Street, New Orleans.
1884 Indicates exhibition at the Cotton Centennial, 1884-1885.
1895 Indicates mention in *Southern Garden* magazine, New Orleans.
1918 Indicates listing in *Bollwinkle Seed Co., Ltd. Catalogue and Garden Guide,* 510
Dumaine Street.

Acidanthera bicolor Hochst. **ACIDANTHERA** Ethiopia. Iris family, corm. Sun. Rich, well-drained soil, lots of water while growing, less during flowering. Gladiolus-like foliage, fragrant white blooms with a brown-purple mark at the base of each petal; open from the bottom of the flower stalk up, June to September. Though hardy here, digging the corms after the foliage dies down and storing through winter is recommended. I have tried leaving them in the ground. I get return growth, no bloom. Plant March-April.

Agapanthus africanus L. Hoffmanns., *A. umbellatus* **LILY OF THE NILE, AGAPANTHUS** South Africa. Tuberous root, Amaryllis family. Dwarf form available. Sun, part shade. Rich, moist, very well-drained soil. Blooms better when roots are crowded. Toward this end, can be planted in pots sunk in the ground. Blooms, in May and June, are large clusters of long lasting flowers with cultivars in white, varying shades of blue. Hardy to 25 degrees. Should come back from the roots if mulched. Plant March-September. Reputedly grown in New Orleans gardens since before 1860. 1895.

A. orientalis Leighton is larger flowered. These two species are often confused.

Albuca nelsonii N. E. Br. **ALBUCA** South Africa. Lily family, bulb. Sun. Well-drained soil. Showy late spring, early summer blooms are racemes of pure white, reddish brown striped blossoms, 3 to 5 feet high; leaves to 3 feet long.

Allium L. species **ALLIUM** The genus which includes the edible onion and garlic. Perennial bulbous herbs, Amaryllis family. Leaves are hollow or flat, usually have an onion odor. Sun. Sandy, well-drained soil. Bloom during spring or summer, form can be a globular cluster or an "umbel" which has the shape of an inverted umbrella, various colors. Plant September-March.

Recommended for New Orleans by my various references are:

A. christophii Trautv. or *A. albopilosum* C. H. Wright **STARS-OF-PERSIA** Asia minor. Flower stalks three feet. Lilac colored flower heads are ten inches across, dry well for use in arrangements. I have tried this one unsuccessfully.

A. neapolitanum Cyr. 'Grandiflorum' **DAFFODIL GARLIC** Southern Europe. Moist soil. Blooms in early spring are beautiful white, starshaped and fragrant in three inch umbels on 12 inch plants. These have naturalized in my garden.

A. sativum L. **GARLIC** Europe, is the cultivated, edible garlic. 2 feet tall. White flowers in globular clusters.

A. schoenoprasum L. **CHIVES** Europe, Asia. Well-drained, slightly acid, rich soil. Plants about eight inches high produce purple cluster flowers. I grow them in pots, harvest the leaves for flavoring in salad, cheese grits, vichyssoise, Hollandaise. Fresh is so much better than frozen, and they're so easy! Bees like the flowers.

A. triquetrum L. Western Mediterranean. Can handle some shade. *"Beautiful drooping white flowers,"* describes Grace Matt Thompson.

The genus *Allium* contains 300 species. The possibility of success with others than the ones named should not be ruled out. Others I have tried are:

A. moly L. **LILY LEEK** Europe. Twelve inches high. Yellow flowers similar to those of *A. neapolitanum* with which I planted them. I saw one year of bloom, then nothing but foliage.

A. *giganteum* Regel. China. Dramatic five inch heads of blue flowers, good for drying. I saw only foliage the first year, then, to my surprise, a flower the second. The third year, there was nothing. Expensive per bulb.

A. *sphaerocephalom* L. **DRUMSTICKS** Europe, Asia minor. Reddish-purple two-inch oval flower heads on two-foot stalks. I have had them repeat a second year in a sunny border. Interesting flowers, worth a try even if they only bloom once.

Alocasia macrorrhiza (L.) G. Don, A. *indica* **GIANT ELEPHANT'S EAR** Southeast Asia. Arum family, bulbous herbaceous perennial. Can reach 6 feet high, form large clumps. Sun, part shade. Fertile, well-drained, moist soil. Flower is the typical Arum flower: a spadix surrounded by a shorter spathe (similar form to that found in the flowers of monstera, anthurium, caladium and the typical Arum flower). Plants are grown for their leaves; large, arrow shaped, with wavy edges. Mulch well. Will die back with frost, return from the root. Caroline Sontheimer uses the leaves in dramatic flower arrangements.

Alpinia zerumbet (Pers.) B. L. Burtt & R. M. Sm., or A. *speciosa* **SHELL GINGER** East Asia. Rhizome, Ginger family. Sun, part sun. Rich, humusy, soil; plenty of moisture. Foliage is attractive, 10 to 12 feet tall; flowers are pendulous clusters of shell pink bracts with yellow and red flowers; blooms in spring the years when there is no freeze or in protected areas. Will return from the roots after freeze, but is slow to do so. Plant March-September. Reputedly introduced to New Orleans gardens between 1830-1840.

Alstroemeria L. species **PERUVIAN LILY** South America. Alstroemeria family, rhizome-like roots. Need filtered shade in our heat. Rich, sandy soil, very good drainage. Bloom in summer, but frequently do not flower the first year after they are planted; resent being disturbed.   Culture described as difficult by some sources. This is borne out by my experience but once they are established, try to get rid of them!   Plant the roots September through January.

A. aurantiaca D.Don ex Sweet. **ALSTROEMERIA** Clusters of two-inch tubular blossoms on two to four foot high stems which may need staking.   Color orange with yellow spots.   Hybrids in pink, yellow, red, solid and spotted. Frequently seen in florists' bouquets.

A. pulchella L.f. **PARROT LILY** Brazil.   Flowers are small dark red tubes with green tips and brown spots inside.   Considered weeds by some New Orleans gardeners, this plant is found in many older gardens around the city.   I have seen its blooms profuse in some very shaded spots, such as in Joel Myers' garden, though my personal experience is that it wants more light to bloom.

X amarcrinum Coutts (*Amaryllis X Crinum*), *XA. memoriacorsii,* or   *A. howardii* **CRINODONNA** Bulb.   Sun, part shade.   Rich, well-drained, but moisture retentive soil. Flowers are four inch fragrant, pink amaryllis-like blossoms on three foot stalks in June. Plant October-June.

Amaryllis belladonna L. **BELLADONNA LILY, AMARYLLIS BELLADONNA** South African bulb which, with its varieties, is the only species of the genus *Amaryllis,* Amaryllis family.   Sun, filtered sun.   Rich, moist soil with very good drainage.   Planted with soil to the neck of the large bulb.   Clusters of fragrant, lily-shaped flowers, three-inches in diameter, appear on three-foot stalks in late summer to early fall.   Varieties in shades of pink to red to purple and white.   Hardy to 25 degrees.   Sometimes called "naked lady" as are *Lycoris* species, because the strap-like leaves appear in the spring and disappear before the flower stalk shoots up out of the ground months later. Should not be moved once planted as it takes time to reach full size.   Bloom is best after a hot summer, but does not bloom every year in New Orleans.   Poisonous. Plant October-April. 1895.

Amomum compactum Soland. ex Maton **AMOMUM** Rhizome. Java. Shade, part sun. Rich, organic, light soil; moist but well drained. Grown for foliage: aromatic, 10-inch leaves grow on stems 2 to 3 feet tall; flowers are brownish-yellow tubular shaped, on a cone-like head beneath the leaves. Leaves may freeze, plant will return from the roots. Plant March-September. 1838.

Anemone coronaria L. **GARDEN ANEMONE, WIND-FLOWER** Mediterranean area. Tuberous root, Ranunculus family. Sun. Slightly acid, fertile, humusy, moist but very well-drained garden soil; raised beds good; moisture is needed through the blooming period. Soak tubers in water 1 hour before planting no more than 1 inch deep on a handful of sand; mix bone meal in the soil; October is traditional planting time here. If well-grown, bloom is prolific. Flowers are poppy-like; single and double; pink, white, red, and blue; bloom late winter through spring; cultivars recommended for New Orleans are: 'St. Brigid' and 'de Caen'. Use as annuals; these plants will not repeat here. Winter rot is very common, so take all above planting suggestions seriously. Plant October-December. 1838, 1884.

A. caroliniana Walt., **WINDFLOWER** is an anemone which is native to Louisiana. Bloom, February to April, is a solitary, white or blue flower.

Arisaema triphyllum (L.) Torr. **JACK-IN-THE-PULPIT** Arum family, bulb. Louisiana woodlands. Fleshy rooted perennial. Shade. Rich, moist, humusy, well-drained soil. Flowers briefly March to May; tubular spathe striped with red and brown lines surrounding a straight spadix; foliage is erect, one foot high; 2 leaves with 3 leaflets each, fruit which follows in autumn is a cluster of bright red berries. Plant October-December.

A. dracontium (L.) Schott **GREEN DRAGON** is taller, has a single leaf with many leaflets; thin spadix protrudes from light green spathe.

A. quinatum (L.) Schott is similar to *A. triphyllum* but has different leaf arrangement; spathe is all green and protrudes above the leaves. Also common in southern woodlands.

All of the above are available from catalogs as nursery grown plants, so there's no need to dig wild ones!

Arum palaestinum Boiss, *A. sanctum* **BLACK CALLA LILY** Shade. Arum family. Moist soil during the growing season. 6 inch long arrow shaped leaves, flowers similar to calla lily, but green with blackish-purple insides; winter blooms are more profuse in pots which Thompson suggests sinking into leaf mold in the garden.

A. pictum L.f. is also called **BLACK CALLA**. It is native to Corsica and Sardinia. Introduction of a black calla (to New Orleans?) was said to have been recent in 1895 *Southern Garden* article. Did it come with the influx of Italian immigrants during that period and earlier?

Belamcanda chinensis (L.) DC **BLACKBERRY LILY** India, southeast Asia, Japan. Tuberous root, Iris family. Sun, part shade. Any soil. Blooms in early summer are orange with red spots, 2 inches wide, in clusters; seeds which follow look like blackberries; foliage is similar to gladiolus, clump-forming. Hardy. See specimens in front of Heymann Conservatory in Audubon Park. Grown by Jefferson in 1766 at Monticello.

Bletilla striata (Thunb.) Rchb.f., *B. hyacinthina* **BLET-ILLA, CHINESE GROUND ORCHID** Temperate areas of China. Tuberous rhizome, Orchid family. Part shade. Moist but well-drained, slightly acidic, fertile soil; good mixture of sand, peat, leaf mold recommended. Thin leaves which form a ground cover send up foot high stems with 6 to 10 pink to purple orchid like blooms in late spring, early summer; cultivar 'Alba' is white. Recommended for planting around azaleas or camellias, as soil requirements are the same. Plant September-April.

Caladium bicolor Ait. Venten, *C. picturatum* C. Koch & Bouche, *C. X hortulanum* Birdsey **CALADIUM** Arum fam-

ily, tuber.   Tropical South America.   Best in shade, morning sun.   Well drained soil high in organic matter, constantly moist; fertilize with bone meal.   I have planted
outdoors as early as March 15 with good results, but rot
from cold, wet soil is a risk before the end of April.
Blooms are typical Arum but insignificant; should be
removed to promote further leaf development.   Depending
on the effect you want, you can cut mammoth or jumbo
sized bulbs into pieces to produce more, but smaller sized
leaves.   Plants are grown for their heart shaped leaves
with many patterns in combinations of shades of red, rose,
pink, white, and green.   Nothing brings out the coolness
of a shady area (even when it is a hundred degrees in the
shade as it gets during New Orleans summers) more than
a planting of white caladiums such as 'Candidum' or
'Aaron'.   My favorite red is 'John Peed'.   Caladiums are
beautiful in pots or in the ground.   Not many plants offer
such a long season of color and beauty for such a small
effort.   They are the only bulb-like plant which I bother to
dig and save each winter.   Even that is easy.   Just make
sure to pull them before the foliage withers away completely so you can't find them.   I dry them, then store in
nylon stockings with labels.   I have compared notes with
those who leave them in the ground.   After a mild winter,
they will return.   Foliage seems to diminish in size each
successive year and they are inexpensive enough to replace, so don't feel slothful if you let them go and buy
new ones. Plant March-August.   1895, 1918.

   Camassia Lindl. species **CAMASSIA** North America.
Bulb, Lily family.   Sun, part sun.   Any soil, normal to wet
in moisture.   Grasslike foliage.   Flowers in spring are blue
to white, star shaped, like little lilies, on spikes.

   C. leichtlinii (Bak.) S. Wats. grows 2 to 3 feet tall, 20
to 40 dainty flowers per spike.

   C. scilloides (Raf.) Cory **WILD HYACINTH** is native to
north Louisiana woods and on the endangered list for this
state. Spikes of 10 to 40 white to light blue flowers on 2

foot stalks in April and May. Should be left where they are, bulbs purchased from cultivated sources.

Canna L. species **CANNA** North and South American tropics and subtropics. Rhizome, Canna family. Foliage similar to banana leaves grows on single stemmed plants which can grow 3 to 6 feet high, depending on the cultivar; rapid growth, clump-forming. Like full sun and heat. Adaptable, but does best in rich, moist, loose soil; fertilize with manure. Will freeze to the ground, return from the roots. Most effective in masses. Major problem with the hybrids is a caterpillar which causes leaf roll. This disfigures the attractive leaves, supposedly can be controlled with weekly spraying with pesticides which I am hesitant to do for fear of hurting the hummingbirds which love the plants. My cannas always look ratty.

C. flaccida Salisb. Native to Louisiana marshes. Small, yellow blooms appear in the fall. Seen occasionally in city gardens.

C. X generalis L. H. Bailey **CANNA HYBRIDS** Developed from South and Central American species. Large, showy blossoms which can be mottled or red, pink, orange, yellow, or white. They bloom from early summer until frost. Foliage can be shades of green to purple and bronze. 1895.

C. X generalis 'Bailey', which has red and yellow spotted flowers, has escaped cultivation and grows wild and well in some fresh water marshes. Should be beautiful in your bog garden.

C. indica L. **INDIAN SHOT** is the reddish flowered C anna which is known to have escaped cultivation in this area at least 100 years ago.[33] The seeds are round and hard, reputed to have been used as shot by West Indies natives, and in dried gourds to make maraccas. 1895.

Clivia miniata Lindl., *C.* hybrids **KAFIR LILY** South Africa. Fleshy rooted perennial, Amaryllis family. Shade. Rich, sandy soil; fertilize with bone meal. Most sources recommend planting in pots as they bloom most freely if roots are crowded. Repot every five years. I submerge my pot in the ground so it can be easily lifted and brought in if very cold weather is predicted or if I want to enjoy the blooms indoors. The clusters of lily-like flowers in April-May are in startlingly intense orange with yellow centers, hybrids in other shades of scarlet to orange and white. The seeds are borne in large red berries which are attractive and sprout readily. Hardy to 25 degrees though one source says 38. Dorothy Gardner has successfully left hers out all year in New Orleans. Grown in breathtaking masses in southern California. 1895.

Colocasia antiquorum (L.) Schott, *C. esculenta* (L.) Schott (both called **ELEPHANT'S-EAR**) Arum family, tuberous root. Tropical Asia, Pacific Islands. Sun, shade. Moist, humusy soil; the greater the fertility, the larger the leaves. Grown for the very attractive foliage. Cold sensitive, but will come back from the roots. Rapid growth and spread. If not contained it can become a pest. Hard to get rid of once established. I have seen them reappear in a spot from which I removed them 5 years earlier. There are several varieties of *C. antiquorum*. *C. esculenta* or taro has the starchy roots from which poi is made in the south Pacific. The presence of elephant ears in French Quarter patios near 1900 has been noted in photos.

Costus speciosus (J. Konig) Sm. **SPIRAL GINGER** East Indies. Rhizome. Sun, part sun. Rich, organic soil; moist but well-drained. Leaves are arranged spirally on stems to 8 feet tall; white flowers with yellow centers protrude briefly from lasting green and red, cone shaped bracts in the fall. Should return from the roots after a freeze. Plant March-September.

C. igneous N. E. Br. **FIERY COSTUS** Brazil. Deep shade. Brilliant orange-gold blooms on 18 inch tall plants. Good in pots.

C. malortieanus H. Wendl. **STEP-LADDER PLANT** Central America. Shade. 3 foot plant with small, red--lipped yellow blooms arising from inconspicuous bracts.

234 THE NEW ORLEANS GARDEN

Crinum L. species **CRINUM** a genus of over 100 species in the Amaryllis family which includes the largest bulbous plants in the world. Native to the Old and New World tropics and subtropics. Sun, light shade. Rich, moist soil. The flowers in late spring and summer are lily-like clusters atop 2 to 3 foot tall stalks, fragrant, in whites; shades of red to pink to wine. Hardy to 28 degrees. Plant with the bulb half out of the ground. Do not like frequent transplantings; may not bloom for several years after being moved. Will form large clumps if left in one place. Common in old New Orleans gardens. Plant October-May.

C. americanum L. **SWAMP LILY, FLORIDA CRINUM** Louisiana swamps. Rich soil, lots of water. White flowers May to November. Spreads. Easy and wonderfully fragrant in my garden pond.

C. asiaticum L. **GRAND CRINUM** Asia. Massive plant with fragrant white flowers, huge root system.

C. hybrids **CRINUM** Many are available.

Crocosmia X crocosmiiflora (V. Lemoine ex E. Morr.) N. E. Br. **MONTBRETIA** is the most widely grown member of a genus related to and sometimes called **TRITONIA**. South Africa. Corms. Part sun, best in full sun. Good drainage, rather dry soil. Orange to scarlet flowers on stalks from 2 to 4 feet, depending on the cultivar. Plant in spring. Intensely colored blooms appear in May through August. Naturalize readily in New Orleans.

Crocus L. species **CROCUS** Most native to Mediterranean regions. Corm. Sun, part sun. Good drainage, fertilize with bone meal. Need refrigeration for 6 to 8 weeks (from the end of October) before planting in New Orleans. Do not freeze them. Will not usually rebloom here, and so should be treated as annuals. I did talk to a gardener from Harahan who digs his crocus bulbs (after the foliage dies back), stores them, rerefrigerates them, and gets 75 per cent rebloom. Low growing plants, attractive in clumps, have wineglass shaped flowers in white, shades of yellow and purple, solid and striped.   Synonomous with spring to many gardeners in Zone 7 and above where they naturalize. Plant October-January. 1857, 1884.

Curculigo capitulata (Lour.) O. Kuntze **PALM GRASS** Asia, Australia.   Star Grass family, rhizome.   Part shade. Moist, but well-drained soil.   3 foot long, 6 inch wide stemless leaves which remind me of corrugated aspidistras. Small yellow flowers are on spikes near the ground and hidden by foliage.   I have seen this plant in many old gardens, often wondered what it was, have never seen it bloom.   Jerome Lebo feels it should be more widely used in New Orleans.   It does not seem to get as ratty looking as aspidistras.

Curcuma species **HIDDEN LILY, SURPRISE LILY** India, Southeast Asia.   Tuberous root, Ginger family. Sun, part shade.   Rich, organic, moist soil.   Names come from the inconspicuous flowers which grow from enlarged bracts which appear before the deciduous leaves in spring (surprise!) or afterwards, directly from the ground, in which case they remain hidden.   Hilda Latapie uses them in bouquets where they always arouse comment.   I have listed only two of the several species available.

C. elata Roxb. To 4 feet or more.   Spring flowers are yellow from violet bracts.

C. petiolata Roxb. **QUEEN LILY** Yellowish-white flowers from rose to purple bracts in summer.

Cyrtanthus mackenii Hook.f. **IFAFA LILY** South Africa. Amaryllis family.   Sun.   Rich, well drained soil; need fertilizer, year round moisture.   Winter, early spring blooms are two-foot long clusters of four to ten tubular, curved flowers each two inches long; ivory, yellow, red; leaves are one foot long, narrow.   Plant just below the soil.   Multiply rapidly; may need annual division of offsets if grown in pots.

DAFFODIL (See *Narcissus*).

Dahlia Cav. hybrids. **DAHLIA** Developed from several species of Mexican origin, the hybrids are almost exclusively grown by gardeners. New introductions available and in and out of fashion frequently. Composite family, tuberous rooted perennial. Height from 2 to 8 feet depending on the variety. Sun. Soil very rich in organic matter, heavily fertilized, constantly watered in depth. Growth and bloom may stop and fail to resume if plants are allowed to go dry. Prepare the bed with organic matter a month ahead, add bone meal to the soil to the depth of a foot to provide long acting food, top dress plants with aged manure. Add a 2 to 3 inch mulch to conserve moisture. Plant the root in a hole 7 inches deep, sideways, with its eye upward and pointed toward a stake (inserted at planting time). Cover with 2 inches of soil. Additional soil should be added as the plant grows. The blooms are the reason this plant has been so popular for so long, inspiring the "great dahlia craze" of early nineteenth century Europe; are every color but blue, sizes from 2 inches to 12, so many shapes that classification by the American Dahlia Society requires 16 categories. Tall varieties need staking, usually are pinched from the time they reach 12 inches until September 1 to encourage bushiness. Tubers should be dug and stored when the foliage dies back. Dwarf dahlias are easy from seed, grown as annuals. Plant March-May. 1838.

Dietes Salisb. ex Klatt. species, also called *Moraea* species **DIETES** South Africa. Rhizome, Iris family. Sun, part shade. Succession of two day blooms form at the tip of the narrow, arrow-like, stiff foliage in spring and early summer. Forms attractive clumps. Foliage may die back in a freeze. Plant September-December.

D. bicolor Sweet or *M. bicolor* (Sweet) Spae has 2 inch yellow blooms with brownish spots at each petal base; needs moist soil. Year round bloom if no frost. Rhizomatous root.

D. vegeta (L.) N. E. Br., *M. iridioides* L. **BUTTERFLY IRIS** has white flowers with brownish yellow and purplish blue spots; can handle dryness or moisture. Rhizome.

Dracunculus vulgaris Schott **DRAGON ARUM** The name means "little dragon". Meditterannean area. Arum family, tuberous perennial. Sun. Acid soil. To 3 feet. Grace Matt Thompson (1947) says: *"Black-purple flowers with bad odor, beautiful foliage."* Hortus Third describes the flower: *"...fls. unisexual, spadix with the zones of female and male fls. contiguous, terminated by a long, exserted, malodorous sterile appendage;..."*[34] I don't know where to buy it or even if I want it, but with such descriptions how could I leave it out?

Endymion hispanicus (Mill.) Chouard, *Scilla campanulata* **SPANISH SQUILL, SPANISH BLUEBELL** Spain, Portugal. Bulb, Lily family. Sun, part shade. Rich, humusy soil. Blooms in spring are blue, pink, or white in small, spiky clusters. Recommended for naturalizing in New Orleans. In my garden, they do rebloom, but their reproductive behavior has not exactly been passionate.

Erythronium californicum Purdy **DOGTOOTH VIOLET, TROUT LILY** Native American woodland flowers. This species from California. Bulb, Lily family. Shade. Requires constant moisture year round; slightly acid soil. A peat moss mulch is recommended. These plants cannot tolerate extreme dryness or heat, which should make them difficult to grow in New Orleans, but one reference reports success. They sound like such beautiful plants. Dainty, scented white flowers, 1 to 3 inches in size, in spring; foliage about a foot high. Should be planted in clusters for best effect, left undisturbed. Maybe they would last in a shaded, brickpatio garden among azaleas and near a cooling fountain.

Eucharis grandiflora Planch. & Linden **AMAZON LILY** Columbia, Amazon River area. Amaryllis family bulb which should be planted with its neck just above the soil. Needs the filtered light it would get on the jungle floor, no direct sun. Rich, humusy, moist, well-drained soil, fertilize with bone meal and well-rotted cow manure. Pot culture recommended; as with *Clivias*, bloom is heavier

when roots are crowded. Four bulbs to an eight inch pot,
six to a ten inch. Repot no more frequently than every
three years.   Flowering is heavier in the spring, can be
stimulated year round by alternating wet and dry periods
if enough time for leaf growth is allowed before withhold-
ing water.   Blooms are fragrant and waxy, white; four to
six on each 18 inch stalk.   Tender, though some report
leaving them out with protection through the winters here.
If you plant them in pots, it is easy enough to bring them
in with your *Clivias*.   Plant March through May, October
through November.   1895.

   Fritillaria meleagris L.   **GUINEA HEN FLOWER,
SNAKE'S HEAD LILY, TOAD LILY** Native to Europe
where they are found naturalized in fields of grass.   Lily
family, bulb.   Shade.   Fertile, moderately moist garden soil
that is very well-drained.   Planting in a pocket of sand is
recommended. Cool location.   Spring flowers are pendulous bell shapes, checkered purple and white, which hang
from 12 inch stems.   Another plant which may not like
the heat of our summers, yet one source reports success.
Crown imperials were offered in newspaper ads, 1857.

   Galanthus nivalis L. **SNOWDROP** Europe.   Amaryllis
family, bulb.   Part shade.   Well-drained garden soil.
Clumps of plants produce white, nodding flowers in the
early spring.   Only one of my sources on New Orleans
recommends them for here.   They are better suited for
northern climes.   The similar **SNOWFLAKE** (*Leucojum
aestivum*) is a superb performer here, naturalizing and
blooming with abandon. 1857.

   Galtonia candicans (Bak.) Decne.   **SUMMER HYA-
CINTH** South Africa.   Bulb, Lily family.   Sun.   Rich, moist
soil; well drained.   Flowers in July and August are bell
shaped, small, white, and fragrant on a 3 to 4 foot spike
which rises from 2 inch wide, thick, fleshy leaves.   Will
rebloom if flowers are cut as they fade.

   Gladiolus X *hortulanus* L. H. Bailey **GARDEN GLADI-
OLUS** Species   are native to Europe and Africa, most gar-

den plants are hybrids. Iris family, corm. Sun. Fertile garden soil, sandy, well-drained; lots of moisture. Plantings can be staggered, February through March, for bloom over a longer period of time. Stakes needed to support the sword-like foliage and heavy flowers which make this plant more attractive in clumps, but still more appropriate for cutting beds than integrated into the garden. Blooms on spikes open from the bottom up in 28 different colors listed by the North American Gladiolus Council. Mine are all descended from a "cheapy" mix of corms from Schwegmann's. They turned out to be yellows with two reds despite the myriad of colors depicted on the package. Left in the ground, they rebloom faithfully. Flowers may have become smaller, I'm not sure; this is what reputedly happens. Should be divided every two to three years, depending on how crowded they become. References suggest buying new corms each year for best results. Thrips and rot are common problems. 1875.

G. byzantius Mill. **WINTER HARDY GLADIOLUS, BABY GLADIOLUS, JACOB'S LADDER** Purple-red flowers with magenta. White form, too.Naturalizes readily; is an old perennial which has escaped cultivation in some areas say Odenwald and Turner. Available in catalogs, today. Sisters' Bulb Farm is a Louisiana source. See RESOURCES.

Gloriosa rothschildiana O'Brien, *G. superba* L. **GLORIOSA LILY, CLIMBING LILY** Tropical Africa, Asia. 4 to 6 foot vine which grows from a tuber, clings by leaf tip tendrils. Lily family. Sun. Rich, moist soil; very sandy for good drainage. Tuber should be planted in a horizontal position, February-May. Summer blooms are yellow and scarlet, lily like, exotic. They like New Orleans. In the right spot they will prosper and proliferate. In the sun, they will grow upright in clumps without support! Hilda Latapie recommends *rothschild* over *superba* for best results.

Habranthus tubispathus (L'Her.) Traub, *H. robustus* **RAIN LILY** Argentina *H. texanus* (Herb.) ex Steud. **COP-PER LILY** Texas. Small bulbs, Amaryllis family. Sun, part shade. Rich, well-drained soil. Small flowers, short lasting but colorful, rose red or coppery-striped purple yellow (*H. texanus*) in April through fall. I saw copper lilies naturalized and blooming near the Texas border in October. Should be grouped for effect. Plant September to December.

Haemanthus katharinae Bak., *H. multiflorus* Martyn. **BLOOD LILY** South Africa. Bulb, Amaryllis family. Culture and requirements same as *Clivia* and *Eucharis* lily. Red and pink blooms in July and August on leafless stalks. Plant February-March.

Hedychium J. Konig. species **HEDYCHIUM** Ginger family. Sun, shade. Rich, organic soil; plenty of moisture. Flowers appear at the end of canes which should be removed after bloom to keep the stand upright and attractive, and to stimulate new growth. Will return after a freeze in New Orleans. Plant March-September. Reputedly introduced to New Orleans gardens before 1860. Do not consider the following list complete:

H. coccineum Buch.-Ham. **RED GINGER LILY** India. Summer flowers are red spikes on 6 foot canes.

H. coronarium J. Konig **BUTTERFLY GINGER** Tropical Asia Very fragrant, white with yellow, butterfly shaped flowers on 6 foot canes, summer-fall.

H. flavum Roxb. **YELLOW BUTTERFLY GINGER** India. Fragrant yellow with orange flowers on 5 foot stalks, summer to fall.

H. gardneranum Roscoe. **KAHILI GINGER** India. Fragrant flower is a long spike of yellow flowers with orange stamens. Bloom begins in July in my garden, always attracts comment.

Hippeastrum advena (Ker-Gawl.) Herb., *H. reginae* L. Herb., *H. vittatum* (L.'Her.) Herb., *H. X johnsonii* (Bury) Herb. **ST. JOSEPH'S LILY** (1799), *Hippeastrum* hybrids.

This is the plant everybody knows as **AMARYLLIS**. Name confusion results from botanists' changes in nomenclature, though it is of the Amaryllis family. The genus is native to South America. Most people today grow the hybrids, many of which come from producers in Holland and South Africa. The amaryllis-like mystery plant with red flowers in the garden beside your old New Orleans cottage may be one of the pure *Hippeastrums* or early hybrids which are more vigorous than the new ones. Sun, part shade. Rich garden soil, good drainage. The large bulb should be planted with its neck out of the soil. Flowers are clusters of three to four huge lily-like blooms on one to two foot bare stalks in colors from white and shades of red, orange in April. Do well outdoors in New Orleans if mulched for winter protection. Can be planted in pots and blooms forced by manipulating moisture to simulate drought and produce dormancy. They do multiply. Small bulbs produced as offsets of larger ones bloom in three years. Plant September-January. 1827 ad in French newspaper in New Orleans listed *"amarillis."* Was it St. Joseph's Lily? 1884: *Amaryllis.* 1895: *A. Johnsonii.*

Hyacinthus orientalis L. and hybrids **DUTCH HYACINTH** Greece, Asia Minor. Bulb, Lily family. Sun. Fertile garden soil with lots of sand and humus, good drainage. Must be chilled in the refrigerator (not freezer) for 6 to 8 weeks before mid-December to January planting (to simulate the cold weather which occurs naturally, elsewhere) for the flower stem to elongate. Very fragrant flowers in spring are shades of blue, pink, red, yellow, and white; clusters of bell-shaped blossoms on 6 to 10 inch spikes; single and double varieties exist. For best results, use as annuals here. Plants will repeat, but flowers are smaller each succeeding year. 1838, 1884.

H. variety *albulus* Bak. **ROMAN HYACINTH** White or blue flowers on 12 inch stalks, looser clustered than the species, on 12 inch stalks. One source reports they naturalize in New Orleans.

Hymenocallis Salisb. species **SPIDER LILY** Amaryllis family, bulb.   Sun, light shade.   Plant just below the surface of rich, moist soil.   Hardy in New Orleans.   Plant year-round.

H. caroliniana (L.) Herb., *H. occidentalis* **SWAMP SPIDER LILY** Southeast U.S., including our swamps. 4 inch wide; spidery, white, fragrant flowers from March to May.

H. narcissiflora (Jacq.) Macbr. *H. calathina* **ISMENE, PERUVIAN DAFFODIL, SACRED LILY OF THE INCAS** Peru.   Flowers in summer are fragrant, white with green stripes, a daffodil-like cup, more complicated structure than our natives.   Needs a dry period in winter and perfect drainage as contrasted with our muck-loving swamp spider lily. Plant February-April.

H. hybrids yellow-flowered 'Sulphur Queen', white flowered 'Daphne' and 'Festalis' with immense white flowers have same culture as the Peruvian daffodil

Ipheion uniflorum (R. C. Grah.) Raf., also called *Triteleia uniflora, Milla uniflora, Brodiaea uniflora* **SPRING STARFLOWER** Peru, Argentina.   Small bulb, Amaryllis family. Sun, part shade.   Any well drained soil.   Low growing foliage appears in the fall, lasts through spring which is when the small, fragrant, pale blue, star shaped flowers bloom. Naturalize readily here, multiplying like crazy!

BULBOUS IRISES

Iris hybrids called **DUTCH IRIS** are a cross between *I. xiphium* and *I. tingitana* **TANGIERS IRIS** Bulb, Iris family. Sun, Part sun. Loose, well-drained, alkaline soil. Plant in September for beautiful flowers in shades of purple, blue, yellow, bronze, white in the spring. Will repeat bloom in New Orleans, but not 100 per cent, and not more than 3 to 4 years in my experience. If you are luckier, and if you provide perfect drainage and lots of sun, you may be; divide them every 3 to 5 years. Plant September-November.

Of the bulbous irises (Dutch, Spanish, and English) Dutch does best in New Orleans.

I. xiphium L. **SPANISH IRIS** France and Portugal. Bulb. White, yellow, and blue flowers with orange patch on the blade bloom later than Dutch iris on taller and weaker stems which can be hidden behind low growing annuals.

I. xiphiodes J. F. Ehrh. **ENGLISH IRIS** Pyrenees. Bulb. Lavender, blue, and white flowers later than the Spanish Iris; larger than Spanish or Dutch. Do not really like our heat.

I. reticulata Blieb. and hybrids **IRIS RETICULATA** Caucasus. Bulb. Sun. Excellent drainage, light, fertile garden soil. Hardy. Graceful foliage on miniature plants, 6 to 8 inches high; early spring blooms described as "velvety" by one catalog, in blues, violets, purples with yellow and yellow with brown.

RHIZOMATOUS IRISES

I. X germanica L., **FLAG, FLEUR-DE-LIS** hybrids of *I. germanica* L., the **BEARDED IRIS** Southern Europe. Rhizome. Sun. Needs excellent drainage, soil heavy in sand and organic matter, alkaline, rather dry; fertilize with bone meal. Performs best in areas unlike New Orleans, with low humidity. Shallow planting of the rhizome is recommended. Flowers are voluptuously petaled, many colored beauties which appear in spring on stems thrust above the sword-like leaves. The "beard" is a fuzzy strip of color on the three outer petals or "falls" of the flower. (The erect petals of the flower are called "standards".) Not to be relied upon in New Orleans. However, if you're ready for experimentation and have money to spare, provide perfect soil conditions and hope for the right weather. The blooms you may get will be breathtaking. 'Tournament Queen' repeated several years for Hilda Latapie. Joel Myers reports a deep purple, planted by the previous owners of her house years ago, which bloomed yearly until she moved it to build a patio.

I. X germanica variety *florentina* (L.) Dykes **ORRIS** The only bearded iris which does well in New Orleans and supposedly the flower on which the fleur-de-lis is based. Rhizomes are the source of orris-root which, powdered, is used in potpourri. Fragrant white flowers tinged with lavender in March, April. Has escaped cultivation in some parts of Louisiana and is still found in old gardens. Mine came from a plantation home in Lockport. Blooms best in established and slightly crowded clumps.

There is disagreement in references as to whether this plant is actually *I. X albicans* J. Lange which comes from Yemen and is used in Mohammedan graveyards. The two are said to be often confused. Another mystery.

I. kaempferi Sieb. ex Lem **JAPANESE IRIS** China, Japan. Rhizome. Morning sun. Requires moist, acidic soil; will grow in a bog garden. Showy, beardless blooms of rose, blue, purple with contrasting mottlings and stripes; April, May. Not really recommended for our area, but they are grown successfully in the sunken garden at Longue Vue, so maybe you can grow them, too.

I. hybrids **LOUISIANA IRIS** are hybrids of five native Louisiana species which do not cross with any others. Rhizomes. Sun, or at least half a day of sun. They grow in water in the swamp, and will grow and bloom beautifully in submerged pots in your garden pool. Within the garden, they will grow best in rich, moist, acidic (pH of 6.5 or lower) soil, high in organic matter, such as camellia or azalea soil. Watering is very important. Do not allow irises to dry out during the growing season. This can mean additional watering during some months, and mulch. Fertilize with azalea-camellia, rotted manure, 8-8-8 or other acid fertilizer in January. Joseph Mertzweiller says to stress this: *"Do not use bone meal or other alkaline fertilizer!"* Do not plant Louisiana irises near trees or plants with root systems which would seriously compete for moisture. The blooms, March through April, are 2 to 8 inches in size; beardless; blue, red, yellow, white, purple, and shades in-between. Plant and divide in late August and September; divide every 3 to 4 years, as crowding creates sparse bloom.

The following plants are the "Louisiana irises" which are the parents of the hybrids. They can be found growing in native habitats, but in fewer and fewer numbers. Plant August-September.

I. brevicaulis Raf. **ZIG-ZAG-STEMMED IRIS** Dwarf with deep blue to white flowers. Found in dryer conditions than the others.

I. fulva Ker-Gawl **COPPER-COLORED IRIS** Rust red, common in south Louisiana swamps.

I. giganticaerulea Small. **GIANT-BLUE IRIS** Found in freshwater marshes in coastal areas. Flowers from blue to purple to white.

I. hexagona Walt. **HEXAGONA** Flowers lilac to white. Found in Southeast U.S. coastal marshes.

I. X nelsonii Randolph **ABBEVILLE RED, SUPER FULVA** A naturally occurring hybrid which breeds true, is only found in southwest Louisiana. Larger than *I. fulva*, colors from red to brown to yellow and deep purple. Can have a yellow or orange mark where the beard would appear in a bearded iris.

I. pseudacorus L., *I. aquatica* **YELLOW FLAG** West Europe, North Africa. Rhizome. Foliage is 1 to 4 feet tall, looks like Louisiana iris. Sun, part shade. Rich garden soil or bog setting. Yellow, beardless flowers are present briefly in April and May. One source says heavy bloom is seen in New Orleans only after a cold winter. Invasive; should not be planted with less competitive plants, such as Louisiana iris. Foliage can be cut back in early winter just before new growth for a fresh look. Widely naturalized around Louisiana waterways. It was grown by Jefferson at Monticello in 1766, *"Flower-de luces."* R. Maitre's 1875 catalogue offers *"Iris, or Fleur de Luce."*

I. siberica L. **SIBERIAN IRIS** Central Europe, Russia. Sun, part sun. Moist but well drained acid soil (pH or 6.5 or lower). Small, beardless blooms in early spring are shades of blue and purple, white (some patterned with gold and black etching on each fall) on slender stems which rise elegantly above the grass-like, clump-forming, arching foliage. Though usually recommended for Zone 8 and north, several have reported success with them here, including me. I bought a mystery plant on sale at a nursery north of the Lake. I guessed it was either an *Iris* or a *Dietes* from the shape of the foliage, which was narrower and less erect than members of those genera I had seen. It bloomed in March, then more prolifically the following March. What beauties the flowers are!

I. spuria L. **SPURIA IRIS** Europe, Asia. Rhizome. 3 foot foliage similar to Louisiana Iris. Sun. Moist, rich, alkaline soil with good drainage. 4 inch blooms, April through June; white, yellows, browns, blues, purples, blends, some veined in different colors. Can take 2 to 3 years to become established after which they should not be disturbed.

I. unguicularis Poir. (*I. stylosa*) Algeria. Rhizome. Sun. Likes poor, dry soil; good drainage. Not hardy, plant in protected spot. Fragrant, lavender blue flowers on dwarf plants in December, January. Does not always last here. Plant October-December.

I. virginica L. **SOUTHERN BLUE-FLAG** Central U.S., Louisiana. Sun. Moist, rich soil. Same culture as Louisiana irises with which it is sometimes confused. It is a vigorous grower with attractive foliage which stays green after Louisiana iris foliage has yellowed. Flowers in March and April are blue or white with lavender or blue lines and yellow patches on the petals.

Ixia L. hybrids **AFRICAN CORN LILY** South Africa. Iris family, corm. Sun. Sandy, very well-drained soil. Spring blooms: 2-inch, star shaped flowers in clusters; red, pink, orange, yellow, cream, with dark centers. Very attractive. Not reliable repeaters in New Orleans as the corms do not ripen well in the moist soil of New Orleans; use as annuals. 1875.

Leucojum L. species **SNOWFLAKE** Europe. Amaryllis family, bulb. Sun, fairly heavy shade. Not picky as to soil conditions, though good drainage and high organic content is recommended; mine have done fine in a low, sometimes mucky spot. Attractive foliage appears in winter, lasts through spring. Hardy in our area; popular for many years in the south; naturalizes readily. The large clumps should be left undisturbed for several years, divided when dormant (after the foliage dies back). There is confusion in the references as to which snowflake is the one commonly grown in New Orleans. This inconsistency of identification is noted by at least one other author (Lawrence, *A Southern Garden*). Plant the bulbs during September to December.

L. aestivum L. **SUMMER SNOWFLAKE** Blooms February to March in New Orleans. Daffodil-like foliage is 12 to 18 inches in height; blooms are small, white, pendulous, with green dots near the tip of each petal; 4 to 9 flowers can be borne on each stem, depending on the variety grown ('Gravetye' is more floriferous). This is the plant I see growing everywhere, including my garden, though some local references call it *L. vernum*. Two sources state that *L. aestivum* is sometimes sold as *L. vernum*, which is where the confusion may have originated.

L. vernum L. **SPRING SNOWFLAKE** Shorter foliage; blooms in early spring are on 6 to 9 inch stems, small white bells, also with green dots at each petal tip; 1 to 2 to each stem. Although *Time-Life* recommends this bulb for Zone 8 and above, a mixture of the two would be worth trying for a succession of bloom if you could could purchase them from a nursery which accurately identified the two separate species.

Lilium L., hybrids **LILY** (The "true" lilies) Lily family. Native to the Northern Temperate Zone around the world. Grows from a scaly bulb which must never be allowed to dry out. Plant ordered bulbs as soon as received. They like sun, but best in shade during the middle of the day in New Orleans. Need very good drainage, raised beds; fertile soil, slightly acid (except *L. candidum* which needs alkaline conditions); fertilize. Should be planted at a depth of 4 to 6 inches, except *L. candidum* which should be covered no more than 1 inch. Roots should be "kept cool" by planting them in a low ground cover such as sword ferns. Plant *L. candidum* in August or September, others in later fall or spring. *Time-Life* recommends digging these bulbs, refrigerating for eight weeks each winter to simulate the dormant phase. I have never done this. But, then the only lily which has repeatedly bloomed and multiplied in my garden is the one which my two "hands on" local references also laud: an Easter lily, *"the so-called 'Creole' bulbs,"* described in *Notes on Gardening in New*

Orleans, of 1921.   Others have lasted one to several years before disappearing.   They are all beautiful while they last. Regardless of whether the plants are supposed to be early, mid-seasonal, or late blooming, all lilies I have grown have bloomed in the spring and early summer.

The North American Lily Society classifies the bulbs in nine divisions based on flower form and origin: ancestral and geographical.   Most of the bulbs sold today are hybrids which make up the first eight divisions and are supposedly of easier culture than the wild species.   Here, I will list the two groups highly recommended to succeed in New Orleans, then others whose prognoses vary.

The "big name" in lily hybridizers is Jan de Graaff, a Dutchman whose farm in Oregon has created more new varieties than anyone else in the world.   I suggest his catalog for additional material.

L. longiflorum Thunb. **EASTER LILY**   Long white trumpets which usually bloom after Easter has passed when in the ground.   Many varieties are available, though the best for New Orleans, the "creole lily" probably must be obtained as a friendship plant.   I haven't seen it for sale.   Variety *eximium* (called variety *harrissii* in early sources) is THE Easter lily.   Foliage which pops up early may be susceptible to freeze damage.   Cover it.   I use inverted flower pots.   1895.

L. formosanum A. Wallace, also called *L. philippinense* Bak. variety *formosanum*, **FORMOSA LILY, PHILLIPPINE LILY, AUGUST LILY** Long trumpet shaped white blossoms in July, August, September.   Hilda Latapie has them in her garden where they have multiplied prolifically, bloom midsummer.   Recommended, but you will probably have to get plants or seeds from an old garden.   I have not found these bulbs offered for sale.   *Formosissima* was recommended, 1895.

Longiflorum Hybrids (Division 5) includes hybrids of the above two species.

L. auratum Lindl. **GOLDBAND LILY** Japanese natives; red-spotted white flowers, each with a yellow stripe down the center, late flowering. I have not tried them. Japan lilies, 1875.

L. candidum L. **MADONNA LILY** Origin is the Middle East, cultivated since 1500 B.C. Yellow throated, pure white flowers. August planting is necessary because the plant produces fall growth, spring bloom. They bombed in my garden. I never saw growth at all and have not tried again.

'Pink Perfection' is an Aurelian hybrid (Division 6). Long, pink trumpets on tall plants. Though my plant has produced one to two flowers, not the 15 to 20 promised, it has repeated several years and I like it. Later flowering.

L. regale E. H. Wils. **REGAL LILY** China, yellow-throated white flowers with purple outsides. Said to be tricky to grow. Super drainage and sun are the keys. I have not tried them.

L. speciosum Thunb. 'Rubrum' **SPECIOSUM LILY** Japan. Pink and white flowers with red spots, dark colored pollen, later blooming. One of my favorites. Repeated for me several years before disappearing. Mike McClung says his are working on their fifth year of repeat bloom in a raised bed with rich, loamy soil dug deep with a layer of sharp sand underneath.

L. superbum L. **TURK'S CAP LILY** Native American Lily which needs moist, acidic soil. Flowers are yellow to red with maroon spots. I haven't tried it. 1838.

L. X testaceum Lindl. **NANKEEN LILY** Said to be the earliest hybrid lily, with yellow, recurved petals spotted red. I have not tried it, but it is available; of historic as well as aesthetic interest if you are experimenting.

L. tigrinum L. **TIGER LILY** China; orange with black spots; gave Mrs. Latapie and me several seasons of bloom.

'Enchantment' is an Asiatic hybrid (Div. 1), one of whose parents is *L. tigrinum*. Flowers are nasturtium-red.

Repeated several years for me. I moved it to a new spot and lost it.

The two lilies which are native to Louisiana, **PINE LILY**, *L. catesbaei* Walt. and **CAROLINA LILY**, *L. michauxee* Poir., are on the endangered list for the state, tricky to transplant, and should be left alone.

Lycoris Herb. species (all also called **NAKED LADY, SPIDER LILY, SURPRISE LILY**) Amaryllis family, bulbs. China, Japan. Sun, light shade, very poor bloom in heavy shade. Need very good drainage; raised beds are good as they should be planted 4 inches deep. Cannot tolerate the heavy clay soil frequently found in our area: amend with sand and organic matter if necessary; fertilize with bone meal; Meerow feels that all *Lycoris* benefit from year round moisture, even while dormant. Popular names derive from the fact the bare flower stalks shoot up from nowhere in the autumn, produce brightly colored flowers with long protruding anthers, and are followed by clumps of arching leaves which wither before summer. Bulbs will become overcrowded and protrude above the surface, diminishing bloom; need to be divided every six years or so. *L. africana* and *L. radiata* are very common in the ground in New Orleans, but one source feels bloom is even more profuse in pots. They should be planted in less heavy and competitive ground covers. Mine disappeared in *Liriope*, proliferates in ajuga. Plant October through April.

L. africana (Lam.) M. J. Roem., *L. aurea* **HURRICANE LILY** Golden-yellow blooms in September. My favorite stand of these is on Jefferson near St. Charles Avenue. Not as reliable a bloomer as *L. radiata* here. Odenwald and Turner feel bloom is better after a dry summer and fall.

L. albiflora G. Koidz. (sometimes listed as *L. alba*) creamy white to light rose blooms in August and September.

L. incarnata Comes ex Sprenger. Salmon to bright rose blooms.

L. radiata (L'Her.) Herb. Coral-red blooms in September and early October. Stewart and Oser feel these bloom better after a wet August, suggest watering if nature does not. Sold by Sisters' Bulb Farm. See RESOURCES.

L. squamigera Maxim. **AMARYLLIS HALLII, HARDY AMARYLLIS, MAGIC LILY** Beautiful fragrant, lilac pink blooms in March. Similar to *A. belladonna* which is a better choice for our climate. Magic lilies are popular and widely available in catalogues. I succumbed during my early days of gardening and get beautiful foliage every year. I have been rewarded with the lovely flowers after a very cold winter, once in thirteen years. Maybe your luck will be different.

L. traubii Hayw. Brilliant orange-yellow color. Meerow states it is frequently sold erroneously as *L. aurea*. Blooms September, October. I think this is the one I have, sold as *L. aurea*, blooming in spectacular color in October.

Moraea Mill. species, **MORAEA**, also called *Dietes* species. South Africa. Iris family, corms. Sunlight, part shade. Succession of 2 day blooms in spring and early summer form at the tip of the narrow, arrow-like, stiff foliage which forms attractive clumps. Foliage may die back in a freeze. Plant March-November.

M. tricuspidata (L.f.) G. J. Lewis, *M. glaucopsis* (DC) Drap. **PEACOCK IRIS** has white flowers with bluish-black petal bases, 1 inch; heaviest bloom in dry soil.

M. neopavonia R. Foster, *M. pavonia* (L.f.) Ker-Gawl. **PEACOCK IRIS** Flowers are red, purple, yellow, or white with dark blotches, 3 and one-half inches; dry soil best.

Muscari Mill. species **GRAPE HYACINTH** Asia minor, Southern Europe. Bulb, Lily family. Sun, shade. Regular garden soil; cool, moist site. Flowers in spring are blue or white, conical shaped clusters of blooms on spikes; each tiny bloom looks like a tiny ball. I have gotton best results by chilling the bulbs with my tulips for eight weeks before planting. I get repeat foliage, not bloom. Plant September-November.

Narcissus L. **NARCISSUS** This Amaryllis family genus includes the many bulbous plants popularly called narcissus, jonquil, and daffodil. Most are native to Europe, some to Asia minor, the orient. Many can be grown in New Orleans for a one-time show; only certain selections will repeat here for more than a couple of years. These are usually the early flowering types. Full sun to part shade is recommended; if you're naturalizing the bulbs, full sun is safest. As soon as an area becomes the slightest bit too shady, you'll lose your blooms. Very well-drained, sandy soil; fertilize with bone meal. Plant September through November; blooms in spring, January through March are white and shades of yellow and orange; peculiar fragrance which I love. Clumps are formed which, after several years need dividing, as flowering will diminish with crowding.

There has been much interbreeding with new varieties developed each year. Original lines are blurred, though "daffodil" should be applied only to large trumpet varieties descended from *N. pseudonarcissus* L.; "jonquil" to descendents of *N. jonquilla* L.; all may be called narcissus. The American Daffodil Society uses a classification system of eleven divisions to organize these plants. These follow with varieties which, according to personal experience and several sources should repeat and naturalize in New Orleans:

Division 1 (Trumpet Daffodils) one flower per stem: 'Mount Hood'. The famous 'King Alfred' and 'Unsurpassable' are in this group. They will not usually repeat bloom in New Orleans but are worth planting as annuals. Kids can't resist sniffing the big trumpets. It's fun to see them pull away with pollen-tipped noses.

Division 2 (Large cupped Daffodils) one flower per stem: 'Carbineer', 'Carlton', 'Fortune', 'Ice Follies'

Division 3 (Small cupped Daffodils) one flower per stem: no New Orleans recommendations. Maybe you'll find one which repeats.

Division 4 (Double Daffodils) more than one layer of petals, may have more than one flower per stem: 'Cheerfulness', 'Twink'.

Division 5 (Tiandrus Daffodils) pendant flowers, elongated cups, one to six per stem: 'Thalia'.

Division 6 (Cyclamineus Daffodils) petals flare backwards; long, slender trumpet: 'February Gold', 'Peeping Tom'.

Division 7 (Jonquilla) two to six flowers per stem, fragrant: 'Trevithian'.

Division 8 (Tazetta Daffodils) cluster flowered, fragrant: 'Geranium', 'Grand Soleil d'Or', 'Silver Chimes'

Division 9 (Poeticus Daffodils): Open for recommendations.

Division 10 (Species and Wild Forms and Wild Hybrids) usually cluster-flowered: *N. tazetta papyraceus* or 'Paperwhite'.

Division 11 (Split-Corona Daffodils and Miscellaneous): open for recommendations.

Some of the national bulb companies offer collections specifically for the south. I have tried one and not gotton 100 per cent repeat bloom. I recommend choosing specific varieties. There is now a Louisiana source of daffodil bulbs--all the ones sold are repeaters at Sisters' Bulb Farm in Gibsland, Louisiana near Ruston. See RESOURCES. 1838, 1884.

Neomarica T. Sprague (sometimes called *Marica*) **NEOMARICA, WALKING IRIS** Brazil. Iris family, rhizome. Sun, part shade. Moist, rich soil. Swordlike leaves in fan shaped clusters 15 to 18 inches tall. Long bloom period. New plants grow readily from the plantlets which form at the tops of flower stems. Can be damaged during severe freezes. Plant March-June.

N. caerulea (Ker-Gawl.) T. Sprague **TWELVE APOSTLES** Fragrant, 4 inch flowers, iris-like, blue with yellow, orange, and brown crests.

N. gracilis (Herb. ex Hook.) T. Sprague **WALKING IRIS** Common name comes from the fact that flowers form at the tips of the leaves which, weighted, tip to the ground and root. White, iris-like blooms with yellow, brown and blue markings.

N. longifolia (Link & Otto) T. Sprague **YELLOW WALKING IRIS** Yellow flowers. Mine came from a cutting from Nancy Weller's garden, seems to bloom all the time, returned from the roots after the severe freeze of Christmas, 1989.

N. northiana (Schneev.) T. Sprague **APOSTLE PLANT** Fragrant white flowers with violet inner segments. On the list of recommendations of the New Orleans Garden Society, Inc., 1921.

Nerine Herb. species **SPIDER LILY** South Africa. Amaryllis family bulbs. Light shade to sun. Any very well-drained soil and setting; require a dry period during dormancy to bloom, fertilize with superphosphate. Plant bulbs with necks barely exposed, clumps form, bloom best when crowded. Pot culture is recommended for all, though Meerow says *N. bowdenii* should naturalize in the coastal deep south. Spidery blooms on leafless stalks in September.

N. bowdenii W. Wats. **CAPE COLONY NERINE** Clusters of 6 to 12 rose-pink spider-like blooms on 18 inch stalks. Dormant and leafless in winter, the opposite of most *Nerines.*

N. sarniensis (L.) Herb. **GUERNSEY LILY** Bright red clusters of 10 blooms on 2 foot stalks. Leaves in winter, needs a dry period during summer dormancy.

Ornithogalum umbellatum L. **STAR OF BETHLEHEM** Europe. Lily family, bulb. Sun. Light, sandy, porous, fertile soil. 1 foot flower stalk with a cluster of white starlike flowers with outer segments striped green; they close at night. Long period of bloom in spring. Sources differ on whether they naturalize in New Orleans, or not. They should.

Oxalis L. species **OXALIS** Found worldwide. Bulbous, tuberous, or rhizomatous roots; Oxalis family. Sun, part sun. Best in moist, fertile soil, but they are not picky. Foliage is usually in clumps, leaves cloverlike. Very difficult to control or eradicate once planted. I have personal experience with only three of the below. Plant in fall. An unidentified species was offered by R. Maitre in 1875.

O. adenophylla Gillies **OXALIS** Chile, Argentina. One and one-half inch flowers in pink. These bloomed once, did not return for me.

O. crassipes Urb. **OXALIS** Probably native to South America. White or pink flowers.

O. deppei Lodd.ex Sweet **GOOD-LUCK PLANT** Mexico. Flowers are red or white.

O. hirta L. **OXALIS** South Africa. Violet, purple, white, or yellow flowers.

O. pes-caprae L., *O. cernua* **BERMUDA BUTTERCUP** South Africa. Showy, yellow flowers are 1 and one-half inches across.

O. purpurea L. **OXALIS** South Africa. Showy , 2 inch flowers in rose, violet, or white with yellow throats. Good for pot culture.

O. regnellii Miq. **OXALIS** South America. Green leaves with purple undersides, white flowers; recommended for cultivation in pots.

O. rubra St.-Hil. **OXALIS** Brazil; escaped cultivation; widespread in Louisiana. Pink to rose flowers with darker veins February to frost. A "weed" in my yard, I have accepted its presence as inevitable, appreciate its delicate flowers; find fault with the unsightliness of the leaves after attack by a disease which presents yellow growth on the undersides, shrivelled appearance above. 'Alba' has white flowers. Was this the species offered by R. Maitre in 1875?

O. stricta L. **YELLOW WOOD SORREL** Europe, found as a weed all over the U.S. The tiny yellow flowers are not that ornamental, but you will most likely see them whether you want to, or not; March-May.

Pancratium maritimum L. **SEA DAFFODIL** Mediterranean area: Spain to Syria. Amaryllis family, bulb. Sun. Sandy, rich soil with very good drainage. Foliage is evergreen; large, white, strongly sweet scented trumpeted flowers on two foot stems in summer. Also good for pot culture. 1895.

X pardancanda Norrisii **CANDY LILY**, offered by Park Seed Company, is a hybrid, which should do well in New Orleans, but has not for me more than one season.

Polianthes tuberosa L. **TUBEROSE** Mexico. Cultivated for so long it is not certain it can be found in the wild. Amaryllis family, tuber. Sun. Fertile, loose, well drained soil, lots of moisture. When planting in spring, push each tuber individually into the ground with the tip slightly protruding. Should be lifted, dried, and stored each year even though they would last the winter, here. They're cheap to purchase, so why bother? Need a long hot season such as we have to bloom. The summer blooms are waxy, white, and exceptionally fragrant ('Pearl' and 'Excelsior' are recommended forms). Fell from popularity after becoming associated with funerals. Each tuber blooms once only. Offsets form rapidly, but can take two years to reach blooming size. Essential for a fragrance garden. Grown by Thomas Jefferson in 1766. 1838, 1875.

Ranunculus asiaticus L. **PERSIAN BUTTERCUP** Southeastern Europe, Asia. Tuberous root, Ranunculus family. Sun. Loose, very well-drained soil; raised beds. Some suggest the same culture as for anemones. *Time-Life* recommends planting be done in bottomless clay pots set into the soil with the rims out one and one-half inches. This will assure soil which is dry around the crown but moist under the roots of the plant. Soak the tubers in water, plant them with their claws down. Plant in October or later for February to April bloom: double 2 to 5 inch flowers in yellow, orange, pink, red, white; many blooms from each plant. Use as an annual. Even if you do everything right, climatic variables can create unpredictable performance in this plant which is worth the trouble for the times you do achieve success. Betty Wood grows the prettiest ones I have ever seen except for Hilda Latapie's. Mrs. Latapie follows no one else's rules: she refrigerates her ranunculus (Giant Strain) with her tulips, plants them in January. 1838, 1884.

Sparaxis tricolor (Curtis) Ker-Gawl, *S.* hybrids **HARLE-QUIN FLOWER, WAND FLOWER** South Africa. Iris family, corm, to 18 inches. Sun. Extremely well drained soil; pot culture is recommended because of our rainy summers. Corms must be kept dry after the foliage dies back. Blooms in spring are spikes of star shaped flowers with yellow throats in orange, red, copper, white, cerise, and yellow. Plant October-December. 1875.

Sprekelia formosissima (L.) Herb. **AZTEC LILY, JACO-BEAN LILY** Mexican. Amaryllis family, bulb. Sun, partial shade. Garden soil, very good drainage. Plant with the neck of the bulb out of the ground. Blooms better when crowded. If crowded and allowed to dry out occasionally, may bloom more than once a season. Flowers (see description in text) are rich red, appear in spring on 12 to 18 inch stems. Hardy to 20 degrees. Plant October-February. Good for pot culture

Strelitzia reginae Ait. **BIRD OF PARADISE** Subtropical South Africa. Rhizome, Strelitzia family. Sun. Sandy, humusy, fertile soil; fertilize (liquid manure recommended). Unusual orange and blue flowers over a long period from fall; banana-tree like leaves form large clumps to 3 or 4 feet. Hardy to 24 degrees. Plant March to September. Described in New Orleans gardens in 1849.

Tigridia pavonia (L.f.) DC. **TIGRIDIA, MEXICAN SHELL FLOWER** Mexico. Iris family, corm. Sun. Fertile garden soil; sandy, well-drained; lots of water while blooming; culture same as that of glads. Blooms from July are yellow, orange, pink, red, & white with spotted centers; each flower lasts a day, but several are produced by each stalk. Have not repeated for me when left in the ground through the winter. I think the corms rot. Plant March-June.

Triteleia laxa Benth. 'Queen Fabiola', also called *Brodieae laxa* SNAKELILY, ITHURIEL'S SPEAR Western North America. Amaryllis family, bulb. Sun. Rich, sandy soil; needs exceptionally good drainage to repeat here. Foliage is grassy. Flowers in spring are tubular, deep blue-violet, many per stem, about twelve inches high. Plant September-December.

Tulbaghia violacea Harv. SOCIETY GARLIC South Africa. Amaryllis family, bulb. Sun. Well-drained soil. Clumps of attractive evergreen foliage. Clusters of lilac colored flowers over a long period, spring through fall. Damage to foliage if temperature drops below 25 degrees, will return. I first saw them in Betty Wood's Metairie garden. Plant September-November, March-May.

Tulipa L. hybrids and species TULIP Most are natives of temperate areas of the Near East and Europe. Lily family, bulb. Sun. Sandy, well-drained, humusy soil; fertilize with bone meal. Spring bloom in New Orleans can be guaranteed only if the bulbs have been precooled (six to eight weeks of refrigeration, not freezing) before planting. Bulbs should not be stored in the same part of the refrigerator as fruit. Traditional planting time in New Orleans is between Christmas and New Year's. I usually order an economy mixture which offers a large number of bulbs for a cheaper price, plus smaller numbers of the exotic but more expensive varieties. I have been lucky with everything I have ordered, including Darwin Hybrids such as 'Apeldoorn' and others in many colors; 'Ballade', a gorgeous Lily-flowered tulip with petals of lavender edged with white; Greigii tulip 'Toronto', a bright, salmon pink; Darwins such as the dark purple 'Queen of the Night' and apricot 'Queen of Bartigons'. "Lucky" means expecting no more than one-time bloom. I do know people who say

they have allowed their tulip foliage to mature and die
back; dug, dried, and stored the bulbs; refrigerated and
replanted them the following year to get smaller blooms
on fifty per cent of the plants.   Is it worth it?   I was
excited to find a mixture of species tulips for naturalizing
in southern climates, since one of them, *T. clusiana*, has
repeated in Baton Rouge gardens.   The small, graceful,
wild blooms of *T. clusiana* DC, *T. clusiana* variety *chrysan-
tha*, *T. sylvestris* L., and *T. saxatilis* Sieber ex K. Spreng.
appeared one year, then no more.   I planted them in
perfect conditions, but my guess is that even with perfect
drainage and a dry year, New Orleans offered them more
moisture than they like.   Ordering different varieties of
tulips affords bloom over a longer period of time, as there
are early, midseason, and latebloomers.   The best sources
of tulip bulbs are the sale catalogs which are issued during bloom season for next year's planting.   The bulbs are
delivered in October to New Orleanians to allow for cooling.   We love tulips!   1838, 1884.

  Veltheimia viridifolia Jacq. **VELTHEIMIA** South Africa.
Lily family, bulbs. I found no data on light requirements.
Needs humusy, sandy soil; perfect drainage.   Three inch
wide strap like leaves from which arises a spike of showy,
pendulous flowers, pinkish purple with yellow spots; late
winter bloom.   Not widely grown in the U.S. except in
California, which makes me wonder if our heavy moisture
would be a problem; but one of my sources reports success with this "very unusual, very beautiful" plant.   For
pot culture, too.

  V. bracteata **WINTER RED HOT POKER260-261** is
offered for southern beds and borders by one catalogue.   I
cannot find this variety in my references so don't know if
it is another name for *V. viridifolia* or something else.

  Watsonia Mill. species and hybrids **WATSONIA, BU-
GLE LILY** South Africa. Corm, Iris family. Sun. Fertile
garden soil; sandy, well-drained; keep moist while growing, need dry soil while dormant.   Blooms in early spring

are bugle shaped on spikes; pink, red, white, lavender, orange. Clump-forming. Mine were beautiful one year, but no more. They repeat well for Hilda Latapie. Plant September-November. Grown at Monticello in 1766.

Zantedeschia K. Spreng. **CALLA LILY** South Africa. Arum family, tuberous rooted perennial. Spring flowers. Bloom best in sun, grow in partial shade; southern exposure best, with protection from summer afternoon sun and winter winds. Lots of water; cool, loose, slightly acid, fertile soil; additional feeding important: either monthly through the growing season with a commercial preparation or through the use of aged manure placed around the plant to be watered in by rains. Mary Stewart and Helen Oser suggest the use of bottom heat: plant the roots over a heavy layer of manure topped with a layer of sand or sandy soil. Blooms in spring and early summer consist of attractive, 4 to 6 inch long spathes wrapped around a long yellow spadix like paper around a bouquet; foliage is arrowshaped, Arum style, 18 to 36 inches tall, dark green. Will die to the ground in a freeze, should return from the roots; may not bloom the season after a freeze. May not bloom heavily until established several years. Plant November to April.

Z. aethiopica (L.) K. Spreng, the **COMMON CALLA,** has white flowers. *Z. albomaculata* (Hook.) Baill., the **SPOTTED CALLA** has creamy white spathes with purple throats; leaves spotted white. *Z. elliottiana* (W. Wats.) Engl., the **GOLDEN CALLA,** has six inch yellow flowers. *Z. rehmannii* Engl., the **RED** or **PINK CALLA** is a foot high plant with white-spotted leaves, four-inch red or pink flowers.

Zephyranthes Herb. species **RAIN LILY** Southern U.S., Mexico, South America. Amaryllis family, bulbs. Sun, part shade. Fertile, well-drained soil, lots of water. Foliage is grass-like; flowers are small, funnel-shaped, colorful; appear May to September, especially after rain.

Naturalize readily in New Orleans. Most common here are Z. *candida* and Z. *grandiflora*. Plant October-February.

Z. X *ajax* Hort. is yellow. Z. *atamasco* (L.) Herb. is a U.S. native with white blooms March to April. Z. *candida* (Lindl.) Herb. is from Argentina, Uruguay; has escaped cultivation, is frequently found wild. It produces white flowers April to May. Z. *citrina* Bak., South America, produces fragrant yellow flowers in midsummer. Z. *grandiflora* Lindl.; Mexico, Guatemala, its large pink blooms are produced, spring and summer.

Zingiber zerumbet (L.) PINE CONE GINGER, SHAMPOO PLANT India. Rhizome, Ginger family. Sun, part shade. Moist, rich, organic soil. Foliage to 6 feet; bloom is a cone of green to red bracts which persist after the small yellowish-white blooms appear briefly in summer on a foot long stalk; when squeezed they ooze a fluid which smells like shampoo. Plant March to November.

BULBOUS PLANTS BY SEASON OF BLOOM

BULBOUS PLANTS FOR SPRING BLOOM

Alpinia zerumbet, Alpinia speciosa SHELL GINGER
Anemone coronaria GARDEN ANEMONE, WINDFLOWER
Arisaema triphyllum JACK-IN-THE-PULPIT
Camassia species CAMASSIA
Clivia miniata, Clivia hybrids KAFIR-LILY
Crocus species CROCUS
Curcuma species HIDDEN LILY, SURPRISE LILY
Endymion hispanicus, Scilla campanulata
     SPANISH SQUILL, SPANISH BLUEBELL
Fritillaria meleagris GUINEA HEN FLOWER, TOAD LILY
Galanthus nivalis SNOWDROP
Hippeastrum hybrids AMARYLLIS
Hyacinthus orientalis and hybrids DUTCH HYACINTH
Ipheion uniflorum SPRING STARFLOWER
Iris species BULBOUS IRISES
Iris species RHIZOMATOUS IRISES
Ixia hybrids AFRICAN CORN LILY
Leucojum species SNOWFLAKE
Muscari species GRAPE HYACINTH
Ornithogalum umbellatum STAR OF BETHLEHEM
Ranunculus asiaticus PERSIAN BUTTERCUP
Sparaxis tricolor, Sparaxis hybrids HARLEQUIN or WAND FLOWER
Sprekelia formosissima AZTEC LILY, JACOBEAN LILY
Triteleia laxa 'Queen Fabiola,'or
     Brodieae laxa SNAKELILY, ITHURIEL'S SPEAR
Tulipa hybrids and species TULIP
Watsonia species and hybrids WATSONIA, BUGLE LILY

BULBOUS PLANTS FOR SPRING-SUMMER BLOOM

Agapanthus africanus, or *A. umbellatus*
     LILY OF THE NILE, AGAPANTHUS
Albuca nelsonii ALBUCA
Allium species ALLIUM
Alstroemeria species PERUVIAN LILY
Xamarcrinum (Amaryllis X Crinum) CRINODONNA
Belamcanda chinensis BLACKBERRY LILY
Bletilla striata BLETILLA, CHINESE GROUND ORCHID
Caladium bicolor, Caladium X hortulanum CALADIUM
Crinum species CRINUM
Crocosmia X crocosmiiflora MONTBRETIA
Dietes species DIETES
Erythronium californicum DOGTOOTH VIOLET, TROUT LILY
Eucharis grandiflora AMAZON LILY
Gladiolus X hortulanus GARDEN GLADIOLUS
Gloriosa rothschildiana GLORIOSA LILY, CLIMBING LILY
Habranthus tubispathus, H. robustus RAIN LILY
Habranthus texanus COPPER LILY
Hymenocallis species SPIDER LILY
Lilium species and hybrids LILY
Moraea species MORAEA, PEACOCK IRIS
Oxalis species OXALIS
Pancratium maritimum SEA DAFFODIL
Tulbaghia violacea SOCIETY GARLIC
Zantedeschia species CALLA LILY

BULBOUS PLANTS FOR SUMMER-FALL BLOOM

Acidanthera bicolor ACIDANTHERA
Amaryllis belladonna BELLADONNA LILY,
    AMARYLLIS BELLADONNA
Caladium bicolor, Caladium X hortulanum CALADIUM
Canna species CANNA
Costus speciosus SPIRAL GINGER
Crinum species CRINUM
Dahlia hybrids DAHLIA
Galtonia candicans SUMMER HYACINTH
Habranthus tubispathus, Habranthus robustus RAIN LILY
Habranthus texanus COPPER LILY
Hedychium species HEDYCHIUM
Hedychium coccineum RED GINGER LILY
Hedychium coronarium BUTTERFLY GINGER
Hedychium flavum YELLOW BUTTERFLY GINGER
Hedychium gardneranum KAHILI GINGER
Haemanthus katharinae, Haemanthus multiflorus BLOOD LILY
Lily formosanum, L. philippinense variety *formosanum,*
    PHILLIPPINE LILY, AUGUST LILY
Lycoris species NAKED LADY, SPIDER LILY,
    SURPRISE LILY
Nerine species SPIDER LILIES
Polianthes tuberosa TUBEROSE
Strelitzia reginae BIRD OF PARADISE
Tigridia pavonia TIGRIDIA, MEXICAN SHELL FLOWER
Tulbaghia violacea SOCIETY GARLIC
Zephyranthes species RAIN LILY

Nancy Weller

Native
Trees and Shrubs

"Whereas the live oak is one of GOD's creatures that has been keeping quiet for a long time, just standing there contemplating the situation without having very much to say, but only increasing in size, beauty, strength, and firmness day by day without getting the attention and appreciation that it merits from its anthropomorphic fellow-mortals and;

"Whereas it has been found that organization and publication are a good means of promoting influence and service in the world; therefore

"This Constitution for an universal association of Live Oaks is hereby ordained and established."

Preamble, Constitution of the Live Oak Society

For years I heard about the club whose members were live oak trees (*Quercus virginiana*), venerated because of their great age. I knew Society membership was a BIG DEAL and that members were held in great esteem. Mention of *Querci* such as the Locke Breaux Oak of Hahn-ville was in tones of reverence. Until its death in 1966 it was the largest oak in Louisiana and president of the Society. Tour guides pointed out esteemed members of the Society on their rounds. Heirs of late and legendary New Orleans preservationist Martha Robinson, as instruc-ted by her will, scattered some of her ashes under the Society member bearing her name on the grounds of Madewood Plantation.

All the obvious questions ran through my mind:
How and where were meetings held?   Did the president
attend?   How was membership attained?   I had a strong
suspicion that human intervention was involved somewhere along the line.   It was more fun not to know until
I began this chapter.

Pat and Dick Johnson's live oak, Chesne, on the corner of Constance and Upperline, wanted to join.   Inves-
tigative phone calls led me from the Cooperative Extension
Service to Edith Pfister, long time past chairman.   She
giggled a little as she referred me on to Mrs. Verlyn
Bercegeay, present chairman and the only human member
of the Society.

The Live Oak Society was founded in 1934 for the
*"promotion of the culture, distribution and appreciation of the
live oak."*   Dr. Edwin Lewis Stephens, President of the
University of Southwestern Louisiana, volunteered his
services as Acting Secretary to assist in formation of the
organization.

Members are live oak trees whose girth, measured
four to four and one-half feet from the ground, is an
average of 16 feet, indicating greater than a century of
age.   There is also a Junior League for trees possessing
"honorable qualifications" but lesser girth.

Officers of the Society include a President, *"some vice-
presidents,...a committee of Elders, and ...a group of illustrious
individual specimens."*

Meetings are *"...held somewhere, semi-occasionally."*

Bylaw number eight is an injunction against "Quer-
cocide", or the killing of live oak trees.   Members are to
be protected from having nails driven into their trunks
and from being whitewashed, a practice of earlier years.

The above standards and more are   defined in the
Constitution and By-Laws of the Live Oak Society which
is presently sponsored by the Louisiana Garden Club
Federation, Inc. From its Louisiana base, membership has

expanded to include over 1900 members in eight states from North Carolina to Texas.

Though today Audubon Park has only five active members, the roster of first officers of the Society included two from there: The George Washington Oak, Second Vice-President (31 feet, 4 inches in circumference at its death in 1974), and The Martha Washington Live Oak, Fourth Vice-President (28 feet, 6 and one-half inches in 1979). There are 245 Society members in City Park which *"houses the largest and most significant collection of mature live oaks in the world."*[35] The Seven Sisters Oak in Mandeville, Louisiana (37 feet), installed in 1968, presides over the Society today.

On Thanksgiving Day, November 24, 1988, in the presence of Pat and Claire Johnson, myself, and Terry Hynes of Atlanta, Dick Johnson and my husband, Jean measured Chesne. She is 15 feet, 4 inches with an 80 foot spread. Thanks to Verlyn Bercegeay, Chesne is now an esteemed member of the Junior League of The Live Oak Society (certificate # 1917). I'll bet she never thought she would achieve such stature in 1915, when she was photographed as a sapling watching trolleys pass on Constance Street! The Johnsons have asked me to be the sponsor. I am deeply honored.

Because of their longevity, trees seem a tie to other times, both past and future. The John McDonough Oak in City Park is thought to be between 600 and 1000 years old. Chesne may be on Constance and Upperline 600 years from now. Remember the furor that was aroused when live oaks were cut down for construction and roadway enlargement on Claiborne Avenue? Though I am not aware of a society for trees other than of live oaks, there is a general affection and reverence for the huge plants that are trees.

Everyone can recite *"I think that I shall never see a poem lovely as a tree...."* The Parkway Commission Report of 1949 described West End Park:

A center row of Magnolia grandiflora trees was planted and dedicated to Joyce Kilmer, the American poet who wrote "Trees." These native magnolias were purchased from an old plantation, long since abandoned, on the West side of the Mississippi River. They cost but $1.50 each.

Arbor Day, a holiday for planting trees, was first celebrated on the treeless plains of Nebraska in 1872 by Julius Sterling Morton who had an interest in nature and missed the forests of the east. Now a tradition in all fifty states (in Louisiana since 1888), Arbor Day is observed in Louisiana on the third Friday in January. New Orleans schools who are members of Parkway Partners are each given a tree to plant on this day.

Aside from their ornamental value, trees are important for the shade they offer, for their role in preventing erosion, and for their assistance in reoxygenating the air. Carbon dioxide and water are raw materials in the process of photosynthesis during which the plant manufactures carbohydrates for food. Oxygen is an important byproduct. With the deforestation and possibly related climatic changes occurring worldwide, the planting of trees becomes even more important. The Arbor Day Foundation and other organizations are gearing up to encourage replanting of trees as a possible antidote to the "greenhouse effect."

Trees and shrubs are either deciduous or evergreen, depending on whether they lose their leaves or not in the fall. The term "evergreen", to me, implies the narrow-leaved varieties, such as conifers. In the south, there are many broad-leaved evergreens, such as the magnolia, myrtle, cherry laurel, ligustrum, pyracantha, and azalea.

The latest tree care theories for home gardeners are described in an article in *American Horticulturist* (September, 1988). They propose creating a situation for the transplant which will allow for the development of a wide, broad root system. In a healthy tree, the roots can extend one and one-half to three times its dripline (the circle formed by water dripping from the outermost leaves and branches of the tree).

1. Dig a satellite-dish shaped hole two to three times the the root ball width. Work soil in for an area beyond to encourage root growth in the right directions. The traditional deep hole is not recommended because it duplicates the containerized conditions of the nursery-grown plant.

2. Transplant your tree at the same level in which it grew in the nursery, or slightly above, on a slight mound of soil. Planting too deeply can cause roots to grow upward.

If the soil around an established tree is disturbed, as by heavy equipment during construction, its root system can be damaged. This can happen if the grade around the tree is lowered and feeder roots in the upper 6 to 8 inches are exposed, if soil is added, covering the feeder roots too deeply, or if soil is heavily packed by construction equipment. In any case, the tree may begin a slow decline leading to death. Louisiana Cooperative Extension's *Protecting Shade Trees Around Your New Home* says: *"It is possible to fill up to 4 inches of a light sandy-loamy soil without killing your trees."* Some trees, such as magnolias, are even more sensitive. Belle Chasse gardener, Be Boe, lost a beautiful live oak to an encircling flower bed which seemed like a good idea when she first thought of it. Once she realized that the layer of soil which supported pansies and caladiums was smothering the roots, it was too late. The tree was dying.

3. Do not amend the soil, as this also creates a situation which mimics a nursery pot, further restricting root spread. However, you must use your judgement. If your soil is hard clay, you have no choice but to work in sand and organic matter.

4. Choose smaller, younger trees. They have an easier time adapting to new environments, so are a better choice than giants. They also cost less.

5. Wait until a year after planting to fertilize a tree. Fertilization may stimulate new growth which cannot be supported.

If a tree or shrub which needs adjustment of pH, is planted, soil modifications may be necessary. This is a reason to give careful consideration to your choice of plants. Complete soil replacement in beds where azaleas, camellias, and hollies are to be planted is standard, and required to provide the acidic medium those plants need to flourish. The same practice for larger trees is very difficult. Information on pH is given in the following plant lists. Some acid-loving plants may be natives growing at the edges of swamps and very well suited to our climate. Your garden or a spot in it may be just right, or you may need to make some changes or choose another plant.

Aluminum sulfate or sulfur will increase acidity. One of them can be worked into the soil to a depth of eighteen inches over a wide enough area to encompass spreading tree roots. Test soil periodically to see if it has reverted to its natural pH and retreat it if it has. As a shrub or tree grows larger, and roots begin to extend into the unaltered soil, problems begin. This is hypothesized to be one of the reasons the beautiful flowering dogwood does not generally do well in New Orleans. Mulch with acidic pine or oak leaves to help maintain the right conditions.

Plants are either monoecious or dioecious, meaning the male flower, which produces pollen, and female which receives pollen are on the same plant or on different ones. In a fruiting tree, whether the fruit is for people, wildlife, or ornament, it is a reason for selecting that species over another. But if the tree is dioecious, two specimens, male and female, are necessary for fruit production to take place. The hollies are the best known examples of dioecious shrubs. Ask your nurseryman whether a fruit bearing tree needs a mate before you buy it.

Local nurseries' stock should be a good indicator of what grows locally, but do some research in other places, too. Your choices may be with you for a while. Literature and catalogs are a source for exotic ideas, local gardens and gardeners are indispensible for accurate data on what grows, and how well it grows in New Orleans. Nurseries are businesses and this fact can affect some of their choices of stock. For instance, a shrub which can be propagated easily and quickly produces many offspring for cheap sale may be more financially lucrative than a slower growing plant. But the less quickly reproduceable shrub may have more ornamental pluses: fruit, attractive foliage, autumn color. Just because plants such as spirea are prevalent does not mean the choice was made by gardeners. It may have been a nurseryman's, and his motive may not have been expansion of plant possibilities.

Though the cold hardiness of a plant is an important factor in whether or not it will thrive in a given area, it is not always the only determining factor. Tolerance of the long, hot and humid summers and limited winters experienced in New Orleans is frequently not reflected in recommendations by mail order nurseries and non-regional literature. There are trees and shrubs which easily live through our coldest temperatures, but do not do their best in our climate because they need a longer period of cold. These plants can exhibit poor disease resistance, sporadic bloom over a longer period rather than intense, briefer bloom, failure to flower as prolifically overall, shorter overall lifespan. You may consider some shrubs so beautiful at their worst that you will choose them, anyway.

Some tropical shrubs will not last through temperatures in the 20's. Though our experience of severe freezes is not frequent, it happens and plants are lost. I offer them anyway because:

1. Some trees/shrubs become less tender as they grow older.

2. In the right spot with the right conditions and protection, a tender tree may make it through harsh weather.
3. Many trees which fall into this category are so beautiful as to be worth the risk of eventual loss. Our "bad" freezes have occurred about every ten years in the past. That's a long time to enjoy a bottlebrush, a silk oak, or a jacaranda.

Before you become too carried away with exotic trees and shrubs, I suggest a basic plan of natives or proven imports so that your poplar performs when your deutzia or duranta doesn't. To allow an easy choice and balance of "safes" and natives, and exotica, I provided a separate chapter for the latter.

The difference between trees and shrubs is supposed to be that shrubs are smaller and have multiple trunks. Some "shrubs" can reach great size and can be trained to "standard" form with a single trunk, and some trees can remain small. Some plants have varying habits and are classified as "trees or shrubs". These inconsistencies are reflected in the lists. When you choose a tree or shrub, consider its ultimate height and spread. It can be helpful to see specimens in established plantings to give you an idea of what your sapling may eventually become. The heights given in the following lists are either the ultimate under perfect conditions or an average. Use these numbers for a general idea of where a plant should be fit into your overall garden scheme. It can be helpful, also, to find out how long it will take the plant to get to its ultimate height. The New Orleans Parkway and Parks Commission can make recommendations of species of trees appropriate for planting near streets, curbs, or sidewalks; as well as planting and maintainence information. Call them. Visit Crosby Arboretum or City Park to see established plants.

Almost all of the following trees and shrubs bloom sometime during spring. Palms and palmettoes follow.

NATIVE TREES & SHRUBS
FOR THE NEW ORLEANS GARDEN

1859 Indicates listing in the catalogue of plants offered for sale by John M.
Nelson at Magnolia Nurseries at Metairie Ridge and at his Plant Depot,
Corner of Camp St. & Lafayette Sq., New Orleans.

1885 Indicates listing in the 1885 *Maitre & Cook Catalogue of Southern Grown Plants*, nurseries on St. Charles at Lower Line.

1921 Indicates inclusion in lists of recommended plants by the New Orleans
Garden Society, Inc. in *Notes on Gardening in New Orleans*. From
Stephen Hand, pp. 183-187.

1935 Indicates listing in *"The Aristocrats of the New Orleans Gardens"* compiled
by landscape architect William A.Wiedorn. From Stephen Hand, pp. 188.

1947 Indicates listing in *Trees, Vines, and Shrubs of New Orleans* which described
plants used in City Parks, Parkways.

DECIDUOUS TREES

Acer rubrum variety *drummondii* (Hook & Arn. ex Nutt.) Sarg. **SWAMP RED MAPLE** Maple family. Southeast U.S., Louisiana swamps. 40 feet. Found in low, moist soils; dryer soils acceptable. Leaves are fuzzy underneath, turn yellow and red in fall. Small but abundant red flowers on female trees in early spring, followed by winged fruit. Silvery-gray bark. A fast growing, relatively short-lived, and very beautiful tree. Nesting site for birds; blossoms attract bees. Other maples are available, but not as well suited to our climate and drainage. 1859.

Amelanchier arborea (Michx.f.) Fern. **SERVICEBERRY** Rose family. Eastern U.S., Louisiana. 10 feet. Sun, part shade. Moist, well-drained soil, slightly acid. Oval, pointed leaves with serrated edges, gray, and with seasonally varying hairiness on upper and lower surfaces. Blooms in March, April are small, in fragrant, white clusters. Purple berries follow in long, drooping clusters; food for birds, small mammals.

Betula nigra L. **RIVER BIRCH** Birch family. Eastern U. S., Louisiana, though not on the Mississippi floodplain. 60 feet. Acid, sandy, moist soil best; adaptable. Finely toothed-edged leaves to 3 inches are symetrically veined, whitish underneath. Bark is papery, reddish-brown, peels off young trees in pretty patterns; becomes scaly in older trees. Catkin flowers followed by winged fruits in spring. Subject to diseases, problems, which can occur when the tree becomes older. Mockingbirds like to nest in the ones the Jordan's planted next door to us.

Carya illinoinensis (Wangenh.) C. Koch **PECAN** North America, Louisiana. Walnut family, 150 feet. Best in rich, moist, deep soil. Long, thin leaflets yellow in fall, late to emerge in spring. The nuts, which everybody knows, are good food for wildlife, people. A good shade tree.

Catalpa bignonioides Walt. **CATALPA** Southeast U.S. Bignonia family, 60 feet. Sun, part shade; any soil. Large, heart-shaped leaves. Beautiful, thick clusters of white, ruffly edged flowers with purple spots and yellow lines in March, April; followed by long seed pods. Host plant for the catalpa moth whose larvae are good fish bait, even though they can denude the tree of leaves. I found a catalpa on State Street near Freret in April by the carpet of fallen flowers on the pavement below. I was startled to find such decorative flowers on a tree so basic. 1859.

Celtis laevigata Willd. **HACKBERRY** North America, Louisiana. Elm family, 100 feet. Grows anywhere. Bright green leaves turn yellow in fall; gray, warty trunk. The nutlike fruits which turn from orange to purple are eaten by 10 or more species of birds. Birds like this tree for nests, too. Easily damaged by wind, either split or up-rooted. Many people call it a "trash tree." I think a big tree is better than no tree. My kids and I used ours for shade, climbing, hanging swings and plants until the wind blew it over into Dr. Leggio's yard, making room for a rose garden.

Cephalanthus occidentalis L. **BUTTONBUSH** North America, Louisiana. Madder family, shrub or tree, 20 feet. Sun, part shade. Fertile, humusy, very moist soil; is naturally found in marshes and is in standing water part of the year. Clusters of 2 inch, round, fragrant, creamy-white flowers with protruding stamens like pins in a cushion, June to September. Foliage becomes raggedy due to chomping insects who love its leaves. A bee plant.

Cercis canadensis L. **RED BUD, JUDAS TREE** Eastern U.S. Pea family, 40 feet. Sun, part sun. Well-drained, rich soil, slightly acid. Heart-shaped, 4 inch leaves turn yellow in fall. Clusters of rose-pink blossoms cover the bare branches in February-March, before leaves appear. Flat seed pods follow. Only lives to 20 years in New Orleans and is susceptible to some diseases. Its beauty makes it worth the trouble. Early blooms are appreciated by bees and winter hummers. 1921.

Chionanthus virginicus L. **FRINGE TREE, GRANCY GRAYBEARD** Eastern U.S., Louisiana. Olive family, 20 feet. Sun, part shade. Fertile, moist but well-drained, acidic soil. 6 to 8 inch clusters of pendulous, fragrant, white flowers appear in April; larger on the male trees than female. On females, bloom is followed in September by clusters of dark blue berries. Late to produce leaves in the spring. Fruits are wildlife food. 1859, 1885.

Cornus drummondii C. A. Mey. **ROUGH-LEAF DOG-WOOD** North America, Louisiana. Dogwood family, 15 feet. Sun or shade. Can handle heavy, wet soils. Leaves are purple in fall. Blooms in April are tiny white flowers in flat clusters. Not as showy as regular dog-wood, but easier to grow, produces small, white berries which are good food for wildlife. Specimens planted in Brechtel Park in Algiers.

C. florida L. **FLOWERING DOGWOOD** American native, found in Louisiana uplands. Part shade; full sun in our hot climate can cause leaf disfigurement. Moist but well drained, loose, acid soil. Tricky to grow in New Orleans: in the wrong pH, in disturbed topsoil, in highly fertilized soils, in the *"hot stress environments of city conditions."*[36] Beautiful in bloom, its flowers in March and April are actually small yellow clusters in the center of four white bracts, followed by red berries. Pink to reddish forms are found, also. When well grown, leaves are emerald green and profuse. Healthy specimens are to be found here and there in New Orleans, as on Leontine off Prytania. Small specimens transplant more successfully. 1859.

Crataegus marshallii Eggl. **PARSLEY HAWTHORNE** Eastern U.S., Louisiana. Rose family, 25 feet. Adaptable to many soil and light conditions, best in part sun, well-drained soil. Incised leaves reminiscent of parsley, yellow in fall; thorny branches. Half inch white to pink clustered flowers in March, April as the young leaves appear. Clusters of red berries follow, last beyond the leaves into autumn, are food for birds and squirrels. Nest site for birds. The most ornamental of the hawthornes for New Orleans planting.

C. opaca Hook. and Arn. **MAYHAW** Eastern U.S., Louisiana. 20 feet. Sun, part sun. Adaptable, but found in wet, acidic soils. 3 inch long, thin leaves; dark green on top, rusty colored and hairy along the veins below. Thorns on newer growth. Clusters of one inch, purple-anthered, white flowers February to March. Followed May to June by small orange berries which are edible: in jellies for people, raw for wildlife. Good nesting and shelter tree for animals.

C. viridis L. **HOGHAW, GREEN HAWTHORNE** Eastern U.S., Louisiana. 40 feet. Sun. Tolerates heavier soil. 2 inch, oblong leaves, wider at the middle, serrated edges; thorns on juvenile growth. Clusters of small white flowers in March, followed by orange or scarlet berries in fall. Food, nestsites for birds.

Diospyros virginiana L. **PERSIMMON** Eastern U.S., Louisiana. Ebony family, 40 feet. Sun. Deep, moist soil best, tolerates dry. 5 inch long, oblong pointy-tipped leaves, shiny and dark green tops; fuzzy bottoms; yellow, red in fall. Bell-shaped female flowers, clustered male; dioecious, so two trees are needed for the 1-2 inch yellow-orange fruit, edible by people or animals.

Fraxinus pennsylvanica Marsh. **GREEN ASH** Eastern North America, Louisiana. Olive family tree, 60 feet. Best in rich, moist soil, but adaptable; found in poorly drained swamp edges. Leaves composed of seven narrow leaflets, dark green; yellow, purple in fall. Small flowers in March, followed by 2 inch long winged seeds. Good for shade, fast growing. Nestsite for birds. Parkway and Park landscapers consider this tree underrated for New Orleans, as well as *F. americana* L., **WHITE ASH**, and *F. tomentosa* Michx. f., **PUMPKIN ASH**. *F. velutina* Torr., **VELVET, ARIZONA ASH**, is a southwestern native, short lived here, but spectacularly chartreuse in early spring.
F. excelsior L. 'Pendula', **EUROPEAN ASH** was available as listed in Magnolia Nurseries catalogue, 1859.

Gleditsia triacanthos L. **HONEY LOCUST, SWEET LOCUST** Pea family, medium to fast growth to 140 feet. Sun, part shade. Any soil, including moderately wet. Compound leaves of fine leaflets, ferny texture. Large spines form on the branches. Small clusters of white flowers are followed by sword-like seedpods. Considered attractive, though lethal and messy by many. New cultivars are available which are thornless and almost seedless. The "unimproved" varieties were reputedly introduced in New Orleans gardens before 1800. Their spines offer safe nest sites for birds. Leaves are larval food for the silver spotted skipper, a small butterfly. Consider one for your wildlife garden. 1859.

Halesia diptera Ellis. **SILVERBELL** Southeast U.S., Louisiana. Storax family tree, 30 feet. Sun, part sun. Best in moist but well-drained, acid soil. 5 inch oval leaves, pointed at the end, slightly toothed; yellow in fall. Flowers, heavier in full sun, March to April, are 1 inch long, white bells issued in clusters of 3 to 6 among the new spring leaves. Oblong, 2 inch, sour-citrusy flavored fruit follows. Best view of the blooms is said to be from underneath the tree, looking up. Hummingbirds may visit. 1859.

Ilex decidua Walt. **POSSUM HAW**   See NATIVE EVERGREEN SHRUBS.

Liquidambar styraciflua L. **SWEET GUM** Eastern U.S., Louisiana. Witch Hazel family tree, 120 feet. Sun, light shade. Moist, rich, deep, and slightly acid soil. Star-shaped leaves with 5 to 7 points, seven inches wide, shiny-topped, maroon or yellow in winter. Yellowish clustered flowers in early spring develop into the one inch prickly balls which turn brown in autumn. Nest sites, food for birds, larval food plant of the luna moth.

Liriodendron tulipifera L. **TULIP TREE, YELLOW POP-LAR** Eastern U.S., Louisiana. Magnolia family tree, 200 feet. Sun. Moist, well-drained, deep soil, neutral to slightly acid. 4 lobed, broad leaves, 5 inches long; bright green, yellow in fall. Flowers (on trees greater than 7 years old) in March and April, are 2 inches, tulip shaped, greenish yellow with orange marks, fragrant. Good shade tree which becomes so tall the flowers are not that visible. Larval plant of the tiger swallowtail butterfly. One grows in the 4900 block of Constance Street. 1859, 1885.

Maclura pomifera (Raf.) C. K. Schneid. **OSAGE ORANGE, BOIS D'ARC** Arkansas, Texas, possibly north-west Louisiana; long cultivated. Mulberry family, fast-growing, to 40 feet. Sun. Rich, moist soil is best; will grow in poor, alkaline. 4 inch leaves are glossy, dark above while paler green below. Open form, pendulous branches, thorny new growth. Dioecious; round, inedible, rough-textured, 5 inch yellow-green fruit on the female trees. Furrowed trunk, orange wood used by Indians for making bows. Traditionally popular clipped, used as hedges. Food for wildlife. Reported in Henry Lawrence's Louisa Street garden in 1841-1866. 1859, 1885.

Morus rubra L. **RED MULBERRY, AMERICAN MUL-BERRY** U. S., Louisiana. Mulberry family, to 60 feet. Sun, light shade. Moist, deep soil is best; will grow in almost any, even alkaline. Some of the 3 to 5 inch leaves are lobed. Small flowers are followed in late spring by one inch red berries, edible. Birds love them. Considered messy by some. There are fruitless varieties of mulberry. Do not buy them by mistake for your wildlife garden. See EXOTIC DECIDUOUS TREES for the WHITE MULBERRY.

Nyssa sylvatica Marsh. **BLACK GUM** Eastern U.S., Louisiana. Tupelo family, 100 feet. Sun, part sun. Rich, moist, slightly acid soil; with plenty of water through dry spells, it can handle any soil. Shiny green elliptical leaves to five inches, orange-red in fall. Dioecious; if both sexes present, small flowers are followed by clusters of dark blue, half inch fruit which the birds love.

N. aquatica L. **TUPELO GUM** 100 feet. Grows in swamps, needs very wet conditions to survive. Trunk is long and slender, tapering from a swollen base. 5 to 12 inch long leaves, oblong and pointed. Bees like the small yellow April flowers. Birds eat the dark purple, one inch long fruits which follow.

Platanus occidentalis L. **SYCAMORE, BUTTONWOOD TREE** U.S., Louisiana. Sycamore family, fast growing to 150 feet. Sun. Adaptable, though best in rich, moist, slightly acid soil. 10 inch leaves which yellow in fall. Fruit is 1 inch hanging brown balls of tightly packed seed clusters. Subject to diseases causing defoliation, shortened life span. My problem with it is that its leaves are too large to integrate well into my garden beds as mulch when they fall in autumn. They blow into my yard from a tree 2 blocks away and just sit there. Nest sites for birds. Reputed to have been planted in Place d'Armes, early 1700's. 1859.

Populus deltoides Bartr. ex Marsh. **COTTONWOOD, POPLAR** Southeast U.S., Louisiana. Willow family, 90 feet. Sun. Adaptable, though rich, moist soil is best. Triangular, dark green leaves to 7 inches, toothed edges. Dioecious, male flowers are drooping, reddish catkins; female are pods which release a cottony material. Fast growing, short lived, trees whose fibrous roots can force

their way into sewage lines and into moist beds to compete with garden plants. Given space, they are pretty
trees, good nest sites for birds, very easy to grow.

P. heterophylla L. **SWAMP COTTONWOOD** is native
to our swamps. Its leaves are greyish underneath.

Prunus americana Marsh. **WILD PLUM** Eastern U.S.,
Louisiana. Rose family, 25 feet. Sun. Needs well-drained
soil. Willowlike, 4 inch, finely toothed leaves. Profuse
display of white, unpleasant smelling, one inch flowers in
February; one inch yellow-red fruits summer, fall. Jellies,
wildlife food.

P. mexicana S. Wats. **MEXICAN PLUM**   Southeast
U.S., Louisiana. 20 feet. Sun. Rich, moist soil, good
drainage. Simple, yellow-green leaves, open, irregular
form. One inch pale pink flowers precede the leaves in
March. One and a half inch purple red fruit in August.
Wildlife food.

P. serotina J. F. Ehrh. **BLACK CHERRY** Eastern U.S.,
Louisiana. 80 feet. Sun, part sun. Acid soil, rich and
moist. Graceful form, foliage described as "lustrous" by
several sources. Profusion of white flowers in drooping
clusters in March. Dark purple, one third inch fruit in
summer; used to make "Cherry Bounce." Birds love them.

Quercus falcata **SOUTHERN RED OAK,** *Q. nigra* **WA-
TER OAK,** *Q. phellos* **WILLOW OAK,** incorrectly called
PIN OAK, see listing under NATIVE EVERGREEN TREES.

Robinia pseudoacacia L. **BLACK LOCUST** East and
Central U.S. Pea family, 80 feet. Sun, part shade. Any
moist, well-drained soil. 14 inch, fine-textured leaves with
many oval, 1 to 2 inch leaflets, thorns at the base of each.
White, fragrant clusters of sweetpea shaped flowers in
spring. Flat, reddish-brown seed pods follow. Pink-flow-
ered cultivars are available, too.

Salix nigra Marsh. **BLACK WILLOW**   Central and
eastern U.S., Louisiana. 5 inch narrow willow-leaves on a
tree upright, frequently leaning and irregular in form.
Same requirements and wildlife attraction as the weeping

willow. (See EXOTIC DECIDUOUS TREES for *Salix babylonica*, WEEPING WILLOW) 1859.

Sassafras albidum (Nutt.) Nees **SASSAFRAS** Eastern U. S., Louisiana. Laurel family tree, 60 feet. 5 inch oval or lobed leaves, turn brilliant yellow, orange, red in fall. Dioecious; female flowers are yellowish clusters which preceed the leaves in spring, are followed by small dark blue fruits on red stalks. We learned from the Choctaw Indians to crush the leaves to make gumbo file, extract oil from the roots to make a tea. A good wildlife tree. 1885.

Taxodium distichum (L.) L. Rich. **CYPRESS, BALD CYPRESS** East, southeast U.S., Louisiana. Taxodium family tree, 150 feet. Sun. Grows in wet soils, streamside; fine in well-drained garden soil, especially if acidic. The trunk is vertically ridged, broadens at the bottom as if to buttress the tree's great height in the swampy muck where it grows naturally; known for the protruberances from its roots called cypress knees. Half inch needles which give the branches a feathery appearance turn yellow in fall. Monoecious; pollen producing cones are clustered at the ends of branches, one inch purple-brown cones bear seeds. Louisiana's State tree. Major source of timber (now depleted) for most older construction in our geographic area. A lovely city tree. 1859.

Ulmus alata Michx. **WINGED ELM, SMALL-LEAVED ELM** Southeast U.S., Louisiana. Elm family tree, 50 feet. Sun. Rich, moist soil. Fine branches and 2 to 4 inch elliptic leaves with finely serrated edges give this elm a lacey look. Small pink flowers in early February, onethird inch "winged" seeds called samaras follow in May. (A samara is a seed enclosed in a paper-like envelope.) Seeds are edible by birds. Elms are also bird nest sites as well as larval food for some butterflies. 1859.

U. americana L. **AMERICAN ELM** Eastern North America to the Rockies, Louisiana. Fast growing to 120 feet. Dark, green leaves to 5 inches have strongly defined veins and serrated edges, turn yellow in fall. Considered one of the most attractive native ornamental trees, but has some problems: is subject to attack by several pests and is susceptible to Dutch elm disease, a fungus spread by beetles. From its introduction to New England in the 1930's, this disease has endangered American elms though it has not reached New Orleans, yet. Clusters of flowers, small but with conspicuous red stamens, appear in early January, followed by samaras. 1859.

   U. parvifolia Jacq. **CHINESE ELM** China, Japan. 35 feet. Leaves to 3 inches; dark green, glossy topped, leathery. Flowers are small, greenish clusters in late summer, fall; seeds in late fall. Susceptible to Dutch elm disease.

   U. pumila L. **SIBERIAN ELM** China. 30 feet. Similar to Chinese Elm and often sold as such. This tree blooms in the spring, not fall. It lives only about 15 years in the South. Though resistant to Dutch elm disease, it hosts other pests. Not as desirable a tree as the above.

DECIDUOUS SHRUBS

   The following are for the most part shrubs, but are interspersed with trees, shrublike perennials, prostrate and spreading shrubs which are useful as groundcovers:

   Aesculus pavia L. **RED BUCKEYE** U.S., Louisiana. Deciduous shrub, Buckeye family, 12 feet. Sun, part shade. Tolerant of soils moist to dry; common in Louisiana pinelands. Coarse leaves. Flowers in March to May are red, one and a half inches long on 10 inch stalks which rise above the foliage, followed by nuts which are poisonous. Considered to be messy shrubs, but butterflies and hummingbirds don't care.

   Callicarpa americana L. **AMERICAN BEAUTYBERRY, FRENCH MULBERRY** Southeast U.S., West Indies. Verbena family, deciduous shrub, 6 feet. Sun, part shade. Tolerant of almost any well-drained soil; best in fertile, slightly acid garden soil. Loose, recurving, irregular branched form. Clusters of pink flowers in summer are followed by clusters of juicy, rosy purple berries which remain after the leaves drop in fall. Stems may die to the ground in cold winters. Short-lived. Berries for birds, blossoms for bees. Probably used in pre-1800 local gardens.

Calycanthus floridus L. **SWEET SHRUB** Southeast U.S., Louisiana. Calycanthus family, deciduous shrub, 10 feet. Light shade best, sun. Moist, humusy, acid soil. Leathery, dark green leaves turn yellow in fall, are fragrant when bruised; bark has a cinnamon-like flavor. Clumpforming plant. Flowers in late spring are 2 inches, with reddish brown ribbonlike sepals; scent like strawberries when new changing to a ripe apple smell. Fragrance is strong during warm, humid weather. 1859, 1885.

Cephalanthus occidentalis **BUTTONBUSH** See NATIVE DECIDUOUS TREES.

Clethra alnifolia L. **SWEET PEPPERBUSH, SUMMER-SWEET, WHITE ALDER** Eastern U.S., reported in the swamps around Lake Pontchartrain. White Alder family, shrub, deciduous, 5 feet. Sun, part shade. Moist, well-drained soil is best; but can handle heavier, poorly drained soil, too. Blooms June to July, 4 to 6 inch spikes of tiny, white, fragrant flowers.

Forestiera acuminata (Michx.) Poir. **SWAMP PRIVET** Louisiana native, found along stream banks and swamp edges. Olive family shrub, deciduous, to 30 feet. Sun or shade. Most soils, moist locations. Small leaves; thickety, wild form. Dioecious, spring blooming; male flowers in yellow clusters, female flowers inconspicuous, followed by small, purple fruit. Wildlife food.

Hydrangea quercifolia Bartr. **OAKLEAF HYDRANGEA** Southeast U.S., Louisiana. Deciduous, 6 feet. Shade, needs sun for profuse bloom. Rich, sandy, acid loam; well-drained. Needs less moisture than garden hydrangea. Large, oaklike leaves are hairy underneath. Foliage colorful in autumn. 10 inch long loose clusters of white blossoms in April to June which persist on the plant as dried flowers. 'Gloster Form' is recommended for the deep south.

Ilex decidua Walt. **POSSUM HAW** Louisiana. Deciduous tree or shrub, 12 feet. Berries on female plants in fall, red to orange; remain on branches after leaves fall. For culture, see *Ilex*, **HOLLY**, NATIVE EVERGREEN SHRUBS.

Itea virginica L. **SWEETSPIRE, VIRGINIA WILLOW** Eastern U.S., Louisiana. Deciduous, to 10 feet. Sun, shade. Any soil, even wet; fertile, moist is best. 2 inch dull green leaves, red in fall, with finely serrated edges on stems which form open clumps. 4 inch spikey clusters of fragrant, white flowers partly droop, partly project above the foliage in April through June. *I. Illicifolia, I. yunnanensis* are Chinese species which have longer clusters of flowers, to one foot.

Lindera benzoin L. **SPICEBUSH** Eastern North America, found in Louisiana. Laurel family, deciduous, 15 feet. Sun, shade. Moist, acid soil best, though adaptable. Yellow-green aromatic foliage which yellows in fall. Fragrant, yellow-green flowers cluster in leaf axils before foliage appears in spring; red berries follow in fall on female plants. Both sexes necessary for fruit. Does not transplant readily, available from nurseries, cuttings. Birds love the berries. It is larval food plant of the spicebush swallowtail butterfly and the promethea moth.

Neviusia alabamensis A. Gray **SNOW-WREATH** Rare, protected in parts of Alabama, Mississippi, Arkansas, Tennessee. Rose family, deciduous shrub, 6 feet. Shade, part shade. Loamy, well-drained, alkaline soil. 3 inch, sharp pointed leaves in clumps of gracefully arching branches. One inch, feathery stamens project from white petal-less flowers in April. Grace M. Thompson grew this shrub in her New Orleans garden in 1946 in sun, dry soil; differing conditions from those recommended above by the Missouri Botanical Garden. Not widely available, though it adapts well to cultivation.

Rhododendron **AZALEA** See *Rhododendron,* EXOTIC EVERGREEN SHRUBS for the following which are native and deciduous, but require the same culture as the exotics: *R. austrinum* **FLORIDA FLAME AZALEA,** *R. canescens* **WILD AZALEA, NATIVE AZALEA, HONEYSUCKLE AZALEA,** *R. serrulatum* **SWAMP AZALEA.**

Rhus copallina L. **SHINING SUMAC** Eastern U.S., Louisiana. Cashew family shrub or tree, deciduous, to 20 feet. Sun. Dry, well-drained soil essential. Coarse foliage, leaves are to a foot, composed of 4 inch leaflets, glossy dark green above, hairy below, bright red in fall. Flowers are greenish-yellow, clustered on spikes which project from stem-tips, late summer. Clusters of fuzzy red berries which turn brown follow in fall and winter. Source of winter bird food.

R. glabra L. **SUMAC** More treelike than the above. Fall color can be inconsistent after a rainy summer or if planted in moist, fertile soil and shade.

Sambucus canadensis L. **ELDERBERRY** Eastern U.S., Louisiana. Honeysuckle family, deciduous shrub, 8 feet. Sun, part shade. Any soil; moist, humusy best. Fern shaped leaves with 5 to 9 pointy tipped, oval, toothed leaves; coarse form. Forms clumps with a spreading canopy which can be demanding of space. Flat topped clusters of white flowers form in June, July, sporadically after. Dark purplish berries follow. Though I have seen this plant for sale in nursery catalogs, it is so common in New Orleans from seeds dropped by birds that I see little need to pay for it. Before the fruit which birds love come flowers for bees.

Spiraea L. species **BRIDAL WREATH, SPIREA** Northern Hemisphere natives. Rose family shrubs, deciduous, from one to twelve feet high, depending on the variety. Sun. Tolerant of soil conditions; fertile, moist but well--drained is best. Not exceptionally attractive as foliage plants, the spireas are disease resistant, long lived, easily propagated; but they do not offer autumn color or berries.

They are planted for their clusters of tiny white or pink flowers which appear in spring. In our mild climate, their bloom is not the big show seen in colder places, but sparser flowers over a longer period. They look wonderful here after a cold winter. Spireas have been popular in the past and are found in a lot of old gardens. 1859, 1885.

Stewartia malacodendron L. **SILKY CAMELLIA, STEWARTIA, WILD CAMELLIA** Southeastern U.S., Louisiana. Tea family shrub, deciduous, 10 feet. Part shade. Deep, well-drained, rich, acidic soil with lots of organic matter and sand. Will not tolerate poor drainage or clay soil. Leaves to 4 inches, oval with toothed edges, pointed tips; smooth above, silky below. White flowers with purple stamens to 4 inches, April to June. Very difficult to grow in New Orleans. It should not be transplanted from the wild. It is available from nurseries. See RESOURCES.

Styrax americanus Lam. **STYRAX, SNOWBELL, STORAX** South east U.S., Louisiana. Storax family, deciduous shrub or tree, 10 feet. Sun, part shade. Rich, loose soil, though tolerates heavier, wetter conditions. Light green, 3 inch oblong leaves with finely serrated edges. Clusters of fragrant, white, half inch bell-shaped flowers which open to reveal yellow stamens, hang like snowdrops from along the branches in April, May.

Symphoricarpos orbiculatus Moench **CORALBERRY, INDIAN CURRANT** Eastern, Central U.S. Honeysuckle family shrub, deciduous, 3 to 7 feet. Sun, shade. Any soil. Spreads by suckers, forming "thickets" of erect and arching branches, elliptic leaves to 2 inches. Clusters of small white flowers in early summer, followed by prolific amounts of coral-red berries which persist for months, are edible by wildlife. Good nest site and cover plant for birds. Leaves are larval food for hummingbird moths.

Vaccinium ashei Reade **RABBIT-EYE BLUEBERRY** Southeast U.S. Heath family, deciduous to semi-evergreen shrub, 4 to 18 feet. Sun. Moist, organic, well-drained, acid soil. Erect or suckering form; oval pale to dark green leaves to two and a half inches. Small pink, white, or red flowers followed by dull, blue-black berries in early summer. Two varieties should be planted near each other for cross pollination. This species is the only one that can successfully be grown in Louisiana. Some cold is required, crops may be sparse or heavy depending on the preceeding winter. Very sensitive to alkalinity: in New Orleans should be planted in containers sunk into the ground and filled with peat moss. Treat with chelated iron if leaves yellow; this is iron chlorosis which can be caused by alkaline ground and tap water. Roots are sensitive. Use fertilizers such as cottonseed meal or azalea-camellia fertilizer spread very evenly to the drip line; do not allow to concentrate. Pruning is important for the best production. Louisiana Cooperative Extension Service has a pamphlet with instructions. Leslee Reed uptown and Pat and John Iwachiw in Kenner have had poor results so far. When berries form, they are good wildlife food if people don't get them first!

Viburnum dentatum **ARROWHEAD** Eastern U.S., Louisiana and *V. nudum* **SWAMP VIBURNUM** are both found in the eastern U.S., Louisiana; are deciduous. Culture is the same as the exotic viburnums. See both under *Viburnum*, EXOTIC EVERGREEN SHRUBS.

EVERGREEN TREES

Gordonia lasianthus (L.) Ellis **BLACK LAUREL, LOBLOLLY BAY** Southeast U.S. Tea family tree, evergreen, 90 feet. Needs protection from the sun when young. Rich, moist, soil is best; can handle low, sandy soil; found in acidic swamps. 5 inch long, pointed leaves; shiny and dark green above, lighter below. Three inch Magnolia-like flowers from July to August. Hard to grow out of its natural setting. Sylvanus spotted this native as a desireable ornamental in 1851, bemoaned its lack of familiarity to nurserymen. 1885.

Ilex opaca **AMERICAN HOLLY** See NATIVE EVER-GREEN SHRUBS.

Juniperus virginiana L. **EASTERN RED CEDAR** North America. Evergreen, 15 to 75 feet. Sun, part sun. Alkaline soil, can handle poor conditions.   Many cultivars available, most are pyramidal in shape, dark green to gray green foliage, bluish cones on female plants.   Reddish, peeling bark on older specimens.   Its heartwood is the aromatic wood of cedar chests. Found in many gardens, old and new. 1859, 1885, 1921, 1935.

Magnolia grandiflora L. **SOUTHERN MAGNOLIA** Southeast U.S., Louisiana. Magnolia family tree, evergreen, 100 feet. Sun, part shade. Deep, moist, acid soil. 10 inch long, 3 inch wide leathery leaves, glossy green above, rusty underneath.   8 inch wide, fragrant, waxy-petaled white blossoms, which everybody knows, April to June, sporadically to November. Cones follow, with crayon-red seeds. Sensitive to depth of planting, fill should not be placed over roots.   A traditional southern shade tree; many cultivars available. 1859.

M. heptapeta (Buc'hoz) Dandy **WHITE SAUCER MAG-NOLIA, YULAN MAGNOLIA** China. 30 feet. Sun, part shade. Deep, moist, acid soil. White, cup shaped flowers, fragrant.

M. macrophylla Michx. **COWCUMBER MAGNOLIA** Southern U.S., Louisiana. 50 feet. Need very well-drained soil. Huge leaves. 12 inch white, fragrant flowers, petal bases blotched purple, April to May.

M. quinquepeta (Buc'hoz) Dandy **TULIP MAGNOLIA** China. Shrub or tree, 12 feet. 5 inch, tulip shaped flowers, purple on the outside, white inside; lemon fragrance.

M. X soulangiana Soul.-Bod. **ORIENTAL** or **SAUCER MAGNOLIA** Hybrid of two Chinese species. Twenty feet. Sun. Humusy, loose, slightly acid soil, good drainage essential.   Light green leaves. Flowers from fuzzy buds form in very early spring on the bare, gray branches. They are cup shaped, 6 inches across, purple outside, white to pink in; fragrant. Many cultivars available with flowers from pure white, shades of pink to rose to purple; blends.

M. virginiana L. (previously *M. glauca*) **SWEET BAY MAGNOLIA** Coastal eastern U.S., Louisiana. Semievergreen tree, 60 feet. 3 inch, cup shaped, lemon scented, white flowers, April to June. Noted by Sylvanus in 1851 as common in the swamps, occasionally planted in New Orleans gardens.

Osmanthus americanus (L.) A. Gray **DEVILWOOD, AMERICAN OLIVE** Southeast U.S., Louisiana. Olive family tree, evergreen, 45 feet. From rich, moist, acidic sites, but is tolerant of other conditions. 4 to 6 inch shiny, oblong leaves; dark green above, lighter below. Small yellow flower clusters in March, April are followed by dark blue, three-quarter inch, large pitted fruit. Available 1859 as *Olea americana*.

Persea borbonia (L.) K. Spreng. **RED BAY, SWAMP BAY** Eastern U.S., Louisiana. Evergreen tree, Laurel family, 40 feet. Sun, part shade. Sandy, moist soil. Aromatic, dark green shiny-topped leaves, 5 inches long, 2 inches wide. Small flowers in May are followed by half-inch, dark blue, fleshy berries. The leaves and those of *P. palustris* (Raf.) Sarg. **SWAMP REDBAY**, are the bay leaves used for flavoring gumbo, red beans, etc. *Laurus nobilis* L. **LAUREL, SWEET BAY, FRENCH BAY TREE** is the evergreen tree or shrub of the Mediterranean from which garlands were made to crown Greek and Roman heroes. Also used as "bay leaf" seasoning, it can reach 30 feet, needs sun, light shade, good drainage. Good for container culture.

Pinus L. species **PINE** The following are North American natives found in Louisiana. Pine family, evergreen. Sun. Well-drained soil, *P. glabra* can handle heavier soil than the others. Pines are good nesting sites for birds;

their cones provide food for squirrels and birds. Those with open forms and high canopies allow successful plantings of shrubs which need indirect light, such as azaleas and camellias.

P. echinata Mill. **SHORTLEAF PINE** 100 feet. Three to five inch needles in pairs. High canopy.

P. elliottii Engelm. **SLASH PINE** 100 feet. 5 inch needles in groups of three. Has a long taproot, therefore does not compete heavily for moisture with plantings under its high canopy. Fast growing.

P. glabra Walt. **SPRUCE PINE** 80 feet. Needles wavy, in pairs to 3 inches long. Low, heavy branches make this not a good tree for underplanting.

P. palustris Mill. **LONGLEAF PINE** 100 feet. Needles to 15 inches long are arranged in threes, grouped in plumelike branch-tip tufts. Open canopy, long taproot.

P. taeda L. **LOBLOLLY PINE** 100 feet. Needles in bundles of 3, to 9 inches long. High branches. Drops lots of needles which are good mulch. Fast growing.

Prunus caroliniana (Mill.) Ait. [*Laurocerasus caroliniana*] **CHERRY LAUREL** Southeast U.S., Louisiana. Evergreen, 40 feet. Sun, part shade. Rich, deep, well-drained soil is best. Glossy, dark green, aromatic, leathery leaves to 4 inches. Tiny white flowers, early spring; small and shiny black berries follow. Dense foliage, used for hedges, reponds well to pruning; fast growth makes it a high maintainence hedge plant if neatness is desired. Volunteers from dropped berries are abundant. Good nest site and food plant for birds. Listed 1859 as *Cerasus carolinana*, 1885. Magnolia Nurseries also offered *P. laurocerasus* **ENGLISH LAUREL, CHERRY LAUREL**, 1859.

Quercus L. species **OAK** Beech family. A large group of trees found around the world in temperate zones of the Northern Hemisphere. The following four are among many found in Louisiana. They require sun, high shade and loose, rich, well-drained soil. Flowers in spring are drooping clusters; fruit is the acorn. Oaks are long lived and grow to great size. (The American Forestry Association keeps statistics on big trees. The "champion" tree reported in Louisiana in 1988 was a live oak in St. Tammany Parish: 36 feet 7 inches in circumference, 55 feet high, 132 foot crown spread.)

They are all important as nest sites for birds and as mammal food. In recent years in New Orleans, the live and water oaks of our city have been threatened by infestations of buck moth caterpillars which feed on the leaves, defoliating and weakening the trees. Orthene is the most effective chemical control against these pests. Yellowbilled cuckoos are natural predators, but, unfortunately enough are not present within the city boundaries. A healthy tree is best equipped to overcome stress, so fertilization and watering is important. 1859.

Q. falcata Michx. **SOUTHERN RED OAK** Deciduous, 80 feet. Leaves have 1 to 3 pairs of lobes, one sickle-shaped, dark green above, lighter below; reddish in fall.

Q. falcata variety *pagodifolia* is called **CHERRYBARK OAK, SWAMP RED OAK**; is found in lower areas.

Q. nigra L. **WATER OAK** Deciduous, 80 feet. Can handle heavy soils better than most oaks. Upright form. Leaves to 3 inches, varied shapes. 1921.

Q. phellos L. **WILLOW OAK**, incorrectly called **PIN OAK**. Deciduous, 60 feet. 2 to 4 inch, willow-like leaves. Found on swamp edges.

Q. virginiana Mill. **LIVE OAK** Evergreen, 60 feet. Broad canopy. Beautiful, traditional southern, New Orleans tree. 1921, 1935.

Sophora secundiflora (Ort.) Lag. ex DC. **MESCAL BEAN, FRIJOLITO, TEXAS LILAC** Texas, New Mexico. Pea family. Sun, part shade. Well-drained soil; found in limestone soils. Compound leaves. Deep-purple 2 to 4 inch long clusters of grape-scented flowers in May to June. Though it is not supposed to grow in New Orleans, there is one on Prytania near Napoleon which was given to the gardener there 20 years ago.

Thuja occidentalis L. **WHITE CEDAR, AMERICAN AR-BORVITAE** North America. *T. orientalis*, **ORIENTAL AR-BORVITAE** Orient. Cypress family, evergreen, 60 feet. Sun. Rich, moist but well-drained soil, acid or alkaline. Conical form, flat sprays of dark green, scale-like leaves; half inch cones on female trees. Considered an "old fashioned" garden shrub which has now been replaced by more attractive and versatile plants. Difficult to control by pruning. Susceptible to attack by diseases, especially in our heat and if drainage is poor. 1859, 1885.

EVERGREEN SHRUBS

Acacia farnesiana (L.) Willd. **SWEET ACACIA** Subtropical America, coastal Louisiana. Pea family, 10 feet, evergreen shrub. Sun. Good drainage, light soil are critical; alkaline pH. Thorny branches, gray green, mimosa-like but finer foliage; April, May blooms are small, fragrant, yellow globes fuzzy with protruding stamens; followed by long seed pods. Hardy to 20 degrees. Stems have long been used as cut flowers in New Orleans (Sylvanus, 1851).

A. baileyana F. J. Muell. **GOLDEN MIMOSA,** which can be seen in the Australian exhibit at Audubon Zoo, is close in appearance.

Hypericum hypericoides (L.) Crantz **ST. JOHN'S WORT, ST.-ANDREW'S-CROSS** Eastern North America, Central America. Evergreen, 2 feet. Part shade, sun. Light, well drained soil. Slender leaves, irregular, spreading form. Large quantities of small, yellow, 4-petaled flowers June to September. A hypericum was offered 1885.

H. densiflorum Pursh. **ST. JOHN'S-WORT** Louisiana. Evergreen, 5 feet. Light shade. Sandy loam. Clusters of small, five-petaled yellow flowers form at the tips of branches, June to September.

Ilex L. species **HOLLY** Western Hemisphere and Asian temperate zones. Shrubs and trees. Sun, light shade, berry production less with shade. Fertile, well drained soil good for all, though swamp species can handle wet conditions. Most require acid soil. Most are dioecious, meaning flowers with male parts (stamens) and female parts (pistils) are on separate plants. Berries are found on the female plant, but unless a male is nearby to provide pollen for fertilization, most hollies will not produce berries. If you want berries, be sure to interview your nurseryman as to whether you are getting a male or female, and whether both are needed for fruit. If you want a female, it is a good idea to buy one with at least a few berries present to make sure. *I. aquifolium*, **EUROPEAN HOLLY**, was offered 1859.

I. X attenuata Ashe 'Fosteri' **FOSTER'S HOLLY** Hybrid of southern U.S. natives. Evergreen, 20 feet. Very good drainage, best in raised beds. Red berries, fall and winter. The cultivar 'Savannah' is widely used by the Parkway and Park Commission for street plantings in New Orleans, does very well here. It is best known for its heavy berry production.

I. cassine L. **DAHOON HOLLY** Louisiana. Evergreen, 10 feet. Moist, acid, soil, as at swamp edges where it grows naturally. Bright reddish orange berries profuse on female plants in fall.

I. cornuta Lindl. & Paxt. **CHINESE HOLLY** China. Evergreen, 8 feet. Sun, thin growth in shade. Large red berries in fall, winter on female plants, only. Cultivar 'Burfordii' produces berries without fertilization by the male plant.

I. decidua Walt. **POSSUM HAW** Louisiana. Deciduous tree or shrub, 12 feet. Berries on female plants in fall, red to orange; remain on branches after leaves fall.

I. glabra L. **INKBERRY, GALLBERRY** Louisiana. Evergreen, 10 feet. Leaves yellow easily (due to iron chlorosis) if acid conditions are not maintained. Flowers in spring attract bees. Berries in fall are black.

I. opaca Ait. **AMERICAN HOLLY** Louisiana. Evergreen tree, 25 feet. Red berries on female plant fall to spring. Male branch is sometimes grafted onto a tree to provide pollen.

I. verticillata L. **WINTERBERRY, BLACK ALDER** Southeast Louisiana. Evergreen, to 10 feet. Grows in swamps and woodlands, acid soil. Foliage turns blackish brown after frost. Red berries in leaf axils and along the bare parts of branches, fall and winter.

I. vomitoria Ait. **YAUPON** Louisiana. Evergreen, 10 feet. Tolerates a wider range of soil conditions than other hollies, including alkaline soils. Large quantities of small red berries fall through winter on female plants. Cultivars with yellow berries, also. Name comes from use of leaves by Indians to make emetic tea.

I. vomitoria 'Nana' is **DWARF YAUPON** To 4 feet. Does not form berries.

Illicium floridanum Ellis. **STAR ANISE** Southeast U.S., Louisiana. Evergreen, 10 feet. Shade, part shade. Found in moist, sandy, acid soils, as along streams; sandy, well-drained, slightly acid soil will do in the garden. Aromatic, 6 inch long leaves are olive green; dark red, with 2 inch flowers, March to May. One source describes the floral aroma as unpleasant. Leslee Reed disagrees. Fruit in fall is star-shaped. 1885. *I. anisatum* L. **JAPANESE ANISE**, and others are available, similar. 1885.

Kalmia latifolia L. **MOUNTAIN LAUREL** North America, found in Louisiana only in Washington Parish. Heath family shrub, evergreen, 10 feet. Found in sandy, peaty, acid soil or moist, swamp edges. Shiny, dark green leaves. Clusters of white to deep pink, purple flecked flowers with fused petals, April to June. A bee's weight on the flower causes a stamen to flip its anther out of a pocket, zap the insect with a load of pollen. Difficult to grow out of its specific environment. Included in original plantings of the Louisiana Swamp Exhibit at the Audubon Zoo, not there now. Acidity is critical. Paul Keith suggests planting in containers in azalea soil. 1885. One source reports local success with *K. augustifolia* L.

Lyonia lucida (Lam.) C. Koch **FETTERBUSH** Southeast U.S., Louisiana. Heath family shrub to 6 feet, evergreen. Part sun. Moist but well-drained, acidic soil with high organic content; soil preparation is important for success in the garden. 3 inch, leathery leaves, mounded form. Small white to pink, bell-shaped flowers in April, May.

Mahonia aquifolium **OREGON GRAPE** Northwest U.S. See *Mahonia*, EXOTIC EVERGREEN SHRUBS.

Myrica cerifera L. **SOUTHERN WAX MYRTLE** Eastern U.S., Louisiana. Bayberry family shrub, evergreen, to 35 feet. Sun, part shade. Rich, moist soil, slightly acid is best; adaptable. Narrow, pointed, resinous leaves, aromatic; dioecious, inconspicuous spring flowers followed by tiny, gray, wax-coated, nuts clustered along the stems of the female plants. Leaves and fruits were the source of wax for bayberry candles. Source of winter food for birds. *Myrica serrata* was offered 1885. 1935.

PALMS AND PALMETTOS

Sabal minor (Jacq.) Pers. **LOUISIANA PALMETTO**
Southeast U.S., Louisiana. Palm family shrub, evergreen, 5
to 10 feet. Sun, shade. Local soil, dry or wet. Grows to
largest size in swampy settings, so in the past was used
as an index of annual flooding. Large, fan-like clusters of
pointed leaves on stalks; can be trunkless or have a foot
in diameter trunk, depending on water conditions. Flowers in spring and summer are small and white, clustered
along stalks to 10 feet long. Half inch black fruits follow.
Hard to transplant. Known in French as latanier, it was
used by Choctaw and Chitimacha Indians for baskets
which used to be sold in the French Market, and by the
French for fans, hats, baskets, brooms, and chair seats.
The *New Orleans Times-Democrat* of October 3, 1891 cites
another use, by *"...devoted Confederate women* (who) *worked
and pleated* (the leaves) *into hats to crown their heads...."*
Available at local nurseries. 1935. *Latania borbonica*, RED
LATAN, an import from the Pacific tropics, was offered
1885.

Sabal palmetto (Walt.) Lodd. ex. Schult. & Schult.f.
Southeastern U.S. Coast. **CABBAGE PALM** Palm family
tree, 90 feet. Sun. Found in sandy coastal soil, usually
with underlying limestone; grows in moist or dry garden
soil. 5 to 6 foot long fan-shaped leaves in a rounded
clump at the top of a long, slender trunk. White flowers
form on prominent stalks, followed by clusters of half inch
black berries.

TREES FOR FALL COLOR

Acer rubrum variety *drummondii* SWAMP RED MAPLE
Celtis laevigata HACKBERRY
Cercis canadensis RED BUD, JUDAS TREE
Cornus drummondii ROUGH-LEAF DOGWOOD
Crataegus marshallii PARSLEY HAWTHORNE
Diospyros virginiana PERSIMMON
Fraxinus pennsylvanica GREEN ASH
Liquidambar styraciflua SWEET GUM
Liriodendron tulipifera TULIP TREE, YELLOW POPLAR
Nyssa sylvatica BLACK GUM
Rhus copallina SHINING SUMAC
Sassafras albidum SASSAFRAS
Ulmus americana AMERICAN ELM

Betsy Ewing

Ferns

"I come from haunts of coot and hern,
I make a sudden sally
And sparkle out among the fern,
To bicker down a valley."

"The Song of the Brook" *Alfred, Lord Tennyson*

The word fern has always made me picture rushing water in cool, wild, remote places. But, as I recall the actual ferns I have seen in the New Orleans area, I realize they have been in not necessarily remote places and it's usually so hot that even the water is sluggish. Most varieties are found in the shade, which is a little cooler than in the sun, even in a humid swamp. Maybe the intense green is what signals coolness. Ferns carpeted the world with green before there were flowering plants. Fossil remains of ferns are found which prove them to be at least 215 million years old. Their allure is that they come from other times as well as places.

To me the SWORD or BOSTON FERN (*Nephrolepsis exaltata* (L.) Schott) is the generic fern. It is the one most often seen in local gardens, both in the ground and cascading voluptuously from hanging baskets. Also long popular as a house plant, it is not a Louisiana native.

Brown and Correll in *Ferns and Fern Allies of Louisiana*
speculate that, as the plant is found growing on the trunks
of Canary Island palms, it may have entered this country
when those trees were brought here many years ago. The
Islenos came here from the Canary Islands during Spanish
Colonial times, around 1780. We don't know if they
brought palms with them that early. We do know that
the sword ferns were found in Dade County, Florida in
1859 and are native in parts of that state[37].

If your garden contains masonry, you will eventually
find specimens of the LADDER BRAKE or BRACKEN
(*Pteris vittata* L.) growing in the cracks. You will also see
this fern high up on the sides of brick buildings and in
the deteriorating tombs of our oldest cemeteries. Those of
its spores which are carried by the wind into pockets of
moist alkaline soil begin the slow and unique process of
fern reproduction called alternation of generations. Originally from China, this fern is another import. When? H.
F. Ransier noted *P. vittata* growing in old cemeteries in
New Orleans in 1927. Brown in *Ferns and Fern Allies...*
said *"Pteris vittata was one of his outstanding finds. He also
reported Adiantum Capillus-Veneris."* These discoveries were
announced in the *American Fern Journal*, 1929.

Maybe bracken were brought to Louisiana as early as
1834 when the Wardian Case (terrarium) was invented and
used for transport and exhibit of plants. They could have
been imported by English plant hunter for Kew gardens,
Robert Fortune who collected many ornamentals from the
Orient during the 1840's and 1850's. Many of his finds,
such as the kumquat, have long been used in New Orleans gardens. Victorian Europeans and Americans had a
fascination for ferns. They displayed their collections in
"Folding stand and Wardian Cases" like the ones offered
in New Orleans in 1875 in R. Maitre's Catalogue, if not
outdoors.

VENUS'-HAIR FERN (*Adiantum capillus-veneris* L.) is a
maidenhair fern found in temperate zones world-wide. It

is not believed to be a Louisiana native even though it is reported to be naturalized around *"the old plantations in West Felicianas Parish"*[38]. I wonder if Martha Turnbull grew this fern at Rosedown in 1835 or later? It frequents the limey crevasses of aging masonry. I have seen luxuriant growths of this plant, whose fragile and delicate appearance deny its toughness, established just under raised uptown cottages, between the brick piers.

The HUGUENOT FERN, or SPIDER BRAKE (*Pteris multifida* Poir. ex Lam.) persists today in the woods nearby and sometimes miles away from the sites of some of the oldest antebellum estates. It must have been imported during antebellum times to have escaped cultivation from plantation gardens long since vanished.

CRETAN BRAKE or AVERY FERN, (*Pteris cretica* L.) is found in parts of Louisiana to which it has spread from Avery Island where it is suspected to have been introduced with plants E. A. McIlhenny imported to his Jungle Gardens in this century. Its origin may be Crete, though it may be indigenous to Florida.

The JAPANESE CLIMBING FERN (*Lygodium japonicum* Swartz.) has appeared on its own in my garden, in moist sites, and in one spot, in conjuction with a ladder brake. It is also called trailing, running, or wild maidenhair. Its origin is the Asian and Australian tropics. We don't know when it first came here. There is no doubt it has naturalized in parts of New Orleans. It has a lovely, delicate appearance, but can be a pest where I don't want it. I can't seem to rid certain spots of it. It has been naturalized in Florida since at least 1932.[39]

A documented example of fern introduction is the discovery by Frank Mackaness, gardener of Kraak's Nursery at Central Avenue in Metairie of the WHISK FERN (*Psilotum nudum* (L.) Griseb.) growing in potting soil brought from Alabama or Mississippi in years previous to 1942. Though it may occur in the wild now, we cannot be sure if it was already there or escaped from the many potted plants sold by the nursery.[40]

What of the native ferns? Some you may not spot as ferns. In addition to those whose fronds in arching clusters or advancing waves signal "fern," there are the floating ferns, ferns which are rooted in muddy bayou bottoms, and an epiphyte which grows along the branches of oak trees. The RESURRECTION FERN (*Polypodium polypodioides* L.) is found other places, too, but I think of it lining the limbs of the massive live oaks in Audubon Park. Its name comes from the fact that it shrivels and turns brown in dry weather, then, after a rain, instantly regreens.

John Steele, in *The Courtyard and Patio Gardens of the Vieux Carre (1718-1860)* suggests that the ferns used in French Quarter gardens were natives, of the *Dryopteris* genus, the southern shield fern and southern marsh fern or *Adiantum capillis-veneris*, maidenhair fern.

A group of plants related to ferns in that they reproduce similarly, are called fern allies. Among others, they are the HORSETAILS, SPIKE-MOSS, QUILLWORTS, and the CLUBMOSSES. They are found in a variety of habitats, some distinctly unfernlike. I love their names, their primitive and bizarre shapes and appearances. Some of these are possibles for garden cultivation, though most will wait to delight the amateur naturalist with his field guide who discovers them on explorative jaunts.

The next time someone tells you they found shamrocks in their yard or gives you a bouquet of four-leaved clovers, tell them "No one is that lucky!" and direct them to look closely for wiry stems and new growth coiled to unfurl. They have, more likely than not, come across a bed of the fern ally, WATERCLOVER. I found it growing by Vance Reynoir's house across the street and transplanted a few sprigs to the edge of my pond. It is common in lawns in the New Orleans area. If allowed its own protected patch, it forms a softly textured cover of rich greens.

Ferns are too free-form for a very structured, formal garden. They are suggested as ground covers, or as underplantings for trees and shrubs, where, being shallowrooted, they will not compete for moisture with the larger plants. The deciduous ferns are effective in bulb beds. Their new fronds unfurl in time to hide the maturing foliage of spring bulbs and lilies after their blooms are spent. Whatever the practical use to which ferns are put, their aesthetic plus is their form; graceful, allowing interplay of light and shade, evoking memories of deep woodsy, quiet, utterly natural places.

CULTURE OF FERNS

However they are used in the garden, most ferns must have moisture and from deep to light shade. A northern exposure or its equivalent in light quality is recommended. The soil in which they are planted must be light and very high in moisture-retentive leafmold or peat, and sand for good drainage. Soggy soil must be avoided. The pH of the soil should be adjusted to accomodate the type of fern planted.

When transplanting a fern from a nursery pot to the ground, or from someone else's garden to yours, it is important to replant at the same level as the plant originally grew. Underground rhizomes should be replanted no more than an inch in depth. As with any transplantation, thorough watering should follow to settle soil around roots and eliminate air pockets.

Sources differ on the best time to transplant ferns: from the spring, to the fall, to anytime but the dead of winter. Cuttings can be taken from ferns which spread by rhizomes in the early spring. To assure success, identify the fern and duplicate its growing conditions in your garden.

As some are endangered, the best policy is not to take wild ferns unless you know their status. Fortunately, the more common ones are also the ones easiest to grow. One way to collect a fern is to wait for its spore cases to ripen (from late spring to late fall, depending on the species) and collect them. Spores cast on moist soil in a covered container kept in bright, but indirect sunlight will sprout in from three weeks to six months, producing a prothallium. This structure produces eggs and sperms and provides the surface on which fertilization takes place. Young maidenhair ferns develop in six months. A staghorn fern (a tropical epiphytic fern used as a houseplant) can take from two to three years. A lot of time and commitment? The reward is a privileged peek at one of nature's secrets. The specifics of propagating some of our native ferns from spores are covered in *Growing and Propagating Wild Flowers* by Harry R. Phillips.

A mulch of leaves helps retain moisture and offers winter protection for your ferns. The fronds which start to brown in the fall should be left until spring to further protect the tender crown.

Which ferns can you choose for your garden? Your selection can be from several sources: nurseries; friends' gardens; cuttings, spores, or specimens from the wild; plant catalogs. I have not had much success with ordered ferns, though with proper selection of species for our climate, there is no reason why this should not be a good source if modern packing materials are placed around the roots to retain moisture during shipping. It is very important to replant the fern before the roots dry out, whether it is ordered or dug in someone else's yard.

The bracken, sensitive, and ostrich ferns are called pests by Broughton Cobb in the *Peterson Field Guide, Ferns*. Once growing, they are difficult to get rid of. This may be an advantage in certain areas of the garden.

If your experience is similar to mine, the ladder brake will appear in your brick walk whether you want it or

not. The brakes are tough ferns with interesting structures. They are as popular in some parts of the world as
houseplants as the Boston fern is in the United States.

The following recommended ferns for New Orleans
gardens are from a survey of local nurseries, The New
Orleans Garden Society, Inc., *Ferns and Fern Allies of Louisiana* and *Louisiana Ferns and Fern Allies*. They are divided
into the two categories used by the authors of the second
work. This is not an exhaustive list.

FERNS FOR THE NEW ORLEANS GARDEN

FERNS WHICH GROW BEST IN THE SHADE AND CAN BE RAISED IN RICH, MOIST, SOIL

Adiantum capillus-veneris L. **VENUS'-HAIR FERN** Native to the south, but probably not to southern Louisiana, as it likes limestone formations, which are not to be found here. Humidity. Needless-to-say, provide alkaline soil which can be done by planting near brick walls. Needs much water until established.

Adiantum pedatum L. **NORTHERN MAIDENHAIR** Native to North America, to Louisiana, not to the New Orleans area. Needs alkaline soil, high humidity, cooler temperatures. Thieret reports it tricky to maintain more than one year outdoors in the heat of south Louisiana, but it has been done in the right setting.

Asplenium platyneuron L. **EBONY SPLEENWORT** Common in Louisiana, evergreen foliage, likes alkaline soil. Can handle dryer conditions. Likes to go dry between waterings.

Athyrium asplenioides Michx. **LOWLAND** or **SOU-THERN LADY FERN** Very common along the Gulf coast in swamps and along streams. Deciduous, grows in compact clumps, likes well-drained, consistently moist soil. Experts disagree on whether it is a separate species or a variety of LADY FERN, *Athyrium filix-femina* L.

Athyrium niponicum pictum **JAPANESE PAINTED FERN** Needs similar conditions to the lady fern. Slow spreading, compact growth. Stalks are reddish colored.

Dryopteris normalis C. Chr. **SOUTHERN SHIELD FERN** Native to Louisiana. Found in swamps and moist woods. Deciduous. Spreads by rhizomes. Easily grown. Can be weedy.

Dryopteris thelypteris L. variety *Haleana* **SOUTHERN MARSH FERN** Native. Found more in south Louisiana than north. Likes swampy areas. Like the southern shield fern, is deciduous, easily grown.

Marsilea uncinata A. Br. **HOOK-SPINE WATERCLO-VER** A waterclover, a fern ally so named because it looks like clover. It is an aquatic plant, but grows easily in moist, sandy soils. Found naturally in Louisiana. Common in New Orleans. You can tell it from clover in your lawn by its wiry stems and the way its new leaves unfurl like fern fronds. It, of course, doesn't bloom.

Polystichum acrostichoides Michx. **CHRISTMAS FERN** A stiff, bushy, evergreen fern which will grow in deep shade. Found in sandy soil in swamps and on the banks of streams. It likes alkaline soil, but does not require it. Its name comes from the fact that it is green at Christmas and is used in decorations for that holiday. Native to Louisiana.

Selaginella apoda L. **MEADOW SPIKEMOSS** A prostrate, mat-forming, moss-like ally suggested for pots, terraria or as a specimen plant. Thieret says it can form an extensive ground cover if not competing with other plants. Needs moist, slightly acidic soil. Naturally it is found in damp, shady wooded places and edging streams and ditches. A Louisiana native. Some spikemosses are endangered. This plant should be purchased rather than collected unless your identification is certain.

FERNS WHICH DO WELL IN THE OPEN, EXPOSED TO THE SUN, IF SUFFICIENT MOISTURE IS AVAILABLE

Cyrtomium falcatum L.f. **JAPANESE HOLLY FERN** An Asian species which is evergreen except during severe freezes. Though the foliage dies to the ground, it always comes back from the roots in my garden. It clumps, has beautifully arched leathery, glossy fronds. Can handle a larger variety of conditions, both moisture and pH-wise than most ferns.

Equisetum prealtum Raf. **TALL SCOURING-RUSH** or **HORSETAIL** An ally which is found in wet places or in well-drained sand or gravel. Spreads by underground stems which need to be controlled in the garden. Planting in containers is suggested. Likes wet, slightly acid, sandy soil and full sun.

Lorinseria areolata L. **DWARF CHAIN FERN** A native which is a deciduous, fast growing, creeper. Likes soil on acid side. Found growing in swamps and low woods.

Nephrolepis exaltata L. **SWORD** or **BOSTON FERN** Native to the tropics and subtropics of the world. Introduced to New Orleans, now naturalized in the city. Sources differ on ideal pH: from acidic to slightly basic.

Osmunda cinnamomea L. **CINNAMON FERN** Native to Louisiana, though not to the New Orleans area. Likes acid soil as is found in the bogs and stream bottoms in pinewoods where it grows wild.

Osmunda regalis variety *spectabilis* L. **ROYAL FERN** Native. Found in swamps, marshes, low woods and creek bottoms. The root mass is sold as "osmunda fiber" as a planting medium for orchids and bromeliads. Likes acid soil; deciduous, turns yellow in fall, grows in clumps.

Onoclea sensibilis L. **SENSITIVE** or **BEAD FERN** A hardy, deciduous, creeping fern which turns yellow in the fall. Invasive. Native to Louisiana. Found along swamp margins in southern parts of the state. Likes slightly acidic soil.

Woodwardia virginica L. **VIRGINIA CHAIN FERN**
Found in swamps and marshes. Native to our area. Can
handle much wetter soil than other Louisiana ferns. Acid
soil. Deciduous. Fast spreading by rhizomes.

The feathery foliaged plant called **ASPARAGUS
FERN** is *Asparagus setaceus (plumosus)*, a tender South African plant in the same family as Asparagus officinalis, the
vegetable. It does not offer edible parts as does its cousin
and it is not a fern at all.

I will not cover ferns as house plants here, except to
say that the same soil, light and moisture requirements as
outside must be met indoors. Humidity can be provided
by misting or by grouping plants together and placing
containers holding water for evaporation in their midst.
Ferns do not mind being potbound. Many tropical ferns
become possible to the enthusiast who wishes to grow
them indoors, in the greenhouse, or in the terrarium.

Pam Kelly Sills

Wildflowers

"Almost every person, from childhood on, has been touched by the untamed beauty of wildflowers: buttercup gold under a childish chin, the single drop of exquisite sweetness in the blossom of wild honeysuckle, the love-me, love-me-not philosophy of daisy petals."

Lady Bird Johnson and Carlton B. Lees
Wildflowers Across America
Copyright © 1988 Cross River Press, Ltd.

Growing wildflowers began for me as a way of coping. I thought that redefining the weedy false garlic (*Nothoscordum bivalve*), yellow wood sorrel (*Oxalis stricta*), pink oxalis (*Oxalis rubra*), dayflower (*Commelina erecta*), buttonweed (*Diodia virginiana*), and doorstep flowers or Mexican petunias (*Ruellia brittoniana*), which are almost impossible to eradicate from my garden, as wildflowers, might help me learn to live with them. It worked. I felt less frustrated by the feeling that my chores had not been done. I even began to appreciate the delicate beauty of the plants.

The frequently used definition of a weed proposes some variation on the idea that if it is growing where someone does not want it, then it is one. So, once I convinced myself that I wanted them, they were no longer, by definition, weeds. The first year I let the wild garlic go instead of pulling it as it appeared, my neighbor Becky Jordan asked what the interesting new flowers were.

With closer examination and reading, I learned that my garden plants are cultivated cousins of the wildflower. What should have been obvious was blocked by the un-thought-out childhood observation that the flowers I saw planted in garden beds and pots were different, almost blatant in their colors and forms, when compared to unassuming wild blooms. Some garden plants have evolved through the manipulations of hybridizers into dramatically showy forms, but the families are the same: Lily, Canna, Amaryllis, Iris, Poppy, Rose, Mallow, Violet, Sunflower. The tiny, yellow-centered white wildflowers which my fieldguide tells me are asters are a far cry from the colorful three to five inch blooms pictured in the *Park Company Seed Catalogue.*

Many of the plants pictured in *Wildflowers of Louisiana* grow in New Orleans gardens. Some of these, the text explains, have escaped cultivation to grow wild. Others have been taken from the swamps for cultivation in the garden. The Louisiana irises are examples of cultivated wildflowers, as are the white rainlily (*Zephyranthes candida*), spiderlily (*Hymenocallis occidentalis*), Hall's honeysuckle (*Lonicera japonica*), butterfly weed (*Asclepias tuberosa*), cypress vine (*Ipomoea quamoclit*), swamp-lily (*Crinum americanum*), and blue phlox (*Phlox divaricata*). Of the above, *Zephyranthes candida* is from South America, *Lonicera japonica* is Japanese, *Ipomoea quamoclit* is a native of tropical America, and the rest are indigenous to the United States. When the word wildflower is used, it does not necessarily follow that the plant is indigenous or native. Many of the flowers found naturalized and growing wild in this country were introduced from other continents, many by the first European settlers. One suggestion for finding period plants for garden restoration in *"Source List for Historic Seeds and Plants"* (Scott Kunst, Old House Gardens) is to: *"Choose species, botanical, or wild forms of garden plants. These are often the same as older garden varieties."* Look for them in catalogues and abandoned homes, old gardens, doorstep gardens, cemetaries or escaped into wild areas around the city.

With increased awareness of wildflowers, I found some gems which I had to have in my garden. Blue-eyed grass (*Sisyrinchium capillare*) is an example. It is in the Iris family. A close look reveals the similarity: the leaves are miniatures of blade-like iris leaves. The flowers which are open in the morning are like tiny jewels in the sunlight. Mine is planted in one of the soil-filled openings of a cinder block so it gets the good drainage it needs to flourish.

Mexican primrose (*Oeonthera speciosa*), the lovely pink flower which some people call buttercup, is a perennial which grows in a bed of liriope in the front of my yard. It has multiplied and blooms prolifically each spring.

When I worked on the westbank, I loved watching the seasonal succession of wildflowers in the field to the right of the street which curved down from the overpass onto General De Gaulle Drive. I don't think it was intended to be a wildflower spot, but Parkway and Park left it to the State which only mowed twice a year, perfect procedure for a wild garden. I saw the bluish flowers, which I later identified as wild petunias (*Ruellia carolinienses*), there. They make interesting small blooms in my front garden, especially with the pink primroses.

Another one of nature's gardens which I would like to duplicate is on the neutral ground along Earhart Boulevard: low growing mimosa, or sensitive plant blooming its small, pink flower puffs among blue wild petunias.

One year in a part of my front yard a plant which formed a dark green mat dotted with little, yellow flowers appeared. It grew thicker each year and bloomed more heavily until sword ferns spread into the area and blotted it out. I learned that it was creeping spot flower (*Spilanthes americana*) when Ranger David Muth identified it on a tour of the swamps of Jean Lafitte Park.

There are several ecological arguments for using wild-flowers. Once established, they require little maintainence except containment of the invasive ones. Energy conservation is a much nicer label for not weeding the garden than laziness. More can be conserved than your personal physical energy by the use of wildflowers. Financial costs are lower with natural plantings. Wildflowers do not usually need additional fertilizer to thrive. They can tolerate our dry spells, saving on the need to water. Water is not the rapidly diminishing resource in New Orleans that it is in other areas. But in taking its presence for granted through careless use, we deny the great expenditure of energy and resources involved in the chemical treatment of water and its transportation through pipes into our homes. Gardening with wildflowers can help build an appreciation for the beauty of our native flora and extend the natural habitats which are being lost to development, therefore helping to preserve our botanical heritage.

Though not an issue in most gardens, the distinction between indigenous and naturalized exotic wildflowers is made more and more when roadside plantings are considered. In parts of the country, invasive introduced plants are not only taking the place of native plants, but also destroying natural ecosystems that they are a part of. The loss of wildflowers means the loss of the natural communities, such as insect fauna, associated with each one. As has been seen with problem alien animals, such as the nutria which supplanted the native muskrat, the exotics don't have the predators that would keep their numbers in balance. If your wildflower garden is part of a native wildlife garden, you may want to stick to indigenous wildflowers.

The definitive source of information on wildflowers is the National Wildflower Research Center in Austin, Texas. It was founded and originally funded by Lady Bird Johnson, for whom highway beautification by preserving and reestablishing natural plantings along national roadways was a personal statement on environmental issues during her husband's term as President of the U. S. in the 1960's.

New Orleanians have access to two good resources for wildflower and native plant information. The Crosby Arboretum, whose Native Plant Center is in Picayune, Mississippi, displays more than 700 plant species in 11 separate natural habitats representative of the Gulf region. The Arboretum's plant sales are a good source of wildflowers.

The Louisiana Nature and Science Center in New Orleans East provides exhibits, tours, lectures, literature, demonstration wildflower plots, and access to experts.

The Nature Center sells wildflower seed mixtures made solely of species which will grow in the soil and climate of Louisiana. Seeds offered in their Louisiana Wildflower Mix #1 are all "Louisiana natives or wildflowers well established in Louisiana." Packets of seeds of individual species can be purchased, too.

Wildflower seed mixes can be ordered from companies, a list of which can be obtained from the National Wildflower Research Center. The mixes advertised in various periodicals frequently contain many grasses. A problem with ordering from non-regional sources is that the mixes contain many non-wildflower seeds, grass seeds, and seeds from some species which will not grow in Louisiana at all. Sticking with local sources is probably more economical in the long run.

A mix will provide a random selection of flowers for an area planting. But, for the purpose of integrating wild specimens into cultivated collections, individual plants are needed. Seed of several the plants in the list below are available in catalogs as the original forms or hybrid versions. Plants can be ordered, too, or purchased at Natives Nurseries. I am starting to see native wildflowers available as plants at other New Orleans area nurseries, too. Look carefully! Wild Seeds, Inc. in Houston offers small quantities of individual seeds. (See RESOURCES.)

If you cannot find a commercial source, taking cuttings or seeds of wildflowers is a better idea than removing the plant, itself. In some parts of the country, digging native plants is illegal. Many are tricky to transplant and digging is tantamount to destroying them. In addition, there are plants which approach extinction due to habitat destruction and overcollection.

Julia Sanders addresses some of the concerns expressed above in her guidelines for transplanting from the wild, *Floral and Faunal Notes: Landscaping with Louisiana Wildflowers, Number 4*, published by the Louisiana Nature and Science Center.

1. Identify the plant since some plants should never be removed (e.g., rare and endangered species). Catesby's lily and wild orchids look exotic and desirable, but are scarce and will not survive the transfer. Butterfly milkweed and other plants with a deep tap root usually cannot survive being dug up and replanted.

2. Check the soil in which the plant is growing and ask if this soil type is in your garden or can be created quickly.

3. Is the plant abundant in the area from which you are removing it? If not, leave it alone. If it is abundant, take only one or two plants. Seeds or cuttings from one plant will yield many plants for the next growing season.

4. It is best to transfer a plant before or after it has flowered.

5. Damage the roots as little as possible. Select a small plant and dig around the outer edge of the root system, keeping soil attached to the roots. Add water to the container or bag in which you have placed the plant.

6. Relocate the plant to your yard or garden as soon as possible. Be on the look-out for areas that are going to be cleared. Check with the owners of the property and rescue wildflowers, shrubs, and young trees.

It is important to duplicate the environment from which the plant comes in terms of moisture, wind, sunlight, and soil. This issue can be approached in one of two ways: by determining what conditions exist in your yard and finding plants which meet those specifications; or by altering the environment in which you wish to place

the plant by using additions to change the moisture retentiveness, drainage, pH, and fertility of the soil. Either
way, for success, information on the needs of each plant is
required. This can be obtained by reading; consulting the
Nature Center or Crosby Arboretum, nurseries, friends;
collecting data of your own (for instance, by pH testing of
the soil and observation); and by joining the Louisiana
Native Plant Society or Project Wildflower.

Julia Sanders continues experimental wildflower planting in her uptown garden. Read her articles in *New Orleans Plant and Garden Magazine* to find the results of her
latest trials. She stresses the importance of duplicating soil
conditions. Frequently, the rich soil of the garden creates
a "legginess" in wildflowers not found in native settings.

The Louisiana Native Plant Society was formed in
1984 for *"the preservation, conservation and study of native
plants in their habitats; the promotion of knowledge of their acceptable utilization; and the education of the public about the
values of native plants and their habitats."* Winter and
summer meetings are held and an informative newsletter
offered for nominal dues.

Louisiana Project Wildflower is an organization which
supports research and projects for highway plantings of
wildflowers. Its newsletter announces conferences, provides much information about wildflower research useful
in your own back (or front) yard.

Even with extensive efforts, you may find that there
are wildflowers which just will not grow in your yard.
There are plants which do well in eastern New Orleans,
but not so well uptown, etc. But the rewards from the
successes are so great! Just consider it a gardening adventure!

Following are some of the wildflowers you can try in
your New Orleans garden. I have included most of the
ones in the Nature Center's mixes, plus some.

WILDFLOWERS FOR
THE NEW ORLEANS GARDEN

1766 Indicates species grown in Thomas Jefferson's garden at Monticello.
1838 Indicates listing in Lelievre's *New Gardener of Louisiana*.
1859 Indicates listing in the catalogue of plants offered for sale by John M.
   Nelson at Magnolia Nurseries at Metairie Ridge and at his Plant Depot,
   Corner of Camp St. & Lafayette Sq., New Orleans.
1883 Indicates listing in *Almanac and Garden Manual for the Southern States*, by
   Richard Frotscher, New Orleans seed merchant.
1916 Indicates listing in *Reuters Seeds for the South*, Spring, New Orleans.
1918 Indicates listing in *Bollwinkle Seed Co. Ltd., Catalogue & Garden Guide*, 510
   Dumaine St.

Achillea millefolium L. **WHITE YARROW** Europe, na-turalized in North America. Herbaceous perennial, Com-posite family. Sun. Will grow in very poor, dry soil. Clusters of small, white flowers on stems to two feet May to July. Foliage is low, fine and feathery, fragrant when crushed; can be used as a ground cover. Cultivar 'Rosea' has pink flowers. Grow from seed or division in early spring. Easy. Grown in European herb gardens for cen-turies.

Amsonia tabernaemontana Walt. **BLUE-STAR** U.S., Lou-isiana. Dogbane family, perennial. Sun, light shade. Rich, moist garden soil, but adaptable. Attractive, clump forming plant to three feet which blooms for two weeks in the spring. Many flowered clusters of light blue blossoms. Seeds or division. Do not expect flowers for two to three years on new plants.

Arisaema dracontium and *A. triphyllum* **JACK-IN-THE-PULPIT** See BULBS.

Asclepias curassavica L. **BLOODFLOWER** South Amer-ica, naturalized in Louisiana. Perennial, Milkweed family. Sun. Well drained soil. Vivid orange-scarlet-gold blooms spring to fall. Attractive pods release tufted seeds from which volunteers arise garden-wide. Monarch butterflies love them. Susceptible to frost damage, but always return in my garden.

A. lanceolata Walt. **RED MILKWEED** U.S., Louisiana. Herbaceous perennial. Sun. Found in wet areas in pine woods and marshes. Reddish flowers on slender four foot stems, May to August. Stems produce milky sap when broken. Flower pods release pretty, feathery tufted seeds when mature.

A. tuberosa L. **BUTTERFLY WEED** U.S., Louisiana. Herbaceous perennial. Sun. Does well in dry, sandy, well-drained soils; alkaline pH. Orange flowers on two foot stems May to July. Hybrids are in reds, yellows, also. Difficult to transplant due to the taproot which the plant sends down deep; seeds or cuttings are better. Division is not recommended. They come up late in spring; site should be marked so they aren't damaged during cultivation. Lacks the milky sap of other milk-weeds, has the same pretty seedpods. In J. B. Russell's 1827 seed catalogue.

Aster species L. **ASTER** Number of native species in Louisiana is unknown. Perennials, Composite family. Sun. Medium-rich, drier soil. Usually flower in summer or fall: yellow centered surrounded by a single row of bristly petals in purple, blue, violet, white. Take cuttings or divisions in spring or sow seed (many more than need-ed since germination rate is low.)

Baptisia species Venten. **WILD** or **FALSE INDIGO** North America. Legume family perennials, several found in Louisiana. Open, sunny setting to light shade. Found in poor, well drained, sandy soil. Pea-like cluster flowers along long stems; white, yellow, blue, depending on the species; April to June. Shrubby habit, dense roots. Seeds slow to germinate; nursery plants are a good idea.

Callirhoe papaver (Cav.) Gray **POPPY-MALLOW** North America, Louisiana. Mallow family, annual. Sun. Well-drained, dryer soil. Bright rose or violet, two-inch flowers on a sprawling plant, March to July. From seed planted in the ground. More common in north Louisiana than

THE NEW ORLEANS GARDEN

south. Les Cambias had some in bloom during my tour of his garden. They were stunning! Available mail-order.

Centaurea cynanus L. **CORNFLOWER** Mediterranean area, escaped cultivation in North America. Annual, Composite family. Sun. Any well-drained soil. Bright blue flowerheads, sometimes pink or white, appear June through September. From seed planted in early spring. 1766, 1838, 1883.

Cichorium intybus L. **COMMON CHICORY** Europe, naturalized in North America. Perennial, Composite family. Sun. Not picky about soil, found in neglected fields and along roadsides, though when cultivated for its roots which are used in New Orleans style coffee and chicory, soil is prepared by deep tilling. Azure-blue, sometimes pink or white flowers from June to October. Grow from seed.

Commelina erecta L. **DAYFLOWER** North America, Louisiana. Spiderwort family, perennial. Sun, part sun. Found in moist places, gardens dry or wet. Brilliant blue flowers in the morning, April to frost. Foliage becomes ratty into the season. The plant is very invasive and difficult to get rid of. Learn to love the flowers; unless you're more meticulous about weeding than I, once they find their way into your garden, and they will, you're stuck!

Coreopsis lanceolata L. **TICKSEED** North America, Louisiana. Composite family, perennial. Sun, light shade. Any well-drained soil. Lots of yellow flowers on stems to two feet from clumps of low foliage, April to June. Bloom can be extended by removing old flowers. It reseeds readily. Easy to grow.

C. tinctoria Nutt. **PAINTED COREOPSIS, CALLIOPSIS** North American plains native, spread elsewhere after escape from cultivation where it was grown for its attractive flowers. Annual, Composite family. Sun, light shade. Will grow in poor, well-drained, sandy soil. Profuse blooms, May into June, are yellow daisies with reddish-purple center blotches, brilliant colors. Easy from seed.

Crinum americanum L. **SWAMP LILY or FLORIDA CRINUM** See BULBS.

Daucus carota L. **QUEEN ANNE'S LACE** Eurasia, naturalized in U.S. Annual, biennial; Carrot family. Half a day's sun, any soil. Ferny clumps of leaves send up flowering stems 3 to 6 feet, producing 4 inch clusters of delicate white flowers summer-fall. Bloom is heavy at first, then sporadic through the rest of the season.

Duchesnea indica (Andr.) Focke **WILD STRAWBERRY, MOCK STRAWBERRY** West Indies or India, depending on the reference. Naturalized in the U.S., Louisiana. Perennial, Rose family. Similar in appearance to the strawberry, *Fragaria*: Is in the same family, different genus and has yellow flowers, not white. Sun or shade. Not picky as to soil; in my yard, does seem to prefer moist spots. Low, trailing plant which forms an attractive ground cover with strawberry like leaves, small five-petaled, yellow flowers in March to April; followed by small, red, tasteless fruit which looks like a strawberry. Division. It just appeared in my garden.

Echinacea purpurea (L.) Moench. **PURPLE CONE-FLOWER** North America, Louisiana. Perennial, Composite family. Sunlight, very light shade. Sandy, humusy, fertile, well-drained but dry soil with neutral to alkaline pH. Blooms, May into June, are unusual, prickly domes in the center of purple petaled flowers which curve backwards. From seed or division of plants in the fall. J.B. Russell's 1827 seed catalogue. *E. pallida* Nutt. **PALE CONE-FLOWER** Another Louisiana coneflower similar to above, narrower petals. Seeds available.

Erigeron philadelphicus L. **DAISY FLEABANE** Indigeneous to, found throughout the U.S. Perennial, Composite family. Sun, light shade. Rich and light, moist, but well-drained soil. December to May blooms are clusters of small, yellow-centered, bristly petaled, pink to white flow-

ers from rosettes of leaves. Division is the best means of
obtaining plants. Cultivated varieties available from seed
companies.

E. *vernus* (L.) Torr. & A. Gray. **ROBIN'S-PLANTAIN**
Louisiana native, found in moist places. Flowers, pink to
white bristles around yellow centers arise from rosettes of
basal leaves February to June.

Erythrina herbacea L. **MAMOU, CORAL BEAN** Southeast U.S., Louisiana. Shrubby perennial from the Legume
family. Full sun, part shade. Best in moist, fertile, sandy,
humusy soil. Red flowers, two inches long and tubular in
form on spikes projecting 8 to 15 inches above the foliage,
April to June. Seed pods split in autumn to expose bright
red beans. Not easily transplanted. Grow from seeds.
Though a freeze will kill the top, it returns from roots.

Eupatorium coelestinum L. **MIST-FLOWER, WILD
AGERATUM** Eastern U.S., Louisiana. Composite family
perennial. Sun, filtered sun. Constantly moist, sandy,
humusy soil; mulch. Flowers August to frost, sometimes
in April are hairy, bright blue to violet in colorful clusters
on plants to two feet. Spreads by underground stems;
seeds itself abundantly.

E. *fistulosum* Barratt **JOE PYE WEED** Louisiana. Perennial, Composite family. Sun, part sun. Moist or wet,
humusy soil. 2 to 9 foot tall plant produces large, rounded clusters of bright pink-purple flowers, July to September. Divide every 2 to 3 years to avoid crowding from
the plant's fast growth.

Eustoma grandiflorum (Raf.) Shinn.[E. *russellianum*; *Lisianthus russellianus*] **PRAIRIE GENTIAN, LISIANTHUS**
North America. Gentian family, annual or biennial. Treat
as annuals. Occasionally return a second year. Sun.
Very well-drained soil. They like our summer heat, not
our humidity. In 1981, Japanese hybridizers returned this
wildflower to the U. S. as an amazingly beautiful garden
plant. Well-known after use, from 1983, at Disney World.
Leathery-gray foliage on plants to 14 inches. Waxy-white,

pink, gentian-purple flowers; single or double. Slender, rose-like buds unfurl into tulip forms then poppy-like blooms. Long-lasting cut. Readily available from nurseries for spring planting, summer bloom. Difficult from seed, but I did it one year! I gave a garden party to show off the rows and rows of flowers.

Gaillardia pulchella Foug. **FIREWHEEL, INDIAN BLANKET** North America, Louisiana. Short lived perennial, Composite family. Full sun. Sandy, well-drained soil. Blooms April to frost are daisy-like with serrated edged petals, purplish-red to red with yellow edges, sometimes all orange or all yellow. Can get leggy in the garden. Reseeds. Easy from seed or cuttings in June. *Gaillardia bicolor* was available in 1883.

Helenium autumnale L. **SNEEZEWEED** North America, Louisiana. Perennial, Composite family. Sun. Rich soil. One inch yellow flowers September to frost on 30 inch, many branched plants. Improved cultivars are available through catalogues. J. B. Russell's 1827 seed catalogue.

Helianthus L. species **SUNFLOWERS** New World. Composite family annuals or perennials. Sun. Average, well-drained soil. Fertile soil can produce weaker stems which require staking. Coarse in form, the plants are grown for their showy yellow petaled flowers with yellow, brown, or purple centers; bloom spring to fall. Though division is best method of increase, stem cuttings before flowering, or seed work, also. See ANNUALS for cultivated varieties. 1883 *H. annuus* L. was grown by American Indians for its seeds. *H. angustifolius* L. **NARROW-LEAVED** or **SWAMP SUNFLOWER** tolerates moist soils. Cut back in summer.

Hibiscus militaris Cav. **HALBERD-LEAVED ROSE MALLOW** North America, Louisiana. Perennial, Mallow family. Sun. Found in wet, heavy, soil. Pinkish-white flowers with a maroon throat bloom from May to October on a shrubby plant to six feet. Grow from seed.

H. lasiocarpos Cav. **WOOLY ROSE-MALLOW** Native perennial. Mallow family. Sun. Wet, clay soil. Large flowers are white (sometimes pink) with red centers, bloom from May to September. Seed. I have seen both of the above growing in the Bonnet Carre Spillway.

Hymenocallis caroliniana **SWAMP LILY** See BULBS.

Ipomopsis rubra (L.) Wherry **STANDING CYPRESS, SCARLET GILIA** North America. Biennial or perennial, Phlox family. Sun. Sandy, well-drained soil. Red and yellow tubular flowers along a stem extending 2 feet above leaves in April on a plant which is a rosette the first year, sends up an 8 foot stem the second. Grow from seed.

Iris fulva, I. X nelsonii, I. brevicaulis, I. giganticaerulea **LOUISIANA IRIS** See BULBS.

Kosteletzkya virginica (L.) Gray **SALT MARSHMAL-LOW** Eastern U.S., Louisiana coastal marshes. Perennial, Mallow family. Sun, filtered sun. Rich garden soil. Blooms are abundant on a much branched stem, to six feet; May to October, 2 to 3 inch delicate, pink mallow form with a column of yellow stamens protruding from the center. Can be found along roads between Highway 51 and Lake Pontchartrain (a good birding spot, also!).

Layia platyglossa (Fisch. & C. A. Mey.) A. Gray **TIDY TIPS DAISY** California. Composite family annual. Sun. Sandy, or humusy, well drained soil, lots of moisture. Yellow, daisy flower heads with white edges; spring and early summer bloom. From seed.

Liatris spicata (L.) Willd. **BLAZING STAR** Eastern U.S. native. Composite family, perennial. Sun. Fertile, slightly sandy, well-drained soil; moisture. Flowers are purple clusters which bloom from the top down along spiky-stalks in August, September. As the seeds can take a year to germinate, it makes sense to buy plants from a nursery.

Other *Liatris* species like drier conditions. Several are found in Louisiana but should be left alone, nursery plants obtained. *L. graminifolia* and *L. tenuis* are on the endangered list for our state.

Lobelia cardinalis L. **CARDINAL FLOWER** North America, Louisiana. Perennial, Lobelia family. Part shade. Fertile, moist, neutral to acid soil, mulch to conserve moisture; found along sandy stream banks naturally. I lost some which I grew from seed during a dry spell one summer. Now I have a drip system which keeps the soil constantly moist; I still loose plants to rot and to the snails which love the tender leaves. Startlingly bright red tubular based flowers around a foot or more long stalk on plants to four feet tall, August to October. Julia Sanders feels rich soil causes the normally erect stems to flop. From seed, never dig from the wild where they are becoming scarce. Mine came from Natives Nurseries and Talen's. 1766 *L. siphilitica* L. **BIG BLUE LOBELIA** Blue flowers on plants to 3 feet. Grows in the Spillway.

Lupinus subcarnosus Hook. **TEXAS BLUEBONNET** Texas. Annual, Legume family. Sun. Well-drained, moderately fertile, neutral to alkaline soil. Bright blue flowers with white or yellow spots, March to April, on plants to 20 inches tall. Seeds should be soaked 24 hours before planting in soil kept moist until the seeds germinate. Once established, they should seed themselves. Pretty even if they don't. Available in nurseries in spring.

Mimosa strigillosa T. & G. **MIMOSA, SENSITIVE PLANT** Tropical America. Legume family, perennial with prostrate stems. Sun. Well-drained soil. Compound leaves fold when touched. The puffball, pink flowers bloom March to September. *M. pudica* 1883, 1766

Mimulus alatas Ait. **MONKEYFLOWER** North America, Louisiana. Snapdragon family, perennial. Sun, part shade. Moist soil, found naturally in marshes and along pond edges. Erect plant one to three feet tall, with lavender flowers which look like little monkey faces, June to September. From seed, cuttings, division. *M. ringens* is similar, on the endangered list for Louisiana.

Monarda citriodora Cerv. **LEMON BEE BALM** North America, widespread in Louisiana. Annual, Mint family. Sun. Dry, well drained soil. Flowers, May to July are white to pink, purple spotted; plants to a yard high. Cut back after flowering. Seed.

M. fistulosa L. **WILD BERGAMOT** or **BEE BALM** Louisiana. Perennial. Sun. Moist, sandy soil with organic matter. Plants to 3 feet produce pink, lavender, purple flowers May to August. Seeds, cuttings, division.

Oenothera speciosa Nutt. **MEXICAN PRIMROSE** North American, Louisiana native. Perennial, Evening primrose family. Sun. Sandy, well-drained soil with high lime content. Plants to 20 inches tall, spreading, produce one to three inch white and pink flowers with bright yellow anthers to October, heavy bloom March to June. Called buttercup by many. Self seeds. Will not flower the first year from seed. Easy. Common in New Orleans.

Oxalis rubra, **OXALIS**, *O. stricta* **YELLOW WOOD SORREL** See BULBS.

Penstemon digitalis Nutt. **BEARDTONGUE** North America, Louisiana. Snapdragon family, perennial. Sun, part sun. Well-drained, dryer soil; though adaptable. 2 to 3 foot stems with showy white flowers April to May. Seed. *P. digitalis* will grow in New Orleans. There are other penstemons native to Louisiana which will grow here. City Park Botanical Gardens grows *P. tubiflorus* Nutt., a white flowered species. *P. laxiflorus* Pennell is delicate lavender. Dorothea Boldt grows it in a raised planter, has seen it naturalized in a lawn on St. Charles Avenue. The western species offered in catalogs need excellent drainage and moisture, but are turned off by wet winters. I have not been successful with any of them.

Phlox divaricata L. **BLUE PHLOX** North America, found in Louisiana. Perennial, Phlox family. Sun to semi-shade. Moist, fertile, well-drained soil; high organic content. A creeping plant which forms a thick mat, pretty and green in the winter, though it gets ratty in summer;

sends up clusters of rich blue to reddish-purple flowers in March to May; white form also. With well-grown plants, enough sun, a solid blanket of color can be formed. Division and stem cuttings are recommended. These plants are readily available in local nurseries where I got mine and where they may be called "Louisiana phlox."

P. pilosa L. **PRAIRIE PHLOX** Also found in Louisiana, is similar to *P. divaricata* but is taller, flowers are pink to dark lavender, sometimes white, bloom April to May; grows in sandier soil.

P. drummondii Hook. **ANNUAL PHLOX** Native to Texas. Sun, very light shade. Good garden soil, very well drained. Bright red, white, pink, or purple flowers bloom on plants 8 to 18 inches tall, March through June. Bloom can be prolonged if old flowers are removed. Seed. Many cultivated varieties of the original Texas wildflower now grow wild in other areas of the South. Seed. Scottish botanist, Drummond, identified it in 1830.

Physostegia virginica (L.) Benth. **OBEDIENT PLANT, OBEDIENCE PLANT, FALSE DRAGON HEAD** North America, Louisiana. Mint family, perennial. Sun, part sun. Moist or dry, rich, welldrained garden soil. Purple spotted pink flowers like snapdragons in spikelike clusters to ten inches long on plants two to four feet tall, summer-fall. Flowers, which are longer at the bottom of the spike, bloom from the bottom up. The name comes from the fact that flower spikes will persist in angles to which they are bent. Cultivars in whites, shades of pink, rose, lavender. Kitten Grote of Covington planted some white plants given her by Miek Laan of Ocean Springs. They are pink in Kitten's garden. She wonders if the acid soil makes the difference. From seed or division of clumps.

Prunella vulgaris L. **SELF-HEAL, HEALALL** Eurasia, widely naturalized in North America. Mint family, perennial. Partial shade. Found in many habitats: apparently adaptable as to soil requirements. Blooms March into June are clusters of violet, pink, white, or bicolored spikes on plants six to twenty inches tall. Seeds or division. Once used medicinally for sore throats. I found it growing on the levee by Audubon Park. Cultivated varieties of other species are offered in some mail-order catalogs. They would be worth trying to see if they would thrive in New Orleans as their wild cousin does.

Ranunculus bulbosus L. **BUTTERCUP** Europe, North Africa, widely naturalized in North America. Crowfoot or Buttercup family perennial. Sun. Found in lawns, old fields, along roadsides, low areas: adaptable as to soil, like moisture. Many one inch yellow flowers on one to two foot stalks rising from basal leaves; April to June. Seed. Invasive.

Several other members of this genus are found in Louisiana, signalled by their flowers with five butter-yellow petals, some tiny in size; creeping or erect form. You'll probably find some growing in your lawn already if you look closely!

Ratibida columnifera (Nutt.) Woot. & Standl. **PRAIRIE CONEFLOWER, MEXICAN HAT** North America, found in Louisiana. Perennial, Composite family. Sun. Any well-drained, neutral to alkaline, garden soil. June to October blooms; flowers have an elongated conical center from which yellow and brown petals droop. Stems to two feet, upper parts leafless. Grow from seed.

R. pinnata (Vent.) Barnh. Thinner yellow petals than above on plants to three feet. Found occasionally in Louisiana.

Rudbeckia hirta L. **BLACK-EYED SUSAN** North America, Louisiana. Short-lived perennial, Composite family. Sun, light shade. Poor, dry, well-drained soil; though adaptable. Flowers, two inches wide, have yellow petals, extended or drooping from conical brown centers; April to July. Plants are coarse, hairy, to two feet high. Easy from seed which should be planted in the fall. Will re-seed if the spot is right.

R. amplexicaulis Vahl. is also classified as *Dracopsis amplexicaulis* (Vahl) Cass. **CLASPING LEAF CONEFLOWER** Louisiana. Composite family, annual. Flowers are similar to the black-eyed Susan but with a more elongated shape. Bloom April to June on plants which can reach five feet. From seed.

R. fulgida Ait. **BRACTED CONEFLOWER** Perennial. Plants to three feet high; flowers May to July have green bracts, elongated and drooping downward under the yellow petals, shallow brown conical centers.

R. maxima Nutt. **GIANT CONEFLOWER** Perennial. Three to six feet. June to September flowers have a long conical brown to black center surrounded by shorter, yellow petals.

Ruellia brittoniana E. Leonard **DOORSTEP FLOWER** Mexico, escaped cultivation, naturalized in the Southeast U.S. Perennial. Bushy plants, to 3 feet. Leaves are purplish in color, long and narrow, willow-like. Flowers from April are one and a half inches long, similar in shape to the *Ruellia*, below, but lavender, plentiful. Spread like a weed all over New Orleans. They eject their seeds with an electrical sounding "ping." For years I didn't know a popular name for this flower, but a friend once told me her father called them "Doorstep Flowers" because you always find them growing by people's doorsteps. I like that better than **MEXICAN PETUNIA**, which is what they are called in Texas. The healthiest stand of them in New Orleans is in Susan LaRocca's wildflower garden on Zimple Street. Probably introduced this century. The Tulane University Herbarium has a specimen collected in Houma in 1914, later ones from New Orleans.

R. caroliniensis (J. F. Gmel.) Steud. **WILD PETUNIA** Perennial, Acanthus family. North America, Louisiana. Sun, light shade. Well-drained, organic, garden soil on the dry side. April to June blooms are trumpet-shaped like little petunias, bluish in color; plants to fourteen inches tall. Cuttings in July, seeds, division. Self seeds readily.

It has moved from my front garden to my husband's studio garden across the street on its own in one season.

Salvia coccinea Juss. ex J. Murr. **TEXAS SAGE, SCAR-LET SAGE, TROPICAL SAGE** Mint family, Perennial. Southern North America and Mexico, West Indies. Best in sun; blooms in shade, too, in my garden. Found in sandy soils; rich soil suggested, but I have found the plant quite adaptable. Spikes of small bright red flowers from April on the square stems typical of salvias, colored black. To 3 feet. Call it wide and spreading, or call it weedy, but if you do not cut it back each year, you will have a plant suitable only for your wild garden. I found my first plant growing in the overgrown back yard of an abandoned uptown house. It transplanted readily, has reseeded even more readily. If you are not truly committed to desiring this flower, watch out! Hummingbird, bee flower. 1883

S. lyrata L. **LYRE-LEAVED SAGE, CANCERWEED** Eastern U.S., Louisiana.   Perennial, mint family. Sun, part sun. Well-drained, sandy, humusy soil. Blooms February through May, are spikes of graceful lavender blue flowers on square stems, one to two feet, sometimes branched; from a rosette of lyre-shaped leaves. From summer cuttings or seeds. Beautiful. Lots of it grows in City Park.

Senecio glabellus Poir. **BUTTERWEED, YELLOWTOP** U.S, Louisiana native. Annual, Composite family. Sun, part sun. Grows in rich, moist or wet soil. Plant, to 3 feet, produces small yellow petaled, yellow centered flowers in clusters which are singly colorful; in masses, breathtaking. Bloom December into May; when at their peak, they turn the roadsides on I-10 to Baton Rouge golden. Seedheads fluffy and white. Volunteered in my husband's studiogarden and by my birdbath.

Sisyrinchium capillare Bicknell **BLUE-EYED-GRASS** U.S., Louisiana. Iris family, perennial. Sun. Moist, sandy soil with some organic matter. Leaves are tufts of thin, flattened iris-like blades with gems of half inch blue flowers tipping tiny stalks, March into May. Open in sunlight. It will thrive in a pot, scaled small to its 6 inch height. There are species with yellow or white flowers, also. I saw blues and yellows in the lawn at F. Edward Hebert Hospital, crouching low to avoid the mower. Cultivated varieties available as seed.

Solidago species L. GOLDENROD Species are native chiefly to North America, several to Louisiana. Composite family, perennials. Full sun, leggy in less. Average, well-drained soil, though enrichment with aged manure and leaf mold enhances growth. Plants from 2 to 8 feet high, depending on the species, produce brilliant yellow flowers in a variety of cluster forms from August to frost. Clumps will encroach on others if not well spaced, growth is rapid under good conditions. Does not cause hayfever. (Ragweed does.) Though usually treated with disdain as weeds in the U.S., Europeans use our native goldenrods as garden ornamentals. Some hybrids have been developed specifically for garden use, also. They may be a better choice for the garden than natives whose great beauty may not compensate for its greater invasiveness.

I left a weed which came up in the corner of the rose bed to see what it would become. It grew into a clump of leafy stalks which became taller and taller without blooming. Finally, in October, greenish buds lining stems protruding from the upper portions of the stalks began to emit fuzzy golden flowers: *S. altissima* L., FIELD GOLDENROD, a nice touch amid all the red and orange of my fall hummer garden!

Spigelia marilandica L. INDIAN PINK, PINKROOT Southern U.S., Louisiana. Logania family, perennial. Sun, part sun. Rich, moist soil. Blooms March into May are tubular, bright red on the outside, opening in five points at the tips to reveal yellow insides; arranged in a cluster along a stem which leans to one side, they open from the bottom up. Flowering period can be extended by removing faded blooms. To 2 feet. Available mail-order. Mine was crowded out before its first bloom by rampant sword ferns, but I plan to try it again.

Spilanthes americana (Mutis) Hieron. **CREEPING SPOT FLOWER** U.S., Louisiana.   Composite family, perennial. Sun, shade.   Moist soil.   Plant creeps over the ground, producing small yellow centered flowers with squarish yellow petals April to frost.   Seeds or cuttings.   Mine just appeared.

Stokesia laevis L'Her. **STOKE'S ASTER, STOKESIA** North America, Louisiana.   Perennial, Composite family. Sun, light shade.   Average garden soil, well-drained.   3 to 4 inch wide flowers, white and blue to purplish blue on stems to 2 feet above the clumps of leathery leaves, May through September.   Seed, cuttings in fall, or division.   Go od drainage is very important.   They hate wet winters. Cultivated varieties are available.   The taller ones can get floppy in the garden. I love them.

Teucrium canadense L. **AMERICAN GERMANDER, WOOD SAGE** Eastern North America, Louisiana marsh margins.   Mint family, perennial to 3 feet.   Sun, part sun. Moist or wet soils.   Erect, hairy stems; sage-like leaves. Spikes of purplish pink flowers July to October.

Thermopsis caroliniana M. A. Curtis **CAROLINA LU-PINE** Eastern U.S. Legume family, perennial, to 5 feet. Sun.   Any well-drained soil.   Gray-green leaves on un-branched stems are attractive.   Yellow half inch flowers on 10 inch spikes last only 2 weeks, spring.

Tillandsia usneoides L. **SPANISH MOSS** North and South America, almost a trademark of southern Louisiana. Pineapple family, epiphyte.   This plant lives on, but not off of other plants: it is not a parasite.   Its coating of greenish-gray scales absorb dust and water from the air for nourishment.   It needs shade, is often seen on oak and cypress trees.   I'll bet you didn't know that it has tiny, emerald green flowers in May!

Tradescantia virginiana L. or *T. X andersoniana* W. Ludw & Rohw. **SPIDERWORT** North America, Louisiana.   Most plants found in old gardens (like mine) are the hybrid, which has escaped cultivation in this area. Spiderwort family, perennial. Partial shade. Moist fertile soil is best, but is adaptable. April to June blooms are violet-blue, rarely pink or white, with tiny, bright golden anthers, three petals, open mornings until noon. Plants are grassy clumps to about two feet tall. Seeds, division. Mine showed up one day, or maybe it was always there with the alstroemeria and I didn't notice. 1921 New Orleans Garden Society list of recommended perennials. Invasive.

Trifolium incarnatum L. **CRIMSON CLOVER** Europe, widely planted in the U.S., Louisiana. Pea family, annual. Two to three inch tapered clusters of dark red flowers bloom from the base up March to June. Only certain strains reseed. Used for soil enrichment and cover. I saw crimson clover in the middle ground on Highway 90 to Houma last year. Discussed as animal forage in *Southern Garden* article, 1894.

T. pratense L. **RED CLOVER** Europe, naturalized in North America. Pea family, short lived perennial. Sun, part sun. Best in moist, rich soil. Its globular, typical clover flowers are magenta, not red, bloom April to June; foliage is rather straggly in form. I have one which has lasted several years in a moist, shady part of the garden. The plants in a sunnier spot produced heavier bloom, but were crowded out. Has agricultural uses; clover seeds available at Feed and Seed stores.

T. repens L. **WHITE CLOVER** Europe, naturalized in the U.S., Louisiana. Pea family, perennial. Sun, part sun. Moist, fertile soil. A creeping plant which, when well grown, has lush clover-leaves, white to pinkish round flower heads January to May. Can die down in the heat of the summer or bloom on until November. Its nitrogen-fixing properties make it useful in lawns.

Verbena canadensis (L.) Brit. **ROSE VERBENA, VERBE-NA** Southeast U.S., Louisiana. Vervain family, perennial, grown as an annual. Spreading plant, to 20 inches high.

Sun. Well-drained soil. Cultivars are available in reddish-purple, lilac, rose, white. Flowers March to June.

V. rigida K. Spreng. **TUBER VERVAIN** South America, naturalized in Southeast U.S. Vervain family, perennial. Sun. Will grow in poor, well-drained, sandy soil. Spreads through underground roots; stems are erect to two feet, leaves thick, hairy, rough with toothed edges. Flowers are deep purple spike-like clusters present April to October. Division or from purchased seed. Mine is planted in my raised rose bed. Its only problem is mildew which makes the foliage ugly through moist periods. I cut it back, start fresh with new spring growth.

V. tenuisecta Briq. **MOSS VERBENA** South America, naturalized in the southern U.S. Vervain family, perennial. Sun. Grows in poor, well-drained, sandy soil; adaptable to other conditions. Low, spreading foliage withan abundance of pretty, purple or white cluster flowers, March to July. Seed.

Vernonia altissima Nutt. **IRONWEED** Perennial, Composite family. Eastern U.S., Louisiana. Sun, part sun. Rich, moist or wet soil. Plants to eight feet, foot wide clusters of purple-blue flower heads in August to October; followed by purple or brown bristled seed. Division, cuttings, seed. Poor germination rate, sow lots of seed. One of the autumn stars of Jean Lafitte Park.

Viola species L. **VIOLET** Temperate regions, worldwide. Species sometimes hard to identify, even for botanists. Several are found in Louisiana. Violet family, perennial or annual. Partial shade. Rich, welldrained, moist soil. Low growing plants form small clumps. Most familiar is the heart-shaped leaf, though there are other forms, too. Delicate, five petaled flowers, in blues to purples, yellow, white; spring to early summer. Seeds, division. Mine reseed readily in non-competitive spots such as the bark path and in the rose bed mulch.

WILDFLOWERS BY SEASON OF BLOOM

SPRING-BLOOMING WILDFLOWERS

Achillea millefolium WHITE YARROW
Amsonia tabernaemontana BLUE-STAR
Asclepias curassavica BLOODFLOWER
Asclepias lanceolata RED MILKWEED
Asclepias tuberosa BUTTERFLY WEED
Baptisia species WILD OR FALSE INDIGO
Callirhoe papaver POPPY-MALLOW
Commelina erecta DAYFLOWER
Coreopsis lanceolata TICKSEED
Coreopsos tinctoria PAINTED COREOPSIS, CALLIOPSIS
Duchesnea indica WILD STRAWBERRY, MOCK STRAWBERRY
Echinacea purpurea PURPLE CONEFLOWER
Erigeron philadelphicus DAISY FLEABANE
Erythrina herbacea MAMOU, CORAL BEAN
Eupatorium coelestinum MIST-FLOWER, WILD AGERATUM
Gaillardia pulchella FIREWHEEL, INDIAN BLANKET
Helianthus species SUNFLOWERS
Hibiscus militaris HALBERD-LEAVED ROSE MALLOW
Hibiscus lasiocarpos WOOLY ROSE-MALLOW
Ipomopsis rubra STANDING CYPRESS, SCARLET GILIA
Layia platyglossa TIDY TIPS DAISY
Lupinus subcarnosus TEXAS BLUEBONNET
Mimosa strigillosa MIMOSA, SENSITIVE PLANT
Monarda citriodora LEMON BEEBALM
Monarda fistulosa WILD BERGAMOT or BEEBALM
Oenothera speciosa MEXICAN PRIMROSE
Penstemon digitalis BEARDTONGUE
Phlox divaricata BLUE PHLOX
Phlox drummondii ANNUAL PHLOX
Prunella vulgaris SELF-HEAL, HEALALL
Ranunculus bulbosus BUTTERCUP
Rudbeckia hirta BLACK-EYED SUSAN
Rudbeckia amplexicaulis CLASPING LEAF CONEFLOWER
Rudbeckia fulgida BRACTED CONEFLOWER
Ruellia caroliniensis WILD PETUNIA
Ruellia brittoniana DOORSTEP FLOWER
Salvia coccinea TEXAS SAGE, SCARLET SAGE, TROPICAL SAGE
Salvia lyrata LYRE-LEAVED SAGE, CANCERWEED
Senecio glabellus BUTTERWEED, YELLOWTOP
Sisyrinchium capillare BLUE-EYED-GRASS
Spigelia marilandica INDIAN PINK, PINKROOT
Spilanthes americana CREEPING SPOT FLOWER

Stokesia laevis STOKE'S ASTER, STOKESIA
Thermopsis caroliniana CAROLINA LUPINE
Tradescantia virginiana SPIDERWORT
Trifolium incarnatum CRIMSON CLOVER
Trifolium pratense RED CLOVER
Trifolium repens WHITE CLOVER
Verbena canadensis ROSE VERVAIN, VERBENA
Verbena rigida TUBER VERVAIN
Viola species VIOLET

SUMMER-BLOOMING WILDFLOWERS

Achillea millefolium WHITE YARROW
Asclepias curassavica BLOODFLOWER
Asclepias lanceolata RED MILKWEED
Asclepias tuberosa BUTTERFLY WEED
Callirhoe papaver POPPY-MALLOW
Centaurea cynanus CORNFLOWER
Cichorium intybus COMMON CHICORY
Commelina erecta DAYFLOWER
Coreopsis lanceolata TICKSEED
Coreopsis tinctoria PAINTED COREOPSIS, CALLIOPSIS
Daucus carota QUEEN ANNE'S LACE
Echinacea purpurea PURPLE CONEFLOWER
Echinacea vernus ROBIN'S-PLAINTAIN
Eupatorium fistulosum JOE PYE WEED
Eustoma grandiflorum PRAIRIE GENTIAN, LISIANTHUS
Gaillardia pulchella FIREWHEEL, INDIAN BLANKET
Helianthus species SUNFLOWERS
Hibiscus militaris HALBERD-LEAVED ROSE MALLOW
Hibiscus lasiocarpos WOOLY ROSE-MALLOW
Kosteletzkya virginica SALT MARSH-MALLOW
Layia platyglossa TIDY TIPS DAISY
Liatris spicata BLAZING STAR
Lobelia cardinalis CARDINAL FLOWER
Mimosa strigillosa MIMOSA, SENSITIVE PLANT
Mimulus alatas MONKEYFLOWER
Monarda citriodora LEMON BEEBALM
Monarda fistulosa WILD BERGAMOT, BEEBALM
Oenothera speciosa MEXICAN PRIMROSE
Phlox drummondii ANNUAL PHLOX
Physostegia virginica OBEDIENT PLANT, FALSE DRAGON HEAD
Ratibida columnifera PRAIRIE CONEFLOWER, MEXICAN HAT
Rudbeckia hirta BLACK-EYED SUSAN
Rudbeckia fulgida BRACTED CONEFLOWER
Rudbeckia maxima GIANT CONEFLOWER
Ruellia brittoniana DOORSTEP FLOWER

Salvia coccinea TEXAS SAGE, SCARLET SAGE, TROPICAL SAGE
Spilanthes americana CREEPING SPOT FLOWER
Stokesia laevis STOKE'S ASTER, STOKESIA
Teucrium canadense AMERICAN GERMANDER, WOOD SAGE
Verbena rigida TUBER VERVAIN
Verbena tenuisecta MOSS VERBENA

FALL-BLOOMING WILDFLOWERS

Aster species ASTER
Centaurea cynanus CORNFLOWER
Cichorium intybus COMMON CHICORY
Commelina erecta DAYFLOWER
Daucus carota QUEEN ANNE'S LACE
Eupatorium coelestinum MIST-FLOWER, WILD AGERATUM
Gaillardia pulchella FIREWHEEL, INDIAN BLANKET
Helenium autumnale SNEEZEWEED
Hibiscus militaris HALBERD-LEAVED ROSE MALLOW
Kosteletzkya virginica SALT MARSH-MALLOW
Liatris spicata BLAZING STAR
Lobelia cardinalis CARDINAL FLOWER
Oenothera speciosa MEXICAN PRIMROSE
Physostegia virginica OBEDIENT PLANT,
       FALSE DRAGON HEAD
Ratibida columnifera PRAIRIE CONEFLOWER, MEXICAN HAT
Ruellia brittoniana DOORSTEP FLOWER
Solidago species GOLDENROD
Spilanthes americana CREEPING SPOT FLOWER
Stokesia laevis STOKE'S ASTER, STOKESIA
Teucrium canadense AMERICAN GERMANDER, WOOD SAGE
Verbena rigida TUBER VERVAIN
Vernonia altissima IRONWEED

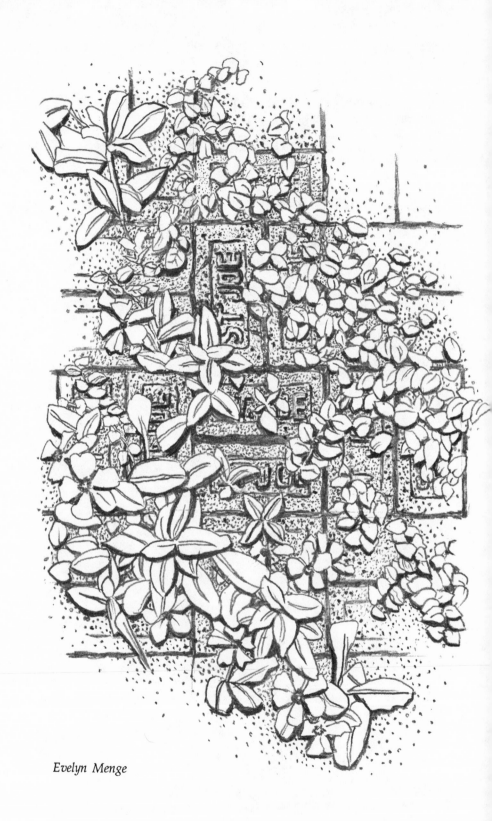

Evelyn Menge

Lawns and Groundcovers

"Shakespeare's lawns, Milton's lawns, were forest glades.
That 'lawn' equals 'grass' is a modern corruption, and I'd be prepared to
bet that before Mr. Edwin Bunning invented the lawn-mower in 1831,
it was an impossibility."

Wilfrid Blunt *Of Flowers and a Village*

What, no grass? That seems a heretical statement for
an American gardener. Though New Orleans gardeners
have a precedence for a break with tradition in the French
Quarter patio garden, the obsession with the lawn is well
entrenched here. The idea was brought to New Orleans
by American entrepreneurs of the Garden District during
the 1840's and later. They copied the fashions of the
wealthy of the northeast U.S. who were oriented toward
English styles, making lawns a part of their gardens.

George Washington Cable made a trip to New Orleans in 1914 during which he saw and commented posi-
tively on local gardens and their lawns. In *The Amateur
Gardener*, he hypothesizes a reason for the importance of
lawns to the American gardener:

...'formal garden', by reason of its initial and continuing costli-
ness, is, and must remain, the garden of the wealthy few, and

*that gardening for the great democracy of our land, the kind
that will make the country at large a gardened land, is 'informal', freehand, ungeometrical gardening....the supreme feature
is the lawn; the lawn mower puts this feature within the reach
of all....*

The lawn can represent everyman's estate around
everyman's castle.   But during the achievment of such
status, Cable warns that the lawn mower can become a
symbol of oppression and an enemy of good gardening.

As is obvious from reading observations of New Orleans gardens and gardening styles through the ages, each
observer has his personal bias determined by his own
cultural background and tastes.   However, there are other
options to the lawn.   There are reasons related to economy
and ecology for choosing other styles than the lawn if one
wishes.

Anne Bradburn's garden is an example of an alternative approach.   After hearing her discuss her garden, I
tried to pick out her house from the description without
knowing the street address. I could. The Bradburn home
is dramatically noticeable in its woodland setting among
others which are beautifully landscaped, but for which the
descriptive comment first out of my mouth was "well tended." Anne's dominant flowering plant is the wild *Tradescantia*, the major ground covering, a mat of oak leaves in
layers of differing stages of decomposition.   A native
azalea gleams golden in the early spring.

Lawns are an integral part of most gardens. I have
great admiration for those with the comittment and organization to maintain and manicure those green expanses
which can provide very appropriate surfaces for recreation
as well as aesthetically pleasing foils for borders, individual plant specimens, and garden architecture.   But I agree
with Cable. What a lot of work they are!

"Mowing the lawn" is a rite of passage for most ado-
lescents: a chore, a way of earning first income, an area
of sibling and parental squabbling.

"The lawn" provides almost as endless a source of conversation topics as the weather; I have heard it discussed over open-heart surgery at Southern Baptist Hospital, during a political party at Gallier Hall, in the checkout line at Schwegmann's, during a barbeque at Ann Morcos' house in Kenner, and by my neighbors sitting on the stoop on Upperline Street.

The lawn can provide a focus for some lives, and a source of tragedy,   comedy, irony.   Miss Maude spent years scavenging discarded sprigs of St. Augustine grass. She hoped to create a real lawn between the street and sidewalk along her house at Upperline and Constance. Mowing and edging the patchy rectangle was part of her rental agreement.   The meticulousness and pride with which she carried out these tasks made the finished product a monument to personal achievement.   A carpet of pure St. Augustine would make such effort worthwhile! The progress of the new grass over the wiry bermuda was a frequent theme of talk in the block (along with the way Mr. Victor treated his wife).   Perfection was achieved shortly before Miss Maude passed on.

The next tenant, male, lowered the blade on the mower, scalped the lawn, killed the St. Augustine.   Miss Mildred commented that her sister would "...roll over in her grave," if she knew. I have to wonder if the grass is what put her in her grave.

Despite the social significance of grass, I do not consider it to be one of the most interesting or enjoyable aspects of gardening (or topics of conversation). I see my being able to admit this as a sign of great personal growth, as I was as much a follower as anyone. My two pregnancies were even planned so I could cut the grass in October when its growth slowed, deliver, and be ready to mow again in the spring when the babies nursed less and the lawn resprouted. (My first husband did not do lawns. Did grass cause my divorce?)

Three grasses commonly used for New Orleans lawns are zoysia, St. Augustine, and bermuda. Consult your favorite nurseryman for further instructions and advice. As my children grew, I discarded their sand box, swing set, rabbit cages, and the grass. My garden, not for everyone, is raised beds and ground covers, living and architectural.

One of the things I love most about old New Orleans is the residue of the past still apparent in wrought iron gates, deteriorating wooden shed walls, six-board fences painted copper-napthalene green and old brick walkways. As most of the living ground covers do not provide a durable or comfortable surface for foot traffic, the favorite local walkway is of old New Orleans brick which can be set in sand or cement. Books on garden design suggest alternatives, many of which can be done yourself: flagstones, concrete stepping stones or walks dressed up with aggregates or imprinted designs, wood decks and pavers. Outdoor flooring can also be provided by organic products such as wood chips, sawdust, bark chunks, shredded bark, and pecan shells.

My beds are edged with liriope, bricks, or lumber. I killed all the grass with "Roundup" and removed it. Then I stretched a synthetic ground cloth (weed mat) which can be purchased locally, over the paths to block plant growth. This, I covered with shredded bark mulch (ordered by the truck load). For the first two years I had some nut grass grow through. I diligently pulled this and seem to have the problem licked. When sprouts do appear in the bark, five minutes with a rake takes care of the whole yard. Some seedlings I leave, thus the clumps of violets and patches of gaillardia, johnny-jump-ups, violets, and mock strawberries here and there in the path.

I faltered at times in my search for a maintainence-free garden. I know now that there is no such thing, even in Anne Bradburn's yard. But there are lower maintainence gardens and plantings which will require less effort with proper installation and early care. Inventive use of ground covers is part of the answer.

I had a scheme for the strip of ground in front of my husband's studio: white clover which (according to the book) dies to the ground in winter in Zone 9 and *Polygonum capitatum* or knotweed, an ornamental ground cover with small pink blooms which is so tough it is used for parking strip planting in California. The combination should be beautiful and so fast growing as to knock out weed growth before it began. My white clover was beautiful in the fall and winter, but died to the ground in summer. Why hadn't I noticed that clover dies in the summer? My knotweed wouldn't sprout at all. I don't know why.

I should not have given up. Mike McClung recently brought by a left over pot from a planting job. Knotweed! I have it now in colorful little patches which seem to migrate into different spots each year.

I finally used liriope across the street. All of it came from divisions from Barbara Blumstein's yard in Port Arthur, Texas. A little bit of liriope goes a long way. Her husband replaced it with violets, an old fashioned favorite ground cover-edger.

Vinca minor, the catalogues told me, is *"One of the finest evergreen ground covers...dotted in early spring with lavenderblue flowers."* I believed. I ordered. One of the excitements of spring was finding the one or two blooms which appeared in the thin mat which I have not seen at all in the past two years. There are those who have had a different experience, but, I would not consider this ground cover to be a sure thing.

Although I would like to see more diversity in New Orleans plantings, the advantages of the most popular ground covers presently in use should be appreciated.

English ivy is considered to be the most versatile ground cover. There are several different species and

varieties available.   They all do well in shade or sun.
They are evergreen.

As with all ground cover plants, weeding is required
until the planting is established.   The rule of thumb according to garden tradition (as told to me by Felicia Kahn
when she gave me my first cuttings of ivy) is: the first
year it sleeps, the second year it creeps, the third year it
leaps. Also according to local tradition, the best time to
start cuttings is winter. But, my neighbor Becky Jordan's,
taken in summer, are right on schedule: creeping in the
second year.

Liriope or lilyturf grows in sun or shade.   It is evergreen.   It will fairly rapidly become a dense, grass-like
mat.   Split clumps into individual plants when setting out
for an even look.   Liriope blooms lilac-colored spikes in
late spring to early summer.   When bloom diminishes, the
plants need dividing.   Mow in January before the new
growth starts to get rid of the old brown leaves.

Ajuga is an evergreen, low-growing ground cover
which produces blue flowers in the spring.   It spreads
rapidly by strawberry-like runners.   It likes shade or sun,
though it always wilts in our summer sun for me.   It is
subject to attack by southern blight. I have found it beautiful in small patches, especially with lady ferns. I don't
seem to be able to maintain it for long without it dying
out in spots.   It divides easily.

Monkey grass is similar to and often confused with
liriope.   It has slender grass-like leaves and is lower growing.   It spreads fast and, like liriope, should be set out by
individual plant rather than in clumps for a more even
look and faster spread.

Confederate jasmine is a fast growing, attractive, evergreen ground cover which does well in sun or shade. It
requires pruning after it becomes established.

GROUND COVERS FOR THE NEW ORLEANS GARDEN

PROSTRATE, SPRAWLING, OR CREEPING TREES OR SHRUBS

Ardisia japonica ARDISIA, MARLBERRY
Carissa grandiflora NATAL PLUM
Cotoneaster species COTONEASTER
Euonymous species EUONYMOUS
Lagerstroemia indica CRAPE MYRTLE
Lantana montevidensis WEEPING or TRAILING LANTANA
Malvaviscus arboreus variety *drummondii* TURK'S CAP
Tecomaria capensis CAPE HONEYSUCKLE
Juniperus species JUNIPER

PERENNIALS AND FERNS

Creeping forms of FERNS
Achillea species   YARROW
Ajuga reptans   AJUGA
Aspidistra elatior   CAST-IRON PLANT
Asparagus densiflorus ASPARAGUS FERN
Chrysogonum virginianum GOLDEN STAR
Coreopsis auriculata cultivar 'Nana' DWARF COREOPSIS
Echeveria secunda HENS-AND-CHICKENS
Evolvulus nuttallianus EVOLVULUS
Gramineae species ORNAMENTAL GRASSES
Hemerocallis species and hybrids DAYLILY
Houttuynia cordata HOUTTUYNIA
Liriope spicata LILYTURF, LIRIOPE, CREEPING LILYTURF
Ophiopogon japonicus MONKEY GRASS, MONDO GRASS
Pachysandra terminals PACHYSANDRA, JAPANESE SPURGE
Polygonum capitatum KNOTWEED
Pseuderanthemum alatum CHOCOLATE PLANT
Setcreasea pallida 'Purple Heart' PURPLE HEART
Viola odorata SWEET VIOLET

VINES

Akebia quinata AKEBIA, FIVE LEAF AKEBIA
Hedera canariensis   ALGERIAN IVY
Hedera helix ENGLISH IVY
Lonicera japonica   JAPANESE HONEYSUCKLE
Thunbergia alata BLACK-EYED SUSAN VINE, CLOCK VINE
Trachelospermum asiaticum DWARF CONFEDERATE JASMINE
Vinca major GREATER PERIWINKLE
Vinca minor COMMON PERIWINKLE

Judy Burks

The
Wildlife Garden

"Everybody's goal should be to live in harmony with the world...."

Dr. Donald M. Bradburn, pathologist, naturalist
WYES-TV documentary, 1989

The wealth of animal life which makes Louisiana a "Sportsman's Paradise" can also make it a paradise for naturalists. By providing food, water, and shelter in our gardens, we can bring this paradise home in the form of birds, both permanent residents and migrants passing through; insect life, including colorful butterflies; reptiles and amphibians such as lizards and toads, and mammals, like gray and fox squirrels and bats.

My favorite reference on the subject is *The Wildlife Gardener* by John V. Dennis.[41] He feels: *"It can safely be said that the compelling reason that turns so many of us into wildlife gardeners is the pleasure of having living animals in the yard."* My experiences with wild creatures in my garden have given me much joy.

Dennis hypothesizes another value of providing for animals which goes beyond pure aesthetics: that we can help wildlife during a time when so many forms are losing their natural habitats and are being exposed to the hazards of pesticides and other pollution. He says:

> Even a very small yard with its plantings and bird feeders helps make up for the loss of natural habitat. When we stop to think of the millions of yards that do offer benefits of this kind, we can take a more optimistic view regarding the future of America's wildlife....when one adds suburban yards to the land that has been set aside as wildlife refuges, nature preserves, and parks, the picture becomes brighter.

Backyard plantings will not make up for the fragmented forests which threaten many of our native songbirds and other wildlife. But the optimism of wildlife gardeners is not misplaced if bringing nature close increases awareness of and concern for issues such as deforestation with its negative ecological consequences.

"Wildlife" is more than the birds and squirrels that come to eat the fruit from your blackberry vines. It means all the animals and plants in a habitat, from minute to massive. "Ecosystem" is the word used to describe flora and fauna and their interrelationship, including the predation necessary to maintain a balance. Natural ecosystems are being recognized and studied even as they are being threatened by invasive introduced plants and animals in some parts of the country. The consequences of disruption of animal-plant associations by the removal of part of the system is dramatically illustrated in the July 22, 1990 article about E. O. Wilson, "The Ant Man" in the *New York Times Magazine*:

> ...ants disperse the seeds of nearly a third of New York's herbaceous plant species. If the 8,800 ant species and their several million invertebrate relatives were suddenly to disappear, the physical structure of the forest would degrade. Most of the fish, amphibian, reptile, bird and mammal populations would crash to extinction for lack of food. 'The earth would rot,' Wilson writes. 'As dead vegetation piled up and dried out, narrowing and closing the channels of the nutrient cycles, other

complex forms of vegetation would die off, and with them the
last remnants of vertebrates.[42]

You may want to choose indigenous plants for your
wildlife garden, though recreating the original setting of
many New Orleans yards would entail making a swamp
or marsh.   Be aware that as you use plants to provide
food and places for larger animals, you are making habitats for the tiny things, too.   Each one has its role in the
system you create.   Your garden is a microcosm of the
world outside.

My wildlife garden is an escape.   I saw my first
hooded warbler there after working a night shift at
Southern Baptist Hospital.   I heard him sing, then saw
him from the deck at the back of my house.   He was
flitting about between the pittosporum and the concrete
birdbath. He was a tiny bird, brilliant yellow, with a black
hood completely encircling his yellow face and forehead.
I grabbed a field guide for identification.   For a while, I
forgot that night shifts existed.   Though my perception
may have been altered by extreme fatigue and my inverted schedule, I still think I have yet to see a bird quite as
beautiful...except, maybe hummingbirds or the black-
throated blue warbler, or....

"Wait until you see the cerulean warbler," said Donald
Bradburn.   He says forty years or more of watching birds
hasn't made it one bit less exciting.   This spring I saw
one! A cerulean warbler! It was beautiful!

Just having the animals would be enough without
them doing all things they do which are intriguing to
watch.   Blue jays hold sunflower seeds in place with one
foot while stabbing the shell open with their sharp beaks.
They grab a few and fly up to a high tree branch, or to
the gutter to shell them.   Sometimes, they spill seeds from
the feeder onto the ground.   This makes the ground feeding mourning doves happy.   I saw one dove try to perch
on a Droll Yankee feeder.   He looked as out of place as

the occasional sparrows who try to hover and drink nectar from hummingbird feeders.

A squirrel used to crawl into the metal seed hoppers on my outside bird cages to get sunflower seed. I snuck up and touched his tail once. It was bristly, not soft as I thought it would be. I blocked the tops of the hoppers with sheet metal covers. The squirrel showed me. He chewed around the circumference of my Droll Yankee feeder, spilling a whole cylinder of seeds (and probably himself) onto the ground. I saw mockingbirds attacking him when he got too close to their nest in the honeysuckle. I don't know what he was after up there.

Cardinals, whose beaks are adapted for quick shelling of seeds, are just as fast at peeling muscadines while clinging to the grape vines hanging over the trellis-roof on the back porch. I find the dried and shredded grape skins they drop on the deck in August and September with occasional slimey pulps which slipped away. Small insects or their larva chew through the skins to eat the juicy fruit, leaving hollow grape-shells behind.

Tiny toads, goal directed, hop lines which continue straight even after quick diversion to zap bugs too small for me to see. Though it is against the rules of taste, mockingbirds in my neighborhood eat toads.

Part of the aesthetic appeal of the garden designed for wildlife is that you can be sure all kinds of animals are there because of your provision for them, even though you can't see them. Dennis mentions night flying moths, small reptiles, toads, and salamanders, which are either nocturnal, underground, or hidden under tangles and debris much of the time. Some insects and amphibians announce their presence by sound. An educated naturalist can identify the species of frog or toad by its croak. The Cornell Laboratory of Ornithology offers recordings of frog and toad calls on a tape called *"Voices of the Night."*

In *The Reptiles and Amphibians of Louisiana,*[43] the authors Dundee and Rossman describe frog songs: The northern cricket frog goes *"gick, gick,gick...."*, the squirrel treefrog goes *"waaak"*, the green treefrog goes *"quonk"*; etc. A good idea, though I still can't tell the difference between a frog, another frog, and a cricket. Dundee and Rossman call frog and toad vocalizations *"a conspicuous part of the nighttime environment in rural and urban Louisiana."* An exhibit of native frogs and toads with button activated recordings of their calls at Audubon Zoo would help. Maybe some day there will be one!

I find the night sounds of insects, birds, and amphibians to be romantic; they help me imagine settings for as yet unlived adventures in places not yet visited. In our city, whose climate encourages nature's encroachment into man's domain, wildlife waits, ready to move in wherever an invitation is extended. I can hear it!

Seamus McAcy described green treefrogs clinging to the windshield of his dad's car each evening on South Carrollton Avenue. I saw one once, on a rainy evening, on a canna leaf in the front yard. As my garden develops, I hear more and different sounds. I hope some of them are frogs, and I hope I get to see them.

Dundee and Rossman report the existence in Audubon Park and in a seven mile radius thereof since 1975 or earlier of the greenhouse frog, *Eleutherodactyus planirostris*. Originally from Cuba, the Cayman Islands, and the Bahamas, this brownish-olive creature has spread throughout Florida from where it is suspected to have traveled to New Orleans in a nursery pot. It lays its eggs in moist soil. Tiny froglets hatch, completely bypassing the tadpole stage. It lives in damp places under debris, except at night and when the weather is wet when it hops about in the open. I listen for the insectlike *"series of four to six faint, whistling chirps uttered at night or in rainy weather,"* trying to determine if its migratory urges have brought it to my garden, yet.

The fun of finding a "frog" hiding in a secret place is a childhood memory for some, and, I believe, a continuing treat for more than will admit to it. Toads are what most city dwellers find, though people frequently call them frogs. I see lots of toads. Though biologists are not that clear on the distinctions; toads are usually short legged, have rough and dryer skins, like dryer habitats, and are members of the family Bufonidae; as compared to the smoother-skinned, longer legged, and sometimes green frogs. Already you know one exception: the non-native greenhouse frog.

Lucky Leslee Reed looked into her pond one day to see a pointy faced pig frog staring back. *Amphibians and Reptiles of Louisiana* says bullfrogs *"...will eventually appear in virtually any artificial pond."* But, in spite of his beautiful song (a piglike grunt), there was no massive movement of lady frogs to his territory. Leslee decided that either Pig Frog was the only one to make it across Napoleon Avenue, or he was what developed from the big tadpole Kit McLellan and I fished out of the abandoned swimming pool by her house in Slidell last year. He died, probably of a broken heart.

The ultimate city dwellers, residents of the highrise condominiums on the Mississippi River near Audubon Park, have been provided a wonderful wildlife garden: by the Audubon Park Commission on one side, and by nature on the other. We went to a party on the eleventh floor one night last year. After it rained, I heard the voices of hundreds of amphibians rising with amazing volume in the darkness from the batture, the area between the riverbank and the levee.

"Frogs!" I proclaimed.

"Toads," corrected Larry O'Meallie.

"Most of those sounds are the Gulf Coast toad," agreed David Muth, who raises frogs and toads in his back yard on Robert Street.

My daughter, Dara, and I explored in the daylight on the weekend, anyway, hoping to find just one frog for our garden. The sounds were gone. Though from the racket I expected the ground to be covered with writhing little creatures, all was still. The nocturnal croakers slept in hidden places.

The river flowed rapidly near its banks. The only standing water was in a few tire-tracks, not enough to meet the needs of frogs whose ties to water are close. We looked under a few logs, but found no frogs, or even toads. A downy woodpecker called. We collected a clump of healall (*Prunella vulgaris*), a perennial European wildflower long naturalized on this continent, and went home.

I heard a chorus from across the levee while eating on the patio at the Dante Street Deli. Was it insects or amphibians, frogs or toads? L. B. Pitts, proprietor, told me that he found frogs in the vegetation during cleanup each night. He promised me some if I came at 10:00 P.M.

"They are frogs, not toads, aren't they?" I asked.

"I don't know," he said. "They're, you know, toad-frogs."

I haven't made it back at ten, but I plan to, sooner or later on a summer night.

Aesthetics aside, and for those who don't see the aesthetic value of small reptiles, toads and frogs, these animals can be very effective in controlling harmful insects in the garden. One toad eats between fifty and one-hundred bugs in one night.

One year a toad spent the summer in a pot of flowers by my front walk. He was so fat, he looked as though his skin would split. He didn't have to move a bit. All his needs were met, down to watering. Actually, it had been a dry season and the regularly moistened earth in the pot may have been what brought him.

More insects in your garden, especially around night lights, will bring Mediterranean geckoes, the funny-looking translucent lizards which arrived on boats from the Old World, to feast. You may find them in your house, too.

Don't step on them as my mother, Dorothy Irwin, does. They will eat the vermin you don't want to admit to.

Though some insects are considered garden pests, the whole class should not be considered villains. Each "bad" bug has its own predators, insect as well as other. If you use pesticides, you will destroy nature's best control of insects, other insects. They may not be as fast as chemical poisons, and plants may get a little ratty looking before the good guys arrive. Gardens and cities are not natural settings, and man's changes have shifted balances, so the system may not work perfectly. If there were more yellow-billed cuckoos in the city to eat buckmoth caterpillars, our oak trees may not be threatened, as they presently are. But cuckoos live in the woods.

In the wildlife garden where chemicals are not used, an increase in insect life of all types will be observed as well as creatures to whom they are a juicy meal. You will find spiders whose wispy, symetrically patterned webs catch morning dewdrops as well as bugs; more amphibians and reptiles, such as skinks, green-brown anole lizards or chameleons and the little brown snakes which also eat worms and slugs. Birds such as purple martins, chimney swifts, and nighthawks pluck flying insects out of the air. As my garden develops, I am sure I hear the buzzy calls of more and more nighthawks flying low overhead to feed at dusk. Mockingbirds, robins, blue jays and seasonal warblers may hop across the ground, peering under leaves to route out subterranean crawling things. Ruby-crowned kinglets, carolina chickadees, and yellow-bellied sapsuckers may quickly investigate tree branches, gobbling insects, their eggs and larvae.

If you leave dying trees in place instead of cutting them down, you will lure downy woodpeckers or northern flickers poking for the bugs inside. Lift the decaying log you placed or left in place to see what creatures you have housed and fed! Lift a leaf or several layers in a decomposing heap to see what scurries or slithers away, all of it food for other wildlife.

Even the soil becomes more alive as natural debris which would be raked up in a manicured garden is left. Minute worms, snails and other molluscs, mites and other arachnids, centipedes, millipedes, and insects who act as scavengers to recycle fallen leaves into humus increase. There are ants and beetles of all shapes and sizes who participate in this process.

Rarely, I find iridescent green backed *Carabidae* beetles who look like relics from *Wonders of the Past*. (They eat caterpillars such as the buckmoth. More of them would be a good thing!) A lone firefly found its way into my garden, but only once. I remember how common they were in Jefferson Parish when I was a teenager. Spraying for mosquitoes has taken its toll, though I have heard it rumored that fireflies are coming back.

Vivid green hopping insects; lacy winged insects; blackdotted orange lady bugs; warring mosquito hawks whose differing races are different colors; red, black, blue, green, or yellow; noisy cicadas; crickets and the debris of metamorphosed bodies and shed skins are only part of the legacy of the insect order to the wild garden.

The evolution of your garden to a wildlife garden will be noticeable. More flowers will bring pollinators such as honeybees, fuzzy bumblebees, and butterflies. The right flowers may attract hummingbirds.

Sugar water feeders will bring your hummers up close. In the winter they may be visited by rust and black feathered orchard orioles, flame-orange and black feathered northern (Baltimore) orioles, and their mates in less brilliant yellows. Orioles came every day to my garden two winters in a row. The sticky drops from a leaky feeder may be lapped up by a butterfly or an anole who may also remain frozen in readiness to prey on sweet-loving ants.

Fruit trees such as the Japanese plum will attract birds, such as the brilliant orange-red male summer tanager and his olive-drab mate, as well as the common mocker, blue jay, and others. They also draw more insects which pollinate the flowers and eat the bruised and rotting fruit. Trees with seeds and nuts, such as the chinese tallow, may bring hordes of robins and yellow-rumped warblers or the ground feeding white-throated sparrow. The squirrel who lives in Chesne, the giant oak tree on the corner who first came to check out my seed offerings also snatches Japanese plums.

Seed feeders will bring the common birds or the uncommon. The pine siskins and American goldfinches which visit Leslee Reed come for the sunflower seed hearts and thistle which she provides in winter. Bird houses and vegetation providing nesting sites brought more birds such as sixteen purple martins to the apartment house perched on our rear roof from March through June, and mockingbirds nesting in the honeysuckle vines.

With more birds come bird predators, even in the city. I saw a kestral (sparrow hawk) in the crape myrtle. It held a dead mockingbird in its talons as it tried to escape from its prey's screaming relatives. Larry O'Meallie said it could have been a sharp-shinned hawk which would be more likely to go after a bird the size of a mocker than the smaller kestral. Red shouldered hawks fly over sometimes, also. Some were nesting on the grounds of New Orleans Adolescent Hospital on Tchoupitoulas Street.

Late joggers in Audubon Park can hear and sometimes see the screech owls which live in the oaks and are found here and there in older sections of the city.

Those who live on the outskirts of the city (Kenner, Harahan, or New Orleans East) may see more mammals in their wildlife gardens or under their houses: eastern cottontails or swamp rabbits, Virginia opossums, northern raccoons, southern flying squirrels, nine-banded armadilloes, marsh rice rats, the fulvous harvest mouse or white-footed or cotton mouse and (if you are near one of the drainage canals or other bodies of water in the area) South American introduced nutria and native muskrats. As late as the 1960's there were deer in what is now Kenner and Metairie near the Lake.

Be and Mich Boe of Belle Chasse express ambivalence about sharing their vegetable garden with opossums and armadillos, but Be speaks with tenderness of the soft-shelled armored armadillo infant they found one day.

I saw a dead opossum on General Meyer near Jo Ellen Smith Hospital in Algiers recently. Donald Bradburn remembers when these animals lived in the underbrush in Audubon Park which has been removed becaused it provided harborage for humans with undesirable habits. My husband, Jean, remembers a visit by an opossum to his Short Street garden in the 1960's. Rabbits have been seen on the levee behind Audubon Park, and raccoons in the vacant St. Elizabeth's home on Napoleon Avenue and Prytania in past months.

If you lived along the wharfs in New Orleans during the days of heavier port activity, your wildlife garden could have attracted mammals who stowed away on ships from faraway places. Lowery reports a Mexican mouse opossum and Alston's mouse opossum from Central America who arrived to the uptown area in a cargo of bananas. Unfortunately, you no doubt already harbour the less glamorous European imports: the Norwegian rat, roof rat, the house mouse.

For a while I kept an eastern box turtle found in the New Orleans Mental Health Center parking lot on the Westbank. It gulped down wiggling earthworms like strands of spaghetti. Four months after turning it loose in my yard, I got a phone call reporting that my turtle was heading down Robert toward Magazine Street. We decided it needed a safer home. Maureen Haney took it to the Science Class at Shaw Elementary School.

Larry and Margie Case had turtles on their Metairie property who would appear on the patio for tidbits of fruit each evening over a period of years.

WATER

The source of water in the wildlife garden can be as simple as the traditional New Orleans concrete birdbath (I got mine at Gentilly Novelty Company), either on a pedestal or ground level. The sides should slope gradually to a depth of no more than three inches. The water should be kept fresh, and the bath clean, all year round. The more consistent you are in the provision of water, the more regular will be the visits of the birds who seek refreshment or a bath.

It seems that, no more than minutes after I clean and refill the bath, house finches, and cardinals edge the rim to take turns splashing. Blue jays will not share. They run all the others off. There is not much which is more fun than watching birds bathe!

My two ground level bird baths serve as artificial puddles for the use of toads, frogs (wishful thinking!), birds, such as my hooded warbler, cardinals and blue jays, butterflies (and, unfortunately, stray cats and river rats). I have seen toads, looking like Jabba the Hut, lounging in the pools at night. Butterflies seem to prefer the wet garden soil in raised flower beds or real puddles.

The fine mist from a garden hose sprayer can provide fun for feathered bathers. Every source I've consulted on luring birds touts the attractive value of dripping water. David Muth hangs a can with a tiny hole in the bottom from a tree branch. He fills the can with water which slowly drips into a plastic children's swimming pool which serves as a bird bath and frog pond. The sound of this small a drip is enough to bring birds.

The means of providing more permanent sources of water in the garden are limited only by the size of your lot, your pocketbook, and your creativity.

Bert and Joel Myers have a decorative concrete pool with a recirculating pump and fountain. It is for water lilies but serves as a breeding spot for toads, too. The tadpoles hatch from eggs, in stringy, gelatinous strands, to become small toads and exit via the lily pads. In the absence of plants, slanting sides are needed to help them to land.

Anthony Eschmann's hand-dug pond is lined with Visqueen sheeting held in place at the edges by bricks. It has a natural look and is perfect for small fish and tadpoles.

My dream is to have the collection of frogs which National Park Service Ranger David Muth has given his wife Wendy. The Muths have a chorus in their yard for months on end, starting with the spring peeper in very early spring. A source of tadpoles in the New Orleans area could also yield green treefrogs, squirrel treefrogs, northern cricket frogs, striped chorus frogs, bronze frogs, southern leopard frogs, eastern narrow-mouthed toads, Woodhouse's toad, bird-voiced treefrogs, and, of course, bullfrogs (a frog for all seasons?). Most of the tadpoles which kids scoop out of inner city and suburban puddles during the spring and summer are of the Gulf Coast toad.

This spring I got tired of waiting for frogs. My husband built a Visqueen lined pond with a brick edge and a drip fountain. I circumvented nature by ordering eggs of the southern leopard frog from the Carolina Biological Supply House catalog. The Reeds, Joel Myers, Larry O'Meallie and Charlie Kahn shared the order with me. The clumps of globular eggs arrived UPS, 200 to a bag. You should have seen me trying to divide them five ways!

I finally had frogs I could see! Donald Bradburn said maybe the frogs will attract the black crowned night herons from Audubon Park, or maybe a great blue heron, to my garden. My husband, Jean, wants owls.

The pond did attract every toad in the vicinity, more than I ever knew existed. Kathy and Mike McClung came over with flashlights to drink beer with us and watch them mate. Toads are not shy. Eight or nine at a time continued singing with a human audience a foot away!

Now I have toads everywhere. Sometimes garter snakes are found in piles of trash in the city. They are one of the few predators of toads. If they don't come on their own, I may have to place another order to Carolina Biological Supply.

SHELTER

Dead and decaying trees, as well as the living can provide shelter for birds and other animals. The fastidious gardener who usually has these chopped up and hauled to the trash pile should reconsider. Left in place, rotting trunks can provide home sites for cavity nesters. Broken branches and fallen leaves left on the ground serve as shelter and as food for insects, arachnids, and molluscs which are, in turn, meals for other animals.

Bird houses are another way of meeting shelter needs in the garden. Jamie Primm, director of the Audubon Zoo Wild Bird Rehabilitation Center, suggests that downy woodpecker houses would be used, as these cavity nesters are relatively common in New Orleans. But since purple martins depend completely on man for nest sites, houses for them would meet a real need.

Bird house designs are specific to the needs of the bird to be attracted. If the specifications are not close to exact, the house may be unused, or used by the wrong bird. Much literature is available on building homes for birds, but my favorite is *Homes for Birds* (Conservation Bulletin 14), printed by the U.S. Department of the Interior and available from the Government Printing Office.

The design for a purple martin house offered therein is one which one author claimed has never failed to attract martins. We shared the plan with Jim and Robin Derbes. Both our houses were full of the reputed mosquito eating birds the very first season they were up!

The purply-black martins settle in our apartments in early March, busily set up housekeeping, rear young, then abruptly leave around July 1. The birds stay in the area in groups, roosting in places like the Causeway over Lake Pontchartrain, where their numbers approach 200,000 in July and where some martins are present from January to August. In late summer they begin fall migration south.

Carlyle Rogillio, expert in the rehabilitation of injured martins, discovered the purple martins on the Causeway in 1983. Through the efforts of his Project Swallow Committee, the Causeway roosting site, one of the largest in North America, has been a declared a bird sanctuary.

We love to watch their activity and hear their gurgling sounds. The males seem to go off during the day while the females tend the nests. When the papas return home at dusk, they are tiny specks high in the sky which circle lower and lower until they swoop in for a graceful landing on their verandas. There is much activity around the house in the evening, as neighborhood insect forays are made among the buzzing nighthawks and chipping chimney swifts. The babies make themselves noticed by popping their heads out the doors jack-in-a-box fashion with yellow beaks open wide to receive the juicy bugs their parents snatch out of the air.

PLANTS

The best way to provide food and shelter for all the wild creatures you hope to attract to your garden is by the appropriate selection and placement of trees and shrubs. Diversity of species and sizes of plants the most important factor. Less than half your space should be lawn. There should be lots of "edge" where plants border on ground cover, lawn, walkway, etc., as these are the points at which the most sunlight is available to plants. In sunlight there is heavier bloom and fruit with its attraction for various types of wildlife craving nectar and fruit; which in turn attract the wildlife which feeds on the wildlife which eats nectar and fruit. Too, sunlight produces heavier foliage growth providing better cover and nesting sites for birds.

The obvious way to plant your garden, if you have a chance to do so from scratch, is to place the taller growing trees at the boundaries with a gradation to shorter trees and shrubs, to perennials, wildflowers, and ground covers. As tall trees do not start tall, you may want include some short-lived fast growers such poplars which will perform while you are waiting for your live oak to reach squirrel-size.

The need for low, herbaceous growth can be met in the New Orleans wildlife garden by a selection of flowering plants which are hummingbird and butterfly attracters. The alternative plants to lawns covered in the chapter on ground covers are also useful as cover, and some for their fruit and flowers.

Pay attention to general soil requirements, including pH; either by choosing plants which meet the conditions of your yard, or by modifying the soil to meet the requirements of the plant. One approach could be to select plants which would naturally be found in one vegetation region, so that soil requirements for all are the same; either the existing conditions of the garden, or one which the entire plot can be modified to meet.

Vegetation regions are discussed in more detail in *Wildflowers of Louisiana.* New Orleans is in the region called "Bottomland Hardwoods and Cypress." Within this area is the alkaline alluvial or floodplain soil of the river; the rich, acidic soil of the swamps, and the variety of consistencies, acidities, etc. which fall inbetween. Levee building has changed the character of the lands along the Mississippi, but the "frontlands", according to Brown, used to support cottonwood, sycamore, red gum, black willow, hackberry, swamp-privet, honey locust, water locust, and green ash.   Tupelo gum, swamp red maple, green ash, American elm, palmetto, water-elm, swamp-privet, pumpkin ash, and, of course, cypress were found in the cypress swamps.

You may wish to encourage a native ecosystem to develop by using indigenous plants in your wildlife garden. Most gardeners use the eclectic approach, integrating wildlife gardening and the desire to decorate, collect, create fantasy environments, or whatever other needs gardening meets for them.

The selection of specific vegetation for your yard can certainly be done on the basis of appearance. A wildlife garden, though usually less manicured than others does not have to be less ornamental.   There are people who may consider many of the plants which make berries or nuts too "messy" to be pretty. I disagree. Neatness may sometimes be a tradeoff for the joy of bringing nature close, but beauty does not have to be.

The following plants should thrive in the New Orleans garden and should provide either food, shelter, or both for wildlife. They are in categories according to the height they will become. This list is by no means complete. Details on the wildlife attractiveness of many trees and shrubs are given in descriptions in their chapters. Flowering plants offer rewards to the pollinating creatures (usually insects) who visit them. Certain early flowering trees are valuable because their blooms offer nectar to bees after the inactive winter and at a time when they are very hungry there is very little else available for them. Most of the exotic shrubs grown in New Orleans are attractive for their flowers.

SOME PLANTS FOR THE WILDLIFE GARDEN

GROUND COVERS, VINES, AND SHRUBS

See LAWNS AND GROUND COVERS
See lists in:
  THE HUMMINGBIRD GARDEN
  THE BUTTERFLY & MOTH GARDEN
  Vitis rotundifolia MUSCADINE GRAPES

LOW SHRUBS

Abelia X grandiflora GLOSSY ABELIA
Cotoneaster species COTONEASTER
Lindera benzoin SPICEBUSH
Rubus species BLACKBERRY
Rubus trivialis SOUTHERN DEWBERRY
Vaccinium ashei RABBITEYE BLUEBERRY

TALL SHRUBS

Aesculus pavia RED BUCKEYE, HORSE CHESTNUT
Callicarpa americana AMERICAN BEAUTYBERRY
Calycanthus floridus SWEET SHRUB
Cephanthus occidentalis BUTTONBUSH
Chaenomeles speciosa FLOWERING QUINCE
Cotoneaster species COTONEASTER
Forestiera acuminata SWAMP PRIVET
Ilex species HOLLY
Juniper chinensis 'Pfitzerana' PFITZER JUNIPER
Juniperus virginiana EASTERN RED CEDAR
Ligustrum amurense PRIVET
Ligustrum sinense COMMON PRIVET
Ligustrum lucidum TREE LIGUSTRUM
Ligustrum japonicum WAX LEAF LIGUSTRUM
Myrica cerifera SOUTHERN WAX MYRTLE
Nandina domestica NANDINA
Photinia serrulata CHINESE PHOTINIA
Podocarpus macrophyllus JAPANESE YEW
Pyracantha coccinea PYRACANTHA
Rhus glabra SUMAC
Sabal minor DWARF PALMETTO
Sambucus canadensis ELDERBERRY
Tetrapanax papyriferus RICE PAPER PLANT
Thuja occidentalis WHITE CEDAR, ARBORVITAE
Viburnum tinus LAURUSTINUS VIBURNUM

SMALL TREES

Amelanchier arborea SERVICEBERRY
Cercis canadensis RED BUD
Chionanthus virginicus GRANCY GRAY-BEARD
Cornus drummondii ROUGH-LEAF DOGWOOD
Crataegus marshallii PARSLEY HAWTHORNE
Crataegus opaca MAYHAW
Crataegus viridis HOGHAW
Diospyros virginiana PERSIMMON
Eleagnus species ELEAGNUS
Ficus carica FIG TREE
Ilex species HOLLY
Juniperus virginiana EASTERN RED CEDAR
Prunus serotina BLACK CHERRY
Pyrus calleryana 'Bradford' BRADFORD FLOWERING PEAR
Prunus caroliniana CHERRY LAUREL
Prunus campanulata FLOWERING CHERRY
Prunus mexicana MEXICAN PLUM
Sabal palmetto CABBAGE PALM

TALL TREES

Carya illinoinenses PECAN
Celtis laevigata HACKBERRY
Cinnamomum camphora CAMPHOR TREE
Fagus grandiflora BEECH
Fraxinus pennsylvanica GREEN ASH
Liquidambar styraciflua AMERICAN SWEET GUM
Morus rubra RED MULBERRY
Nyssa sylvatica BLACK GUM
Pinus species PINE
Quercus virginiana LIVE OAK
Quercus falcata SOUTHERN RED OAK
Sapium sebiferum CHINESE TALLOW TREE
Ulmus parvifolia CHINESE ELM
Ulmus pumila SIBERIAN ELM

THE HUMMINGBIRD GARDEN

"These are the birds of the gods, the dancers of the air."

Tony Keppelman in *Hummingbirds*
Little, Brown and Company, Publishers, 1988

Birding is an adventure in nature. We're in the woods and marshes so wildflowers are abundant. We never know what birds we'll see. When there is a rare change of topic from birding issues (Is the belly band diagnostic of the red-tailed hawk? Will Leslee ever see a purple gallinule again?) we share secrets about gardening and plants or people.

Mary Joe Krieger recounts the life histories of the Fabulous Five of St. Joseph's Academy in Waveland; like Sheila Gottschalk who lived with Mrs. Nix on Carrollton Avenue (in a house Leslee says was designed by Frank Lloyd Wright but Jean says wasn't) while she went to medical school. Of the Five, only Mary Joe grew up to bird.

Sometimes we try to figure out what the enigmatic president of the Louisiana Ornithological Society and master birder, does for a living. No one seems to know.

"He is very mysterious," says Gloria McKinnon. "But I think all he does is bird."

He ate breakfast with us one morning in Lafayette. Every time someone was about to ask him what he did, he changed the subject to sandhill cranes.

Part of the appeal of hummingbirds is their intimacy with the flowers I love and that they dare to become quite intimate with people, affording a closeness to nature not quite like any other experience. They bring the excitement and adventure of the birding trip home.

They are a well kept secret which I would like to tell everyone. I am surprised at the number of people who say they have lived in New Orleans all their lives and never seen one.

I first noticed hummers at the four o'clocks. I've never lost the excitement I first felt at viewing the tiny, iridescent creatures hovering and darting with breathtaking rapidity among the flowers.

After doing some reading, I knew that hummingbirds were attracted by trumpet-shaped flowers, preferably red or orange colored. I collected a few plants fitting this description. My sister Judy Keim, sent me a ceramic feeder from Arizona, which I filled with sugar water and hung in the garden.

How to Attract Birds (Ortho Books) as well as other sources told me that, "...(The rubythroated) *is the only hummingbird that breeds in the eastern United States, and the only one we are likely to encounter in gardens there.*"

I followed the admonition not to leave feeders up past October. This, I was told, could cause the birds to stay, rather than migrate, thus meeting death in the first freeze of the winter. I compulsively took down my feeders until reading in *Bird Watcher's Digest* (November-December, 1986) that *"To presume that a bottle of sugar water supplied by mere mortals could alter a force as powerful as the migratory urge is a conceit, and in most cases, conjectural."*

The rubythroated hummingbird returns from its wintering grounds in Central America in late February to early March. Most of the ones seen in gardens in New Orleans are passing through, on their way north, or in the fall, on their way south. The movements of the birds correlate with the flowering times of the wildflowers which are the important sources of nectar-food in different geographical areas. Though there are breeding populations in the New Orleans area, the city itself cannot provide the insect population necessary for feeding baby hummers. Nancy Newfield, New Orleans hummingbird authority, conjectures that settings like Audubon Park may offer breeding habitat for a few pairs, but wooded areas around the city are more likely sites for most Louisiana rubythroats. During mid-May to the first week in July, the birds are not seen in the city. Nancy speculates that is when they're parenting in the swamps.

I first heard about winter hummingbirds from a birdwatching friend, Larry O'Meallie. A lecture by Nancy Newfield told me how to attract them to my garden. Some of these birds are the rubythroated. Others are western and northwest coast birds which winter on the Gulf Coast in numbers described as "rare" and "casual" by the fieldguides: the blackchinned, the broad-tailed, the rufous, allen's, buff-bellied, anna's, and calliope.

Only the most recent editions of birding field guides mention hummers other than the rufous as winterers in this area. Johnsgard's *The Hummingbirds of North America* (1983) documents earlier the Gulf coast excursions of several varieties, as does Lowery's *Louisiana Birds* (1955). Is there better observation and documentation than in previous years, or are there more birds? One feeling is that the birds are migrating here in greater and greater numbers each year. Ron Stein, hummingbird expert from LaPlace, theorizes that this displacement of migrant hummers is due to habitat destruction in the usual wintering grounds in Central and South America.

Whatever the true explanation of their presence, the nice thing about the cold-weather hummers is that they stay all season. Nancy Newfield's talk told me the secret of enticing them to my yard: I needed to expand my plantings to include more fall and winter-blooming nectar plants. She also reassured me that hummers, though they can be killed by severe enough temperatures over a long enough time span, can tolerate more cold than one would think. (Keep those feeders up!)

My first rufous chose my yard as the center of his territory. I could find him there at almost any time I chose to visit. He stayed three months, headquartered in the 'Lady Banksia' rose by the back fence. He came

Christmas day in nondescript plumage and left at the end of March in full courtship colors. He was quite feisty for three inches long. To my chagrin, he chased off all other hummers.

I can watch hummingbird antics endlessly. They divebomb into a mass of lantana and salvia from a perch atop the large crape myrtle. (Some people are surprised that the birds perch rather than hovering eternally.) They slide through the early morning dewdrops pooled in the grooves of the large leaves of a rice-paper plant for a bath or a fun splash, who knows which? They either ignore me or fuss with metallic clicks when I enter the garden. They whir through the corridor which is my side yard shooting straight up to avoid the clump of shell ginger. They pluck tiny insects out of the air.

One October day a fearless rubythroat zipped onto our backyard deck to hover at the feeder, inches from my husband Jean's face. We held our breaths and watched as, glistening green, she moved on to the cigar flowers and firespike. "It's like being in an enchanted garden!" Jean said.

The key to having hummers year-round is lots of attractant plants blooming each season. In summer, feeders can be used to supplement flower nectar, and to entice the birds to appropriate spots for good viewing. In winter, the maintainence of feeders is especially important in the event of a freeze when plant sources of nectar and insects disappear.

The suggested formula for feeders is: one part granulated sugar to three parts water. (Some sources say one part sugar to four parts water during the warm months.) I find hot tap water dissolves the sugar fine, though some people boil the water. If I make the procedure too complicated, I find myself not changing the feeders as often as I should. Nancy adds Vodka, 1 to 2 Tablespoons per mix, to her sugar solutions to keep them from freezing when the temperature drops to 32 degrees.

Do not use honey. It can cause a fatal fungus disease in the birds. Red food coloring is not necessary in the sugar water, especially if the feeder has red parts. I add it because I like the way it looks and I think hummers might, too. The contents of the feeder must be changed every three to four days and the feeder scrubbed with a bottle brush and cleaned with vinegar, or soaked in clorox to kill bacterial growth and mold.

Feeders should not be hung in bright sunlight, as the expansion caused by the sun's heat causes the sugar water to drip. So can the buffeting which occurs when the feeder is hung in a windy spot. Problems with insects can be thwarted by smearing vaseline around base of the wire from which the feeder is suspended, though this does not always work. We're trying a product from the hardware store called Tanglefoot Pest Barrier, now.

The first winter I planted my yard and left feeders out, I had a winter visitor. I had an advantage in that I live between two other birders, Leslee Reed and David Muth, who had established hummer gardens. Seen in our gardens in the winter of 1987-88 were the rufous, black-chinned, buff-bellied, and ruby-throated hummingbirds.

A list of best hummingbird plants for almost year-round bloom in the New Orleans area follows. Most of these are from Nancy Newfield's list. The plants marked with asterisks are the essentials for a New Orleans hummingbird garden because they will give you the prerequisites: exhuberant bloom over lengthy periods of time. If you are serious about hummers, a few sparsely flowering plants won't do. The other plants attract hummers, but should be secondary because of short bloom periods or other reasons.

PLANTS FOR THE HUMMINGBIRD GARDEN

VINES

Bougainvillea hybrids BOUGAINVILLEA
Campsis radicans TRUMPET VINE, TRUMPET CREEPER *
Ipomoea coccinea, Quamoclit coccinea RED MORNING GLORY *
Lonicera japonica halleriana JAPANESE HONEYSUCKLE *
Lonicera sempervirens CORAL HONEYSUCKLE *
Manettia cordifolia FIRECRACKER VINE *
Phaseolus coccineus SCARLET RUNNER BEAN
Quamoclit pinnata CYPRESS VINE *
Wisteria sinensis WISTERIA, CHINESE WISTERIA

EXOTIC TREES & SHRUBS

Abelia X grandiflora GLOSSY ABELIA
Abutilon pictum FLOWERING MAPLE, CHINESE BELLFLOWER *
Aesculus pavia RED BUCKEYE (Native)
Albizia julibrissin MIMOSA, SILK TREE
Beloperone gutatta SHRIMP PLANT *
Buddleia species BUTTERFLY BUSH
Callistemon citrinus, Callistemon rigidus BOTTLEBRUSH *
Camellia species CAMELLIA
Citrus species CITRUS
Clerodendrum philippinum CASHMERE BOUQUET, GLORY BOWER
Clerodendrum paniculatum, or *C. speciosissimum* GIANT SALVIA,
    JAVA SHRUB, PAGODA FLOWER
Cuphea micropetala MEXICAN CIGARFLOWER *
Eriobotrya japonica JAPANESE PLUM, LOQUAT
Erythrina crista-galli CORAL TREE, CRY-BABY TREE
Hibiscus syriacus ALTHAEA, ROSE-OF-SHARON
    (single flowers best)
Hibiscus rosa-sinensis CHINESE HIBISCUS
Lantana camara HAM AND EGGS
Malvaviscus arboreus or *grandiflorus* GIANT TURK'S CAP *
Malvaviscus arboreus variety *Drummondii* SULTAN'S TURBAN *
Musa species BANANA
Odontonema strictum FIRESPIKE, THE HUMMINGBIRD PLANT *
Russellia equisetiformis FOUNTAIN PLANT *
Tecomaria capensis CAPE HONEYSUCKLE
Weigela hybrids CARDINAL SHRUB, OTHERS

PERENNIALS

Agave species AGAVE
Aloe species ALOE
Aquilegia species COLUMBINE
Kniphofia uvaria RED-HOT-POKER, TRITOMA
Hemerocallis (reds and oranges) DAYLILY
Hibiscus coccineus SCARLET ROSE MALLOW,
    TEXAS STAR HIBISCUS
Leonotis leonurus LION'S EAR
Mirabilis jalapa FOUR O'CLOCK
Pentas lanceolata PENTAS, EGYPTIAN STAR CLUSTERS *
Phlox paniculata PERENNIAL PHLOX, SUMMER PHLOX
Salvia elegans or *rutilans* PINEAPPLE SAGE *
Salvia ambigens ANISE SAGE *
Schlumbergera bridgesii CHRISTMAS CACTUS

WILDFLOWERS

Cirsium species THISTLES
Ipomopsis rubra STANDING CYPRESS, SCARLET GILIA
Lobelia cardinalis CARDINAL FLOWER *
Monarda fistulosa WILD BEEBALM *
Phlox divaricata BLUE PHLOX
Salvia coccinea TROPICAL SAGE or TEXAS SAGE *
Spigelia marilandica INDIAN PINK

ANNUALS

Alcea rosea HOLLYHOCK
Cleome hasslerana CLEOME, SPIDER FLOWER
Impatiens hybrids IMPATIENS HYBRIDS *
Impatiens balsamina GARDEN BALSAM *
Nicotiana glauca TREE TOBACCO
Nicotiana species FLOWERING TOBACCO
Perilla frutescens PERILLA
Salvia splendens RED SALVIA *

BULBS

Alstroemeria species PERUVIAN LILY
Canna species CANNA
Gladiolus X *hortulanus* GARDEN GLADIOLUS
Iris hybrids and species IRIS
Strelitzia reginae BIRD OF PARADISE

Birding during spring migration in Cameron parish, I saw so many hummers zooming around the banks of honeysuckle, I thought they would collide!

"I wish they would all come to New Orleans," I mused.

"We could seed all of uptown with salvia!" suggested Larry O'Meallie. "But people would just cut it down because they didn't know what it was."

But maybe they wouldn't! Seeding the city would be a big task, but we could do it if we got everybody to help. If we told them how, everyone could plant his own hummingbird garden. Of course it may be conceit or conjectural to think it possible, but perhaps, with hummingbird gardens all over the New Orleans area, we could change the migratory habits of a few more hummers. More people could experience the delight and awe of nature which these wonderful little creatures inspire! The whole city of New Orleans could become an enchanted garden!

THE BUTTERFLY AND MOTH GARDEN

"Quis lot colorum e schematum elegantias naturae suis divinae artis vestigia eis impressa agnoscat et miretur?"

Ludwig von Reizenstein
Catalogue of the Lepidoptera of New Orleans and its Vicinity
New Orleans: Isaac T. Hinton, 1863

I remember the passion vine with its elaborate flowers growing in the woods on the outskirts of Jackson, Mississippi where I lived before the age of eleven. Miss Maude grew one on her page fence on Constance Street. She warned me against them because they "draw terrible stinging caterpillars."

Leslee Reed and I toured the Butterfly Garden which is part of the Botanical Garden at City Park. As we passed the passion vine, a larval food of the Gulf fritillary butterfly, I quoted Miss Maude.

"Gulf fritillary caterpillars don't sting," said Leslee. "I'm sure they don't."

"They look like they would," I responded.

How would we find out? We could touch one or we could ask someone who knows. But then, how do they know unless they handled the red and black striped, spiny creatures long enough to either get stung or not get stung?

Leslee's friend, Margaret Seale, who raises butterflies, knows the answer: They do have spines which feel rubbery when touched, but they do not sting! She touches caterpillars all the time.

It is funny how myths begin and are passed on. Anything which looks different is subject to suspicion. A Hammond native told me that the intensely red-purple berries of an American beautyberry (*Callicarpa americana*), in the woods around his home are poisonous. They aren't. Ask any mockingbird. Similarly, the reputation of caterpillars for stinging and other bad deeds is usually undeserved. Most of the serious defoliation which occurs is the work of larval moths, not butterflies; and very few of the moths, at that.

Looking at the bristly or smooth, striped or spotted or solid, bright or dull, ominous or cartoonish caterpillars, undulating along a leaf, it is easy to forget that they are part of the process of metamorphosis, which begins and ends with the lovely butterfly. The garden which is to have the nectar-drinking beauties should also provide for the sometimes unappealing babies by offering the specific and different plants which serve as "larval foods." The parent butterfly lays its eggs on the plants whose leaves are food for the hatching caterpillars. They repeatedly eat and molt, growing fat, then encasing themselves in the protective chrysalis from which, transformed into winged graces, they emerge.

Though the nectar-full butterfly flowers will provide food for the adults, if the plants on which they lay their eggs are not available, there will be few and eventually no butterflies. The grasses and many of the wildflowers considered as weeds are, unfortunately or not, depending on your outlook, the appropriate ones to do the job. As man expands into the swamps and marshes, or even mows the levees surrounding New Orleans, he destroys the wild patches which provide butterfly habitat. Planting for butterflies can help provide for the survival of threatened native species as well as attracting even more beauty to your New Orleans garden.

An irony is that the levees in Jefferson Parish have won awards for being the most beautiful in the State of Louisiana: the best kept, most neatly mowed. All those acres of smooth, green grass are completely devoid of the beautiful, colorful butterflies which would be plentiful if the levees were left to the original wildflowers and native grasses. If patches of unmowed areas were left on the levees, as plots of wildflowers have been planted in parks in New Orleans and on I-10 enroute to the airport in Jefferson, the bonus would be butterflies!

The monarch is the most famous butterfly. Most people know that the black and orange winged insect is migratory, and that its wintering grounds in fir forests of Mexico and California are endangered. Flocks of monarchs can be seen crossing the Lake Pontchartrain Causeway in diagonal paths or flying through the streets of New Orleans in March and October. Everyone knows that the monarch lays its eggs on milkweed; that the caterpillars which hatch are black, white, and yellow striped; the chrysalis-casing which is the third stage of metamorphosis is bright green, spotted yellow. Many kindergarten classes have observed the emergence of the new butterfly, fragile and impotent until body fluids surge through the crumpled wings which expand into organs of flight.

"Bye butterfly!" say the children.

"Butterfly flowers, as they are called, are tubular, rich in nectar, often fragrant, and have a flat rim where the butterfly can perch while it feeds," explains Dennis in *Wildlife Gardening.* In addition to proper plants, the garden for butterflies should offer protection from wind and sources of moisture. A puddle, ground level bird bath, or moist earth can be the water source. Breezes can be blocked to make a still feeding place by situating the flowers near your house, a fence, or encircling them by taller plants or shrubs. Enclosure also holds the scents emitted by the flowers, allowing an accumulation of fragrance. Ironically, the smells of rotting fruits and manure will be just as effective in luring butterflies. Such indelicate tastes for such refined creatures!

Further sources of information on butterfly gardening in the New Orleans area are the City Park Botanical Garden, the Louisiana Nature and Science Center, a lecture by Ms. Frances Welden, or questioning your children who have learned about butterflies, moths, and their larvae, caterpillars from Margaret Seale at their schools. She does demonstrations for kids as well as workshops for teachers so they can encourage in their young students the sense of wonder about the natural world which is lost in so many by the time they reach adulthood.

Margaret "raises" butterflies. She has purposefully planted a garden of larval foods as well as nectar sources. Sometimes she brings butterfly chrysalises, moth cocoons or caterpillars from other places to her garden or to jars which line her window sills so she can observe their development or emergence close-up.

Some butterflies which will come to your New Orleans garden and the plants which serve as food sources for their larvae, from Frances Welden's "Butterfly Gardens in New Orleans," *Floral & Faunal Notes*, Number 6, Louisiana Nature and Science Center are:

RED ADMIRAL: *Urtica species* NETTLE
BUCKEYE: *Agalinis* PURPLE GERADIA, *Antirrhinum* species SNAPDRAGONS
MONARCH: *Asclepias* species MILKWEED
GULF FRITILLARY, VARIEGATED FRITILLARY: *Passiflora* PASSION VINE
PAINTED LADY: *Helianthus* species SUNFLOWERS
QUESTION MARK: *Celtis laevigata* HACKBERRY
RED-SPOTTED PURPLE: *Salix* species WILLOW, *Crataegus* species HAWTHORNE
SNOUT: *Celtis laevigata* HACKBERRY
CLOUDLESS SULFUR: *Cassia alata* CANDELABRA PLANT, *Cassia marilandica* WILD SENNA
SPICEBUSH SWALLOWTAIL: *Camphor* or *Sassafras*
BLACK SWALLOWTAIL: *Umbelliferae* PARSLEY, DILL, CARROTS
GIANT SWALLOWTAIL: *Citrus* species CITRUS
TIGER SWALLOWTAIL: *Liriodendron* TULIP TREE/YELLOW POPLAR
PIPEVINE SWALLOWTAIL: *Aristolochia* PIPEVINE
VICEROY: *Salix* WILLOW

MOTHS

"Charlotte! Come out here quick...and bring a flash-light!" yelled my husband. "There's a hummingbird in the four o'clocks!"

"At ten o'clock at night?" I asked. "It's got to be a moth."

We focused the light on the hovering form which when dimly lit by the moon looked exactly like a hummingbird. "You're right...." Jean said incredulously. "It's a moth!"

The fascinating faker has fooled more than one person. It is an argument for not discounting all moths from your wildlife garden because of the destructive habits of a few. The group of moths named sphinx moths for the sphinx-like attitude sometimes assumed by their larvae, are further called either hawk moths for their swooping flight, or hummingbird moths, because they hover like their namesakes. The actual hummingbird moth, or common clearwing (a sphinx) feeds by day.

The several night flying sphinxes are part of the mystery of the night! In your nocturnal New Orleans garden you can see or imagine them as well as the giant silk-worm and royal moths with dramatically eye-spotted or streamer-tailed wings, velvety-haired bodies and names which insinuate their secret lives on the other side of day: Io, polyphemus, cecropia, luna, promethea, imperial or royal walnut.

The tiger moths, most common of which is the great leopard, metamorphose from fuzzy wooly-bear caterpillars. These were my children's favorites, either curled into hairy balls clearly revealing the crimson rings between their segments, or undulating quickly along the ground toward the next food source. David and Dara told me from experience they didn't sting. We hatched several in jars through the winter. The adult moth has black rings and spots on its white upper wings.

Other tigers have fuzzy larvae in different colors. Margaret Seale says the white-hairy tussock moths are fun for children to play with. No, they don't sting!

Rather than assume all caterpillars sting, become familiar with the four types found in New Orleans which do. Notice that they are all moths, not butterflies. Make sure of your identification before touching anything, however!:

1.   The plume moth whose larva looks like an oval shaped clump of brownish hair.

2.   The saddleback caterpillar, a type of slug caterpillar moth. It is bright green with an oval brown spot on its back, horn like projections on each end, covered with tufts of spines.

3.   The caterpillar of the beautiful Io moth, green with two narrow brown and white stripes extending its length. Its spines are in little clumps on each segment.

4.   The buck moth caterpillar, dark and fuzzy, has a-chieved local fame because of its threat to our oak trees. Its black and white winged adult form, the buck moth, can be seen flying on December days. By April, the tiny caterpillars have grown large enough to be seen everywhere. If native predators: tiny wasps, certain beetles, and birds such as the yellow-billed cuckoo were plentiful enough, the buck moths would not be a problem. In 1990 City recommendations changed from the traditional two sprayings of infested oaks to one spraying in the last week of March, first of April when the caterpillars are all hatched but before they begin to leave the trees. Maybe the monarchs migratory in March will pass through early enough to avoid being unintended casualties of spraying.

Many times, moths and butterflies are difficult to distinguish. Some moths are dayflying like butterflies, though more are creatures of the night. Moth antennae are usually feathery, rather than club-like as is the butterfly's. The butterfly larva forms a chrysalis, the moth may weave a silken cocoon, or pupate on or under the ground. There are other differences which you can discover in the reference which Margaret Seale recommends as best for beginners: *Butterflies and Moths* by Golden Press.

The larval forms of butterflies and moths are usually called caterpillars, but can also be known as worms, slugs, or borers. The catalpa sphinx, whose larva, the catalpa worm is used as fish bait, is an example. Though the worms can defoliate a catalpa tree, their parasitic wasp-predator should keep many of them from completing their cycles. More moths than butterflies are known for the damage caused by their larvae, but there are more harmless than harmful.

Many trees and shrubs serve as larval food for moths. You will probably want to focus on planting the flowers that will attract moths as pollinators. The choices for butterflies will please the dayflying moths. To attract the night flying sphinx moths, make sure you plant:

Heliotropium arborescens COMMON HELIOTROPE
Ipomoea alba MOONVINE
Jasminum officinale COMMON JASMINE
Mirabilis jalapa FOUR O'CLOCK
Nicotiana affinis FLOWERING TOBACCO

The following are butterfly plants for the New Orleans garden. Some provide nectar, others larval food. Your goal should be as many flowers as possible for as much of the year as possible so that any day when temperatures are mid-60 and above, butterflies will find food in your yard. Margaret Seale describes the best butterfly day as one which is "nice, sunny, and warm, about 80 to 85 degrees." She has seen fifteen species in her small garden at once. She says butterflies attract other butterflies. The more the merrier as far as I'm concerned!

PLANTS FOR
THE BUTTERFLY AND MOTH GARDEN

ANNUALS, PERENNIALS, BULBS

Ageratum houstonianum AGERATUM, FLOSS FLOWER
Allium schoenoprasum CHIVES
Callistephus chinensis CHINA ASTER, ANNUAL ASTER
Chrysanthemum X *morifolium* FLORIST'S, GARDEN
    CHRYSANTHEMUM
Chrysanthemum carinatum, Chrysanthemum coronarium, Chrysanthemum
    segetum and their hybrids ANNUAL CHRYSANTHEMUM
Chrysanthemum nipponicum NIPPON OXEYE DAISY
Coreopsis species COREOPSIS
Coreopsis tinctoria CALLIOPSIS
Cosmos sulphureus YELLOW AND ORANGE COSMOS
Dianthus species PINKS
Helianthus species SUNFLOWER
Hemerocallis species DAYLILY
Iberis amara ROCKET CANDYTUFT
Iberis umbellata GLOBE CANDYTUFT
Impatiens wallerana IMPATIENS, SULTANA
Impatiens balsamina GARDEN BALSAM
Lantana camara HAM AND EGGS
Lantana montevidensis WEEPING, TRAILING LANTANA
Lobularia maritima SWEET ALYSSUM
Lycoris species NAKED LADY, SPIDER LILY
Matthiola incana STOCK
Pentas lanceolata EGYPTIAN STAR-CLUSTER
Petroselinum crispum PARSLEY
Petunia X *hybrida* PETUNIA
Phlox drummondii ANNUAL PHLOX
Rudbeckia fulgida BRACTED CONEFLOWER
Rudbeckia hirta BLACK-EYED SUSAN
Rudbeckia laciniata CUTLEAF CONEFLOWER
Salvia farinacea MEALY-CUP SAGE
Salvia splendens SCARLET SAGE
Scabiosa atropurpurea PINCUSHION FLOWER
Tagetes species MARIGOLD
Tithonia rotundifolia MEXICAN SUNFLOWER
Tropaeolum species NASTURTIUM
Verbena X *hybrida* GARDEN VERBENA
Verbena peruviana PERUVIAN VERBENA
Verbena canadensis ROSE VERBENA
Verbena bonariensis PURPLE-TOP
Viola species VIOLETS

WILDFLOWERS

Achillea millefolium WHITE YARROW
Ageratum houstonianum AGERATUM
Asclepias curassavica BLOODFLOWER
Asclepias tuberosa BUTTERFLY WEED
Asclepias lanceolata RED MILKWEED
Echinacea purpurea PURPLE CONEFLOWER
Erigeron philadelphicus DAISY FLEABANE
Eupatorium fistulosum JOE PYE WEED
Eupatorium coelestinum WILD AGERATUM
Helianthus species SUNFLOWER
Ipomopsis rubra STANDING CYPRESS
Liatris spicata BLAZING STAR
Lobelia cardinalis CARDINAL FLOWER
Monarda fistulosa WILD BERGAMOT, BEEBALM
Oxalis rubra OXALIS
Oxalis stricta YELLOW WOOD SORREL
Prunella vulgaris SELF-HEAL, HEALALL
Salvia lyrata LYRE-LEAVED SAGE, CANCERWEED
Salvia coccinea TEXAS SAGE, SCARLET SAGE
Scabiosa atropurpurea PINCUSHION FLOWER
Solidago species GOLDENROD
Tradescantia species SPIDERWORT
Trifolium pratense RED CLOVER
Trifolium repens WHITE CLOVER
Vernonia altissima IRONWEED

VINES

Dolichos lablab HYACINTH BEAN
Ipomoea coccinea RED MORNING GLORY
Ipomoea purpurea MORNING-GLORY
Ipomoea quamoclit CYPRESS VINE, CARDINAL CLIMBER
Wisteria floribunda JAPANESE WISTERIA
Wisteria sinensis WISTERIA, CHINESE WISTERIA

EXOTIC SHRUBS

Abelia X *grandiflora* GLOSSY ABELIA
Buddleia species BUTTERFLY BUSH
Cinnamomum camphora CAMPHOR TREE
Citrus species CITRUS
Clethra alnifolia SWEET PEPPERBUSH, WHITE ALDER
Lantana camara HAM AND EGGS
Raphiolepis indica INDIAN HAWTHORNE
Raphiolepsis umbellata YEDDA HAWTHORNE
Rhododendron species AZALEA

NATIVE TREES & SHRUBS

Aesculus pavia RED BUCKEYE
Calycanthus floridus SWEET SHRUB
Celtis laevigata HACKBERRY
Lindera benzoin SPICEBUSH
Liriodendron tulipifera TULIP TREE, YELLOW POPLAR
Prunus mexicana MEXICAN PLUM

THE BEE GARDEN

"Today, about 250,000 beekeepers, most of them hobbyists, manage over 4 million colonies in every state though most honey bees are kept in rural settings, hives are often seen in backyards, on roof tops, and even on the balconies of high-rise apartments."

Dale K. Pollet, *Bee Ready*, L.S.U. Extension, September, 1989

Honeybees and bumblebees are important because of the role they play in plant reproduction. Though there are many other species of bees and other insects, as well as other animals, like hummingbirds and bats, which pollinate plants; because of their numbers, the honeybees and bumblebees carry the greatest responsibility for this function throughout the whole world.

In the process of collecting pollen for food, they spread the yellow substance from part to part within flowers and from flower to flower. The fact that without pollination there can be no seed production in plants, makes it an extremely important agricultural function. Vegetable gardeners and those with fruit and berry trees and shrubs need pollinating insects, also.

Since most ornamental gardeners are not too concerned with whether their plants produce seeds, and even take steps to prevent the plants from "going to seed" to extend bloom, why should they care if they have bees in their gardens?

Aesthetics? If the little insects had no functional value, the aesthetic one would be good enough for me. I like to hear the sounds of the bees. When my peach angel's trumpet is blooming, they disappear into the huge flowers which amplify their sounds. The whole tree seems to be buzzing.

I like to see them traveling from blossom to blossom. I like to wonder where the hive is where honey is being made from the nectar collected from my flowers.

When johnny-jump-ups, torenia, or zinnias volunteer from seeds dropped the previous season, and when the fig and Japanese plum trees bear fruit I know that the bees did their job.

I always think of bumblebees as connected to a flower. They are wonderful to look at no matter which blossom they are probing. One of the most memorable sights of all my years of gardening was the bumblebees in their gold and black striped fuzziness picking their ways about the bright golden centers and vivid orange petals of Mexican sunflowers.

Honeybees are European imports. Their origin is probably southeast Asia, but they are the dominant pollinators in spots world-wide where they have been taken by travelers.

Native American bumblebees seem to be decreasing in number, probably due to habitat destruction. Before the honeybees were imported, bumblebees took care of most pollination of flowering plants on this continent.

Bumblebee nests are either established by the queen in the ground in burrows abandoned by rodents or mice or on the ground in a cavity which she hollows out. An undisturbed grassy or brambly area in a large garden may be suitable. Every time I see bumblebees coming from within the clump of holly fern, I hope they have chosen my garden as a homesite. So far they seem to prefer the more isolated spots which probably exist in the swamps and marshes around the city and maybe in empty lots and abandoned buildings.

We owe thanks to the beekeepers in our vicinity who keep hives for honeybees. A small yard could support one or two hives. There are local outlets for supplies. Louisiana Cooperative Extension offers a publication called *Bee Ready* free to those interested.

Bees are necessary in home and commercial gardens for pollination of fruit trees and vegetables. Though whatever flowers are planted will attract bees, the best plants for honey production are the clovers and herbs:

Trifolium repens L. **WHITE CLOVER** The all time best honeybee flower, this perennial grows best in moist, fertile soil in sunny spots. It is not a native, but is found in many lawns where its nitrogen-fixing properties make it useful. My experience with this plant in New Orleans has been that it dies back during the heat of summer. I have used it as a ground cover among Liriope plugs until the latter filled in the gaps.

Trifolium pratense L. **RED CLOVER** Another imported perennial, this plant's longer flower tubes make it more suitable for the longer nosed bumblebees than for the short nosed honeybees. (Even though a recent postage stamp was issued showing a honeybee on red clover.) Its flowers are typical clover flowers, but magenta in color, not red. I have one which has lasted several years in a moist, shady part of my garden. The ones in a sunnier spot which were crowded out by lantana and scarlet sage bloomed more prolifically. Clover seeds can be purchased at a Feed and Seed store.

The other best bee plants are the garden herbs, specifically:

Salvia elegans PINEAPPLE SAGE
Salvia officinalis GARDEN SAGE
Origanum marjorana SWEET MARJORAM
Melissa officinalis LEMON BALM
Thymus species THYME
Mentha species MINTS

BATS IN THE NEW ORLEANS GARDEN

"Fillet of a fenny snake,
In the cauldron boil and bake,
Eye of newt and toe of frog,
Wool of bat, and tongue of dog. "

Remember the witches from Shakespeare's Macbeth? No wonder bats have such a bad image. Their P. R. through the ages has been the pits.

Nearly one-quarter of the world's species of mammals are bats. Forty per cent of American species are endangered or close. Their numbers are dwindling rapidly due to the same habitat destruction which has affected other wildlife. In addition, the use of chemicals as preservatives and insecticides in human habitats has removed some traditional homesites.

Led by ecologist, Merlin Tuttle, a movement to reverse that trend (under the name Bat Conservation International, Inc.) is underway. Why? If you do not find bats to be fascinating creatures as I do, you may be impressed by the fact that (in Mr. Tuttle's words):

Nearly everywhere, bats play an essential role in the control of nocturnal insects, but they are particularly crucial elements in tropical forests and savannas because they pollinate and disperse the seeds of many plants, including key species upon which other forms of life are dependent.

Periodically bats make the news in New Orleans. An article in the *Times-Picayune* (January 21, 1989) reported health concerns by citizens when a colony of 300 bats was found under the arched roof of the cafeteria-auditorium at the Carver Middle School on Higgins Boulevard; 200 in an attic at Palmer Elementary School on Clouet Street, and 50 in an uptown school attic. People either think rabies or vampires when they hear the word "bat." City health officials reassured citizens that New Orleans bat species are not disease carrying. Dr. Brobson Lutz, Director of the

Health Department, confirmed the absence of diseases attributable to bats within the City of New Orleans.

Rabies is much more likely to be contracted from a pet in our area, though in the Western United States, the picture is different. In the wild, this viral disease is found more frequently in skunks and raccoons than bats. Precautions make sense. Any wild animal which behaves in an abnormal way, such as not exhibiting appropriate fear of humans, should be avoided. No wild animal should be picked up or kept as a pet, which is illegal without a permit, anyway.

The bats which are common in New Orleans are all insectivores. They eat lots of insects, including mosquitoes, fleas, and Formosa termites. One mouse-eared bat can eat as many as 600 mosquitoes in an hour. That should make them very desirable!

Because of their contributions to man, they should not be killed. If you don't want bats in your belfry, attic, etc., seal it off. Blocking the attic in an older New Orleans home is much easier than the installation of rat guards, which no one with a raised house considers not doing!

Some bats, such as the red bat, the seminole bat, the northern yellow bat, and occasionally the eastern pipistrelle, roost singly in trees or clumps of Spanish moss. Colony nesters can be found in the eaves or attics of old buildings or in whatever crevices they can find within the city. These can include the southeastern myotis or mouse-eared bat, eastern pipistrelle, big brown bat, evening bat, Rafinesque's big-eared bat, and the Brazilian free-tailed bat.

To make your wildlife garden complete, you may want to install a bat house. These specially designed boxes with partitions to simulate the crevices in which the animals naturally roost are popular in Europe. If you do not have the courage to be unconventional, even for this worthy but not yet popular cause, be encouraged by the fact that most people would never figure out what your bat house was. Plans can be obtained from Bat Conservation International, or in *International Wildlife* (January-February, 1986). Bob Thomas of the Nature Center says the ones installed there are unused. He feels that New Orleans offers enough real eaves without the provision of artificial ones.

Some people, like Susan and C. H. Palm stage backyard "batwatches." You may have seen the flying mammals at dusk snapping up insects from around street lights. Most people, including myself, haven't. But, we're in for a treat once we decide to train our eyes in the right direction.

George H. Lowery,, Jr. in his *The Mammals of Louisiana and its Adjacent Waters* gives much more information about bats and the other mammals you may find in your New Orleans wildlife garden and elsewhere in the state. He follows his comments on the economic and aesthetic value of bats with what I will allow too be my last words on the subject:

> *Anyone who fails to derive some pleasure from watching one of these marvelously agile creatures feeding at twilight must indeed be a callous individual unperceptive of the beauties of the world of nature that surround us.*[44]

So there!

Andree B. Carter

Special Gardens

"There are as many kinds of gardening as of poetry."

Joseph Addison
18th century English gardener

Growing things, designing a garden can be a creative outlet, a personal statement. Different needs are met and different styles expressed through gardening by different people. I feel the only rules or garden design should be the ones you make or choose for yourself. Though *"House and Garden: The Magazine of Creative Living"* offers some interesting ideas, it need not be a standard. I believe the tiny doorstep gardens found throughout the New Orleans area offer as much pleasure to their creators as do the elaborate and expansive spreads pictured in the magazines, maybe more. The diversity which has been a part of New Orlean's past should be as much a part of its future.

Anthony Eschmann has refined the concept of fantasy gardening. He created on his ninth ward estate (somewhat smaller than Henry Lawrence's or Valcour Aime's), a lush retreat with brick pathways winding through colorful blooming plants. A garden swing sits at the edge of a shallow pond (excavated by hand and lined with plastic sheeting) on which water lilies float and in which fish and tadpoles swim. Amphibian noises abound at night. He tried ducklings for a short time. They gobbled up his expensive Japanese koi and started on the vegetation. I gave him a pair of floating duck candles in memoriam.

Nancy Newfield's garden in Metairie is shrubby-- "scrubby" she corrects--with what she calls in her lectures "old lady plants," salvias, lantana, four o'clocks, turk's cap, Mexican cigar, shrimp plant. They have all been grown in New Orleans gardens for a long period of time (hence the name) and can all be spreading in form. Nancy achieves her gardening purpose, which is not decoration. She attracts the jewels of the bird world in droves! She has created a hummingbird heaven!

Caroline Sontheimer's Carrollton gardens are elegant and stylish, full of not uncommon local plants arranged in a very distinctive way by Natives Nursery's John May- rone. Her front yard is part lawn and includes white Madagascar periwinkle, red balsam, daylilies, ardisia, Chin- ese hibiscus, gingers, papyrus, iris, bananas, giant elephant ears, swamp magnolia, and more. She has bloom almost all year round and very low maintainence. Her garden and others are a source for the dramatic arrangements she creates with parts of plants no one else would think to use and exotic and native flowers. She brings her garden inside her house and others'.

Ernestine Hopkins would politely call my garden "ca- sual." Pat Johnson calls it "an English country garden." A lady up the street calls it a weed patch. It is a collection of wildflowers and cultivated plants of native and exotic origin whose overall style has evolved through trial and error. There is no way my garden would make it to *House and Garden*. My own garden fantasies for a while related to incorporating domestic wildlife into the back- yard world. I lost three camellias to my children's scratching, overgrown Easter chicks before I put hardware cloth on the ground around the roots for protection. The chicks were eventually eaten by a roving pack of Uptown stray dogs. I thought guinea fowl would be quaint garden decoration. I pictured them perching in my loquat and warning me when intruders approached. I purchased a series of pairs from Joe Kuhn on River Road in Destrehan. They were compatible with the garden, but not with city living. Invariably they would fly over the fence and visit neighbors where they weren't known. I would hear through the grape vine later that the birds ended up in a gumbo pot: one of the hazards of being a loose fowl in uptown New Orleans.

There are gardens I have observed for years. I feel lucky when I stop for a peek and get caught. That almost always means a tour. I ask lots of questions. Ernestine Hopkins on Valmont Street has a "friendship garden" of plants collected over a long period of time. Her calla lilies came from a dime store 60 years ago. The old-fashioned multiflora petunias in lavender, hardier than newer hybrids, return year after year, as do larkspur volunteers (grown in Louisiana gardens in 1838) and magenta summer phlox. 'Queen Elizabeth' (1954) and 'Peace' (1945) Roses, a Grandiflora and Hybrid tea which are among the better performers in New Orleans, are in raised beds with pink impatiens, rex begonias, red and white geraniums (the pelargonium offered by local nurseries at least since 1859). Potted sedums and echeverias (hens and chickens) are placed here and there on the patio. The pale pink crape myrtle standards herald each spring in the pastel garden. Crape myrtles have been essential in local gardens since their introduction in the 1830's. Ms. Hopkins remembers many of the friends who are the sources of her seeds, cuttings, or plants. It is the softness of this garden I like and its constancy.

Louise Ewin came out to work in her garden on Freret Street one December day. She caught me parked, gazing across the lawn at the semicircular bed in front of her raised cottage. She explained her goal: "...just a little color." She pointed out her favorite spuria iris, not yet blooming. Lots else was, a mixture of modern and traditional varieties. I saw annual blue ageratum; red salvia; nasturtiums in orange, yellow, red; pink petunias, yellow and purple pansies; perennial red pentas; shrub sasanquas with pink blossoms and dark blue berried dwarf Indian hawthorne. Almost any time of the year I drive by, I see color. Ferns are a common green thread. Mrs. Ewin has planned and achieved a full and luxuriant, while casual, natural look reflecting the early 20th century English influence of Gertrude Jekyll.

"Survival of the fittest" determines what you see growing in Les Cambias' garden, he says. Even so, his plot is a well-ordered series of raised beds with labeled plants. He experiments with hybridization of salvias and liriopes as a volunteer at City Park Botanical Garden and in his own yard, called "The Green Empire" by neighbors for its trees and shrubs . He grows many plants from seed. You won't find the species he recommends in every garden: barbados cherry, abelia, society garlic, scabiosa, natives such as oakleaf hydrangea, poppy mallow, echinacea, coreopsis, stokesia, physostegia, penstemon digitalis, and milkweeds.

CONTAINER GARDENS

Among the earliest ornamental gardens described by travellers to New Orleans are container gardens, the "gallery gardens" reported in 1804: *"galleries enclosed in wrought iron over which vines climbed and within which flowers were planted."*[45] By 1938 (in the *W. P. A. Guide*) they are described as *"the 'hanging gardens' on the iron balconies of some of the French Quarter homes...."*

They persist today, throughout the city. At Mardi Gras the ones overlooking parade routes are are planted in green, purple, gold: with deep green foliaged purple petunias and golden yellow marigolds. I'll bet you can think of other combinations. Carolyn and Albert Brown's gallery garden in the Pontalba Apartments has crape myrtles, asparagus fern, climbing and trailing moonvine, caladiums.

Plants can be grown in an enormous variety of clay pots in standard to exotic shapes, boxes, tubs, barrels, in window boxes, or hanging containers. This style of horticulture can be a form of decorating at one extreme and experimental gardening at the other, since pot mobility allows climatic control and the latitude for trying all kinds of tropicals from seed. Lighter weight pots make the introduction of tender plants into the garden with hasty retreat indoors possible when the temperature drops. They allow you to provide instant color indoors or out and to rearrange it when you get bored. Immovable containers allow control over soil type and provide the good drainage of raised beds more aesthetic choices of appearance.

The Mediterranean herbs are particularly well suited to containers. Even the apartment dweller with a sunlit windowsill can have fresh herbs.

RULES FOR CONTAINER GARDENING

1. Regular watering on a more frequent basis than if the plants were in the ground is essential.

2. Soil should be porous and fast-draining.

3. Regular feeding during the growing season is important because nutrients are quickly lost from the soil with heavy watering.

4. Plants need to be repotted when the roots fill the container. Use a fresh soil mix.

Many annuals and bulbs, some perennials and flowering shrubs are appropriate for containers. My lists have designated those especially suited to or benefitting by being root-bound in pots. Don't forget exotics such as bromeliads, orchids, and the wonderful rhizomatous achimenes which thrive outdoors most of our year but are not freeze tolerant.

The hanging basket of ferns is a beautiful way to display these graceful plants. Doing it yourself can save lots of money: Purchase a wire basket designed for the purpose at a nursery. Line it with sphagnum moss. Fill the interior with soil. Keep moist. The plants will grow and spread around the outer surface of the basket, eventually forming a solid ball of fern. It must be brought indoors during a freeze.

Ferns which lend themselves to such treatment are:

SWORD or BOSTON FERN
JAPANESE CLIMBING FERN
RESURRECTION FERN (will grow in sphagnum alone)
CHRISTMAS FERN

WATER GARDENS

The fountains so often thought of as traditional, in French Quarter gardens, at least, were rareties before the modernization of plumbing systems. The last outbreak of yellow fever in New Orleans was in 1905. By 1920, the open cisterns offering breeding places for yellow fever carrying mosquitoes had been done away with and water supplied through pipes and under municipal water pressure substituted. With the change, fountains with their flowing, spouting, spraying, running water became possible and popular.

The fountain of the Victorian age was a cast iron basin with cast iron statuary perched centrally. Richard Koch's Spanish colonial influenced designs of the 1920's and 1930's were much copied, both the masonry and tile b asined and wall-hung styles. Large concrete fountains in Audubon and City Parks were built during the 1930's. Fountains on Lakeshore Drive date to the 1960's.

The large old metal pots used in sugar cane processing are popular as fountain basins in modern gardens. Your garden may or may not include a fountain. If it does include water in a container much larger than a bird bath or even a very wet spot, it can also include some unique flora. That special moist spot under the dripping air conditioner or around a leaky spigot can be capitalized upon as a microcosm perfect for certain plants which can also be grown in the naturally wet area around the pond, in your wildlife garden, or in your pond or fountain, itself.

Call American Aquatic Plants and the Louisiana Pond Society in RESOURCES for expert advice in such areas as acid-base balance when you set up your pond. A circulating pump may be necessary for aeration. Fish or frequent changes of water will prevent mosquito proliferation.   Chloramine is used in the purification of modern water supplies.   It is poisonous to fish, but will disappate with time, or with the addition of appropriate chemicals a vailable where aquarium and pond supplies are sold.   If you build your own pond, an invaluable tip from expert Bert Myers which we followed is to provide a constant drip source of water to replace that which rapidly evaporates on hot summer days.   Make sure the on-off valve is within view of the spigot for easy regulation of drop size. The addition of a few drops at a time will not upset the chloramine balance.

SPECIAL RULES FOR WATER PLANTS

1.   At least 5 hours a day of sun.
2.   Water near the plants should be still.
3.   2 to 18 inches should be provided from the top of the container to the water surface.
4.   Use heavy garden soil with some clay, not commercial potting mixes.
5.   Cover soil surface with pebbles.

WATER & BOG PLANTS

Alocasia macrorrhiza ELEPHANT EAR
Canna hybrids CANNA
Cyperus papyrus PAPYRUS
Eichhornia crassipes WATER HYACINTH, RICHARDSON LILY
Eleocharis montevidensis SPIKE RUSH
Iris hybrids LOUISIANA IRIS
Nelumbo species WATER LOTUS
Nuphar luteum SPATTERDOCK, YELLOW COWLILY
Neomarica gracilis WALKING IRIS
Nymphaea species WATER LILIES
Orontium aquaticum GOLDEN CLUB
Pontederia cordata PICKEREL WEED
Sagittaria latifolia ARROWHEAD
Sagittaria graminea variety *platyphylla* DELTA ARROWHEAD
Saururus cernuus LIZARD'S TAIL
Victoria amazonica VICTORIA LILY
Pistia stratiotes WATER LETTUCE

FRAGRANCE GARDENS

EXOTIC TREES & SHRUBS

Aloysia triphylla LEMON VERBENA
Azara microphylla BOXLEAF AZARA
Brugmansia X candida ANGEL'S TRUMPET
Buddleia species BUTTERFLY BUSH
Carissa grandiflora NATAL PLUM
Cestrum diurnum DAY BLOOMING JESSAMINE
Cestrum nocturnum NIGHT BLOOMING JESSAMINE
Choisya ternata MEXICAN ORANGE
Citrus reticulata SATSUMA, MANDARIN ORANGE
Coronilla valentina CROWN VETCH
Escallonia mutis ESCALLONIA
Eucalyptus cinerea SILVER DOLLAR TREE
Gardenia jasminoides CAPE JASMINE, COMMON GARDENIA
Jasminum floridum FLORIDA JASMINE
Jasminum polyanthum PINK JASMINE
Lantana camara HAM AND EGGS
Ligustrum japonicum WAX LEAF LIGUSTRUM
Michelia figo, Magnolia fuscata BANANA SHRUB
Osmanthus fragrans SWEET OLIVE
Philadelphus coronarius MOCK ORANGE
Pittosporum tobira JAPANESE PITTOSPORUM
Rosa species ROSE
Royena lucida AFRICAN EBONY TREE
Tabernaemontana divaricata CRAPE JASMINE
Viburnum tinus LAURUSTINUS VIBURNUM

NATIVE TREES & SHRUBS

Cephalanthus occidentalis BUTTONBUSH
Magnolia grandiflora SOUTHERN MAGNOLIA
Magnolia virginiana SWEET BAY MAGNOLIA
Persea borbonia RED BAY, SWAMPBAY
Calycanthus floridus SWEET SHRUB
Illicium floridanum STAR ANISE
Itea virginica SWEETSPIRE, VIRGINIA WILLOW
Myrica cerifera SOUTHERN WAX MYRTLE

ANNUALS, PERENNIALS, BULBS

Achillea millefolium WHITE YARROW
Amaryllis belladonna BELLADONNA LILY
Amomum compactum AMOMUM
Cheiranthus cheiri WALLFLOWER

Cleome hasslerana CLEOME, SPIDER FLOWER
Crinum species CRINUM
Eucharis grandiflora AMAZON LILY
Galtonia candicans SUMMER HYACINTH
Hedychium coronarium BUTTERFLY GINGER
Hedychium flavum YELLOW BUTTERFLY GINGER
Hedychium gardneranum KAHILI GINGER
Heliotropium arborescens HELIOTROPE
Hyacinthus orientalis and hybrids DUTCH HYACINTH
Hymenocallis caroliniana SWAMP SPIDER LILY
Hymenocallis narcissiflora ISMENE, PERUVIAN DAFFODIL
Iberis amara ROCKET CANDYTUFT
Ipheion uniflorum SPRING STARFLOWER
Lathyrus odoratus SWEET PEA
Lobularia maritima SWEET ALYSSUM
Matthiola incana STOCK, GILLYFLOWER
Mirabilis jalapa FOUR O'CLOCK
Narcissus species NARCISSUS, DAFFODIL, JONQUIL
Pancratium maritimum SEA DAFFODIL
Perilla frutescens PERILLA
Petunia X hybrida PETUNIA (The purples)
Polianthes tuberosa TUBEROSE
Reseda odorata COMMON MIGNONETTE
Viola odorata SWEET VIOLET

HERBS

Melissa officianalis LEMON BALM
Mentha species MINT
Monarda citriodora LEMON BEEBALM
Rosemarinus officinalis ROSEMARY
Salvia officinalis SAGE
Santolina chamaecyparissus LAVENDER COTTON

VINES

Clematis dioscoreifolia JAPANESE CLEMATIS
Clematis virginiana VIRGIN'S-BOWER
Gelsemium sempervirens CAROLINA JESSAMINE
Ipomoea alba or *Calonyction aculeatum* MOONFLOWER
Jasminum species JASMINES
Lonicera japonica JAPANESE HONEYSUCKLE
Millettia reticulata EVERGREEN WISTERIA
Quisqualis indica RANGOON CREEPER
Trachelospermum jasminoides CONFEDERATE JASMINE
Wisteria sinensis WISTERIA, CHINESE WISTERIA

THE SHADE GARDEN

PLANTS FOR SHADE, FULL SHADE, DENSE SHADE

EXOTIC TREES & SHRUBS

Azara microphylla BOXLEAF AZARA
Ardisia crenata CORALBERRY
Aucuba japonica AUCUBA
Eranthemum pulchellum BLUE SAGE
Fatsia japonica JAPANESE ARALIA
Hydrangea macrophylla GARDEN HYDRANGEA
Indigofera kirilowii INDIGO
Justicia carnea FLAMINGO PLANT
Mahonia bealei OREGON GRAPE HOLLY
Malvaviscus arboreus TURK'S CAP, SULTAN'S TURBAN
Nandina domestica NANDINA, SACRED BAMBOO
Odontonema strictum FIRESPIKE
Podocarpus macrophyllus SOUTHERN YEW, JAPANESE YEW
Tetrapanax papyriferus RICE PAPER PLANT

FERNS

Adiantum capillus-veneris VENUS'-HAIR FERN
Asplenium platyneuron EBONY SPLEENWORT
Athyrium asplenioides LOWLAND or SOUTHERN LADY FERN
Athyrium niponicum pictum JAPANESE PAINTED FERN
Dryopteris normalis SOUTHERN SHIELD FERN
Dryopteris thelypteris variety *haleana* SOUTHERN MARSH FERN
Marsilea uncinata HOOK-SPINE WATERCLOVER
Polystichum acrostichoides CHRISTMAS FERN
Cyrtomium falcatum JAPANESE HOLLY FERN

WILDFLOWERS

Duchesnea indica WILD STRAWBERRY, MOCK STRAWBERRY
Lobelia cardinalis CARDINAL FLOWER
Prunella vulgaris SELF-HEAL, HEALALL
Spilanthes americana CREEPING SPOT FLOWER
Tillandsia usneoides SPANISH MOSS
Tradescantia virginiana SPIDERWORT

ANNUALS

Digitalis purpurea variety 'Foxy' FOXGLOVE
Impatiens wallerana IMPATIENS, SULTANA
Lobelia erinus EDGING LOBELIA

Myosotis sylvatica GARDEN FORGET-ME-NOT
Torenia fournieri TORENIA, WISHBONE FLOWER
Salvia splendens SCARLET SAGE

PERENNIALS

Ajuga reptans AJUGA
Aspidistra elatior CAST-IRON PLANT
Begonia species WAX, ANGEL-WING, REX, BEEFSTEAK BEGONIAS
Justicia brandegeana, Beloperone guttata SHRIMP PLANT
Ligularia tussilaginea LIGULARIA
Liriope LILYTURF, LIRIOPE
Nierembergia hippomanica variety *violacea* CUPFLOWER
Nierembergia scoparia TALL CUPFLOWER
Ophiopogon japonicus MONKEY GRASS, MONDO GRASS
Pachysandra terminals PACHYSANDRA, JAPANESE SPURGE
Pseuderanthemum alatum CHOCOLATE PLANT
Setcreasea pallida 'Purple Heart' PURPLE HEART
Polygonum capitatum KNOTWEED
Saxifraga stolonifera STRAWBERRY GERANIUM
Tradescantia albiflora WANDERING JEW

BULBOUS PLANTS

Amomum compactum AMOMUM
Arisaema triphyllum JACK-IN-THE-PULPIT
Arum palaestinum or *sanctum* BLACK CALLA LILY
Bletilla striata BLETILLA, CHINESE GROUND ORCHID
Caladium species and hybrids CALADIUM
Clivia miniata and *Clivia* hybrids KAFIR-LILY
Colocasia species ELEPHANT'S-EAR
Curculigo capitulata PALM GRASS
Eucharis grandiflora AMAZON LILY
Leucojum species SNOWFLAKE

VINES

Aristolochia durior DUTCHMAN'S PIPE
Bignonia capreolata CROSS VINE, TRUMPET FLOWER
Dioscorea alata POTATO VINE, AIR POTATO
Ficus pumila FIG VINE
Hedera canariensis ALGERIAN IVY
Hedera helix ENGLISH IVY
Monstera deliciosa MONSTERA, SPLIT-LEAVED PHILODENDRON
Trachelospermum asiaticum DWARF CONFEDERATE JASMINE

NATIVE SHRUBS

Cornus drummondii ROUGH-LEAF DOGWOOD
Forestiera acuminata SWAMP PRIVET
Illicium floridanum STAR ANISE
Itea virginica SWEETSPIRE, VIRGINIA WILLOW
Lindera benzoin SPICEBUSH
Sabal minor LOUISIANA PALMETTO

PLANTS FOR HALF-SHADE, PARTIAL SHADE, SEMI SHADE, LIGHT SHADE

EXOTIC TREES & SHRUBS, DECIDUOUS

Musa species BANANA
Vitex agnus-castus CHASTE TREE, VITEX
Caesalpinia gilliesii BIRD OF PARADISE
Clerodendrum species CLERODENDRUM
Cuphea micropetala MEXICAN CIGARFLOWER
Jasminum floridum FLORIDA JASMINE
Kolkwitzia amabilis BEAUTY BUSH
Philadelphus coronarius MOCK ORANGE
Punica granatum POMEGRANATE
Weigela florida OLD-FASHIONED WEIGELA

EXOTIC TREES & SHRUBS, EVERGREEN

Cinnamomum camphora CAMPHOR TREE
Eriobotrya japonica JAPANESE PLUM, LOQUAT, MESPILUS
Grevillea robusta SILK OAK
Brunfelsia australis YESTERDAY, TODAY, AND TOMORROW
Buxus microphylla variety *japonica* JAPANESE BOX
Camellia species CAMELLIA
Cestrum diurnum DAY BLOOMING JESSAMINE
Cestrum nocturnum NIGHT BLOOMING JESSAMINE
Choisya ternata MEXICAN ORANGE
Cocculus laurifolius COCCULUS, MOONSEED
Cycas revoluta SAGO PALM
Escallonia species ESCALLONIA
Fortunella japonica KUMQUAT
Gardenia jasminoides CAPE JASMINE, COMMON GARDENIA
Ligustrum species PRIVET
Malpighia glabra BARBADOES CHERRY
Michelia figo BANANA SHRUB
Myrtus communis MYRTLE
Nerium oleander OLEANDER

Osmanthus fragrans SWEET OLIVE
Pittosporum tobira JAPANESE PITTOSPORUM
Rhododendron species AZALEA
Tabernaemontana divaricata CRAPE JASMINE
Trachycarpus fortunei WINDMILL PALM
Viburnum tinus LAURUSTINUS VIBURNUM

WILDFLOWERS

Amsonia tabernaemontana BLUE-STAR
Baptisia species WILD OR FALSE INDIGO
Commelina erecta DAYFLOWER
Coreopsis lanceolata TICKSEED
Coreopsis tinctoria PAINTED COREOPSIS, CALLIOPSIS
Erigeron philadelphicus DAISY FLEABANE
Erythrina herbacea MAMOU, CORAL BEAN
Eupatorium fistulosum JOE PYE WEED
Mimulus alatus MONKEYFLOWER
Penstemon digitalis BEARDTONGUE
Phlox divaricata BLUE PHLOX
Physostegia virginica OBEDIENT PLANT, FALSE DRAGON HEAD
Rudbeckia hirta BLACK-EYED SUSAN
Ruellia caroliniensis WILD PETUNIA
Salvia coccinea TEXAS SAGE, SCARLET SAGE, TROPICAL SAGE
Senecio glabellus BUTTERWEED, YELLOWTOP
Spigelia marilandica INDIAN PINK, PINKROOT
Stokesia laevis STOKE'S ASTER, STOKESIA
Teucrium canadense AMERICAN GERMANDER, WOOD SAGE
Trifolium pratense RED CLOVER
Trifolium repens WHITE CLOVER
Vernonia altissima IRONWEED
Viola species VIOLETS

ANNUALS

Ageratum houstonianum AGERATUM, FLOSS FLOWER
Anchusa capensis BUGLOSS, CAPE FORGET-ME-NOT
Bellis perennis ENGLISH DAISY
Browallia speciosa BROWALLIA
Callistephus chinensis CHINA ASTER, ANNUAL ASTER
Capsicum annuum ORNAMENTAL PEPPERS
Catharanthus roseus or *Vinca roseus*
        MADAGASCAR PERIWINKLE
Cheiranthus cheiri WALLFLOWER
Chrysanthemum hybrids ANNUAL CHRYSANTHEMUM
Cuphea platycentra CIGAR FLOWER, FIRECRACKER PLANT
Cynoglossum amabile CHINESE FORGET-ME-NOT

Dianthus species PINKS
Heliotropium arborescens HELIOTROPE
Iberis species CANDYTUFT
Impatiens balsamina GARDEN BALSAM, LADY'S SLIPPERS
Malva sylvestris ZEBRINA, FRENCH MALLOW
Matthiola incana STOCK, GILLYFLOWER
Nicotiana alata and hybrids FLOWERING TOBACCO
Salpiglossis sinuata SALPIGLOSSIS, PAINTED TONGUE
Viola cornuta VIOLA, *Viola* X *wittrockiana* PANSY
Viola tricolor JOHNNY-JUMP-UP

BULBOUS PLANTS

Agapanthus africanus LILY OF THE NILE, AGAPANTHUS
Alocasia macrorrhiza GIANT ELEPHANT'S EAR
Alpinia zerumbet SHELL GINGER
Alstroemeria pulchella PARROT LILY
X *Amarcrinum (Amaryllis x Crinum)* CRINODONNA
Amaryllis belladonna BELLADONNA LILY
Belamcanda chinensis BLACKBERRY LILY
Costus speciosus SPIRAL GINGER
Crinum species, native & exotic CRINUM
Curcuma species HIDDEN LILY, SURPRISE LILY
Dietes species DIETES
Endymion hispanicus, Scilla campanulata
        SPANISH SQUILL, SPANISH BLUEBELL
Habranthus tubispathus, Habranthus robustus RAIN LILY
Habranthus texanus COPPER LILY
Hedychium species HEDYCHIUM
Haemanthus katharinae, Haemanthus multiflorus BLOOD LILY
Hippeastrum hybrids AMARYLLIS
Hymenocallis species SPIDER LILY
Ipheion uniflorum SPRING STARFLOWER
Iris hybrids DUTCH IRIS
Leucojum aestivum SUMMER SNOWFLAKE
Lilium and hybrids LILY
Lycoris species NAKED LADY, SPIDER LILY, SURPRISE LILY
Moraea MORAEA, also called *Dietes* species, PEACOCK IRIS
Muscari species GRAPE HYACINTH
Narcissus species NARCISSUS
Neomarica species NEOMARICA, WALKING IRIS
Nerine species SPIDER LILIES
Oxalis species OXALIS
Sprekelia formosissima AZTEC LILY, JACOBEAN LILY
Zantedeschia species CALLA LILY
Zephyranthes species RAIN LILY
Zingiber zerumbet PINE CONE GINGER, SHAMPOO PLANT

THE NEW ORLEANS GARDEN

PERENNIALS

Aquilegia species COLUMBINE
Chrysogonum virginianum GOLDEN STAR
Dichorisandra thrysiflora BLUE GINGER
Echinacea purpurea PURPLE CONEFLOWER
Gerbera jamesonii GERBERA DAISY, TRANSVAAL DAISY
Liatris species BLAZING STAR, GAYFEATHER
Libertia species LIBERTIA
Lythrum salicaria PURPLE LOOSESTRIFE
Mirabilis jalapa FOUR O'CLOCK
Physalis alkekengi CHINESE LANTERN PLANT
Reinwardtia indica YELLOW FLAX
Rudbeckia species CONEFLOWER
Salvia species SAGE
Salvia farinacea MEALY-CUP SAGE
Strobilanthes isophyllus BEDDING CONEHEAD
Trachelium caeruleum THROATWORT
Viola odorata SWEET VIOLET

VINES

Akebia quinata AKEBIA, FIVE LEAF AKEBIA
Clitoria ternatea BUTTERFLY-PEA
Clytostoma callistegioides BIGNONIA, ARGENTINE TRUMPET VINE
Cocculus carolinus COCCULUS, CAROLINA MOONSEED
Gelsemium sempervirens CAROLINA JESSAMINE
Ipomoea coccinea RED MORNING GLORY
Jasminum species JASMINES
Lathyrus latifolius PERENNIAL SWEET PEA
Lonicera japonica JAPANESE HONEYSUCKLE
Quisqualis indica RANGOON CREEPER
Stigmaphyllon ciliatum BUTTERFLY VINE
Thunbergia alata BLACK-EYED SUSAN VINE, CLOCK VINE
Trachelospermum jasminoides CONFEDERATE JASMINE
Tropaeolum peregrinum CANARY-BIRD VINE, CANARY CREEPER
Solanum jasminoides POTATO VINE
Vinca major GREATER PERIWINKLE

NATIVE TREES & SHRUBS

Aesculus pavia RED BUCKEYE
Amelanchier arborea SERVICEBERRY
Callicarpa americana AMERICAN BEAUTYBERRY,
    FRENCH MULBERRY
Calycanthus floridus SWEET SHRUB
Cephalanthus occidentalis BUTTONBUSH

Cercis canadensis RED BUD, JUDAS TREE
Clethra alnifolia SWEET PEPPERBUSH, WHITE ALDER
Cornus florida FLOWERING DOGWOOD
Halesia diptera SILVERBELL
Ilex species HOLLY
Lyonia lucida FETTERBUSH
Myrica cerifera SOUTHERN WAX MYRTLE
Persea borbonia RED BAY, SWAMP BAY
Sambucus canadensis ELDERBERRY
Styrax americanus STYRAX, SNOWBELL, STORAX

THE HERB GARDEN

"The old-time garden herbs are part of every well-regulated Creole kitchen garden. Thyme, Sage, Rosemary, Mint, Sweet Marjoram, Basil, Lavender, Anise, Caraway, Bene, Borage, Catnip, Coriander, Dill, Fennel, Hoarhound, Pot Marigold, Pennyroyal, Rue, Summer Savory, Tansy, Tarragon, Wormwood--all these thrive in our gardens, and are used by the Creole housewives, some for culinary, others for medicinal, purposes".

The Picayune Creole Cook Book, 1901.

Whoever wrote that lavender and borage should thrive in our gardens could not have been a gardener! The traditional herbs are of Mediterranean origin. Needless to say, the climate of New Orleans is far from ideal for many of them. With the same ifs, ands, and buts as in all the other chapters, most of those recommended above can thrive here. For some, planting in the fall to beat the summer heat works, or in modified soil in raised beds to provide perfect drainage, but, there will always be casualties of the hot, wet season.

"Herb" is a culinary term, not a botanical one. The plants used as herbs can be herbaceous perennials, bulbs, annuals, or evergreen shrubs. Their status as herb is earned by their function: as seasonings or decoration in cooking or for medicinal purposes. They are usually aromatic. Most of them are in the Mint and Parsley families.

Generally, their culture involves:
1.   Superb drainage in raised beds.
2.   Neutral to slightly alkaline soil (pH between 6.0-7.0).
3.   Six to eight hours a day of full sun.
4.   Spacing of plants to allow for good air circulation (12-18 inches apart).
5.   Poor to average soil fertility to produce higher concentrations of the essential oils which are the sources of flavor and fragrance.
6.   Mulch to prevent competitive weeds and hold in moisture.

Aromatic herbs should be harvested when concentrations of oils are highest, in the morning after the dew has evaporated. They can be dried, stored in non-porous glass containers for later use; or used fresh. A selection of mints for use fresh in tea, or basil for pesto or fresh in salads are delights which the smallest garden can easily provide!

Herbs can be integrated into your regular plantings, but not where you use poisons for pest and disease control. The "Herb Garden" is a design category in itself, with its own traditions and styles through the ages. Use creole boxwood or santolina for edges if you decide to go formal.

The kitchen and herb garden in descriptions of old New Orleans gardens was either separate (in the back yard as opposed to the front) from ornamental plantings or integrated (as in some courtyard gardens). Most of the herbs are attractive for the textures and colors of their foliage rather than their flowers, and can be arranged in formal or informal decorative patterns. Most do well in pots; making a container herb garden a mobile and attractive proposition for a patio or "hanging or gallery garden". Dr. Nia Terezakis lives in a "sky house" with sunny balconies where she integrates herbs with shrubs or annuals in great concrete and earthenware pots. She harvests her cooking needs with scissors.

As sachets and potpourris are one of the uses of fragrant herbs, the combination of scented roses and herbs is logical to provide the raw materials for these products. Since poisons must be used in New Orleans to maintain new varieties of roses, the more disease resistant antique roses (fragrant varieties) would be a better selection for this use. Orris Root is the powdered rhizome of *Iris germanica* variety *florentina*, the white flowered bearded iris which is the only member of its group to repeat reliably in New Orleans. It is used as a fixative in potpourri and

is traditionally included in herb gardens.   Some sources
say the iris that grows here is *I. X albicans*.

The root of vetiver *(Vetiveria zizanioides)*, an Old
World grass brought to New Orleans from the East Indies,
was used by creole ladies as a sachet in linen closets.   Its
eight foot high clumps were found naturalized in stands
around Covington and Hammond in 1938.

Karen Eberle grows vetiver in her Upperline Street
garden.   It is an interesting substitute for pampas grass
and perfect in the spacious New Orleans potpourris garden.   It is not reliably hardy in our nastiest freezes.

Bill Van Calsem of Hove' Parfumeur, 824 Royal
Street,   mysteriously describes his source of vetiver as
"upriver."   Since 1931, Hove' has sold vetevir in ribbon-
wrapped bundles, and marketed traditional local scents in
colognes, perfumes, potpourri: honeysuckle, tea olive,
heliotrope, vetevir, and even camellia, though *Camellia
sasanqua*, I'm sure!   We all know *Camellia japonica* has no
scent!

Another oversized addition to a local herb garden
could be a source of bay leaves.   *Laurus nobilis* is the
Mediterranean import, the laurel, sweet bay, or French bay
tree grown in New Orleans gardens since 1731.   However,
it is the leaves of the Louisiana native swamp redbay or
swampbay *(Persea palustris)*,   which are traditionally used
to flavor gumbo.   To meet all your needs for creole cook-
ery, you could include sassafras *(Sassafras albidum)*, the
native tree whose crushed leaves are used to make gumbo
file', the thickening agent in file' gumbo (as opposed to
okra-based gumbo).   Its roots provide an oil used in
sassafras tea.

Some herbs should be a part of any wildlife garden.
The usually small, spikey flowers are rich in nectar for
bees.   Parsley is the larval plant of black swallowtail
butterfly.

The L.S.U. Agricultural Center research station at Burden Research Plantation in Baton Rouge initiated a project

during 1987 to test the adaptability of species of herbs and perennial plants to Louisiana soil and climatic conditions and how well they survive through winters and summers. The ten which they feel are almost certain to succeed in our area are: the mints, thyme, basil, oregano, Greek oregano, parsley, dill, fennel, catnip, and lemon balm. The New Orleans Garden Society, Inc. also suggests anise, borage, coriander, caraway, chives, sweet marjoram, rosemary, rue, sage, and summer savory.

ANNUAL HERBS

Anethum graveolens L. **DILL** Old World native. Parsley family annual, to 3 feet. Sun. Rich, moist, well-drained soil. Should be grown from seed sown directly in the ground as it does not transplant well, fall or early spring. May need staking. The threadlike foliage is used in cooking, as are the seeds. The flowerheads, flat yellow clusters, are used in pickling. Dill tends to go to seed as soon as the heat hits here, so early sowing is important.

Borago officinalis L. **BORAGE** Europe, North Africa. Borage family, annual to 2 feet. Sun, part sun. Dry, well-drained soil, low in fertility. Seeds should be sown in the ground in very early spring. I have found this plant does not last well in the humidity of our summers. Pretty star-shaped flowers, intensely blue, are cucumber-flavored, can be candied, floated in wine or fruit juice for decoration, eaten on tomatoes. Leaves become hairy with maturity, when young and tender are good in salad.

Calendula officinalis L. **CALENDULA, POT MARIGOLD** See ANNUALS.

Coriandrum sativum L. **CORIANDER, CHINESE PARSLEY** Southern Europe. Parsley family annual to 3 feet. Sun. Rich, well-drained soil. Ferny foliage, flowers are pink to lavender to white clusters. Fast-sprouting seeds should be sown directly in the ground in early spring. Has a taproot which does not transplant well. Citrusy

414 THE NEW ORLEANS GARDEN

seeds are used in baking. Fresh leaves are strong flavored, used in Chinese, Mexican, Mediterranean cooking.

Helianthus species. **SUNFLOWERS** See ANNUALS, WILDFLOWERS. I insert sunflowers here because of a surprising medicinal use suggested for New Orleans gardeners by the August, 1895 issue of *Southern Garden* magazine: *"Those of our readers who live in a malarial neighborhood, will find it greatly beneficial to their health by planting Sunflowers on or near their premises."* The author probably meant *H. annuus*, the large seeded sunflower.

Ocimum basilicum L. **BASIL** Old World tropics. Mint family, annual, to 2 feet. Sun, part sun. Moist, well-drained soil. Many varieties are available. Easy to grow from seed planted in spring. Leaves are fragrant when bruised. Flowers are small, white or pink spikey clusters. Leaves are used in cooking or fresh in salad and pesto.

Perilla futsecens (L.)Britt. **PERILLA, SHISHO.** See ANNUALS.

Petroselinum crispum (Mill.) Nyman ex A. W. Hill **PARSLEY** Old World. Biennial grown as an annual, Parsley family. Shade. Rich, moist soil. Several varieties. Must be started from seed or set out as purchased plants in the fall in New Orleans. May meet its demise with summer heat. Pinching bloom stalks can prolong growth, but butterflies like them. Parsley is the larval food of the black swallowtail butterfly. Leave some for the caterpillars!

Pimpinella anisum L. **COMMON ANISE** From Greece to Egypt. Annual, Parsley family. Sun. Light, well-drained soil, regular watering. To 2 feet. Delicate flowers clusters to 2 inches in summer. The licorice-flavored seeds and leaves are used in baking, cooking. Sow seed in early spring where plants are to grow. They do not transplant well. Slow to sprout.

Satureja hortensis L. **SUMMER SAVORY** Mediterranean region. Mint family, annual, to 18 inches. Sun. Well-drained, rich organic soil. Sow seed directly in the ground in early spring. Successive sowings can lengthen harvest time. Tiny pink flowers. Leaves should be cut for drying before flowers appear. Fresh leaves are used in salad, cooking, added to vinegar.

Sesamum indicum L. **SESAME, BENE, BENNE** Tropical Africa and Asia. Pedalium family, annual, to 3 feet. Easy to grow from seed sown in spring. Sun. Well-drain ed soil. The plants like our long hot summers, have naturalized in parts of the south. The leaves are shiny, 3-lobed, to 5 inches long. Flowers in summer are rose or white, 1 inch long, followed by the famous seeds. It is not really feasible to grow your own supply, as it takes 20 to 30 plants to produce a cup of seed, though a bene plant in the garden was considered good luck by slaves.[46] Seeds were brought to Louisiana either by slavers[47] or by slaves, as were okra seeds. Have traditionally been used on or in breads, cookies, candy such as pralines.

PERENNIAL HERBS

Allium sativum L. **GARLIC** Europe. See BULBS.

A. schoenoprasum L. **CHIVES** Europe, Asia.   See BULBS.

Aloysia triphylla (L'Her.) Britt.[*A. citriodora*] **LEMON VERBENA** Argentina, Chile. Shrub, Verbena family, to 10 feet. Sun. Any well-drained, good garden soil. Narrow leaves to 4 inches long on a plant which can become rangy. Grown for the wonderfully strong lemony scent of its leaves. They can be used in drinks, cooking, potpourris. The insignificant, white and mauve flowers form on a spike in the summer. The plant was reputedly introduced in this country by the Spanish explorers. It was reported in New Orleans gardens in 1849 by Alexander Gordon. Hardy to 10 degrees.

Artemisia absinthium L. **WORMWOOD, ABSINTHE** Europe. Perennial, Composite family, to 4 feet. Sun, light shade. Well-drained soil, can tolerate drought. Silvery gray, fuzzy, finely divided leaves on erect stems which form beautiful wide-spreading stands. Insignificant yellow flowers late summer-fall. Seeds are slow, grow from rooted cuttings. Bitter-tasting herb with past medicinal uses; currently used in absinthe, beers, vermouth, perfumes. Ornamental. See it in the Botanical Garden at City Park.

A. dracunculus L. **FRENCH TARRAGON** Europe, Asia, parts of Southern U.S. To 2 feet. Sun, part shade. Rich, well-drained soil. Excellent in containers. Narrow, shiny green, aromatic leaves grow on a plant which spreads by rhizomes. Tiny flowers may not appear at all. Divisions or cuttings necessary, as seeds are sterile, if formed. If you find seeds offered for sale, they are probably of *A. dracunculoides*, **RUSSIAN TARRAGON**, related, but not nearly as flavorful.

Carum carvi L. **CARAWAY** Europe. Biennial, Parsley family. Small white to pink flowers are formed the second year, followed by the seeds which are harvested, used as seasoning. Sow seeds in ground in fall.

Foeniculum vulgare Mill. **FENNEL** Old World. Perennial, Parsley family. 3 to 5 feet high, may need staking. Should be cut to the ground once the seeds are harvested. Several varieties of common or sweet fennel are grown for their seeds and leaves. Sow seeds in spring.

F. vulgare variety *azoricum* **FLORENCE FENNEL, FINOCCHIO, SWEET ANISE** is grown for its stems and bulbous base which can be eaten like celery. It needs cool weather to form, seeds should be sown in fall.

Lavandula species L. **LAVENDER** Mediterranian regions. Mint family shrubs to 3 feet. Sun. Very well-drained light, sandy soil. Dry climate and poor soil fertility create the most aromatic lavender. Our moist conditions usually do this plant in. It has been very short lived in the gardens where I have seen it grow at all. It is known as the most delightfully fragrant of all the herbs. The narrow green to grayish leaves are as attractive as the

spikes of purple or pink flowers.   Several species to try.
Maybe you will be successful.

Marrubium vulgare L. **COMMON HOREHOUND,
HOARHOUND** Mediterranean region, Europe and Asia.
Mint family perennial to 2 feet.   Sun.   Poor sandy, dry
soil.   Wooly, grayish-green, crinkly leaves on a clump-
forming plant which can be weedy.   Past uses were medicinal and in candy.   The scent was thought to discourage
flies.

Melissa officianalis L. **LEMON BALM** Europe, Eurasia.
Mint family, perennial.   Needs part shade.   Cutting back
will promote denser growth.   Grow from seeds or cuttings.   Easy.   Use for tea, salads, potpourri.

Mentha L. species **MINT** Old World.   Mint family, pe
rennials.   Will grow in part shade.   Moist, fertile soil.
Spread by underground stolons, containment is necessary
to control invasive tendencies.   I have found when I mixe
d two varieties one would eventually dominate, the other
disappear.   They bloom tiny spikes if given a chance.
Many species and varieties used in teas and cooking.
Very easy to grow, easier to use.   Vegetative reproduction
recommended over seeds.   Try spearmint, peppermint,
applemint, orange mint, pineapple mint, pennyroyal,....

Nepata cataria L. **CATNIP, CATMINT** Eurasia.   Mint
family, perennial, to three feet.   Rich, sandy soil.   Sun,
part sun.   Purple to white flower spikes borne in late
summer, fall.   Reseeds.   Can be invasive.   Should be
severely cut back in summer.   Used in tea by humans, but
known mostly for its effect on cats.

Origanum species **OREGANO** Mediterranean Europe.
Mint family, perennial.   Grows in part shade.   Experimentation with the many species and varieties is recommende
d to find the best flavor, as this varies with soil and
climate.   There are also unrelated plants with similar
flavors which are called oregano, **MEXICAN OREGANO,**
Lippia graveolens L., a Verbena family member; *Coleus am-*

boinicus Lour., **SPANISH THYME** or **CUBAN OREGANO**, Mint family.

O. majorana L. **SWEET MARJORAM** Africa, Asia. Mint family, tender perennial, sometimes grown as an annual. Leaves used for flavoring. Flavor is sweeter, more delicate than oregano.

Pelargonium species **SCENTED GERANIUMS** See PERENNIALS. These delightful plants are poorly suited to our heat and humidity, do not do well in the New Orleans garden.

Rosemarinus officinalis L. **ROSEMARY** Mediterranean regions Portugal, Spain. Mint family, evergreen shrub, 2 to 4 feet. Leaves are used fresh or dried for flavoring. Many different varieties with subtly varying foliage, flowers from white through shades of blue to lavender. I have been successful with rosemaries planted in cinder blocks.

Ruta graveolens L. **RUE** Southern Europe. Rue family semi-evergreen perennial to 3 feet. Sun, part shade. Slightly acid soil, poor to average in fertility. Tiny leaves on a bushy plant, small yellow flowers summer to fall. Medicinal and cooking uses; can be toxic in large amounts; flowers are ornamental. I have never tried this one. It can be used as a substitute for citrus in your butterfly garden as a larval plant food for the giant swallowtail butterfly.

Salvia officinalis L. **SAGE** Mediterranean area. Mint family, perennial, to 2 feet. Sun. Well-drained soil. Very sensitive to soggy soil or overwatering, a downfall in New Orleans. I usually loose my garden sage during wet weather. Gray, gold, variegated white or purple foliage with white to purple spikes of flowers, wonderfully flavored. Used dry or fresh in cooking.

Santolina chamaecyparissus L. **LAVENDER COTTON** Spain, North Africa. Composite family, evergreen shrub to 2 feet. Sun. Very well-drained, rich soil. Drought tolerant. Fragrant, silver-gray foliage, yellow button-shaped flowers in summer. Prune in spring, though never cut to the ground and never prune in fall, as growth appears on old wood. Suggested as a border plant for the formal herb garden.

Tanacetum vulgare L. **COMMON TANSY** Europe, Asia. Composite family perennial to 3 feet. Sun. Any well-drained soil. Spreads by underground stems to form clumps of ferny, camphor-scented foliage. Yellow flowers form in summer. Recommended for dried arrangements. No longer used in food or tea due to the discovery that it contains a toxic oil.

Thymus vulgaris L. **GARDEN THYME** Mediterranean. Mint family, perennial, upright to 12 inches or creeping in form. Many varieties produce the tiny leaves, which, dried or fresh, are essential in cooking.

Tulbaghia violacea Harv. **SOCIETY GARLIC** See BULBS. Is not a garlic, though its leaves can be used in soups and salads. It is recommended as an herb garden border plant.

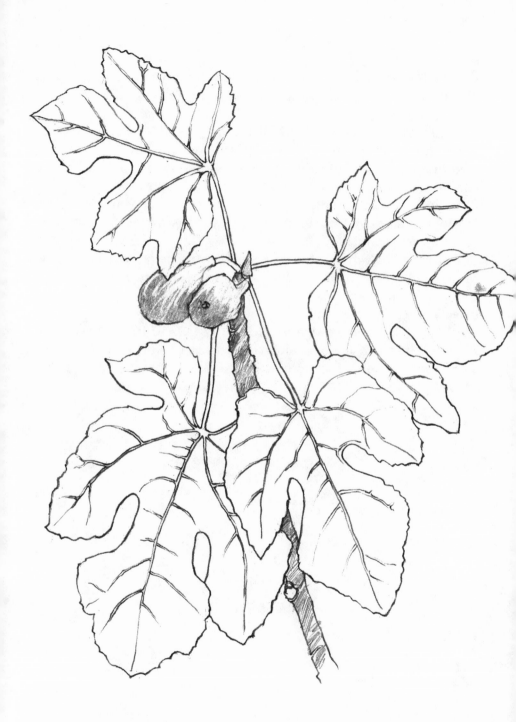

Harriet Hazlett

Historic Gardening

New Orleans chooses to garden,
"...and garden with exceptional grace."

George Washington Cable
The Amateur Garden, 1914

There are so many digressions to make in learning about gardening in New Orleans: taxonomy, garden design, and most exciting of all, tracing the origins of our ornamental plants which came from other places during other times, and the secret pasts of older gardens!

In the absence of records, you may be able to find clues which tell you about your old garden. The evidence is there, among the weeds. We bought our Upperline Street house from the Ostendorfs, a family whose men had personally built the camelback addition to the three room barge-board house when they purchased the property in 1891. As we peeled off layers, sheet-rock over beaded board over wallpapers, we found old newspapers underneath, corroborating the date. Miss Claire, in her 80's, returned to tell us what it had been like when she lived there as a child. She grew up and moved to Kenner. When we bought the house in 1972, it was enveloped in cat's claw vines, the "yellow bignonia" whose brilliance was praised in the 1938 *W. P. A. Guide to New Orleans*. Pink crinums bloomed on stalks which rose from nondescript clumps. Four o'clocks, recommended for Louisiana gardens by Lelievre in 1838, grew out of an upright piece of glazed ceramic sewer-pipe. We never figured out whether it was art deco or an accident, but our neighbor, Miss Maude, said it had been there forever. My kids collected seeds from lavender, white, and yellow to go with the more common magenta.

The small-flowered *Canna indica* or Indian shot (available 1885 from Maitre and Cook nurseries on St. Charles and Lower Line), predecessor to the lushly flowered modern hybrids, produced hard, round seeds like the four o'clocks, which my children dumped into tin cans to make rattles. Tradescantia, clerodendrum, and alstroemeria flowered under more Japanese plum trees (grown here since the early 18th century) than anyone would have chosen to plant. The house is on the site of orchards of orange, pecan, persimmon, and plum (Japanese or wild?) trees planted before 1840 surrounding the Avart Plantation home. I wonder if the huge pecan tree on Robert off Magazine and all the loquats in the neighborhood are descendents?

Japanese climbing fern gracefully ascended the page fence. "You'll never get rid of it," said Miss Maude. Do I want to? St. Joseph's lilies (an Amaryllis hybrid introduced in 1799, popular before the flamboyant *Hippeastrum* of today) lined a rear extension. We found mounds of oyster shells, over old automobile parts, over horseshoes. Under the house, the children dug up old bottles whose glass shimmered rainbow hues in the light. It was all in ruin, the debris of old gardens and lives and the embryo of new.

So much of the past is everywhere, yet the ties are tenuous. While exploring the newspaper files at the New Orleans Public Library for local secrets, I found a report of

an unusual bloom, called the "Sacred Lily of India" in a
yard at 732 Aline Street. On April 1, 1949, Mrs. George
Buse showed her prize to the press. Apparently an Arum
family member, it had thrived for twenty years near a bed
of wood fern under a pear tree. Its *"...huge ungainly bloom
spike with a head hooded like a cobra..."* produced a *"totally
obnoxious odor."* The reporter called it *"...remarkable for its
unuusal appearance rather than for its endearing qualities,"* an
appropriate topic for April Fool's day coverage. Also
growing in her garden were shrimp plant, daisies, butterfly lilies and iris, a plum tree, a French bay tree. I left
the library and headed for Aline Street. The shotgun
camelback single house was vacant, being renovated. No
one was looking, so I quickly slipped through the gate.
The grassy lawn was edged with elephant ears. Cat's
claw grew up the fence and over a pile of old brick and
rubble at the back. On July 1, 1989 there were no traces
of the plants of forty years before.

Descriptions of some New Orleans gardens have been
well-recorded. The house at 1239 First Street dates to
1859. It has usually been called by the name of the current owner, which makes it presently the Stan and Ann
Rice House. During 1942, when it was owned by Dr. and
Mrs. Frank Bostrom, the garden's tall orange trees near the
house and an *"impressive bay tree on the river side of the
garden"* were considered *"outstanding plants of considerable
age."*[48] There were palms, oleanders, an inga, banana, fig,
elderberry, pyracantha, tree dahlias, pomegranate, and
plumbago. Beds contained gerberas, day lilies, crinums,
amaryllis, callas, white and red four o'clocks, and butterfly
lilies. Monkey grass edged beds of maidenhair and sword
ferns and others of creole box, low azaleas, and cherry
laurels. Mr. and Mrs. John Minor Wisdom were residents
from 1947 to 1972. Mrs. Wisdom reports that the crape
myrtles still there today were planted by Mrs. Emory
Clapp who lived in the house 65 years, died in 1934. The
"last sour orange tree in the city" was in this yard until

the 1950's. The Wisdoms say Harry Daunoy, local garden
consultant, theorized that the lowered water table caused
its demise.[49]   In 1961 Samuel and Samuel described Mrs.
Wisdom's garden: a Japanese viburnum, which was es-
timated to be around 40 years old in 1973; a cocculus, a
Rangoon creeper so beautiful it was photographed for Kew
Gardens in England by Mr. Daunoy, and bottle-brush
(*Callistemon lanceolatus*, now *Callistemon citrinus*) planted by
Mrs. Wisdom, all of which disappeared in the 1963 freeze;
barberries, which don't last in New Orleans and didn't in
this garden, though they show up repeatedly in nursery
catalogues through the years; and loquat, cherry laurels
(*Prunus Laurocerasus*), yews (*Podicarpus*), myrtles, white
azaleas, boxwood, a seasoning bay tree (*Laurus nobilis*),
shrimp plant, Confederate jasmine. She planted a rose
garden of polyanthas following the soil modification direc-
tives of Mr. Daunoy.[50]   Formal hedges, flagstone paving,
boxwood edged parterres, raised beds, classical statuary
were part of the design in 1961. When Arlene Mmahat
moved in in 1973, she and Rene Fransen, landscape architect, planned a new garden of old plants common in
New Orleans around the plants still present from earlier
gardens: camellias, crape myrtles, sweet olives, and one of
the oldest and largest *Magnolia fuscatas* in the city. During
the 1970's the Mmahats added modern 'Pristine' hybrid tea
roses and a swimming pool.[51] From 1950 until 1989, a
charmed purple-flowering bougainvillea reached the second
floor gallery in front of the house. It lasted through
several harsh winters, but not the freeze of 1989. By June,
1990, it had not returned.

   If you want to return not only your old house in Orleans Parish, but also your garden to the period during
which it originated, the Notarial Archives are a good
starting place. Before photography came into use in 1880
watercolor paintings were used to record architectural
details of houses and sometimes gardens and garden
layouts around properties which were sold at judicially

ordered auctions and subdivisions of plantations. The information was presented on posters displayed, then folded in large planbooks and saved as legal documents. Now dusty and yellow with age, they are under the protection of archivist Sally Kittridge Reeves in the basement of the Civil Courts Building by City Hall. If you cannot find specific information on your house, other houses of the same period and neighborhood may be better recorded. The Archives contain architectural plans, drawings, and watercolor paintings from between the years of 1803 and 1880. Banana trees are the only definitely identifiable plant in the paintings. They do give a feel of the gardens. There is enough information to encourage speculation and allow informed guesses about tree and shrub identity. Plans only were included before 1803 and back into the 1700's.

Other resources for the historic gardener:
1. The several volume series of books on *New Orleans Architecture* (Pelican Press) which includes many reproductions of material from the Notarial Archives.
2. *The Historic New Orleans Collection* which has slides of watercolors from the Archives as well as other original sources.
3. Louisiana State University's School of Landscape Architecture, and its expert in Landscape History, Suzanne L. Turner.
4. Gallier House Museum, tours of the restored house and garden, archives.
5. Hermann-Grima House, tours of the restored house and garden.
6. Tulane University Library: The Louisiana Collection and The Garden Library of the New Orleans Town Gardeners, Southeastern Architectural Archive, where I found old garden catalogues and historic garden documents such as:

Affleck, Thomas. *Affleck's Southern Rural Almanac and
Plantation and Garden Calendar* for 1854 which lists plants
and culture for New Orleans gardens.
Lelievre, J. F. *Nouveau jardinier de la Louisiane,* 1838.
7.   The Southern Garden History Society, whose purpose
is: *"to promote interest in Southern garden and landscape
history, in historical horticulture, and in the preservation and
restoration of historic gardens and landscapes in the South."*
8.   The Preservation Resource Center, 604 Julia Street,
sponsors lectures and seminars, programs on historic
gardens, a Gardens and Archaeology Committee which
offers assistance in obtaining grants for research for restoration of the gardens of historic homes.

To find historic plants:
1.   First look carefully at what is already growing in your
yard and neighboring old yards as I did.   Some of the
past may still be present.
2.   Look for wild garden plants in abandoned yards, old
gardens, doorstep gardens, cemetaries, or in wild areas
around the city.   Many wildflowers are European imports
for ornamental use which long ago escaped cultivation.
3.   Allow plants to reseed on a year to year basis.   They
should revert to more old-fashioned forms.
4.   Order species or botanical forms of garden plants, not
modern hybrids, from catalogues.   In my plant descriptions I have indicated the species whose historic use is
documented and the date of introduction and source of
historic listing for as many ornamentals as I could find.
5.   Collect seed catalogues and read them carefully.   Many
offer historic plants, though they may not be identified as
such.
6.   The Thomas Jefferson Center for Historic Plants provides source lists for historic plants and reference books
on plants and gardens.   Write them for information as
well as the other sources of Historic Seeds and Plants
listed in RESOURCES.

7. Other sources of information on historic plants are: *Landscapes and Gardens for Historic Buildings*, by Rudy J. Favretti and Joy Putnam (Nashville, Tennessee: The American Association for State and Local History, 1978). Newly released is *For Every House a Garden*, by Rudy and Joy Favretti (University Press of New England, Hanover, New Hampshire, 1990).

PLANTS IN TRADITIONAL NEW ORLEANS GARDENS

From four sources:
1. Ewan, Joseph. *Introduction of Plants into New Orleans Gardens: a putative list arranged by dates.* November, 1969. "New Orleans" embraces plantation plantings of south Louisiana. Species for which substantial evidence exists are listed.
2. Steele, John. "Plants found in Vieux Carre Gardens 1803-1860". *The Courtyard and Patio Gardens of the Vieux Carre (1718-1860).*
3. Gallier House Museum. *Putative List of Plants Grown in the Gallier House Garden, 1850's.*
4. Gordon, Alexander. "Remarks on Gardening and Gardens in Louisiana." *The Magazine of Horticulture* XV (1849): 245-49. From John Steele.

THE GARDEN OF 1799

Aloysia triphylla LEMON VERBENA
Broussonetia papyriferus PAPER MULBERRY
Buxus sempervirens COMMON BOX
Callicarpa americana FRENCH MULBERRY,
    AMERICAN BEAUTY BERRY
Cercis siliquastrum JUDAS TREE
Citrus sinensis ORANGE TREES
Eriobotrya japonica JAPANESE PLUM, MESPILUS, LOQUAT
Ficus carica FIG
Gardenia jasminoides CAPE JASMINE, COMMON GARDENIA
Gleditsia tricanthos HONEY LOCUST

Hibiscus rosa-sinensis CHINESE HIBISCUS
Hibiscus syriacus ALTHEA
Hydrangea macrophylla HYDRANGEA, HORTENSIA
Jasmine multiflora and other species JASMINE
Liriodendron tulipifera TULIP TREE, YELLOW POPLAR
Magnolia grandiflora SOUTHERN MAGNOLIA
Michelia fuscata BANANA SHRUB
Myrica cerifera WAX MYRTLE
Nerium Oleander OLEANDER
Opuntia ficus-india PRICKLY PEAR
Osmanthus fragrans SWEET OLIVE
Phoenix daytylifera DATE PALM
Punica granatum POMEGRANATE
Rosa species ROSE
Taxodium distichum BALD CYPRESS
Vitex agnus-castus CHASTE TREE
Vitis species GRAPES
Yucca species YUCCA

THE GARDEN OF THE 1830's COULD HAVE ALSO INCLUDED

Agave sisalana SISAL
Albizia julibrissin MIMOSA, SILK TREE
Arbutus unedo STRAWBERRY TREE
Ardisia crenata ARDISIA
Caesalpinia pulcherrima PRIDE OF BARBADOS, FLOWERFENCE,
    POINCIANA
Camellia japonica CAMELLIA
Camellia sasanqua SASANQUA
Dryopteris species NATIVE FERNS
Hemerocallis species DAYLILY
Hippeastrum johnsonii ST. JOSEPH'S LILY
Iris hybrids LOUISIANA IRIS
Ligustrum lucidum TREE PRIVET
Lagerstroemia indica CRAPE MYRTLE
Nandina domestica NANDINA
Pittosporum tobira JAPANESE PITTOSPORUM
Rhododendron species AZALEA
Wisteria sinensis WISTERIA

BY THE 1850's, REPUTED NEW INTRODUCTIONS INCLUDED

Abelia grandiflora GLOSSY ABELIA
Adiantum capillus-veneris MAIDENHAIR FERN
Agapanthus species AGAPANTHUS
Agave americana CENTURY PLANT
Alpinia zerumbet MEXICAN SHELL GINGER

Ardesia crispa ARDESIA
Aspidistra elatior ASPIDISTRA
Aucuba japonica AUCUBA
Beloperone guttata SHRIMP PLANT
Brugmansia arborea ANGEL'S TRUMPET
Brunfelsia species YESTERDAY, TODAY, OR TOMORROW
Centaurea cineraria DUSTY MILLER
Cestrum nocturnum NIGHT-BLOOMING JASMINE
Cestrum diurnum DAY-BLOOMING CESTRUM
Clerodendrum bungei CASHMERE BOUQUET
Crinum amabile CRINUM
Crinum americanum NATIVE CRINUM
Cycas revoluta SAGO PALM
Cynodon dactylon HYBRID BERMUDA GRASS
Duranta repens DURANTA
Ervatamia coronaria FLEUR D'AMOUR
Erythrina crista-galli CORAL TREE, CRY-BABY TREE
Ficus pumila FIG VINE
Fortunella japonica KUMQUAT
Hedera helix IVY
Hedychium species BUTTERFLY, GINGER LILY
Hibiscus species HISBISCIS, MALLOW
Lantana camara LANTANA
Lilium longiflorum EASTER LILY
Liriope muscari CREEPING LILYTURF
Magnolia virginiana SWEET BAY
Manettia species FIRECRACKER VINES
Mentha species MINT
Musa sapientum BANANA
Narcissus pseudonarcissus NARCISSUS
Neomarica gracilis WALKING IRIS
Ophipogon japonica MONKEY GRASS
Phoenix canariensis PALM
Plumbago capensis PLUMBAGO
Pyrus communis PEAR
Rosmarinus officinalis ROSEMARY
Rosa banksia LADY BANKS ROSE
Russellia equisetiformis CORAL, FOUNTAIN PLANT
Strelitzia reginae BIRD-OF-PARADISE
Tetrapanax papyriferus RICE PAPER PLANT
Trachelospermum jasminoides CONFEDERATE JASMINE
Viola odorata OLD FASHIONED VIOLETS
Yucca gloriosa YUCCA
Zantedeschia aethiopica CALLA LILY
Zephyranthes species RAIN LILIES

"Creole Camellias": Cultivars listed in the *Catalogue of Fruit, Shade, and Ornamental Trees, Evergreens, Roses and Miscellaneous Plants Cultivated and for sale by John M. Nelson* and available at the Magnolia Nurseries at Metairie Ridge and at Mr. Nelson's Plant Depot at the corner of Camp Street and Lafayette Square in New Orleans in 1859 were *Albo Pleno (Alba Plena?), Alexina, Caleb Cope, Candidissima, elata, Fimbriata, Fordii, Feastii, Henre Favre, imbricata, incarnata, Lady Hume's Blush, Mrs. Cope, Queen Victoria, Reine des Fleurs, speciosa.*

Edging for Parterres: Boxwood: "creole box" was introduced to the U.S. in 1860, possibly available as early as 1874 in Mobile. Common box available in 1859 in New Orleans and undoubtedly earlier, used since 1760 in the U.S., for centuries in Europe. *Ligustrum vulgare* is another traditional European hedge plant available in this country from an early date. *Ligustrums*, species unidentified, are listed in catalogues from 1859.

ANNUALS, PERENNIALS, BULBS RECOMMENDED FOR LOUISIANA GARDENS IN 1838

by J. F. LELIEVRE, Ex-Jardinier-Agriculteur du Gouvernement Francais pour les Colonies

Nouveau Jardinier de la Louisiane, contenant Les Instructions Necessaires Aux Personnes qui s'occupent de Jardinage.

Nouvelle-Orleans: Chez J. F. Lelievre, Libraire, Encoignure Royale et Ste.-Anne, 1838.
(Translation from Gallier House Museum, Tulane University, New Orleans)

ANNUALS

Chinese Hollyhock: *Alcea rosea* HOLLYHOCK
Amaranth, Tasselflower, Tricolored Amaranth, Amaranthus tricolor: *Amaranthus caudatus* LOVE-LIES-BLEEDING, GIANT
    AMARANTH, JOSEPH'S COAT and other *Amaranthus* species
Snapdragon: *Antirrhinum majus* SNAPDRAGON
Campanula, Bellflower: *Campanula medium* CANTERBURY-BELLS
Cockscomb: *Celosia cristata* COCKSCOMB
Cornflower, "Bluebottle": *Centaurea cynanus* CORNFLOWER
Wallflower: *Cheiranthus cheiri* WALLFLOWER
Larkspur: *Consolida orientalis* LARKSPUR, ANNUAL DELPHINIUM
Pinks, Sweet William: *Dianthus species* PINKS, SWEET WILLIAM,
    SPANISH CARNATION, CARNATIONS
Sunflower, Mirasole: *Helianthus annuus, Helianthus divaricatus*
    SUNFLOWERS
Heliotrope: *Heliotropium arborescens* HELIOTROPE
Candytuft: *Iberis umbellata* GLOBE CANDYTUFT
Immortelle: *Helichrysum* species IMMORTELLE, EVERLASTING
    Xeranthemum annuum IMMORTELLE
Balsam: *Impatiens balsamina* GARDEN BALSAM, LADY SLIPPERS
Alyssum: *Lobularia maritima* SWEET ALYSSUM
Stocks, Gillyflower: *Matthiola incana* STOCK
Ice Plant: *Mesembryanthemum crystallinum* ICE PLANT
Primula: *Primula vulgaris* PRIMROSE
Poppy: *Poppy orientale* ORIENTAL POPPY *Poppy rhoeas* SHIRLEY
    POPPY, FIELD or FLANDERS POPPY
Mignonette: *Reseda odorata* COMMON MIGNONETTE
Scabious: *Scabiosa atropurpurea* PINCUSHION FLOWER
Marigold: *Tagetes patula* FRENCH MARIGOLD, *Tagetes erecta*
    AFRICAN or AZTEC MARIGOLD
Nasturtium: *Tropaeolum* NASTURTIUM

Verbena: *Verbena* species VERBENA
Tricolored violet: *Viola tricolor* JOHNNY-JUMP-UP
Pansy: *Viola Xwittrockiana* PANSY
Zinna: *Zinnia* ZINNIA

PERENNIALS

Columbine: *Aquilegia canadensis* COLUMBINE, AMERICAN,
    Aquilegia vulgaris COLUMBINE,EUROPEAN
Garden Chrysanthemum, Keelshaped Chrysanthemum:
    Chrysanthemum species CHRYSANTHEMUM
Cacalia: *Emilia javanica* TASSEL FLOWER, FLORA'S PAINTBRUSH
Lavender: *Lavandula* species LAVENDER
Sensitive plant: *Mimosa pudica* SENSITIVE PLANT, SHAME
    PLANT, MODEST ACACIA
Marvel of Peru: *Mirabilis jalapa* FOUR O'CLOCK, MARVEL-OF-
    PERU
Cactus: *Opuntia species* PRICKLY PEAR CACTUS
Geranium: *Pelargonium zonale* ZONALE GERANIUM
Fragrant Violet: *Viola odorata* SWEET VIOLET

BULBOUS PLANTS

Amomum: *Amomum compactum* AMOMUM
Anemone: *Anemone coronaria* ANEMONE, WINDFLOWER
Dahlia: *Dahlia* DAHLIA
Hyacinth: *Hyacinthus orientalis* DUTCH HYACINTH
Lily: *Lilium superbum* TURK'S CAP LILY

VINES

Convolvulus: *Calystegia sepium [Convolvulus sepium]* BINDWEED
    This is the species native to Louisiana.
Dolichos: *Dolichos lablab* HYACINTH BEAN
Jasmine: *Jasmine officinale* COMMON WHITE JASMINE
Honeysuckle: *Lonicera sempervirens* HONEYSUCKLE
Passion Flower: *Passiflora incarnata* MAYPOP, PASSION FLOWER

SHRUBS

Camellia: *Camellia japonica* CAMELLIA
Flowerfence, or Poinciana?:   *Caesalpinia pulcherrima* PRIDE OF
    BARBADOS, FLOWERFENCE, POINCIANA
Hortensia, Hydrangea: *Hydrangea macrophylla* HYDRANGEA
Oleander, Rose-bay: *Nerium oleander* OLEANDER
Pomegranate: *Punica granatum* POMEGRANATE
Roses: *Rosa* species ROSES

THE PRINCIPAL BORDER PLANTS
FOR THIS LOCALITY
(From a July 1, 1895 article in *Southern Garden* magazine)

Alternathera, different varieties: *Amaranthus* species JOSEPH'S
　COAT, COPPERLEAF, SUMMER POINSETTIA
Alyssum Benthamii: *Lobularia maritima* SWEET ALYSSUM
Adiantum capillus-veneris: *Adiantum capillus-veneris* SOUTHERN
　MAIDENHAIR FERN
Ageratum mexicanum: *Ageratum houstonianum* AGERATUM, FLOSS
　FLOWER
Achyranthus vershaffeltii aureus: *Amaranthus* species
Begonia discolor: *Begonia grandis* HARDY BEGONIA
Bellis perennis: *Bellis perennis* ENGLISH DAISY
Boussingaultia baselloides: *Andredera baselloides,* probably *Andredera
　cordifolia* MADEIRA VINE, MIGNONETTE VINE
Cineraria maritima: *Centaurea cineraria* DUSTY MILLER
Browallia elata major: *Browallia americana* cultivar 'Major'
　BROWALLIA
Coleus: *Coleus* species COLEUS
Dianthus heddewigii: *Dianthus chinensis* DIANTHUS
Dianthus plumarius: *Dianthus plumarius* COTTAGE PLUMARIUS,
　GRASS PLUMARIUS
Geranium Zonale: *Pelargonium zonale* ZONALE GERANIUM
Iresine Lindenii: *Iresine lindenii* BLOODLEAF
Iberis amara: *Iberis amara* CANDYTUFT
Lobelia erinus: *Lobelia erinus* EDGING LOBELIA
Lantana hybrid nana: *Lantana camara* cultivars LANTANA
Myosotis palustris: *Myosotis scorpioides* FORGET-ME-NOT
Petunia: *Petunia* dwarf and tall growing PETUNIA
Phlox suffriticosa: *Phlox carolina* THICK-LEAF PHLOX
Portulaca hybrids: *Portulaca grandiflora* MOSS ROSE
Pyrethrum parthenoides aurea: *Chrysanthemum partheniifolium*
Reineckia carnea: *Reineckia carnea,* similar to and confused with
　Liriope
Sanchezia nobilis: probably *Sanchezia speciosa* SANCHEZIA
Tagetes dwarf varieties: *Tagetes* dwarf varieties MARIGOLD
Torenia Fournierii: *Torenia fournieri* TORENIA, BLUEWINGS
Verbena hybrids: *Verbena* hybrids VERBENA
Viola odorata: *Viola odorata* SWEET VIOLET

Some suggested bedding combinations using the above plants:

1. blue torenia bordered with *Alternanthera ficoidea* cultivar *Versicolor*, COPPER ALTERNANTHERA, copper or red leaves,

2. *Browallia americana* cultivar 'Major', blue-purple, bordered with red ALTERNANTHERA,

3. blue ageratum bordered with *Tagetes tenuifolia*, SIGNET MARIGOLD,

4. For a shady bed: HARDY BEGONIA or REX BEGONIA bordered with MAIDENHAIR FERN,

5. Dark leaved *Canna indica* bordered with *Sanchezia nobilis* (red flowers),

6. Varieties of dracaenas bordered with *Sanchezia nobilis*,

7. *Canna,* variety *Madame Crozy*, bordered with *Iresine*, BLOODLEAF.

A HISTORY

What I really wanted was a list which told me when all the exotic plants in New Orleans were introduced. I had a picture in my mind of how it would look: a ditto of about 23 pages with the scientific name of each plant and a year within parentheses following. The search for this list lead me from one place to the next and from one fact to the next until I had the following story. Now I know that New Orleans gardening history isn't in one place. It's fragmented into the bits and pieces of personal letters, archives, and paragraphs and articles in published accounts here and there.

There's been research. John Steele, *The Courtyard and Patio Gardens of the Vieux Carre (1718-1860)*, and Stephen Hand, *The Courtyard and Patio Gardens of the Vieux Carre (1861-1982)*, wrote their landscape architecture theses on French Quarter gardens. Landscape historian Suzanne Turner is analyzing data from the notarial archives for a book on New Orleans garden history. I can't wait! Certain names recur as authorities on old gardens: botanist, Joseph Ewan, architects, Sam Wilson, Jr. and Christopher Friedrichs. Joe Ewan calls them all hortohistorians.

There are many gaps in the story and lots we'll never know for sure. It is easier to figure out what was probably grown in the past than to know exactly how shrubs, trees, flowers were placed within a landscape.

U. P. Hedrick, in *A History of Horticulture In America* says: *"One suspects that until cotton brought wealth in the nineteenth century, horticulture received scant attention in New Orleans."*[52] This may be true if "horticulture" or gardening is defined by a huge variety of imported species or confined to solely ornamental or "pleasure" gardening. I am expanding the definition to include all the doorstep gardens, which can be as little as one beloved rose bush grown from a cutting, one "lily" or native iris transplanted from the swamp or cutting flowers tucked at the edge of the vegetable or herb garden. It's hard NOT to garden in New Orleans. If you do nothing, nature will eventually provide her own garden. Today, in one way or another, everybody gardens.

In New Orleans, modern gardening themes were probably themes in the past, too: the battle against the native climate and terrain to control indigenous flora which constantly threatens encroachment, the search for plant materials which will adapt to conditions here or the modification of conditions to allow non-native plants to bloom, the integration of indigenous with exotic plants, the acceptance of indigenous encroaching flora. Through time, as economics and economies change, as sources of labor (slave, professional gardener, teenaged kids) are available or not, as leisure time and income expand or contract, gardens change in selection of plant material as well as size and elaborateness of style.

THE COLONIAL ERA (1718-1803)

We know what was here first: the river, the swamp and the marsh. Cottonwood, sycamore, red gum, black willow, hackberry, swamp-privet, honey locust, and green ash grew on the lands fronting the river. Floods added rich silts to the soil where goldenrod, asters, ironweed, sennas, bitterweed, and dogfennel grew. In the cypress swamp were tupelo gum, swamp red maple, American elm, palmetto, pumpkin ash, Virginia willow, buttonbush. Flowers bloomed: swamp-lily, pickerel-weed, irises, white water-lilies, fragrant ladies' tresses orchids. Fresh or brackish marshes depending on their salinity supported grasses, rushes, mangrove, elder, aquatic plants, some flowering. On higher grounds and at marsh and swamp margins were live oaks, redgum, bitter pecan, persimmon, cherrybark oak, water oak, Nuttall oak.

Man was present in these lush natural gardens as the Indian. As Hedrick said: *"Few Whites now know anywhere near so many wild plants as every North American Indian had to know in order to live.*"[53]   He used the bark, roots, leaves, and wood for food, medicines, clothing, shelter.

In 1718 the French came.   They brought the culture of their homeland with them, including the plants and gardening styles: the formal patterns of parterres inspired by the gardens at Versailles.   During the French and Spanish colonial periods, to 1803, exotic plants used in Louisiana gardens came directly from France or Spain or via the French West Indies.   The oleander, sweet olive, gardenia, and michelia or banana shrub we think of as belonging to New Orleans were some of these early imports, along with other favorites such as vitex, chinese hibiscus, althea, and hydrangea.   The prickly pear cactus and peppers, both among the first New World plants introduced by the Spaniards to Europe, probably arrived in New Orleans during Spanish colonial times.[54]   By the end of this period, Louisiana trees and shrubs--southern magnolia, oak, wax myrtle, cypress, and "French" mulberry were probably all grown in local gardens.[55]   There is a story that three rows of native sycamore trees were planted on the St. Peter and St. Ann Street sides of Place d'Armes in the early 18th century to shade French or Spanish soldiers resting between drills.[56]   The Louisiana iris, crinum, and spiderlily growing in swamps around the city are too pretty not to have been collected by some early doorstep gardener, though John Steele hypothesizes that imports were the norm.

The Africans who were brought to Louisiana as slaves were chosen because of their agricultural talents. They were the labor force which made the grand-scale agriculture of plantations feasible.   They did the planting and garden maintainence, probably including the ornamental.   Louise Hanchey in *How We Cooked* records the origin of "gumbo" in the words of four West African coast dialects for okra.   She repeats a tale which she says has become a part of the folklore of southwest Louisiana: *"It has been said that the slaves brought the seeds of the okra plant with them in their hair.*"[57]   A New Orleans tour guide who begged to remain anonymous says the captives hid seeds in their ears.   (Jane Stewart said she heard the same stories, but with different orifices!)   They're great stories, but I really can't imagine stuffing okra seeds anywhere while being dragged away into slavery!   "*...the West Africans were noted for their ingenious and resourceful ways of using the ingredients available in any particular region....*" for cooking.   This resourcefulness could have been applied to horticultural practices in many New Orleans area gardens, but from what I've found, it seems contributions of blacks to early garden history are greatest in the area of herbs and herbal medicine.   Open activity was suppressed by restrictive laws.   Slaves or slavers are credited with the introduction of sesame seed or bene, as well as okra, to the New World.[58] They probably brought many other plants, too.   The Pharmacy Museum is a source of further information.

The evidence that blacks gardened is in the doorstep gardens of some present-day descendents of Africans. They nurture the plants of Lelievre: Cherokee and other old roses, four o'clocks, perennial verbenas, bird of paradise which is poinciana, not strelitzia, balsam called lady slippers, and Japanese plum called mespilus.

Father Pierre Francois-Xavier de Charlevoix, a priest who recorded his experiences during a visit to New Orleans shortly after it was founded in 1718 saw:

> *...about a hundred huts set down among trees and under-brush....Later, the yards, surrounded by sharp-pointed picket fences, were well planted with fruits, shrubs, and flowers,* (door-step gardens?) *with vegetables in a rear garden. The streets were planted with sour orange trees, which loaded the hot, moist air with heavy perfume. Slaves vended fruits and vegetables from near-by plantations....*[59]

If we choose the version presented in the *Official Catalogue of the World Industrial and Cotton Centennial Exposition in 1884*:

> *...we see the trading post described by the priest-chronicler, Charlevoix, in 1721, as a place of one hundred wretched hovels, in a malarious, wet, thicket of willows and dwarf palmettos, infested by serpents and alligators....*

The first European plants tried in Louisiana were fruit trees such as oranges, figs, peaches, and apples. Attempts to grow olives, dates, and European grapes were unsuccessful.

The first Botanical Garden in the New World[60] was built in 1731 at the uptown river corner of Chartres and Ursulines Streets on the grounds of the Ursuline Convent. The nuns experimented with fruits, medicinal herbs, and fragrant ornamentals: orange trees, French bay tree, yew, fig, Japanese plum, pomegranate, madonna lilies, rosemary, lavender, ivy, thyme, cabbage, mint, strawberries, stock, onions, garlic, parsley, artichokes, and roses.[61] The West Indian Company provided the seeds and plants.

For years after 1718, the French Quarter was New Orleans. John Steele describes the early development of New Orleans gardens in his thesis. They were no tourist attraction back then! In 1721, city engineers De Pauger and De la Tour planned lots large enough for a garden *"...which here is half of life,"*[62] at the rear. Walled gardens originated because the government required some sort of enclosure which city fathers hoped would give the city "an urban character."[63] Raised planting beds were laid out in the formal styles of France, though I'm sure local gardens fell short of the degrees of refinement reached by their French models. Fragrant herbs and ornamentals, especially spring blooming orange and lemon trees, were very popular, but not for romance. Something was needed to block the stink of the densely populated, poorly drained place where animal dung and other refuse was left lying in the

streets.   Scented, shady courtyards may have been cool
retreats from the city's heat and noise.   But with more
shade comes less bloom.   The most fragrant flowering
plants couldn't have completely masked odors of the chickens and pigs which often shared the yard with children
playing and women doing wash and household chores.

Romance came later.   Back then, the courtyard garden
was usually a service yard and combined ornamental and
kitchen garden.   It was paved with brick in a herringbone
pattern and after 1800 with ballast stones from ships and
Blue River flagstone.   I can picture the post-rain quagmire
in the unpaved yards!   Until 1905, each garden even had
its cistern.   After the devastating fires of 1788 and 1794,
the Quarter was rebuilt with more masonry.   The new
buildings blended Spanish traditions and some American
influences with the French.   John Steele says,

> While the basic size and location of the gardens date to the
> early French Period, the Mediterranean influences of patio
> type gardens which include inward orientation, paved areas,
> and container plantings are a direct result of the Spanish
> culture in the Vieux Carre.

THE ANTEBELLUM ERA (1803-1860)

Botanist Joseph Ewan defines periods of New Orleans
garden history by the horticulturists most responsible for
the discovery and/or introduction of the popular new
plants of that era.   I have used his outline as a structure
for this history.   He calls 1785-1820 the Michaux Period.

The Botanic Garden of Andre' Michaux in Charleston,
South Carolina was entry and distribution point for imported ornamentals and fruits throughout the south from
1787 until after Michaux's death in 1802.   The famous
French botanist collected American plants to take to Europe, too.   We are not sure if the first crape myrtle arrived
in New Orleans this early, but we owe him for its impor-

tation to Charleston before 1802. He also introduced the chinaberry, ginkgo, mimosa or silk tree, native spice bush, and many varieties of azaleas, possibly the first in the south.

The most noted ornamental plants in the accounts of travelers to New Orleans around 1803, the date of the Louisiana Purchase, were native live oaks, magnolias, and wax myrtles, imported oranges in groves and roses in *"prodigal abundance."*[64] There were sub-tropical vines[65] and *"gallery gardens"* full of flowers, too.[66] Plantations such as those of Pierre Foucher and Etienne de Bore', now Audubon Park, lined the Mississippi River. De Bore' developed the process for granulating sugar in 1795. With the sweets of his success, he built an estate with large, beautiful gardens described by historian Charles Gayarre' in 1812:

> *Flowers of every description perfumed the air. Extensive orchards produced every fruit of which the climate was susceptible. By judicious culture there had been obtained remarkable success in producing an abundance of juicy grapes, every bunch of which, however, when they began to ripen, was enveloped in a sack of wire to protect them from the birds.*[67]

(European grapes in this climate would be remarkable!) A boat ride upriver allowed views of shady corridors and gardens inspiring the streams of adjectives only 19th century writers can spew.

During the period between 1820 and the Civil War (1861), cotton and sugar planters around New Orleans and 130 miles upriver became enormously rich. More than half of America's millionaires during the 1850's lived along this stretch of the Mississippi. They built grand homes surrounded by splendid gardens, perfect settings for the interesting new plants being collected all over the world by European and American botanists. How did the plants get here?

We know from ads like the one in the February 14, 1825 *Louisiana Courier for the Country* that garden specimens were shipped from Europe for direct sale in New Orleans:

THE FRENCH FLORIST GARDENERS

Have the honor of informing the public of their arrival in this city from Paris, with a beautiful collection of exotic plants, fruit trees of all kinds, shrubs, 150 varieties of the rose, hyacinths, daffodils, jonquils, tuberoses, amarillis (very scarce), imperial crowns, a complete assortment of flower and kitchen vegetable seeds, a quantity of other plants and bulbous roots, too long to mention, and the catalogue of which, explaining the names and colours in both French and English, may be seen at their store,in Mr. Andry's house, Toulouse street.[68]

The roses could have been newly introduced oriental species or new varieties being developed by French hybridizers. The 'Banksia' roses, white (1807) and yellow (1825), are still popular in New Orleans, today.

During the 1830's, a plant introduction center was formed by the United States government at the tip of Florida. Henry Perrine, former consul to Mexico began a program there to test subtropical plants as economic crops. His work and life were cut short in 1840 by a Seminole Indian raid. Perrine brought many plants, including the avocado or alligator pear and sisal, to the United States through Florida. Joseph Ewan feels that some of Perrine's introductions were planted in New Orleans, and that *"Had...he survived...the history would have been so rich and whereas he is all but unknown, he would be rightly remembered."*[69]

One of the most significant events in horticultural history took place in 1834 with the invention of the "Wardian Case" by Nathaniel Ward of England. It was just a terrarium. But, it supplied a protected world for seeds and seedlings which had not previously survived the trip to Europe via the slow sea going vessels of the day. The Wardian Case took the risk out of the plant importation business. Wonderful new species poured into European botanical centers, and filtered to America through several different channels.

Robert Fortune was one of the most active botanical collectors during the 1840's-1850's. He returned to Kew Gardens in England from an 1845 oriental trip with 18 Wardian cases full of plants and seeds! He introduced several plants which found their ways into New Orleans gardens: the kumquat, new azaleas, new chrysanthemum varieties, and weigela, winter jasmine, plum species, and forsythia.[70] The beautiful yellow flowered forsythia needs cooler weather than ours to do well, but New Orleanians keep trying! It was offered by Magnolia Nurseries in 1859 as a new plant and can be found in nurseries today!

Planter Valcour Aime of St. James Parish began his gardens in 1842. Alexander Gordon of Baton Rouge, a botanical collector and writer described them as *"Unsurpassed, if unequalled by any in the Union."*[71] They were different from those of other fine estates because they followed the looser style of English landscaping rather the formal French. Aime's gardener, Monsieur Muller, was from Paris, a graduate of the Jardin des Plantes, a botanical center since the mid 18th century. Hortohistorians speculate that he may have fed Aime's insatiable desire for exotic plants through botanical connections direct to Robert Fortune in the Orient.[72] One of Aime's prizes was supposedly the first camphor trees in this country--from Korea.[73]

Some American nurserymen were active in the distribution of new plant discoveries as well as offering their own developments. Prosper J. A. Berckmans of Augusta, Georgia was famous in the south for fruits and exotic ornamentals including azaleas and camellias. Henry Lyons of Columbia, South Carolina exerimented with fruits and flowers.

Between 1828 and the Civil War, Landreth Nurseries of Charleston specialized in roses, camellias, azaleas, magnolias, and the native osage orange or bois d'arc, whose

seed Lewis and Clark brought east from Arkansas and
Kansas. For a while, the osage orange, a tree used in
hedgerows, was one of the cheapest and commonest nursery plants sold in the eastern United States.[74] I found it in
New Orleans catalogues dated 1859, 1885, and in an article
from *The New Orleans Times*, July 30, 1866 which described
Mr. Henry Lawrence's garden at the time of its destruction. Its first plantings dated to 1841, and included
"*...plants brought from islands washed by the Carribean Sea
stand*(ing) *side by side with the jujube, the apple, the crabapple,
the pineapple, the lemon, the rose tree, the creole orange, the
osage orange, the peach, the fig, the nectarine,*" as well as the
first banana trees introduced in this climate, magnolias,
orange trees, and Lebanon cedars. It was at Louisa Street
fronting on Desire, "*in the shadow of the Touro Almshouse.*"

Harriet Martineau wrote about the New Orleans area
in *Retrospect of Western Travel* in 1837. She was impressed
by the gardens of roses she saw on the way to the Battlefield of New Orleans. Neither she nor the newspaper
reporter above mention camellias or azaleas, so accepted
as a part of Louisiana and New Orleans garden tradition
as described by Hedrick:

> *...the elaborate gardens of the rice and indigo plantations, with
> their parterres, avenues of live oaks, formal beds, walks bor-
> dered with box, and masses of azalea; or plantings of camel-
> lias, crape myrtles, jasmines, and other flowers and shrubs--a
> blaze of color.*[75]

When did they first appear in New Orleans gardens?

The first traders who brought camellias to Europe
from China and Japan in the 1700's were more interested
in *C. sinensis*, the source of tea than in *C. japonica* and its
cousins. It did not take long for them to see the ornamental and economic potentialities of the camellia as garden plant. The East India Company brought a pale flesh-
colored *C. japonica* to England in 1794 for botanical en-

thusiast Lady Hume.   It was named for her, 'Lady Hume's Blush' (variety *incarnata*).[76]

The first camellia in France was a gift to the Empress Josephine just before 1800.   She grew camellias (and roses) in her gardens at Malmaison.   The two other species which have been grown in New Orleans arrived in Europe from the Orient in 1811, *C. sasanqua*, and 1820, *C. reticulata*. Camellias became enormously popular, reaching their peak of popularity in Europe around 1840.[77]

Hedrick says the first camellia to reach America came via Europe around 1798 to a John Stevens in New Jersey. Stevens acquired the white flowered 'Alba Plena' in 1800.[78] It is still available and popular today. I wonder if the 'Albo Pleno' offered in John Nelson's Magnolia Nurseries Catalogue, New Orleans, 1859 is 'Alba Plena'?   'Lady Hume's Blush' was listed then, too.

J. F. Lelievre recommended camellias in *Noveau Jardinier de la Louisiane* of 1838.   He did not mention azaleas. Because of close French ties, it would seem someone must have brought the plants to New Orleans well before this date, but if so, I didn't find documentation of the event.

Martha Turnbull of Rosedown Plantation in St. Francisville is said to have been among the first amateur horticulturists to bring camellias to Louisiana.[79] *Gardens of Louisiana* says:

> *Despite the long-standing legend that a Parisian landscape architect designed the gardens, it was the belief of the late Mrs. Milton Underwood, who was responsible for Rosedown's restoration, that Martha Turnbull herself planned the remarkable gardens. Meticulous garden diaries and invoices left by Mrs. Turnbull bear out Mrs. Underwood's theory....Her records reveal that she imported azaleas for Rosedown in 1836,....*[80]

That was the the year the newlywed Turnbulls returned from their Grand Tour of Europe.[81]

The *W. P. A. Guide to New Orleans* of 1938 describes Mrs. David Pipes' garden at 1238 Philip Street. It contained camellias grown from cuttings made about 1915 *"...of the first plants brought over from France....One variety, in which the owner takes especial pride, was transplanted from an ancestral home in West Feliciana Parish."*

"My grandfather (Pipes) was related to the Turnbulls," says Mrs. Edmund Wingfield, who lived in the Philip Street house for thirty years.[82] The "ancestral home" mentioned above was Catalpa Plantation, built in 1835, near St. Francisville. The main house burned down in the early part of this century. Mrs. Wingfield's family history substantiates that West Felicianas Parish and the beautiful gardens of her ancestor's homes are points of early introduction of camellias and azaleas into Louisiana.

During 1912, Mr. and Mrs. Edward Butler, (part of the Pipes extended family), lived at Catalpa Plantation and continued a horticultural tradition. Joseph Ewan says the Butlers were *"...hosts to many botanists* (such as C. S. Sargent of the Arnold Arboretum of Harvard University) *at their plantation where there was once a hothouse three stories high in which pineapples ripened and many exotics flourished."*[83]

Gumbo Ya-Ya, Folk Tales of Louisiana a Work's Progress Administration, Louisiana Writers' Project publication of 1945, describes The Shadows in New Iberia, home of Weeks Hall: *"In the east garden is a clump of camellia trees planted when the house was built* (1830-31). *Nowhere in the state do camellias flourish better than in New Iberia, to which these natives of China were brought from France."*

A January 20, 1842 advertisement in the *Courier de la Louisiane* verifies the arrival of camellias and azaleas in New Orleans by that date, if not earlier: *"shipment from Havre:*
300 Camellia Japonica 12-15 varieties, Roses, Azaleas, Daphnes, Indica."[84]

During the prosperous years between 1830 and the Civil War, the creoles of the French Quarter were more conservative than the plantation masters. John Steele feels they clung to old styles and colonial plants, developing only a few favorites among the many new species of ornamentals introduced.[85] Camellias were supposedly one of these, though the apellation "creole camellia" must have developed later. The term may apply to varieties popular among creoles, but from the above evidence, though the first of the ornamentals may have come from France, they were fancied equally by gardeners of all descents.

Sheared hedges edged the parterres or walks in courtyard gardens.[86] Though *Buxus microphylla* variety *japonica* is called creole box and thought of as the traditional shrub for parterre borders, it was not introduced to this country from Japan until 1860.[87] *Buxus sempervirens*, the common box of Europe, was the boxwood used in Louisiana from before 1800. It does not last in the southern climate.   Even so, two cultivars, the tree form, 'Aborescens' and 'Dwarf box' were listed in the Magnolia Nurseries catalogue of 1859.   So was *Ligustrum vulgare*, common privet, for centuries a European hedge plant. These are the likely candidates for antebellum New Orleans borders.

The Beauregard-Keyes House at 1113 Chartres Street (1830's), Gallier House at 1132 Royal Street (1860), Hermann-Grima House and Courtyard at 820 St. Louis Street (around 1860) are restorations, open to the public today, which offer examples of the typical gardens of well-to-do Vieux Carre families before the Civil War.

The creoles who left the Quarter built homes downriver and out the Esplanade Ridge.   The uptown area known as the Garden District was laid out in the 1830's and built beginning in the 1840's by Americans, whose settlement had started at the upriver edge of the French Quarter (presently the Central Business District) and spread further upriver with time. The wealth of American entrepreneurs who capitalized on opportunities available during the boom period before the War was displayed in

grand homes and plantings in the area between Jackson
and Louisiana Avenues, Magazine Street and St. Charles
Avenue. S. Frederick Starr in *Southern Comfort: The Garden
District of New Orleans, 1800-1900,* suggests that *"the term
garden in the name 'Garden District' was taken in the English
sense as meaning the entire yard,"* rather than ornamental
plantings and landscaping. The information he discovered
implies more informal than formal planting. He found
examples of gardens laid out on axial plans with herring-
boned brick walks like the ones in the French Quarter, but
more which were *"designed in the informal English style, with
meandering paths and picturesquely natural planting."* [88]

To the fashion-conscious newly wealthy in booming
northern American cities, gardens in the style of the English landscape gardening school were "the latest thing."[89]
The attempt to present a romanticized natural setting in
the garden was a reaction to formal French design. American counterparts in French-influenced New Orleans followed suit. Expansive lawns, made possible by the invention of the mower in 1831, and layout may have mimicked
the English style, but a purely New Orleans flavor probably dominated with the luxuriant growth of plants in this
climate plus the addition of semi-tropical species such as
banana trees and the Chinese fan palms available around
1850. Some of the labeled plans from the Notarial Archives show traditional fragrant orange and other fruit
trees. Kitchen gardens of vegetables and herbs, which
must have reinforced a semi-rural atmosphere, were a
frequent part of these estates. Yards were enclosed by
picket or horizontal board fences, then eventually by the
wrought and cast iron which is still seen today.[90]

The George G. Westfeldt house and garden at 2340
Prytania Street was built in 1838. The garden's naturalistic
plantings are described, in *The Great Days of the Garden
District and the Old City of Lafayette.*[91] Some plants there
today may persist from the date the raised cottage was
constructed: a member of the Live Oak Society[92] named

after the Livaudais family whose 18th century plantation was in the vicinity, southern magnolias, sweet olive trees, crape myrtles, azaleas, camellias, yaupon, the native holly whose female plant is covered with red berries in the fall, and other fruit and flowering trees. In 1942 an ailanthus, Tree of Heaven grew there, too.[93] On January 21, 1990, I also noted cherry laurel, ginger, aspidistra, and bamboo, a later introduction.

Many Garden District residents were different from other Louisiana wealthy in that they had hired servants, not slaves to perform gardening tasks. Three-fourths of the professional gardeners recorded in the 1860 Census for the Garden District were German or Irish immigrants.[94] The luckier and more industrious of these probably became the nurserymen of the post Civil War era whose German named businesses are listed in City Directories and clustered in the Carrollton area around Cherokee Street on both sides of St. Charles Avenue on Sandborne Insurance Maps of the 1880's. I will have more to say about them later.

For all the focus on gardening, there were critics of New Orleans area gardens. Their comments make the French/American dichotomy in the city obvious, as well as the effect of cultural background and taste on personal perspective; another reason it is difficult to know for sure what gardens were like in the past. A journalist who wrote under the pen-name Sylvanus said in 1851:

> As you approach New Orleans, descending the river, the view on either bank is quite attractive. You can scent the odor of the flowers....But the admiration you feel and express, is, I think, more the result of contrast with the dull and heavy wilderness through which you travel for several days before you reach what is called the coast. Though nature has done much to adorn the scene, art has done little or nothing. And your admiration should you chance to stop at any of the numerous plantations, would cease. You would be astonished at the few varieties of trees and shrubs, and flowers, you would meet with, and surprised at the meagreness of what

seemed so powerfully attractive in the approach....Landscape Gardening is half a century behind the age....Even with the wealthiest planters...a garden seems a superfluity, except...a kitchen garden....The French Creoles are fond of gardening, but it is in a small way, and indeed, their fondness for it is more connected with the idea of profit than of pleasure. There are many families...who make a handsome support from the products of their gardens....But their flowers are usually of the most ordinary kind...such as roses, acacias, violets, and camellias....[95]

The sentiment was echoed by another journalist in *The Horticulturist* in 1858 who also commented that there were no good public gardens and no horticultural society. Hedrick blamed stodgy creoles who preferred their traditional designs and plants.[96] I suppose they were not impressed with the efforts of Baroness Pontalba who converted Place d'Armes, fenced since the 1820's, into Jackson Square, a public garden in the 1850's.

Sylvanus felt most antebellum New Orleanians were more concerned with the pleasures of eating, drinking, and gathering dollars than in growing flowers. There are certainly those, today. He allowed that *"there are many quiet, snug little gardens and delicious retreats, scattered here and there, through the city and its suburbs,..."* but his anti-creole bias showed when he commented that New Orleans lacked architectural beauty except in public buildings and further when he said the city seemed to be developing more taste as it became Americanized: as trees and shrubs were planted, and as houses were built back from the street. With those attitudes, I wonder how many creole plantations or courtyard gardens he ever got invited to see? Could his opinions be the reason he couldn't write under his own name?

Charles and A. J. Downing of New York ran a nursery which offered broad selections of ornamentals, but was better known because of the popularity of A. J.'s *Treatise on the Theory and Practice of Landscape Gardening*, 1841. He was considered the most influential American horticulturist during the period--and after. Edited and expanded reprints of the book were issued as late as 1967. A writer in New Orleans' Reuter Seed Company's monthly newsletter of 1932 cited Downing via this book as the *"ranking authority."* Ornamental planting on private residential properties became standard practice in the northern United States after the publication. It was probably an influence on Sylvanus.

Louisiana had its own book, the first to address the unique issues of gardening here. It was *Noveau Jardinier de la Louisiane (The New Gardener of Louisiana)* written in 1838, in French, by J. F. Lelievre, former Agricultural-Gardener of the French Government for the Colonies. Its suggestion for the arrangement of plants in ornamental beds is timeless:

> ...it suffices to raise plants as has been told heretofore and to put them in place symmetrically on flowerbeds or in a garden plot varying the colors and arranging the plants according to their order in natural size and succession, putting the larger at distances sufficiently remote to place in the intervals those of less elevation and to be sparing in all parts of the planting of flowers that are to succeed others so as not to see one end of a flower bed unfurnished while the other is covered with flowers.[97]

The ordinary gardener could have expanded his horizons beyond the local scene. Beginning in 1851 Thomas Affleck of Natchez published an almanac which included facts on flower and vegetable cultivation in New Orleans and information about catalogues and mail order sources of seeds and plants not available locally.[98]

John M. Nelson's catalogue of stock available at his Magnolia Nurseries at Metairie Ridge and at his Plant Depot, Corner of Camp Street and Lafayette Square in 1859 included many varieties of roses, camellias, hardy deciduous shrubs, hardy evergreen trees and shrubs, evergreen and deciduous vines, fruit trees, bulbs, dahlias, chrysanthemums *"of Pompone and Daisy varieties,"* and limited numbers of *"Bedding Out Plants"*: petunias, salvias, heliotrope, scarlet geraniums, and cuphea platycentra (Mexican cigar).

"Carpet-bedding," derived from the *"...parterres, geometric beds and ribbon borders in hectic displays of carpet bedding"* of Victorian England and popular in the northeast before and after the civil war,[99] was a labor-intensive style which consisted of masses of low growing brightly colored foliage or flowering plants which were cropped into geometric patterns. Sometimes taller plants were used as center pieces. All of the limited number of bedding plants offered by Magnolia Nurseries were among those popular for use in geometric bedding in the northeast. For New Orleanians up on the latest American fads and with the money or energy to fight the climate to maintain order, the plants were there.

Vines and flowering shrubs were probably more important as a source of color than flowers in the garden in New Orleans, and maybe everywhere during this period. Carpet bedding plants aside, Hedrick said in 1950:

> The culture of hardy annuals and perennials in flower gardens is now so general that it is hard to believe they were little grown a hundred years ago, or not widely grown until the end of the nineteenth century.

Stephen Hand, whose thesis continues Steele's research on French Quarter gardens,[100] feels that English trends were reflected in gardening habits of New Orleanians. He noted changing styles in at least one Notarial Archives Planbook garden layout in the French Quarter showing rounded beds.[101] Rounded corners on long raised parterres are shown in an 1869 plan of a garden district yard.[102] Garden ornaments such as cast iron fountains with statues on pedestals rising out of basins are another Victorian inspiration. Many people think of fountains as part of Vieux Carre gardens, but they were not that common anywhere until there were municipal water systems with consistant supply and increased water pressure (1860 in New Orleans).

ERA OF THE COTTON EXPOSITION (1860-1900)

After the Civil War, the slave labor used to carry out the meticulous chores required to maintain an elaborate formal garden was no longer available. Styles must have rapidly become 'informal'. For a long period of time gardening was not a priority, as seen by the article in *The New Orleans Times*, July 30, 1866 which dramatically recounts the destruction of the gardens of Mr. Henry Lawrence by the Reconstructionist government to make way for the track of the Levee Railroad. They were *"...by a decree of government...mutilated in form and feature...."*

The plants commonly found in cultivation after the war were the old favorites: *"Michelia fuscata, gardenia, Grand Duke and arabian jasmine, plumbago, zonale geraniums, a few varieties of Hybrid, Hybrid Perpetual, Noisette, and Bourbon Roses and a few hardy shrubs."* Camellias, considered difficult to manage, were less extensively grown. A few spring annuals were planted.[103]

The iron fences surrounding Lafayette Square, Tivoli (Lee) Circle, and Coliseum after the Civil War were, according to the Parkway Commission historian who wrote the 1949 *Report*, more than Victorian ornamentation and not a sign of renewed interest in gardening. He said:

> The War Between The States brought poverty to once wealthy citizens, but the 'carpet bag' administration of the Reconstruction period learned how to manipulate bond issues and how to profit on contracts for so-called 'public improvements' (of which iron fences were a favorite form).

Joseph Ewan describes the Civil War and Reconstruction as *"a kind of paralysis"* followed by a new period of plant introduction (1883-1900) stimulated by the Cotton

Centennial and the efforts of local nurserymen and citizen-amateur horticulturists such as Dr. and Mrs. Tobias Richardson. *"Recovery was slow. Encouragement came from the North."*[104]

The Gardener's Mutual Protective Association was founded July 11, 1875, by nurseryman. There was a German Gardeners Club, possibly this early. There is an increase in *City Directory* listings of plant and seed sources from seven in 1870 to thirty in 1880.

Reinhardt Maitre, *"a scientific German gardener,"*[105] (an emigre from Baden Germany) had a seed store at *"No. 631 Magazine Street, Nurseries and Green-houses at 976 (two squares above Louisiana Avenue)."* In 1875, he published a 125 page catalogue which offered: *"Vegetable and Flower Seeds, Holland or Dutch Bulbs, Tuberous and Perennial Plants, Green-house Hot-house and Bedding Plants, Ornamental and Evergreen Trees, Flowering Shrubbery, Camellias and Roses, Vases and Garden Statuary, Trellises and Frames, Fancy Flower Pots and Urns for Parlor Decorations, Garden Implements, and other Garden Requisites."* There were 9 pages of roses.[106]

By 1885, the catalogue of Maitre & Cook, located on Magazine Street with nurseries on St. Charles at Lower Line, included eighteen pages of roses, eighty-seven varieties of *Camellia japonica*, thirty-two varieties of *Azalea indica* among other expansive listings. Even though these changes indicate an increase in gardening activity, Maitre & Cook conclude the catalogue with a comment on the need for further horticultural progress and their hope that:

> With the return of prosperity, the people of this state will display as much good taste for all sorts of improvements as their more lucky and prosperous brethren of other states in the union....[107]

The "World's Industrial and Cotton Centennial Exposition" of 1884-1885 presented an *"infinite variety of rare tropical and semi-tropical plants, flowers, shrubbery,"* as well as displays of flora from Mexico, Central America, the West Indies, and different states of the Union. Horticultural Hall, the huge greenhouse which held the exhibits, was topped by a 90 foot high tower roofed with glass.[108] It was a part of Audubon Park until damaged by a tornado in 1909 and finally destroyed by a hurricane in 1915.[109]

The *Premium List of the Department of Horticulture* for the Exposition described prizes for winners in the plant competition planned *"...for the purpose of making the most comprehensive possible exhibition of the valuable fruits and plants of all nations."* A list of the categories tells which plants were in style. Fruit trees were predominant. Our Japanese plum, *"Japan Medlar,"* was one. Ornamental trees and shrubs were of groups traditionally represented in New Orleans gardens, then and now. Other categories defined for entrance and competition were:

> Roses: *Bourbon, China, Hybrid, Noisette, Tea. Palms and cycads, ferns, orchids, carniverous plants, achimines, agave, anthurium, begonia, chrysanthemums, crotons, cactus, dracaena, gloxinia, maranta (prayer plants), pelargonium.* "Bedding Plants": *abutilon, achyranthes, alternanthera, canna, coleus, gernanium--zonale, heliotrope, lantana, salvia, verbena.*

The grounds were planted with pampas grass, which was almost unknown in New Orleans before its use at the Exposition but popular afterward and today.[110] The century plant, *Agave americana*, reputedly grown locally since the 1840's was used, too.

New Orleanians who visited the Cotton Centennial must have been turned on by all the new garden plants as well as ornamental natives they saw there. According to D. Clive Hardy, *"...in addition to the general public, the displays drew a large attendance of prominent horticulturists when the Mississippi Valley Horticultural Society held its annual meeting at New Orleans in January of 1885."*[111] Was this the stimulus for the formation of the New Orleans Horticultural Society? We know it was founded around this time,

as a clipping announcing its second annual exhibition to
be held April 3-5, 1888 is described in *The Garden Library
of the New Orleans Town Gardeners Southeastern Architectural
Archives Catalog.*

Today, if people think of the Cotton Exposition, it is
in the context of the story that the water hyacinth, that
lovely purple-flowering noxious pest, escaped into the
bayous after being taken home as a souvenir from one of
the pavillions.   One story cites the Japanese Pavillion.   I
couldn't find verification of this tale in Catalogues of
Centennial exhibits.   They detail every item down to the
six stuffed Quetzals in the Guatemalan exhibit, but fail to
mention water hyacinths anywhere.   Don Schmitz of Florida's Bureau of Aquatic Plant Management, now involved
in efforts to control this plant-gone-crazy, notes that the
*"...first, and earliest, references pointing to the Japanese as
accountable* (for introducing the water hyacinth at the Exposition)..." is a paper by J. N. Gowanloch in 1944 in the
Louisiana Conservationist.   Schmitz says:

> *Coincidentally, it should be noted that anti-Japanese public
> sentiment was high when these papers were published....
> Another version is they were brought into New Orleans by a
> sea-captain who returned from Venezuela with the lavender-
> flowered waterhyacinth as a gift for his wife sometime in the
> 1880's.   His wife was very successful in cultivating the
> species and eventually sold the waterhyacinth at the exposi-
> tion.*[112]

I found another explanation of the introduction of the
Tropical American *Eichhornia crassipes* in the following
story told in a 1942 guide to the Garden District.   The
house which used to be at 2426 Prytania was once called
"Palm Villa" because its garden contained a collection of
palms from all over the world, possibly among the first
planted in the Garden District, along with *"...tall ferns,
majestic trees and strange and curious flowers...,"*[113] and *"...a
greenhouse with costly orchids."*[114]

Once, this house was surrounded by an elaborately beautiful garden....Dr. Richardson introduced here plants foreign to this section and although the fact has been denied by local scientists, legend has it that our aesthetic bayou pest, the delicately lovely water hyacinth, is an importation of Dr. Richardson's; an old resident even claims it was known for a while as the Richardson lily.[115]

Dr. Tobias G. Richardson (1826-1892) was Dean of the Tulane School of Medicine from 1865 to 1885. (Ivy Day for senior medical students was initiated in 1909 when the building on the uptown campus was named for him.) He and his second wife Ida Richardson (nee' Slocum) travelled extensively, to Mexico, the Sandwich Islands, the Amazon, Peru, the Orient, Europe. Both were amateur botanists. There is documentation that Dr. Richardson introduced *Ipomoea paniculata*, a tuberous rooted morning glory with pinkish-purple or pink flowers, to New Orleans around 1879 through London from India. It was first grown by Joseph Muller, formerly gardener at the old fair grounds who became a "well-known florist." [116]

Headlines in the *Times-Democrat* and the *Daily Picayune* of August 30, 1890 announced the bloom of another "Richardson lily", one of the only two specimens of *Victoria regia (V. amazonica)* in the United States at that time:

THE QUEEN OF THE NYMPHACEAE--AN EXQUISITE BLOOM IN THE GARDENS OF DR. RICHARDSON

THE MONSTER SOUTH AMERICAN WATER LILY TO BLOOM TONIGHT IN DR. RICHARDSON'S GARDEN

The smaller species described surrounding the giant plant in its "artificial lake" included the water hyacinth. Which was the real "Richardson lily"?

Joseph Ewan offers further confirmation of the Richardsons' plant introduction activity in his article, "Letters from C. S. Sargent (Director of the Arnold Arboretum of

Harvard University) to Reginald Somers-Cocks, 1908-1926."
He says:

> ...It is notable that, on several occasions, Sargent mentions
> sending seeds or plants of foreign introductions, recently
> grown at the Arnold Arboretum, as possible additions to New
> Orleans gardens. This was in the spirit of Ida Richardson
> who is credited, and with good evidence, for the introduction
> of Cocculus laurifolius, Siphonanthus indicus (Clerodendrum
> indicum), and other exotics (such as Quisqualis indicus or
> the Rangoon creeper) into local gardens and patios....[117]

Until her death in 1910, Mrs. Richardson was active in
horticultural and philanthropic concerns.

By the 1880's many gardeners shared Dr. Richardson's fascination with the palm and palm-like plants available in New Orleans from the 1850's and much earlier.
Specimens have disappeared to time and weather, but
some very large ones remain from this period, today,
especially in the garden district. Dr. Richardson's palms,
listed in a Times Democrat article, October 3, 1891, included
tender specimens: the Hawaiian Pritchardia gaudichaudii,
Archontophoenix alexandrae of Queensland, and Stevensonia
grandiflora of Seychelle Island. In recent years native varieties, the sabal palm and palmetto, more likely to withstand our occasional severe freezes, are more often planted. Palms are still very much a part of the "look" of New
Orleans.

W. H. Coleman in his Historical Sketch Book and Guide
to the Environs of New Orleans, 1885, described a great
change in gardens as contrasted with the average garden
of fifteen years earlier, which was twenty years after the
devastating War.

> In former days...a few clipped bushes, a bit of lawn, with
> angular flower-beds dotting it, here and there a few white and
> red roses, constituted what was called a pretty garden in the
> city. The varieties of roses seldom exceeded half a dozen, and
> some of these most mediocre, to which were added a Grand

Duke jasmine, a mignonnette, trimmed pittosporum or ligustrum nepalensis.[118]

Coleman said the new gardens were *"overrun"* with varied rose cultivars, a selection of palms, coleus, hibiscus abutilus[119], and *"artistically kept"* lawns, neatly edged. New roses and more colorful plants were added to Jackson Square. Coliseum, Annunciation, Clay, and Washington squares were improved. Oak trees, umbrella china trees, flower beds, ponds, and grotto replaced Spanish Fort's earlier *"shabby orange grove."* West End, previously wild, sported *"long parterres on the revetment, rockeries, puzzle labyrinth, leafy arcades and lily ponds."* He reported private gardens worth viewing along many streets including Prytania, St. Charles, and Esplanade.[120]

The French Quarter garden changed during the latter 19th century. As their fortunes declined, older families moved out of their ancestral properties, converting them to apartments or boarding houses. They constructed shotgun houses on the garden lots which adjoined some old homes for rental to the wave of Italian immigrants of the 1880's. Where new enclosures or replacements for deteriorating brick walls were needed, horizontal board fences (the traditional six-board fence) were used. Not until the 1930-1950 restorations in the Quarter was masonry substituted for the last of those wooden barriers.[121]

As modern plumbing was installed, the 'ollas' or large earthenware jars which were used as water carriers and purifiers in French Quarter courtyards stayed as decorative planters. New plants were integrated into the creole gardens. The walls may have been ivy-clad. Cannas, caladiums, palms, elephant ears, and yuccas appeared in the old raised beds among traditional citrus trees, pittosporum, sweet olive, banana plants, fragrant myrtle, gardenia, amaryllis, jonquils, lilies and sweet violet edging.[122]

In 1894, a monthly magazine called *Southern Garden, Horticulture, Floriculture, Truck Farming and Gardening in*

General in the South was published as the "official organ of the New Orleans Horticultural Society and the Gardener's Mutual Protective Association". Subscription was: *"$1.00 a year in advance."* Its first issue voiced the same complaint of Maitre & Cook in 1885 -- that the progress of gardening in the south was slow compared to other parts of the country.

> *The culture of flowers has progressed slowly here, and may yet be considered partly in its infancy, although of late more interest is being taken, owing principally to the existence of a Horticultural Society and exhibitions.*

In the northeast, annual flower exhibitions or flower shows had been held since at least 1830, to show the public the new varieties of plants discovered and developed for introduction into home gardens.

The 1894-1895 volume of the magazine may have been the first and last. It is the only one I found. A list of its topics gives a picture of what was popular in gardening at the time.

Chrysanthemums were big! Caladiums were reviewed as bedding and pot plants. *"The Principal Border Plants for this Locality"* were listed and illustrated in a drawing showing a yard with borders around its edges and circular beds dotting the lawn. All were filled with an amazing clutter of plants, the *"carpet beds of showy designs"* felt by the editor to be an improvement over the few spring blooming annuals of earlier years.

Hoya carnosa, the wax plant, a tender plant for indoor use was described as *"an old vine much esteemed by our Creole families."* Vines suggested for outdoors were passion flower, the morning glories (*Ipomoea* species), Chinese wistaria, several clematis species, crossvine *(Bignonia capreolata)*, and Cherokee roses. Rosa Montana or coral vine *(Antigonun leptopus)*, so widely planted in the 1930's,

"Although not a novelty, is comparitively scarce in the city, rarely cultivated in the country."
The cosmos introduced in Europe in 1799 was reportedly attracting a lot of attention in New Orleans. Spring and summer bulbs were covered in an article which described cyclamens as difficult, but which recommended *"Amaryllis Johnsonii, Formosissima and Belladonna lilies, Pancratium, Clivia, Eucharis Amazonica, Agapanthus umbellatus, Montbretia, calla lilies"*. The black calla (an arum) was said to have been *"introduced of late years."*

Bedding cannas, admired by a reader at the Chicago World's fair, were new in New Orleans. "Indian Shot", the ordinary variety with the pellet-like seeds now found naturalized all over the city, was called a weed then, too. Asparagus fern *(Asparagus plumosus)* and ferns, crotons, pansies, crimson clover were featured.

There were several articles on bamboo. Dr. G. Devron wrote about the hardiness of cluster growing varieties whose new growth occurs in fall and winter making the plants susceptible to winter kill.

...I know of at least one cluster growing Bamboo that has resisted our winters for more than 18 or 20 years, in a neglected garden of this city where it forms clusters of 10-20 feet wide, with canes 1 and a half to 2 inches in diameter, and 25-30 feet high....This bamboo is seen in the rear and uncultivated portions of the Fasnacht garden (a commercial nursery on New Shell Road near Metairie Road) adjoining the former 'Half-way-house', near the Metairie Cemetary.

Articles on lilies and suggested rose varieties for cemetary planting were presented by Mrs. Georgia Torey Drennan. She listed *"...some of the loveliest and best suited to sacred purposes."* In 1912 she wrote *Everblooming Roses For the Outdoor Garden of the Amateur,* an out of print classic now little-known by New Orleanians.

Mr. Harry Papworth, English gardener to Mrs. Ida Richardson and an expert on chrysanthemums planned a book on their culture.

THE MODERN ERA (1900-1990)

During the late 19th century beautification became important. Citizens formed independent commissions to improve their own streets or avenues. In 1909, the Parkway and Park Commission was formed (originally the Parking Commission of New Orleans), to take over this task: "...to plant, maintain, protect and care for trees and shrubs and other plants, in all of the public highways of this City." Its first focus was shade trees, its first plantings, 170 elms set out on Orleans Avenue in 1914. (They had been destroyed by windstorms and replaced by camphors by 1949.) By 1930, responsibility extended to beautification and grass cutting of all parks, places and parkways and all the street trees and palms, except in Audubon Park, City Park, and the shores of Lake Pontchartrain,[123] which had their own Commissions.

Reginald Somers-Cocks was an English botanist who came to New Orleans via Canada. Ida Richardson established the Richardson Chair in Botany at Tulane University because of her interest in his work. He held that position from 1908 until he died in 1927. He was important for building the herbarium at Tulane (though Joseph Ewan made more contributions in this area after 1947), the discovery of 30 new native trees, several of which bear his name, and the founding of the New Orleans Garden Society.

From a letter dated December 3, 1913 from C. S. Sargent of the Arnold Arboretum it seems that the Arnold Arboretum shared plants for public planting with New Orleans through Cocks:

> I am glad to...hear that the plants arrived safely. Although I wrote both to the Superintendent of the Park and to the Chairman of the Park Commission I have never heard a word from either of them. They seem to have curious ways in your town....[124]

The Audubon Park Commission was established in 1886. Cocks served on its Board of Commissioners during the early 1900's.

George Washington Cable in *The Amateur Garden* in 1914 wrote on winter gardens of New Orleans in an essay in which he says New Orleans gardens *"with exceptional grace."* Of the many yards he saw, *"thousands of them, prettily planted, are extremely small."* He was impressed with the number of flowers present in January of what must have been a year with a mild winter or a late freeze, and with the contrast with small gardens in the rest of the country which were mainly lawn. He said, the:

> ...'formal garden', by reason of its initial and continuing costliness, is, and must remain, the garden of the wealthy few, and that gardening for the great democracy of our land, the kind that will make the country at large a gardened land, is 'informal', freehand, ungeometrical gardening....the supreme feature is the lawn.

He further expressed:

> ...that those gardens of New Orleans are as they are, not by mere advantage of climate but for several other reasons. Their bounds of ownership and privacy are enclosed in hedges, tight or loose, or in vine-clad fences or walls. The lawn is regarded as a ruling feature of the home's visage, but not as its whole countenance--one flat feature yet never made a lovely face. This lawn feature is beautified and magnified by keeping it open from shrub border to shrub border, saving it, above all things, from the gaudy barbarism of pattern bedding; and by giving it swing and sweep of graceful contours. And, lastly, all ground lines of the house are clothed with shrubberies whose deciduous growths are companioned with broad-leafed evergreens and varied conifers, in whatever proportions will secure the best midwinter effects without such abatement to those of summer as would diminish the total of the whole year's joy....In New Orleans virtually every home, be it ever so proud or poor, has a fence on each of its four sides...they clothe them with shrubberies and vines--a lawn whose dimensions are enlarged....around meandering shrubbery borders-- made affable and entertaining by Flora's versatilities.[125]

National interest in beautification of the urban landscape was mobilized by the Garden Club Movement in
1891. The first garden club was formed that year in Athe
ns, Georgia. Not until 1919 was the New Orleans Garden
Society, still in existence today, founded by Reginald
Somers-Cocks. His enthusiasm during the time he served
as president from 1919-1922 and from 1924-1925[126] was
contagious. He involved the group in some unusual
activities for garden clubs as described in C. S. Sargent's
letter of April 8, 1920:

> I read in a Boston paper that Louisiana is to be hunted from
> end to end for a mysterious species of Aronia and for an Ash-
> tree, and that the New Orleans Garden Club has been called
> on by Harvard to perform this service, so I suppose great
> results can be expected. In the meantime I wish you would
> dry for me flowers of as many of the different Azaleas cul-
> tivated in the old Louisiana gardens as you can reach....We
> are interested to know...which were the Azaleas cultivated in
> the southern states....I should think that this would be a
> subject in which the members of your Garden Club would be
> interested; still if they want to hunt swamps for a missing
> Ash-tree I would not discourage them.

In addition to Professor Cocks who was president,
some of the other first officers of the Society were nurserymen C. W. Eichling and E. A. Farley, Mrs. Hunt Henderson, Miss Grace King, Mrs. Isidore Newman. By 1923
the roster of members had expanded and included Paul A
bele, who had been secretary of the N. O. Horticultural
Society in 1894-5, Charles Mauthe, caladium hybridizer,
Chris Reuter, seedsman, Martin Behrman of Algiers, Mrs.
Emory Clapp, Joseph and John Fabacher of 5705 St.
Charles Avenue, Richard Koch, Mrs. D. W. Pipes, Mrs.
George Westfeldt. By 1927, additional prominent nursery-
man/florists and citizens had joined: Mr. and Mrs.
Bollwinkle, Mr. P. A. Chopin, Mr. George Eberle, Mrs.
Mary Frotscher, and Mrs. Henry Kraak, Mrs. Ole' Olsen,
landscape architect, Mr. George Thomas, Superintendent of

the Parkway Commission, Mrs. Monte M. Lemann. These were serious gardeners! Among the founding objectives established by the club were:

> To encourage and promote the beautification of our City Parks under the direction of the Parking Commission; to make New Orleans the Garden City of the country; to hold annually a Flower Show.

Mary Stewart presented the 1921 annual report to the group: *Notes on Gardening in New Orleans* based on information collected from members. It discussed Mrs. Stewart's preference for the English style or naturalesque garden as influenced by Gertrude Jekyll as compared to the "old fashion formal garden". (Jeckyll's innovation was borders of largely perennial plants with large drifts of flowers planted in planned color schemes.) The article included a list of flowering annuals, perennials, shrubs, and vines for this region arranged according to season of bloom to make it easier to plan continuous color in the garden.[127]

In the twentieth century, the introduction of new species and varieties of plants into our gardens lost some of its aspect of adventure, but not necessarily its glamour. Scientific agencies and commercial seed houses and nurserymen have played the most significant role. Modern transportation has made faraway places not so far.

In 1910, David G. Fairchild established the Brookville Plant Introduction Garden in Miami, the first official United States Department of Agriculture plant introduction station since the one attempted in the 1830's by Henry Perrine. Fairchild was one of this century's most famous and most active "plant hunters." His introductions through the U.S.D.A. included fruits, food plants such as water chestnut, zoysia grass and the plant-pest, kudzu vine.

One of the significant figures in the introduction of exotics in south Louisiana from 1900 until his death in 1949 was a wealthy private collector who was also a scientist and one of the earliest recognized conservationists in the U. S. for his work with the snowy egret. Edward A. "Ned" McIlhenny of Avery Island considered himself a plant lover and an experimenter in growing and hybridizing plants. He created "Jungle Gardens", a collection of plants from the world over which ultimately included 30,000 azaleas, over 400 varieties of camellias, 65 kinds of bamboo and many more exotics. In a 1927 talk to the New Orleans Garden Society he described his work with the United States Bureau of Plant Industry of the U.S.D.A. which provided him with plants and descriptions of their soil and climatic origins so that he could attempt duplication. His greenhouse capacity was 750,000 plants. The result of his years of activity was a list of recommended plants for use in Gulf-coastal landscapes. He worked with many genera of trees and shrubs already used, identifying species or varieties best for our gardens. Some of the ones he mentioned are noted in landscapes today: ligustrum (*Ligustrum* species), viburnum (*Viburnum* species), Chinese cinnamon (*Cinamomum cassia*), Chinese photinia (*Photinia serrulata*), escallonia, (*Escallonia asiatica, E. berteriana*), cocculus (*Cocculus laurifolia*), the bottlebrushes (*Callistemon lanceolatus* and *Melaleuca* species), nandina (*Nandina*), ardesia (*Ardisia crennulata*), arborvitae (*Thuja* species), tung oil tree (*Aleurites fordii*), *Cedrela sinensis, Manihot Carthagensis*, soapberry (*Sapindus saponaria [S. Indicus]*), jobo or yellow mombin (*Spondias mombin [S. axillaris]*), Chinese parasol tree or Japanese varnish tree (*Firmiana simplex, [Sterculia plantanifolia]*), Chinese weeping elm (*Ulmus parvifolia*), Chinese tallow-tree (*Sapium sabiforum*), acacia (*Acacia species*), parkinsonia (*Parkinsonia aculeata*), bamboos.

Nurseries and florists made new plant introductions available to the public. Elmer A. Farley, Sr. and Henry

Kraak were two of the leaders in the nursery business in New Orleans.

Henry Kraak was a German gardener who learned his craft in Kew Gardens in England, the Tuilleries of Paris, as well as Germany. He was among the gardeners commissioned by the French government to recreate the Tuilleries at the Louisiana Purchase Exposition in St. Louis in 1904. He did not want to return to Europe at the end of the fair, but spoke no English and couldn't stay without a job. He picked a streetcar at random and rode to the end of the line. He got off at the Annheuser-Busch Brewery where he found a job shoveling hops, and soon after, Joseph Fabacher, who shaped the rest of his life! Fabacher owned Jax breweries in New Orleans. He had a better use for Kraak's talents, and his shovel, as gardener at the Fabacher estate, 5705 St. Charles Avenue in New Orleans. The gardens there are said to have been memorable!

Kraak continued to be a man of action all his life. He knew the young German maid who came to work in the Fabacher household for only three weeks before he made her his wife. The same year, 1906, not too long after he arrived in New Orleans, he borrowed $500.00 from Mr. Fabacher, bought a home at Nashville and Pitt, and began his nursery and landscaping business at 1019 Central Avenue in Jefferson. Around 1913, Mrs. Kraak opened her florist shop at 1425 Eleanore Street where she specialized in coursages and bouquets.

The Kraak family figured prominently in the horticultural and floral life of New Orleans until the nursery closed in 1973. Henry's son, Bill, with E. A. McIlhenny planned plantings for Huey Long's new state capitol building in 1935. Kraak landscaped, but refused to guarantee plantings for Charity Hospital, built over an eight year period in the 1930's, because, as Dorothy Dubourg nee' Kraak says, "Those doctors wouldn't change out the soil in the beds." By then everyone knew the importance of soil replacement. Henry Kraak died at age 78 in 1955 the day the New Orleans Horticultural Society was to award him, its oldest member, his 50 year membership placque.

Other accomplishments of the Kraak family were promotion of some of the most lavish flower shows in the city's history, introduction of houseplants such as pink anthuriums, spathiphyllum, dracaena, dieffenbachia from Guatemala and Puerto Rico, and, as Joseph Ewan remembers *"...that Eleanore shop used to supply the chaps with corsages for the Newcomb debutantes!"*[128]

E. A. Farley, Sr., pioneer florist and nurseryman native to New Orleans, died in 1958 at age 69.   At that time, his company at 3333 Gentilly Boulevard was one of the south's largest.   *"From his small nursery in Gentilly, begun in a cow pasture without even a street leading into town, Mr. Farley became a giant of the florist industry in New Orleans."*   Obituary notices in the *New Orleans Item* and *Times-Picayune* cited his contributions to the beautification of the streets of the city when he served as treasurer and chairman of the board for the New Orleans Parkway and Park Commission.   He introduced the beautiful Chinese elm for street plantings.   Active in civic affairs, he also served as Commissioner of City Park Board and the New Orleans Horticultural Society.   From 1948 to 1958, to celebrate the Christmas season, he created glorious displays in his greenhouses, orchid shows and a fairyland of flowers!

Flower shows have always been a part of the agenda of the Horticultural Society.   They are not consistently documented in the newspaper index files at the New Orleans Public Library after 1895.   The early shows were held at Odd Fellows Hall and the Washington Artillery Hall.   Shows were apparently not held during the wars.   I don't think the peaks of pagentry of the three-day extravaganza of 1949 have been reached again.

E. A. Farley was general chairman of the 1949 event, called "Spring Flower and Fashion Show."   It was staged at the Municipal Auditorium whose floor was *"...carpeted with 10,000 square feet of grass grown on burlap matting."*[129]

There were many floral displays: "*Rare orchid and rose gardens, tulips from Holland, and exotic Chinese landscapes....*"[130]   High school girls named for different flowers were queen and maids for "Spring Fiesta day" celebrated with a grand march down Canal Street.   Henry Kraak, in charge of decorations for the show, converted downtown New Orleans into a "Floral Trail" of evergreens and azaleas.   Kraak called the show the "*...finest and most colorful ever presented here.*"   The *Times-Picayune* said it was the first show of its kind since 1939.

The romance between New Orleans and the azalea did not really begin until the 1920's.   In 1921, Mary Stewart wrote:

> *The splendid demonstration made by Mr. Fabacher along his terrace is interesting the whole city in azaleas, and we are vastly indebted to him.   In this case too, it was believed that only a few could have the joy of growing these wonderful plants.   While Mr. Fabacher and Mr.[Eugene H.] Roberts, and others, who have taken great pains to use acid earth, and to keep their plants well shaded, have done a great service...*[131]

The awareness that most soil in the city was alkaline and the lovely flowering shrubs needed acidic conditions led to experimentation by nurserymen such as George Thomas of the Parkway Commission.   Techniques for culture were developed which proved successful to the point that by 1940 it was "*...almost impossible to stand on any street in the city during February and March and be out of sight of a blooming azalea.*"[132]

New procedures also made it possible to grow a wider variety of roses.   Harry L. Daunoy was well known by New Orleans gardeners for his work in the area of soil analysis.   His ad in the *New Orleans Garden Society Yearbook, 1935-1936* read:

H. L. Daunoy, Garden Consultant, Soil Test $2.00 each
Plant and Garden Examination, by agreement
Minimum charge $5.00

In an article, Mr. Daunoy repeated comments repre-
senting themes among local gardeners: "Roses no longer
do well in New Orleans," and "Roses won't grow in New
Orleans." His belief was that a change in the soil had
taken place in the city within the previous 25 to 30 years.
Could the change have been in the varieties of roses used,
instead? He attributed the death of many old specimens
of orange trees and problems with live oaks to the lowered water table.[133] He developed a system for rose culture
which enabled New Orleanians to grow the finicky newer
Hybrid Teas. It incorporated fertilization, insect control,
and most importantly, acidification.

The W. P. A. Guide to New Orleans[134] describes three
kinds of gardens in New Orleans in 1938: the French
Quarter garden; the old-fashioned southern type with
camellias and fragrant magnolias, sweet olive, jasmine; the
newer landscaped type, *"almost continuously vivid with roses,
lilies, irises, cannas, azaleas, poinsettia, wistaria, and a variety of
showy annuals."* During the 1930's, azaleas and boxwood
in formal hedges were the most fashionable plants to use t
houghout the city. Vines such as rosa montana, cat's
claw, purple bignonia and trees such as mimosa and parkinsonia, were popular for their colorful displays.

Gardens from all sections of the city were chosen for
the New Orleans Garden Society tours conducted yearly
on the Sunday before Mardi Gras and in early April. *The
W. P. A. Guide* describes plantings from each area, a written tour of the 1938 garden! You can do the tour yourself
to compare then with today.

FRENCH QUARTER: The renovation of Le Petit
Theatre in 1919 and design of its courtyard in an architectural style related to Spanish Colonial times, signaled a
revival of interest in the deteriorating historic section and

efforts to preserve the old styles began. Architect Richard Koch's interpretation of the local tradition included elements from the Spanish Colonial period in New Orleans (1769-1802) and the gardens of 16th century Spain. Koch's designs were employed in many other restorations and his ideas copied by others over the next several decades, especially as new residents moved into the Quarter.

Beginning in the 1930's there was a renewed interest in ornamental courtyard gardening in the Vieux Carre. Fountains, based on Koch's Spanish influenced design with octagonal shaped, tile or stucco faced basins capped with flagstones, or wall fountains of the type he conceived in the patio of what is now Pat O'Brien's became increasingly common. More relaxed plantings were seen in Quarter courtyards; trellised vines, potted plants, ferns, and tender exotics. Stone and iron sculpture and iron garden furniture became popular garden ornaments, along with the traditional 'ollas'. Cast iron railings, grilles, lace verandas from demolished old homes in other parts of the city, recycled as flower pot holders became essential decorative items. The balconies of some French Quarter apartments overlooking the streets continued to hold the collections of potted ornamental plants, called "hanging gardens."[135]

Some of the plants seen in patio gardens of the 1930's: southern magnolias, palms, banana trees, crape myrtles, altheas, pomegranates, pittosporum, Japanese plum, sweet olive, *Magnolia fuscata*, oleanders, gardenias, camellias, creole box, azaleas, hydrangeas, ferns, irises, lilies, English ivy, climbing roses such as 'Lady Banksia', trellised vines such as star jasmine, coral honeysuckle, cat's claw.

"Traditional" courtyards of the French Quarter, today, copy Koch's creations, the "restored" patios of the 1930's.

GARDEN DISTRICT: In 1938, the garden of Mrs. David W. Pipes at 1238 Philip Street was full of camellias, including ante-bellum favorites, collected after 1915, the year she and her husband moved to New Orleans from

Hollygrove Plantation in Clinton. She grew some of them from cuttings from camellias reputed to be among the first brought to Louisiana to Catalpa Plantation, a family home, some 75 to 100 years earlier. Creole boxwood hedges encircled the camellias, azaleas, sweet olive, crape myrtle, pear, Japanese plum, and coral trees. Beds held irises, daylilies. Climbers such as bougainvillea, purple blossomed solanum, lavender bignonia, 'Yellow and White Lady Banksia' roses and wisteria mounted walls, lath houses and iron fences. There was a greenhouse where Mrs. Pipes propagated her plants. Mrs. Edmund Wingfield, granddaughter of Mrs. Pipes (who lived in the house for the 30 years preceeding 1969 with her husband, the late Judge Wayne Borah) said her grandmother hybridized chrysanthemums, also. An active gardener, herself, during our phone interview of July 26, 1990, she discussed preparations for a coming Garden Club of America meeting to be held in New Orleans. Her present garden has no camellias. "I'm camellia-d out!" she said.

The Philip Street garden seemed unmodified in a 1970's description. Ownership had changed. A very tall palm was there, though gone by January of 1990, when I peeked through the wrought iron enclosure of what was still the home of Mrs. James Gundlach and her family. Blooming daffodils, emerging Dutch iris and hyacinth were clustered under the still present camellias, boxwood, and other shrubbery. When I toured the garden on July 26, 1990, I saw that the entire yard was a brick-edged bed raised above the level of the walkways and patio along the house. A grassy expanse of lawn met borders of trees and shrubs which included the above mentioned plants and southern magnolia, hydrangeas, and pittosporum. Borders and island beds in the lawn and pots contained caladiums, Canna indica (the weedy kind), clumps of solid and variegated liriope, aspidistra, crinum, lady and holly ferns, camellia sasanquas, ivy, confederate jasmine, impatiens, petunias, begonias, and chrysanthemums.

AUDUBON PARK DISTRICT: The Park itself was described as being filled with typical southern garden flowers, an abundance of dwarf orange and banana trees, arborvitae, magnolias, mimosas, crape myrtles, magnificent live oaks, and an iris study field. On July 29, 1989 in front of the Heyman Conservatory I noted magnificent live oaks, a crape myrtle whose bloom was finished leaving capsules swollen with seed, beds bordered with liriope in heavy bloom, its purple spikes like a regiment of soldiers in parade around rounded edges. Mounds of yellow blossomed lantana, *Duranta repens* drooping clusters of golden berry-laden branches and sky blue flowers and blue plumbago grew behind bronze leaved cannas with salmony-orange flowers, purslane with flowers of yellow or yellow-centered rose, blue stokesia, lavender-purple echinacea with center-cones of gold-tipped bristles.

Audubon Place was in 1938 and remains a private street. I did not gain entry for a closer look than from the entrance gates on St. Charles Avenue and Freret Streets. The neutral ground, as now, contained palms, water oaks, evergreens, well-maintained lawns. At No. 27, Mr. and Mrs. Henry Flonacher's garden contained a Spanish patio and rockery around which grew weeping willow, fan palms, banana clumps, East Indian bamboo, a camphor tree, cedars, Chinese paper plants, oleanders, crotons, kumquat, Japanese plum, yellow jasmine, flowering almond.

At 1912 State Street, was Mrs. C. S. Williams' typical New Orleans winter garden of January-blooming azaleas and camellias with border plantings of narcissus and violets. In 1990, we drove into the driveway for a look. The azaleas and camellias were there. The heavy freeze on Christmas Eve had played havoc with bloom messages of plants. Though elsewhere in the city, camellias were blooming, not in this garden. Border plantings seemed to have disappeared since 1938. The house was for sale.

3008 Calhoun was the private experimental garden of George Thomas, who died in 1934. He grew plants unusual in Louisiana, including summer-blooming bulbs, Texas and Mexican shrubs. On June 5, 1990, I was given a tour and history by George B. Atkins who has been in the house since childhood. He came from England with his parents to "live in" with the widowed Thomas, an English horticulturist, who "did" gardens in the uptown area, including St. Charles Avenue. He is listed in the New Orleans City Directory at 3008 Calhoun Street in 1910. Back then his property covered more of the block and included a greenhouse, potting shed, wagons and space for horses. His "experiments" included work with soils for azaleas and roses and the introduction of plants he collected from wild areas around the city. He discovered the first yellow *Iris fulva*. Louisiana iris once grew along the iron fence which fronts the property. Neutral ground plantings of azaleas and the Sunken Gardens on Canal Boulevard were his ideas. A small placque imbedded in a granite boulder in the second block of Canal Boulevard near City Park Avenue is a tribute:

In appreciation
of the fine work of
George Thomas
Supt. New Orleans
Parkways Commission
1925 to 1934
Towards the Greater
Beauty of this City
N.O. Parkways commission
N.O. Horticultural Society
N.O. Garden Society
N.O. Botanical Society

Now, the smaller yard, non-gardened contains an original azalea and camellias, old roses, crinum and a free-standing clump of gloriosa lilies. Doorstep flowers (*Ruellia brittoniana*) and Peruvian lilies (*Alstroemeria pulchella*), considered uptown weeds, and firespike (*Odontonema strictum*) "come up in the lawn". Could this yard be where they began their spread to New Orleans gardens?

CITY PARK AND GENTILLY: City Park, in 1938 as now, offered a rose garden. A flame vine bloomed in March. A large *Monstera deliciosa* bore fruit some years. Beautiful old live oaks, the Dueling Oaks, and mixed native and imported irises are still there.

The New Orleans Parkway Commission Nurseries on Gentilly Road had materials for planting in parks and neutral grounds: cedars, Japanese plums, willows, palms, pines, sycamores, chinaberries, azaleas. In a pool were lotuses which bloomed masses of white in May. There was an azalea trail. A current tour of these nurseries comes later.

METAIRIE: Mrs. Edgar B. Stern at 11 Metairie Lane had an *"old-fashioned creole garden"* with azaleas and camellias, orchid greenhouses.

In 1990, though Mrs. Stern is deceased, her Longue Vue Gardens live on at 7 Bamboo Road as a public garden run by a Board of administrators. Landscape architect Ellen Biddle Shipman designed the gardens in 1942. The Spanish garden was redone in 1966 by William Platte after he and Mrs. Stern visited the Generalife Gardens in Spain. Inspired by the 13th century moorish gardens of the Alhambra, it is surrounded by several smaller gardens, each with its own theme. There is a wild garden of Louisiana natives. This is a wonderful place to learn about plants and garden design, to see plants in bloom: roses, pansies, sweet peas, geraniums, snapdragons, zinnias, marigolds, camellias, azaleas, firespike, jasmine, wild azaleas, dogwoods.... Longue Vue is in and of New Orleans, yet it transcends New Orleans. It is a national gardening treasure.

The modernization of drainage systems over a period of years resulted in covering over the open drainage canals which lay in the center of many avenues, to form even more of the "neutral grounds" so perfect for the floral decoration famous in New Orleans in the coming years. In 1935 the Parkway Commission used federal money available through the Works Progress Administration to create jobs for the unemployed in beautification of the city with flowers and shrubbery. Until then, the neutral ground plantings were of a few broadleaf and conifer groups with limited plantings of annual and perennial flower gardens. Over the next decade and more, efforts by public and private interests toward creation of The Floral Trail resulted in sixty miles of horticultural splendor along the avenues of the city. Continuous bloom was planned beginning with camellias, dogwood, and red bud in February, followed by azaleas, then mimosa, magnolia, parkinsonia, oleander, crape myrtle. A release by The Parkway Commission in 1941 pictured that year's Queen and her court planting an azalea and presented a history of the Trail and an announcement:

> In 1941 the Floral Trail backers, with the New Orleans Horticultural Society and Home Gardening magazine as teammates, began vivid demonstrations to encourage residents in the city's modest cottages and mansions too extend and widen the Floral Trail with private plantings. On the theory that everyone with any land around their premises would like to add floral beauty to their home settings, several model gardens were installed around homes to prove that with a little effort and at nominal cost every New Orleans home could add its own flowers to the community's growing wealth of natural beauty. With this essential minimum of guidance scores of new gardens have been developed from spots that were barren and ugly before the activity began.

The Fortieth Anniversary Report of the Parkway Commission in 1949 describes a wonderland of gardening: five large greenhouses of the finest type in the south, a separate propagation house, 67 acres of nursery. The staff was responsible for tree planting, care, and removal, spraying for diseases and insects, grass cutting, parkway planting of annuals, trees, shrubs grown from seed or cuttings on the Commission grounds. Changes were made seasonally of beds of such annuals as petunias, phlox, snapdragons, alyssum, zinnias, marigolds, calendulas, godetia. Tender, but colorful plants such as chenille and painted copperleaf (*Acalypha hispida, A. wilkesiana*), jatropha (probably coralplant, *J. multifida*), redbird slipperflower (*Pedilanthus tithymaloides*), croton, mother-in-law's tongue (*Sansevieria*), and ginseng (*Panax*) were set out around the city in the spring; stored on view to the public in greenhouses during the winter. Potted plants were provided as decoration for city functions.

The dominant shade tree was the live oak; others used and recommended for property owners who planted their own: camphor, ash, sweet gum, sycamore, hackberry, elm, native magnolia, sterculia (Chinese parasols?), orchid (*Bauhinia purpurea*), weeping willow, ligustrum, golden rain, crape myrtle, and less commonly, the maidenhair tree or gingko, called "an odd type." Palms included the washingtonia, phoenix, sabals, chamerops, cocos australia, and sago and were placed "*in great numbers along the parkways, especially along Elysian Fields Avenue....also on Canal Boulevard and Carrollton and St. Bernard Avenues.*"[136]

A publication of 1947 called *Trees, Vines, and Shrubs of New Orleans* listed other plants used by Parkways as well as by City and Audubon Parks: "angel's trumpet (*Datura arborea*), bamboo (*Dendrocalamus latiflorus*), banana, bougainvillea (*B. spectabilis*), *Camellia reticulata*, fountain grass (*Russellia equisetiformis*), gardenia, *Duranta repens*, *Vitex agnuscastus*, *Hibiscus mutabilis*, Japanese magnolia, oleander, *Parkinsonea aculeata*, pomegranate, rosa-de-montana, sweet olive, yaupon, Spanish bayonet (*Yucca aloifolia*)."[137]

New Orleanians have shown their interest in horticulture during the period from 1940 to the present through support for publications and by broad involvement in organizations.

Home Gardening magazine (endorsed by the New
Orleans Garden Society) and published at 10 cents a copy
or $1.00 a year was available from 1941 through 1952.
The editor was Camilla Bradley who since April, 1952 has
authored the monthly, now bimonthly, "New Orleans Garden" in the insert which Orleans Parish residents receive
with their utility bills. The Garden Club of America honored her with a Horticultural Award for 1976 for *"kindling
enthusiasm in the pursuit of practical and informed horticulture
as a lecturer, columnist, editor-in-chief of a southern gardening
magazine, and introducer of foreign flora."*

In 1947 *A Garden Book of Old New Orleans* by Grace
Matt Thompson, former owner of the Cottage Flower Shop
was published. It is a description of the author's patio
garden which contained an enormous variety of trees,
shrubs, perennial, annual, and bulbous plants. She recommends cultural practices based on her own experience.
Many of her sources were California nurseries. She was
an avowed experimenter with techniques as well as varieties. She also grew all the traditional local plants. The
book may not have been a bestseller, but it is a gem as a
source of new plant ideas, an example of the interest in
botany of some New Orleans gardeners[138] and the focus on
California as one of the sources of new plant introductions
during this period. She used accurate botanical names to
describe her plants.

French Quarter residents of 1950's formed the Patio
Planters, a garden club which focused on sharing new
plants. The Planters brought tropical and semi-tropical exotics resisted by antebellum creoles to their courtyards.
Pineapples and other bromeliads and orchids grew with
more traditional banana trees, oleander, althea, ginger
plants, rice paper plants. Fig and other vines were espal-
iered against masonry walls which replaced the last of the
horizontal board fences left from the 1880's.[139]

Gardening in New Orleans was written by Mary
Stewart and Helen Oser of the New Orleans Garden Socie-

ty, Inc. in 1952. It was based on the hands-on experiences of club members and was the first comprehensive book on gardening in New Orleans. It did not list the boxwood popular in the 1930's, though it continued to emphasize azaleas, camellias, and roses. Stephen Hand sees in the book an indication of *"lingering formality* [in local garden design] *though there was a loosening up in terms of planting design and plants used"*[140]. The only plant listed for use as a ground cover was ivy. Lawn grasses were stressed: *"...your garden is only as beautiful as the lawn which it frames...."*[141]

Mrs. Stewart also wrote extensively for the *Times-Picayune*, appeared on local radio and television, and went on to write *The Southern Gardener*.

The severe freeze of 1962 curtailed experimental urges in local gardeners for a while. Coldhardy and evergreen plants filled the gaps left by the weather: viburnums, ligustrums, camellias. But before long, even the monkey puzzle, sold during 1858 could be found again.

By the 1970's, an interest in native plants was expressed in renewed used of the wax myrtle, American holly, red maple. A focus on textures in selection of plants for landscaping was exemplified by Audubon Park plantings: the river birch (common in Louisiana, though not on the Mississippi floodplain) with its reddish brown, paper-like, exfoliating bark; the traditional exotic crape myrtle with smooth beige bark; and the coarse textured, smooth, shiny, greenish barked Chinese parasols. The Japanese pagoda tree *(Sophora japonica)*, a Legume family member with interesting bark and foliage, showy flower clusters was re-introduced. It had been available in 1885 from Maitre & Cook Nurseries in New Orleans. Palms again became popular, and urges to try the risky semi-tropicals returned.

By 1980, the private Vieux Carre garden contained less formal arrangements of palms and bananas, hibiscus, althea, lantana; while the "New Orleans Courtyard Style" supposedly of Spanish colonial origin but actually more related to romantic recreations of the 1930's had become legend: *"raised brick planters, a fountain on a wall or at the intersection of two paths, and strict symmetry and balance throughout the garden."*[142]

The 1984 World's Fair held on the Riverfront in Downtown New Orleans had no Horticulture Hall, but it did have plants. Many people first saw and were charmed by the beautiful pink flowering vine, Mandevilla, and the yellow allamanda used abundantly there. Crape myrtles were named the official flower of the Fair. They were everywhere, in lavender, red, pink, as the "Miniature Weeping Crepe Myrtle" developed by nurseryman David Chopin of Baton Rouge. He provided more than 8,000 of them for planting in hanging baskets, whiskey barrels, clay pots, and in the landscape as groundcovers and borders. The Louisiana Cooperative Extension Service conceived two native plant exhibits, one of aquatic plants such as bald cypress, Louisiana iris, water lilies, and cattails; the other of trees, such as oaks, maples, southern magnolias, shrubs and wildflowers.

Today gardeners who choose to mail-order can pick from an enormous variety of plants from all over the world. Most local nurseries do not usually stock more esoteric exotics, a change from twenty years. Nurserymen I interviewed felt this to be a function of the present economy. Plants not sold by the time winter comes and whose hardiness is questionable are at risk of loss during winter holdover outdoors. But there are some adventurers.... I have heard of a nursery in Abita Springs...

The Parkway and Park Commission of 1990 as described by landscape architects Skip Treme' and Keith Bleichner is a stark contrast to that of the *Report of 1949*.[143] The green space maintained by the Commission has increased more than 50 per cent since 1958, while the maintainence staff has been reduced by 100 employees. Just keeping the grass cut involves most of their time and

energy much of the year. Shrubs are less frequently planted than in the past because they require greater maintainence, they block the view of drivers in the many more
automobiles which exist now, and because of the perception that shrubs offer cover for lurking criminals. Future
plantings of azaleas will be made only where underground
watering systems exist, such as the one installed on St.
Charles Avenue. Camellias are not being used as they
require too much care in mass plantings to look good.
The Lotus Pool of 1938 is gone. Only a few plants are
left which are remnants of the Floral Trail, so glorious
forty years ago. Even the Azalea Trail on the Commission
grounds has almost disappeared.

Major trees used in plantings today must be hardy
and disease resistant because the budget for replacement is
so tight. Predominant trees planted today are: crape
myrtle, live oak (though there are those who decry this
traditional beauty because of the damage to sidewalks by
the root systems of ancient specimens), southern magnolia,
Chinese elm, the deciduous oaks, red maples, the hybrid
Savannah holly, yaupon (another native holly), Japanese
magnolias, the native red bud, bald cypress, green ash.
Limited plantings of Frazer's Chinese photinia are found
on St. Charles Avenue. It has been decided that summer
lilac (*Vitex agnus-castus*), which was planted up until three
years ago, is scraggly in winter and lacking in refined
character when out of bloom, though there are plantings
in Joe Brown Park. Formosan golden raintrees have not
been heavily planted since the 1983 freeze. The arching
yellow primrose jasmine (*Jasminum Mesnyi*), cassias such as
the candelebra plant, the Himalayan cocculus and other
tropicals and subtropicals of questionable hardiness but
unquestioned beauty are not used. The old fashioned
arborvita, Chinaberries and cedars are not be used today.

It is hoped that with progress in genetic engineering
some of our tender subtropicals will be hardier in the
future. Also, with the avoidance of the "monoculture"

which can result in mass destruction after a freeze or species specific disease, the tender but beautiful aliens can be slipped in with hardier plants. Their loss may be just as painful sentimentally, but less financially.

The severity of present economic problems has exposed the city's deep comittment to gardening. Through the innovative leadership of Florence Schornstein, Superintendent of the Parkway and Park Commission and original financial contributions of the Council of Jewish Women and the Junior League, the Parkway Partners Program was developed. Since its formation in 1983, it has involved volunteer private citizens, neighborhood groups, schools, businesses, and, of course, garden clubs in taking on many of the maintainence and beautification chores of the Commission. From the basics such as watering, grass cutting, weeding, picking up litter, to the planting and maintainence of flower beds on neutral grounds, the planting of trees and shrubs, and landscaping, activities of volunteers, (10,000 in 1990), have made possible projects which would have been impossible for the financially strapped city whose boundaries now extend all the way to Venetian Isles. Fund raising projects to finance the landscape renovation of Jackson Square was undertaken by the New Orleans Town Gardeners. The flowers at Lee Circle are changed four times a year thanks to the New Orleans Town Gardeners and the Garden Study Club. The Sunken Gardens on Canal Boulevard, a Works Progress Administration project of the 1930's abandoned in the '60's was restored in the 1980's. For the Papal visit in September, 1987, sabal palms and sagos were planted on Carrollton Avenue.[144]

The new American garden in New Orleans is evolving from a past rich in contributions of diverse cultural groups, each of which imposed its own favorite plants and design variations on the French Formal, English Romantic and later English styles prevalent historically and on the levees, the swamp and the marsh which we know were here first. There are more challenges to be met by private gardeners than ever before. The gauntlet to experiment and change in such a way that our natural and historical past is preserved must be carried by a city without the wealth of Valcour Aime, on a public or private level. Today's gardener from doorstep on up can make an important contribution to the city through participation in Parkway Partners and involvement in civic beautification projects through garden clubs. Return to the past through focus on native plants and natural gardens may be an economic move both in terms of finances and ecology; an aesthetic move in terms of the beautiful birds and butterflies which will appear in the expanded habitat you provide. There are elements of French Quarter Courtyard styles in Ottesen's description: "...--*the new American garden features functional paved areas with flowing interlocking masses of native plants or flowering garden subjects on a scale effective in the landscape.*"[145]   Maybe the new American garden of the next century will look south to the New Orleans garden!

Allison Crutcher McAshan

Appendices

NOTES

SELECTED BIBLIOGRAPHY

BOTANICAL NAMES

RESOURCES

INDEX

NOTES

1. *The New American Garden* by Carole Ottesen (Macmillan, N.Y., 1987), p. 1. Reprinted with permission.
2. Reprinted by permission of Louisiana State University Press from *Wildflowers of Louisiana and Adjoining States* by Clair A. Brown, 1972, xxix.
3. Parkway Commission of New Orleans. *Fortieth Anniversary Report, 1909-1949*, p. 19.
4. See Louisiana State University Cooperative Extension's pamphlet called *Composting*.
5. Roberts, Eugene H. "Conscripts and Volunteers." *Notes on Gardening in New Orleans. 1923.* Louisiana Collection, Howard Tilton Memorial Library, Tulane University.
6. From *The Time-Life Encyclopedia of Gardening: Perennials.* By James Underwood Crockett and the Editors of *Time-Life Books Inc.*
7. Bradley, Camilla. "New Orleans Garden." *Homemaking.* New Orleans Public Service, Inc., November, 1975.
8. Sylvanus. "Random Notes on Southern Horticulture." *The Horticulturist and Journal of Rural Art and Rural Taste.* 6 (January to December, 1851), p. 220. Gallier House Museum, Tulane University, New Orleans, Louisiana.
9. From *A Garden Book of Old New Orleans,* by Grace Matt Thompson, 1947, used by permission of Milburn Calhoun, Pelican Publishing Company, Inc.
10. Reprinted by permission of Louisiana State University Press from *Wildflowers of Louisiana and Adjoining States* by Clair A. Brown, 1972, xxix.
11. Hedrick, U. S. *A History of Horticulture in America to 1860.* Portland, Oregon: Timber Press, 1988, p. 351.
12. Hedrick, p. 353.
13. Samuel, Martha Ann Brett and Ray Samuel. *The Great Days of the Garden District and the Old City of Lafayette, 1978,* p. 20. Used with permission of Parent's League of the Louise S. McGehee School, New Orleans.
14. Parkway Commission of New Orleans. *Fortieth Anniversary Report, 1900-1949.*
15. Editorial. *Southern Garden, Horticulture, Floriculture, Truck Farming and Gardening in General in the South.* New Orleans, Louisiana: Vol. 1 (November 1, 1894). Louisiana Collection, Howard Tilton Memorial Library, Tulane University.
16. Gallier House Museum. Tulane University, New Orleans, Louisiana.
17. Interview with Dorothy Dubourg nee' Kraak, June, 1990.

18. *The Optimist's Daughter*, by Eudora Welty. Copyright 1978, Random House, Inc.
19. Reddell, R. "In Defense of Modern Roses." *American Horticulturist.* August, 1989, pp. 33-42.
20. Drennan, Georgia Torrey. "Spring Planting of Roses for the Cemetary." *Southern Garden.* Volume 1, March 1, 1895. Louisiana Collection, Howard Tilton Memorial Library, Tulane University. Mrs. Drennan was the author of *Everblooming Roses for the Outdoor Garden of the Amateur, 1912.*
21. LeBreton, Dagmar Renshaw, Ethel Wight Usher, Marcelle Peret. *A Tour of the Garden District.* American Association of University Women, 1942, p. 7. Louisiana Collection, Howard Tilton Memorial Library, Tulane University.
22. Hedrick, U. P. *A History of Horticulture in America to 1860.* Portland, Oregon: Timber Press, 1988, p. 264.
23. McIlhenny, E. A. "Variety in Landscape Work for the Southern Coast Country." *Yearbook of the New Orleans Garden Society, 1927.* p. 23. Louisiana Collection, Howard Tilton Memorial Library, Tulane University.
24. Pizzitti, Ippolito and Henry Cocker. *Flowers, A Guide for Your Garden.* New York: Harry N. Abrams, Inc., p. 165.
25. See *A Garden Book of Old New Orleans, by Grace Matt Thompson*, p. 58, picture, p. 45. Reprinted with permission of Milburn Calhoun of Pelican Publishing Company.
26. Reprinted from *Perennials for American Gardens* by Ruth Rogers Clausen and Nicholas H. Eckstrom, copyright © 1989, with permission of Random House.
27. Oser, Elizabeth H. and Mary B. Stewart. *Gardening in New Orleans.* New Orleans: Robert L. Crager & Company, 1952.
28. Meerow, Alan. "Tropical Bulbs for Southern Gardens." *Horticulture, The Magazine of American Gardening.* Vol. LXI, No. 11 (November, 1983): 24-29. "From Amaryllis to Zephyranthes." Vol. LXII, No. 10 (October, 1984): 40-46.
29. Caillet, Marie & Joseph Mertzweiller. *The Louisiana Iris: The History and Culture of Five Native American Species and Their Hybrids.* A Publication of the Society for Louisiana Irises. 1988. p. 3.
30. Caillet, & Mertzweiller, p. 3.
31. Caillet, & Mertzweiller, p. 6.

488   THE NEW ORLEANS GARDEN

32. *The Works Progress Administration Guide to New Orleans: The
     Federal Writers' Project Guide to 1930's New
     Orleans.* Reprinted by Pantheon Books, 1983,
     p. 225.
33. Louisiana State University Press. *Wildflowers of Louisiana and
     Adjoining States,* by Clair A. Brown, 1972, p. 23.
34. *Hortus Third, A Concise Dictionary of Plants Cultivated in the
     United States and Canada* edited by Ethel Zoe
     Bailey (Macmillan, N. Y., 1976).
35. Gambel, Betsie. "Roots of a City." *The Times-Picayune.*
     August 2, 1989.
36. Odenwald, Neil G. and James R. Turner. *Identification,
     Selection, and Use of Southern Plants for Landscape
     Design.* Baton Rouge: Claitor's Publishing
     Division, 1987, p. 139.
37. Austin, Daniel F. "Exotic Plants and Their Effects in
     Southeastern Florida." *Environmental Conservation.*
     Vol. 5, No. 1, Spring 1978, p. 29.
38. Brown, Clair A. and Donovan S. Correll. *Ferns and Fern Allies
     of Louisiana.* Baton Rouge, Louisiana: Louisiana
     State University Press, 1942, p. 98.
39. "Pestiferous Spread of Many Ornamental and Fruit Species in
     South Florida." *Proceedings Florida State
     Horticultural Society* 89: 1976, 352.
40. Brown, Clair A. and Donovan S. Correll. *Ferns and Fern Allies
     of Louisiana.* Baton Rouge, Louisiana: Louisiana
     State University Press, 1942, p. 147.
41. Material from *The Wildlife Gardener* by John V. Dennis © 1985
     used with permission of Alfred A. Knopf Inc.,
     publisher.
42. Reprinted by permission of the publishers from *The Ants* by
     Bert Holldobler and Edward O. Wilson,
     Cambridge, Massachusetts: Harvard University
     Press, Copyright © 1990 Bert Holldobler and
     Edward O. Wilson.
     Royte, Elizabeth. "The Ant Man," *The New York Times
     Magazine,* July 22, 1990. Copyright © 1990 by
     The New York Times Company. Reprinted by
     permission.
43. Reprinted by permission of Louisiana State University Press
     from *The Amphibians and Reptiles of Louisiana* by
     Harold A. Dundee and Douglas A. Rossman.
     Copyright © 1989 by Louisiana State University
     Press.
44. Reprinted by permission of Louisiana State University Press
     from *The Mammals of Louisiana and its Adjacent
     Waters* by George H. Lowery, Jr. Copyright ©

1974 by George H. Lowery, Jr.

45. Hedrick, p. 352.

46. From Louise Hanchey's notes for pamphlets on cooking for The Lafayette Natural History Museum and Planetarium, Lafayette: *Charleston Receipts, Recipes collected by Junior League of Charleston, South Carolina.* Published by Walker, Evans & Cogswell Co., p. 246.

47. Lovelock, Yann. *The Vegetable Cook: An Unnatural History.* New York: St. Martins Press, Inc., 1972. From Louise Hanchey's notes.

48. LeBreton, Dagmar Renshaw, Ethel Wight Usher, Marcelle Peret. *A Tour of the Garden District.* American Association of University Women, 1942, p. 8. Louisiana Collection, Howard Tilton Memorial Library, Tulane University.

49. Telephone interview with Mrs. John Minor Wisdom, June, 1990.

50. Telephone interview with Mrs. Wisdom, June, 1990.

51. Telephone interviews: Arlene Mmahat, January 26, 1990 and Renee Francen, January 29, 1990.

52. Hedrick, U. P. *A History of Horticulture in America to 1860.* Portland, Oregon: Timber Press, 1988, p. 349.

53. Hedrick, p. 4.

54. Hawks, Ellison. *Pioneers of Plant Study.* New York: Macmillan, 1928, pp. 119-120.

55. Ewan, Joseph. *Introduction of Plants into New Orleans Gardens: a putative list arranged by dates.* November, 1969. He says: " 'New Orleans' embraces plantation plantings of south Louisiana. Species for which substantial evidence exists are listed."

56. Parkway Commission Report, 1949.

57. Hanchey, Louise. *How We Cooked, Some Old Louisiana Recipes.* Lafayette, Louisiana: National Endowment for the Humanities, the City of Lafayette, and the Lafayette Natural History Museum Association, 1976, pp. 6, 10.

58. Lovelock, Yann. *The Vegetable Cook: An Unnatural History.* New York: St. Martins Press, Inc., 1972. From Louise Hanchey's notes.

59. Hedrick, p. 349.

60. Steele, John. *The Courtyard and Patio Gardens of the Vieux Carre (1718-1860).* Thesis. Louisiana State University, 1976, p. 101.

61. *Times-Picayune,* March 17, 1941 article reported the discovery of the orignal garden plans in the archives of the Ursulines Convent by Sam Wilson, Jr.

62.   Wilson, Samuel, Jr. *The Vieux Carre New Orleans: Its Plan, Its Growth, Its Architecture.* New Orleans: Marcow O'Leary and Associates, 1968, in John Steele, p. 22.
63.   Wilson, Samuel Jr. in John Steele, p. 27.
64.   Hedrick, p. 351.
65.   Some vines available in the early 1800's were morning glories, purple or white Dolichos or hyacinth bean, honeysuckle, passion flower, jasmines.
66.   Flowers could have been violets, alyssum, geraniums, nasturtiums, marigolds, zinnias.
67.   Hedrick, p. 352.
68.   From Joseph Ewan.
69.   From Joseph Ewan.
70.   Whittle, Tyler. *The Plant Hunters.* New York: PAJ Publications, 1988, pp. 125-129, 178-179.
71.   Hedrick, pp. 355-356.
72.   "Louisiana's Golden Age of Valcour Aime." *Louisiana Historical Quarterly.* 10 (1969): 211-22, from John Steele, p. 76.
73.   Kane, Harnett T. *Plantation Parade, The Grand Manner in Louisiana.* New York: William Morrow and Company, 1945, pp. 30-33.
74.   Hedrick, pp. 204, 333.
75.   Hedrick, p. 353.
76.   Pizzetti, Ippolito and Henry Cocker. *Flowers, A Guide for Your Garden.* New York: Harry N. Abrams, Inc., p. 161.
77.   Pizzetti and Cocker, p. 160, 161.
78.   Hedrick, p. 222.
79.   *Rosedown Plantation and Gardens, A Portrait of the Past.* Brochure provided for tour of Rosedown Plantation, St. Francisville, Louisiana.
80.   From *The Pelican Guide to Gardens of Louisiana,* by Joyce Yeldell LeBlanc, Copyright 1974, 1989 by Joyce Yeldell LeBlanc, used by permission of the publisher, Pelican Publishing Company, 1974.
81.   Kane, Harnett. *Plantation Parade, The Grand Manner in Louisiana.* New York: William Morrow and Company, 1945, p. 295.
82.   Telephone interview with Mrs. Edmund Wingfield nee' Pipes, widow of Judge Wayne G. Borah, July 25, 1990.
83.   Ewan, Joseph, editor. *Letters from Charles Sprague Sargent to Reginald Somers Cocks, 1908-1926.* Reprint from *Journal of the Arnold Arboretum,* Volume 46, 1965, p. 144.
84.   Gallier House Museum. Tulane University. New Orleans, La.

85. See PLANTS FOR TRADITIONAL NEW ORLEANS GARDENS.
86. From Steele, John. *The Courtyard and Patio Gardens of the Vieux Carre (1718-1860)*. Thesis. Louisiana State University, 1976.
87. *Wyman's Gardening Encyclopedia*, pp. 158-159.
88. Starr, S. Frederick. *Southern Comfort: The Garden District of New Orleans, 1800-1900*. Massachusetts Institute of Technology, 1989, p. 177.
89. Newton, Norman T. *Design on the Land: The Development of Landscape Architecture*. Cambridge, Mass.: The Belknap Press of Harvard University Press, 1971, p. 259.
90. Starr, p. 64.
91. Samuel, Martha Ann Brett and Ray Samuel. *The Great Days of the Garden District and the Old City of Lafayette, 1978*, p. 50-51. Used with permission of Parent's League of the Louise S. McGehee School, New Orleans.
92. See NATIVE TREES AND SHRUBS and RESOURCES for a discussion of the Live Oak Society.
93. LeBreton, Dagmar Renshaw, Ethel Wight Usher, Marcelle Peret. *A Tour of the Garden District*. American Association of University Women, 1942, p. 11. Louisiana Collection, Howard Tilton Memorial Library, Tulane University.
94. Starr, p. 181.
95. Sylvanus. "Random Notes on Southern Horticulture." *The Horticulturist and Journal of Rural Art and Rural Taste*. (January to December 1851): 220-224. Gallier House Museum. Tulane University. New Orleans, Louisiana.
96. Hedrick, p. 357.
97. Lelievre, J. F. *Nouveau Jardinier de la Louisiane, Contenant les instructions necessaires Aux Personnes qui s'occupent de Jardinage*. New Orleans: Chez J. F. Lelievre, Libraire, Encolgaure Royale et Ste.-Anne, 1838, p. 156. In English: New Gardener of Louisiana, Containing instructions necessary for persons occupied in gardening. By J. P. Lelievre, former Agricultural Gardener of the French Government for the Colonies. At the Bookstore of J. P. Lelievre, Corner of Royal and Ste. Anne. 1838. Translation from Gallier House Museum. Tulane University. New Orleans, Louisiana.
98. Affleck, Thomas. *Affleck's Southern Rural Almanac and Plantation Garden Book*. New Orleans: Picayune

Company, 1851. The Garden Library of the New Orleans Town Gardeners, Southeastern Architectural Archive, Tulane University Library.

99. Scott-James, Anne and Osbert Lancaster. *The Pleasure Garden*. London: Penguin Books, 1979, p. 70.

100. Hand, Stephen B. *The Courtyard and Patio Gardens of the Vieux Carre (1861-1982)*. Thesis, Louisiana State University, 1982.

101. New Orleans, Louisiana. *Notarial Archives Planbooks, Book 5, Folio 19, 1868.*

102. New Orleans, Louisiana. *Notarial Archives Planbooks, Book 97, Folio 18, 1869.*

103. Editorial. *Southern Garden, Horticulture, Floriculture, Truck Farming and Gardening in General in the South*, A monthly Journal published at New Orleans, Louisiana and the official organ of the New Orleans Horticultural Society and The Gardeners Mutual Protective Association. Volume 1, November 1, 1894. Louisiana Collection, Howard Tilton Memorial Library, Tulane University.

104. Ewan, Joseph. Letter to Charlotte Seidenberg, Mary 21, 1990.

105. LeBreton, Dagmar Renshaw, Ethel Wight Usher, Marcelle Peret. *A Tour of the Garden District*. American Association of University Women, 1942, p. 26. Louisiana Collection, Howard Tilton Memorial Library, Tulane University.

106. Copies from R. Maitre's 1875 catalogue and the following information are from Joseph Ewan:
Maitre tomb in Metairie Cemetary at circle of tomb of Army of Northern Virginia; Reinhardt Maitre born in Kuohlinsbergen, Baden, Germany; 1830-1898 Christina Maitre nee' Rehm: 1842-1906 (of the family which owned Rehm Nurseries?)

107. Hand, p. 45.

108. *Visitors Guide to the Industrial and Cotton Centennial Exposition*. Louisville, Kentucky: Courier-Journal Job Printing Co., 1884.

109. Forman, L. Ronald and Joseph Logsdon. *Audubon Park, An Urban Eden*. New Orleans, Louisiana: Friends of the Zoo, 1985.

110. *Southern Garden*. Volume 1, August 1, 1895. Louisiana Collection, Howard Tilton Memorial Library, Tulane University.

111. Hardy, D. Clive. *The World Industrial & Cotton Centennial Exposition, 1884-85*. Thesis, Tulane University, 1976.

112. Schmitz, Don C., Brian V. Nelson, Larry E. Nall, and Jeffrey D. Schardt. *Exotic Aquatic Plants in Florida: A Historical Perspective and Review of the Present Aquatic Plant Regulation Program, Abstract.* Tallahassee, Florida: Florida Department of Natural Resources, Bureau of Aquatic Plant Management, 1988, pp. 5-6.

113. "Dr. Richardson's Victoria Regina." *Times-Democrat.* August 30, 1890. Page 3, column 5. New Orleans Public Library.

114. "The Monster South American Water Lily to Bloom Tonight in Dr. Richardson's Garden." *The Daily Picayune.* August 30, 1890, p. 8, column 3. New Orleans Public Library.

115. LeBreton, Usher, & Peret.

116. *Southern Garden.* Volume 1, April 1, 1895. Louisiana Collection, Howard Tilton Memorial Library, Tulane University.

117. Ewan, Joseph. "Letters from Charles Sprague Sargent to Reginald Somers Cocks, 1908-1926." *Journal of the Arnold Arboretum.* Volume 46, 1965, p. 5.

118. Coleman, William H. *Historical Sketch Book and Guide to New Orleans and Environs.* New York: Coleman Publisher, 1885, pp. 253-254. Gallier House Museum. Tulane University. New Orleans, Louisiana.

119. *Hibiscus abutiloid* is an orange flowered Hawaiian shrub which is used in the city today. *Abutilon* is flowering maple, another mallow family shrub. Coleman could have meant both or either depending on whether he left out a comma. They were both available in 1885.

120. Coleman, 253-254.

121. Hand, Stephen B. *The Courtyard and Patio Gardens of the Vieux Carre (1861-1982).* Thesis, Louisiana State University, 1982.

122. Hand, pp. 39-50.

123. Parkway Commission of New Orleans. *Fortieth Anniversary Report: 1909-1949.*

124. Ewan, Joseph. "Letters from Charles Sprague Sargent to Reginald Somers Cocks, 1908-1926." *Journal of the Arnold Arboretum.* Volume 46, 1965, p. 5. p. 27.

125. Cable, George Washington. *The Amateur Garden.* 1914. Rare Books and Manuscripts, Howard Tilton Memorial Library, Tulane University.

126. Oser, Elizabeth H. and Mary B. Stewart. *Gardening in New Orleans.* New Orleans: Robert L. Crager & Company, 1952.

127. New Orleans Garden Society, Inc. *Notes on Gardening in New Orleans.* New Orleans: 1921. From Stephen Hand, pp. 183-187.

128. Ewan Joseph. Letter to Charlotte Seidenberg, May 21, 1990.

129. "Spring Flower and Fashion Show." *Times-Picayune.* March 11, 1949. New Orleans Public Library.

130. *Times-Picayune.* March 12, 1949. New Orleans Public Library.

131. Stewart, Mrs. Andrew. "Garden Notes for New Orleans." *Notes on Gardening in New Orleans.* New Orleans Garden Society, 1921, p. 22.

132. *New Orleans Garden Society Yearbook, 1940,* p. 25.

133. Interview with Mrs. John Minor Wisdom, June, 1990.

134. *The W. P. A. Guide to New Orleans: The Federal Writers' Project Guide to 1930's New Orleans.* New York: Pantheon Books, 1983.

135. Hand, Stephen.

136. *Parkway Commission Report, 1949.*

137. Forrest, Lee. *Trees, Vines, and Shrubs of New Orleans.* City Park, Audubon Park, Parkway Commission, 1947.

138. *A Garden Book of Old New Orleans,* by Grace Matt Thompson, Used with permission of Milburn Calhoun of Pelican Publishing Company.

139. Hand, p. 104.

140. Hand, p. 113.

141. Oser, Elizabeth H. and Mary B. Stewart. *Gardening in New Orleans.* New Orleans: Robert L. Crager & Company, 1952.

142. Hand, p. 139. Quote from Friedrichs, Christopher A., Landscape Architect, New Orleans, Louisiana, 13 August 1982.

143. Interview with Steve Treme' and Keven Bleichner of the Parkway and Park Commission, February 6, 1990.

144. Interview with Florence Schornstein, Superintendent and Brenda Pumphrey, Coordinator of Volunteer Services, New Orleans Parkway & Park Commission, March, 1990.

145. *The New American Garden* by Carole Ottesen (Macmillan, N.Y., 1987), p. 2. Reprinted with permission.

SELECTED BIBLIOGRAPHY

BOOKS AND PAMPHLETS

NEW ORLEANS AND LOUISIANA

Brown, Clair A. *Ferns and Fern Allies of Louisiana*. Baton
Rouge: Louisiana State University Press, 1942.

Brown, Clair A. *Louisiana Trees and Shrubs*. Baton Rouge: Louisiana
State University Press, 1965.

Brown, Clair A. *Wildflowers of Louisiana and Adjoining States*. Baton
Rouge: Louisiana State University Press, 1980.

Caillet, Marie and Joseph Mertzweiller. *The Louisiana Iris: The
History and Culture of Five Native American Species and
their Hybrids*. A Publication of the Society for Louisiana
Irises. Waco, Texas: Texas Gardener Press, 1988.

Dorman, Caroline. *Natives Preferred*. Baton Rouge: Claitor's
Bookstore, 1965.

Duncan, Wilbur H. and Leonard E. Foote. *Wildflowers of the
Southeastern United States*. Athens: University of Georgia
Press, 1975.

Forman, L. Ronald and Joseph Logsdon. *Audubon Park, an Urban
Eden*. Tokyo: Toppan Printing Company, 1985.

Hand, Stephen B. *The Courtyard and Patio Gardens of the Vieux
Carre (1861-1982)*. Thesis, Louisiana State University, 1982.

Harvey, Barbara S. *Walled Gardens of the French Quarter*. New Orleans:
The Garden Study Club of New Orleans, 1974.

Leavitt, Mel. *A Short History of New Orleans*. San Francisco:
Lexikos, 1982.

LeBlanc, Joyce Y. *The Pelican Guide to Gardens of Louisiana*.
Gretna: Pelican Publishing Co., 1974.

Louisiana State University Cooperative Extension.
*Amaryllis, Azaleas, Chrysanthemums, Composting, Crape Myrtles,
Daylilies, Ground Covers, Grow Annuals for Year-Round
Color, Growing Rabbiteye Blueberries in Louisiana,
Herbaceous Perennials for Louisiana Landscapes, Louisiana
Iris, Protecting Shade Trees Around your New Home,
Roses, Vines for Louisiana*

Odenwald, Neil G. and James R. Turner. *Identification, Selection, and
Use of Southern Plants for Landscape Design*. Baton Rouge:
Claitor's Publishing Division, 1987.

Oser, Elizabeth H. and Stewart, Mary B. *Gardening in New Orleans*.
New Orleans: Robert L. Crager & Company, 1952. This classic was the first comprehensive book on local gardening.
There is a reprint available which does not include material
of historic interest: the lists of past presidents of the
N. O. Garden Society and the members whose experiences
were the basis of the book. The cover photos were taken in
my garden. Lest my credibility be compromised, I would
like to note that sun-requiring plants tucked into the shade
on the front are potted. The stage was set while I was away!

River Oaks Garden Club. *A Garden Book for Houston and the Gulf Coast.* Third Revised Edition. Houston, Texas: Pacesetter Press, 1975

Samuel, Martha Ann Brett and Ray Samuel. *The Great Days of the Garden District and the Old City of Lafayette.* New Orleans: Parent's League of the Louise S. McGehee School, 1978.

Schlesinger, Dorothy G., Robert J. Cangelosi, Jr., Sally Kittredge Reeves. *New Orleans Architecture, Volume VII: Jefferson City.* Gretna: Pelican Publishing Company, 1989.

Southeastern Architectural Archive Tulane University Library. *The Garden Library of the New Orleans Town Gardeners. A Catalog.* New Orleans: 1988.

Starr, S. Frederick. *Southern Comfort: The Garden District of New Orleans, 1800-1900.* Cambridge, Massachusetts: Massassachusetts Institute of Technology Press, 1989.

Steele, John Sidney. *The Courtyard and Patio Gardens of the Vieux Carre' (1718-1860).* Thesis, Louisiana State University, 1976.

Thieret, John W. Louisiana. *Ferns and Fern Allies.* Lafayette: Lafayette Natural History Museum Published in Conjunction with The University of Southwestern Louisiana, 1980.

Thompson, Grace Matt. *A Garden Book of Old New Orleans.* New Orleans: Pelican Press, Inc., 1947.

Trimble, Genevieve Munson et al. *The How to Grow Better Day-by-Day Gardener's Guide.* New Orleans: The Garden Study Club of New Orleans and the New Orleans Town Gardeners, 1987.

United States Department of Agriculture in cooperation with the Louisiana Agricultural Experiment Station. *Soil Survey of East Bank of Jefferson Parish, Louisiana.* Jefferson Parish: 1980.

United States Department of Agriculture in cooperation with the Louisiana Agricultural Experiment Station. *Soil Survey of West Bank of Jefferson Parish,* Louisiana. Jefferson Parish: 1980.

The W.P.A. Guide to New Orleans: The Federal Writers' Project Guide to 1930's New Orleans. New York: Pantheon Books, 1983.

Welch, William C. *Perennial Garden Color for Texas and the South.* Dallas, Texas: Taylor Publishing Company, 1989.

GENERAL GARDENING

Baron, Robert C. *The Garden and Farm Books of Thomas Jefferson.* Golden, Colorado: Fulcrum, Inc., 1987.

Brooklyn Botanical Garden. *Herbs and Their Ornamental Uses.* Special Printing of Plants and Gardens, Vol. 28, No. 1, 1972.

Bubel, Nancy. *The New Seed-Starters Handbook.* Emmaus, Pennsylvania: Rodale Press, 1988.

Clausen, Ruth R. and Nicolas Ekstrom. *Perennials for American Gardens.* New York: Random House, 1989.

Cornell University, Staff of the L. H. Bailey Hortorium. *Hortus Third, A Concise Dictionary of Plants Cultivated in the United States and Canada.* New York: Macmillan Publishing Company, 1976.

Damrosch, Barbara. *Theme Gardens.* New York: Workman Publishing, 1982.

Feltwell, John. *The Naturalist's Garden.* Topsfield, Massachusetts: Salem House Publishers, 1987.

Hedrick, U. P. *A History of Horticulture in America to 1860.* Portland, Oregon: Timber Press, 1988.

Johnson, Hugh. *The Principles of Gardening.* New York: Simon and Schuster, 1979.

Lathrop, Norma Jean. *Herbs, How to Select, Grow and Enjoy.* Tuscon, Arizona: H. P. Books, 1981.

Lawrence, Elizabeth. *A Southern Garden, A Handbook for the Middle South.* Chapel Hill: University of North Carolina Press, 1942, 1967, 1984.

Meeuse, Bastiaan and Sean Morris. *The Sex Life of Flowers.* New York: Facts on File, 1984.

Ottesen, Carole. *The New American Garden.* New York: Macmillan Publishing Company, 1987.

Phillips, Harry R. *Growing and Propagating Wild Flowers.* Chapel Hill and London: The University of North Carolina Press, 1985.

Pizzetti, Ippolito and Henry Cocker. *Flowers, A Guide for Your Garden.* New York: Harry N. Abrams, Inc., 1968.

Scott-James, Anne and Osbert Lancaster. *The Pleasure Garden.* London: Penguin Books, 1979.

Time-Life Encyclopedia of Gardening. New York: Time-Life Books, 1971-1978.

Whittle, Tyler. *The Plant Hunters.* New York: PAJ Publications, 1988.

Wyman, Donald. *Wyman's Gardening Encyclopedia.* New York: Macmillan Publishing Co., Inc., 1977.

DAYLILIES

American Hemerocallis Society. *Daylilies, Everything You've Always Wanted to Know About Daylilies.* 1978.

Webber, Steve. *Daylily Encyclopedia.* Damascus, Maryland: Webber Gardens, 1988.

Stout, A. B. *Daylilies: The Wild Species and Garden Clones, Both Old and New, of the Genus Hemerocallis.* Milkwood, New York: Sagapress, Inc., 1986.

WILDLIFE

Boone, D. Daniel. *Homes for Birds: Conservation Bulletin 14.*
    Washington, D. C.:   U. S. Department of the Interior, Fish
    and Wildlife Service, 1979.
Dennis, John V. *The Wildlife Gardener.* New York: Alfred A. Knopf,
    1985.
Dundee, Harold A. and Douglas A. Rossman. *The Amphibians and
    Reptiles of Louisiana.* Baton Rouge and London: Louisiana
    State University Press, 1989.
Holldobler, Bert and Edward O. Wilson. *The Ants.* Cambridge,
    Massassachusetts: Harvard University Press, 1990.
Johnsgard, Paul A. *The Hummingbirds of North America.*
    Washington, D. C.: Smithsonian Institution Press, 1983.
Keppelman, Tony. *Hummingbirds.* Boston: Little, Brown &
    Company, 1988.
Lowery, George H., Jr. *Louisiana Birds.* Baton Rouge, Louisiana:
    Louisiana Press, 1974.
Lowery, George H., Jr.   *The Mammals of Louisiana and its Adjacent
    Waters.* Baton Rouge, Louisiana: Louisiana State University
    Press, 1974.
McKinley, Michael. *How to Attract Birds.* San Francisco: Ortho
    Books, 1983.
Mitchell, Robert T. and Herbert S. Zim.   *Butterflies and Moths.* New
    York: Golden Press, 1987.
National Geographic Society. *Field Guide to the Birds of North
    America.* Washington, D.C.: National Geographic Society,
    1987.
Newfield, Nancy L. *Attracting Hummingbirds to Your Garden.*
    Orleans Audubon Society.
Newfield, Nancy L. "When To Take Down Your Hummingbird
    Feeder." *Birdwatcher's Digest.* (September-October, 1989),
    p.80-83.
Skutch, Alexander F. *The Life of the Hummingbird.* New York:
    Crown Publishers, Inc., 1973.
Stokes, Donald and Lillian. *The Hummingbird Book, The Complete
    Guide to Attracting, Identifying, and Enjoying Hummingbirds.*
    Boston: Little, Brown and Company, 1989.

ROSES

Beales, Peter. *Classic Roses.* New York: Holt, Rinehart and
    Winston, 1985.
Crockett, James U. *Roses.* New York: Time-Life Books, 1975.
McNair, James K. *All About Roses.* San Francisco: Ortho Books, 1976.
Phillips, Roger and Martyn Rix. *Roses.*

PERIODICALS

NEW ORLEANS AND LOUISIANA

Bradley, Camilla. "New Orleans Garden." *Homemaking.* New
Orleans: New Orleans Public Service, Inc., monthly 1975- .
New Orleans Plants and Gardens. New Orleans: LaCoste
Publishing Corporation, bi-monthly, 1989- .
Louisiana Conservationist. Department of Wildlife and Fisheries,
P. O. Box 98000, Baton Rouge, Louisiana 70898, bimonthly.

GENERAL GARDENING

American Horticulturist. American Horticultural Society, 7931 East
Boulevard Drive, Alexandria, Virginia 22308, issued 6 times
a year as a magazine and 6 as a news edition.
Harrowsmith-Country Life. The Creamery, Charlotte, Vermont 05445.
Bimonthly.
Horticulture, The Magazine of American Gardening. P. O. Box 53879,
Boulder, Colorado 80321, monthly.
National Gardening, The Gardener's Newsmagazine. National
Gardening Association, 180 Flynn Avenue, Burlington,
Vermont 05401, monthly.
Flower & Garden, The Home Gardening Magazine. Modern Handcraft,
Inc., 4251 Pennsylvania, Kansas City, Missouri 64111, monthly.

WILDLIFE

Bird Watcher's Digest. Pardson Corporation, P. O. Box 110,
Marietta, Ohio 45750-9977, bimonthly.
National Wildlife. National Wildlife Federation. 8925 Leesburg Pike,
Vienna, Virginia, 22184. Bimonthly.
Purple Martin Update. The Purple Martin Conservation Association.
Institute for Research & Community Services, Edinboro
University of Pennsylvania, Edinboro, Pennsylvania 16444.
Four times a year.

BOTANICAL NAMES

Jean and I stopped to admire a red-leaved plant in a Sicilian garden. The only understandable word in the stream of Italian which effused from the gardener's mouth was *Amaranthus*. All the Italian versions of common names for Amaranths: Love Lies Bleeding, Joseph's Coat, Tasselflower, etc., would not have given me a clue as to what it was. The botanical name was what I needed!

A common system of nomenclature has a practical value to people who grow or study plants, or who just like them: accuracy of identification. I have included the scientific names of plants along with their popular names in my listings.

The Plant Kingdom is divided and subdivided by a system which shows the biological relationships of plants within the different groups. As research continues, knowledge increases, changes are made. I used as a source of scientific names: *Hortus Third: A Concise Dictionary of Plants Cultivated in the United States and Canada.* It lists botanical names as assigned by the rules of the *"International Code of Botanical Nomenclature."*

I have given the family name (common version) and the genus and species name of every plant I describe in my text. For instance, *Amaranthus tricolor* is a member of Amaranthaceae or the Amaranth family.

Genus: *Amaranthus*
Species: *tricolor*

Among species there are natural varieties and man made varieties which can be called hybrids, garden hybrids, cultivars, or indicated to be "of garden origin." Following are some of the ways these subdivisions are described:

Amaranthus tricolor variety *salicifolius*
Amaranthus tricolor var. *salicifolius* cv. 'Splendens'
'Splendens'

Hybrids are designated by "X": X *Amarcrinum*, crinodonna.

It gets even more involved! The scientific name of a plant also includes the name, usually abbreviated, of the person who identified and named the species. In:

Ilex opaca Ait.

"Ait." is for William Aiton, who lived 1731 to 1793 and gave American holly (*Ilex opaca*) its scientific name. Though these citations are frequently not used, I have included them because part of a species' history is missing when they are omitted.

In many plant names, the author cited (by "L.") is Carl Linnaeus, the Swedish biologist who devised the above system of taxonomy, called binomial nomenclature, in 1753:

Ilex cassine L.(dahoon holly)

Other citations represent characters who, far from being dry classroom botanists, suffered incredible privations in the search for new and exotic plants: from loneliness to death from starvation, fever, dysentery, or being shot with poisonous arrows and chopped to bits by Tibetan monks. Tyler Whittle tells their tales in *The Plant Hunters*.

The intricacies of the naming procedure are reflected in the variations you will see in my text. If you are interested in further explanation, *Wyman's Gardening Encyclopedia* (under "Nomenclature") is a good place to start.

RESOURCES

The How to Grow Better Day-by-Day Gardener's Guide, a compilation of information in calendar form for the New Orleans gardener.

New Orleans Plants and Gardens, New Orlean's bimonthly gardening magazine offers up-to-date information on all types of modern garden interests from antique roses, to butterfly gardens, to organic gardens, to garden design. To subscribe, send $5.50 per year to: LaCoste Publishing Corporation, P. O. Box 19389, New Orleans, Louisiana 70179.

The Times-Picayune, New Orlean's daily newspaper offers:

"Gardening", a weekly column by Severn Doughty, Ph.D, who is the Louisiana Cooperative Extension Service horticultural agent for the five-parish area including Orleans and Jefferson. Each week he presents a calendar of current events and announcements for New Orleans gardeners.

"One Gardener", a twice monthly column of essays on gardening in New Orleans by Marty Ross.

"Yearly Gardening and Outdoor Living Tabloid" and a Club Directory as well as coverage of special events in gardening throughout the year.

LOUISIANA COOPERATIVE EXTENSION SERVICE, a branch of the Louisiana State University Agriculture Center, provides educational information to the general public in several areas, including horticulture and agriculture, current events in gardening and information about organizations.

Staff of professionals available by telephone for information in offices in each parish.

TeleTips is a free call-in service which plays tape-recorded messages with "how to" information on many gardening topics such as soil testing.

New Orleans 486-9711   Slidell 649-1648

Publications offering "how to" information are distributed through parish Extension offices.

Spring Garden Show, An Educational Experience for the Home Gardener and the Professional, sponsored in cooperation with the Metro Area Horticulture Committee Foundation and the New Orleans Botanical Garden, held each year at City Park.

NEW ORLEANS PARKWAY & PARK COMMISSION should be consulted for questions on tree planting and maintainence, including recommended   species for given locations in New Orleans.   Its Superintendent, Florence Schornstein and Coordinator of Volunteer Services, Brenda Pumphrey offer Orleans Parish residents a way to make the whole City a garden with two unique programs.

The Plant-a-Tree Trust Fund accepts tax-deductible donations as gifts or memorials to help fund the planting of trees and beautification of New Orleans.

Parkway Partners Program, A Joint Venture of the City of New Orleans and Parkway & Park Commission is an organization of volunteers who Adopt a park, playground, or portion of neutral ground for which they provide maintainence or beautification services as mutually agreed upon a yearly basis.   The Partner's area is identified by a sign announcing their status as a Parkway Partner.

THE LOUISIANA NATURE & SCIENCE CENTER in New Orleans East offers exhibits, tours, lectures, literature, demonstrations on topics related to nature and science. Environmental issues are stressed.   Under the direction of Robert A. Thomas, Ph.D, The Nature Center can show as well as tell you how to live and garden in harmony with nature through gardening for wildlife and with wildflowers. The wildflower demonstration plot, bird feeding stations, hummingbird plantings are of special interest. Join for acess by pass and newsletter.

LOUISIANA WILDLIFE & FISHERIES MUSEUM at 303 Williams Blvd. in Kenner is managed by The Louisiana Nature & Science Center.   Similar programs are offered.

COLLEGES AND UNIVERSITIES are a good source of information, through their libraries, or actual coursework and depending on your area of interest.

Delgado Community College offers programs in horticulture and houses Louisiana Cooperative Extension's Urban Gardening Office.

Louisiana State University School of Landscape Architecture is a good source on landscape gardening history.

The L.S.U. Department of Agriculture sponsors experiments with ornamental garden plants.

The L.S.U. Department of Botany maintains a Herbarium, a collection of dried plant specimens used in taxonomic studies.

L.S.U. was the home of Clair Brown, known for his works on ferns, trees, and wildflowers of Louisiana. A significant contribution of L.S.U. to the study of native plants was the commissioning of British botanical artist Margaret Stones to execute drawings of 200 Louisiana plants for the bicentennial.

Southeastern Louisiana University in Hammond offers a Horticulture curriculum through the Department of Biological Sciences.

Tulane University houses The Garden Library of the New Orleans Town Gardeners in the Southeastern Architectural Archive in the basement of Howard Tilton Memorial Library.

Tulane's Botany Department maintains a Herbarium and the Koch Botanical Library.

University of Southwestern Louisiana in Lafayette has a Horticulture Center which contains an extensive library, tropical botanical gardens and an experimental garden.

ARBORETA are botanical gardens for woody plants which will grow in a given area. They are for educational and scientific use. Each plant should be labeled with botanical and popular names. There is no arboretum in New Orleans, but two are close by.

The Crosby Arboretum, P. O. Box 190, Picayune, Mississippi 39466. It has plant sales! (601) 798-6961.

Cohn Memorial Arboretum, 12056 Foster Road in Baton Rouge.

Gloster Arboretum, Gloster, Mississippi.

Hilltop Arboretum, Highland Road, Baton Rouge.

Louisiana State Arboretum is at Chicot State Park near Opelousas.

GARDENS

Audubon Zoological Garden is a zoo for plants, too. Within Audubon Park across Magazine Street from the Zoo is Leon Heymann Conservatory. Its greenhouse of exotics is surrounded by plantings of native and exotic species.

Beauregard-Keyes House, 1113 Chartres Street, New Orleans French Quarter. Parterre and herb garden restored to the 1830's.

Burden Research Plantation, at Essen Lane and I-10 in Baton Rouge, is the site of the Rose Test Garden and the Louisiana State University Experimental Station and Annuals and Herb Test Gardens.

City Park, New Orleans. The whole park is a garden of ancient oaks, azaleas, camellias, native iris. Within is the New Orleans Botanical Garden and rose garden. Educational programs on gardening topics are given weekly as announced in the Times-Picayune.

Gallier House Museum, 1118-1132 Royal Street, French Quarter home and courtyard restored to 1857.

Hermann-Grima House and Courtyard, 820 St. Louis Street offers a restoration of a Vieux Carre garden circa 1860.

Historic New Orleans Collection Museum/Research Center, 533 Royal Street, courtyard gardens.

Longue Vue Gardens, 7 Bamboo Road, 8 acre estate of the late Mrs. Edith Stern which contains a series of magnificent and meticulously tended gardens in different styles and color schemes.

Pitot House, 1440 Moss Street, parterre and other gardens with traditional Louisiana garden plants.

Zemmurray Gardens, near Hammond, are worth a visit during camellia and azalea bloom season.

ORGANIZATIONS

The address for many organizations changes with election of new officers which can be on a yearly basis. Louisiana Cooperative Extension Service (Jefferson: 341-7271, New Orleans: 486-3736, Plaquemines: 682-0081, St. Bernard: 279-9402), The Louisiana Nature & Science Center (246-5672), the *Times-Picayune* Club Directory and gardening column are sources of current contact information for groups whose focus is gardening or nature.

American Hemerocallis Society, write Elly Launius, Executive Secretary, 1454 Rebel Drive, Jackson, Mississippi 39211.

Bayou Gesneriad Society of Louisiana

Bat Conservation International, P. O. Box 162603, Austin, Texas 78716, (512) 327-9721.

Crescent Bird Club

Delta Daylily Society, write to 1304 Pleasant Street, New Orleans, Louisiana 70115-3429.

Gulf States Mycological Society

International Cycad Society, call Dr. Severn Doughty at 486-3736.

Louisiana Chapter of the International Palm Society, Wilbur Le Gardeur, 6661 Manchester Street, New Orleans, Louisiana 70126.

The Live Oak Society of the Louisiana Garden Club Federation, Inc. If you know a live oak tree who wants to join, have them call or write (or you call or write for them): Mrs. Verlyn T. Bercegeay, 112 Bellewood Drive, Hammond, Louisiana 70401, (504) 542-4729.

Louisiana Fern Society

Louisiana Native Plant Society, 239 Pomeroy, Shreveport, Louisiana 71115. Newsletter. Information on regional conferences.

Louisiana Ornithological Society

Louisiana Pond Society. Call Richard Sacher at 827-0889.

Louisiana Project Wildflower, Lafayette Natural History Museum, 637 Girard Park Drive, Lafayette, Louisiana 70503. Annual meeting, newsletter.

Louisiana Society for Horticultural Research, University of Southwestern Louisiana. Bulletin. Members are given plants to try in their gardens, report results. Annual meeting.

The Men's Amaryllis Club of New Orleans, Inc.

Orleans Audubon Society, P. O. Box 4162, New Orleans, Louisiana 70178-4162.

The Louisiana Nature Conservancy, P. O. Box 4125, Baton Rouge, Louisiana 70821. (504) 338-1040.

New Orleans Rose Society

The Potted Plant Club

Preservation Resource Center, 604 Julia Street, 581-7032.

Society for Louisiana Irises, Elaine Bourque, 1812 Broussard Road East, Lafayette, Louisiana 70508. Bulletin.

Southern Garden History Society, Old Salem, Inc., Drawer F, Salem Station, Winston-Salem, North Carolina 27108.

Rara Avis, whose motto is "**Rainforest conservation for profit**", is an experiment whose purpose is to develop income producing uses of the rainforest which do not entail its destruction. Tourism is, of course, one. The journey to Rara Avis gives new meaning to the phrase "roughing it", so this trip is not for everyone. If your interest in garden and house plants extends to seeking their origins in a more active way than reading, a visit to the Central American jungle is it! The ultimate adventure is available for the truly committed amateur naturalist: an intimate view of the upper reaches of the forest from Don Perry's Automated Web for Canopy Exploration. Amos Bien, plant ecologist, is Presidente. To join or visit, write Amos: Apartado 8105, San Jose 1000 Costa Rica, Telefono 53-08-44.

PLANT & SUPPLY SOURCES

I have never found a nursery I didn't like. I recommend checking out all the ones in the Metropolitan Area yourself. What fun! The following are specialized sources in Louisiana. Call or write them to find out if they offer catalogues or price lists:

Amaryllis Incorporated, E. M. Beckham, P. O. Box 318, Baton Rouge, Louisiana 70821, (504) 924-5560.

American Aquatic Gardens, 621 Elysian Fields, New Orleans, 827-0889.

Gentilly Novelty Company, 1700 Benefit, New Orleans, 949-5195. Concrete birdbaths, readymade or customed to your needs.

Natives Nurseries, John Mayronne, P. O. Box 2355, Covington, Louisiana 70434, Highway 1082 outside Covington. (504) 892-5424. Native plants.

Louisiana Nursery, the Durio family, Rt. 7, Box 43, Opelousas, Louisiana 70570, (318) 948-3696. The price of the catalogue will be refunded when you order: Magnolias and other Garden Aristocrats, $5.00, magnolias, hydrangeas, many other ornamental trees, shrubs, vines, bulbs, water and bog plants, native and exotic, many "traditional Southern plants". Daylilies and Louisiana Iris, $3.00, named cultivars of daylilies and Louisiana Iris species and hybrids, as well as other Iris species and many hard to find bulbs. Crinum List, $2.00, crinum, amarcrinum, cannas, rainlilies.

Louisiana Nature and Science Center, P. O. Box 870610, New Orleans, Louisiana 70187. Wildflower seeds and mix for Louisiana.

Prairie Bass, Bill Fontenot, Route 2, Box 491F, Carencro, Louisiana 70520. Native plants.

Sisters' Bulb Farm, Route 2, Box 170, Gibsland, Louisiana 71028. Celia Jones and Jan Jones Grigsby have revived their grandmother's daffodil farm. They sell the species, natural hybrids and pre-1940 varieties which have repeated there for years. Others bulbs, also.

DAYLILIES

Celia Krebs' Fort Isabel Nursery, Rt. 1, Box 309, Bogalusa, Louisiana 70427, (504)735-7371. Write for list.

Crochet Daylily Garden, Clarence & Beth Crochet, P. O. Box 425, Prairieville, Louisiana 70769. Free price list.

The Hobby Garden, Lee Gates, 38164 Monticello Drive, Prairieville, Louisiana 70769. 673-3623.

Guidry's Daylily Garden, Lucille S. Guidry, 1005 E. Vermilion, Abbeville, Louisiana 70510. Catalogue, $2.00.

Mrs. W. M. (Elsie) Spalding, Iowa, Louisiana.

LOUISIANA IRIS

Bay View Gardens, Joseph Ghio, 1201 Bay Street, Santa Cruz, California 95060. Catalog, $.50.

Bois D'Arc Gardens, Ed and Rusty Ostheimer, P. O. Box 485, Houma, Louisiana 70361.

Caldwell Nursery, Jim & Jenny Caldwell, Route 2, Box 3584, Coldspring, Texas 77331. Daylilies, too.

Deep South Garden, Dorman Haymon & Sandy Duhon, 1218 Duhon Road, Duson, Louisiana 70529.

Albert C. Faggard, 3840 LeBleu Street, Beaumont, Texas 77707. Daylilies, too.

Gatewood Gardens, Richard Goula, 113 Acacia Drive, Lafayette, Louisiana 70508.

Tim and Cathy Hebert, 117 Reams Boulevard, St. Martinville, Louisiana 70582.

CATALOGUES

The following are some of my special favorites among mailorder catalogues from sources outside of Louisiana. My suggestion for getting the myriad of seed and bulb catalogues available is to subscribe to one of the national gardening magazines (See Bibliography) and write to sources advertised on its pages. Also, just wait. The mere fact of your subscription will put you on mailing lists to receive catalogues if you do nothing.

GENERAL SEED CATALOGUES

Park Seed Company, Cokesbury Road, Greenwood, South Carolina 29647-0001.

Burpee, W. Atlee Burpee & Co., 300 Park Avenue, Warminster, Pennsylvania 18991-0003.

Thompson & Morgan, P. O. Box 1308, Jackson, New Jersey 08527.

SPECIALTY CATALOGUES

Antique Rose Emporium, Old Roses, Beautiful catalogue. Rte. 5, Box 143, Brenham, Texas 77833.

Carolina Biological Supply Company, Burlington, North Carolina 27215, 1-800-334-5551.

The Crow's Nest Birding Shop, Cornell Lab of Ornithology, 159 Sapsucker Woods Road, Ithaca, New York 14850, (607) 254-2400. Books, gear, gifts for bird and nature enthusiasts, including frog and toad voice tapes!

Jackson & Perkins Roses, Medford, Oregon 97501.

Lilypons Water Gardens, P. O. Box 188, Brookshire, Texas 77423. Water plants, tadpoles, pool supplies. Catalogue, $5.00.

Logee's Greenhouses, Rare Plants, 55 North Street, Danielson, Connecticut 06239.

McClure & Zimmerman, Quality Flowerbulb Brokers, 1422 West Throndale, Chicago, Illinois 60660.

Oregon Bulb Farms, 14071 N.E. Arndt Rd., Dept. MO, Aurora, Oregon 97002, 1-800-328-2852. Source of lilies hybridized by Jan deGraaf.

The Plumeria People, Tropical Plant Specialists, P. O. Box 820014, Houston, Texas 77282 (713)496-2352.

Sandy Mush Herb Nursery, salvias and other herbs, Route 2, Surrett Cove Road, Leicester, North Carolina 28748.

Sunnybrook Farms, salvias and other herbs, perennials, P. O. Box 6, Chesterland, Ohio 44026.

Wild Seed, Inc., 1101 Campo Rosa Road, P. O. Box 308, Eagle Lake, Texas 77434. Offers individual wild flower seeds in small quantities.

HISTORIC SEEDS AND PLANTS

The Thomas Jefferson Center for Historic Plants, P. O. Box 316, Charlottesville, Virginia 22902. Seed list and bibliography.

Scott G. Kunst, Old House Gardens, 536 Third Street, Ann Arbor, Michigan 48103. Send $1.00 and a business-sized self-addressed stamped envelope for a source list and suggestions for finding plants.

Select Seeds, Fine Seeds for Old-Fashioned Flowers, 180 Stickney Hill Road, Union, Connecticut 06076. Catalogue $2.00.

GARDEN CLUBS

An incomplete list of garden clubs in the "Times-Picayune" in 1987 recorded fifty clubs in the New Orleans area. The formation of clubs shows not only the spread of interest in horticulture, but also the growth of the city:

New Orleans Garden Society, Inc., N. O. (1919)
Buena Vista Garden Society, Old Metairie (1936)
Lake Vista Garden Club, N. O. (1949)
Aurora Garden Club in Algiers (1950)
Green Thumb Garden Club in Arabi (1950)
Pontchartrain Garden Club, N. O. (1951)
Aurora Plantation Garden Club, in Algiers (1953)
Jefferson/Lakeshore Garden & Study Club, Metairie (1954)
Twilight Gardeners in Gretna (1954)
Colonial Garden Club in Harahan (1957)
Terrytown Garden Club in Gretna (1962)
Les Jardiniers de Bissonet Garden Club in Kenner (1962)
The Ivy Garden Guild in Metairie (1963)
Metairie Ridge Garden Club in Metairie (1966)
Lake Forest Garden Club East N. O. (1971)

Some groups are independent. Most are associated with a larger organization on a national level, such as Garden Club of America and the National Council of State Garden Clubs, Inc.

The Garden Club of America has two local affiliates. The Garden Study Club of New Orleans and the New Orleans Town Gardeners. These groups, combined, conducted the first public tours of Longue Vue Gardens in 1968, produced the *"Gardeners Guide for New Orleans and the Gulf South"* a calendar and compendium of advice essential to the New Orleans gardener. Both groups have been important in fund-raising for city beautification projects. Garden Study Club members were responsible for the publication of *Walled Gardens of the French Quarter* by Barbara S. Harvey, 1974.

One of the most important local gardening projects of recent years is The Garden Library of the New Orleans Town Gardeners at Tulane University. Members of the New Orleans Town Gardeners lead by Mrs. M. Truman Woodward, Jr. and Mrs. Charles N. Monsted began the collection which was originally kept in Mrs. Woodward's home. In order to make it more assessible and promote its use, it was donated to Southeastern Architectural Archive at Tulane in 1986. It is an extensive and growing collection of publications on gardening, but with an emphasis on Southern, Louisiana, and New Orleans gardening. It includes some historically important material. As knowledge of its existence spreads, I would hope that more donations of personal material, such as grandma's gardening diary or ancient seed catalogues, will make this collection even more of a resource for those trying to piece together our gardening past.

Many local garden clubs are affiliates of the Louisiana Garden Club Federation, Inc. and, at a national level, the National Council, as was the original New Orleans Garden Society and as is the Live Oak Society. Members of the Federated groups provide information to members on horticulture, landscape design, and floral arrangement through educational programs. They also encourage, through cash awards and scholarships, involvement of their members and others in projects related to beautification, conservation, litter control, energy awareness, environmental education, litter control, energy awareness, environmental education, roadside improvement, butterfly conservation, birds, Arbor day planting of trees, and Garden Therapy as rehabilitation.

New Orleanian Dorothea Boldt, founder of the Delta Daylily Society, president of the American Hemerocallis Society and elected 1980 "Woman of the Year" by the California Garden Clubs, asserted that many of the above issues which are now concerns of environmentalists on a national level have been tackled as projects by "garden club ladies" for years. Brass markers designating "Blue Star Highway" were part of garden club project of maintained highway plantings in honor of American Servicemen. You have probably noticed these, as I have, without knowing their significance. South Claiborne Avenue and Jefferson Highway are the locations of two in the New Orleans area.

With our economy as it is today, the work of Garden Clubs is more important than ever if the city is to maintain its hard-won reputation as a garden spot.

INDEX

Abelia 85
Abelmoschus 157
ABSINTHE 415
Absolute Restaurant 146
Abutilon 85
Acacia 104,294,466
Acalypha 477
Acer 275
Achillea 182-183,320
Achyranthes 433
Acidanthera 225
Acmena 98
ADAM'S NEEDLE 209
Adiantum 304,308,433
Aesculus 284
Affleck, Thomas 426,451
AFRICAN CORN LILY 247
AFRICAN EBONY TREE 104
AFRICAN DAISY 158
Agapanthus 225
Agave 183
Ageratum 157
Ailanthus 75
Aime', Valcour 393,443
AIR POTATO 136
Ajuga 183-184
Akebia 131
Albizia 75
Albuca 225-226
Alcea 157
Aleurites fordii 466
Allamanda 130,141
ALLIGATOR PEAR 103,144
Allium 226-227,415
Alocasia 227,400
Aloysia 415
Alpinia 227
Alstroemeria 227-228,422
Alternathera 433
ALTHAEA 92,157
ALYSSUM 168
Amaranthus 158
AMARYLLIS HALLII 252
AMARYLLIS BELLADONNA 228
Amaryllis 228
AMARYLLIS 241
AMAZON LILY 237
Amelanchier 275
AMERICAN BEAUTYBERRY 284-285
AMERICAN ELM 283
AMERICAN GERMANDER 334
AMERICAN HOLLY 296
AMERICAN OLIVE 291
Amomum 229
Amsonia 320
Anchusa 158
Andredera 131,433

ANEMONE 229
Anethum 413
ANGEL'S TRUMPET 86
ANISE SAGE 204
ANNUAL ASTER 159
ANNUAL CHRYSANTHEMUM 161
ANNUAL PHLOX 171,329
Annuals, culture 154-156
Antigonon 131
Antirrhinum 158
APOSTLE PLANT 255
Aquilegia 184
Araucaria 98-99
Arbor Day 270
ARBORVITAE, AMERICAN 294
ARBORVITAE, ORIENTAL 294
Arctotis 158
Ardisa 105
ARGENTINE TRUMPET VINE 134
Arisaema 229-230
Aristolochia 131
Arnold Arboretum 157,446,462
ARROWHEAD 122,289,400
Artemisia 415-416
Arum 230,423
Asarina 132
Asclepias 320-321
ASH, ARIZONA 279
ASH, EUROPEAN 279
ASH, GREEN 279
ASH, PUMPKIN 279
ASH, VELVET 279
ASH, WHITE 279
ASIAN JASMINE 146
Asparagus 184,311
ASPARAGUS FERN 184
Aspidistra 185
Asplenium 308
ASTER BUSH 91
Aster 321
Athyrium 308
Atkins, George B. 474
Aucuba 105
Audubon Wild Bird Rehab. Center 362
AUSTRALIAN BRUSH CHERRY 104
AUSTRALIAN FLAME TREE 76
AUTUMN SAGE 205
AVOCADO 103
Azalea Trail 481
AZALEA 118-122
AZALEA, cultivars 121-122
AZALEA, culture 119
AZALEAS, NATIVE 120
Azara 99
AZTEC LILY 258

BABY GLADIOLUS 239
BABY'S BREATH 165

BACHELOR'S BUTTON 160
BALD CYPRESS 283
BALLOON FLOWER 202
BALLOON VINE 133
BALSAM 166
BALSAM APPLE 142
BAMBOO 185
Bambusa 185
BANANA 81
BANANA SHRUB 116
Baptisia 321
BARBADOES CHERRY 115
BASIL 414
Batwatch 391
Bauhinia 76,86
BEAR-GRASS 209
BEARDTONGUE 328
Beauregard-Keyes House 447
BEAUTY BUSH 93
BEDDING CONEHEAD 206
BEE BALM 198,328
Begonia 185-186
Belamcanda 230
BELLADONNA LILY 228
Bellis 158,433
Beloperone 193
BENE, BENNE 415
BENGAL CLOCK VINE 145
BENGAL TRUMPET VINE 145
Bercegeay, Mrs. Verlyn 268-269
BERGAMOT 198
BERMUDA BUTTERCUP 256
Betula 275-276
BIG BLUE LOBELIA 327
Bignonia 132
BIGNONIA 134-135
BIRD OF PARADISE 86,258
BITTERSWEET 133
BLACK ALDER 296
BLACK CALLA 230
BLACK CHERRY 282
BLACK-EYED SUSAN 203,330
BLACK-EYED SUSAN VINE 145
BLACK GUM 281
BLACK LAUREL 289
BLACK LOCUST 282
BLACK WILLOW 282-283
BLACKBERRIES 144
BLACKBERRY LILY 230
BLANKETFLOWER 190
BLAZING STAR 194,326
BLEEDINGHEART 134
Bleichner, Keith 22,125,480
Bletilla 230
BLOOD LILY 240
BLOODFLOWER 320
BLOODLEAF 433
BLUE-BOTTLE 160
BLUE DAWN VINE 138
BLUE DAZE 190
BLUE-EYED-GRASS 332

BLUE GINGER 189
BLUE PASSION FLOWER 143
BLUE PHLOX 328
BLUE SAGE 91
BLUE SKY VINE 145
BLUE-STAR 320
BLUE THUNBERGIA 145
BLUEWINGS 173
Blumstein, Barbara 345
Boe, Be 49,144,148,271,359
Boggs, Lindy 51
BOIS D'ARC 280
Boldt, Dorothea 209,212
BORAGE 413
Borago 413
Borah, Judge Wayne 472
Bostrom, Mrs. Frank 423
BOTTLEBRUSH 106-107
BOUGAINVILLEA 132
Boussingaultia 131,433
BOXLEAF AZARA 99
BOXWOOD 106,411,424,430,447,472,479
Brachychiton 76
Bradburn, Anne 55,72,342,344
Bradburn, Dr. Donald M. 128,349,351,361
Bradley, Camilla 44,95,139,223,478
BRAZILIAN PEPPER TREE 104
BREATH OF HEAVEN 89
BRIDAL WREATH 287
Brodieae 242,259
Brookville Plant Introduction Garden 465
BROOM 90
Broussonetia 477
Browallia 159,433
Brown, Clair 27,41,208
Brugmansia 86
Brunfelsia 105
BUCKEYE, RED 284
Buddleia 86
BUGLE LILY 260-261
BUGLOSS 158
Bulbous plants, culture 219-222
BUNYA-BUNYA 99
Burden Research Plantation 412
Buse, Mrs. George 423
Butler, Mr. & Mrs Edward 446
BUTTERCUP 330
BUTTERFLY BUSH 86
BUTTERFLY GINGER 240
BUTTERFLY IRIS 235
BUTTERFLY PEA 134
BUTTERFLY TREE 76
BUTTERFLY VINE 145
BUTTERFLY-WEED 321,332
BUTTERWEED 332
BUTTONBUSH 276-277
BUTTONWOOD TREE 281
Buxus 106

Cable, George Washington 341-342,421,463

CADENA DE AMOUR 131
Caesalpinia 86
Caladium 230-231
Calendula 159,413
CALICO FLOWER 131
CALIFORNIA PEPPER TREE 104
CALIFORNIA POPPY 164
CALLA LILY 261-262
Calliandra 87
Callicarpa 284-285
CALLIOPSIS 162, 322
Callirhoe 321
Callistemon 106-107
Callistephus 159
Calodendrum 77
Calonyction 137
Calycanthus 285
Calystegia 432
Camassia 231
Cambias, Les 322,396
Camellia107-108,412,430,444-445,447,453,
    471
Camellia, culture 107-108
Campanula 159
CAMPHOR TREE 100
Campsis 132
CANARY-BIRD FLOWER 174
CANARY-BIRD VINE 146
CANARY CREEPER 144,146
CANCERWEED 332
CANDLESTICK 87
CANDY LILY 257
CANDYTUFT 166
Canna 232,400
CANTERBURY-BELLS 159
CAPE CHESTNUT 77
CAPE COLONY NERINE 255
CAPE FORGET-ME-NOT 158
CAPE HONEYSUCKLE 97
CAPE JASMINE 112
CAPE LEADWORT 95
Capsicum 159
CARAWAY 416
CARDINAL CLIMBER 138
CARDINAL FLOWER 327
Cardiospermum 133
Carissa 108
CAROLINA JESSAMINE 136
CAROLINA LUPINE 334
CAROLINA MOONSEED 135
Carpet-bedding 190,451
Carriere, Miss Olive 72
Carthamus 160
Carum 416
Carya 276
Case, Larry & Margie 360
CASHMERE BOUQUET 88
CASSAVA 94
Cassia 87
CASSIA BARK TREE 100
CAST-IRON PLANT 185

CAT'S CLAW 140,422,423
Catalpa 276
Catalpa Plantation 446
Caterpillars, stinging 381
Catharanthus 160
CATHEDRAL BELLS 135
CATMINT 417
CATNIP 417
CEDAR OF LEBANON 100
Cedrela 466
Cedrus 99-100
Celastrus 133
Celosia 160
Celtis 276
Centaurea 160-161,206,322,433
CENTURY PLANT 183
Cephalanthus 276-277
Ceratostigma 87
Cercis 77,277
Cestrum 109
Chaenomeles 88
CHAIN OF LOVE 131
Chamaerops 125
Chamelaucium 88
Charlevoix 438
CHASTE TREE 84
CHERRY LAUREL 292
CHESTNUT DIOON 123
CHILEAN JASMINE 141
CHILEAN PINE 98
Chimonanthus 88
CHINA ASTER 159
CHINABERRY 81
CHINA FIR 101
CHINESE CINNAMON 100
CHINESE DATE 85
CHINESE FORGET-ME-NOT 163
CHINESE GROUND ORCHID 230
CHINESE HIBISCUS 113
CHINESE HOLLY 102,295
CHINESE LANTERN PLANT 201-202
CHINESE PARASOL 79
CHINESE PHOTINIA 117
CHINESE PLUMBAGO 87
CHINESE PRIVET 114
CHINESE RED BUD 77
CHINESE SCHOLAR TREE 84
CHINESE TALLOW 83
CHINESE WISTERIA 147-148
Chionanthus 277
CHIVES 226
CHOCOLATE PLANT 203
Choisya 109
Chopin, David 80
Chopin, Mr. P. A. 464
Chorizema 109
CHRISTMAS-BERRY TREE 104
Chrysanthemum 161,187-188
Chrysogonum 188
Cichorium 322
CIGARETTE PLANT 89-90

CIGARFLOWER 163
Cineraria 206,433
Cinnamomum 100
Cirsium 374
Cistus 109
Citrus 100
Clapp, Mrs. Emory 423,464
Clarkia 161
Clematis 133-134
Cleome 161
Clerodendrum 88-89,134
Clethra 285
CLIMBING HYDRANGEA 137
CLIMBING LILY 239
CLIMBING SNAPDRAGON 132
Clitoria 134
Clivia 232-233,237-238
CLOCK VINE 145
CLOVER, CRIMSON 335
CLOVER, RED 335,388
CLOVER, WHITE 335,388
CLUSTERBERRY, RED 110
Clytostoma 134-135
Cobaea 135
Cocculus 110,135
Cocks, Reginald Somers 462
COCKSCOMB 160
Coleman, W. H. 458
Coleonema 89
Coleus 162
Colocasia 233
COLUMBINE 184
Commelina 322
COMMON ANISE 414
COMMON BOX 106
COMMON CHICORY 322
CONEFLOWER 203-204,330-331
CONEFLOWER, PURPLE 190,323
CONFEDERATE JASMINE 146
CONFEDERATE ROSE 92
CONFETTI BUSH 89
CONFUCIOUS VINE 144
Consolida 162
COPPER LILY 240
CORAL BEAN 324
CORALBERRY 105,288
CORAL PLANT 96,477
CORAL TREE 78
CORAL VINE 131
Coreopsis 162,188-189,322
CORIANDER 413
Coriandrum 413
CORNFLOWER 160,322
Cornus 277-278
Coronilla 89
Cortaderia 189
Cosmos3 162-163
COSMOS, EARLY 163
COSMOS, YELLOW & ORANGE 163
Costus 233
Cotoneaster 109-110

COTTAGE PLUMARIUS 433
Cotton Centennial, 1884 454-455
COTTON ROSE 92
COTTONWOOD 281-282
Council of Jewish Women 482
Courier de la Louisiane 446
CRANESBILL 191
CRAPE MYRTLE 80
Crataegus 278
CREEPING SPOT FLOWER 334
CREEPING ZINNIA 172
CREOLE BOX 106
CRINODONNA 228
Crinum 234,323
Crocosmia 234
Crocus 234-235
CROSS VINE 132
CROTON 477
CROWN VETCH 89
CRY-BABY TREE 78
CUNNINGHAM FIR 101
Cunninghamia 101
CUP & SAUCER VINE 135
CUPFLOWER 198
Cuphea 89,90,163,189
Curculigo 235
Curcuma 235
Curcurbitaceae 135
Cycas 123
Cydonia 77
Cynoglossum 163
CYPRESS VINE 138
CYPRESS 283
Cyrtanthus 235
Cyrtomium 310
Cytisus 90

Daboecia 110
Daedalacanthus 91
DAFFODIL GARLIC 226
DAFFODIL 235
DAGGER PLANT 209
Dahlia 235-236
DAHOON HOLLY 295
Daily Picayune 457
DAISY FLEABANE 323
Dante Street Deli 132,355
Datura 90
Daucus 323
Daunoy, Harry L. 424,469-470
Davis, Dan 43
DAWN REDWOOD 72
DAY BLOOMING JESSAMINE 109
DAYFLOWER 322
DAYLILY 192
DAYLILY, culture, history 209-214
de Bore', Etienne 441
Delphinium 163-164
DELPHINIUM, ANNUAL 162
DELTA ARROWHEAD 400
DEODAR CEDAR 99-100

Detweiler, Maureen 55,62,64,66
Deutzia 90-91
DEVIL'S TRUMPET 90
DEVILWOOD 291
DEWBERRY, SOUTHERN 144
Dianthus 164,433
Dichorisandra 189
Dietes 236,252
Digitalis 164
DILL 413
Diodia 313
Dioon 123
Dioscorea 136
Diospyros 278
Dipladenia 141
DOGTOOTH VIOLET 237
DOGWOOD,FLOWERING 277-278
Dolichos 136
DOORSTEP FLOWER 331
Dorman, Caroline 134
Downing, A. J. 450
Dracunculus 237
DRAGON ARUM 237
Drennan, Georgia Torey 64,461
DRUMSTICKS 227
Dryopteris 304,308
Dubourg, Dorothy 467
Duchesnea 323
Duranta 110
DUSTY MILLER 160,206
DUTCH HYACINTH 241
DUTCHMAN'S PIPE 131
DWARF HOLLY 115
DWARF YAUPON 296

EASTERN RED CEDAR 290
Eberle, Karen 412
Eberle, George 464
Echeveria 188-189
Echinacea 190,323
Echinops 190
Ecosystems 316,365
EDGING LOBELIA 168
Edging for parterres 430,447
EGYPTIAN STAR-CLUSTER 200
Eichhornia crassipes 400,456
Eichling, C. W. 464
ELDERBERRY 287
Eleagnus 91,111
Eleocharis 400
ELEPHANT EAR 227,233,400,423
ELM, CHINESE 84,284,466,468
ELM, SIBERIAN 84,284
ELM, SMALL-LEAVED 283
ELM, WINGED 283
Emilia 432
Endymion 237
ENGLISH DAISY 158
ENGLISH LAUREL 292
Equisetum 310
Eranthemum 91

Erigeron 323-324
Eriobotrya 101
Erythrina 78,324
Erythronium 237
Escallonia 111
Eschmann, Anthony 361,393
Eschscholzia 164
Eucalyptus 102
Eucharis 237
Euonymous 111
Eupatorium 324
Euphorbia 91
EUROPEAN HOLLY 295
Euryops 112
Eustoma 324
EVENING PRIMROSE 198
EVERGREEN WISTERIA 142
Evolvulus 190
Ewan, Joseph 86,208, 427,435,440,442,446,
        453,457,462,468
Ewin, Louise 395-396

Fabacher, Joseph 464,467
Fabulous 5, St. Joseph's Academy 368
Fairchild, David G. 465
FALSE DRAGONHEAD 329
Farley, E. A., Sr. 466-468
Farnsworth, George 48
Fasnacht Garden 461
Fatsia 112
Feijoa 112
Felicia 91
FENNEL 416
Ferns 301-311
FERNS, culture 305-307
FETTERBUSH 297
FEVERFEW 161
Ficus 78,136
FIERY COSTUS 233
FIG TREE 78
FIG VINE 136
FINOCCHIO 416
FIRECRACKER VINE 141
FIRECRACKER PLANT 163
FIRESPIKE 94
FIREWHEEL 325
Firmiana 79
FIVE LEAF AKEBIA 130
FLAME PEA 109
FLAMEGOLD 80
FLAMINGO PLANT 113
FLORA'S PAINTBRUSH 432
Floral Trail 469,476,481
FLORENCE FENNEL 416
FLORIDA CRINUM 234
FLORIDA JASMINE 93
FLORIDA YEW, STINKING CEDAR 118
FLOSS FLOWER 157
FLOWER-FENCE 87
Flower show, 1949 468-469
FLOWERING MAPLE 85

FLOWERING QUINCE 88
FLOWERING TOBACCO 169
Foeniculum 416
Forestiera 285
FORGET-ME-NOT 169
Forman, McLain J. 127
Fortune, Robert 443
Fortunella 112
FOSTER'S HOLLY 295
Foucher, Pierre 441
FOUNTAIN PLANT 96
Fountains 399,452,471
FOUR O'CLOCK 197
FOXGLOVE 164
FRANGIPANI 95
Fransen, Rene 424
Fraxinus 279
Freeze, plant care during & after 39-40
French Quarter Gardens 439,446,452,470,
    478-479
FRENCH BAY TREE 114,291
FRENCH MALLOW 169
FRENCH MULBERRY 284
FRENCH TARRAGON 416
Friedrichs, Christopher 435
FRIJOLITO 293
FRINGE TREE 277
Fritillaria 238
Fuchs, Dr. Edwin 168

Gaillardia 190,325
Galanthus 238
GALLBERRY 296
Gallier House Museum 425,447
Galphimia 91
Galtonia 238
Galvezia 112
Garden Club Movement 464
Garden Club of America 478
Garden Study Club 482
Gardener's Mutual Protective Association
    454,459
Gardenia 112-3
Gardening in New Orleans 478
Gardner, Dottie 22,72,189,209,212,214,233
Garic, William 34
GARLIC 226
Gauthier,Terry 83
Gayarre', Charles 441
GAYFEATHER 194
Gazania 164
Gelsemium 136
Genista 90
GERALDTON WAX PLANT 88
Geranium 191
GERANIUM 199-200
Gerbera 191
GERBERA DAISY 191
German Gardener's Club 454
GIANT SALVIA 89
GILLYFLOWER 168

Ginkgo 79
Ginseng 477
GLADIOLUS 238-239
Gleditsia 279
GLOBE AMARANTH 165
GLOBE CANDYTUFT 166
GLOBE THISTLE 190
GLORIOSA LILY 239
GLORY BOWER 89
GLOSSY ABELIA 85
GODETIA 161
GOLDEN MIMOSA 105,294
GOLDEN RAIN TREE 80
GOLDEN CLUB 400
GOLDEN WONDER 87
GOLDEN SHRUB DAISY 112
GOLDEN STAR 188
GOLDEN DEWDROP 110
GOLDENROD 206,333
GOLDMOSS 205
Gomphrena 165
GOOD-LUCK PLANT 256
Gordon, Alexander 427,443
Gordonia 289
Gottschalk, Sheila 368
GOURD FAMILY 135
Gramineae 191
GRANCY GRAYBEARD 277
GRAPE HYACINTH 252
GRAPES 147
GRASS PLUMARIUS 433
GRASSES, ORNAMENTAL 191
GREATER PERIWINKLE 146-147
GREEN DRAGON 229
Green, Roger 51
Grevillea 102
Grote, Kitten 329
GUERNSEY LILY 255
GUINEA HEN FLOWER 238
Gumbo Ya-Ya 446
Gundlach, Mrs. James 472
Gysophila 165

Habranthus 240
HACKBERRY 276
Haemanthus 240
HALBERD-LEAVED ROSE MALLOW 325
Halesia 279-80
Halimium 113
Hall, Weeks 446
HAM AND EGGS 93
Hanchey, Louise 437
Hand, Stephen 435,452,479
Haney, Maureen 360
Hanging gardens 397,471
HARDY AMARYLLIS 252
Hardy, D. Clive 455
HARDY ORCHID TREE 76
HARDY BEGONIA 185,433
HARDY GERANIUM 191
HARLEQUIN FLOWER 258

HAWTHORNE, GREEN & PARSLEY 278
HEALALL 329
HEART-OF-MAN 143
HEART-SEED 133
Hedera 137
HEDGEHOG 183
Hedrick, U. P. 435-436,444-445,450,452
Hedychium 240
Helenium 325
Helianthus 165,325,414
Helichrysum 165
HELIOTROPE 166
Heliotropium 166
Hemerocallis 192
Hemerocallis, culture, history 209-214
Henderson, Mrs. Hunt 464
HENS & CHICKENS 188-189
Hermann-Grima House 425,447
Hibiscus 92,113,192,325-326
HIDDEN LILY 235
Hippeastrum 240-241
HOARHOUND 417
HOGHAW 278
HOLLY 295-296
Hollygrove Plantation 471
HOLLYHOCK 157
HONEY LOCUST 279
HONEYBUSH 197
HONEYSUCKLE, CORAL 140
HONEYSUCKLE, JAPANESE 140
HONG-KONG ORCHID 76
Hopkins, Ernestine 394-395
HORN-OF-PLENTY 90
Horticulturist, The 450
Hosta 192
Houttuynia 193
Hove' Parfumeur 412
How We Cooked 437
Hummingbird Bar & Grill 21
HURRICANE LILY 251
HYACINTH BEAN 136
Hyacinthus 241
Hydrangea 92,137,285
HYDRANGEA 92
Hymenocallis 242
Hypericum 294

Iberis 166
ICE PLANT 169
IFAFA LILY 235
Ilex 102,286,295-296
Illicium 113,296
Impatiens 166
IMPATIENS, NEW GUINEA 166
INDIA RUBBER TREE 78
INDIAN BLANKET 325
INDIAN CURRANT 288
INDIAN HAWTHORNE 118
INDIAN PINK 333
INDIAN SHOT 232
INDIGO 93

INDIGO, WILD or FALSE 321
Indigofera 93
Inga 87
INKBERRY 296
Ipheion 242
Ipomoea 137-138
Ipomopsis 326
Iresine 433
Iris 242-247,400
IRISES, BULBOUS 243
IRISES, LOUISIANA, culture 245-246
IRISES, RHIZOMATOUS 244-247
IRISH HEATH 110
IRONWEED 336
IRONWOOD 103
Irwin, Dorothy 356
ISLAND SNAPDRAGON 112
ISMENE 242
Itea 92,286
ITHURIEL'S SPEAR 259
IVY, ALGERIAN 137
IVY, ENGLISH 137
Iwachiw, Pat & John 289
Ixia 247

Jacaranda 79
JACK-IN-THE-PULPIT 229,320
JACOB'S LADDER 239
JACOBEAN LILY 258
JAPANESE ANISE 113
JAPANESE ARALIA 112
JAPANESE BOX 106
JAPANESE CLEMATIS 133
JAPANESE FLOWERING CHERRY 82
JAPANESE PAGODA TREE 84
JAPANESE PITTOSPORUM 117
JAPANESE PLUM 101
JAPANESE SPURGE 199
JAPANESE VARNISH TREE 79
JAPANESE WISTERIA 148
JAPANESE YEW 118
Jardin des Plantes 443
JASMINE, ARABIAN 139
JASMINE, CHINESE 139
JASMINE, ITALIAN 139
JASMINE NIGHTSHADE 145
JASMINE, PINK 93
JASMINE, SPANISH 139
JASMINE, WINTER 139
Jasminum 93,138
JATROPHA 477
JAVA SHRUB 89
Jekyll, Gertrude 465
JERUSALEM THORN 82
JOBO 466
JOE PYE WEED 324
JOHNNY-JUMP-UP 174-175
Johnson, Pat, Dick, Claire 268-269,394
JOSEPH'S COAT 158
Josephine, Empress of France 52,445
JUDAS TREE 77,277

JUJUBE 85
Jungle Gardens 466
Junior League 482
JUNIPER 102
Juniperus 102,290
Justicia 113,193
KAFIR-LILY 332-333
KAHILI GINGER 240
Kahn, Charles N., Jr. 361
Kahn, Felicia 107,346
Kalanchoe 194
Kalmia 297
Keim, Judy 40,369
Keith, Paul 297
Keppelman, Tony 368
Kew Gardens 75
Kilmer, Joyce 269
Kniphofia 193
KNOTWEED 202
Koch, Richard 464,470
Kochia 167
Koelreuteria 80
Kohlmeyer, Ida 51,55
Kolkwitzia 93
KOREAN BOX 106
Kosteletzkya 326
Kraak, Henry family 464,466-467
Krieger, Mary Joe 368
Kudzu 465
Kuhn, Joe 395
KUMQUAT 112

Laan, Miek 329
LADY'S SLIPPERS 166
Lafaye, Susan 48
Lagerstroemia 80
Landreth Nurseries 443
LANTANA, WEEPING or TRAILING 93
Lantana 93
LARKSPUR 162
Latapie, Hilda 17,19,39,132,144,223,235,
    238,239,244,249,250,253,258,261
Lathyrus 140,167
LAUREL 114,291
Laurocerasus 292
Laurus 114,291,412
LAURUSTINUS VIBURNUM 122
LAVENDER 416
LAVENDER COTTON 418
Lawrence, Henry 444,453
Layia 326
LEATHERLEAF MAHONIA 114
Lebo, Jerome 89,180
Lelievre, J. F. 422,426,431-432,438,451
LEMON VERBENA 415
LEMON BEE BALM 328
LEMON BALM 417
Leonotis 194
LEOPARD PLANT 195
Leptospermum 102
Leucojum 238,247-248

Liatris 194,326
Libertia 194-195
Ligularia 195
Ligustrum 114
LIGUSTRUM, WAX LEAF 114
Lilium 248-251
LILLYPILLY TREE 98
LILY LEEK 226
LILY OF THE NILE 225
LILY 248-251
LILYTURF 195-6
Limomium 167
Linaria 167,195
Lindera 286
LION'S EAR 194
Lippia 415
Liquidambar 280
Liriodendron 280
LIRIOPE 195-196
Lisianthus 196, 324
LISIANTHUS 324
Livaudais family 448
Live Oak Society 268-269,448
LIVE OAK 293
Livistonia 124
LIZARD'S TAIL 400
Lobelia 168,327
LOBLOLLY BAY 289
Lobularia 168
Longue Vue Gardens 475
Lonicera 140
LOQUAT 101
Lorinseria 140,310
Louisiana Courier for the Country 441
Louisiana Conservationist 456
LOUISIANA IRIS, culture 245-246,326
LOUISIANA IRIS, history 223-224
Louisiana Ornithological Society 368
LOUISIANA PHLOX 200
LOVE-IN-A-MIST 169
LOVE-IN-A-PUFF 133
LOVE-LIES-BLEEDING 158
Lowery, George H., Jr. 359,370,391
Lupinus 327
Lutz, Dr. Brobson 389
Lycoris 251-252
Lygodium 303
Lyonia 297
Lyons, Henry 443
LYRE-LEAVED SAGE 332
Lythrum 196

Macfadyena 140
Maclura 280
MADAGASCAR PERIWINKLE 160
MADEIRA VINE 131
Madewood Plantation 267
MAGIC LILY 252
Magnolia 81,94,290-291
Magnolia Nurseries 451
MAGNOLIA, COWCUMBER 290

MAGNOLIA, ORIENTAL 81,291
MAGNOLIA, SAUCER 81,291
MAGNOLIA, SOUTHERN 290
MAGNOLIA, STAR 81
MAGNOLIA, SWEETBAY 291
MAGNOLIA, TULIP 81,94,290
MAGNOLIA, WHITE SAUCER 81,291
MAGNOLIA, YULAN 81,290
MAGUEY 183
Mahonia 114-115
MAIDENHAIR TREE 79
Maitre, Reinhardt 454
Maitre & Cook 454,460,479
Malpighia 115
Malva 168
Malvaviscus 94,115
MAMOU 324
MANDARIN ORANGE 100
Mandevilla 141
Manettia 141
Manihot 94
MARGUERITE 187
MARIGOLD 173
MARLBERRY 105
Marrubium 417
Marsilea 309
Martin, Karen & Phil 68
Matricaria 161
Matthiola 168
Maurandia 132
MAYHAW 278
MAYPOP 143
McAcy, Seamus 353
McClung, Mike & Kathy 26,31,142,250,
    345,362
McIlhenny, E. A. 100,103,107,116,185,303,
    466,467
McKinnon, Gloria 368
McLellan, Edward & Kit 25,36,354
MEALY-CUP SAGE 204
Melaleuca 116
Melampodium 197
Melia 81
Melianthus 197
Melissa 417
Mentha 417
Merremia 142
MESCAL BEAN 293
Mesembryanthemum 169
MESPILUS 101
Metasequoia 72
Metrosideros 103,107
MEXICAN BUSH SAGE 205
MEXICAN CIGARFLOWER 89-90
MEXICAN FLAME BUSH 87
MEXICAN FLAME VINE 144
MEXICAN HAT 330
MEXICAN HEATHER 189
MEXICAN ORANGE 109
MEXICAN PALO VERDE 82
MEXICAN PETUNIA 206,331

MEXICAN PLUM 282
MEXICAN PRIMROSE 328
MEXICAN SHELL FLOWER 258
MEXICAN SUNFLOWER 173
Michaux, Andre'440
Michelia 116
MIGNONETTE VINE 131
MIGNONETTE, COMMON 171
MILKWEED 320-321
Millettia 142
MIMOSA 75,327
Mimulus 327
MINT 417
Mirabilis 197
MIRASOLE 165
MIRLITON 144
MISSOURI PRIMROSE 198
MIST-FLOWER 324
Mmahat, Arlene 424
MOCK ORANGE 94
MOCK STRAWBERRY 323
MODEST ACACIA 432
MOMBIN, YELLOW 466
Momordica 142
Monarda 198,328
MONDOGRASS 198-199
MONKEY PUZZLE TREE 22-23,72-74,98
MONKEY FLOWER 327
MONKEY GRASS 198-199
Monstera 142
MONTBRETIA 34
MOONFLOWER 137
MOONSEED 110
Moraea 236,252
Morcos,Ann 82
MORNING-GLORY 137-138
Morton Julius Sterling 270
Morus 81,280-281
MOSS ROSE 171
MOSS PINK 200
MOSS VERBENA 336
MOUNTAIN LAUREL 296-297
MOUNTAIN BLUET 161
MOUNTAIN FLAX 200
MULBERRY, RED or AMERICAN 280
MULBERRY, WHITE 81
MULLEIN 207
Muller, V. Aime's gardener 443
Muller, Joseph 457
Musa 81
MUSCADINE GRAPES 147
Muscari 252
MUSK MALLOW 157
Muth, David & Wendy 315,354,360,
    361,372
Myers, Joel & Bert 228,244,361,400
Myosotis 169,433
Myrica 297
MYRTLE 116
Myrtus 116

NAKED LADY 219,251
Nandina 116
Narcissus 253-254
NASTURTIUM BAUHINIA 76,86
NASTURTIUM 174
NATAL PLUM 108
NEEDLE PALM 209
Nelumbo 400
Neomarica 254-255,400
Nepata 417
Nephrolepis 301,310
Nerine 255
Nerium 116-117
NETTLE 379
Neviusia 286
New Orleans Garden Society 470,477
N. O. Horticultural Society 455,459,468
New Orleans Item 468
N. O. Parkway & Park Commission 468
New Orleans Town Gardeners 482
Newfield, Nancy 98,198,369,370-372,394
NEW ZEALAND CHRISTMAS TREE 103
NEW ZEALAND FLAX 200
NEW ZEALAND IRIS 195
Nicotiana 169
Nierembergia 198
Nigella 169
NIGHT BLOOMING JESSAMINE 109
NIPPON DAISY 187
NIPPON OXEYE DAISY 187
NORFOLK ISLAND PINE 99
NORTHERN GOLDEN RAIN TREE 80
Notarial Archives 424
Noveau Jardinier de la Louisiane 426
Nuphar 400
NUTALL'S WEED 162
Nymphaea 400
Nyssa 281

O'Meallie, Dr. Lawrence P. 22,127,354,
   358,361,370,375
OAK 292-3
OAKLEAF HYDRANGEA 285
OBEDIENT PLANT 202,329
Ochsner, Dr. Rise 203
Ocimum 414
Odontonema 94
Oenothera 198,328
OKRA 437-438
OLEANDER 116
Olsen, Mrs. Ole' 464
Onoclea 310
Ophiopogon 198
Opuntia 199
ORCHID TREE 76
OREGANO, CUBAN 418
OREGANO, MEXICAN 417
OREGON GRAPE HOLLY 114
Origanum 417
Ornithogalum 255
Orontium 400

ORRIS ROOT 411
OSAGE ORANGE 280
Oser, Helen 252,261,478
Osmanthus 117,291
Osmunda 310
Oxalis 256
OXEYE DAISY 187
OZARK SUN DROP 198

P. J.'s Coffee & Tea Co. 21
Pachysandra 199
PAGODA FLOWER 89
PAINTED COPPERLEAF 477
PAINTED COREOPSIS 322
PAINTED TONGUE 171
PALM, BUTIA 123
PALM, CABBAGE 298
PALM, CHINESE FAN 124
PALM, COCOS 123
PALM, DATE 124
PALM, DESERT FAN 125
PALM GRASS 235
PALM, MEDITERRANEAN FAN 123
PALM, MEXICAN WASHINGTON 125
PALM, THREAD 125
Palm, Susan & C. H. 391
PALM, WINDMILL 124
PALMETTO, LOUISIANA 298
PAMPAS GRASS 189
Panax 477
Pancratium 257
PANSY 174-175
Papal palms, 1987
Papaver 170
PAPER MULBERRY 77
Papworth, Harry 461
PAPYRUS 400
PARADISE FLOWER 145
Parkinsonia 82
Parkway Partners Program 482
PARROT LILY 228
PARSLEY 414
PARSLEY PLANT 195
Parthenocissus 142
PARTRIDGEBERRY 197
Passiflora 143
PASSIONFLOWER 143
Patio Planters 478
PEACOCK IRIS 252
PEAR 83
PEAR, FLOWERING 83
PECAN 276
Pedilanthus 477
Pelargonium 191,199-200,418
Penstemon 200,328
Pentas 200
PEONIES 179-180
PEPPERS,ORNAMENTAL 159
PERENNIAL PHLOX 200-201
PERENNIAL SWEETPEA 140
Perennials, culture 180-182

Perilla 170,414
PERIWINKLE, COMMON 147
Perrine, Henry 442,465
Persea 103,291,412
PERSIAN BUTTERCUP 257-258
PERSIMMON 278
PERUVIAN LILY 227
PERUVIAN PEPPERTREE 104
PERUVIAN VERBENA 174
PERUVIAN DAFFODIL 242
Peterson, Joy 99
Petroselinum 414
Petunia 170-171,433
Pfister, Edith 268
Pharmacy Museum 438
Phaseolus 143
Philadelphus 94-95
PHILODENDRON, CUT-LEAF 142
PHILODENDRON, SPLIT-LEAF 142
Phlox 171,200-201,328-329
Phoenix 124
Phormium 200
Photinia 117
Physalis 201-202
Physostegia 202,329
PICKEREL WEED 400
Pimpinella 414
PINEAPPLE GUAVA 112
PINCUSHION FLOWER 172
PINE CONE GINGER 262
PINE, LOBLOLLY 292
PINE, LONGLEAF 292
PINE, SHORT LEAF 292
PINE, SLASH 292
PINE, SPRUCE 292
PINK FLAMETREE 76
PINK ROOT 333
PINK STERCULIA 76
PINKS 164
Pinus 292-293
Pipes, Mrs. David W. 445,471
Pistia 400
Pittosporum 117
Pitts, L. B. 355
PLAINTAIN 82
Plantago 202
PLANTAIN LILY 192
Platanus 281
Platte, William 475
Platycodon 202
Plumbago 95
Plumeria 95-96
Podocarpus 118
Poinciana 86
POINSETTIA 91
Polianthes 257
Polygala 96
Polygonum 202
Polypodium 304
Polystichum 309
POMEGRANATE 96

Pontalba, Baroness 450
Pontederia 400
POPCORN TREE 83
POPLAR 281-282
POPPY-MALLOW 321
POPPY, FIELD 170
POPPY, FLANDERS 170
POPPY, ICELAND 170
POPPY, OPIUM 170
POPPY, ORIENTAL 170
POPPY, SHIRLEY 170
Populus 281-282
Portulaca 171
POSSUM HAW 286,295
POT MARIGOLD 159,413
POTATO VINE 136,144-145
PRAIRIE PHLOX 329
PRAIRIE GENTIAN 324
PRICKLY PEAR CACTUS 199
PRIDE OF BARBADOS 87
Primm, Jamie 362
PRINCES FEATHERS 158
PRIVET 114
PRIVET, AMUR 114
PRIVET, CHINESE 114
PRIVET, SWAMP 285
Project Swallow Committee 363
Prunella 329
Prunus 82,282,292
Pseuderanthemum 203
Psilotum 303
Pteris 302-303
PTERIS FERN 96
Punica 96
PURPLE LEAF PLUM 82
PURPLE LOOSESTRIFE 196-197
PURPLEHEART 206
PURPLE-TOP 174
PURSLANE 171
PUSSY WILLOW 96
Pyracantha 118
Pyrethrum 433
Pyrus 83

QUEEN LILY 235
QUEEN ANNE'S LACE 323
Quercus 292-293
QUINCE,COMMON 77
Quisqualis 143

RABBIT EARS 162
RABBIT-EYE BLUEBERRY 288-289
RAIN LILY 240,261-262
RANGOON CREEPER 143
Ranunculus 257-258,330
Raphiolepis 118
Ratibida 330
RATTLEBOX 97
REDBAY 291
REDBIRD SLIPPERFLOWER 477
RED BUD 277

RED GINGERLILY 240
RED-HOT-POKER 193
RED MORNING GLORY 138
Reed, Leslee 129,198,203,223,289,296,354,
   358,368,372,376,381
Reeves, Sally Kittridge 425
Reineckia 433
Reinwardtia 203
Reseda 171
Reuter Seed Company 451
Rhododendron 119-120,287
Rhus 287
RICE PAPER PLANT 97
Rice, Stan & Ann 423
Richardson, Dr. Tobias G. 453,456-458
Richardson, Ida 453,457
RIVERBIRCH 275-276
Roberts, Eugene 469
ROBIN'S-PLAINTAIN 324
ROBIN-REDBREAST BUSH 116
Robinia 282
Robinson, Martha 267
ROCKET CANDYTUFT 166
ROCKROSE 109
Rogillio, Carlyle 363
ROMAN HYACINTH 241
ROSE-OF-SHARON 92
ROSE BANANA 82
Rosedown Plantation 445
ROSE MALLOW 192
Rosemarinus 418
ROSEMARY 418
Rosenzweig, Dara 37,175,219,380,422
Rosenzweig, David 37,219,380,422
ROSE OF MONTANA 131
Roses, culture 55-60
Roses, modern 67
Roses, old 65
ROSE VERBENA 174,335
ROUGH-LEAF DOGWOOD 277
Royena 104
RUBBER PLANT 78
Rubus 144
Rudbeckia 203,330-331
RUE 418
Ruellia 204,331
Russelia 96
RUSSIAN TARRAGON 416
RUSSIAN OLIVE 91
Ruta 418

Sabal 298
SACRED BAMBOO 116
SACRED LILY OF INDIA 423
SACRED LILY OF THE INCAS 242
SAFFLOWER 160
SAGE 204-205,418
Sagittaria 400
SAGO PALM 123
ST. ANDREW'S CROSS 294
ST. JOHN'S WORT 294

St. Joseph's lily 240
Salix 83,96,282-283
Salpiglossis 171
SALT MARSH-MALLOW 326
Salvia 172,204-205,332,418
Sambucus 287
Sanchezia 433
Sanders, Julia 318-319,327
Santolina 411,418
Sanvitalia 172
Sapindus 466
Sapium 83
Saponaria 205
Sargent, Charles Sprague 446,464
SASANQUA 108
Sassafras 283,412
SATSUMA 100
Satureja 414
Saururus 400
Saxifraga 205
Scabiosa 172
SCARLET FIRETHORN 118
SCARLET GILIA 326
SCARLET ROSEMALLOW 192
SCARLET RUNNERBEAN 143
SCARLET SAGE 172,332
SCENTED GERANIUMS 418
Schinus 104
Schmitz, Don 456
Schornstein, Florence 482
Scilla 237
SCOTCH PURSE 115
SCUPPERNONG 147
SEA DAFFODIL 257
Seale, Margaret 376,378-379,382
Sechium 144
Sedum 205-206
Seidenberg, Jean 25,26,37,61,81,269,359,362,
   368,371,380
Selaginella 309
SELF-HEAL 329
Senecio 144, 206,332
SENNA 87
SENSITIVE PLANT 327
SERVICEBERRY 275
SESAME 415
Sesamum 415
Sesbania 97
Setcreasea 206
Shadows, The 446
SHAMEPLANT 432
SHAMPOO PLANT 261
SHASTA DAISY 188
SHELL GINGER 227
SHINING SUMAC 287
Shipman, Ellen Biddle 475
SHISHO 414
SHOWER OF GOLD 91
SHOWY SEDUM 205
SHRIMP PLANT 193
SIBERIAN LARKSPUR 163-164

SILK OAK 102
SILK TREE 75
SILK TASSEL TREE 76
SILKY CAMELLIA 288
SILVER DOLLAR TREE 102
SILVER BELL 279-280
Sisyrinchium 332
SNAKE'S HEAD LILY 238
SNAKELILY 259
SNAPDRAGON 158
SNEEZEWEED 183,325
SNOW-WREATH 286
SNOWBELL 288
SNOWDROP 238
SNOWFLAKE 238,247-248
SOAPBERRY 466
SOAPWORT 205
SOCIETY GARLIC 259,419
Soil, Kenner & Little Woods 28
Soil testing 29-30
Solanum 144-145
Solidago 206,333
Sontheimer, Caroline 394
Sophora 84,293
Southern Baptist Hospital 351
SOUTHERN DEWBERRY 144
Southern Gardener, The 479
SOUTHERN RED OAK 293
SOUTHERN YEW 118
Spanish Fort 459
SPANISH BLUEBELL 237
SPANISH-DAGGER 209
SPANISH MOSS 334
SPANISH SQUILL 237
Sparaxis 258
SPATTERDOCK 400
SPEEDWELL 207-208
SPICE BUSH 286
SPIDER FLOWER 102,161
SPIDERLILY 242,251,255
SPIDERWORT 334
Spigelia 333
SPIKE RUSH 400
Spilanthes 334
Spiraea 287
SPIRAL GINGER 233
Spondias 466
SPREADING DEUTZIA 91
Sprekelia 258
SPRING STARFLOWER 242
STANDING CYPRESS 326
STAR ANISE 296
STAR JASMINE 146
STAR MORNING GLORY 138
STAR OF BETHLEHEM 255
Starr, S. Frederick 447
STARS-OF-PERSIA 226
STATICE 167
Steele, John 427,435,437,439,440,446
Stein, Ron 370
STEP-LADDER PLANT 233

Stephens, Dr. Edwin Lewis 268
Sterculia 79
Stern, Mrs. Edgar B. 475
Sternberg, Dr. Will 72
Stewart, Jane 438
Stewart, Mary 252,261,465,469,478,479
Stewartia 288
Stigmaphyllon 145
STOCK 168
STOKE'S ASTER 206,334
Stokesia 206,334
STONECROP 205
STONECROP,WHITE 205
STORAX 288
STRAWBERRY GERANIUM 205
STRAWFLOWER 165
Strelitzia 258
Strobilanthes 206
Styrax 288
SULTAN'S TURBAN 94
SULTANA 166
SUMAC 287
SUMMER CYPRESS 167
SUMMER HYACINTH 238
SUMMER LILAC 84
SUMMER PHLOX 200-201
SUMMER POINSETTIA 433
SUMMER SAVORY 414
SUMMERSWEET 285
SUNDROP 198
SUNFLOWER 165,325,414
Sunken Gardens, The 482
SURPRISE LILY 235,251
SWAMP BAY 291
SWAMP COTTONWOOD 282
SWAMP LILY 234
SWAMP PRIVET 285
SWAMP RED BAY 291
SWAMP RED MAPLE 275
SWAMP RED OAK 293
SWAMP SPIDER LILY 242
SWAMP VIBURNUM 122,289
SWEET ACACIA 294
SWEET ALYSSUM 168
SWEET ANISE 416
SWEET BAY 114,291
SWEETGUM 280
SWEET LOCUST 279
SWEET MARJORAM 418
SWEET OLIVE 117
SWEET PEA 167
SWEET PEPPERBUSH 285
SWEET SHRUB 285
SWEETSPIRE 92,286
SWEET SULTAN 161
SWEET VIBURNUM 122
SWEET VIOLET 208
SWEET WILLIAM 431
SYCAMORE 281
Sylvanus 449-450
Symphoricarpos 288

Syzygium 104

Tabernaemontana 122
Tagetes 173
TAIWAN CHERRY 82
TALL CUP FLOWER 198
Tanacetum 419
Tansy 419
TASSELFLOWER 158
Taxodium 283
TEA OLIVE 117
TEA PLANT 108
TEA TREE 102
Tecomaria 97
Terezakis, Dr. Nia 127,411
Tetrapanax 97
Teucrium 334
TEXAS BLUEBONNET 327
TEXAS LILAC 293
TEXAS STAR HIBISCUS 192
TEXAS SAGE 332
Thermopsis 334
THICK-LEAF PHLOX 433
THISTLES 374
Tithonia 173
Thomas, George 65,464,469,473,
Thomas, Robert "Bob" 391
Thompson, Grace Matt 38,712,74,76,85,88,
    90,99,100,179,226,230,237-238,286,478
THORNY ELEAGNUS 111
THRIFT 200
THROATWORT 207
THRYALLIS 91
Thuja 294
Thunbergia 145
THYME 419
Thymus 419
TICKSEED 322
TIDY TIPS DAISY 326
Tigridia 258
Tillandsia 334
Times-Democrat 457-458
Times-Picayune 468-470
TOAD LILY 238
TOADFLAX 167,195
TOADLILY 238
Torenia 173,433
Torreya 118
Trachelium 207
Trachelospermum 146
Trachycarpus 124
Tradescantia 207,334
TRANSVAAL DAISY 191
TREASURE FLOWER 164
TREE-OF-HEAVEN 75
TREE LIGUSTRUM 114
Trees and Shrubs, culture 270-274
TREE TOBACCO 169
Treme', Skip 22,77,125,162,480
Trifolium 335,388
TRINIDAD FLAME BUSH 87

Triteleia 242,259
TRITOMA 193
TRITONIA 234
Tropaeolum 146,174
TROPICAL SAGE 332
TROUT LILY 237
TRUMPET VINE 132
TRUMPET CREEPER 132
TRUMPET FLOWER 132
TUBEFLOWER 89
TUBER VERVAIN 336
TUBEROSE 257
Tuilleries 467
Tulbaghia 259,419
TULIP 259-260
TULIP TREE 280
Tulipa 259-260
TUNG OIL TREE 466
TUPELO GUM 281
TURK'S CAP 94,114
TURK'S-TURBAN 89
Turnbull, Martha 445-446
Turner, Suzanne L. 425,435
Tuttle, Merlin 389
TWELVE APOSTLES 255

U.S.Department of Agriculture 465-466
U.S.Bureau of Plant Industry 466
Ulmus 84,283-284
Ursuline Convent Botanical Garden
    52,439
Urtica 379

Vaccinium 288-289
Van Calsem, Bill 412
VARNISH TREE 79
Veltheimia 260
Verbascum 207
Verbena 174,207,335-336
Vernonia 336
Veronica 207-208
VETEVIR 191-192,412
VIBURNUM SUSPENSUM 123
Viburnum 122-123,289
VICTORIA LILY 400
Victoria 400
Vinca 146-147,160
Viola 174-175,208,336
VIOLET, SWEET 208
VIOLET 208,336
VIRGIN'S BOWER 134,144
VIRGINIA WILLOW 286
VIRGINIA CREEPER 143
Vitex 84
Vitis 147

W. P. A. Guide to N. O., 1938 422,445
WALKING IRIS 254-255
WALL-FLOWER 161
WANDERING JEW 207
WANDFLOWER 258

Ward, Nathaniel, Wardian Case 442
Washingtonia 125
WATER HYACINTH 400
WATER LETTUCE 400
WATER LILY 400
WATER LOTUS 400
WATER OAK 293
Watsonia 260-261
WAX MYRTLE, SOUTHERN 297
WEEPING LANTANA 93
WEEPING WILLOW 83
Weigela 97-98
WEIGELA, OLD-FASHIONED 97-98
Welden, Frances 378-379
Weller, Nancy 255
Wells, Paul 99,123
Westfeldt, Mrs. George 448
WHITE ALDER 285
WHITE CEDAR 294
WILD AGERATUM 324
WILD BERGAMOT 328
WILD BLUE PHLOX 200
WILD CAMELLIA 288
Wildflowers, transplanting 318-319
WILD HYACINTH 231
WILD INDIGO 321
WILD PETUNIA 204,331
WILD PLUM 282
Williams, Mrs. C. S. 473
WILLOW OAK 293
Wilson, Sam, Jr. 435
WINDFLOWER 229
Wingfield, Mrs. Edmund 446,472
WINTER RED HOT POKER 260
WINTER HARDY GLADIOLUS 239
WINTERBERRY 296

WINTERSWEET 88
Wisdom, Mrs. John Minor 423
WISHBONE FLOWER 173
Wisteria 147
WOOD SAGE 334
WOOD ROSE 142
Woodwardia 311
WOOLY ROSE-MALLOW 326
World's Fair, 1984 480
WORMWOOD 415

Xeranthemum 175

YARROW 182-183,320
YAUPON 296
YEDDA HAWTHORNE 118
YELLOW BUTTERFLY GINGER 240
YELLOW COWLILY 400
YELLOW FLAX 203
YELLOW MANDEVILLA 141
YELLOW MOMBIN 466
YELLOW POPLAR 280
YELLOWTOP 332
YELLOW WALKING IRIS 255
YELLOWWOOD SORREL 256
YESTERDAY,TODAY,TOMORROW 105
Yucca 209

Zantedeschia 261-262
ZEBRINA 168
Zemurray, Sam 28
Zephyranthes 261-262
Zingiber 262
Zinnia 175
Ziziphus 85
Zoysia grass 465